TIME, PROCESS AND STRUCTURED TRANSFORMATION IN ARCHAEOLOGY

ONE WORLD ARCHAEOLOGY

Series Editor: P. J. Ucko

TIME, PROCESS AND STRUCTURED TRANSFORMATION IN ARCHAEOLOGY

Edited by

Sander van der Leeuw and
James McGlade

London and New York

First published 1997
by Routledge
11 New Fetter Lane, London EC4P 4EE

Simultaneously published in the USA and Canada
by Routledge
29 West 35th Street, New York, NY 10001

Typeset in Bembo by Florencetype Ltd, Stoodleigh, Devon

Printed and bound in Great Britain by
Redwood Books, Trowbridge, Wiltshire

British Library Cataloguing in Publication Data
A catalogue record for this book is available from the British Library.

Library of Congress Cataloguing in Publication Data
A catalogue record for this book has been requested.

ISBN 0-415-11788-7

Contents

List of figures

List of tables

List of contributors

Peter M. Allen, International Ecotechnology Research Centre, Cranfield University, Cranfield, Beds. MK43 0AL, UK.

Graham P. Chapman, Department of Geography, University of Lancaster, UK.

Jim Doran, Department of Computer Science, University of Essex, Wivenhoe Park, Colchester, Essex CO4 3SQ, UK.

Harry R. Erwin, TRW Systems Division, PO Box 10400, Fairfax, VA 22031, USA.

Henri-Paul Francfort, UPR 315, C.N.R.S., 27 rue Damesme, 75013 Paris, France.

Natalie S. Glance, Xerox PARC, 3333 Coyote Hill Road, Palo Alto, CA 94304, USA.

Bernardo A. Huberman, Xerox PARC, 3333 Coyote Hill Road, Palo Alto, CA 94304, USA.

Geoffrey C. P. King, Institute de Physique du Globe, Université de Paris 6 (Pierre et Marie Curie), 4 Place Jussieu, 75005 Paris, France.

Sander E. van der Leeuw, Université de Paris I (Panthéon-Sorbonne), Institut d'Art et d'Archéologie, 3 rue Michelet, 75006 Paris, France.

Allan G. Lindh, United States Geological Survey, Stop 977, 345 Middlefield Road, Menlo Park, CA 94025, USA.

James McGlade, Institute of Archaeology, University College, London, 31–34 Gordon Square, London WC1H 0PY, UK.

Steven J. Mithen, Department of Archaeology, University of Reading, Whiteknights, Reading RG6 2AA, UK.

Tim Murray, Department of Archaeology, LaTrobe University, 3083 Bundoora, Victoria, Australia.

Denise Pumain, Equipe P.A.R.I.S., 13 rue du Four, 75006 Paris, France.

Robert G. Reynolds, Department of Computer Science, Wayne State University, Detroit, MI 48226, USA.

Robert Rosen, Department of Physiology and Biophysics, Dalhousie University, Halifax, Nova Scotia, Canada.

H. Martin Wobst, Department of Anthropology, Machmer Hall, University of Massachusets, Amherst, MA 01003, USA.

Ezra Zubrow, Department of Anthropology, State University of New York, Buffalo, NY 14261 USA.

Preface

Although some of its roots go even further back in time, the immediate origins of this book bring us back to 1986/87, when the two editors met in Cambridge. Each had been working independently towards applying some of its basic ideas in archaeology. Each had felt the loneliness of working in isolation in an archaeology which at the time was primarily swinging towards the post-modernist and deconstructionist paradigms. Each had experienced the excitement and challenge of contact with colleagues in other disciplines.

Peter Allen and Colin Renfrew were the 'godfathers' of that meeting. The contact between them, established in the late 1970s, drew us both into this area of research, and ultimately to Cambridge. In a conducive environment collaboration between us rapidly widened the scope of our plans and deepened the nature of our commitment to developing non-linear simulation approaches for archaeology. The Conference from which all of the chapters in this volume are drawn was a first step in that direction, bringing together the authors in this volume and a number of other scientists from different disciplines. Thanks to the generous support of the Wenner-Gren Foundation for Anthropological Research, the McDonald Fund for Archaeological Research and the Cultural Service of the French Embassy in London, we were able to meet and discuss in December 1990 for four days in the pleasant, leafy surroundings of St John's College, Cambridge.

The Conference was intended as a forum to acquaint archaeologists with some of the modelling going on in other disciplines. Its multi-disciplinarity was at once its richness and its main hurdle. Four days are not much time to bridge some of the conceptual chasms, or even to learn how to understand each other's language. The papers reflected a wide range of occupations, many of them in the social sciences, but the list of participants is more representative of the impact of physicists and mathematicians on the non-linear modelling that goes on in that area.

The practical difficulties of multi-disciplinary work became even clearer to us in the process that led to this – partial – publication of the conference. To make a long story short, it turned out to be impossible, mainly for commercial reasons, to publish a set of papers of the scope and kind we intended for an archaeological readership. As a result, and to our great regret, a number of very interesting contributions which were not directly related to acknowledged issues in archaeology had to be omitted. The final selection was made in close collaboration with the editor of the present series, Peter Ucko, whom we wish to thank very warmly for his willingness to see as much of the project into print as was possible. Other things being equal, we have favoured those papers by non-archaeologists which are closest to our discipline and/or concerning work which had not been published elsewhere in one form or other.

We hope therefore that the conference may still serve its original purpose: to draw attention to what we feel is a very interesting way of thinking about natural and social processes, and a set of potentially creative techniques to study aspects of complex processes by simulation. We hope that this book will provide an introduction for those of our colleagues who wish to explore non-linear modelling. For those interested in pursuing the issues raised we have included some references to recent publications of those participants in the conference whose papers we were not able to include in this book.

There are many people to whom we would like to express our gratitude for contributing time, money, encouragement, help, advice and more intangible things to this venture. First there are the 'godfathers' whom we have already mentioned. Peter Allen was, and is, a friend and partner in many discussions. He helped our efforts by his encouragement, by employing one of us, and by making IERC into a focus for multi-disciplinary efforts at modelling. Colin Renfrew, as co-organizer of the Conference and as Director of the McDonald Fund for Archaeological Research, contributed time, money, advice, hospitality and constructive criticism whenever his many other activities and initiatives permitted. Sydel Silverman, as President of the Wenner-Gren Foundation for Anthropological Research first challenged one of us to organize a conference on this topic, then helped us find the best format. The Foundation she presides over bore the lion's share of the costs, and 'bailed us out' when that most non-linear of all processes which dictates currency exchange rates threatened our solvency.

At the Conference, our thanks evidently go first and foremost to those fellow academics who accepted an invitation from an unexpected quarter, who turned up in Cambridge on a very wet and snowy evening in December, and who lived with us through the ups and downs of four days of intense conversations. Very heartfelt apologies go to those among them whose papers could in the end not be included in the volume. The only consolation we can offer them is that their contributions were important in kindling our interest, and that the fact that they were not considered as directly relevant to archaeology as other papers is archaeology's loss. But our thanks go equally to all who made running the conference a pleasure, in St John's College as well as in the Department of Archaeology.

In the four odd years between the Conference and the writing of this preface, we owe thanks to the nameless editors and reviewers who could not oblige, but kept encouraging us to strive for publication. And of course to Peter Ucko, Diana Grivas and Routledge for all the stages in the production of a book, from first acceptance to finished product. But we also wish to extend our thanks to those whom we first met in connection with the Conference, and who have since sent us many interesting papers, or with whom we have collaborated quite closely. Among these, we would exceptionally like to mention Denise Pumain, Ezra Zubrow and Harry Erwin by name, as they have contributed most directly to our growing sense that it is all worth the effort. And finally, our thanks go to the ARCHAEOMEDES team who have responded so wonderfully to our ambition to apply some of these ideas in truly interdisciplinary research.

Sander E. van der Leeuw
James McGlade

1   Introduction: Archaeology and non-linear dynamics – new approaches to long-term change

JAMES MCGLADE AND
SANDER E. VAN DER LEEUW

Social evolution is not continuous, nor linear, and cannot be reduced to a general tendency to growing differentiation, complexity and flexibility (Touraine 1977, p. 5).

Introduction

In the last twenty years archaeology has changed fundamentally. What probably strikes the interested lay reader most is the enormous quantity of data which have been obtained through punctilious and systematic fieldwork, and the continued integration between the discipline and a wide range of others, from the natural sciences through the social sciences to the humanities. Physics and chemistry (radiometric dating, dietary reconstruction through trace-element analysis), ecology and the life sciences, medicine (palaeo-pathology and palaeo-epidemiology) ethnography and social theory are among the outstanding contributors.

Indeed, one cannot deny that our knowledge about, and understanding of the prehistoric past have grown almost exponentially. At the same time, we have become aware of many more of our biases and of the limitations of our discipline. Much of that has been achieved through a dialectic between what might be described as three schools, 'Positivist', 'Marxist' and 'Structurationist'. On the other hand this book is born from an increasing frustration with the narrow, pitched epistemological and ideological battle which has been a ravaging side-effect of this dialectic over the last decade.

Any nation, any discipline and any 'school' characterizes and distinguishes itself by retaining, and propagating, a caricature of its neighbours and competitors. In order to change the course of (intellectual) history, it seems often necessary to reduce 'the other' to a fixed point which provides leverage against the current dynamic. Once a new approach, a new 'school' or a new paradigm have been established, the situation often becomes more relaxed, and elements of seemingly opposing ideas contribute to a more mature discipline. In archaeology, the different approaches have succeeded each other so rapidly that the more mature phase of each has not really been reached. The rather reductionist nature of the discipline as a whole, working as it does from an almost infinite number of very partial and often ambiguous data towards very general and global ideas, is possibly responsible for that, at least in part.

It seems to us that a more pluralistic approach is called for, one which recognizes process and event as complementary aspects of human history and tries to steer a course between the oversimplification which is inherent in so-called 'laws of human behaviour' and the limitations of extreme contextualism. In effect an attempt at understanding the past which accepts its own inherent limitations and foibles and notably does not try to explain everything from the same point of view, but makes a virtue of polyocularity.

There are categories of problems raised by our past as it is observed in archaeology, such as those raised in this book, which could benefit from the fact that in a number of neighbouring disciplines the study of the relationship between the recurring and the unique has led to unsuspected and often counterintuitive results, linking phenomena at the microscopic level (in our case that of the individual) to those at the macroscopic level (in our case that of the society) and explaining the spontaneous emergence of qualitative transformations.

In this book we explore some aspects of these developments which have aimed at describing the non-recurrent, the unstable and the unpredictable in formalized and relatively simple terms. In his lecture to the Nobel prize committee (1978), Prigogine characterizes this approach in very simple terms. Commonly, he argues, one describes a (convection) flow as a *disturbance* in an otherwise stable system, the basin full of liquid in which it occurs. But a very different perspective results when one takes the flow to be a (temporarily stable) structure in a basin full of random movement. Then, irreversible direction (and thus change) becomes the focus, rather than undirectedness or reversibility (1978, p. 779). Along with the perspective, the questions which one asks change as well, as do the kinds of data which one collects, indeed the kind of phenomena which arouse interest.[1]

One aspect of this wide field has become known in archaeology through the efforts of Renfrew, Cooke, Zubrow and a few others as 'Catastrophe Theory' (Renfrew and Cooke 1979). Another aspect has in the last few years had much publicity under the popular title 'Chaos Theory' after the fact that one is sometimes able to describe apparently incoherent (chaotic) behaviour in deterministic terms (e.g. Gleick 1987). But in much more encompassing terms, what is at stake is the realization that many phenomena are in part or as a whole due to non-linear dynamics, sudden accelerations or decelerations in certain parameters, which make this field the area of the study of the change of change, and one of its primary formal tools the calculus of difference and differential equations (Renfrew *et al.* 1982, Part III).

Our exploration into the non-linear properties resident in societal systems is a first and tentative one. We hope it will provoke a level of reflection and debate within archaeology similar to that which is going on in a wide range of disciplines, from medicine and tectonics to ecology and meteorology, via urban studies and the science of organizations.

Archaeology and long-term change

Archaeological research is, by definition, fundamentally concerned with dynamical description and interpretation, and particularly with questions relating to the long-term evolution of societal structures. However, the processes which are ultimately responsible for structuring long-run societal dynamics are both elusive and unpredictable. At the root of this problem lies the difficult task of unravelling the complex array of micro-macro interactions which link individual purposive action to the larger-scale collective processes that produce societal change; in short, we have a somewhat less than perfect understanding of cultural dynamics.

A measure of this difficulty is the fact that our ability to account for the dynamical properties at the heart of social transformation is severely constrained by questions of causality; thus, while there is ample evidence for the propensity of human social groups to generate complex adaptive solutions to the plethora of social, political and economic problems with which they are faced, equally there are many instances in which disorder and collapse can emerge as unanticipated consequences from well-ordered and apparently stable organizations.

A key question that arises from such observations is whether an understanding of the structural relations surrounding societal dynamics, and their reproduction through time, can be attained. Within contemporary archaeology a variety of theoretical approaches, positivist, Marxist, structuralist and post-structuralist, have attempted to address this issue, each one in turn essentially obscuring the intrinsic complexity of the problem by superimposing a single theoretical lens through which the data are to be viewed. Epistemological purity is deemed eminently preferable to any attempts at trans-disciplinary or integrated frameworks; under this rubric, pluralistic approaches are intellectually suspect. Yet, as we shall argue here, the future of archaeology as a more effective contributor to debate within the human sciences rests precisely in the contact and enrichment provided by research areas beyond the narrow confines of archaeological theory. The present book is intended as a step in this direction.

What is at issue is the need for an appropriate research strategy that will facilitate an appreciation not only of the structural relations involved in societal reproduction but equally of their place in the long-term behaviour of societal systems. That the interrelationship of these two scales is far from obvious is readily borne out by a continuing debate within archaeology, as a variety of theoretical approaches have sought to establish a working definition of cultural evolution (e.g., Hodder 1986, 1987a, 1987b; McGlade 1990; Shanks and Tilley 1987a, 1987b; Renfrew 1982, 1985, 1987; van der Leeuw 1982, 1989, 1990a). Despite the epistemological and methodological diversity represented by these orientations, they all articulate a common concern; i.e., is it possible to construct convincing models of social change which adequately account for the status of individual events and the role of human agency, and if so, what is the precise relationship between these microscopic levels of description and the '*longue durée*' of historical evolution?

While Braudel's (1973, p. 1244) injunction that 'the long-run always wins in the end' has a deterministic appeal which is not entirely spurious, it is a philosophical position which effectively misrepresents the 'active' nature of individual participation in culture. Clearly, we must acknowledge the power of 'directed, intentional behaviour' as capable of producing structural change, though whether this can ever be regarded as a *primary* motive force, as some have suggested (e.g., Hodder 1986, p. 41), is debatable.

Some measure of the complexity of this problem is to be found in the fact that while social change proceeds through the conscious choices exerted by human actors at the household, community and urban levels of interaction, equally, the trajectory of history is strewn with discontinuities and abrupt transitions which are a consequence of the unintentional and the idiosyncratic, of the curious power of unanticipated or random events to alter and reshape the social trajectory.

Understanding the processes which generate both continuous and discontinuous change in the dynamical evolution of complex socio-cultural systems is thus of critical importance for archaeology. Its contribution to the construction of long-term history is predicated on its ability not only to isolate the key processes involved in structural transformation, but also to provide interpretive and analytical frameworks for their elucidation.

The fundamental problem is of a dual nature; on the one hand, there is a need at the micro-level to come to terms with the role of agency in societal reproduction, while on the other hand, at the larger macro-level, archaeology needs to assess the contribution of such behaviour to the long-term structuring of societal organization and vice versa.

Temporalities and structure

Order, disorder and continuity

Conventional archaeological description of the long-term is generally biased towards the notion of continuity, as though it were a prerequisite for the construction of narratives. A prominent aspect of such attempts at historical reconstruction is the implicit belief that once we can 'fix' events in time, then somehow we can 'know' them, or extract meaning; we can then logically fit them together and organize them into a coherent classificatory sequence.

Taxonomic ordering thus becomes the key to the establishment of a secure chronology and ultimately to evolutionary understanding. Central to such a preoccupation is the need for finer and finer temporal discriminations and it is here that the chronometric techniques of archaeological science (e.g., C^{14} dating) are seen to fulfil the need to fix even more securely a linear, temporal event sequence.

This century-old preoccupation with chronological ordering has been eminently successful, if we are to measure it against the proliferation of narratives that account for socio-cultural evolution – especially those which have been concerned with establishing history as a gradual unfolding of events that is consistent with a 'simple to complex' progression. Central to such a view is that disjunctions or discontinuities in our chronological sequence are simply hiccups – gaps awaiting the inevitable arrival of new data sets. The almost unconscious desire to construct a developmental ordering of events means that should the appropriate data not be forthcoming, then it is a question of 'papering over the cracks'; we can then proceed with the business of constructing 'seamless narratives'.

The rather obvious fear is that without these narrative structures, archaeology will fail in its self-appointed role of reconstructing long-term history. It will founder, lost amidst an inchoate mass of material, in which the spectre of disorder and chaos looms large. Archaeological studies are, moreover, predicated on one of the most enduring of anthropological myths: that of *cultural coherence*. Under this rubric there persists 'an archetype of culture as the perfectly woven and all-enmeshing web . . . the central notion of culture as an integrated whole' (Archer 1988, p. 2). One of the most obvious manifestations of this notion of cultural consistency is to be seen in the archaeological description of a distinctive Neolithic, Bronze or Iron Age society. This effort to create a convincing and identifiable cultural identity – one united by a series of shared beliefs and traditions – has generally been promoted by minimizing *difference* and *anomaly*. A 'smoothing' process emphasized the apparent consistency in material culture and settlement morphology characteristic of each archaeological 'age'.

It is thus that our western intellectual heritage has conditioned us to pursue *coherence* and *similarity* as the mainsprings of classification: disorder, discontinuity and difference have no place in this scheme; they are aberrant categories which must be underplayed or judiciously edited out of interpretive and explanatory discourse. Elsewhere (McGlade 1990, p. 71) it has been pointed out that this conventional emphasis on similarity and concordance effectively distorts the archaeological record. We are led further and further away from the diversity in the data; its intrinsic complexity is homogenized, reduced to manageable classificatory entities, all in the service of convincing narrative construction. Instead, we might do well to heed van der Leeuw's (1989, 1991, pp. 35–6) injunction and attempt to discover more and more dimensions of variability in our data, rather than fewer and fewer.

We argue that it is precisely the aberrant, the discontinuous and the 'different' categories of data which form the rudiments of an alternative theory of change – one predicated on the importance of *instability* rather than stability as the basis from which a more insightful understanding of historical process can emerge.

From a methodological perspective we are seeking insight into the structure of the spatio-temporal mosaic that is presented to us as the residue of extinct patterns and processes. This has long been the special preoccupation of the structuralist tradition in the social and historical sciences. Emphasis has principally focused on those long-run continuities in the history of the large-scale geographic, economic and cultural currents that underpin local events such as politics, wars and other short-run phenomena. For the French Annales School originating in the 1920s in the work of Fèbvre, Bloch and (later) Braudel, such structures were essentially independent of the details of individual, conscious action, and in effect autonomous. From our perspective, what is of particular interest in the work of Braudel is his attempt to reconcile the methods of sociology and history in a totalling vision; central to this project is the role assumed by the co-evolution of time and structure. To achieve this he identified three distinct levels of temporality: the event, the 'conjoncture' (or cyclical phase) and the long-term (Braudel 1973). Structure is thus seen to reside in the coalescence of these inter-temporal events.

While there are a number of problems in the practical application of these ideas, what is important in the contribution of Braudel is the attempt to redefine time in terms of alternating rhythms and periodicities, as opposed to its conventional linear representation. The need to realign and, indeed, to re-theorize our concept of time within archaeology has been advocated by a number of authors (e.g., Bailey 1983; Shanks and Tilley 1987a; Bintliff 1992) and more recently, within the context of the present book's concern with periodicity and non-linear evolution (e.g., van der Leeuw 1990b; Picazo 1993; McGlade, in prep, Picazo and McGlade *in press*). The manifest difficulty in generating debate on such issues within contemporary archaeological theory is a clear demonstration of the embeddedness of time as chronometric sequence, and ultimately of the dominance of linear, deterministic approaches to social evolution.

Positivist versus intentionalist approaches

How then does archaeology deal with issues relating to time and structural transformation? For the purpose of discussion we can with some justification characterize current archaeological theory as being dominated by two principal approaches to the development of an evolutionary epistemology. In a sense, it can be construed as a 'materialist/idealist' debate; on the one hand, cultural evolution and the construction of long-term history is dealt with from an evolutionist perspective that privileges concepts such as adaptation and equilibrium as the principal focus of societal change (e.g., Binford 1977;

Christenson and Earle 1980). By contrast, idealist-inspired approaches subscribe to a post-modernist world-view in which the roles of ideology, power and social action are seen as central to any understanding of societal process, and formative constituents of the meaning structures which shape people's lives (e.g., Hodder 1982, 1986; Shanks and Tilley 1987a, 1987b).

Indeed, the epistemological premises upon which both arguments are based are mutually exclusive to the point that they can reasonably claim alternative paradigmatic status. Moreover, their avowed philosophical divergence has over the past two decades succeeded in generating a debate which is increasingly characterized by empty rhetoric and hermeneutic circularity (e.g., contributions in Bapty and Yates 1992). Perhaps most damaging of all is the fact that much of it is fuelled by the intransigent attitudes of its practitioners, in their self-conscious pursuit of a dubious philosophical goal: the chimera of epistemological purity.

But this clearly is more than an archaeological debate – it is at root symptomatic of a wider cleavage which splits the world of academic discourse, effectively partitioning the acquisition of knowledge into two ideologically separate camps: one oriented towards the natural sciences with its *explanatory* framework and deductive nomological referents, and the other organized around an interpretive framework based on the hermeneutic methods of social theory in which the impossibility of explanation is a *sine qua non*. However, it needs to be pointed out that this dichotomous situation is based on a dubious interpretation of science – one whose definitional criteria are rooted in nineteenth-century empiricist positivism. The invocation of such a model by post-processual practitioners is particularly odd given the fact that it had been jettisoned by the leading practitioners in the natural sciences many years ago, in favour of the concepts of time, space and causality reflected in quantum physics and probability theory.

As with most polarized dialogue, neither side can lay exclusive claim to 'truth'; in this case both the empiricist attitude to natural causation, or alternatively, wholly intentionalist accounts of human causation, are themselves insufficient. Ultimately, neither positivist nor intentionalist explanations are adequate descriptions of the complexity of historical process. While it might be legitimately claimed that the post-modern agenda, with its reinstatement of agency, has been instrumental in rescuing archaeology from the worst excesses of positivist 'explanation', what it has manifestly failed to provide is a series of methodological bridgeheads from which we might renegotiate the relationship between human intentionality, structure, and long-term change. The renewed emphasis on the recursive, structural properties of societal systems has been achieved at a cost. While human actors have been resurrected from a predominantly passive role, and reinstated as 'knowledgeable agents', this has been carried out at the expense of alternative levels of description – the possibility that some of the variability resident in human social organization may conceal underlying structural similarities is dismissed as being redolent of the 'covering law' approaches of the New Archaeology.

There is no necessary connection between the search for generic structures and positivism *per se*; thus, contrary to recent pronouncements by adherents of post-processual orthodoxy, the search for large-scale event sequences, recurrent cycles or oscillations over the long-term, need not have any relationship with the scientistic pronouncements of positivist philosophy.

Thus, while claims for the existence of law-like attributes within socio-cultural systems are clearly unwarranted, it is quite another thing to deny the validity or indeed the descriptive power of pattern formation at the supra-community or macroscopic level. For example, Leach's (1954) study of social transformation among the Kachin of Burma revealed that particular developmental sequences were subsumed by a larger, long-term oscillatory dynamic. This underlines the fact that apparently discrete event sequences within a particular social trajectory may in fact be masking the existence of broader structures operating at a higher level of aggregation (cf. Rowlands and Gledhill 1977, p. 156).

Moreover, it should be noted that societal systems are characterized by highly non-linear interactions, and that the recent discovery of chaotic trajectories within the time evolution of non-linear systems has caused a revision of our long-held assumptions on the *existence*, *nature* and *meaning* of structure itself. Many systems − climatic, physical, chemical, biological and physiological − display a range of behaviours which, while superficially resembling non-periodic, disorganized states, on closer inspection reveal subtly ordered structures; what appears to be erratic and unpredictable in reality is a *highly structured* form of disorder (chaos in the sense in which it is used in this book).

The importance of such findings lies in the way in which they throw light on the problematic relationship between micro and macro levels of description; thus the global behaviour of the system may not only differ from, but actively contradict local event sequences.

We need to reassess this relationship and look for frameworks which seek to integrate micro and macroscopic perspectives within models which are simultaneously morphogenetic *and* structurationist; i.e., questions of structural transformation must be tackled from an interactive dynamical perspective within which human agency and decision-making are wedded to larger scale macro-structural events.

Theoretical advance is only possible if we are prepared to realign the conceptual roots upon which cultural evolutionary theory is founded, not so much by a dismissal of evolution, but rather by its redefinition. The most important part of such a realignment is to actively supplant evolutionary ideas of *progressive unfolding* in favour of models which recognize the non-linear dynamical aspects of structures, and thus underline the importance of *instability* and *discontinuity* in the process of social transformation. Additionally, rather than considering the evidence of the natural and physical sciences as antithetical, positivist and thus intellectually inadmissible, we must adopt a more catholic standpoint and recognize that the manifest complexities of human societal systems can only be sensibly approached by the admission of as many and varied levels of description as possible into our theoretical frameworks (van der Leeuw 1989, p. 306). Thus we assert the heuristic potential of a measure of *theoretical plurality* as a necessary step in the construction of an alternative approach to the dynamics of change.

The evolution of complex systems

Spontaneous social orders

We have seen that the problem of understanding the long-term behaviour of societal systems is inextricably bound up with questions of 'origins' and 'innovation' (van der Leeuw 1990b), which we might more generally and neutrally subsume under the heading *structural transformation*. From this it follows that the central issue in any discussion of cultural dynamics concerns the problem of *emergence*: i.e., the role of phenomena such as collective action or the spontaneous generation of new modes of behaviour; particularly the propensity for social groups and organizations to generate options which are the result of unplanned or unanticipated outcomes. As archaeologists we should be fundamentally concerned with the structural development of emergent phenomena, for herein lies the key, not only to a better characterization of social complexity, but to an understanding of the relationship between order and disorder. Moreover, to a large extent, it is these processes which are implicated in the construction and evolution of the *spatial inhomogeneity* which we recognize in the archaeological landscape.

Any attempt to deal with the morphogenetic properties of social systems must acknowledge the important role played by unforeseen events and the fact that actions often combine to produce unintended consequences (Boudon 1982). Such processes can generate a whole class of phenomena we might define as the *spontaneous structuring of social order*. Such ideas have formed core research interests within sociology, but have had, as yet, little impact in either anthropology or archaeology.

Much of the impetus for the study of spontaneous social orders can be traced back to the work of Scottish Enlightenment figures such as David Hume (1711–76), Adam Ferguson (1723–1816), and Adam Smith (1723–90). Ferguson's approach to the subject is characteristically perceptive:

> Every step and every moment of the multitude, even in what are termed the enlightened ages, are made with equal blindness to the future; and nations stumble upon establishments, which are indeed the result of human action, but not the execution of any human design.
>
> (Ferguson 1767, p. 122)

But perhaps the most familiar manifestation of this tradition is to be found in the writings of Adam Smith, particularly his oft quoted 'invisible hand' explanation of market dynamics. Thus although an individual participant in the market 'intends only to his [or her] own gain . . . he [or she] is in this, as in many other cases, led by an invisible hand to promote an end which was no party of his [or her] intention' (Ferguson 1767, p. 214).

Smith's ideas were to exert a significant influence on the nineteenth century, largely through the works of the economist Carl Menger (e.g. 1982), who made an important contribution to the spontaneous order tradition with his invisible-hand account of the origins of money. Before Menger's intervention, it was a commonly held assumption that money owed its origins to a deliberate invention of the state, or was the product of social convention (Cronk 1988, p. 291). Continuing this economic theme, more recently Mary Douglas has postulated what can be described as a spontaneous order explanation for the operation of an exchange rate system among the Lele:

> In such transactions there is an appearance of centrally imposed control, but it is deceptive. No central governing body imposes the rates of exchange. The exchange control emerges by the decisions of individuals striving to hold to their position of advantage in a particular social structure.
>
> (Douglas 1967, p. 145)

However, the most prominent exponent of spontaneous organization within societal structures has been F.A. Hayek (1948, 1977, 1983). His main contribution has been directed at the role of knowledge and the way in which it generates coherent structure within social institutions, even though separate individuals possess different and incomplete fragments of the pool of available knowledge at any one time. Like Smith and Menger before him, Hayek also saw the marketplace as the quintessential example of spontaneous social order.

It was for these reasons that Hayek was convinced that the vast majority of human institutions which have formed the core of societal organization throughout history have emerged 'without a designing and directing mind' (1948, pp. 6–7): it is in this sense that they are self-producing and self-organizing systems. Such views are entirely consistent with those of Touraine (1977), who has stressed the fact that first and foremost society is an agent of its own self-production, and that embedded in this process, we encounter unintended and spontaneous social arrangements. We are thus led to the fact that we must consider the emergent properties latent in all human social organization as a fundamental self-organizing principle.

The evolutionary importance of instability

As with the social sciences, the capacity of many physical, chemical and biological systems to spontaneously generate structure is well known (e.g., Turing 1952; Haken 1977; Nicolis and Prigogine 1977), but it has received scant attention in archaeology and the social sciences generally (cf. Renfrew *et al.* 1982; McGlade 1990). A great deal of research has shown that a wide diversity of natural organizations ranging from cells to ecosystems, comprises regimes that may be triggered by instability. The observation that spatio-temporal patterning can occur in systems far from equilibrium, first made by Rashevsky (1940) and Turing (1952), has more recently been developed by Prigogine and co-workers who have coined the term 'order through fluc-tuation' to describe the process (e.g. Nicolis and Prigogine 1977). The fundamental point is that *non-equilibrium* behaviour – as an intrinsic property of social systems – can act as a source of *self-organization*, and hence may be the driving force behind qualitative restructuring as the system 'evolves' from one state to another.

These types of evolved structures, 'dissipative structures' as they are known, rely on the action of fluctuations – which are damped below a critical threshold and have little effect on the system but become amplified beyond this threshold and generate new macroscopic order. Thus, within this paradigm, evolution occurs as a series of *phase transitions* between disordered and ordered states; successive bifurcations generating new ordered structure. The critical role accorded to non-equilibrium depends on the interaction between perturba-tions which are endogenously created, and random fluctuations which are created by the environment.

It is argued here that the dissipative structures approach to evolutionary change is conceptually superior to the linear and step-wise solutions of conven-tional neo-evolutionary schemes, and is potentially a useful analogue for some aspects of societal development. It presents us with a morphogenetic metaphor which lends itself to the description and interpretation of discontinuous patterns of change. This metaphor places emphasis on the essential *disequilib-rium* properties at work within social systems, allowing us to focus on *thresholds* which may be identified as precursors of social transformation. As a conse-quence, evolution may proceed precisely because of the *non-adaptedness* or *non-optimal* states within system structure (cf. Allen and McGlade 1987a, 1987b, 1987c, 1989).

Instability, far from being an aberration within a 'stable' system, becomes fundamental to the reproduction of the social order. The long-term evolu-tion of societal structure can be seen as a history of discontinuity in social space; i.e., history not as a finely spun homogeneous fabric, but as being punctuated by a sequence of phase changes as the result of both conscious and unintended actions. Such discontinuities are in fact thresholds of change, where the role of human agency and/or idiosyncratic behaviours assumes paramount significance in the production and reproduction of societal struc-tures. At the highest level of transformation, these bifurcations represent fundamental changes in perception.

Clearly the conditions around which social configurations become unstable and subsequently reorganize or change course have no inherent predictability; the diversity which characterizes all human behaviour guarantees this. It is this diversity which is critically important from an evolutionary perspective, for it accounts for the system's 'evolutionary drive' (Allen and McGlade 1987c,

p. 726). The existence of idiosyncratic and stochastic risk-taking behaviours acts to maintain a degree of evolutionary 'slack' within social systems; error-making strategies are thus crucially important. In fact, without the operation of such *non-optimal* and unstable behaviours, we effectively reduce the degrees of freedom in the system and, hence, severely constrain its creative potential for evolutionary transformation.

Order, disorder and chaos

One of the enduring issues isolated by the above methods is the importance of positive feedback or self-reinforcing mechanisms as Arthur (1988, p. 10) has characterized them. Processes such as reproduction, co-operation, and competition at the interface of individual and community levels can, under specific conditions of enhancement, generate unstable and potentially trans-formative behaviour. Instability is seen as a product of self-reinforcing or autocatalytic structures operating within sets of human relationships and at higher aggregate levels of societal organization. This is clearly the case both in population dynamics and within complex exchange and redistribution processes. Of crucial importance to an understanding of these issues is the fact that networks of relationships are prone to collapse or transformation, independent of the application of any external force, process or information. Our earlier point is worth reiterating: instability is an *intrinsic* part of the internal dynamic of the system.

The complexity of social systems is in large part a consequence of the existence of multiple modes of operation, and hence of multiple sets of decision-making criteria. Thus, much of the inherent instability in, for example, exchange systems reflects the dominance of highly non-linear inter-actions. It is the role of such non-linearities which has led to observations on the emergence of erratic, aperiodic fluctuations in the behaviour of bio-logical populations (May and Oster 1976) and in the spread of epidemics (Schaffer and Kot 1985a, 1985b). These highly irregular fluctuations (often dismissed as environmental 'noise') are manifestations of *deterministic chaos*. First described in a seminal paper by Lorenz (1963) and later given formal definition by Li and Yorke (1975), the important contribution of this work was in demonstrating that chaotic behaviour was a property of, among others, purely *deterministic* systems, i.e., systems unperturbed by extraneous noise.

As a result of subsequent observations in the physical, chemical and bio-logical sciences, there is now emerging something of a consensus on the role of chaotic dynamics in the time evolution of systems as diverse as global climatic regimes and physiological processes such as blood flow. We now know with some certainty that the seeds of aperiodic, chaotic trajectories are embedded in all self-replicating systems, and these intrinsic non-linear inter-actions have become the object of intensive study. Such systems have no inherent equilibrium but are characterized by the existence of multiple equi-libria and sets of coexisting attractors to which the system is drawn and between which it may oscillate.

An equally important characteristic displayed by all chaotic systems, whether biological or physical, is that, given any observational point, it is impossible to make accurate long-term predictions (in the conventional scientific sense) of their behaviour. This property has come to be known as 'sensitivity to initial conditions' (Ruelle 1979, p. 408), and simply means that nearby trajectories will diverge on average exponentially.

For biological, ecological, and by implication social systems, the discovery of self-induced complex dynamics is of profound importance, since we can now identify a powerful source of *emergent behaviour*. The root of the heterogeneous and asymmetric behaviours observed in the archaeological landscape may not prove as intractable as they appear; the creation of spatially inhomogeneous structures may indeed have chaotic origins. Far from promoting any pathological trait, the aperiodic oscillations resident in chaotic dynamics may yet perform a significant operational role in the evolution of the system, principally by increasing the degrees of freedom within which it operates. This is another way of saying that chaos promotes *flexibility*, which in turn promotes *diversity*.

These findings throw light on some of the problems inherent in the concept of adaptation – as we have seen already, a little-understood concept in sociocultural evolution. Briefly put, since the existence of chaos severely calls into question concepts such as density dependent growth in human and biological populations, we might be able to see a theoretical solution in the coexistence of multiple attractors defining a flexible domain of adaptation, rather than any single state. We thus arrive at a paradox where chaos becomes responsible for enhancing the *robustness* of the system.

Modelling complex societal systems

Linear versus non-linear systems

If we are to understand complex societal systems as essentially the product of non-linear evolution, then we must first make clear the basic difference between linear and non-linear processes.

Until relatively recently the pre-eminence of physics within western scientific thought – particularly under the influence of Newtonian mechanics – meant that 'explanation' was resident in a kind of mechanical causality. In effect, this explanatory paradigm was merely a descriptive exercise such that understanding system behaviour became synonymous with the enumeration of a set of functional relationships (cf. Allen 1985). The linear consequences of this type of causality were, moreover, enshrined in the goal of prediction. A useful example of such linearity can be seen in conventional systems theory, where the output of a process or behaviour is directly proportional to the input; as a practical example, we might take the first law of thermodynamics, which is a statement of energy conservation, and represent it as a balance equation, thus:

$$\text{change in state} = \frac{\text{inputs} - \text{outputs}}{\text{unit time}}$$

where the state variable could be an expression of mass, energy or momentum. Another way of conceptualizing these ideas of proportionality is to say that the response (R) of a physical system is linear, for example, when it is directly proportional to some applied force (F); algebraically we have:

$$R = \mu F + \beta$$

where μ and β are constants. When there is no response in the absence of applied force, then we have $\beta = 0$. Our linear system, then, can be described as one where two distinct forces F_1 and F_2 are applied and which has the response $S = \mu_1 F_1 + \mu_2 F_2$, where μ_1 and μ_2 are independent constants.

From our current perspective, perhaps the most serious limitation of a linear world-view is that it actively precludes or misrepresents the evolutionary potential of all natural and social systems – particularly the propensity of complex systems to generate emergent unanticipated behaviours (Allen and McGlade 1986, 1987c). These occur precisely as a consequence of the non-linear couplings which are embedded in the system.

From a philosophical perspective, it might be said that the first thing that a non-linear dynamical perspective does is to effectively destroy historical causation as a linear, progressive unfolding of events. It forces us to reconceptualize history as a series of contingent structurings which are the outcome of an interplay between deterministic and stochastic processes. The material residue of these structurings and restructurings comes down to us as the archaeological record and we are faced with the daunting task of interpreting not just a physical palimpsest, but also the symbolic and cultural conventions within which the material remains are situated.

In doing so, moreover, we have to take into account the difference between *complication* and *complexity*, the fact that the principal distinguishing feature of any complex system is that it is fundamentally irreducible – it is more than the sum of its component parts. The existence of non-linear interactions at the heart of complex systems actively precludes any reductionist epistemology.

The manifest equilibrium tendencies of linear systems concepts as they are used in archaeology (e.g., linear programming and optimal foraging models) also stand in contrast to their non-linear counterparts by virtue of the latter's ability to operate beyond the bounds of a single steady state; i.e., non-linear systems possess the ability to generate emergent behaviour and have the potential for multiple domains of stability. Non-linear systems can thus be described as occupying a state space or 'possibility space' within which multiple domains of attraction are possible. For societal systems, this is a consequence of the fact that (a) they are governed by feedback or self-reinforcing processes, and (b) they are coupled to environmental forces which are either stochastic or periodically driven.

Dynamical systems

Before discussing the question of dynamical systems and their evolution, we might first introduce an important distinction; i.e., the difference between dyna*mic* systems concepts and their use in archaeology and dyna*mical* systems theory or qualitative non-linear dynamics.

In the context used here, *dynamic* models include all models which are explicitly concerned with the time evolution of a set of events or processes. Indeed, within archaeology, such formal modelling approaches may be said to emanate from the important contributions provided by Doran (1970) and Clarke (1968, 1972), who not only argued for the utility of explicit modelling procedures but, more importantly, emphasized the broad, *heuristic* nature of such enterprises. Additionally, we can identify a number of studies spawned by these exemplars which sought to use simulation modelling as a means of generating quantitative prediction (e.g., Thomas 1972; Hodder 1978; Renfrew and Cooke 1979; Sabloff 1981). In this book, Mithen's contribution (Chapter 7) is generally following this line of argument to simulate the relationship between hunter-gatherer decision-making behaviour and mammoth population dynamics.

An implicit assumption in many of these modelling exercises was that simulation constituted an imitation of 'reality', and that there existed a linear correlation between the amount of data included and the model's successful representation of that reality (McGlade 1987, p. 24). This philosophy aligned itself with a desire for larger and ever more complex models as the route to sophisticated prediction. In fact such a strategy runs directly counter to sound modelling wisdom, which is consistent with the principle of parsimony of Occam's razor: less is more.[2]

As we have seen, *dynamical* modelling approaches operate from a radically different set of epistemological assumptions, eschewing the search for quantitative prediction in favour of identifying the qualitative dynamics underpinning system evolution, and defined by particular attractors which characterize non-linear system behaviour. One of the main contributions of dynamical systems methods has undeniably been in the detection of turbulent aperiodicities which we associate with chaos, since such behaviour effectively undermines the goal of prediction – for so long the *raison d'être* of much scientific enterprise.

The inherent *unpredictability* of non-linear systems was first alluded to long ago by Poincaré: 'It may happen that small differences in the initial conditions produce very great ones in the final phenomena. A small error in the former will produce an enormous error in the latter. Prediction becomes impossible' (Poincaré 1899, *passim*).

Poincaré's precocious insights were, however, to remain virtually unknown until the early 1960s, when significant advances in the power of computers 'rediscovered' deterministic chaos. Importantly, high-speed computation not only provided insights into the structure of previously intractable mathematical problems, but, more significantly, it allowed system trajectories and their topological structure to be realized as geometric objects in state space. An additional offshoot of increased computing power is that it has finally laid to rest Laplace's vision of infinite predictability; rather than increasing our predictive capabilities in non-linear systems the reverse has occurred, for it has been shown that the motion of relatively simple dynamical systems cannot be unfailingly predicted into the future because of their susceptibility to chaos (Lorenz 1963).

Generally speaking, when we define a dynamical system we are referring to a system whose time evolution from some initial state can be described by a set of rules, which can be expressed as mathematical equations. The evolution of such a system is acted out in so-called *phase space*. These ideas can be illustrated by considering the simple example of the motion of a pendulum. If a pendulum is allowed to move back and forth from some initial starting condition as described in Figure 1.1, we can describe its initial state by recourse to speed and position. From whatever starting values, of position and velocity, it returns to its initial vertical state, damped by air resistance and other forms of energy dissipation – a classic dissipative structure. The two-dimensional phase space in which the pendulum dynamics are acted out, is defined by co-ordinates, displacement and velocity. All motions converge asymptotically towards an equilibrium state referred to as a *point attractor*, since it 'attracts' all trajectories in the phase space; moreover, the system's long-term predictability is guaranteed.

A second type of attractor common in dynamical systems is a *limit cycle*, which we have already encountered in our discussion of organizational ecologies. The representation of a limit cycle in phase space indicates periodic motion (Figure 1.2) and, like the point attractor, this type of attractor is stable

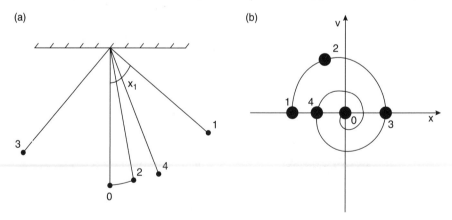

Figure 1.1 Diagram showing a well-known example of a point attractor. The pendulum in (a) swings from 1 to 3 and back, but eventually it loses its momentum and comes to focus on a single point (0). (b) shows the trajectory as a relationship between v (speed) and x (position) in relation to 0.

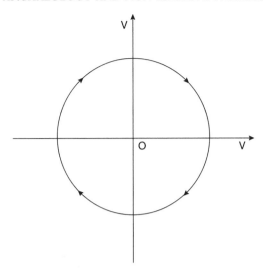

Figure 1.2 Diagram of a limit-cycle attractor. The point (ideally) follows the circle around point 0 forever.

and hence guarantees long-term predictability. A third form of attractor is known as a *torus* and resembles the surface of a doughnut (Figure 1.3). Systems governed by a torus are quasi-periodic; i.e., one periodic motion is modulated by a second one which is operating on a different frequency. This combination produces a time-series whose structure is not clear and in some circumstances can be mistaken for chaos; this is illusory, however, since the torus is ultimately governed by wholly predictable dynamics. An important facet of toroidal attractors is that although they are not especially common, quasi-periodic motion is often observed during the transition from one typical type of motion to another. As Stewart (1989, p. 105) points out, they can

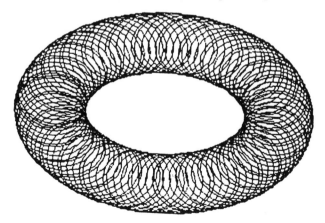

Figure 1.3 Diagram of a torus-shaped trajectory which is the result of a combination of two oscillations with different periodicities.

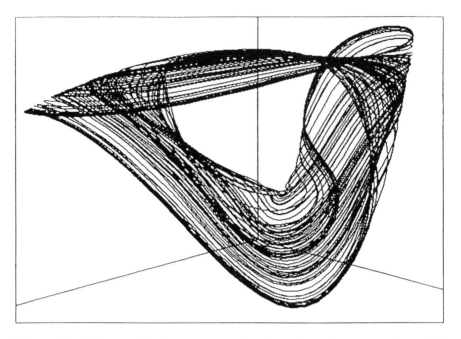

Figure 1.4 Diagram of a 'strange attractor', where the trajectory remains within certain limits, but never repeats itself.

provide a useful point of departure for analyses of more complex aperiodicities such as chaos. Lastly, we encounter the most complex and bizarre attractor of all, the so-called *strange* or chaotic *attractor*[3] (Figure 1.4). This species of attractor is characterized by motion which is neither periodic nor quasi-periodic, but completely aperiodic such that prediction of the long-term behaviour of its time evolution is impossible. None the less, over long time periods, regularities may emerge giving to the attractor a degree of global stability, even though at a local level it is completely unstable. In this respect Schaffer and Kot have noted that: 'To the extent that these regularities can be detected in real world data, it follows that fluctuations heretofore believed due to chance are in fact deterministic' (1986, p. 342).

An additional feature of chaotic attractors is that they are characterized by non-integer or fractal dimensions (Farmer *et al.* 1983). Each of the apparent lines in the phase space trajectory, when greatly magnified, is seen to be composed of additional lines which themselves are structured in like manner. This infinite structure is the hallmark of fractal geometries.

As a final observation in this classification of dynamical systems and attracting sets (which is dealt with in more detail in Erwin's contribution, Chapter 3), we should note that beyond the complexity of low-dimensional strange attractors we encounter the full-blown chaos characterized by *turbulence*; indeed, to a large extent, the quintessential manifestation of chaotic behaviour is to be found in turbulent flows. As demonstrations of this highly erratic state, we might cite the motion of a rising column of smoke, the eddies behind a boat or an aircraft wing as providing particularly graphic examples.

Above all, the important point distinguishing these chaotic phenomena from random or stochastic processes is that they contain no unpredictable inputs or parameters. Their overriding attribute is their sensitive dependence on initial conditions (Ruelle 1979, p. 408); i.e., the chaotic state is locally unstable such that the smallest microscopic perturbation can result in a new trajectory which diverges exponentially from the initial starting point.

Implications for the human sciences

We argue that dynamical systems approaches have a great deal to contribute to our understanding of societal structuring, and particularly social process viewed as a non-linear evolutionary phenomenon.

In searching for correspondence between models of natural and social process, it is clear that at a macroscopic level both share discontinuous properties defined by symmetry-breaking instabilities. Discontinuity promoted by non-linear interactions operates to generate novel structural possibilities both at the molecular level and at a corresponding societal level. Sudden changes of state or qualitative transformations form an integral part of all social processes (cf. Weidlich and Haag 1983); indeed, interest in the dynamics which generate structural change has recently attracted a great deal of attention as a consequence of the profound social and political changes occurring in central Europe, particularly the rise of democratic social movements within totalitarian communist states.

However, a crucial distinction must be made here when employing natural science metaphors or analogies: human populations which are affected by discontinuities and perturbations constantly alter their behaviour and hence affect the phenomenon itself in a self-reinforcing manner. It is this ability – the hallmark of social action – which creates the fundamental distinction separating the social from the natural sciences (Mayntz 1989). Additionally, while human social organizations may be said to share some characteristics with their biological counterparts, they are not organisms. One single human being, for example, is capable of radically influencing and altering the behaviour, attitudes and ideological motives of another – something not possible in the animal kingdom.

The conceptual shift implied by an emphasis on discontinuous, emergent properties of societal systems is attractive precisely because of its emphasis on social structures as self-organizing entities within complex open systems; it calls into question conventional attitudes to the homogeneity of time and space. Thus we move from a world defined by classical symmetric properties to one in which the reality of non-equilibria at the heart of societal organization acts to promote symmetry-breaking instabilities.

From an evolutionary perspective – defined here as *structural elaboration* rather than developmental complexity – this means that the process of structural transformation can result in a wide diversity of evolutionary patterns; indeed, a whole behavioural spectrum is possible, ranging from equilibrium and homeorhetic states on the one hand to an array of complex unstable trajectories on the other.

Perhaps the most important contribution to an understanding of such discontinuous dynamics is provided by the kinds of structured disorder represented by chaotic behaviour. That the seeds of chaos are potentially resident in even the most elementary positive feedback mechanisms is of undoubted significance from our perspective. Societal systems abound with such self-reinforcing connections, especially since their evolution is articulated by processes such as reproduction, co-operation and competition. Under these conditions, the generation of unstable dynamics is readily explicable; the potential for social transformation is thus intrinsic to the system. What needs to be 'explained' is stability rather than change.

Some issues

We end this introduction with an overview which touches upon the main issues raised in the following chapters, highlighting some aspects and placing some notes at the end of each chapter. It is worth pointing out that the book comprises three parts. It begins with four chapters which discuss aspects of dynamical approaches proposed outside archaeology. They present a general background, focus on some of the different kinds of non-linear dynamics which have thus far been recognized in a range of disciplines, on some of the limitations of the approach, and they present some examples. Their centre of gravity is, however, methodological. Next are eight chapters which apply various kinds of modelling techniques. Most of these touch on subjects or discussions which are familiar to archaeologists, and many have been written by, or together with, archaeologists. The final section discusses issues relating to the place and role of modelling in (archaeological and social science) research.

Each of the three parts of the book is introduced by a few pages written by the editors which, we hope, serve to facilitate reading of the chapters by archaeologists who do not have the requisite theoretical background.

The general perspective

A critically important message (and one conveyed in many of the succeeding chapters) is that a mature theoretical archaeology – one divested of the spurious and self-conscious processual/post-processual dichotomy – with its sights set on an understanding of long-term societal development, cannot afford to ignore recent research in the natural sciences; their summary proscription to the realms of the 'illegitimate' or the 'irrelevant' implied by adherents of post-processual orthodoxy, is both naive and ill-considered. It represents not only the promotion of an exclusive epistemological arena within which archaeological interpretation takes place but, more importantly, a serious misconception of the intrinsic complexity of human systems, for example with respect to human/environmental interaction. Issues such as social change cannot be successfully constituted as the sole preserve of reflexive social action, but rather as a dynamic interaction in which social agency, decision-making and societal organization are seen to be embedded in the natural world. This set of structuring relations can be illuminated by the application of models and insights derived from non-linear dynamical approaches.

It follows from its cross-disciplinary nature that the application of a non-linear approach to questions in archaeology depends on the successful transfer of concepts between disciplines. To those who question such a strategy, we would respond that in our opinion the use of transferred concepts is not necessarily less appropriate, or less efficient than the use of concepts developed within the discipline concerned. One can indeed question whether a discipline which strives to study human behaviour in the past, using relatively scarce material remains as its principal source, is indeed in a position to develop all its own concepts and approaches. Neither does it seem possible, or even desirable, to keep such a discipline free from ideas developed in other fields of research endeavour which have human behaviour as their subject. The critical element is the way in which the concept travels, how it is made to feel at home in its new environment, and how it is used, intelligently or not. Inevitably there are difficulties, but these should not be a reason to abandon the exercise altogether. It serves no purpose whatsoever to judge a discipline or an intellectual venture by its worst examples.

Yet it is important to be aware of some fundamental differences between the disciplines in which dynamical modelling was first developed and those in which we wish to use the approach. In the former, and notably the natural sciences, the phenomena studied are relatively easily 'objectifiable': observations can be repeated and in a sense the process of gathering knowledge about them is one of reaching agreement on an intersubjectively acceptable way of describing and controlling them in the present and the future. Transposing such ideas to the description of social processes in the modern world seems within reach, as some of the following chapters show (e.g., Pumain, Chapter 4).

In archaeology, however, control is out of the question, firstly because the phenomena concerned had their role in the past, and are infinitely more complex. Moreover, the density of data is so much less that underdetermination (cf. Atlan 1992) of the theories does not allow us to perceive more than a *pointillé* outline of past dynamics. There is as yet no question of scrutinizing any dynamics in such detail that intersubjectivity is attainable to the degree it is in the natural sciences. Rather than building up knowledge about the past, we are trying to *understand* the past by linking the different bits of *pointillé* into a configuration.[4] From that perspective, it seems that archaeology's discussion about acceptable epistemologies is premature, and that an equally serious discussion about the ontology of archaeological data is long overdue (cf. Murray, Chapter 17). Nowhere is that more clear than when archaeologists are confronted with the ethnographic realities of cultural systems which have fundamentally different spatial, temporal and causal perceptions, and in which individuals therefore make their decisions along lines which we often cannot even fathom. The absence of a discussion on ontology in the context of structuration is, in our opinion, one of the major deficiencies of the theory of post-processualist archaeology.

Models and modelling

The next set of questions touches on the admissibility of modelling and the status of models. One of the principal aims of the present book is the assertion of both the utility and the importance of formal modelling procedures as a means of elucidating some of the non-linear interactions that underwrite the processes that are ultimately responsible for structuring evolutionary dynamics. Although much controversy surrounds the idea of modelling itself, it is in our opinion largely through the construction of models – as a continuous activity – that we as humans understand and impose a coherent rationale on knowledge structures, behaviour and events. Models in the sense used here follow Waddington's (1977) definition in which they are conceived as 'tools for thought'. They help us to uncover some of the more complex patterns and processes, otherwise imperceptible by conventional statistical analytical methods.

However, it is critically important to realize that whereas models act as descriptive analogues of real world phenomena, they must not – nor should they ever – be confused with explanations of these (McGlade 1987, p. 22). The real world is too complex to be modelled. All that we can hope to do is to model small areas or aspects of it and hope thus to enhance our understanding. Hence our stress on poly-ocularity and the need to search for ever more dimensions of variation behind the phenomena observed.

Following some of the remarks on migrant concepts just presented, one might distinguish between those models which serve to reduce observed complexity and those that serve to enhance it. In the physical and formal sciences the tendency has been to strip observations further and further down, to formalize maximally, in order to allow for discussion without misunderstanding. In archaeology phenomena cannot be stripped, they have to be dressed in order to reconstruct the reasons for the particular configurations of remains we have found. The essence of the social phenomena responsible for them is their complexity. Thus formalization has a different function – not to create intersubjectivity but to explicate intuition. Even a model which uses formalization is in many cases necessarily a metaphor in archaeology.

Models can come in all kinds and sizes (Apostel 1960), and many of the choices which a researcher makes in building one depend on the future model's function. We argue here for the importance of a modelling perspective that operates at a high level of abstraction, as being particularly suited to understanding long-term dynamical processes. Sanders (1992, p. 33) cogently argues that a high level of abstraction has the advantage of making calibration easy and, while leaving a wide gap between the model and any potential 'reality', allowing very flexible and insightful application to a wide range of situations. Realistic and detailed models on the other hand, ready for use by planners and decision-makers, are very difficult to calibrate because they include so much detail and are much less flexible and therefore not usable in such a wide range of cases for heuristic purposes.[5]

In this book, several authors raise important issues about the adequacy and status of formal models. Chapman (Chapter 15) first examines the different levels of complexity of phenomena, and comments on the way dynamics and structure relate at these different levels. Next, he considers some implications of these ideas for the modelling of dynamics and structure. The second part of his chapter looks at a specific way of describing complex hierarchies and its utility in considering a restricted range of phenomena in the social sciences. He then examines a particular rigorous definition of structure and asks whether it is useful for classifying structures into groups which have a similar structure vector, with the aspiration that they might also have similar patterns of dynamics.

Rosen's chapter (Chapter 14) is concerned with an aspect of the following question: what kinds of models can a system generically have? Usually, it is tacitly supposed that models must be simulable, or computable, or formalizable. He argues that this is, in fact, an exceedingly non-generic property to require of a putative model, and that it can hold only for systems which are themselves highly exceptional (non-generic). We call a system for which every model is computable a simple system, or mechanism. A system which is not simple, and hence has non-computable models, we call complex.

He explores one aspect of complexity, and its implications for modelling, by looking at dynamical systems, which are always computable. In particular, he asks 'what is a generic perturbation of a dynamical system?' and shows that computability (i.e., simplicity) is not preserved by such perturbations and concludes by suggesting that complex systems may be regarded as limits of their simple models.

Notwithstanding Rosen's cogent argument, it seems to us that the encoding of, for example, human/environmental relations as formal mathematical models may provide us with a set of exploratory tools that allow us to grasp the qualitative dynamics which may be said to form the 'deep structure' of any non-linear system. Additionally, these analytical methods may be thought of as potential bridging mechanisms; i.e., better able to articulate the relationship between micro and macroscopic processes. Ultimately, what we have is an alternative evolutionary dynamic (Allen, Chapter 2) in which concepts of order and disorder within socio-cultural systems are no longer conceived as diametrically opposed, but rather as different facets of a non-linear continuum. McGlade (Chapter 12) presents an instructive example of the inherent transitions between order and chaos, and argues that within this inter-structural reality resides much of the dynamics we encounter as the archaeological record.

The processes

We thus reiterate the need for a shift in our perceptions away from the temporal and structural frameworks which are currently employed in archaeological approaches to the long term. Van der Leeuw (1990b, p. 92) (paraphrasing the nineteenth-century historian Schlegel) has compared the archaeologist to a prophet standing with his back to the future and looking into the past predicting the origin of known phenomena from a perspective diametrically opposed to that within which humans in the past made decisions about their future. He concludes that the archaeologist should, as it were, travel back in time and look forward with those being studied.

This clearly has consequences for a number of the questions we usually ask of archaeological data. We have already referred to the fact that the success of this approach in representing hitherto inexplicable behaviour of a wide range of systems sheds a different light on one of the fundamental assumptions underlying most scientific explanation, the concept of causality. McGlade (Chapter 12) and others show how unexpected system behaviour, which does not fit the usual idea of cause-and-effect, can 'suddenly' occur in an otherwise regular process.

As Allen shows in Chapter 2, the theoretical and methodological tools provided by a dynamical systems approach allow us to reconceptualize the evolutionary behaviour of complex human systems from a non-linear dynamic perspective – one in which discontinuity and bifurcation are seen as intrinsic properties of open, dissipative systems. Systems which depend for their resilience and continued existence as much on non-replicative behaviour as they do on replication.

The focus on system *resilience*, that is the capacity of a system to survive by changing 'in tune' with its environment, not only draws attention to the importance of non-replicative ('innovative') behaviour, but also to the fact that from this perspective it is change which is assumed and stability which is questioned, rather than vice versa. As change is assumed to occur non-linearly in many cases, it is often important to have an idea of the *change of change* before change itself can be qualified and/or quantified at any point of the system's trajectory. This has fundamental consequences for many disciplines, of the general nature outlined by Pumain (Chapter 4), who tries to reconstruct long-term models of urban development.

Although such very long-term models often are virtually impossible to formalize in a testable manner, they ought to be present in the back of our minds when we formulate ideas concerning shorter-term developments. It probably serves an important purpose that such models are made explicit and subjected to scrutiny.

The transitions (bifurcations) between system states which are themselves dominated by various kinds of attractors are in effect expressions of existing fields of tension between those attractors, as is lucidly outlined by Erwin (Chapter 3) in his description of various classes of system behaviour.

His contribution places Renfrew and Cooke's (1979) approach to 'Catastrophe theory' in a wider perspective, sketching the many other kinds of bifurcation which could occur, and thus enriches our dialogue with the archaeological record.

The focus on non-linear dynamics has also changed our perspective on space and time. McGlade (Chapter 12) refers to the fact that our awareness of non-linear phenomena puts density-dependent spatial phenomena in a new light, and our conception of time is reviewed by Murray (Chapter 17), who argues that the growing importance of radiometric dating is one example of the kind of contraction and impoverishment of the archaeologists' perspective which we have already mentioned: it implies the imposition of a universal, external, analytical dimension on what is a highly individual non-linear phenomenon which is dependent on experiential and highly contextual attributes.

In ecology, awareness of this problem has led to a focus on the range of temporal rhythms occurring in any ecosystem, and to the changes which the symbiosis with humans imposes on those rhythms. Van der Leeuw argues (1990a, pp. 307–8) that these changes are to a considerable degree, if not entirely, responsible for unexpected occurrences in the human/environmental co-evolution.

The data

Wobst evaluates (Chapter 16) the metrologies of the early New Archaeology and the early post-processual archaeology for their sensitivity to change and variation in the terms of their respective paradigms. He suggests that despite massive paradigm changes over the last thirty years there has been relatively little change in metrology, and even less of that change in metrology has been theorized in the terms of the given paradigms. It is our understanding that this may well have been the most fatal flaw of archaeological theory in the last three decades. Quite often, the metrology turns out to have been contradictory if not inimical to the understanding of change and variation. This is shown most clearly at the lowest level of analysis, where both maintained the 'type' concept, even though the kinds of types they defined did change. By maintaining the basic procedure of archaeological data collection, they continued the systematic suppression of information which is inherent in that approach, and consequently inhibited the development of methods to elicit data which would corroborate or falsify the ideas (van der Leeuw 1991, p. 28). Wobst concludes that if we want to better understand change in human systems, in a framework of agency and structuration, we need to take theoretical control of all aspects of our research enterprise. This includes theorizing even the most 'non-sexy' aspects of mensuration, lest we contribute unthinkingly to the naturalization of distasteful 'structures of measurement' and, thus, to our own material enslavement. Such theorizing should, among other things, pay much more attention to the problem of levels of generalization and the appropriate resolution of mensuration at each of these levels.

Pumain (Chapter 4) shows how the overall pattern of a size hierarchy in heterarchical systems remains stable, while the position of the individual cities is only comprehensible when viewed at a smaller, more local scale.

This problem is in part congruent with that of model calibration in archaeology. Those involved in non-linear modelling know that it is difficult to calibrate many models even under the best of circumstances, and that without careful calibration the non-linear nature of many relationships in such models may very easily lead to fallacious models or unrealistic system behaviour in view of the sensitivity to initial conditions. In archaeology, such calibration is at present only possible in extraordinary circumstances. This may for the moment well be the main constraint in the use of formal non-linear models in the discipline, limiting our capacity to answer many questions, and confining us in many instances to metaphoric use and/or the investigation of generic models. But in our opinion it would be wrong to ignore the potential of the non-linear approach for such reasons as long as the metrology has not been developed to deal with variation and diversity in archaeological data in an enriching way (cf. van der Leeuw 1991).

New areas of research

The relationship between data and theories in archaeology is at present one of overwhelming underdetermination of theories. But we assert that this is probably to a large extent due to a century's attempt to systematically impoverish the information delivered by the archaeological record through universal stress on similarities, averages and 'types'. We suspect that asking different questions, looking for different relationships, we might well find whole areas of archaeology where underdetermination is not necessary in view of the enormous – and growing – effort put into excavation and survey on all sides.

A number of contributions in this book suggest that we might profitably look to the area of learning and cognition for a way forward. Doran (Chapter 11), for example, attempts to model the behaviour of a number of individual agents in the Upper Palaeolithic on a Distributed Artificial Intelligence testbed. In his case, however, it is not clear to what extent exactly the behaviour of these agents depends on their perception, cognition or decision-making behaviour. All three are implicated in what is essentially a behaviouristic attempt at modelling.

Both King and Lindh (Chapter 9) and Reynolds (Chapter 10) attempt to gain a better understanding of the role of learning and cultural transmission of information against the background of the genetic transmission of information. King and Lindh do this by designing an automaton which simulates features of the transfer of information between generations of a species. It illustrates that strategies of information transfer that involve sexual transfer of information including recessive information (strategies that we term 'Darwinian'), are more effective than Lamarckian strategies when coping with a fractally varying environment. Reynolds (Chapter 10) approaches essentially the same question by building an 'autonomous learning system'. He demonstrates through running simulations on it that a hybrid system which includes both genetic and cultural information transmission is indeed more effective than any system which uses but one of these transmission modes. But whereas King and Lindh are primarily concerned with diversity of response (and thus adaptability) in the face of an environment, Reynolds is concerned with rates of learning.

Mithen's contribution (Chapter 7) is concerned with the effect of human choice (between predation strategies) on the population dynamics of mammoths in the Palaeolithic, and demonstrates effectively that a change in strategy can explain mammoth extinction just as effectively as any environmental fluctuation or other exogenous factor. Glance and Huberman (Chapter 5) and van der Leeuw and McGlade (Chapter 13) discuss the importance of information processing at yet another level, that of the society as a whole. Much of Huberman's work to date has focused on eliciting the topological constraints underlying multiple-actor information processing structures, and the phase transitions between what might in our context be called 'egalitarian', 'hierarchical' and 'market' modes of information processing. These ideas are employed by van der Leeuw and McGlade in their attempt to retrace some of the steps which have led to fundamental changes in social structure through the ages, and notably in approximating the dynamics which led to the emergence of towns. In Chapter 5, Glance and Huberman turn their attention towards the relationship between present and future, studying the impact of different ways of generating expectations about the future on a system of individuals. One of their conclusions is similar to their earlier work: variation in expectations makes for a more stable system than uniformity.

Finally, it should be stated that what we are presenting is not so much a coherent agenda for archaeological theory and practice; our aim is simply to demonstrate the great potential of non-linear dynamics as a way of reconceptualizing long-term history, and thus to provide archaeology with a new set of tools with which to interrogate the past.

Notes

1   Hence the name 'flow structure approach'. Such 'flow structures' exist by virtue of the fact that they dissipate excess entropy (randomness), and can spontaneously organize themselves under certain conditions of positive feedback. This explains two other names this approach carries: 'dissipative structure approach' or 'self-organizing systems approach'.

2   In presenting such a critique, however, we must acknowledge the context – cultural and scientific – within which this work is situated. The era to which most of these simulations belong was that of the New Archaeology; a period dedicated to reformulating archaeology in a new deductive-nomological guise, so as to conform to the 'classical' natural science traditions. Thus, the twin tools of hypothesis testing and its corollary, prediction, were regarded as pre-eminent goals to which a mature archaeology should aspire. In commenting on this kind of

'science-envy', it is somewhat ironic that the extreme form of deductivism to which archaeology aspired had long ago been jettisoned by the biological and physical sciences. For example, while the natural sciences were busy grappling with post-positivist, relativistic and probalistic models ushered in by the break-throughs of a post-Einstein universe (a universe defined by its uncertainty), archaeology was expending an enormous amount of energy searching for theo-retical structures which would enshrine models of scientific enquiry whose hallmark was their aspiration to objective *certainty*.

3   In a technical sense these attractors are not topological submanifolds of the total available space, but are fractals (Mandelbrot 1983; Tsonis and Tsonis 1987).

4   The difference between the two terms is here used to indicate the difference in the degree of determination of theories by facts.

5   To some extent, subsequently stripping a model or adding detail may fudge the issue, but it cannot fundamentally change the situation because an abstract heuristic model defines its constituent parts in terms much more removed from the 'observed decisions' than a decision-making model does.

References

Allen, P.M. 1985. Towards a new science of complex systems. In *The Science and Praxis of Complexity*, S. Aida, P.M. Allen and H. Atlan (eds), 307–40. Tokyo: United Nations University Press.

Allen, P.M. and J.M. McGlade 1986. Dynamics of discovery and exploitation: the Scotian shelf fisheries. *Canadian Journal of Fisheries and Aquatic Science* 43, 1187–200.

Allen, P.M. and J.M. McGlade 1987a. Modelling complex human systems: a fish-eries example. *European Journal of Operations Research* 30, 147–67.

Allen, P.M. and J.M. McGlade 1987b. *Managing Complexity: a fisheries example*. Report to the United Nations University, Tokyo.

Allen, P.M. and J.M. McGlade 1987c. Evolutionary drive: the effect of microscopic diversity, error making and noise. *Foundations of Physics* 17, 723–38.

Allen, P.M. and J.M. McGlade 1989. Optimality, adequacy and the evolution of complexity. In *Structure, Coherence and Chaos in Dynamical Systems*, P.L. Christiansen and R.D. Parmentier (eds), 3–21. Manchester: Manchester University Press.

Apostel, L. 1960. Towards the formal study of models in the non-formal sciences. *Synthese* 12, 125–61.

Archer, M. 1988. *Culture and Agency*. Cambridge: Cambridge University Press.

Arthur, W.B. 1988. Self-reinforcing mechanisms in economics. In *The Economy as an Evolving Complex System*, K.J. Arrow, P.W. Anderson and D. Pines (eds), 9–31. New York: Addison-Wesley.

Atlan, H. 1992. Self-organising networks: weak, strong and intentional. The role of their underdetermination. *La Nuova Critica N.S.* 19–20, 51–70.

Bailey, G.N. 1983. Concepts of time in quaternary prehistory. *Annual Review of Anthropology* 12, 165–92.

Bapty, I. and T. Yates (eds) 1992. *Archaeology after Structuralism: archaeological discourse and the strategies of post-structuralism*. London: Routledge.

Binford, L.R. 1977. *For Theory Building in Archaeology: essays on faunal remains, aquatic resources, spatial analysis and systematic modeling*. New York: Academic Press.

Bintliff, J.L. (ed.) 1992. *The Annales School and Archaeology*. Leicester: Leicester University Press.

Boudon, R. 1982. *The Unintended Consequences of Social Action*. London: Macmillan.

Braudel, F. 1973. *The Mediterranean and the Mediterranean World in the Age of Philip II*. London: Collins.

Christenson, A.L. and T.K. Earle 1980. *Modelling Change in Prehistoric Subsistence Economies.* New York: Academic Press.

Clarke, D.L. 1968. *Analytical Archaeology.* London: Methuen.

Clarke, D.L. 1972. Models and paradigms in contemporary archaeology. In *Models in Archaeology,* D.L. Clarke (ed.), 1–60. London: Methuen.

Cronk, L. 1988. Spontaneous order analysis and anthropology. *Cultural Dynamics* 3, 282–308.

Doran, J.E. 1970. Systems theory, computer simulations and archaeology. *World Archaeology* 1, 289–98.

Douglas, M. 1967. Primitive rationing. In *Themes in Economic Anthropology,* R. Firth (ed.), 119–47. London: Tavistock.

Farmer, J.D., E. Ott and J.A. Yorke 1983. The dimension of chaotic attractors. *Physica* 7D, 153–80.

Ferguson, A. 1767. *An Essay on the History of Civil Society.* [reprint: Edinburgh: Edinburgh University Press, 1966).

Gleick, J. 1987. *Chaos: making a new science.* New York: Viking Penguin Inc.

Haken, H. 1977. *Synergetics – an introduction.* Berlin: Springer-Verlag.

Hayek, F.A. 1948. *Economics and Knowledge. In Individualism and Economic Order,* F.A. Hayek (ed.), 33–56. Chicago: University of Chicago Press.

Hayek, F.A. 1977. The creative powers of a free civilization. In *Essays on Individuality,* F. Morley (ed.), 259–89. Indianapolis: Liberty Press.

Hayek, F.A. 1983. *Knowledge, Evolution and Society.* London: Adam Smith Institute.

Hodder, I. (ed.) 1978. *Simulation Studies in Archaeology.* Cambridge: Cambridge University Press.

Hodder, I. (ed.) 1982. *Symbolic and Structural Archaeology.* Cambridge: Cambridge University Press.

Hodder, I. 1986. *Reading the Past.* Cambridge: Cambridge University Press.

Hodder, I. (ed.) 1987a. *Archaeology as Long-term History.* Cambridge: Cambridge University Press.

Hodder, I. 1987b. *The Archaeology of Contextual Meanings.* Cambridge: Cambridge University Press.

Leach, E. 1954. *Political Systems of Highland Burma: a study of Kachin social structure.* London: Bell.

Li, T.Y. and J.A. Yorke 1975. Period three implies chaos. *American Mathematics Monthly* 82, 985–92.

Lorenz, E.N. 1963. Deterministic nonperiodic flow. *Journal of Atmospheric Science* 20, 130–41.

McGlade, J. 1987. Chronos and the oracle: some thoughts on time, time-scales and simulation. *Archaeological Review from Cambridge* 6, 21–31.

McGlade, J. 1990. The Emergence of Structure: social transformation in later prehistoric Wessex. Unpublished Ph.D. dissertation, University of Cambridge.

McGlade, J., in prep., Transactional dynamics and prehistoric exchange: spatial outcomes.

Mandelbrot, B.B., 1983, *The Fractal Geometry of Nature.* San Francisco: W.H. Freeman.

May, R.M. and G. Oster 1976. Bifurcations and dynamic complexity in simple ecological models. *American Naturalist* 110, 573–99.

Mayntz, R. 1989. Social discontinuity. *Interdisciplinary Science Review* 14, 4–15.

Menger, C. 1982. On the origin of money, *Economic Journal* 2, 239–55.

Nicolis, G. and I. Prigogine 1977. *Self-Organization in Non-Equilibrium Systems.* New York: Wiley Interscience.

Picazo, M. 1993. Hearth and home: the time of maintenance activities. Unpublished paper presented to the TAG Conference, Durham (UK), December 1993.

Picazo, M. and J. McGlade, in press. Los tiempos del espacio: temporalidades y reproduccion social. *Revista de Arqueologia del Poniente.*

Poincaré, H. 1899. *Les méthodes nouvelles de la mécanique céleste.* 3 vols. Paris: Flammarion.

Prigogine, I. 1978. Time, structure and fluctuations. *Science* 201, 777–85.

Rashevsky, N. 1940. Advances and applications of mathematical biology. *Bulletin of Mathematical Biophysics* 1, 15–25.

Renfrew, A.C. 1982. Socio-economic change in ranked societies. In *Ranking, Resource and Exchange,* A.C. Renfrew and S.J. Shennan (eds), 1–8. Cambridge: Cambridge University Press.

Renfrew, A.C. 1985. *Approaches to Social Archaeology.* Edinburgh: Edinburgh University Press.

Renfrew, A.C. 1987. Problems in the modelling of socio-cultural systems. *European Journal of Operational Research* 30, 179–92.

Renfrew, A.C. and K.L. Cooke (eds) 1979. *Transformations. Mathematical approaches to culture change.* New York: Academic Press.

Renfrew, A.C., M.J. Rowlands and B.A. Segraves (eds) 1982. *Theory and Explanation in Archaeology: the Southampton conference.* London: Academic Press.

Rowlands, M.J. and J. Gledhill 1977. The relationship between archaeology and anthropology. In *Archaeology and Anthropology,* M. Spriggs (ed.), 143–58. Oxford: British Archaeological Reports, British Series 19.

Ruelle, D. 1979. Sensitive dependence on initial conditions and turbulent behaviour of dynamical systems. *Annals of the New York Academy of Sciences* 316, 408–16.

Sabloff, J.A.(ed.) 1981. *Simulations in Archaeology.* Albuquerque, N.Mex.: University of New Mexico Press (School of American Research Advanced Seminar Series).

Sanders, L. 1992. Modèles de la dynamique urbaine: une approche critique. In *Temporalités Urbaines,* B. Lepetit and D. Pumain (eds), 3–41. Paris: Anthropos.

Schaffer, W.M. and M. Kot 1985a. Nearly one-dimensional dynamics in an epidemic. *Journal of Theoretical Biology* 112, 403–27.

Schaffer, W.M. and M. Kot 1985b. Do strange attractors govern ecological systems? *Bioscience* 35, 342–50.

Schaffer, W.M. and M. Kot 1986. Differential systems in ecology and epidemiology. In *Chaos,* A.V. Holden (ed.), 158–78. Princeton, N.J.: Princeton University Press.

Shanks, M. and C. Tilley 1987a. *Re-constructing Archaeology. Theory and practice.* Cambridge: Cambridge University Press.

Shanks, M. and C. Tilley 1987b. *Social Theory and Archaeology.* Cambridge: Polity Press.

Stewart, I. 1989. *Does God Play Dice?* Oxford: Blackwell.

Thomas, D.H. Jr. 1972. A computer simulation model of Great Basin Shoshonean subsistence and settlement systems. In *Models in Archaeology,* D.L. Clarke (ed.), 671–704. London: Methuen.

Touraine, A. 1977. *The Self-Production of Society.* Chicago: University of Chicago Press.

Tsonis, P.A. and A.A. Tsonis 1987. Fractals: a new look at biological shape and patterning. *Perspectives in Biology and Medicine* 30, 355–61.

Turing, A. 1952. The chemical basis of morphogenesis. *Philosophical Transactions of the Royal Society of London* B 237, 37–72.

Van der Leeuw, S.E. 1982. How objective can we become: some reflections on the relationship between the archaeologist, his data and his interpretations. In *Theory and Explanation in Archaeology: the Southampton conference,* A.C. Renfrew, M.J. Rowlands and B.A. Segraves (eds), 431–57. London: Academic Press.

Van der Leeuw, S.E. 1989. Risk, perception, innovation. In *What's New? A closer look at the process of innovation,* S.E. van der Leeuw and R. Torrence (eds), 300–29. London: Unwin and Hyman.

Van der Leeuw, S.E. 1990a. Rythmes temporels, espaces naturels et espaces vécus. In *Archéologie et Espaces,* J.L. Fiches and S.E. van der Leeuw (eds), 299–346. Antibes: APDCA.

Van der Leeuw, S.E. 1990b. Archaeology, material culture and innovation. *SubStance* 62/63, 92–109.

Van der Leeuw, S.E. 1991. Variation, variability and explanation in pottery studies. In *Ceramic Ethnoarchaeology*, W.A. Longacre (ed.), 11–39. Tucson: University of Arizona Press.

Waddington, C.H. 1977. *Tools for Thought*. St. Albans: Paladin.

Weidlich, W. and G. Haag 1983. *Concepts and Models of a Quantitative Sociology*. Berlin: Springer-Verlag.

Part I

DYNAMICAL APPROACHES TO SOCIAL PROCESSES

The identification and description of cultural dynamics is a primary concern of archaeological theory and practice; for this reason, we introduce a set of chapters in the first section of this book, which, although not specifically archaeological, nevertheless provide a useful starting point and provide a number of different examples of the operation of non-linear dynamics in societal systems.

A central theme of these contributions concerns the role of discontinuous transitions, a subject which is of fundamental concern to the interpretation of human history, and not surprisingly is an omnipresent theme in archaeological discourse. From a long-term perspective, the collapse of complex societal systems is of course a ubiquitous occurrence, and it has spawned an entire research industry attempting to explain such 'aberrant' behaviour. There is often an implicit assumption that such phenomena can be understood by the isolation and analysis of key variables such as climatic events, population pressure, warfare, invasion, etc. This quest for determining variables as part of a deductive explanatory method is still a fundamental constituent of most models of culture change.

Such models portray 'collapse' as a radical departure from some hypothesized equilibrium state to which society is said to aspire. Frequently, the image used is one of pathological decline and/or discontinuity – a period of chaos during which societies enter a 'dark age'. Thus it is that we have the trajectory of history neatly summarized as a binary opposition between periods of high civilization and culture (order) contrasted with dark ages during which confusion and disorder (chaos) flourish.

Such a dichotomous model is, of course, an illusion, and it is in many ways a hangover from the origins of archaeology in the nineteenth-century, when the discipline was wed to the kinds of evolutionary ideas which are embedded in the philosophy of progress. One of the major critical thrusts of this volume is that such schemes – still prevalent in an implicit way in archaeological theory – are ultimately of little use in coming to grips with the essentially non-linear processes which articulate societal production and reproduction. From this it follows that models of social transformation must be recast so as to incorporate discontinuity as part of the *intrinsic* dynamic of complex socio-natural systems.

This question of qualitative structural change is the core of Allen's contribution (Chapter 2). In searching for correspondence between models of natural and social process, he argues that at a macroscopic level both share discontinuous properties defined by symmetry breaking instabilities; thus, self-reinforcing properties (positive feedback) promoted by non-linear interactions operate to generate novel structural possibilities both at a molecular level and at a corresponding societal level.

Sudden changes of state, or qualitative transformations, form an integral part of all social processes; indeed, interest in the dynamics which generate structural change has recently attracted a great deal of attention as a consequence of the profound changes occurring in central Europe, particularly the rise of democratic social movements within totalitarian communist states. However, a crucial point must be made when employing natural science metaphors or analogies: people who are affected by discontinuities constantly alter their behaviour and hence affect the phenomenon itself. It is this ability, the hallmark of social action, which marks the fundamental distinction separating the social from the natural sciences.

The conceptual shift implied by an emphasis on discontinuous, emergent properties of societal systems is useful precisely because in emphasizing social structures as self-organizing entities within a complex open system, conventional attitudes to the homogeneity of time and space are effectively redundant. This is precisely the point being made by Peter Allen. Thus we move from a world defined by classical symmetric properties to one in which there is the possibility that non-equilibria at the heart of societal organization generate symmetry-breaking instabilities.

In the final analysis, Allen's message is an evolutionary one, defined here as *structural elaboration* rather than developmental complexity. What this means is that the process of structural transformation can result in a wide diversity of evolutionary patterns; indeed a whole behavioural spectrum is possible, ranging from homeorhetic states on the one hand to an array of complex unstable trajectories at the other extreme.

For example, from this perspective, the collapse of social systems such as Mycenae or Wessex II − whatever their precise contextual details − can be understood as a bifurcation in societal ideology and organization, followed by the establishment of an unstable threshold, after which the system may move along one of a number of possible trajectories − pathways running the gamut from order to chaos:

> Social processes turn erratic in this period, with old regularities
> disappearing and new ones not yet developed; usually impeded
> forces become virulent, normally controlled interaction is replaced
> by collective behaviour and because of the general disorientation

and menace, human beings behave in a more emotional and opportunistic manner. Under these conditions the future is especially
open and undetermined and may be steered by more or less accidental events in very different directions.

(Mayntz 1989, pp. 9–10)

It is clear that no general theory relating to these types of qualitative change,
or phase transitions, can ever be contemplated for social structures. Nevertheless, much is to be learned from the generic behaviours of analogous
structures and organizational evolution in the natural sciences. This is the
position adopted by Harry Erwin (Chapter 3) who extends the general points
made by Allen on the importance of structural stability and emergent behaviour. Erwin adopts a more pedagogic approach, and presents a series of
modelling approaches within the context of an introduction to dynamical
systems. The object of this exercise is to assess the utility of non-linear
analytical tools for a better understanding of the dynamics of social processes.
Of key importance, here, are the limits to modelling non-linear behaviour,
in the sense that not all non-linear behaviours can be successfully 'tracked'
or mapped. In addition there is the problem of calibrating a system with
imperfect knowledge of its dynamics, i.e., if its topology is unstable. It is
indeed one of the fundamental lessons of non-linear systems that prediction
is not possible in such circumstances.

Since the main substance of Erwin's presentation rests on the issue of
structural stability, he naturally devotes substantial space to the question
of bifurcations, and provides us with a useful classificatory sequence so as to
underline the possible relationships between mathematical abstraction and
social phenomena. A valuable demonstration of the dynamics of such
phase transitions is attempted with reference to Colin Renfrew's (1986)
identification of 'peer polities' in the archaeological record. Erwin argues
that the urban/rural dynamics which characterize peer polity growth and
interaction (i.e., population, trade/exchange, warfare, and political control)
can be understood within the 'attractor' paradigm of classical dynamical
systems.

The largely theoretical emphasis of the first two chapters in this introductory section is effectively complemented by Denise Pumain (Chapter 4),
who provides a concrete example of the kinds of long-term socio-economic
structuring discussed by Erwin. This focuses particularly on the interaction
of 'slow' and 'fast' dynamics and their role in the generation of urban evolution. Using data from French cities over the last two centuries, she presents
an elegant demonstration of the way in which the growth of urban settlement displays two distinct dynamics depending on the chosen scale of
observation. For example, at a macroscopic level which includes the entire
system of cities, the hierarchical size distribution remains largely unchanged
over time; however, at the scale of the individual city a wide variety of
fluctuations can be perceived in the process of its evolution.

What Pumain shows is that these spatio-temporal dynamics can be collapsed into a single explanatory framework by recourse to the paradigm of open, dissipative systems. Thus, the urban hierarchy can be viewed as an attractor for the rapid dynamic that is represented by individual urban centres competing for population migration. The global stability of the relative positions of settlements in an urban hierarchy reflects a kind of inertia which is readily visible in urban systems which are the product of a long historical evolution; for example, the original hierarchical structuring of the cities of the Roman Empire is today still largely intact in Europe. Pumain points out that this structural invariance can be seen with respect to major innovation cycles such as with the first industrial revolution in England, where, even though the geographical structure of the urban system changed, the original hierarchical structure remained largely intact.

An important issue foregrounded by the chapters in this section is the way in which explorations of complex, non-linear phenomena necessarily utilize the power of computer simulation to generate possible dynamic futures to which socio-natural systems are prone. The probability of occurrence of these future scenarios is, of course, a debatable point, but one which has no solution. Nevertheless, this is precisely the question being addressed by Natalie Glance and Bernardo Huberman (Chapter 5) in the last chapter of this section. These authors attempt to generate insight into decision-making problems faced by humans in their quest to anticipate outcomes. However, rather than dealing with issues of prediction, the emphasis is on the effect of agents' expectations on the system's dynamical behaviour. These outcomes, which are unstated, may be thought of as being analogous to social or economic phenomena.

Analysis was carried out with respect to two different systems of future projection; the first representing agents who believe that the system changes very little over time, and the second dealing with those who put faith in relatively short-term trends.

Simulation experiments show that agents characterized by identical levels of uncertainty can support a population with relatively long time horizons, provided the population is small; thus, instability and potential chaos occur when population density exceeds some threshold. However, broadly speaking, the practice of making long forecasts acts as a destabilizing element.

Perhaps the most interesting result of these experiments with the behaviour of expectations is that the most stable system occurs as a result of the coexistence of divergent expectation strategies – agents that are rewarded as a result of successful strategies increase at the expense of others. This is reflected in the global behaviour of the system as cyclical dynamics punctuated by sudden crashes. The diversity that this produces in system dynamics effectively underwrites the system's long-term survival. Thus, the selection for any single 'optimal' solution leads to instability and collapse. Interestingly, this result lends confirmation to Allen's general point on the importance of diversity for the long-run survival of evolutionary systems. It presents the growing differentiation and specialization which we often see in the past, wherever large numbers of individuals interact, from a different angle; not as a wilful choice by the individuals in such a population, but as an inherent dynamic in the interaction of groups beyond a certain size. As such the chapter presents a useful perspective on one of the phenomena which inevitably accompanies urbanization.

In conclusion, the chapters presented in this introductory section demonstrate the power of dynamical description as an important exploratory and analytical tool. They suggest a variety of ways in which the complexity of human societal systems can be investigated; more specifically, they provide a series of approaches which are potentially useful in the interpretation of specific archaeological problems – particularly those relating to questions of structural transformation.

Reference

Mayntz, R. 1989. Social discontinuity. *Interdisciplinary Science Review* 14 (1), 4–15.

2 Models of creativity: towards a new science of history

PETER M. ALLEN

Introduction

Archaeology is about the description and understanding of *qualitative*, structural change in human systems of the past, and real understanding is usually related to *scientific* knowledge. However, when these two ideas are brought together, they raise some unresolved, fundamental issues. What is the science of change? What is the science of evolution? And what is therefore the relationship of science to ourselves?

One way to look at these questions is to address the nature of the relationship between physics, the fundamental study of physical phenomena, and the science of living beings. After all, if we accept that we are the fruit of the evolutionary processes of biology acting upon underlying physical mechanisms, then a satisfactory science of the living world, and our place within it, can only come from an understanding of biological and socio-cultural evolution which is based on the fundamental laws of physics – a reconciliation of Newton and Darwin. And yet they are seemingly fundamentally opposed to each other, since the first has traditionally seen the world in terms of a mechanical system running for ever according to fixed laws, while the second describes a world of increasing complexity, with emergent and changing organisms, structures and interactions.

Our quest for a scientific approach to archaeology therefore leads us to the problem of the relationship between the laws of physics and chemistry and those applying to the living world of evolutionary change. And the underlying paradox here is clearly that the power of physics, particularly its ability to make predictions and hence to understand history as a *necessary* system trajectory, is founded on fundamental laws which are independent of time, laws of conservation and of symmetry, while evolution is about change, and the emergence of new forms and entities.

The only 'law' in physics which clearly addresses the question of change and the direction of time is the second law of thermodynamics. But this is not really a 'law' like the others, since in fact it merely *accepts* the existence of time's arrow, of irreversibility, but neither proves that this must result from more fundamental laws, nor shows exactly how this can be reconciled with them. Evolution and change are concepts that the physical sciences have traditionally been unable to deal with satisfactorily. This is related to the choice of mathematics as their preferred language of expression. Equations merely express the fact that the left and right hand sides must be equal, and therefore that they are merely two different ways of saying the same thing. The 'trick' used to deal with systems and their change through time is to suppose that the left and right hand sides of an equation might correspond to later and earlier times respectively. In this way, the assumption of some 'law of conservation' means that earlier and later values must be identical, and therefore that if the number of something in one part of a system increases, then there must be a compensatory decline elsewhere.

But such a perspective denies the existence of creativity and innovation, seeing everything in terms of some elementary particles swirling around in space according to fundamental mechanical laws. The application of this traditional kind of science to the real world is thought to simply require a suitable definition of the appropriate elementary particles conserved over time, in order to write down equations which allow prediction. Change, in this view, is the superficial transfer of these components from one part of the system to another.

But change and transformation, the emergence and evolution of complex living beings and societies, do not merely concern the changing numbers produced by some mechanical representation. Instead, they concern the spontaneous appearance of new structures and states of organization, implying that we must recognize at least two levels of description for our system: that of its elementary components subject to an accounting principle, and that of the structure or organization within which they exist. Our science must aim at understanding the relation between these two levels if it is not to be trivial. It is the mutual co-evolution of these two levels of description that is at the heart of the matter, and our focus of concern is the emergence of such new entities, with new powers and needs, which open new dimensions of experience.

According to the view to be presented here, change is not just an occasional and rare phenomenon, but instead change and, more importantly, the *capacity to change* play a greater role than previously believed in explaining the diversity we observe around us. The stability of any existing macroscopic form (or description) is permanently tested by the experiences of each local context. Thus, the evolutionary process itself necessarily leads to systems which possess both the ability to evolve and the capacity to adapt and change in response to the uncertainties of the real world.

In this chapter, it is argued that this ability ultimately resides in the internal diversity and variability of living populations. According to this view, the present was not an inevitability, but was created by its particular history, a history marked by creativity and the emergence of new forms, functionalities and organizations. The natural environment of humanity has been constantly changing, either on its own or as a result of human activities, and of course the human environment of humans (socio-cultural behaviour) has also been changing over time. The long-term survival (or extinction) of any particular group of humans therefore is perhaps more related to its ability to cope with uncertainty and change, and to generate responses, than to the optimality of its precise behaviour at a given time.

The mechanical paradigm

The basis of understanding in the natural sciences has traditionally been the mechanical model (Prigogine and Stengers 1984, p. 54). In this view, the behaviour of a system could be understood, and anticipated, by classifying and identifying its components and the causal links, or mechanisms, that act between them. In physical systems, the fundamental laws of nature such as the conservation of mass, momentum and energy govern these mechanisms, and determine entirely what must happen.

By isolating or closing a system so that no new matter or energy could flow in to disturb it, such limits are placed on its possible behaviour that classical physics was able to predict the properties of the final state quite generally for almost any system, however complex. The final state was that of thermodynamic equilibrium, and the properties of matter that would characterize it could be calculated in a very wide range of problems. This was such a triumph for classical science, that it was believed (erroneously) that analogous ideas must apply in the domains of biology, ecology, the human sciences, and particularly of course, economics (cf. Arrow and Debreu 1954; Debreu 1959).

But such ideas were misguided. In fact systems encountered in ecology and economics are always open to flows of matter and energy, and only attain thermodynamic equilibrium with death. Ironically, the mathematics and the methods borrowed from all-conquering physics have largely been utterly inappropriate when applied to the living world. Living systems are in constant dialogue (not equilibrium) with their environment and, even when not visibly evolving, they maintain the capacity to evolve and change which is related to their underlying diversity. Although biological, ecological or human systems are discussed in terms of the characteristic behaviour of the typical elements, or stereotypes, which make up the classificatory scheme that has been decided upon, underneath any such scheme there is always the greater particularity and diversity of reality.

In the classical scientific view, the future of a system is predicted by the simple expedient of considering the behaviour of the equations which govern its motion. Explanation is in this case an illumination of how a system functions, rather than of why the system is as it is. But while it is easy to write down the equations of mechanics for imaginary point particles, when considering a real system it is always necessary to make approximations in order to arrive at mechanical equations which are supposed to govern its motion. The assumption that must be made is that the elements which make up the variables (individuals within a population, firms in a sector, etc.) are all identical and of the *average* type. In that case, the model reduces to a 'machine' which represents the system in terms of a set of differential (perhaps non-linear) equations which govern its variables. This Newtonian vision views the world as a vast and complex clockwork mechanism.

In this perspective, predictions are made by simply running the model forward in time, and statements about the future are, under given conditions, made by studying the types of solution that are possible for the equations in the long term. Scientific explanation of this kind is based on the inevitability of a system's final state. The idea of 'equilibrium' comes from the simplistic assumption that there will only be a single solution to these equations – a point attractor – and therefore that whatever happens the system will eventually finish up with that solution's values. This 'point attractor' solution of the differential equations is viewed as expressing some maximum or minimum of some potential function. In physics, for example, the dissipative forces of friction and viscosity work to lead any mechanical system to a thermodynamic equilibrium expressing maximum entropy.

But this is completely false for open systems. Even in systems which we would all agree were purely physical, when open to flows of energy and matter, there is no longer necessarily a unique final state expressing some 'optimal' principle. We now know that systems of non-linear differential equations can have a whole multiplicity of possible solutions, from stationary homogeneous kinds, through chaotic, heterogeneous ones to ordered spatial and temporal structures. The external experimental conditions therefore no longer suffice to determine a unique future, as such systems can structure in a variety of ways which depend on the internal details of their constituent components – details which cannot be controlled from outside the system.

In other words, there is a single, predictable outcome – thermodynamic equilibrium – to experiments on isolated systems, but not for open systems where matter and/or energy can flow into, and out of, the system. This profoundly changes both our notion of 'explanation' and of scientific understanding.

When non-linear mechanisms are present, the system may continue to change indefinitely – either executing a cyclic path of some kind, or possibly even a chaotic movement around a 'strange attractor'. More importantly, its evolution may involve structural changes of spatial and hierarchical organization, in which qualitatively different characteristics emerge. New problems, satisfactions and issues can spontaneously be generated by the system.

This capacity for structural change is not contained in the dynamical equations. They are capable of functioning but not of evolving. Evolutionary change must result from what has been 'removed' in the reduction to a deterministic description, i.e., the non-average. The system is driven by two kinds of terms: deterministic average mechanisms operating between typical components, and non-average local behaviour which, in non-linear systems, can be amplified and can lead to qualitative structural changes in the average mechanisms.

Evolutionary drive

In some recent papers (Allen and McGlade 1987a, 1987b, 1987c, 1989) mathematical simulations have been made of this new evolutionary dialogue between 'average' (macro) processes and the 'non-average' (micro) detail. This led to the new concept of evolutionary drive.

The interesting idea here was to define a 'possibility space', a space representing the characteristics and behaviours that could potentially arise for the different types of individuals present. In practice, of course, this is a multidimensional space of which we would only be able to anticipate a few of the principal dimensions. However, it is nevertheless extremely instructive to think about the evolutionary process in these terms. The central problem of change is that of understanding how, over time, the kinds of behaviour present in a system can actually increase and complexify. In terms of possibility space, we may say that if, initially, there is a single type of individual present, occupying a single cell of this space, then how can new populations appear?

The answer clearly is that this possibility space will be explored by individuals if their behaviour is flexible in some way. In biological evolution, we know that not only are there mutations but more importantly that sexual reproduction leads to the production of offspring which are not exact copies of either of their parents. The genetic mechanism is precisely such that a large space of possibilities is explored, and offspring, offspring of offspring and so on, spread out over time from any pure condition.

Physical constraints mean that some behaviours do better than others, and so there is a differential rate of survival and of reproduction. If the possibility space is seen as a kind of 'evolutionary landscape', with hills representing behaviours of high performance, then our simulations lead to the amplification of populations which are higher on the hill, and the suppression of those which are lower down (Figure 2.1).

These papers showed how imperfections in the reproduction of populations provided a capacity for the latter to climb the hills of the adaptive landscape. By making populations with different intensities of 'error-making' or 'imperfect reproduction' it was possible to find the best amount of non-replication to ascend a given slope. This corresponds to the selection of 'diversity creating' mechanisms in the behaviour of populations, initially involving genetics, and later cognitive processes. Evolution was thus shown to select for populations with the ability to learn, rather than for populations with optimal behaviour, a result reminiscent of the 'Red Queen Hypothesis' (Van Valen 1973, pp. 1–30).

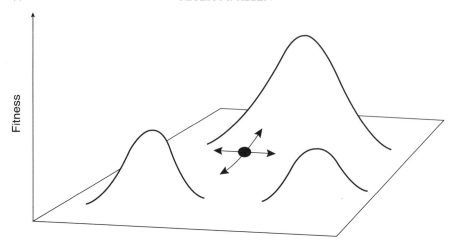

Figure 2.1 In possibility space, an initially pure population will diffuse outwards as a result of sexual reproduction, mutations, and entropic processes. Differential success makes it climb hills.

This view of evolution also allows us to understand how it was that neo-Darwinism came to resemble the old ideas of equilibrium physics. In the hill-climbing simulations, we found that if a population got to the top of a hill, then in fact it was advantageous to suppress error-making and imperfect reproduction. Evolution was 'over' and there was nowhere better to evolve to, and nothing to learn. If this were the case, then obviously, instead of performing complex calculations of populations in possibility space, with imperfect reproduction, the final state of the system could have been predicted *if* the position of the hill tops could be calculated a priori. These would mark the inevitable end point of evolution, and the equilibrium solution.

However, in this perspective one does not take into account that the shape of the hills in possibility space reflects the position of all populations that happen to be present in the 'landscape'. In other words, the advantage to be gained from a particular behaviour depends on which other behaviours are present at the time. The hills, and the populations, co-evolve (Figure 2.2). A mixture of exploratory diffusion of individuals in some behaviour space, and their differential successes, thus makes the difference between what is 'organic' and what is merely 'mechanical'. The core of our new understanding is the occurrence of a process of simultaneous stretching and squeezing of populations in the space of possible behaviours.

This view, of course, bears a striking resemblance to the ideas of Yin and Yang, and of 'dialectics', but in our case we not only have a vision of such a process, we also have mathematical equations which can represent it (Figure 2.3).

In further (unpublished) computer experiments, it was found that if some characteristic or strategy could exist which would result in self-reinforcement,

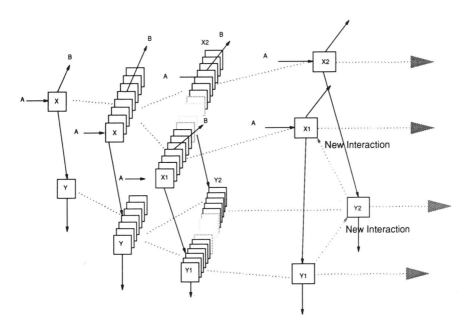

Figure 2.2 Evolution corresponds to the simultaneous stretching and squeezing of populations that we show here.

then once it emerged it could trap the population and block evolution at least for some time. An example of this from biology is the peacock's tail, where a gene produces the beautiful tail in the male, and makes such a tail attractive to the female. In sexual reproduction, anything which enhances the probability of mating produces a positive feedback on its own population dynamics, and fixes itself. However, it is at the expense of functionality with respect to the external environment. A peacock's tail is not an aid to finding its food better, or escaping predators, but simply the mark of a positive feedback trap.

In human systems such positive feedback systems abound. Much of culture may well be behaviour which is fixed in this way. In most situations imitative strategies cannot be eliminated by the evolutionary process, and so fashions, styles and indeed cultures rise and decline without necessarily expressing any clear functional advantages. Indeed, 'culture' could be viewed not so much as being 'the best' way of doing things somewhere, but perhaps as resulting from ignorance of other ways of doing things. Human activities in general, from fishery science to Patagonian folk dance, exhibit these properties of autocatalytic self-organization, where ritual and shared ideology emerge and serve as the identity and focus of a social group, irrespective of

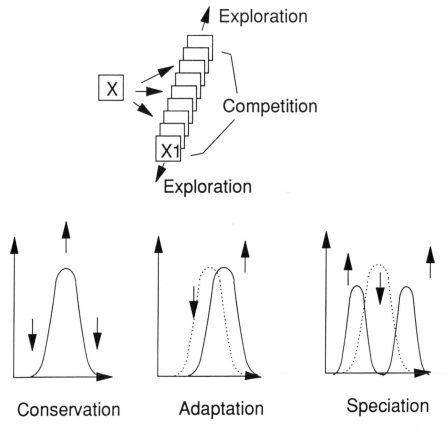

Figure 2.3 The explicit presence of stretching and squeezing generates a latent adaptability.

the precise merits or truth of the ideology itself. Much of human attention is focused on playing a role in groups where values are generated internally, and the physical world outside is largely irrelevant.

The work above has been further extended to show how 'adaptive land-scapes' are really generated by the mutual interaction of populations. In the space of possibilities, closely similar populations are most in competition with each other, since they feed off the same resources and suffer from the same predators, but there is some distance in character space, some level of dissim-ilarity, at which two populations do not compete with each other.

Initially, a population grows until it reaches the limits set by the compe-tition for underlying resources. At this point, there is a positive pay-off for error-makers, who escape somewhat from competition. We could say that although initially there was no hill to climb, the population effectively digs a valley for itself, until there is a hill to climb on either side of the present

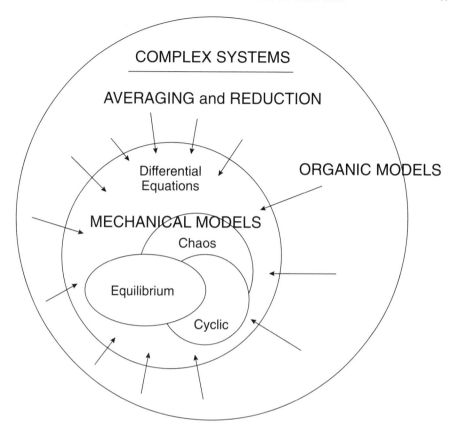

Figure 2.4 Models based on differential equations are an approximation to the broader class of complex systems.

character centroid (which represents the present way of 'doing things'). However, over some distance in this space the population growth is restricted because of the 'competitive shadow' of the original population, and so the 'dissidents' diffuse in only very small numbers up the slope away from the original type. After a certain time, however, small populations arise which are sufficiently different from the original type that they can grow and multiply on the basis of some other resource.

In its turn, this new population increases until it too is limited by internal competition for the limiting resource, and once again there is a pay-off for deviants, particularly for those on the outside of the distribution, as they climb another hill towards unpopulated regions of character space. In this way, well-defined populations appear successively, and colonists diffuse out from each of them as they reach a competitive limit, gradually filling character space with a set of populations separated approximately by some distance

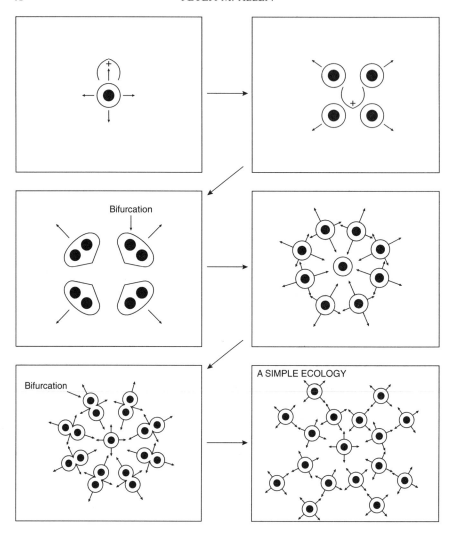

Figure 2.5 The working of the evolutionary process leads to the emergence of an ecology. The identities of the populations are interdependent, and the response to any perturbation is more than mechanical.

which is characteristic of the resource diversity which can be tapped (Figure 2.4).

From a single population our model generates a simple ecology (Figure 2.5), and a dynamic one since the identity of each population is maintained by the balance between a continued diffusion of deviants outwards into character space, and the differential reproduction and survival that is due to the presence of the other populations. Random events which occur during the 'filling' process will affect which populations arise, and so it is not true that the evolution represents the discovery of pre-existing niches.

Such a system operates beyond the mechanical paradigm, because its response to external interventions can involve changes in the structure and of the 'identity' of the populations in the system. Harvesting particular populations in such a system, as in fishing for example, will provoke a complex response from the other populations. The identity of each species depends on that of the others, and on the accidents of its particular history. Removing, or severely depleting, one or several populations will therefore set in motion a series of responses and changes in behaviour of other species which may look very much like (and indeed be) a form of learning. Deviant behaviour which hitherto encountered a negative pay-off may instead be reinforced, and in addition the responses may be essentially unpredictable (Allen 1990).

Models of complexity: from settlement to finance

If the preceding sections have helped to clarify why scientific theories about living systems have failed, we would like to show next that the ideas discussed above can actually help us in a practical way. To do so, this section will present a brief discussion of three examples which have been drawn from the present, all of which have relevance for archaeology. The first of these is concerned with subsistence strategies, and notably with fishing as an example of a strategy where the (human) predator population has only partial knowledge of the dynamics of the (animal) prey population. The next is concerned with the dynamics of trade, and the last with the processes responsible for urbanization.

Management of natural resources

The same evolutionary approach was used to develop dynamical models for the management of natural resources (McGlade and Allen 1985). This work has been discussed elsewhere in detail, but it is worth summarizing some of the main conclusions.

The essential point that emerged was that success in fishing, as in life, requires two almost contradictory facets of behaviour. First, the ability to organize one's behaviour so as to exploit the information available concerning net benefits (to be rational) which we have called 'Cartesian' behaviour. More surprisingly, however, a second ability is required, that is to be able to ignore present information and to explore beyond present knowledge. We have called these kinds of fishermen 'Stochasts'. The first makes good use of information, but the second generates it! At the root of creativity is always this second type.

In the short term it is always true that the more rational actor must outperform the less rational one, and therefore that for example taking steps to maximize present profits must, by that yardstick, be better than not doing so. Nevertheless, over a longer period the best performance will not come from the most rational but instead from behaviour which is some complex compromise. For example, a fleet of Cartesians which goes where available information indicates highest profits will in fact lock into zones for much too long, remaining in ignorance of the existence of other, more profitable zones simply because there is no information available concerning 'other zones': 'You don't know what it is you don't know.'

New information can only come from boats which have chosen not to fish in the 'best' zones, or which do not share the consensus values, technology or behaviour, and hence who generate information. They behave like risk-takers, but may or may not see themselves as such. They may act as they do through ignorance, or through a belief in some myth or legend. Whatever the reason, or lack of it, they are vital to the success of the fishing endeavour as a whole. It is their exploration that probes the value of the existing pattern of fishing effort, and lays the foundations for a new one.

As information is generated concerning the existence of new, rich fishing grounds, so the value of this information starts to fall as the news spreads, and exploitation rates increase in those locations. We see a cyclic pattern in the discovery of value in a zone, the spread of information and with it the saturation or exhaustion of the discovery, calling for fresh explorations (Allen and McGlade 1986, 1987a).

The model can either be used as a simulator, for the overall management of the fishery, or for the benefit of any particular fleet wishing to improve its performance. The parameter values which appear in the mechanisms governing the decision-making of fishing boats are calibrated so as to give realistic behaviour (Allen and McGlade 1987b). It is also possible to make a model which will run competing strategies against each other, and eventually discover for itself the robust and successful sets of strategies – generating an 'ecology' of fishing strategies.

Evolutionary economics

The idea that economics should be thought of in biological terms occurred to authors as far back as Darwin, who was partially inspired by the ideas of Adam Smith. However, for various reasons (amounting to a kind of 'physics envy'), economics adopted the equilibrium perspective of a mechanical system that has come to rest. Economists such as Schumpeter (1934) and Goodwin (1951), who attempted to introduce dynamical considerations and non-linear effects, were not followed by the mainstream. Many of the points that are being made in this present chapter have been pointed out before (e.g., Boulding 1981; Nelson and Winter 1982). However, the mathematical models presented here offer a new practical path forward.

In earlier papers, a description has been given of the self-organization of a market system, where the possibility space is in fact that of the possible products that could be supplied by firms for a particular end use or function. It shows how this end use can be viewed in a 'quality space', and how strategies can be explored by competing firms, using a simulation model. It also shows how evolution will create a 'market ecology' as a result of the

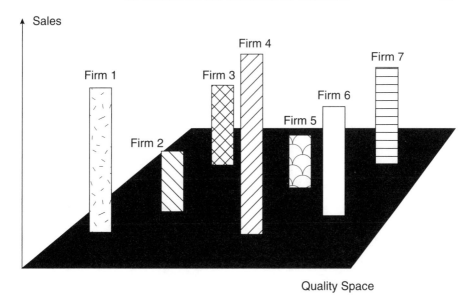

Figure 2.6 A self-organizing model of a market system leads to an ecology of firms.

evolutionary process of research, development and economic competition (Figure 2.6).

Another set of models has recently been used to study the behaviour of financial markets (Allen, 1990). In these, the speculative game of investment is simulated by considering that the differences between actors' perceptions, requirements and beliefs allow transactions to take place. Whether a given asset is considered to be over or under-priced depends on the beliefs that a given actor has about the alternatives. The parameters that characterize an actor are therefore those which capture the manner in which s/he forms her/his beliefs, and updates them in the light of events.

The model can include 'fundamentalists' who try to really assess future values, speculators who try to anticipate events, and 'technical analysts' who try to ignore the real complexity and extract buy and sell signals from some time-series data about, for example, changing prices. Our models are capable of simulating behaviour and market structure in a realistic and useful way. Once again, it is the diversity of different actors that allows the whole system to function at all, and what we see emerging is a 'business (or trade) ecology'. A similar approach has been developed in papers by Arthur (1988, 1990).

Settlement patterns

In the very first applications of non-linear ideas to human systems (Allen and Sanglier 1979a, 1979b, 1981), a non-linear dynamical system of equations

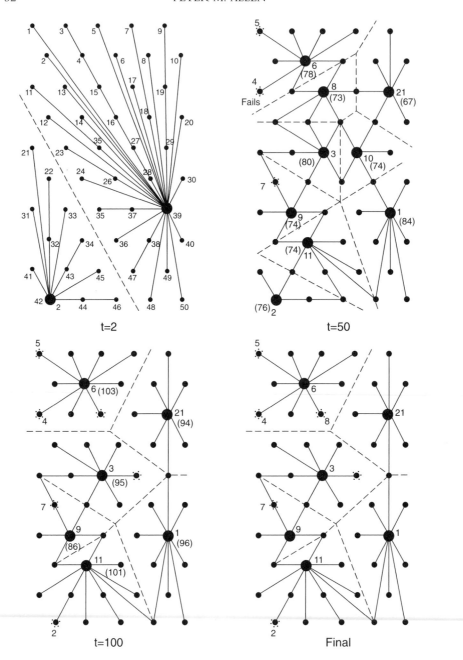

Figure 2.7 Successive market areas and centres resulting from the dialogue between average dynamics of supply and demand (with non-convex functions) and random occurrence of entrepreneurs.

expressing the supply and demand of different products was made to evolve by the random occurrence of entrepreneurs at different points and times in the system. The supply side was characterized by a non-convex production function for different economic activities, and consumer demand was assumed to reflect relative prices. The random parachuting of entrepreneurs on to the plain of potential demand resulted in the gradual emergence of a stable market structure and pattern of settlement.

As discussed in the previous section, we find positive feedback traps, where the system can get itself locked into a somewhat unsatisfactory market structure, as a result of a particular history. Basically, a very large number of possible stable structures could result from the experiment, involving different numbers of centres in different locations, and necessarily not offering the same level of efficiency.

Even in this very preliminary form the models already showed many important principles: many final states are possible, precise prediction in the early stages is impossible, approximate rules appear (centre separations etc.) but there is always considerable deviation and local individuality present. The results are affected by the particularities of the transportation system, as well as by information flows affecting the mental maps of consumers (Gould and White 1974). Also, the evolution of structure as a result of changing technology, transportation, resource availability, etc., can be explored, as the changing patterns of demand and supply affect each other in a complex dynamic spatial process.

The fundamental basis for the models are the decisions of the different types of individual actors considered, which reflect their values and functional requirements. These may be represented by very simple rules. However, the spatial dynamics give rise to very complex patterns of structure and flow, and to a structural emergence and evolution at the collective level. In such systems the microscopic and macroscopic levels are not related in a simple fashion. It is not true that the large structure is simply the small writ large. This is because macroscopic structure emerges, and this affects the circumstances of the microscopic parts, as they find themselves playing a role in a larger, collective entity. Each actor is co-evolving with the others.

New models (Figure 2.7) have been continuously developed from these early simulations in order to provide realistic tools for understanding regional and urban evolution, in which the patterns of structure and flows are the result of an ongoing evolutionary process of self-organization (Allen 1985; Sanglier and Allen 1989). Applications of these ideas have been made in the USA, Belgium, Holland and France, as well as in understanding intra-urban evolution in cities of Belgium and France (Sanders 1992).

Discussion

Instead of viewing evolutionary dynamics as the progress of a population up a pre-existing (if complex) landscape, our models show how the landscape itself is produced by the populations in interaction, and how the detailed history of the exploration process itself affects the outcome. Paradoxically, uncertainty is therefore inevitable, and we must face up to this. Long-term success is not just about the solving of optimization problems, but also about the optimization problems posed to the other parts of the system. An ecology consists of self-consistent sets of populations, both posing and solving the problems and opportunities of their mutual existence.

Innovation occurs because of non-average individuals and initiatives, and whenever this leads to an exploration into an area where positive feedback outweighs negative, then growth will occur. We assign value afterwards, which may well be the role of historical and archaeological studies. It is only when we wish to rationalize what we see that we insist that there was some pre-existing niche which was revealed by events. The future, then, is not contained in the shape of the hills, since they are fashioned by the explorations of their climbers.

Does this mean that there is no overall effect of evolution? Is no function (thermodynamic?) maximized or minimized by it, which would characterize climax ecosystems and mature societies? Indeed, do climax ecosystems and mature societies really exist or is evolution actually continuing under an apparently stable envelope?

The answer suggested by our work is that stability is a mask that hides evolutionary potential. Only if deviant behaviour is constantly suppressed by selection do the existing structure and organization appear to be stable. But, in fact, there is a pool of hidden adaptability in the system, which allows the ecosystem to adjust and restructure in an organic and non-mechanical way. Sustainability is linked to these properties of hidden adaptability rather than to the attainment of some stationary, stable optimal. Evolution gives rise to a nested hierarchy of spatio-temporal structures, from microbes to Gaia, which continue to evolve.

In human systems, at the microscopic level, decisions reflect the different expectations of individuals, based on their past experience. The interaction of these decisions actually creates the future, and in so doing fails to fulfil the expectations of many of the actors. This may either lead them to modify their (mis)understanding of the world, or, alternatively simply leave them perplexed. Evolution in human systems is therefore a continual, imperfect learning process, spurred by the difference between expectation and experience, but rarely providing enough information for a complete understanding. It is this very ignorance, or multiple misunderstanding, that allows exploration, and hence learning. In turn, the changes in behaviour that are the external sign of that learning induce fresh uncertainties in the behaviour of the system, and therefore new ignorance. This offers a much more realistic picture of the complex game that is being played in the world, and one which our models can begin to quantify and explore.

Instead of the classical view of science eliminating uncertainty, the new science of history accepts uncertainty as inevitable. Rather than viewing this with dismay, however, our new understanding of evolutionary processes tells us that this is quite natural and normal. Evolution is not necessarily progress and neither the future nor the past is/was preordained. Creativity really exists, and evolution both encourages and feeds on invention. Recognizing this, the first step towards wisdom is the development and use of mathematical models which capture this truth.

References

Allen, P.M. 1985. Towards a new science of complex systems. In *The Science and Praxis of Complexity*, S. Aida, P.M. Allen and H. Atlan (eds), 307–40. Tokyo: United Nations University Press.

Allen, P.M. 1990. Why the Future is not what it was. *Futures* 22, 555–70.

Allen, P.M. and J.M. McGlade 1986. Dynamics of discovery and exploitation: the Scotian shelf fisheries. *Canadian Journal of Fisheries and Aquatic Science* 43, 1187–1200.

Allen, P.M. and J.M. McGlade 1987a. Modelling complex human systems: a fisheries example. *European Journal of Operations Research* 30, 147–67.

Allen, P.M. and J.M. McGlade 1987b. *Managing Complexity: a fisheries example*. Report to the United Nations University, Tokyo.

Allen, P.M. and J.M. McGlade 1987c. Evolutionary drive: the effect of microscopic diversity, error making and noise. *Foundations of Physics* 17, 723–38.

Allen, P.M. and J.M. McGlade 1989. Optimality, adequacy and the evolution of complexity. In *Structure, Coherence and Chaos in Dynamical Systems*, P.L. Christiansen and R.D. Parmentier (eds), 3–21. Manchester: Manchester University Press.

Allen, P M., and M. Sanglier 1979. Dynamic models of urban growth. *Journal of Social and Biological Structures* 2, 269–78.

Allen, P M. and M. Sanglier 1979a. Dynamic model of growth in a central place system. *Geographical Analysis* 11, 256–72.

Allen, P M. and M. Sanglier 1981. Urban evolution, self-organization and decision making. *Environment and Planning* A 13, 167–83.

Arrow, K. and G. Debreu 1954. Existence of an equilibrium for a competitive economy. *Econometrica* 22, 265–90.

Arthur, W.B. 1988. Self-reinforcing mechanisms in economics. In *The economy as an evolving complex system*, K.J. Arrow, P.W. Anderson and D. Pines (eds) 9–31. New York: Addison-Wesley.

Arthur, W.B. 1990. Positive feedbacks in the economy. *Scientific American* 263, 94–9.

Boulding, K. 1981. *Evolutionary Economics*. Beverly Hills, Calif: Sage Publications.

Debreu, G. 1959. *Theory of Value*. New York: John Wiley and Sons.

Goodwin, R.M. 1951. The non-linear accelerator and the persistence of business cycles. *Econometrica* 19, 1–17.

Gould, P., and R. White 1974. *Mental Maps*. Harmondsworth: Penguin Books.

McGlade, J.M. and P.M. Allen 1985. *The Fishing Industry as a Complex System*. Ottawa: Ministry of Fisheries and Oceans (Canadian Tech. Fisheries and Aquatic Science No. 134).

Nelson, R.R. and S.G. Winter 1982. *An Evolutionary Theory of Economic Change*. Cambridge Mass.: Belknap Press.

Prigogine, I. and I. Stengers 1984. *Order out of Chaos.* New York: Bantam Books.

Sanders, L. 1992. Modèles de la dynamique urbaine: une approche critique. In *Temporalités Urbaines,* B. Lepetit and D. Pumain (eds), 3–41. Paris: Anthropos.

Sanglier, M. and P.M. Allen 1989. Evolutionary models of urban systems: an application to the Belgian provinces. *Environment and Planning* A 21, 477–98.

Schumpeter, J. 1934. *The Theory of Economic Development.* Cambridge, Mass.: Harvard University Press.

Van Valen, L. 1973. A new evolutionary law. *Evolutionary Theory* 1, 1–30.

3   The dynamics of peer polities

HARRY R. ERWIN

The purpose of modelling is insight, not numbers (Hamming 1962)

Introduction

Our understanding of human systems is in the middle of a revolution. There is an emerging consensus that many human systems are non-linear and that they may transition to irregular or aperiodic dynamics when stressed or forced. This realization has destroyed our hopes for a predictive theory of social evolution, but in return we are now gaining a deeper insight into how social systems actually evolve. This chapter is a bridge between the mathematical dynamicists and the social scientists: it examines the limitations of modelling technology for non-linear systems and then uses case studies of peer polity evolution to gain an understanding of the power of non-linear social models in understanding the evolutionary dynamics of social systems.

Limits on modelling

Webster's Collegiate Dictionary defines a model as a representation of a thing. For the applied scientist this definition becomes more specific: a model is an abstract representation of a system that provides useful estimates for parameter values of interest. These estimates need not be correct – insight is often all that a model is intended to provide – but they should at least represent the behaviour of the real system. In archaeology, where systems are often non-linear and data noisy, the question of whether a model or representation is valid becomes important (cf. also Rosen, Chapter 14 this volume).

The author's position is that a *valid* model is one that provides useful insights, desirably but not necessarily in the form of numerical predictions or statistical distributions. This pragmatic definition avoids arguments over the validity and equivalence of abstract models, since a formal or more rigorous definition of model validity can result in a situation where the only valid model of a system (particularly one with continuous dynamics) is the system itself.[1]

An important problem which the social scientist should be aware of is that not all non-linear systems can be modelled – some have behaviour that cannot be predicted by any model. This occurs even in computer systems, which might be regarded as highly predictable. Computer system models are built from elements that describe how individual hardware and software components behave in response to digital stimuli. Although these models lack minor details, most systems analysts believe that they need only provide additional detail to duplicate exactly the operation of the computer they are studying. Practical experience on the other hand has shown that computer simulations are often inaccurate, and the added detail frequently increases the inaccuracy. These inaccuracies have been found to reflect computer behaviour that depends sensitively on non-linear analogue phenomena and the resolution of low level race conditions (cf. Erwin 1988, 1989).

To understand how that can happen, consider the purpose of the model. It is intended to replicate the behaviour of a real computer system with some degree of accuracy. This runs into the following set of problems:

1 The completion times of individual computer operations can vary in a way that depends sensitively and non-linearly on the input scenario, component interactions, and the initial values of internal, often non-observable, parameters.
2 Because of the resolution of race conditions, system response times can change discontinuously as inputs and internal parameters are varied by small amounts. This is particularly important in distributed systems with multiple processing elements running asynchronously.
3 To provide valid predictions, a model has to be insensitive to small errors in its input data, whilst the real system shows discontinuous behaviour as those data are varied.

Unless there is some way of showing that observed model behaviour matches that of the real system, such models cannot be safely used even for insight.

Luckily, there are ways around this problem, but they require an understanding of how non-linear models fail. Research work during the last thirty years has provided some of the necessary insight. The underlying problem is that the evolution of two nearby system trajectories (representing slightly different initial conditions) can diverge in state space, growing apart exponentially, and eventually becoming uncorrelated. When that happens, it may be impossible to calibrate a system model to provide adequate predictions. A model has to have dynamics similar to those of the real system, but when nearby trajectories diverge in this fashion, the system – the best possible model – lacks self-similar dynamics when critical parameters change. The dynamics of the computer simulation then diverge from the real dynamics of the system

time

Figure 3.1 The pattern generated by strongly non-linear dynamics in a discrete flow.

for some parameter values. This phenomenon, termed 'sensitive dependence on initial conditions', is a key idea in non-linear systems theory.

A system with sensitive dependence on initial conditions is a difficult problem for the analyst – there is an absolute limit to the accuracy with which *any* model (including the system itself) can replicate observed system behaviour for him or her given the unavoidable inaccuracy of measurement data. This strange property is basic to how chaos occurs in deterministic systems.[2]

Deterministic chaos can be induced in both discrete and continuous dynamic systems in several ways, including:

1 Strongly non-linear dynamics – seen, for instance, in difference equation models of population dynamics in ecology (May 1987, pp. 35–9). Strong non-linearity results in dynamic processes that merge distinct initial states into the same terminal state, while spreading nearby initial states over the entire state space.[3] Figure 3.1 illustrates the typical pattern for a discrete flow.

2 Intermittency – dynamic systems which flow smoothly at most times, but sometimes show rapid fluctuation and divergence. The periods of rapid fluctuation inflate small neighbourhoods in state space, so that the eventual return to smooth flow finds that system state information has been lost.[4] Figure 3.2 illustrates a sample pattern for this occurring in a continuous flow.

3 Multiple interfering periodicities – where the periodic or cyclic processes interact non-linearly, the periodicities interact and the non-linearity folds the interactions so that state history is lost (Newhouse *et al.* 1978). Figure 3.3 illustrates this pattern for a discrete flow.

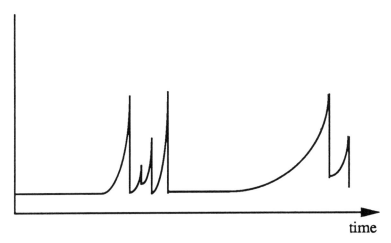

Figure 3.2 The pattern generated by intermittent dynamics in a continuous flow.

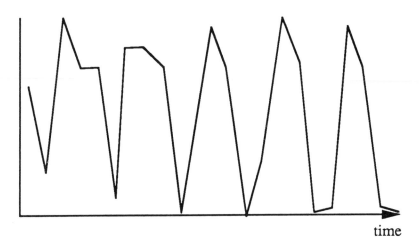

Figure 3.3 The pattern generated by quasiperiodic dynamics in a discrete flow.

4 Non-dissipative chaos, e.g., Arnold's 'Cat maps' (1978) and circle maps:

$$(x) = ((\alpha x + \beta) \text{ modulo } 1) \text{ for } a > 1.$$

Information is lost at each iteration as points which are an integer distance apart are folded together by the modulo operation. Pseudo-random number generators and ergodic processes belong to this category.

Chaotic processes now appear to be ubiquitous, and mathematical dynamicists have a suspicion that they include nearly all macroscopic low-dimensional 'random' processes. Even in systems with randomness, interaction between statistical noise and non-linear dynamics can be remarkably complex.

Mathematical dynamics

When a system has chaotic dynamics, measurement noise can lead to invalid model results despite having an accurate representation of the system dynamics. But problems also occur if the topology of the system is unstable, since the model itself is now unavoidably inaccurate. This problem is quite old; Jules Henri Poincaré first encountered it in his studies of the stability of orbits during the late nineteenth century. The field that developed from his work, now called global dynamics, describes how the topology of a continuous dynamical system can change as critical parameters are varied (Abraham and Shaw 1982–8, Parts 1–4).[5]

The idea of structural stability provides a useful organizing paradigm for dynamic systems and evolutionary models. Guckenheimer and Holmes (1983, sects. 1.7 and 5.4) define a dynamical system to be structurally stable when small C^1 (i.e., continuous, once differentiable) perturbations yield topologically equivalent dynamics (dynamics that can be related to those of the original system by a continuous one-to-one and onto mapping). Models of structurally unstable systems are suspect because they may have dynamics significantly different from those of the system they simulate. Although structurally speaking, stability is generic in such systems (i.e., structurally unstable dynamics are a set of measure zero in parameter space), if the boundary between the regions dominated by different dynamics is fractal, the true dynamics of a system may still be effectively indeterminate.[6] Note also that although these problems are clearly related to the problem of sensitive dependence on initial conditions for chaotic processes, there are types of chaos that are structurally stable. These factors make an early understanding of the underlying dynamics of a system crucial in developing a valid model.

This can be illustrated by an example. The better adapted the social system, the slower it changes, and slow enough change is indistinguishable from stability. This can result in models that are topologically invalid. Classical civilization survived with many of its institutions intact for 1,500 years (800 BC to AD 700) in the Eastern Mediterranean. Some historians have conjectured that it was inherently stable and would have survived indefinitely in isolation. As urban civilization in the Arab Near East seemed to maintain further continuity of development to about AD 1500, there is some evidence for that belief. The dynamic model for the classical city that results might be characterized by stability at a fixed point or small limit cycle. Yet, that model omits a significant detail. Russell (1987, *passim*) shows that there were five centuries of population decline in Europe from AD 200 to 700, and in the

Near East the decline may have continued for another 300–500 years. Evidently, since the cities survived throughout this period, their rural hinterlands became depopulated.

Hodges and Whitehouse (1983, pp. 58–60) have evidence that regional populations recovered in Tunisia and Italy once the cities disappeared, strongly suggesting a causal connection between urbanization and rural depopulation in the classical *polis*. Their data suggest that classical civilization was unstable and that long-term models that ignore the interaction between the city and the local rural population may have the wrong dynamics. In omitting such a significant detail, those models cannot be safely used for long-term predictions.

General models of dynamical systems

The critical issue here is that the dynamics of a system must be understood in the context of potential alternatives. Significant insight into this can be provided by analysis of a given model as a member of a one-parameter family of dynamic models. For instance, when a social system shows behaviour transitioning smoothly between convergence to a fixed point and periodicity, it can be studied as a Hopf bifurcation. Such schemes of related topological systems are perhaps the most general models that can be applied to dynamic systems, and mathematicians have classified them into a number of generic bifurcations of dynamical schemes (continuous collections of dynamical systems or flows).

Some mathematical concepts and terminology will be useful in this discussion. A *generic property* is one that has a significant (i.e., non-zero) probability of being observed. For example, the occurrence of simultaneous *independent* cultural change in two areas – when neither change is viable alone – is non-generic since the probability of its occurrence is vanishingly small. Such non-generic events can occur, but simultaneous changes usually have a common cause.

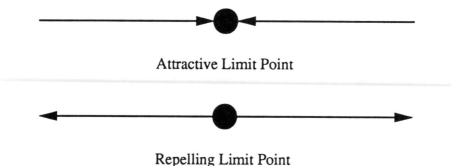

Attractive Limit Point

Repelling Limit Point

Figure 3.4 The generic limit points for one-dimensional flows.

A second basic concept is that of limit points and limit sets. A *limit point* of a dynamical flow is a point fixed under the action of the flow. Similarly, a *limit set* is a collection of points mapped into itself by the flow. Attractive limit sets are called attractors, while limit sets that repel nearby points are called repellers. The *inset of a limit set* is the set of points that converge to the limit set under the action of the flow. If a flow is time-reversed, with attractors becoming repellers, the result is also a flow, and the outset for the original flow is the inset for this time-reversed flow. In one dimension, all generic limit points of dynamic flows are either attractive or repelling (see Figure 3.4).

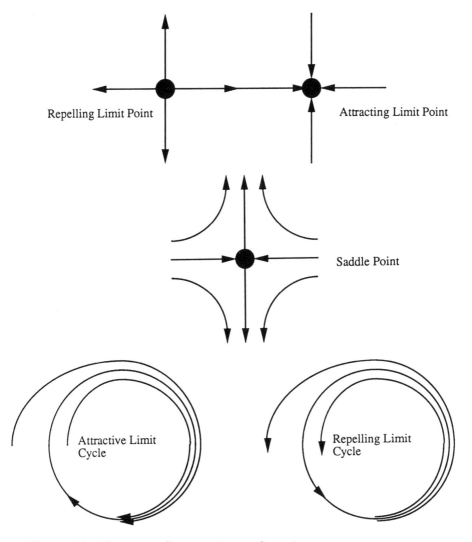

Figure 3.5   The generic limit sets in two dimensions.

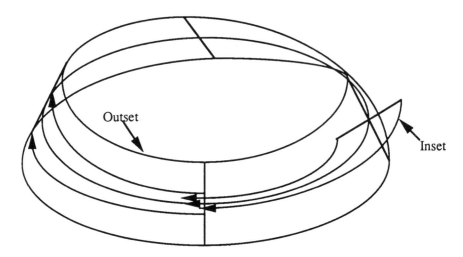

Figure 3.6 A saddle cycle in three dimensions with an inset and an outset forming Möbius strips.

In two dimensions, there are several additional types of generic limit sets (see Figure 3.5). The attractive and repelling limit points in one dimension generalize naturally, and attractive and repelling limit cycles appear. Finally, there is a new type of limit point, the saddle point, which attracts in some directions and repels in others.

In three dimensions, it becomes yet more complicated, but the processes by which limit points were generalized for two dimensions still apply. The various types of two-dimensional limit points, in particular, now spawn collections of three-dimensional attracting, repelling, and saddle cycles, with the insets and outsets spiralling an integral number of times as the flow passes around the cycle. If the integer is odd, the insets and outsets for those cycles form Möbius strips (see Figure 3.6).

One of the ways to spawn higher dimensional dynamics is by introducing the suspension operator. A suspension of a dynamic flow is a dynamic flow of one dimension higher. For each point in the original space, the suspension substitutes a unit circle, S^1, with a circular flow. Two continuous projection maps can be defined which preserve the dynamics on the suspension, one mapping to a non-zero flow on the unit circle and the other to the original dynamics (see Figure 3.7). In this manner, one can generalize a dynamic flow.

Abraham and Shaw (1982–8, Part 4) identify three major categories of dynamical schemes that depend on a single control parameter: subtle bifurcations, catastrophic bifurcations, and explosive bifurcations. These categories have the characteristics described in the following subsections. Also described is a fourth category: fractal bifurcations.

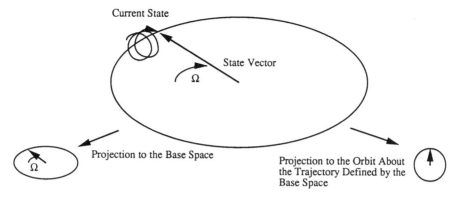

Figure 3.7 The solenoid, a suspension of the unit circle. The system state is restricted to a 2-torus.

Subtle bifurcations

The subtle bifurcations show a gradual transition between distinct types of dynamic attractors. Included in this category are the following:

1 **The first excitation or 'Hopf bifurcation'**, characterized by an attractive fixed point spawning a small attractive limit cycle that grows gradually as the control parameter is increased. The Hopf bifurcation is one model for the gradual emergence of periodic dynamics from a fixed point. In economic and governmental systems, this can occur as the time lag between information acquisition and policy action grows. No hysteresis is present, i.e., the transition point between the fixed point and the limit cycle is independent of whether the control parameter is increasing or decreasing. The dynamics change gradually as a basin of attraction slowly grows from a point attractor. Such models are robust and control theory can be used to analyse the transition process (see Figure 3.8).

2 **The second excitation**, where a process similar to that described in 1 above spawns doubly periodic dynamics from an existing limit cycle (see Figure 3.9). The configuration that is generated is called a solenoid.

3 **The octave jump in two dimensions or period doubling bifurcation**. This occurs when a periodic attractor at the middle of a Möbius band splits into two. The attractor is replaced by a repeller at the middle of the band and a single attractor twice as long on each side of the repeller. The experiment of cutting a Möbius band in half lengthwise gives insight into the process underlying this bifurcation. This bifurcation can also appear from a repelling limit cycle (see Figure 3.10).

4 **The octave jump in three dimensions**, which is an extension of 3 to three dimensions, in which the two-dimensional limit cycle is replaced by a three-dimensional saddle cycle.

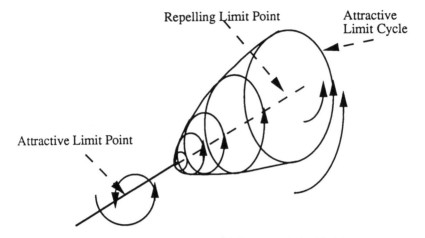

Figure 3.8   The first excitation or Hopf bifurcation imbedded in parameter space.

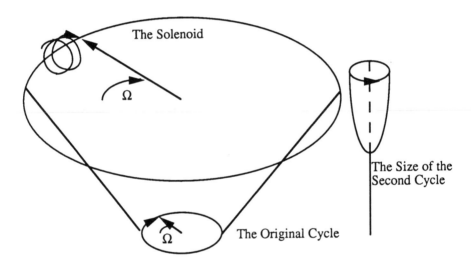

Figure 3.9   The second excitation imbedded in parameter space.

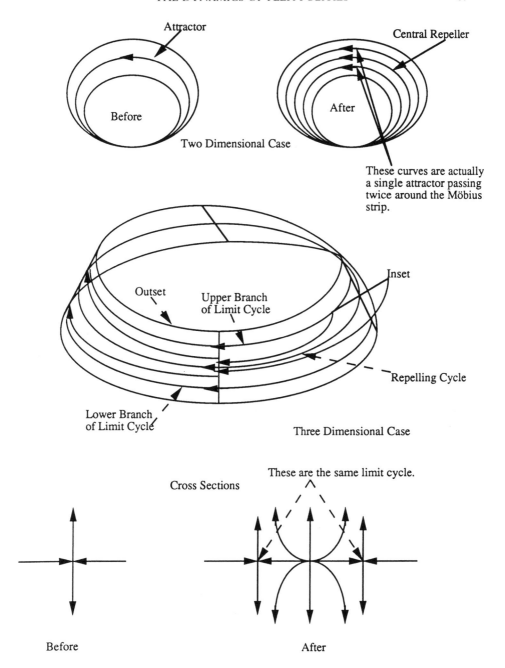

Figure 3.10 Octave jump in two and three dimensions.

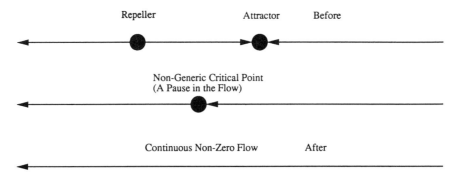

Figure 3.11   The static fold catastrophe.

Catastrophic bifurcations

The second major category of bifurcations is made up of the catastrophic (fold, pinch, and basin) bifurcations and is the domain of elementary catastrophe theory (Thom 1975). In a catastrophic bifurcation, as a control parameter changes in value, the system dynamics suddenly shift and a new attractor and its basin of attraction simultaneously appear. Then, if the direction of change of the control parameter is reversed, the attractor remains present for some time past the transition point before it disappears, leading to hysteresis – the transition point depending on the direction of evolution. Key characteristics of these bifurcations are that the attractor forms or disappears at the boundary of its basin, and that the dynamics of the attractor reflect pre-existing dynamics in the earlier system. Chaos is observed in such cases – A.E. Woodcock (1990), among others, has interesting results in this area – which implies that models involving catastrophes have to be carefully assessed for robustness. Some bifurcations in this category include the following:

1   The **static fold in one dimension**. This dynamic system is a flow on the real line to the right or left as it approaches infinity, but there are two finite limit points with an opposite direction of flow in the intervening segment. Figure 3.11 illustrates such a system. In the figure, the left-hand point happens to be a repeller and the right hand point an attractor. The middle segment is a barrier to leftward flow. The bifurcation occurs when the length of the middle segment becomes zero. First, there is a momentary pause in the flow as the limit points merge. Then the pause disappears, and a non-zero flow to the left exists throughout the real line. This dynamic system thus describes the disappearance of a local stable point and it is one possible model for technological innovation or the disappearance of a barrier to trade or migration.[7]

2   The **static fold in two dimensions** (see Figure 3.12.). This is a two-dimensional version of the previous example. An attractive fixed point

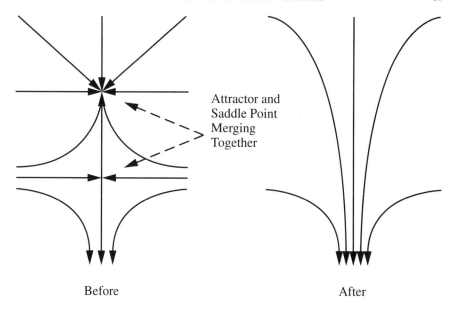

Figure 3.12   Static fold in two dimensions.

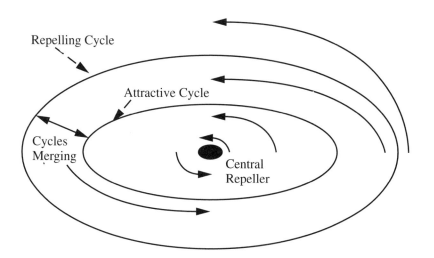

Figure 3.13   Periodic fold in two dimensions – before.

and a saddle point mutually annihilate each other, and the system now converges to a distant attractor. The reverse process can create a pair of limit points in a region previously characterized by a non–zero flow.

3   The **periodic fold in two dimensions** (see Figure 3.13). Here, there are two concentric limit cycles around a central fixed point, one cycle attracting and the other repelling. (Note that a computer simulation would only see the attractive cycle and possibly the fixed point.) There is an intermediate flow that passes from one cycle to the other and two concentric basins of attraction. As one limit cycle changes its radius to approach the other, the interval between them disappears (see Figure 3.14). The resulting system has a single basin of attraction and a single fixed point. This is one possible model for the disappearance of a large cycle and its basin.

There are two ways to interpret this bifurcation in a social system model. The first is as a dynamic flow that circles an attractive centre, but which is prevented from reaching the centre by a repulsive force. Over time, as the force weakens, the orbit disappears and the flow can reach the fixed point at the centre. The second model is the evolution of a dynamic flow repelled by a central fixed point but prevented from escaping too far by a centripetal force. As the centripetal force weakens, the flow is no longer bounded and can escape to infinity.

4   The **periodic fold in three dimensions** is a simple generalization of the two-dimensional case.

5   '**Pinch catastrophes**' are time-reversals of the corresponding subtle bifurcations, where insets become outsets and attractors become

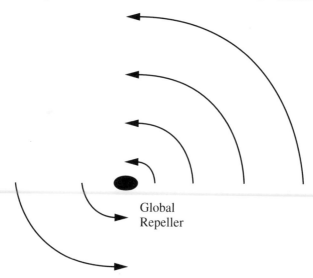

Figure 3.14   Periodic fold in two dimensions – after.

repellers. For example, the **spiral pinch** is a time-reversed Hopf bifurcation, in which a point repeller is spawned by the merger of the repelling limit cycle with the point attractor within the cycle. The catastrophe is associated with the disappearance of the point attractor.

6   The **basin bifurcation in two dimensions** is an interesting catastrophe with relevance to historical patterns. If a trajectory leaving one saddle point arrives at another saddle point, it is termed *a heteroclinic trajectory* (Figure 3.15). If it forms a loop, returning to the initial saddle point, it is called *a homoclinic trajectory* (Figure 3.16). The process whereby one saddle point momentarily passes another is illustrated by the heteroclinic trajectory in Figure 3.17. This results in a right–left swap of basins of attraction between the saddle points, the basin bifurcation. A good historical example illustrating this process is the Arab capture of Syria, breaking Constantinople's land communications to Egypt, and eventually detaching the whole of Northern Africa from

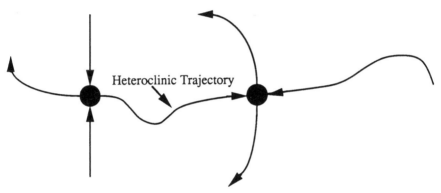

Figure 3.15   A heteroclinic trajectory connecting two saddle points.

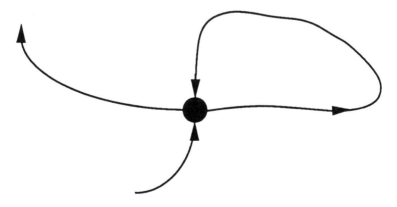

Figure 3.16   A homoclinic trajectory.

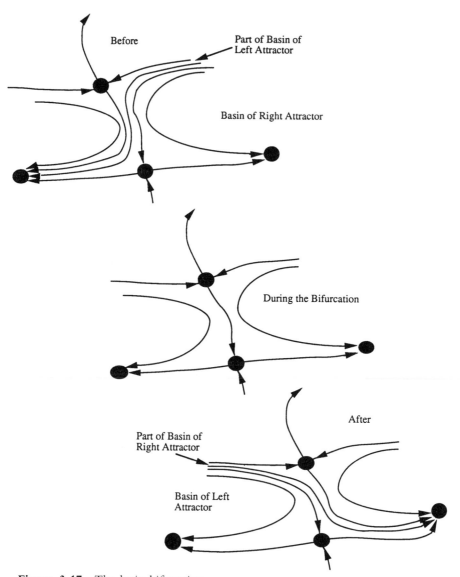

Figure 3.17 The basin bifurcation.

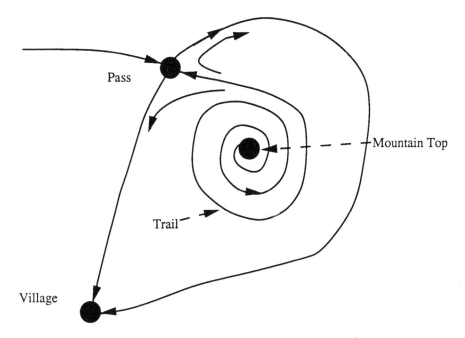

Figure 3.18 'Before' topology for 'periodic blue sky' catastrophe.

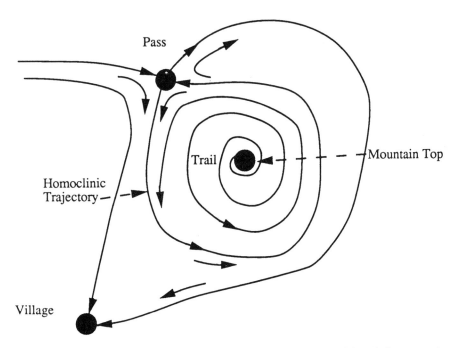

Figure 3.19 The homoclinic trajectory stage in the 'periodic blue sky' catastrophe.

Byzantine rule. The key here was the sudden transfer of a large region
between capitals, without any prior long-term encroachment in the
area.

7 **'Periodic blue sky' in two dimensions**. Here, a periodic attractor
appears *out of the blue*. This can best be illustrated by an intuitive
example. Imagine being on top of a mountain (Figure 3.18). A trail
spirals down from the mountain, crosses on to a ridge, and eventually
reaches a pass. The ridge trail continues on, but a path travels down
from the left side of the pass into a valley to a village. The valley
extends around the mountain so that the path down the right side of
the pass arrives at the same village. The mountain top is a fixed point
repeller, the pass is a saddle point, and the village is a fixed point
attractor. Now fill the valley to be even with the pass. Build a one-
way loop trail around the mountain, level with the pass and reconnect
the left-hand valley trail so it avoids the pass. The one-way loop trail
forms a homoclinic trajectory (Figure 3.19). Continue by filling the
valley until a second ridge rises outside the loop trail, which now leads
down to the pass. Build a trail along the outer ridge leading to the
pass and have the old left-hand valley trail spiral down to the loop trail
(Figure 3.20). The loop trail is a long-period cyclic attractor that *has
suddenly appeared*. This is a second model for the sudden appearance of
large-scale periodic dynamics in a previously stable dynamic system. It

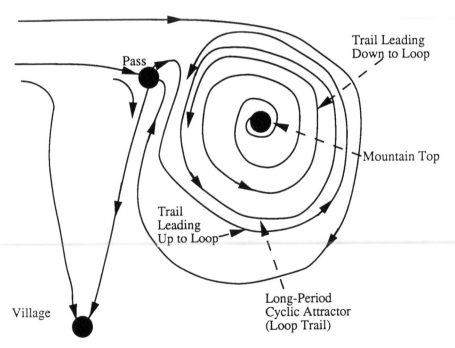

Figure 3.20 Final stage of the 'periodic blue sky' catastrophe.

differs from the periodic fold catastrophe in the special role of the saddle point.

8   **'Chaotic blue sky' in three dimensions**. The periodic blue sky catastrophe cannot be trivially suspended in three dimensions. Instead, a chaotic interval with an infinity of bifurcations is required to take the system from stable singly periodic dynamics to doubly periodic dynamics. These and similar chaotic catastrophes are possible models for periods of civil war. A social system passing through such a period would have an unpredictable history, since each decision point would have large consequences. Rössler (1976) identified two related catastrophes, the **band**, resulting from the forced Duffing equation, and the **funnel**, seen in human heart and brain function.

Explosive bifurcations

The third category of bifurcations is that of the explosive bifurcations, defined by Smale in 1967. These are discontinuous like catastrophes, but lack hysteresis. Instead, an attractor changes type within its undisturbed basin of attraction. There are few common examples, but the following are important:

1   **'Blue loop' in two dimensions**. Consider an attractive fixed point in its basin of attraction. Also present in the basin is a repelling fixed point and a saddle point. One trajectory leads from the repelling fixed point to the saddle point. The two trajectories leaving the saddle point eventually arrive at the attractive fixed point (Figure 3.21). Now allow the attractive fixed point to approach the saddle point. Eventually the points merge, leaving an attractive periodic trajectory surrounding the repelling fixed point (Figure 3.22). The basin of attraction is the same,

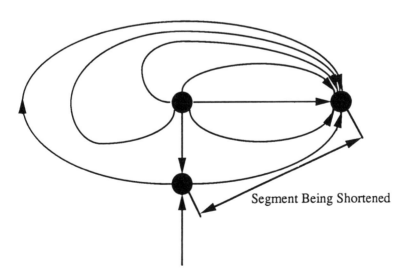

Figure 3.21   Blue loop in two dimensions – before.

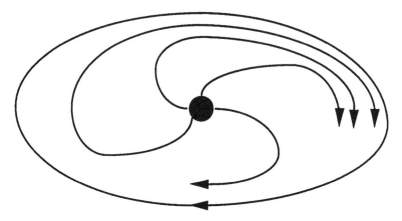

Figure 3.22   Blue loop in two dimensions – after.

but the attractor is now a limit cycle, a different type. This process models the sudden appearance of periodic dynamics in a pre-existing basin of attraction. An interesting example, concerning economic models for peer polity evolution, will be discussed later. (see pp. 78–82)

2   **Blue loop in three dimensions**. This is the suspension of the previous example.

3   There also are some **chaotic explosions**. These are characterized by the fact that the system's history is sensitively dependent on many individual decisions.

Fractal bifurcations

Abraham and Shaw (1982–8, Part 4) also describe several fractal bifurcations, where a dynamic system evolves through an infinite number of bifurcations arrayed in sheets. These include Rössler's octave cascade, the noisy cascade, the braid bifurcation, and the tangle bifurcation. Due to their complexity and the lack of evidence for fractal patterns of social evolution, these are not very useful as models for social systems.

Peer polities from the viewpoint of the dynamicist

The discussion so far may have given the impression that modelling of non-linear systems is complicated, or that it has little value; but that misreads the evidence. Modellers who seek predictive results are indeed asking the wrong question much of the time, and instead should be seeking insight into their system. Although the numerical predictions that emerge in modelling are frequently wrong, a number of researchers have shown that the patterns seen are frequently representative of the real system. Also, if a chaotic or structurally unstable component of the system dynamics is small or not physically relevant, approximate results are reliable (Guckenheimer and Holmes 1983, sect. 5.4). A third factor allowing use of non-linear models is that many chaotic processes are intermittent and remain well-behaved for long periods of time. When chaotic intervals will occur, and what the nature is of short- to medium-term dynamics during non-chaotic periods are questions of natural interest to social scientists, and recently Weigend *et al.* (1990) have shown that neural net algorithms can track those systems, even through the chaotic periods, and can be used to predict when chaos will occur. Modelling of non-linear systems, used with an awareness of its power and weaknesses, has much to offer the student of human systems.

To show the reader in more detail how to build models of non-linear processes, and how such models may contribute to our insights, the second part of this chapter will be concerned with elaborating a series of models for one particular archaeological phenomenon: 'peer polities'.

Renfrew (1986, p. 15), noting that early civilizations usually had a uniform structure of about a dozen independent 'Early State Modules,' each of about 1,500 km^2 area, defined the 'peer polity' to describe the elementary unit of that common structure. These peer polities were characterized by the following:

- closely similar political institutions;
- a common set of weights and measures;
- a common system of writing (if literate);
- shared religious beliefs;
- shared language; and
- shared culture;
- while remaining fiercely independent and competitive.

The interactions among these peer polities included:

- warfare;
- competitive emulation;
- symbolic entrainment;
- transmission of innovation; and
- increased flow in the exchange of goods.

Richard Hodges (1986) provides an evaluation of this paradigm for Anglo-Saxon England:

1. He confirms that multiple centres of comparable size and organization were characteristic of the peer polities.[8] Still, he notes that the number of polities decreased over time from many small tribal territories in the earliest period to the two kingdoms of the Viking age. This implies a secular growth of polities over time.
2. He confirms that organizational change was simultaneous, although he feels that it was perhaps due to general Frankish influence on the entire region.

3. Innovation development was distributed throughout the area.
4. The interactions among the peer polities which he can identify included competition and symbolic entrainment, but there was no sign of increased flow in the exchange of goods.
5. There was no sign of economic transformation associated with the intensification of production and the further development of hierarchical structures. At the point of political transformation, production remained continuous but the management of resources appeared to change. Intensification did occur during the tenth century when the centralized state was created. This implies that the economic transition associated with urbanization involved the production of only a small quantity of urban goods.

Peer polity systems have interesting non-trivial dynamics. Understanding them would give insight into the dynamic evolution of more complex societies and might provide some explanation for the collapse phenomena seen in some societies. Major puzzles in this area include:

• Why were cyclical dynamics so common?
• Why multiple peer centres?
• Why cultural co-evolution?
• How did the transition from the preceding culture to peer polities occur?
• Why did the transition to a centralized state occur when it did?
• Why was rapid appearance and collapse so typical of these systems?

The cross-cultural nature of this pattern of a dozen or so small independent urban communities sharing a common cultural heritage suggests that the underlying dynamics should be simple and part of our human heritage. This chapter examines some classes of models for the insight they can give into these questions. The models examined include economic models, population migration models, and political models.

Economic models for peer polities

In *The Economics of Feudalism*, Rader (1971) develops general market equilibrium models of slave and feudal economies. His use of the Poincaré–Bendixsen theorem is flawed when he attempts to prove that rural and urban populations can be expected to cycle, but his results are recoverable with some additional assumptions, and his model for the feudal economy can be extended to peer polity systems. He assumes self-sufficient regional economies, extensive economic obligations to local elites, and free individual agriculture, limited by labour availability and the fertility of the land. He notes that the short-run interest of the elites is in maximizing the supply of elite goods produced in 'urban' workshops. In Figure 3.23, that preference defines a relationship S between rural population (R) and urban population(U) that lies

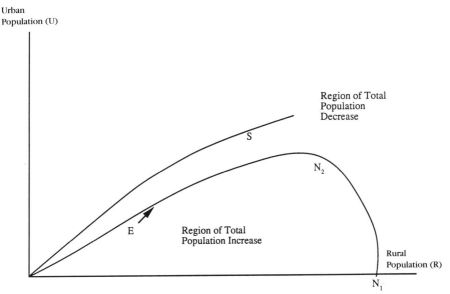

Figure 3.23 Rader's basic model.

above the region where the population is stable or increasing. The locus E in the figure represents the combinations of urban and rural populations that result in a stable total population.[9] The elite preference for elite goods, combined with the relative ease of collecting taxes and tribute from controlled urban areas, leads to short-run policy-making that favours rural-to-urban migration. Rader notes that due to disease and crowding, the death rate in pre-modern urban populations usually exceeded the birth rate, resulting in a negative U component in the vector of population change.[10] On the other hand, rural populations below the Malthusian limit should tend to see a secular population increase.[11] If sufficient rural–urban migration occurs so that the population is near the locus S, then the change in total population is negative, leading to a long-term drift towards zero total population.

Without enforced migration, the urban population can be expected to be small (due to the high death rate) and the total population can be expected to increase until the population vector approaches a purely agricultural limit point at N_1.[12] Since the maximum population for a society with both rural and urban elements exceeds the total population at N_1, some natural rural-urban migration can be expected as the population approaches N_1 and the population vector then drifts towards a limit at N_2 (Figure 3.24). As that drift begins, the first formation of craft villages, the nuclei of peer polities, is seen.

The critical consideration in determining whether peer polities will form from the craft villages is whether the power of the village and regional elites is sufficient to enforce rural to urban migration in excess of the natural level, moving the population vector over to the locus S. Cultural factors contributing

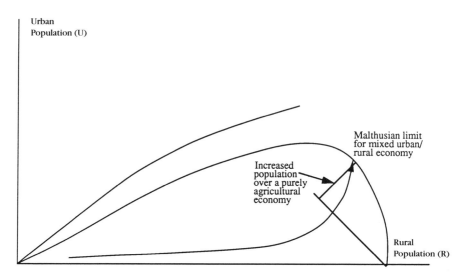

Figure 3.24 Population dynamics in the absence of elite pressure.

to that power may include the following: control over manpower, tribute collection, control of trade, and control of elite goods.

Given the assumption that the elites can mobilize enough power to control the agricultural population once the craft villages grow large enough, it is clear why cyclical dynamics characterize peer polities. The scenario is shown in Figure 3.25: an agricultural population grows, and craft villages form. Those craft villages provide a power base for village elites, and their policies encouraging urban goods production lead to a rapid population shift from the rural to the urban sector. That moves the community into a zone of net population decrease, but elite control over the increased urban population gives them enough power to continue to shift enough population out of the rural sector to maintain the urban sector. Regional population decrease continues until control of the urban sector is no longer enough to maintain control over the agricultural sector, and the population rebels or emigrates to the countryside. System collapse takes place, the urban centres rapidly disappear, and the system returns to an agricultural economy and the first stage of the cycle.[13]

Non-linear dependence of political power on urbanization is necessary to create the observed dynamics, especially the rapidity of de-urbanization. If political power were linearly dependent on urbanization, stability would be associated with the ratio of urban to rural population, not with the population size in either category. Given that assumption, as an urbanized society lost population, the elites could (and would want to) enforce an evolutionary trajectory that eventually would arrive at zero population. The historical pattern of system collapse at a non-zero regional population would not occur

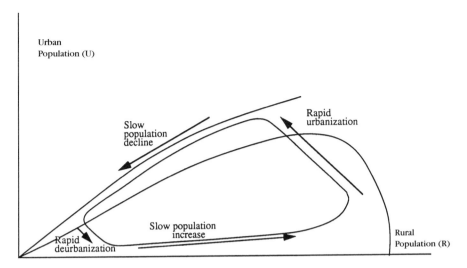

Figure 3.25   Population dynamics with elite enforcement of urbanization.

(Cherry and Renfrew 1986, 152–4). The dynamics seen in the historical record instead appear to be a 'blue loop' explosive bifurcation in two dimensions (see p. 76), analogous to a Van der Pol system ($x'' + \alpha\varphi(x)x' + x = \beta\varphi(t)$) with large α and zero forcing, β. This has some interesting implications. If a sufficiently large forcing function is applied to this type of system (representing large-scale migrations generated by the population dynamics of neighbouring polities), chaotic dynamics can be generated (Guckenheimer and Holmes 1983, sect. 2.1), with elites, urban groups, and rural groups all playing a role. These dynamics would make long-term planning impossible for the elites and would disrupt social and political relationships. For instance, if a population movement reduced the size of an urban community below the urbanization threshold, the peer polity could be destroyed. By implication, co-operative control over population movements should be a primary concern of elites.

The model derived here exhibits several desirable characteristics, including cyclical population dynamics, cyclical urbanization, association of urbanization with elite goods production, rapid urbanization and de-urbanization, with slow population change at other times. Analysis suggests that:

1   Irregular urbanization/de-urbanization dynamics will be seen in polities exposed to uncontrolled population movements.
2   The urban population required to set off formation of the peer polity should be about the same size as the total urban population at the time of systems collapse.
3   The ratio of urban population to rural population should be increasing or stable at the time of systems collapse.

4   Polities with elite policies that avoid a high level of urbanization should
    last longer and may avoid systems collapse.

Some preliminary work provides additional insight into these dynamics.[14]
A spreadsheet model of the economy of the Minoan palace of Mallia was
constructed to examine the factors leading to urbanization and population
change. This model was set up as a time-stepped simulation with an integration step size of one year. Each year's production was simulated, and the
resulting changes in capital goods, population element sizes, and productivity
were fed back to provide the basis for the following year's economic activities. Non-linear production functions were used, and non-linear interactions
between economic sectors were also modelled. The resulting dynamics were
extremely complicated, although recognizably related to those discussed in
this case study. The lessons learned include:

1   The palace was dependent on sea-borne trade for survival. The
    maximum population of the district (5,000–10,000) appears to have
    been between two and four times the population that could be
    supported by local agriculture.
2   The system was difficult to manage without a market and price mech-
    anism. The input–output matrix had to be inverted in some fashion
    to determine the desired production of each sector for each year.
    Without a price mechanism in the model, there was a tendency for
    the size of the elite to rise. Pregnancy rates for elite women were high
    due to good nutrition, and the birth rate for the group exceeded the
    replacement rate. Even though death in childbirth continuously reduced
    the number of elite women, they were replaced through recruitment
    from lower status groups. This led to a continuous population increase
    in the elite group.
3   The sub-system that produced goods for trade showed interesting behav-
    iour. It was modelled as a six-stage cascaded distribution system with
    lags, and inventories fluctuated wildly, as Mosekilde and Larsen's results
    suggest would be the case (Mosekilde and Larsen 1988; Larsen and
    Mosekilde 1990).
4   Rural-to-urban migration had to be carefully managed to avoid contrac-
    tion of the agricultural sector.
5   Elite control was necessary to the survival of the system, but a balance
    between the cost of maintaining the elites and the benefits they provided
    was hard to establish. An interesting question is whether the fully devel-
    oped palace system was near stability or whether its appearance already
    reflected runaway dynamics leading to the collapse of the system.

Population migration models

Population migration processes are another source of non-linear models. The inhabitants of an area controlled by a set of peer polities can be regarded as constituting an open system, with each family group optimizing its adherence to a specific polity. Huberman and Hogg's analysis (1988) can be applied to identify the migration dynamics for the population in the absence of coercion. The following cases are typical:

1 The pay-off for belonging to polity i is proportional to $\mathbf{K}_i/\mathbf{P}_i$, where $\mathbf{K}_i$ represents the total resources of the polity, and $\mathbf{P}_i$ the population of the polity. Migrants have perfect knowledge of their potential pay-offs.

2 The pay-off for belonging to polity i is proportional to $\mathbf{K}_i/\mathbf{P}_i$, where $\mathbf{K}_i$ represents the total resources of the polity, and $\mathbf{P}_i$ the population of the polity. Migrants have imperfect or delayed knowledge of their potential pay-offs.

3 The polities are assumed to form coalitions. The coalition with the largest total population rules. The pay-off for belonging to polity i is now proportional to $(\mathbf{K}_i/\mathbf{P}_i + \mathbf{V}\phi(i)/(\phi(i)\mathbf{P}_i))$, where $\mathbf{V}$ is the total pay-off for membership in the ruling coalition, $\phi(i)$ is the characteristic function for the ruling coalition, and the sum is over all polities. Migrants have perfect knowledge of their potential pay-offs.

4 The pay-off for belonging to polity i is the same as in case 3, but migrants have imperfect or delayed knowledge of their potential pay-offs.

In case 1, the system converges to an evolutionarily stable strategy with the population of each polity proportional to the resources of the polity. Huberman and Hogg have analysed case 2 for computational ecologies and show that the resulting population shifts can show periodic and chaotic dynamics, depending on the recency and correctness of the information available on pay-offs, the complexity of the strategies employed by the migrants, and the magnitude of the pay-offs. Case 3 has several general solutions, most characterized by shifting coalitions (as polities change sides in return for side-payments).[15] Case 4 is similar to case 2, with cyclic and chaotic population shifts clearly possible. If resources are scarce (for instance, if there are local food shortages), this can result in chaotic political conditions, raiding, peasant revolts, and civil war as peasants, urban craftsmen, and elites move to areas with food and other resources. Local elites can be expected to respond by closing polity borders, trading for resources, raiding neighbours, and co-operating to control resources.

This can be integrated with Rader's economic model. If the regional population has decreased to the point that urban centres are weak and the population is restive, loss of control over the population in one polity can spread rapidly. The scenario could unfold as follows: the local urban centre is sacked and many of the elite are killed, and the population then flees elite control. With no one left to rule, remaining local elite groups begin hiring mercenaries to help them take over areas in better shape.[16] The loss of elite control over large portions of the countryside gives the peasantry refuges against tribute collection and elite control, leading to further migration and further decrease of the population of the remaining elite centres. Eventually, only locations isolated from the population movements or attractive to population can maintain the old civilization.

The factors that would lead to chaos in this system are the relative pay-off sizes and the availability of information. For instance, significant chaos can occur in a 'gold rush' situation due to the high pay-offs associated with being present for the initial discoveries in an area. Chaos can also occur in a civil war, due to the high uncertainty about which faction is likely to prevail. The requirement for this mechanism to operate is that migration be an individual or small group decision, rather than one taken collectively by the community. Validation of these models is difficult since systems of this type are highly susceptible to noisy inputs, masking the underlying dynamics.

Political decision-making models

A third source for non-linear models is power politics. Socio-biologists have some interesting results from studies of territoriality, but the dynamics of social evolution are intrinsically different from those seen in biological evolution, and analogies between the two must be drawn with care.[17] Social systems are characterized by high complexity and directly adaptive change, rather than a winnowing of randomly generated variation, changing the evolutionary dynamics in unexpected ways and generally decreasing the chances of the system having a fixed point or terminal cycle. For instance, the game that underlies interpersonal conflict shows distinctly different patterns of evolutionary dynamics depending on whether the behaviour is learned or inherited.[18]

To see this, consider the two-person non-zero-sum game with information collection, which underlies interpersonal conflict. The following summarizes the rules of the game. Two players compete for a resource, with each player having a resource-holding potential (RHP)[19] known to her or him but unknown to her or his opponent. The game is ended by one or the other player quitting (resigning) at some point or by the player with the higher RHP winning by force. At any decision point, both players have the strategies of playing on (collecting noisy information, expending energy, and risking defeat by force) or resigning (abandoning the game and avoiding defeat by force). The pay-offs are ordered with:

$$\text{Pay-off}_{\text{loss by force}} < \text{Pay-off}_{\text{resign}} < \text{Pay-off}_{\text{win}}$$

There are several ways to analyse this game. Socio-biologists normally take the approach of directly solving the evolutionary dynamics for the stable points and terminal cycles (the evolutionarily stable strategies, ESSs), but that approach is difficult when a system lacks closed form solutions or when the dynamics are chaotic. Analytic approaches to solving this game have not been successful, and simulation techniques have been required for insight. The approach described here models the game as a series of bouts that provide information on relative RHP. The modelling assumptions include:

1. Before each bout, either player can choose to end the game (resign) with victory going to the other side. If both players resign, a compromise pay-off is awarded to each. If neither resigns, the game can be resolved during the bout by force, or it can continue to the next bout with no decision.
2. Bouts with no decision provide noisy information to both sides on relative RHP.
3. Pay-offs are defined for victory, resignation, compromise, and loss by force.
4. Each player knows a priori her/his ranking in the population, but not that of her/his opponent. Their relative ranking determines the winner when the game is decided by force.
5. After a fixed number of bouts, if both players are still present, the game is decided by force. (This finite horizon assumption is necessary for the simulation.)

Several simulation studies have provided insight into the stable population strategies for this game:

1. *The one-sided version of the game* (predator versus prey), where the attacker controls whether the game continues, is easy to solve and yields the following 'threshold' strategy: if the latest estimate of the probability of success exceeds an a priori threshold, continue, otherwise quit.[20] This model does not yield a good model for two-sided conflicts between nearly equal opponents.
2. *Darwinian evolution*: Using a genetic algorithm (random variation and natural selection) for strategy evolution, J.A. Erwin conducted simulation studies under the author's direction during the period 1987–8. He modelled a large population of asexual clones competing according to initial selections from a cycle of strategies, each defined so that it exploited the previous one. Mutation rates for the encoded strategies were selected to be realistic for *E. coli* and other bacteria. He found that selection rapidly eliminated those strategies that were temporarily inferior. The population strategy then homed in on the most effective remaining strategy. He also conducted studies of the effect of varying the mutation rate (using rates representative of those naturally occurring in bacteria) and discovered that random mutations were usually sufficiently inferior in scale for the high mutation rates to drop out of the population rapidly, so that the population strategy then locked in

on one of the strategies associated with the lowest available mutation rate. He did note mutations accumulating in the portions of the genetic code not subject to selection.

3   *Evolution by learning, discrete ranking*: The author conducted a series of simulation studies in 1989 of the case where there were a finite number of RHP values, and the population strategy evolved through periodic generation of a consensus strategy. Here, the population strategy eventually became cyclic, although the length and complexity of the terminal cycle was very sensitive to the maximum time horizon for the game.

4   *Evolution by learning, continuous ranking*: The author also conducted a series of simulation studies in 1989–90 of the case where ranking was continuous and the population strategy evolved through periodic generation of a consensus strategy. This case was felt to be representative of the evolution of culturally defined group behaviour. Here, the evolutionary dynamics of the game showed structural instability, and evidence of chaotic evolution was seen for some values of the input parameters (see Table 3.1 in the appendix). The evolutionary dynamics were also very sensitive to the maximum time horizon of the game. In one case when the horizon was 4 bouts, the population strategy converged to a 4-cycle, while with a 5-bout horizon, it converged to a 48-cycle. With shorter horizons, the population strategy rapidly fixated for most parameter values, but for longer horizons fixation on a terminal point or cycle took markedly longer.

The structural instability and chaos seen in the fourth study were due to sensitive dependence of the evolutionary histories on the relative magnitude of the expected pay-offs for alternative strategies. The preference function discriminating between the two strategies of resign or continue is non-linear or even discontinuous. This association of non-linearity with chaos is commonly seen in other contexts, including computer systems and networks, computational ecologies, and open systems (Erwin 1989; Huberman and Hogg 1988; Kephart *et al.* 1989).

The assumption that the population strategy evolves through periodic generation of a consensus is not required. Huberman and Hogg's analysis (1988) of open system dynamics can be adapted to model individual learning, with the result that the population strategy can evolve chaotically for some choices of game parameters.

These results have some interesting implications. Although stability can be expected for territorial behaviour in animal populations, the population consensus strategy for handling rank and resource disputes in human social systems need not be structurally stable and may evolve chaotically. Small perturbations, noise, and errors in perception can result in wildly divergent results. Strategies of this sort underlie such phenomena as decisions to resort to violence in peer-polity disputes, maintenance of social order, individual morale in combat, and decision in battle.

The evolution of social systems can be expected to be correspondingly unpredictable. In particular, the dynamics of human decision-making appear not to be structurally stable, and so cannot be modelled predictively. This model also makes the following quantitative predictions:

1 As risk per bout increases, with information and pay-offs held constant, players will leave the game earlier and earlier. Also, the population strategy will evolve more chaotically and bluffing strategies will become more popular.

2 As information per bout increases, with risk and pay-offs held constant, players will be more willing to compete in the first case, although length of time in the game will not change dramatically. Bluffing strategies will not be popular, and the population strategy will be more stable.

3 As pay-offs for winning increase relative to those for losing by force or resigning, players will remain in the game for longer periods. Bluffing strategies will become more popular and the game will evolve more chaotically.

Among others, these results clarify the traditional military difference between 'shock' (high tempo, hence high risk and a low rate of information collection) and 'attrition' (low tempo) combat. But they also imply the following for our particular study:

1 Even in the absence of external change, the level of violence in society will vary irregularly over time. This irregular variation will reflect changes in the pay-offs for co-operative, aggressive, and bluffing strategies.

2 An increase in the pay-off for winning will increase the level of violence in society.

3 A decrease in the information initially available on relative resource-holding power (for instance after the death of a strong leader) will increase the use of bluffing strategies, resulting in an increase in the number of disputes resolved by force.

4 An increase in the risk associated with collecting information on relative resource-holding power will reduce the level of violence. But it also will increase the use of bluffing strategies.

5 High levels of information on relative resource-holding power will reduce the level of violence.

Finally, these results imply that historical regularities may be limited to levels where the individual decision-process cannot inject irregularity. Predictable dynamics may occur, but the identity of the leadership groups that emerge, depending as it does on the outcome of political processes, will not be predictable. Since the formation of the centralized state appears to involve the resolution of political conflict, this result suggests that state formation might be expected to be an irregular and perhaps chaotic process.

Peer polities – a summary

The cyclical dynamics seen in peer polities appear to reflect a dynamic system with the following elements:

1   urban areas with a birth rate below the replacement rate – hence serving as population sinks;
2   rural areas with a birth rate potentially exceeding the replacement rate – thus potential sources of population; and
3   a non-linear function of the size of the population under elite control defining the power of urban elites to control migration between the countryside and the urban communities.

The initial emergence of the peer polity system appears to be a 'blue loop' explosive bifurcation in two dimensions (see p. 76). Initially, specialization was minimal, groups had to migrate to exploit alternative resources, and there was a stable population. Once the system could generate a surplus, it was able to support specialized craft villages, which increased the stable population. With further increases in the craft village populations, which increased elite power non-linearly, the local elites gained control over-urbanization. That destroyed the fixed point solution, and the interaction of the local elite power and preferences with rural and urban population densities then resulted in the cyclical process seen in the archaeological record.

Multiple peer centres with a common culture rather than a single city appeared in each region. This reflected the necessity to organize the region co-operatively with a common elite culture to stabilize local polities against emigration. The requirement for multiple peer centres (rather than a single centre) was due to the limited span of control of local elite groups – without co-operation between local elite groups in neighbouring areas, agricultural-ists had the option of migrating away. The urban system at this stage of development could not produce enough surplus to support additional levels of hierarchy and centralized control – that would not be available until the introduction of the market system.

The transition to a centralized state involved power politics and individual initiative and was much more irregular and chaotic. The independence of the individual peer polities had to be overcome, and they had to be inte-grated rapidly into a market economy to generate the additional surplus needed to support centralized rule. In some cases, this process was catalysed by income generated by external trade (Wessex) or by an external threat (classical Greece). In the absence of external stimuli, it required a leader who simultaneously combined brilliant leadership skills, political power, and effec-tive personal control over mobilizable resources. The low probability of that combination and the chaos of power politics to be overcome are possible explanations for the infrequency of the transition to the centralized state and market economy.

Conclusions

The non-linear systems revolution provides a set of new paradigms for the social sciences:

- A stronger awareness of the need for model validation,
- More rigorous methods for selecting models to use,
- New approaches to modelling, and
- A deeper awareness of the possibility of non-linear and irregular dynamics in human systems.

This chapter has provided an introduction to the ideas and issues involved in non-linear models of human systems and has discussed some of the dangers of modelling. Use of non-linear models clarifies the occurrence of both regular and irregular (chaotic) dynamics in the archaeological and historical record. Regular dynamics are associated with linear and near-linear systems, and, in particular, systems where the political decision process cannot inject irregularity. Irregular dynamics are seen in strongly perturbed non-linear systems where rapid response and adaptation is required. Model reliability depends on the regularity of the dynamics, and careful validation is critical to the understanding of model results. However, despite these known risks, non-linear models founded on real data, if carefully validated to overcome their potential weaknesses, can give valuable insight into social system evolution.

Appendix: modelling technology

Categories of models
Symbolic models can be divided into the following four categories:

1a Analytical (mathematical) models – these express a continuous process as a set of differential or difference equations. Since these models are usually linear, they give better insight into linear systems than complex or non-linear systems. Analytic models for non-linear systems remain an open research area. This is a well-understood, mature technology.
1b Topological models – these examine an evolutionary process by considering the vector field that defines the system flow in the state space of the system. These models can be continuous or discrete. These are usually calibrated only in the grossest of senses, but they do give insight into the applicable analytical and descriptive models.
2a Static descriptive models – these are usually based on statistical or queuing-theoretic analysis techniques and often are carried out in spread-sheet form. Generally these models give good insight into discrete (as opposed to continuous) processes, but, being primarily concerned with steady-state dynamics, they are poor at dealing with complex systems or transient behaviour.

2b Dynamic descriptive models – these are simulations in the strict sense. These are based on explicit models of object behaviour and may be continuous, discrete, or semi-continuous (mixed). These are good at giving insight into complexity or non-linearity, but their predictive value is often limited by the issues that have been discussed above. Approaches to validation are not well understood.

Model definition

There are five steps in model definition:

- system identification;
- system representation;
- model design;
- model implementation;
- model validation.

System identification establishes the relationships between an observer and some relevant part of reality, with a system defined as a collection of objects and their relationships and relevant behaviour. Applied scientists proceed by 'scoping the system'. They select a set of interesting objects and interrelationships that appear to be isolated and reflect the issues they are addressing. They then place the system boundaries where object interactions involve no significant feedback on the time-scale of the model. For instance, the solar system is typically studied as an isolated gravitational system, since gravitational interactions with other stars and gas clouds are weak and proceed on a long time-scale.

During *system representation* the analyst binds symbolic images of system elements on to her/his problem-solving paradigms. This is the step where s/he initially defines the model topology. S/he approaches this process by dropping irrelevant detail and defining functional interactions between system elements using mathematical or behavioural descriptions (protocols). For instance, the symbolic representation of the solar system might be a collection of point masses under the influence of the standard inverse square law.

The elements of the system representation should be selected to have measurable inputs, behaviour, and outputs; i.e., a tie to reality, since without that initial linkage of pattern and process it will be very difficult to validate the evolving model. For instance, an information processing model for a community should not be concerned with abstract information flow, which is very difficult to measure even in existing systems, but instead treat the individual actors, the messages they exchange, and the resources they use.

Similarly, when modelling energy flow, some way of relating energy to measurements of food production or human labour is needed. The resulting system may be more complicated than is immediately obvious. For instance as discussed earlier, birth rates in hunter-gatherer societies may have more than one stable state. Analysts usually imagine that those societies have a low per capita labour output – although still high enough to collect the food required to ensure that enough children are born and raised to maintain the population. That would imply the caloric input of the average adult female to be at or below the level required for maximum fertility, but Dobe !Kung women show a different pattern. Although well-nourished, their labour output is comparable to that of female athletes and ballet dancers, and their fat percentage (20.6 per cent) is so low that first menstruation is delayed to 16.6 years of age, first pregnancy occurs at about 19, and inter-birth intervals are 40 per cent greater than those in more sedentary !Kung groups (Harris and Ross 1987, pp. 23–4). That stable state is a possible alternative to the low labour output state usually assumed in analyses. Therefore, delayed marriage (seen for instance in many peasant societies) need not necessarily imply malnutrition; it also can be consistent with good nutrition and high labour output.

The *model design* is an 'appropriate' representation of the system for study. It implements the system objects and their behaviour in design elements. This is a preliminary software design consisting of the modules, interfaces, and adaptation parameters necessary to reflect the assumed topology. In a simulation of the solar system, this stage would be concerned with defining the characteristics of the software objects representing the planets and their interactions.

Model implementation consists of writing the simulation – programming in the strict sense. Typical simulation tools and languages that can be used in this include the following:

1   Standard programming languages, including FORTRAN, C, BASIC, Pascal, Ada. These languages handle the representation of simulation object behaviour with difficulty and are awkward to use in simulation applications.
2   Object-oriented general purpose programming languages, including Smalltalk, C++, Eiffel, and Lisp. These languages are designed to support the easy definition of objects and object behaviour and can usually be extended to provide basic simulation components such as processes, co-routines, and semaphores. An extensive, but reusable, infrastructure of intermediate simulation components is usually required before the simulation itself can be built in these languages.
3   Simulation languages – SIMULA, DYNAMO, GASP, GPSS, SIMSCRIPT, SLAM, etc. These languages provide the necessary simulation infrastructure and extensive support and analysis tools. Often these languages support only a few types of models, and sometimes there is significant lack of programming flexibility. Cost can be high.

4   Simulation packages – NETWORK II.5, for example. These support specific simulation applications, usually in engineering, computer capacity planning, or system design. These are expensive (\$15,000 or more for a licence) and generally do not support scientific research models.

The author prefers to use a simulation language or an object-oriented language that can be easily adapted for simulation purposes. Object-oriented languages are more flexible, but simulation development in those languages often requires high quality programming skills. (Based on the author's experience developing a multi-process simulation package, simulation programming in C++ is comparable in difficulty to programming in assembly language, requiring about three times the effort that would be needed for a comparably sized standard C program. This is primarily due to the strong type checking, which is an obstacle in simulation programming. Most applications programmers find C++ easier to check than standard C.) Simulation languages are easier to use, but most existing languages are oriented towards engineering problems that may have little common ground with social science. So, experienced modellers learn to maintain a mix of tools and languages to support their activities.

Model validation is the last and hardest step and so is often omitted. This is bad, since simulations of non-linear systems should be carefully tested to confirm that their dynamic behaviour is consistent with that of the real system. The techniques used in validation range from observation and simple statistical comparisons to sophisticated mathematical analyses. The candidate model should be validated against benchmark data, other models (both implicit and explicit), and internally against itself, and, always, sensitivity studies are necessary.

1   Validation against benchmark data. This is the most reliable approach when the data can be made available.
2   Validation against other models. Multiple models representing different approaches and addressing different issues should be used to avoid the risk of models having the same blind spots. Analytical validation also should be an element of this approach.
3   Internal validation. In this approach to validation, the researcher conducts multiple simulation runs, varying key parameters (or random number seeds) and looking for consistent outputs. This approach gives only limited confidence that a model is realistic, but discontinuities and irregular behaviour can diagnose chaos and lack of structural stability in the system being simulated. Table 3.1, discussed in more detail above, illustrates typical problem behaviour.

It is easy to err during model validation since non-linear dynamic systems can violate the analyst's assumptions. For instance, dissipative chaotic processes are frequently non-ergodic (non-stationary). When that occurs, any statistical

Table 3.1 Simulation results.

V	C	R	L	G	B	D	Iterations	Results
4	3	2	0	0.4	0.2	0.4	500	A 6-cycle
4	3	2	0	0.4	0.32	0.28	1030	A 4-cycle
4	3	2	0	0.45	0.36	0.19	1030	A 6-cycle
4	3	2	0	0.5	0.3	0.2	500	A constant
4	3	2	0	0.499	0.4	0.101	1030	A 3-cycle near the baseline case
4	3	2	0	0.4999	0.4	0.1001	1030	A 6-cycle near the baseline case, but running in the opposite sense
4	3	2	0	0.5	0.399	0.101	1030	A 6-cycle
4	3	2	0	0.5	0.4	0.1	500	The baseline case, a 3-cycle
4	3	2	0	0.5001	0.3999	0.1	1030	An 80-cycle
4	3	2	0	0.501	0.399	0.1	1030	A 20-cycle
4	3	2	0	0.501	0.4	0.099	1030	A 36-cycle
4	3	2	0	0.505	0.404	0.091	2030	Acyclic Continuous FFT. Autocorrelation goes to zero. Chaos or long-period cyclic
4	3	2	0	0.51	0.408	0.082	1000	Acyclic. Continuous FFT. Autocorrelation goes to zero
4	3	2	0	0.515	0.412	0.073	1000	A constant
4	3	2	0	0.52	0.416	0.064	1000	A 169-cycle
4	3	2	0	0.525	0.42	0.055	700	A 32-cycle
4	3	2	0	0.53	0.424	0.046	1000	A 36-cycle
4	3	2	0	0.6	0.3	0.1	500	A 4-cycle
6	2	2	0	0.5	0.4	0.1	500	An 84-cycle

V – Pay-off for victory
C – Pay-off for compromise (simultaneous resignation)
R – Pay-off for resignation
L – Pay-off for losing by force
G – Probability of a correct measurement during a bout
B – Probability of an incorrect measurement during a bout
D – Probability of a decision during a bout (prior to the last bout)

Note: The depth of game simulated was four information collection bouts, although the program supports other values. Iterations were generally continued until cyclic behaviour appeared.

measurements provided by the model reflect transient behaviour that may not reflect the long-term dynamics of the system. Another potential problem is that while chaos in the model is highly correlated with chaos in the system, it is possible for either to be present independently. For instance, the mapping $x_{n+1} = (2{\star}x_n) \bmod 1$ is a well-known example of non-dissipative chaos.

Yet, in a computer with a finite word length, the result of repeatedly iter-
ating this mapping is not chaos but convergence to a fixed point, normally
0.0 or 1.0. A model also can exhibit chaos when the real system is well-
behaved, and if a system is not structurally stable the model and the system
can have very different dynamics.

Notes

1 There are even cases where the system cannot be used to model itself. These
   issues have also defined the author's position on formalism in software engineering. Formal methods (proofs of correctness, exhaustive testing, formal
   specifications), while useful, are inadequate to address the correctness of systems
   whose dynamics are unpredictable. In particular, the correctness of distributed
   and parallel processing architectures and the performance of real-time and near-
   real-time systems cannot be demonstrated a posteriori using formal methods unless
   they were originally designed to have correctness demonstrated.
2 It usually reflects a 'folding' of the system dynamics (i.e., trajectories with different
   histories land on the same point) and a simultaneous loss of information about
   the initial system state as the evolutionary paths of nearby points diverge exponentially (see Schuster 1988 for an excellent survey). In dissipative systems (those
   that do not conserve energy) this process results in fractal patterns, since the initial
   error volumes associated with input parameters become spread out in some dimensions, while at the same time becoming reduced in total volume.
3 M.J. Feigenbaum (1978) developed the theory for this 'route to chaos'.
4 This route to chaos was first proposed by Manneville and Pomeau (1979).
5 Although the techniques in this field were originally oriented towards continuous dynamic flows, averaging techniques have been developed more recently
   which allow the study of discrete systems (Guckenheimer and Holmes 1983,
   Chapter 4).
6 Note that people tend to design symmetric systems, which are usually structurally
   unstable. See Mosekilde and Larsen (1988) and Larsen and Mosekilde (1990).
7 In real systems the barrier region has to be fairly wide, otherwise random fluctuations will 'tunnel' through it.
8 There is an unresolved question here as to whether the urban centres in peer
   polities follow Zipf's Law.
9 Rader does not model the decrease in fertility associated with high levels of
   labour output
10 This could be due to a depressed birth rate in urban areas.
11 There is a difference of opinion in this area. See Harris and Ross (1987) for an
   extended discussion. Simulation work conducted under the author's direction by
   J.J. Erwin in 1991 suggests that convergence may be to a population density high
   enough to reduce the birth rate, but not so high that the standard of living is
   dramatically depressed. In any case, Rader's model requires only homeostatic
   regulation of the population at some level between malnutrition and starvation.
   Interestingly, if labour output is proportional to calorie intake, and a Cobb–
   Douglas production function is assumed, net income is maximized for farmers at
   low levels of calorie intake rather than at high levels.
12 Given the data in Harris and Ross (1987), there are probably additional attractors, but these may not be accessible for a system with high population.
13 S.E. van der Leeuw (discussion with the author, December 1990) notes that
   emigration and colony formation in the classical Greek period were elite-
   controlled, suggesting that this model may be applicable.

14 Performed by J.J. Erwin in January–February 1991, under the author's direction.
15 See, for example, Moulin (1982, Part 2).
16 Based on an early date for the Achaean take-over in Crete. That process may have occurred on the periphery even when the core areas were stable. Viking and Norman activities throughout Europe showed the same pattern.
17 Biological evolution of social behaviour is constrained by the limited information content of the genome. Biologically determined behaviour will lack flexibility and have cruder mechanisms than learned behaviour. Behaviour which is rich, reflects subtle mechanisms, and adapts relatively easily to changing circumstances, is likely to be learned behaviour.
18 For related results, see Hines and Bishop (1983).
19 Or 'combat power' in military terminology.
20 Directly solved by the author in 1983 and presented at the 1983 Animal Behaviour Workshop at the University of Guelph. John Bather (pers. comm. 1984) later pointed out that a basic theorem in dynamic programming also implied the result.

References

Abraham, R.H., and C. Shaw 1982–8. *Dynamics – the Geometry of Behaviour*, Parts 1–4. Santa Cruz: Aerial Press.

Arnold, V.I. 1978. *Mathematical Methods of Classical Dynamics*. New York: Springer-Verlag.

Cherry, J.F. and A.C. Renfrew 1986. Epilogue and prospect. In *Peer-Polity Interaction and Socio-Political Change*, A.C. Renfrew and J.F.Cherry (eds), 149–58. Cambridge: Cambridge University Press.

Erwin, H.R. 1988. Performance engineering techniques for complex dynamic systems. In *CMG '88 Proceedings*, 1–4. Chicago: Computer Measurement Group.

Erwin, H.R. 1989. Mixing and sensitive dependence on initial conditions in computer systems. *CMG Transactions* 65, 3–5.

Feigenbaum, M.J. 1978. Quantitative universality for a class of non-linear transformations. *Journal of Statistical Physics* 19, 25–52.

Guckenheimer, J. and P. Holmes 1983. *Non-linear Oscillations, Dynamical Systems, and Bifurcations of Vector Fields*. New York: Springer-Verlag.

Hamming, R.W. 1962. *Numerical Methods for Scientists and Engineers*. New York: McGraw-Hill.

Harris, M. and E.B. Ross 1987. *Death, Sex, and Fertility*. New York: Columbia University Press.

Hines, W.G.S. and D.T. Bishop 1983. On learning and the evolutionarily stable strategy. *Journal of Applied Probability* 20, 689–95.

Hodges, R. 1986. Peer polity interaction and socio-political change in Anglo-Saxon England. In *Peer Polity Interaction and Socio-Political Change*, A.C. Renfrew and J.F. Cherry (eds), 69–78. Cambridge: Cambridge University Press.

Hodges, R. and D. Whitehouse 1983. *Mohammed, Charlemagne and the Origins of Europe*. London: Duckworth.

Huberman, B.A. and T. Hogg 1988. Behaviour of computational ecologies. In *The Ecology of Computation*, B. A. Huberman (ed.), 77–115. Amsterdam: North-Holland.

Kephart, J.O., T. Hogg and B.A. Huberman 1989. Dynamics of computational ecosystems. *Physics Review* 40A, 404–21.

Larsen, E.R., and E. Mosekilde 1990. *Chaotic Dynamics Produced by Human Decision Making Behaviour*. Working Paper 1–90, Institute of Economics, Copenhagen Business School.

Manneville, P. and Y. Pomeau 1979. Intermittency and the Lorenz model. *Physics Letters* 75A, 1–10.

May, R.M. 1987. Chaos and the dynamics of biological populations. In *Dynamical Chaos*, M.V. Berry, I.C. Percival, and N.O. Weiss (eds), 27–42. Princeton, N.J.: Princeton University Press.

Mosekilde, E. and E.R. Larsen 1988. Deterministic chaos in the beer production–distribution model. *System Dynamics Review* 4, 131–47.

Moulin, H. 1982. *Game Theory for the Social Sciences*. New York: New York University Press.

Newhouse, S., D. Ruelle and F. Takens 1978. Occurrence of strange Axiom-A attractors near quasi-periodic flow on T^m, $m \leq 3$. *Communications in Mathematics and Physics* 64, 35–40.

Rader, T. 1971 *The Economics of Feudalism*. New York: Gordon and Breach.

Renfrew, A.C. 1986. Introduction: peer polity interaction and socio-political change. In *Peer Polity Interaction and Socio-Political Change*, A.C. Renfrew and J. Cherry (eds), 1–18. Cambridge: Cambridge University Press.

Rössler, O.E. 1976. Different types of chaos in two simple differential equations. *Zeitschrift für Naturforschung* 31, 1664–70.

Russell. J.C. 1987. *Medieval Demography*. New York: AMS Press.

Schuster, H.G. 1988. *Deterministic Chaos* (2nd rev. edn). Weinheim: VCH.

Thom, R. 1975. *Structural Stability and Morphogenesis*. Reading, Mass.: W.A. Benjamin.

Webster's Collegiate Dictionary 1939 (5th edn). Springfield: Merriam.

Weigend, A.S., B.A. Huberman and D.E. Rumelhart 1990. Predicting the future: a connectionist approach, XEROX PARC Research reports SSL-90–20/P-90–00022.

Woodcock, A.E. 1990. Revolutions, catastrophes, and chaos: the role of chaotic attractors in political and military behaviour. Paper presented at the Smithsonian Institution, Washington, DC., 26 February 1990.

4   City-size dynamics in urban systems

Denise Pumain

Introduction

The distribution of population over a territory always leads to aggregates of various sizes: households, hamlets, villages, towns and cities. There is in the long-run a trend towards an increase in the size and the concentration of the population in the aggregates. This evolution has not always been continuous in the past. However, the process of concentration of the population has been almost continuous and of an unprecedented intensity since at least two centuries in many developed countries: more than 80 per cent of the total population is now concentrated in the largest towns and cities, against about 20 per cent before AD 1800.

Several theories have been developed about the causes and consequences of the urbanization process, mainly understood as the transformation of a rural into an urban population. Explanations have put forward the relationships with economic development, demographic growth, improvement of agricultural productivity, rural depopulation, and technical progress improving our capacity to manage larger and larger cities as well as the speed of communications between cities. The distribution of urban growth among cities has mostly been studied in a 'comprehensive' way, by establishing relationships between the growth of cities and the diffusion of innovations (Morrill 1965; Pred 1966). This was first seen mainly as a 'filtering' process down the urban hierarchy and later as a result of more complex network structures in the urban system (Pred 1977, p. 79).

We suggest in this chapter that it would also be interesting to build a theory of the historical development of urban systems, which would be perhaps less ambitious, but which could integrate some of their significant dynamic properties, as they have been revealed by the systematic statistical analyses of the distribution of urban growth in a large number of cities and over long periods of time. Such studies are no longer so rare: after the pioneer work by Madden (1955) for the United States and the book by Robson about Great Britain (1973), the work of Vlora on Italy (1979), Pumain (1982) and Guérin-Pace (1993) for France and Matthiesen for Denmark (1985) has increased the material required for comparisons.

In the territorial distribution of urban growth, major regularities can be observed. The most important feature, at the macroscopic scale of the entire system of cities, is the persistence of the spatial and hierarchical configuration of the system: despite the growth of the urban population and the increase in the number and sizes of cities, the general spatial pattern and the statistical form of the size distribution of cities is preserved over time. Such results suggest that the dynamics of a system of cities could be formalized in using analogies with other open systems situated 'far from equilibrium' and whose spatio-temporal dynamic properties have been investigated in the physical sciences.

Can we consider the shape of the urban hierarchy as an *attractor* for the state of any urban system? How is this *structural stability* compatible with the permanent *fluctuations* in the size of the individual cities at the meso-level, and with the even more rapid changes among the individuals who compose the urban population at a micro-level? A dynamic theory of urban systems should connect the *slow dynamic* of their city-size distribution with the more *rapid dynamic* of the *individual cities competing to attract population*. But it should also integrate a few specific properties of urban systems, as both geographical and historical objects.

The concept of a system of cities

In opposition to villages which exploit the resources of their site, cities have been conceptualized as entities which benefit from their location by exchanging and accumulating the wealth of several distant areas. This is possible through the various kinds of flows (of materials, people, information, etc.) which connect cities to each other. The importance of those relationships for the functioning and the evolution of cities has led us to conceive of a set of cities, in a regional or in a national territory, or even in a larger framework, as a system of interdependent units.

Archaeology will tell us if, from the very beginnings, the city existed as an isolated entity or as a node in a network of cities. Whatever the theory about the origins of urban functions, political and religious control over a society and its territory, handicraft production (Duby 1986, vol. 1, p. 14), or economic trade and exchange (Bairoch 1985, p. 37), it seems very difficult to imagine an isolated city. Following Berry (1964, p. 150), it is necessary to conceive of any town as 'a system within a system of cities'. In any case, the specificity of the urban growth of the last two centuries has led us to individualize urban systems by describing them as distinct from the rest of the settlement systems.

In many studies, urban systems are supposed to be delimited by the national boundaries, which usually strongly reduce the number of interactions between cities. The delimitation of an urban system remains a difficult problem however – one which has not thus far been solved in a satisfactory way. We know from empirical observation and from urban theory that the sphere of relations of any city is highly dependent upon its size. Small towns may well have relationships of interdependence only at a regional scale, whereas medium-size ones will be more strongly connected at a national level, and large cities at a supranational level. The delimitation of the relevant urban system should therefore vary according to the size of the cities being considered, as well as according to the growth of the network of inter-urban links. This kind of variable geometry for the space concerned has not yet been satisfactorily integrated into any model. We will therefore provisionally consider a set of cities, as defined in a national framework, as an urban system.

In a most formal and parsimonious way, urban systems can be conceptualized as hierarchical open systems (Prigogine and Stengers 1979, p. 184). They are hierarchical in the sense that they can be described at three significant levels: the elements are the individuals, the urban residents (urban households could also be used to define that elementary level); the subsystems are the individual cities, which are defined only by the number of elements that they contain, and this measure of their size strongly differentiates them (usually from a few thousands to several millions of people); the whole system is the total set of cities, where exchanges of elements between sub-systems are taking place. Urban systems are also open systems, since they exchange individuals with their environment, for instance migrants to and from rural areas or other countries.

Such a theory is not as poor a description for an urban system as it could seem at first sight. In a very general sense, a city can be defined as a permanent agglomeration of many people over a limited space. Of course, this definition is too simple and a minimum size and minimum density of the aggregate, which may not always be the same, has also to be considered. On the one hand, when describing a city simply by its number of inhabitants, it becomes less unreasonable to compare cities through centuries and from one civilization to another. On the other hand, population size is indeed a very synthetic description of the relative importance of a city as compared with others, since it is very often rather closely correlated with many other social, economic and cultural indicators. It is very often considered as the first 'dimension', i.e., the most important differentiating factor among a set of cities (Parr and Reiner 1980, p. 224). A dynamic theory of urban size in urban systems can then be expected to help our understanding of the logic of the process of urbanization.

The hierarchy of urban sizes: an attractor?

Usually, the cities belonging to the same region or to the same country are strongly differentiated according to their size. There is strong evidence about a certain invariance in the statistical distribution of city sizes. The size distribution is highly skewed, with many small towns located close to each other, less and more distant medium-sized cities and only a few very large cities which are generally located far away from each other. The number of cities is roughly in an inverse geometrical relationship to their size. This distribution was identified (by Le Maître in 1682) and formalized (Auerbach 1913) a long time ago. It is usually known as the 'rank-size rule' as described by Zipf (1949, pp. 417–41): when plotted on logarithmic co-ordinates, the population size of a city is a linear function of its rank in the urban hierarchy. The cumulative frequency distribution of the sizes of cities is also similar to a Pareto function (Simon 1957, p. 148) or to a lognormal distribution (Gibrat 1931, p. 280). The slope of the Pareto distribution and the dispersion of the lognormal function are both indicators of the degree of concentration of urban populations (in other words, a measure of the inequalities in size among cities).

Such types of city size distributions can be found everywhere in the world (Zipf 1949; Rosen and Resnick 1980; Parr 1985; Moriconi 1993). They seem to maintain the same shape for a very long time. Despite the numerous difficulties in evaluating the number of their inhabitants, it is thought highly probable by several historians that the hierarchical organization of French cities has existed at least since the Roman Empire. The existence of the hierarchy is not linked to demographic growth, since it has maintained itself even during the regressive periods of the Middle Ages.

For the development of a dynamic theory of settlement systems, it would be important to know whether other kinds of distributions have been observed. This is a question which archaeology might help answer: do we, for instance, have examples of a normal distribution of settlement sizes? Such a distribution would suggest that there is an optimal size for human settlement, depending upon the availability of resources at a given distance and/or upon the internal management capacities of the group. The occurrence of a normal distribution of city sizes would imply that under such circumstances a permanent settlement is not viable below or above a given threshold of size.

If such settlement size distributions could be found, for instance for agricultural communities, an explanation would have to be sought in the specificity of the urban functions. But if it is impossible to find evidence for the existence of a normal distribution of settlement sizes, our explanation of the lognormal distribution may be more general, invoking and analysing the aggregation of the population over a territory. The universal occurrence of this configuration leads us in any case to think of it as a very strong and stable attractor in the dynamics of the urbanization process.

From static to dynamic interpretations

Several kinds of theories have been put forward to explain the distribution of city size in urban systems (for a review, see Pumain 1982, pp. 15–72 or Sheppard 1982, pp. 127–51). This distribution was at first considered to be an expression of an equilibrium. Zipf, for example, considered the 'rank-size distribution' to be the result of an equilibrium between two counterbalancing forces, a 'force of concentration' and a 'force of diversification' (Zipf 1949, p. 359). Both forces resulted from the 'law of least effort', tending either to concentrate people and activities of production and consumption in the same place, in order to avoid transportation costs, or to locate production and consequently consumption in the vicinity of the natural resources to be exploited, resources whose distribution is likely to be rather dispersed. However, he did not really argue why the two forces would equilibrate in order to produce the perfect regular size distribution of cities.

Tentative explanations of city size distribution as the most probable state of an urban system are not convincing either. Berry and Garrison (1958, p. 86) have suggested, without demonstration, that the Pareto distribution would correspond to a state of maximum entropy within the urban system. Curry (1964, p. 145) has derived a skewed distribution of city sizes from the principle of entropy maximization (in the sense used in information theory) in a process of allocating individual cities among the various possible city sizes. However, many weaknesses have been found in his interpretation: the distribution which results from the application of the theory is rather different from the observed ones (Haran and Vining 1973, p. 304); moreover, the model supposes a closed urban system (Chapman 1970, p. 331), and shifts from invoking the size distribution itself towards invoking the constraints which have to be defined to get this particular outcome of the process (Pumain 1982, p. 48).

Central place theory provides a static explanation for the size, spacing, and hierarchical functional organization of cities.[1] 'Sociability' (according to Reynaud 1841, p. 38), or 'centrality' (according to Christaller 1933, p. 671), are key concepts in understanding the grouping of population and of non-agricultural activities in the most accessible, central, places. A regular pattern of nested urban levels is considered to represent an equilibrium between supply and demand of goods and services. Supply is limited by a minimum threshold in the number of consumers required for its profitability, whereas demand is limited in extent by a decreasing accessibility around the centres and a corresponding increase in the relative transportation cost.

In this model, the theoretical distribution of city sizes is supposed to be discontinuous, like a staircase where each level corresponds to a specific bunch of urban functions. Several authors have tried to make it compatible with a rank–size distribution by introducing stochastic variations in the hierarchical levels (Beckmann 1958; Beguin 1979). One may indeed argue that several independent and random factors are blurring the size limits of each level and smoothing the size distribution: the location of industrial functions, which does not depend on city size, and local variations in the demand per capita and in the elasticity of the relationship supply–profit are the main explanatory factors for such a randomization of the model. However, Parr (1970) argues that the rank–size distribution has a larger validity, because it contains all the plausible hierarchical distributions, whereas not all hierarchical structures which are derived from central place theory are compatible with the actual size distributions of cities.

An interesting development has been proposed by Allen and Sanglier (1979, p. 260), with a dynamic model of a central place system. When experimented over fictitious data, this model produces satisfying results, especially as far as the distribution of city sizes is concerned. However, this type of model could only be verified by testing it against the historical development of a real urban network. That in turn requires a major effort of data collection, a well-known problem for complex dynamic models (Pumain 1989, p. 167). If we believe in experimentation as a cornerstone in any assessment of the usefulness of theories, we must first look for simpler, but more easily verifiable, dynamic models.

Of particular interest are the models which derive a skewed distribution of sizes from the growth process of the population of cities. Several models of the distribution of growth among cities have been designed in order to demonstrate how they could lead to a Pareto distribution (Steindl 1965, pp. 297–8; Simon 1955, p. 430) or to a lognormal distribution (Gibrat 1931, Ch. VI) of city sizes. Most of them were stochastic models. Their specifications differed, but they were all based on the same main hypothesis. Gibrat demonstrated that any distribution of city sizes will become a lognormal distribution if the following characteristics of the growth process are observed:

- at each small time interval, cities are growing with a number of inhabitants which is proportional to their size (or, in other words, the growth *rates* of cities are independent of their sizes).
- the distribution of growth rates among cities is *independent* from one time interval to another.

In other words, Gibrat's 'law of proportional effect' assumes that the causes of urban growth are diverse and numerous, that the effect of one of them is small when compared to the total effect of all causes, and that this global effect is multiplicative, and proportional to the size of the cities.

It is with this model that we have experimented here. The model seems at first a simple statistical interpretation of the distribution of city size in an urban system, probably too simple for a dynamic description of an urban system. But testing it against real empirical data can nevertheless suggest improvements for the design of more sophisticated models of urban dynamics. On the basis of our findings concerning the structure of urbanism in France, we would like to present some issues in the formalization and modelling of the evolution of sets of cities, when such modelling is undertaken in the framework of the theory of self-organizing systems.

Quasi-stochastic dynamic properties of urban systems

Experimentation with this model has required the construction of a large database on the evolution of the French urban system (Pumain 1982; INED 1984). The first reliable data concerning the population of cities are to be found in the 1831 census. Censuses occurred afterwards every five years (but with breaks in 1916 and 1941 due to the wars) and with a different periodicity from 1946 up to now: 1954, 1962, 1968, 1975 and 1982. In the censuses, population figures are only given for administrative units, the communes, which are rather small (15 square kilometres on average). Communes are considered to be urban when they include more than 2,000 inhabitants. Thus, towns and cities have been defined as 'agglomerations' or urban areas. This was done to be able to keep the concept of 'city' consistent over this long period of time. The urban agglomerations were reconstituted in the database on the basis of contiguity, including all neighbouring urban communes.

From 1831 to 1982, the French urban population increased sixfold, from 6.5 to 39.6 million, the number of urban communes from 854 to 4,888 (5.7 times), the number of urban agglomerations from 617 to 1,782

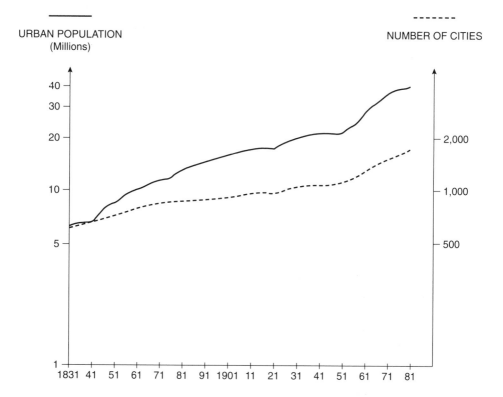

Figure 4.1 Evolution of the size of the urban system.

(2.9 times) and the mean population size of an agglomeration from 9,500 to 22,300 inhabitants (2.3 times; Figure 4.1). In comparison with the urbanization of other, similar, countries, the French process appears to have been rather slow and belated: during all of the nineteenth century, whereas the mean annual growth rate of the urban population was more than 2 per cent in Great Britain, it was about 1 per cent in France. The urbanization rate, which was already much lower in France than in Great Britain at the beginning of the nineteenth century (20 per cent versus 44 per cent in 1831) passed beyond 50 per cent only as late as the 1930s. It is only after the Second World War that urbanization accelerated, with mean growth rates of the urban population above 2 per cent per year. Still, in comparison with Great Britain and even with Germany, very few new towns were created during this expansionary stage of the urban system, even during the first Industrial Revolution.

Structural stability

Despite the dramatic growth of the urban population and of the number and size of cities, the urban system has remained remarkably stable in its geographical and dimensional configuration. The maps (Figure 4.2) show that the sites and the relative sizes of cities do not exhibit large changes between the beginning and the end of this period of almost two centuries. The correlation between the ranks of cities in the urban hierarchy is surprisingly high: 0.71 from 1831 to 1982 and 0.83 from 1911 to 1982.

This inertia in the relative positions of cities in the urban hierarchy is characteristic of urban systems which have a long history. The ordering of cities of the Roman Empire is still largely observable today, two thousand years later; according to R. Etienne (1988, p. 90) 'the modern urban network is already designed, the hierarchy of cities is confirmed [in the Roman Empire]'. Among the 107 capitals of roman '*pagi*' located within the modern boundaries of France, eighty-five are still larger than 5,000 inhabitants. Thirty-seven of the fifty-five largest urban agglomerations of today were Gallo-Roman cities.

In countries whose settlement system is younger, as for instance in the United States, the correlation between the current rank of cities and the one they had in the last century is highly negative (Moore 1958). In France, among the forty-three towns with more than 20,000 inhabitants in 1831, thirty-seven are still today among the top forty-three. The remaining six, which have lost a part of their relative importance, still appear above the seventy-ninth rank. All the cities which have now more than 100,000 inhabitants were already larger than 10,000 in 1831.

The general translation of the whole urban hierarchy towards larger sizes is well illustrated by a transition matrix of cities from one population size class to another between 1831 and 1982 (Table 4.1). Most cities have either remained in the same size group (this is the most frequent case for towns smaller than 10,000 inhabitants) or have increased their size by one level

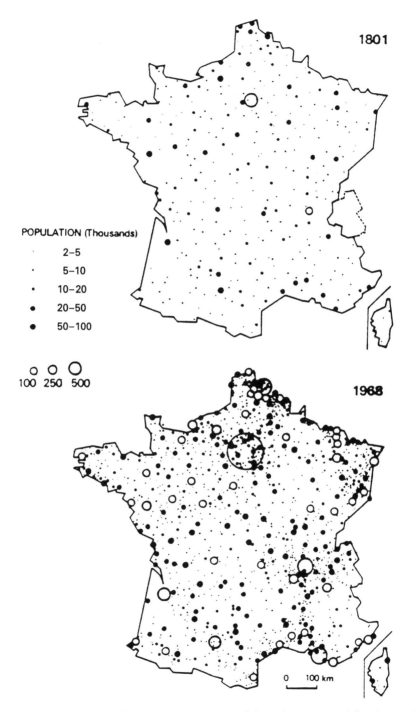

Figure 4.2 Persistency of the spatial structure of the urban system (after Fontanel and Peseux 1976).

Table 4.1 Transition matrix (1831–1982) by hierarchical levels, reflecting the proportion of cities in each size class in 1831 which belonged in a particular size class in 1982.[2]

1982 / 1831	0	1	2	3	4	5	6	7	8
0	0.1	0.6	0.2	0.1	0	0			
1	0.1	0.5	0.3	0.1	0	0			
2		0.1	0.5	0.3	0.1	0			
3			0.1	0.3	0.5	0.1	0		
4					0.2	0.4	0.3		
5						0.3	0.4	0.3	
6							0.3	0.5	0.3
7									1

Hierarchical levels (size classes)

0 = < 2,500   5 = 40,000 – 80,000
1 = 2,500 – 5,000   6 = 80,000 – 160,000
2 = 5,000 – 10,000   7 = 160,000 – 320,000
3 = 10,000 – 20,000   8 = > 320,000
4 = 20,000 – 40,000

(especially when they were larger than 10,000 inhabitants in 1831) but very few have changed in size by more than one hierarchical level and almost none by three or four. Robson (1973, pp. 56–9) has found very similar transition matrices for England and Wales during the nineteenth century.

The shape of the distribution curve of city sizes has also remained very stable (Figure 4.3). The high level of primacy, which is a well-known specificity of the French urban system (the population of the Paris agglomeration is six to seven times the one of Lyon, which is in second place), has kept about the same intensity since at least the beginning of the nineteenth century, and very likely since long before.

The French settlement system, then, has maintained its main structural properties and its specificity for two centuries (or more), through two or three industrial revolutions, rural depopulation, during stagnation in the interval between the two wars, as well as during the demographic and economic boom and the rapid urbanization period of the last forty years. The urban system responded to the strong constraints imposed by industrial revolution, railway construction, diffusion of car transportation or the final stages of rural depopulation, by changing its configuration only minimally.

Fluctuations in growth of individual cities

Such stability is all the more surprising, as urbanization is in itself a very fluctuating process. It fluctuates in time: the mean annual growth rates of the urban population oscillated between 0.5 per cent and 2.8 per cent during the twenty-six census intervals (exclusive of negative rates in the war periods, and of exceptionally low and high rates in the periods 1836–41 and 1841–6 due to a systematic bias in the census data for 1841). The values exhibit

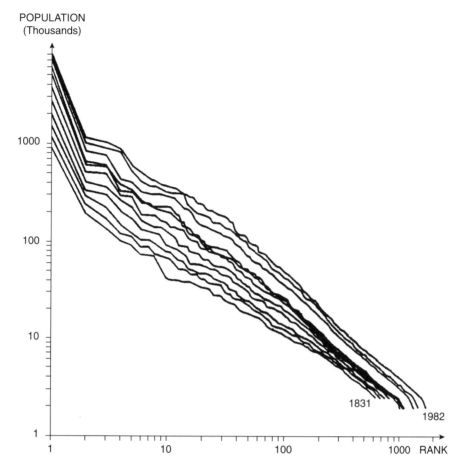

Figure 4.3 Rank–size distribution of French urban agglomerations.

cyclical fluctuations with periodicities of twenty to fifty years; these are roughly followed by fluctuations in the growth rate of the number of cities (that is, in the number of settlements whose population passes over or below the threshold of 2,000 inhabitants (Figure 4.4). In each period, there are very large variations in the intensity of growth among cities: the statistical distributions of the growth rates are almost normal but their standard deviation values are usually about three times the mean value. For each town, there are large fluctuations of growth from one census interval to another.

Is urban growth a purely random process?
The test of Gibrat's model against French data leads us to conclude that its main hypothesis converges with the ones put forward by Madden (1955, p. 241) and Robson (1973, p. 83):

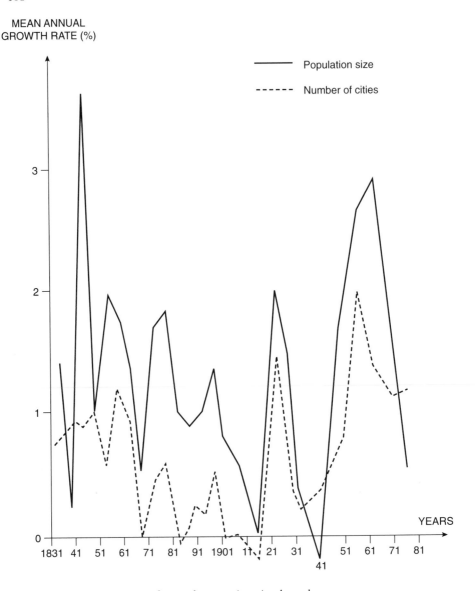

MEAN ANNUAL
GROWTH RATE (%)

Figure 4.4 Fluctuations of growth over time in the urban system.

1   The 'law of proportional effect' gives a proper description of the process
    of urban growth. On the one hand, the variations in the number of
    inhabitants of a city are − on average − roughly proportional to its size
    (or, in other words, in the urban system as a whole, urban growth
    rates are randomly distributed among cities, irrespective of their size).
    On the other hand, the spatial distribution of the growth rates is rather

variable from one period to another. Both rules hold for the largest part of the growth process in any urban system.

2   It may be added that, despite non-negligible fluctuations in the ratio between the growth rates of the urban population and of the number of cities, respectively, there is a rather strong parallelism in the evolution of both rates (Figure 4.4). Consequently, the hypothesis that there is a rather stable relationship between those two processes of expansion in urban systems can also hold true. Of course, this last observation relies upon the precise geographical definition delimiting urban sub-systems. In simpler words, the dynamic of the rural settlements whose population is large enough to let them grow above the threshold of urban size is similar to the dynamic occurring in cities already belonging to the urban system.

Why does urban growth follow the two fundamental hypotheses of the process described by Gibrat? It is understandable that cities grow on average at the same speed: as they are all connected in the same system, they are all submitted to the same general conditions (demographic and economic growth, socio-economic and technical innovations, etc.) which are responsible for the urbanization process. The variety of local conditions and the slight differences in the timing of the diffusion of innovations may explain the quasi-random fluctuations in the growth rates of individual cities.

What remains to be explained is why urban growth is proportional to urban size. Urban growth has two components, natural growth and net migration. The natural growth of populations is always multiplicative, and proportional to their initial size: when there are no limitations on resources, such growth is exponential, otherwise it follows a logistic curve. It would require a very peculiar segregation of the age groups among cities, according to their size (for instance all young people in small towns and older folk in the largest cities) to change this.

Net migration is also roughly proportional to city size, as long as the in-migration and out-migration flows are also proportional to this size. This is normally the case, as is described in the analogue models of gravitation which are used most of the time to adjust the observations of migratory flows or to predict them. According to spatial migration theory (Courgeau 1980, Ch. XI), interaction flows between various places are proportional to the probability of contacts of their residents, and this probability is a function of the size of the places.

It is, then, the multiplicative aspect of the spatial process of agglomeration of population which has to be explained, in order to find a proper explanation of the size distribution of cities.

The main characteristic of urban systems is their hierarchic structure, which reveals an organizational principle operating at the macro-level; it can be interpreted as resulting from a specific process of interactions between the individuals at the micro-level which define the spatial variations in their reproductive and migratory behaviour. There is no explicit intentionality with respect to city-size distribution in the behaviour of the individuals. In that sense, urban systems can be described as self-organized systems. If one or both of the behavioural features of urban populations would change from what they used to be during the centuries of slow and then rapid urbanization, or if they ceased to be rather homogeneous over space, the evolution and the structure of urban systems could become very different.

Geographical dynamic properties of urban systems

However, like Robson (1973, p. 86), we have observed systematic deviations from the stochastic process described by Gibrat. This should lead to a reformulation of a dynamic model, including hypotheses which would take into account the specific nature of urban systems.

Urban systems are geographical systems
A first kind of deviation from Gibrat's model is the existence of a slight positive correlation between growth rates and the size of cities. This correlation is higher with the logarithm of size than with size itself, so that the trend towards a growth rate increasing with city size is a non-linear one (Figure 4.5). It is responsible for a larger increase in the slope of the rank–size distribution (absolute value) than would be expected from Gibrat's model (Figure 4.6). The largest French cities have then taken a greater advantage of the urbanization process than the smallest. The correlation between city growth and city size was, on the contrary, negative in a developing urban system like the American during the nineteenth century (Madden 1955, p. 244); it has also become negative during the last fifteen years in the most urbanized countries, leading to a slight decrease in the concentration of city sizes (Figures 4.5 and 4.6). This trend was interpreted by several scholars as a complete reversal, called 'counter-urbanization', which, they argued, would reduce the inequalities in size among the cities. However, this interpretation is at variance with the observations for the 1980s and the previsions made for the 1990s, at least in Europe, which show again a trend towards an increasing concentration of urban population.

A second type of deviation from a random process is less frequent and seems less continuous in time, but may have stronger effects on the geographical structure of urban systems: city growth rates are not always independent from one time interval to the next, they exhibit a slight temporal autocorrelation (Figure 4.5). In France, this correlation was rather high at the end of the nineteenth century, and during the last forty years. Instead of a random distribution, there is then a trend for a geographical selectivity in urban growth. This last process is totally independent of the previous one, since it occurs in all classes of population size. It may have contributed to a reinforcement in the concentration of city sizes in the urban system, but it

**CORRELATION BETWEEN LOG OF POPULATION SIZE
AND GROWTH RATES**

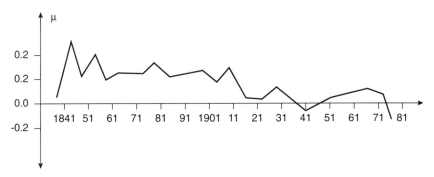

CORRELATION BETWEEN SUCCESSIVE GROWTH RATES

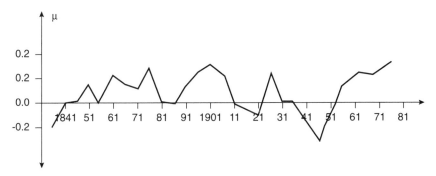

Figure 4.5 Two deviations from Gibrat's process of urban growth. (a) Correlation between the logarithm of the population size and growth rates. (b) Correlation between successive growth rates.

is also compatible with de-concentration (as observed during the period 1975–82 in France (Figures 4.5 and 4.6). It corresponds to the introduction of innovations whose diffusion has been limited in space, for specific reasons (non-substitutable resources, location close to mountains or to the sea). Detailed studies of the distribution of growth in such regions which have been momentarily favoured show that they are subject to the same general stochastic process, with large inequalities in the growth rates of individual cities at any time. Only the average rate of growth is higher.

Whereas the 'law of proportional effect' can be seen as a very general description of the evolution of any hierarchical open system, trivial since it only explains the Pareto-type structure, the selectivity in the growth process, related to size or to other properties of the cities, appears to be a specific feature of the evolution of the urban systems. We want to show that this can no longer be considered as a residual in a stochastic theory of the growth of cities, but that it has to be integrated in a dynamic model.

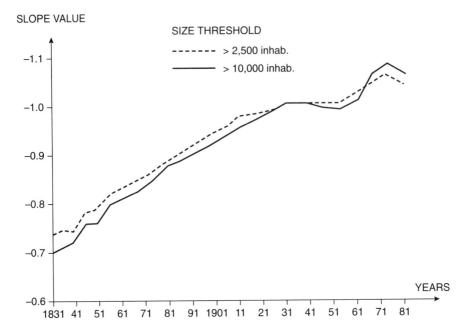

Figure 4.6 Evolution of the slope of the rank–size distribution between 1831 and 1982.

Inter-urban competition

We have pointed out that large-scale interaction is a specific property of cities, and that the organization of urban systems in hierarchical networks is 'self-organized' rather than the result of any planning. This structure has progressively emerged from a continuous process of competition between cities. For instance, when studying the construction of the national road-system in France during the eighteenth century, Lepetit (1988, p. 185) found that at that time the very concept of a road network did not exist. But there was already at a local scale a very strong competition between neighbouring cities for attracting the infrastructure. Other well-known examples of such inter-urban competition for development, for instance, concerned the choice of the capitals of the *départements* in 1793, or more recently the location of industrial zones, the creation of airports or of technopoles.

As a result of the competitive process, not only is the demographic growth on average equal among cities over long periods of time but also the same kinds of socio-economic changes occur everywhere, at about the same pace. In French cities, during the period 1950–80, the tertiarization of the economy, the substitution of new types of activities for older ones, and the modifica-tions in social structure have, for instance, been very general. This explains why very old differentials in the socio-economic profiles of cities, like the

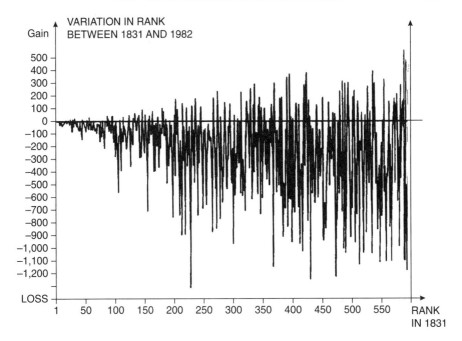

Figure 4.7 Competition in the urban hierarchy (after Guérin-Pace 1993).

ones induced by the industrial revolution of the last century, have remained almost unchanged since that time (Pumain and Saint-Julien 1978, p. 53). Imitation of what has been done elsewhere and anticipation about getting a better position in the urban hierarchy, are permanent and very old concerns for public and private local authorities. Both processes have been quoted by Allen (1978, p. 17) as being responsible for non-linearities in self-organizing social systems. Those processes play an important role in the systems of cities, because information has been circulating in urban networks for a long time, as soon as cities became interconnected.

Illustrating the effects of such inter-urban competition are the graphs which show the changes in the rank held by cities in the urban hierarchy at different dates (Figure 4.7). Except for a dozen of the largest cities, for which the changes are fewer and of lesser amplitude, the rises and falls in rank are distributed throughout the urban hierarchy, over long periods of time as well as for shorter intervals.

Shrinking space and urban hierarchy

If the competition unfolded under perfect circumstances it would lead only to random fluctuations and, on average, the growth rate of cities would be the same. This explains the important role of a stochastic process like the one defined by Gibrat. But the process of urban change is not perfectly ubiquitous, as one would expect from any simple theory of the diffusion of

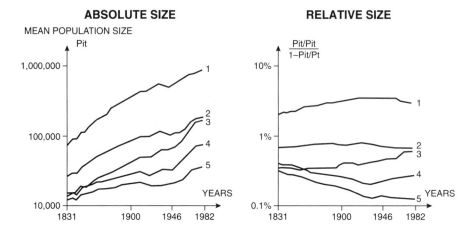

Figure 4.8 Types of urban growth 1831–1982.

innovations in space. A hierarchical diffusion process gives an initial advantage to the largest cities.

Two effects can explain the advantage of the largest cities. First their large size increases the probability of appearance and use of innovations, and especially of associations of innovations. Second, because of their size, they have more interactions in the urban network and can capture the innovations which come from elsewhere.

This explains the systematic advantage of the largest cities in the competition for urban growth, at least at the beginning of any cycle of innovation–diffusion. The stages during which smaller cities grow faster may be regarded as periods at the end of the overall process (Robson 1973, p. 213).

There is a third reason for the fact that large cities have an advantage. We have classified the curves representing the evolution of the population of cities in five types (Figure 4.8). Despite general growth, the relative importance of at least two categories in the urban system decreases. Those cities whose share in the total urban population is decreasing are on average smaller than the growing ones. Their geographical distribution is rather regular, dispersed all over the country, in all regions, usually in the interstices between the larger and more rapidly growing cities. This can be interpreted as the result of the net shrinkage of space due to the increasing speed of communications (Janelle 1969, p. 361). In due course, the range of the largest cities is thus extended in such a way that the smaller cities are short-circuited, even for low-level functions. As inter-urban competition is taking place in a shrinking spatio-temporal framework, contrasts in the urban hierarchy tend to become more and more pronounced.

Conclusion: modelling the urban system

The 'normal' evolution of an urban system tends to preserve its structure; that is, the hierarchical organization, the position of cities in the hierarchy of sizes, and also the main socio-economic differences. This evolution is produced by a combination of two processes which causes considerable fluctuations in the short term, but which has a rather regular effect in the long term: the fact that population growth is proportional to the size of cities, and the very rapid diffusion of qualitative changes and innovations within every town.

Each time an innovation cycle occurs in a concentrated space, as in the first industrial revolution, or today in the 'sun-belt' developments, it may change the relative position or the 'weight' of sub-systems of cities, and then change the geographical structure of the urban system, without necessarily changing its hierarchical structure very much. This happens when the initial advantages or the expected benefits of concentration are stronger than the spontaneous trends to regulation in the urban system (imitation and competition between cities).

If a dynamic model of city sizes in urban systems is to be conceived in the framework of self-organizing systems theory, it will have to derive the macro-level hierarchic structure of the system from a micro-level process of interactions between the individuals. Even if this interactive process is reduced to hypotheses concerning natural growth and migratory behaviour of individuals, this process cannot be defined independently of the previous state of the system: the behaviour of individuals is influenced by the size of the settlements and by the relative location of cities. The advantage which is given to the largest cities is not only a matter of size but is also due to 'shrinkage' in the spatial organization of the system.

This may increase the inertia of the urban system. Such inertia is certainly another characteristic of urban dynamics, and it can be explained by the fact that a city is not only an aggregate of inhabitants but that it also has a material, built-up structure. This 'concrete' inscription of past processes of accumulation of wealth and values slows down the momentary trends which would tend to change the ordering of the cities in the urban hierarchy. Few major bifurcations may be expected in the historic trajectory of urban systems. It may be that any modelling which uses only a conceptualization of cities in terms of aggregation of people will prove irrelevant.

This kind of formalization could, however, provide measures of the degree of freedom of local and national governments when they pretend to intervene in the distribution of population over a territory. We should answer such questions as: is a hierarchical organization of city sizes the only possible state for an urban system? Is the trend towards a higher concentration of urban population unavoidable? Dynamic modelling of urban systems would help us to explore and to measure the 'costs' of other possible solutions. Experiments with computer simulations are (almost) painless for the inhabitants!

Notes

1 Central place theory may not have been invented by Christaller (1933) but by Reynaud (1841), as discovered by Robic (1982).
2 All the calculations and figures in this chapter have been prepared with the collaboration of F. Guérin-Pace of the Institut National des Etudes Démographiques (INED), Paris.

References

Allen, P.M. 1978. Dynamique des centres urbains. *Sciences et Techniques* 50, 15–19.
Allen, P.M. and M. Sanglier 1979. Dynamic model of growth in a central place system. *Geographical Analysis* 11, 256–72.
Auerbach, F. 1913. Das Gesetz der Bevolkerungskonzentration, *Petermans Mitteilungen* 59, 74–6.
Bairoch, P. 1985. *De Jéricho à Mexico*. Paris: Gallimard.
Beckmann, M.J. 1958. City hierarchies and the distribution of city size. *Economic Development and Cultural Change* 6, 243–8.
Beguin, H. 1979. Urban hierarchy and rank-size distribution. *Geographical analysis* 11, 149–63.
Berry, B.J.L. 1964. Cities as systems within systems of cities. *Papers and Proceedings of the Regional Science Association* 13, 147–63.
Berry B.J.L. and W.L. Garrison 1958. Alternate explanations of urban rank–size relationships. *Annals of the Association of American Geographers* 1, 83–91.
Chapman, G.P. 1970. The application of information theory to the analysis of population distribution in space. *Economic Geography* 2, 317–33.
Christaller, W. 1933. *Die Zentralen Orte in Süddeutschland*. Jena: G. Fischer.
Courgeau, D. 1980. *Analyse quantitative des migrations humaines*. Paris: Masson.
Curry, L. 1964. The random spatial economy: an exploration in settlement theory. *Annals of the Association of American Geographers*, 54, 138–46.
Duby, G. (ed.) 1986. *Histoire de la France urbaine*. Paris: Seuil.
Etienne, R. 1988. Gaule romaine. In *Histoire de la population française*, J. Dupâquier (ed.), vol. I, 65–118. Paris: Presses Universitaires de France.
Fontanel, C. and C. Peseux 1976. Potentiel de population et réseau urbain en France. *L'Espace Géographique*, no. 4.
Gibrat R. 1931. *Les inégalités économiques*. Paris: Sirey.
Guérin-Pace, F. 1993. *Deux siècles de croissance urbaine*. Paris: Anthropos.
Haran E.G.P. and D.R. Vining 1973. On the implications of a stationary urban population for the size distribution of cities. *Geographical Analysis*, 5, 296–308.
INED 1984. *Fichier de l'urbanisation de la France*. Paris: INED.
Janelle, D.G. 1969. Spatial reorganization: a model and concept. *Annals of the Association of American Geographers* 21, 348–68.
Lepetit, B. 1988. *Les villes de la France moderne*. Paris: Albin Michel.
Madden, C.H. 1955. On some indications of stability in the growth of cities in the United States. *Economic Development and Cultural Change* 4, 236–52.
Matthiesen, C.W. 1985. *Danske byers vaekst*. Copenhagen: Reitzel.
Moore, F.T. 1958. A note on city size distributions. *Economic Development and Cultural Change* 7, 17–37.
Moriconi, F. 1993. L'urbanisation du monde. Paris: Anthropos.
Morrill, R. 1965. *Migration and the Spread and Growth of Urban Settlement*. Lund: University of Lund Press (Lund Studies in Geography, series B, 26).

Parr, J.B. 1970. Models of city size in an urban system. *Papers and Proceedings of the Regional Science Association* 25, 221–53.

Parr, J.B. 1985. A note on the size distribution of cities over time. *Journal of Urban Economics* 18, 199–212.

Parr, J.B. and T.A. Reiner 1980. A note on the dimensions of a national urban settlement system. *Urban Studies* 2, 223–30.

Pred, A.R. 1966. *The Spatial Dynamics of US Urban-Industrial Growth, 1800–1914: interpretive and theoretical essays*. Cambridge, Mass.: MIT Press.

Pred, A.R. 1977. *City Systems in Advanced Economies*. London: Hutchinson.

Prigogine, I. and I. Stengers 1979. *La nouvelle alliance*. Paris: Gallimard.

Pumain, D. 1982. *La dynamique des villes*. Paris: Economica.

Pumain, D. 1989. Spatial analysis and urban models. In *Urban Dynamics and Spatial Choice Behaviour* J. Hauer, H. Timmermans and N. Wrigley (eds), 155–73. Dordrecht: Kluwer.

Pumain, D. and T. Saint-Julien 1978. *Les dimensions du changement urbain*. Paris: CNRS.

Reynaud, J. 1841. Villes, article de l'Encyclopédie Nouvelle. In *Deux siècles de géographie française,* Ph. Pinchemel, M.C. Robic and J.L. Tissier (eds), 29–35. Paris: CTHS.

Robic, M.C. 1982. Cent ans avant Christaller, une théorie des lieux centraux. *L'Espace Géographique* 1, 5–12.

Robson, B. 1973. *Urban Growth. An approach*. London: Methuen.

Rosen, K.T. and M. Resnick 1980. The size distribution of cities: an examination of Pareto's law and primacy. *Journal of Urban Economics* 8, 165–86.

Sheppard, E. 1982. City size distribution and spatial economic change. *International Regional Science Review* 7, 127–51.

Simon, H.A. 1955. On a class of skew distributions. *Biometrika* 42, 425–40.

Simon, H.A. 1957. *Models of Man*. New York: Wiley.

Steindl, J. 1965. *Random Processes and the Growth of Firms*. New York: Hoffner.

Vlora, N.R. 1979. *Città e territorio*. Bologna: Pàtron.

Zipf, G.K. 1949. *Human Behaviour and the Principle of Least Effort*. Cambridge, Mass.: Addison-Wesley.

5   Expectations and social outcomes

NATALIE S. GLANCE AND
BERNARDO A. HUBERMAN

Introduction

In most social systems, expectations about the future, along with imperfect knowledge about the present and the past, determine individual choices. Stock trading, currency markets, and the planning of production cycles provide a few examples of such behaviour. Expectations form as a result of the intentional nature of social agents, a property which is absent in the objects that are the purview of physics and chemistry. It is because of this that a dynamical formulation of social interactions entails a different approach, one in which the future enters explicitly in the equations describing the evolution of the system.

Previous work on the dynamics of interacting processes in computational ecosystems (Huberman and Hogg 1988; Kephart *et al.* 1990: Hogg and Huberman 1991) took into account their ability to project past trends into the present and examined the behaviour that results when the perceived pay-off differs from the actual pay-off. It also showed how rewards can stabilize the system without resorting to complex control algorithms. Equally important, these studies provide a starting point for using the dynamics of computational processes to gather quantitative insights about social and biological organizations.

In order to have a more realistic economic model of a system of agents competing for resources, we now incorporate several features that are essential for understanding the dynamics of expectations. Among them, we introduce the notion of transaction costs, and allow the agents to make decisions based on future preferences along with present ones. This is particularly relevant when the cost of moving between resources becomes high compared to instantaneous pay-off. Only when the accumulated utility becomes large enough to justify the transaction cost do agents change strategy.

We consider two types of expectations, both very simple. We are not interested here in how agents might predict the future, but rather in the effect of their expectations on the system's dynamical behaviour. Our focus thus follows the recent interest in economic research on the role of psychological forces in market movements (e.g. Day and Huang 1990). The two scenarios are:

1 Flat expectations in which each agent assumes that the system remains essentially constant; thus its prediction for the future state of the system is simply the present state. Since its information is delayed, the present state is actually the state of the system some time in the past;

2 Linear extrapolations in which each agent expects the system to follow its present trend. Again, because the agent's information is delayed, the agent's decisions are actually based on the trend perceived at some delayed time in the past.

Besides transaction costs and future expectations, we also include discounts as an essential variable in our study. Discounts mean that a dollar now is worth more than a dollar in the future. Since an agent could place its money in the equivalent of a bank and let it grow at interest rates, economic rationality dictates that future pay-offs be discounted with respect to immediate pay-off.

This chapter presents the results of such a study. We show how long forecasts tend to destabilize the system (see pp. 123–8), and obtain a phase diagram that exhibits a sharp boundary separating stable equilibria from complex dynamics as the horizon length increases. We also demonstrate the existence of an optimal strategy for flat expectations, in the sense that profits are maximized and behaviour is stable. Rising expectations in time are seen to lead to a crash whereby the fixed point gives way to wild oscillations. In the case of trendy agents (discussed in on pp. 133–5), we obtain qualitatively similar behaviour to that of flat predictions, but with a more pronounced tendency for expectations to destabilize the system.

The more striking result appears on pp. 135–8. There, we show how a diversity of expectations among the agents, coupled to reward mechanisms in which those agents that do well increase at the expense of the others, leads to overall dynamics characterized by cycles of almost stable behaviour interrupted by sudden crashes. This process is accompanied by an ever-changing diversity in the composition of the system.

Before closing this section, we mention that there is a major difference between this approach and other studies on the effect of expectations on collective games of co-operation and competition (Axelrod 1984). For example, research on the logic of ongoing collective action has elucidated how expectations about the future determine the types of mixed strategies that are optimal for the system (Bendor and Mookherjee 1987). Although important in determining the kind of behavioural rules that ensure overall co-operation, such results have little dynamical content, and thus cannot explain how those mixed strategies emerge. In contrast, we consider the full dynamical evolution of the system, and show how rising expectations lead to the replacement of evolutionarily stable strategies with complex oscillations and chaos.

Modelling expectations

The basic model considered in this chapter consists of N agents which are free to choose among R resources according to the *perceived* (i.e., not necessarily correct) expected pay-off for using each resource. Competition and co-operation among the agents are taken into account by allowing the pay-off for using a particular resource to depend on the number of agents already using it. For example, in a purely competitive environment, the pay-off for using a particular resource i would decrease monotonically with the fraction of agents already using it, $f_i(t)$. Alternatively, the agents using the same resource could assist one another, and in this case, the pay-off might increase as more agents used that resource. Each agent evaluates the pay-off associated with each resource asynchronously at an average rate α and switches to the resource with the highest pay-off under the constraint that the benefit obtained by switching be greater than the transaction cost for switching. To account for the fact that an agent's information about the current state of the system can be somewhat imperfect and delayed, we add a normally distributed quantity with zero mean and standard deviation σ to each (instantaneous) pay-off, and delay the information available to each agent by a time τ.

In evaluating the perceived expected pay-off for using each resource, agents take into account future anticipated earnings as well as present perceived earnings. The agents discount future earnings expected at a time s from the present time t at a rate $e^{-s/H}$, reflecting their bias to the present, where $\mathbf{H}$ is constant in time and is the agents' horizon length. The instantaneous perceived density-dependent pay-off is defined to be $\mathbf{G}(\mathbf{f}(t))$. $\mathbf{f}(t)$ is a vector describing the fraction of agents using each resource at time t and has scalar components $f_i(t)$ corresponding to the fraction of agents using resource i. Now let $f_i^\star(t+s)$ be a vector describing the expected behaviour of the system at time s from the present. (The components $f_i^\star(t + s)$ represent the expected fraction of agents utilizing resource i at time s from the present.) This vector function $\mathbf{f}^\star(t + s)$ represents the mathematical expression of the way in which agents form expectations about the future. In principle it could depend on the system's entire past history as well as additional information made available to the agents. Under the simplifying assumptions of this chapter, it will be seen that $\mathbf{f}^\star(t + s)$ depends only on the delayed values $\mathbf{f}(t - \tau)$ and $\mathbf{f}'(t - \tau)$. the vector with components $f_i'(t - \tau)$. The time rate of change of the fraction of agents using resource i at the delayed time $t - \tau$.

Each agent then expects the instantaneous pay-off density for resource i at a time s from the present to be $G_i(\mathbf{f}^\star(t + s))$. The agent's anticipated pay-off, $g_i(\mathbf{f}^\star, t)$, at time t for the ith resource is then the discounted time integral of the expected instantaneous pay-off density:

$$g_i(\mathbf{f}^\star, t) = \int_0^\infty G_i\ (\mathbf{f}^\star(t + s))\ \exp[-(s/H)]\ ds \qquad (5.1)$$

At this point, we specialize to the case of a system with two resources. The scalar function of time $f(t)$ is defined to be the fraction of agents using resource 1 at time t ; then $1 - f(t)$ is the fraction using resource 2. Similarly, $f'(t)$ is the time rate of change of the fraction of agents using resource 1 and $1 - f'(t)$ is the time rate of change of the fraction of agents using resource 2.

Two very simple models of expectations are (1) flat expectations and (2) linear extrapolation, both based on the agent's delayed information about the state of system (see above). Flat expectations describes agents who believe the system to be changing very slowly. In this case, the expected future behaviour of the system is simply the past observed behaviour, or

$$f(t + s) = f(t - \tau) \tag{5.2}$$

for all $s \geq 0$, where τ is the delay. The expected pay-off can be evaluated trivially since the instantaneous pay-off at all future times is constant:

$$g_i^{flat}(f(t - \tau)) = HG_i(f(t - \tau)) \tag{5.3}$$

Here, the explicit time-dependence has dropped out, since the expected pay-off depends on time only implicitly through $f(t - \tau)$.

The second type of expectation reflects the agents' belief that the system will continue to follow the observed trend. As a result, their expectations depend both on the state of the system $f(t - \tau)$ and on its trend, or slope, $f'(t - \tau)$, the time rate of change of the state. Agents assume that the system will continue to follow the trend observed at the delayed time. They extrapolate to the present and then to the future (we assume agents are aware of the time lag of their information), allowing their predictions to decay asymptotically to the boundaries at $f = 0$ and $f = 1$ for the sake of continuity. We can then write for the expected evolution of f,

$$f^{\star}(t + s) = \theta - (\theta - f(t - \tau)) \exp\left[\frac{f'(t - \tau)}{\theta - f(t - \tau)}(s + \tau)\right] \tag{5.4}$$

where

$$\theta = \begin{cases} 1, f'(t - \tau) > 0 \\ 0, f'(t - \tau) \leq 0 \end{cases} \tag{5.5}$$

Specifically, the agents' expectations are such that they match actual behaviour at time $t - \tau$, that is $f^{\star}(t - \tau) = f(t - \tau)$, $f^{\star\prime}(t - \tau) = f'(t - \tau)$, and for small $\tau + s$, the extrapolation is linear; that is

$$f^{\star}(t + s) = f(t - \tau) + (s + \tau) f'(t - \tau) \tag{5.6}$$

Note that when $f'(t - \tau) = 0$, $f^{\star}(t + s) = f(t - \tau)$, for all future times s, reducing to the case of flat expectations.

The pay-off expected by trend-followers depends on the functional form of the instantaneous resource pay-offs. Taking the case of quadratic pay-offs (i.e., pay-offs which have both a co-operative and a competitive component),

$$G_i(f(t)) = a_i + b_i f(t) + c_i f^2(t) \tag{5.7}$$

the agent's total accumulated pay-off then becomes:

$$g_i^{trend}(f(t-\tau), f'(t-\tau)) = H\left\{a_i + \theta(b_i + c_i)] - \frac{(b_i + 2\theta c_i)(\theta - f(t-\tau))^2}{Hf'(t-\tau) + \theta - f(t-\tau)}\right. \tag{5.8}$$

$$\left.\exp\left[-\frac{f'(t-\tau)}{\theta - f(t-\tau)}\right] + \frac{d_i(\theta - f - \tau))^3}{2Hf'(t-\tau) + \theta - f(t-\tau)}\exp\left[-\frac{2f'(t-\tau)}{\theta - f(t-\tau)}\tau\right]\right\}$$

In spite of its complicated structure, this equation yields the result that when the slope is zero, i.e., $f'(t - \tau) = 0$, then $g_i^{trend}(f(t - \tau)) = HG_i(f(t - \tau))$, again reducing to the case of flat expectations.

Transaction costs enter whenever an agent evaluates the difference in pay-off between two resources. Since an agent switching resources incurs a transaction cost, the benefit of switching must overcome this cost. Thus, in the absence of uncertainty, an agent will move to another resource j only when

$$g_j(f^\star, t) - g_i(f^\star, t) > T \tag{5.9}$$

T being the transaction cost. In general, however, the agents' knowledge will be imperfect which in the computational ecosystem model is incorporated through an uncertainty parameter σ characterizing the average size of the errors in the agents' perceptions of the instantaneous resource pay-offs G_i. The agents' uncertainty in the expected pay-off for using resource i, g_i is then $H\sigma$, since no new information is gained by projecting into the future. The probability that an agent will choose to switch between two resources is then given by

$$\rho_{i \to j}(f^\star, t) = \frac{1}{2}\left\{1 + \text{erf}\left[\frac{g_j(f^\star, t) - g_i(f^\star, t) - T}{2H\sigma}\right]\right\}, i \neq j \tag{5.10}$$

while the probability that it does not switch is simply

$$\rho_{i \to i}(f^\star, t) = 1 - \rho_{i \to j}(f^\star, t) = \frac{1}{2}\left\{1 - \text{erf}\left[\frac{g_j(f^\star, t) - g_i(f^\star, t) - T}{2H\sigma}\right]\right\} \tag{5.11}$$

For both flat and trendy expectations, $\rho_{i \to j}(f^\star, t)$ will have no explicit time dependence since the anticipated pay-offs $g_i(f^\star, t)$ depend on time only implicitly through the delayed values $f(t - \tau)$ and $f(t - \tau)$. In the case of zero uncertainty ($\sigma = 0$), $\rho(f^\star, t)$ reduces to a step function, for example:

$$\rho_{i \to j}(f^\star, t) = \begin{cases} 1, & g_j(f^\star, t) - T > g_i(f^\star, t) \\ 0, & g_j(f^\star, t) - T < g_i(f^\star, t) \end{cases} \tag{5.12}$$

Note that transaction cost adds asymmetry to the dynamics of the system since $\rho_{i \to j}(t) + 1 - \rho_{j \to i}(t)$.

Finally, the dynamics of a system of identical agents choosing between two resources is described by the dynamical equation derived by Huberman and Hogg (1988, pp. 77–115).

$$\frac{df(t)}{dt} = - \alpha[f(t) - f(t) \, \rho_{1\rightarrow1} (f^\star, t) - (1 - f(t)) \, \rho_{2\rightarrow1} (f^\star, t)] \tag{5.13}$$

where $f(t)$ is the fraction of agents using resource 1, α is the rate at which agents re-evaluate their preferences, $\rho_{i\rightarrow j}(f^\star, t)$ is given by Equation 5.10 (above), and $g_i(f^\star, t)$, the accumulated expected pay-off is given by $g_i^{flat}(f(t - \tau))$ of Equation 5.3 (above) for the case of flat expectations and by $g_i^{trend}(f(t - \tau), f'(t - \tau))$ of Equation 5.8 for the case of trend-followers. In a later section, where rewards are introduced we will consider a more complex system made up many different types of agents, but still limited to two different kinds of resources or strategies. At that point we will need to generalize Equation 5.13.

The past is the present is the future

The simplest and most straightforward incorporation of expectations into the computational ecosystem model is to assume that the agents expect the behaviour of the system to remain roughly constant. Given naïve agents with little insight into the dynamics of the system, this simple mechanism is quite reasonable. However, it is not the predictive abilities of the agents that interest us here, but rather the effect of the agents' expectations on overall behaviour.

Long forecasts destabilize
It seems intuitively obvious that for short horizons, transaction costs will tend to stabilize the system, forcing it into an equilibrium which might not be optimal. However, it is important to determine both how far into the future agents can look for a given fixed transaction cost without creating instabilities, and to establish how the maximum stable horizon length scales with the agents' uncertainty and the transaction costs.[1]

For a given system characterized by a set of pay-offs, re-evaluation rate, delay, and uncertainty, we can map out stability boundaries in the space σ versus H/T (H = horizon length, T = transaction cost). Note from Equations 5.3 and 5.10 that the stability boundaries in the case of flat expectations will depend only the ratio H/T that is, at fixed s, the maximum stable horizon will scale linearly with increasing transaction costs. We also expect the functional form of the boundary to have the same qualitative features when considering other two-resource computational ecosystems with flat expectations.

Linear stability analysis of the dynamical equation (Equation 5.13) gives us an implicit solution to the functional form of the stability boundary. We linearize Equation 5.13 in the neighbourhood of a fixed point f_o, letting $\delta(t) = f(t) - f_o$. Then, with

$$\gamma_{1\rightarrow1} = \frac{d\rho_{1\rightarrow1}}{df} (f)| \, (f = f_o)$$

and

$$\gamma_{2 \to 1} = \frac{d\rho_{2 \to 1}}{df} (f) \mid (f = f_o)$$

we obtain:

$$\frac{d\delta}{dt} = \alpha\{\delta(t)[\rho_{1 \to 1}(f_o - \rho_{2 \to 1}(f_o) - 1] + \delta(t - \tau)$$
$$f_o[\gamma_{1 \to 1} - \gamma_{2 \to 1}] + \delta(t - \tau)\gamma_{2 \to 1} \tag{5.14}$$

The behaviour of the solutions to this equation can be characterized by making the substitution $\delta(t) = \exp(-\alpha s t)$, giving the following equation in the complex variable s:

$$[f_o(\gamma_{1 \to 1} - \gamma_{2 \to 1}) + \gamma_{2 \to 1}]e^{-\beta s} + \rho_{1 \to 1}(f_o) - \rho_{2 \to 1}(f_o) - s - 1 = 0 \tag{5.15}$$

where $\beta \equiv \alpha\tau$. There are an infinite number of roots to the above exponential equation; the system is stable to perturbations about the fixed point only if ·the largest real part of all roots is less than zero (Bellman and Cooke 1963).

In the limit $\mathrm{Re}(s) \to 0$, an analytic expression can then be derived from Equation 5.15, giving the stability boundary $\sigma(H/T)$ implicitly in terms of the accumulated pay-offs g_i that enter the ρ functions through Equations 5.3 and 5.10:

$$\beta = \{[f_o(\gamma_{1 \to 1} - \gamma_{2 \to 1} + \gamma_{2 \to 1}]^2 - [1 - \rho_{1 \to 1}(f_o) + \rho_{2 \to 1}(f_o)]^2\}^{-1/2} \cos^{-1}$$
$$\left[\frac{1 - \rho_{1 \to 1}(f_o)\rho_{2 \to 1}(f_o)}{f_o(\gamma_{1 \to 1} - \gamma_{2 \to 1}) + \gamma_{2 \to 1}}\right] \tag{5.16}$$

In order to solve for $\sigma (H/T)$ we also need the fixed point f_o, given by the solution to

$$f_o\rho_{1 \to 1}(f_o) + (1 - f_o)\rho_{2 \to 1}(f_o) = f_o \tag{5.17}$$

Solving Equations 5.16 and 5.17 simultaneously for σ and f_o gives the limiting value of the uncertainty at which $\mathrm{Re}(s) \to 0$ for fixed H/T and the system becomes unstable. We find that when the uncertainty is large enough, the system is stable for all values of H/T, and that for increasing H/T very small amounts of uncertainty cause instability. The results for the choice of resource pay-offs, $G_1 = 4 + 7f - 5.333f^2$ and $G_2 = 4 + 3f$, $\alpha = 1$, $\tau = 6$ and $\sigma = 0.5$ are shown in Figure 5.1. As can be seen, the system is unstable for all choices of initial conditions within region A, delineated by the curve $\sigma(H/T)$ derived above.

Thus far, we have described the region in phase space for which the system is definitively unstable, but we have yet to investigate the surrounding region. In region C, all fixed points of the system are repellers ($\mathrm{Re}(s) > 0$). Below, in region B, some fixed points are attractors, some are repellers. That there exist multiple fixed points for some pairs of horizon and transition cost can be seen by graphical solution of the dynamical equations. For some initial

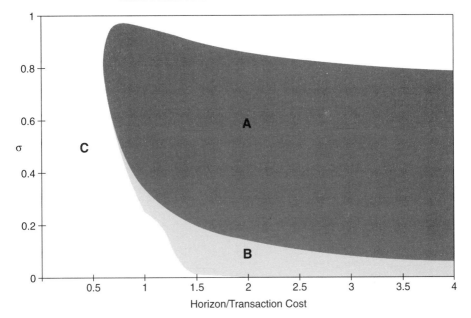

Figure 5.1 Stability portrait in the phase space H/T vs. σ for a system with resource pay-offs $G_1 = 4 + 7f - 5.333f^2$ and $G_2 = 4 + 3f$, $\alpha = 1$, $\tau = 6$. System is always unstable in region A and always stable in region C. In region B, system either relaxes to a fixed point or is pulled into a limit cycle, depending upon the initial conditions. The boundary to region A was derived analytically, while the lower boundary to region B was found by repeated numerical integration of the dynamical equation.

conditions, the system relaxes to a fixed point. Alternatively, for others the system is pulled into a limit cycle. As a result, the behaviour of the system depends strongly on the initial conditions. Figure 5.2 demonstrates this dependence. The same system relaxes to a fixed point for one set of initial conditions but gets pulled into a limit cycle for another. We further add that although the system can be chaotic for large enough values of H/T in region A, within region B the uncertainty is small enough that no chaotic behaviour is observed.

Region C of Figure 5.1 gives the values of σ vs. horizon/transaction cost for which the system always relaxes to a fixed point. However, it can take a prohibitively long time to do so, depending on the initial conditions – see, for example, Figure 5.3. In this example, the system is trapped for a long time at the almost-fixed point $f = 0$. The slow rate of escape is caused by the barrier to switching erected by the transaction costs. For vanishing transaction costs, the rate of transitions between resources

$$\alpha(f\rho_{1\to2} + (1 - f)\rho_{2\to1}) \tag{5.18}$$

is on the order of the re-evaluation rate α. However, for transaction costs such that $T/H \gg |G_1(f) - G_2(f))|$,

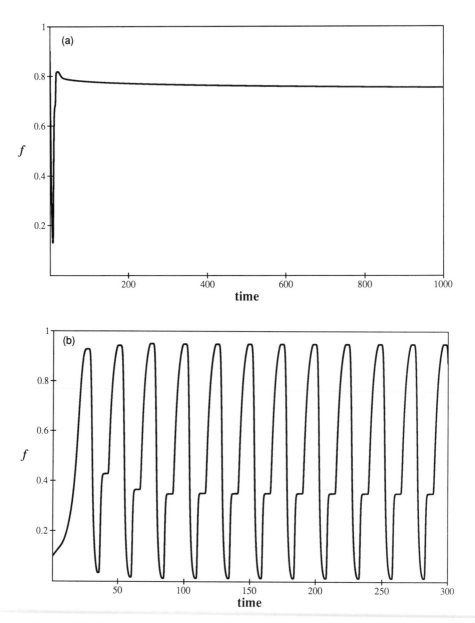

Figure 5.2 Same resource pay-offs. $H/T = 1.2333$, $\alpha = 1$, $\tau = 6$, and $\sigma = 0.135135$. System in region B of phase diagram of Figure 5.1, where different initial conditions can lead to different types of behaviour. (a) Initial condition $f = 0.9$; the system relaxes very slowly to a fixed point at $f_o = 0.74424$ (after over 8,000 time-steps); (b) Initial condition $f = 0.1$; the system oscillates. Apparently sharp corners due to transaction costs.

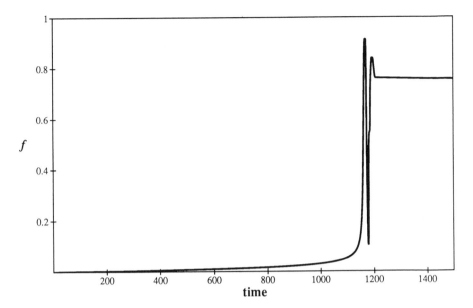

Figure 5.3 Same resource pay-offs. $H/T = 1.2$, $\sigma = 0.13889$, $\alpha = 1$, $\tau = 6$. System in region C of H/T phase diagram of Figure 5.1. Initial condition $f = 0$. System takes a very long time to escape the almost fixed point $f = 0$ and overcome the cost barrier erected by the transaction costs.

$$\rho_{1\rightarrow 2} \approx \rho_{2\rightarrow 1} \propto \exp\left[\frac{-T_2}{4H^2\sigma^2}\right]$$ (5.19)

and consequently the transition rate is also reduced from α by a factor proportional to $\exp(-T^2/4H^2\sigma^2)$. In the example shown, $G_1 = G_2$ at $f = 0$ and thus the transaction costs trap the system in a suboptimal state for a length of time roughly exponential in the square of the transaction costs.[2] Also note that if the uncertainty vanishes, the system will be trapped forever in the suboptimal metastable state $f = 0$. This is another manifestation of the persistence of non-optimal strategies as demonstrated in Ceccato and Huberman (1989).

As mentioned earlier, the stability boundaries mapped out in Figure 5.1 depend only on the ratio $H{:}T$; thus, from this figure we know the linear stability boundaries $H(T)$ for different values of the uncertainty σ. Specifically, when σ is small, the slope of $H(T)$ becomes very steep and only very large horizons destabilize the system at a fixed transaction cost. Consequently, when σ vanishes, infinitesimally small values of T are sufficient for the fixed point to be stable at all values of the horizon length H. This observation can be understood as follows: agents with perfect information will resist any movement away from the fixed point when there are transaction costs. Therefore, the combination of non-zero transaction costs with perfect information effectively erects an insurmountable transition barrier. Note, however, that the fixed point is still unstable when there are no transaction costs (when $H/T \rightarrow \infty$). Lastly, we observe the anomalous behaviour seen for $\sigma \sim 0.9$: as H/T increases the system passes successively through a stable regime, an unstable regime, and then a second unstable regime.

Optimal horizons

We have established that for a fixed transition cost there is a range of possible horizon lengths that lead to stable behaviour, defined as relaxation to a fixed point. However, the location of the fixed point varies with horizon length. We now define the optimal horizon length as being the horizon for which a system yields the highest performance under time and stability constraints. The choice of performance measure is somewhat arbitrary; we choose to equate performance of the system with the average earnings per agent in analogy to a market economy. There are two contributions to the average amount earned per agent at any given time: the average instantaneous pay-off received per agent and the mean transaction cost incurred per agent. The average system pay-off is simply the sum of the actual pay-offs accrued by the entire system per unit time, i.e.,

$$\text{Pay-off } (t) = f(t) \, G_1(f(t)) + (1 - f(t)) \, G_2(f(t)) \tag{5.20}$$

while the mean transaction cost per unit time at time t is the fraction of agents switching between resources per unit time multiplied by the transaction cost, or

$$\text{Cost } (t) = \alpha T[f(t)\rho_{1 \rightarrow 2})f(t - \tau)) + (1 - f(t)) \, \rho_{2 \rightarrow 1}(f(t - \tau))] \tag{5.21}$$

In general, even at a stable fixed point agents are still switching back and forth between resources, incurring small, but non-zero transaction costs. Finally, the amount earned per agent is the pay-off per agent minus transaction cost per agent, i.e.,

$$\begin{aligned}
\text{Earnings } (t) &= \text{Pay-off } (t) - \text{Cost } (t) \\
&= f(t)G_1 \, (f(t)) + (1 - f(t))G_2(t) - \\
&\quad \alpha T[f(t)\rho_{1 \rightarrow 2}(f(t - \tau)) + (1 - f(t))\rho_{2 \rightarrow 1}(f(t - \tau))]
\end{aligned} \tag{5.22}$$

Notice that at a fixed point, earnings are accrued at a constant rate. When there are multiple fixed points, the performance of the system depends upon which fixed point is attained. The fixed point which yields the highest performance is defined as the optimal fixed point, and for our previous choice of pay-offs is located at $f = 0.75$.

In the dynamics of expectations, there is a trade-off between performance and response time in determining the optimal horizon length. With increasing horizon lengths, stability decreases in the sense that $\text{Re}\,(s) \rightarrow 0$ and accrued transaction costs increase. Thus, the maximum performance of a system is always greater for smaller horizons. However, the response of the system to

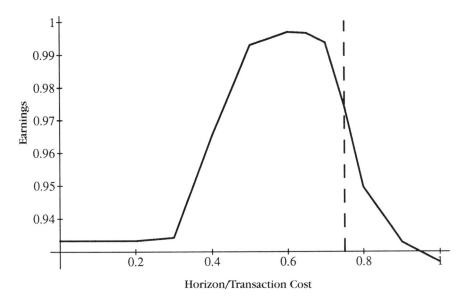

Figure 5.4 Normalized mean earnings per agent as a function of horizon length. Pay-offs are the same as for Figure 5.1 with T =1, τ = 6, α = 1, and σ = 0.5. For these parameters the fixed point is stable to the left of the dashed line and unstable to the right of it. Earnings are averaged over the first 100 time-steps, with the initial condition f = 0.5.

excursions away from the fixed point improves as the horizon gets longer (see Equation 5.19), so that if the performance is averaged over the initial response, the optimal horizon at a fixed level of uncertainty depends strongly on the initial conditions. Consider, for example, a system with the resource pay-offs G_1= 4 + 7f – 5.333f^2,G_2 = 4 + 3f.

In Figure 5.4, the normalized average earnings of the system (averaged over the first 100 time-steps, with the initial condition f = 0.5) is plotted vs. the horizon length of the agents' expectations. In this case, the system is stable for horizon lengths less than 0.75, and unstable at horizons greater than this value. The optimal horizon in this case is H = 0.6, although perfor-mance can be marginally greater at shorter horizons given an ideal choice of initial conditions. At this horizon length, the average earnings are about 99.7 per cent of maximum.

Crash of rising expectations

We next consider a society of agents which, unaware of (or indifferent to) the trade-off between stability and response time, plays a dangerous game. Intent on maximizing performance, these agents slowly increase the horizon into the future for which they trust their expectations to remain reliable. As the horizon length of their flat predictions increases, the respective perfor-mance of the system also improves, until the optimal horizon length is reached.

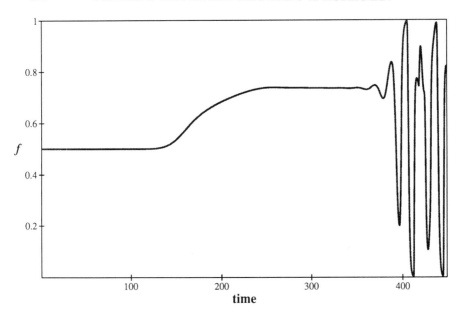

Figure 5.5 Horizon length of agents increases linearly with time from $H = 0$ to $H = 2.25$. Instability first hits at $H = 1.7$, but is not noticeable until $H \gg 1.85$. As the horizon increases the distribution of agents approaches its optimal value, reaching its maximum at the horizon length which best counters the trade-off between stability and response time. As the horizon increases further, performance is only slightly compromised, but eventually the horizon becomes large enough that the system destabilizes. Resource pay-offs are as in previous figures, $T = 1$, $\alpha = 6$, and $\sigma = 0.2$.

At this point, since the system is very near an optimal fixed point, increasing the horizon further will not deteriorate performance significantly and greedy agents might unwisely choose to extend the horizons even further. Soon enough the system becomes unstable and begins to oscillate.

Imagine that the horizon length increases linearly with time starting with a zero value horizon. Figure 5.5 shows the dynamical approach of the system to the optimal fixed point (corresponds to optimal performance) followed by the inevitable crash. In this example, the transition cost is 1, the uncertainty 0.2, the delay 6 time units, and the re-evaluation rate is 1, with the same resource pay-offs introduced earlier. The horizon length was made to increase slowly at a rate of 0.005.

Curiously, the point at which the system becomes unstable is not what might have been predicted from examination of Figure 5.1. Instead of crossing over at $H = 1.5$ into the instable region A, the system remains stable until $H \approx 1.7$. Furthermore, if we were to next imagine the oscillating agents to start decreasing the horizon length as soon as they observed instability, say when $H = 1.9$ (after 380 time-steps) the system would not restabilize (determined here by absence of fluctuations) until $H \approx 0.9$.

What is causing the hysteresis in stability as a function of horizon length? To understand this effect, first note that even with increasing horizon H, the unstable fixed point is only marginally unstable. Thus, instabilities grow very slowly when the system is near one of these unstable fixed points. Since the fixed point changes continuously with horizon length, the system remains near the instantaneous fixed point. However, once the system becomes unstable, it takes a long time to restabilize as the fixed point is weakly attractive just below the outside stability boundary.

Interestingly enough, a stable system of agents can support a sub-population of agents with indefinitely increasing expectations. As long as the sub-population is small, the system may remain stable, but at a new fixed point. However, once the sub-population becomes large enough, rising expectations once again cause a transition to instability.

Follow the trend

In the previous section we postulated agents which believe that system averages remain roughly constant over time and persist in this belief despite evidence to the contrary. If the environment in which the system resides varies little with time, a stable system will be better able to profitably use the resources than an oscillating one. Thus, in this case, the agents' flat expectations are counterproductive in that they create instability out of a stable environment.[3]

This motivates us to introduce a new type of agent, the trend-followers. These agents not only have access to the delayed (and again, imperfect) state of the system, but can also recall the state of the system back to some point in the past, giving them knowledge of the derivative at the delayed time. We further specify that these agents have short memories, on the order of a few delays, and consequently follow short-term trends as opposed to long-term trends. Examining the dynamical behaviour of trend-followers will elucidate the effect of this second type of expectations.

Recalling Equations 5.13 and 5.17, we see that $df(t)/dt$ is now a function of both $f(t - \tau)$ and $df(t - \tau)/dt$ so that the evolution of the state of the system depends on both the delayed value and the delayed derivative. This type of differential equation is called a neutral equation as it contains both delayed and advanced terms (a delayed derivative is equivalent to an advanced term). If we had chosen to give the agents perfect forecasting abilities so that $f^\star(t + s) = f(t + s)$, then we would have had a very complicated advanced equation, known to be always unstable (Bellman and Cooke 1963). Fortunately, self-fulfilling behaviour is very unlikely and we need not consider it in this context.

Long forecasts still destabilize

Once again, linear stability analysis can be used to give an implicit solution to the functional form of the stability boundary. Following the approach taken in the previous section (which is also valid for neutral differential-difference equations), the following characteristic equation for s is obtained, valid for all negative values of s:

$$\rho_{1\to2}(f_o) - \rho_{2\to1}(f_o) - 1 + \exp(-\beta s)[1 + \alpha s(H + T)]$$
$$[f_o(\gamma_{1\to1} - \gamma_{2\to1})\ \gamma_{2\to1}] - s = 0 \tag{5.22}$$

This differs from the characteristic equation for the case of flat expectations only in the factor of $[1 + \alpha s(H + \tau)]$, which arises from combining terms involving $\gamma = \delta\rho/df \mid f = f_o,\ f' = 0$ and $\xi\ \delta\rho/df \mid f = f_o,\ f = 0$. (It turns out that $\xi = (H + \tau)\gamma$ for quadratic resource pay-offs.) In the limit $\mathrm{Re}(s) \to 0$ an analytic expression for the stability boundary $\sigma(H)$ at fixed transaction cost, T, follows and is given by solving the following system along with Equation 5.17. (which gives f_o implicitly):

$$[f_o(\gamma_{1\to1} - \gamma_{2\to1}) + \gamma_{2\to1}][\cos \beta s_2 + \alpha s_2(H + \tau)\ \sin\beta s_2] +$$
$$(\rho_{1\to1}(f_o) - \rho_{2\to1}(f_o) - 1) = 0 \tag{5.23}$$
$$[f_o(\gamma_{1\to1} - \gamma_{2\to1}) + \gamma_{2\to1}][\sin \beta s_2 + \alpha s_2(H + \tau)\ \cos \beta s_2] + s_2 = 0$$

Unfortunately, the above expressions also depend on the imaginary part of the root, s_2, and we must solve the system for many values of s_2, since the stability boundary is given by the largest unstable region delineated by $\sigma(H)$.

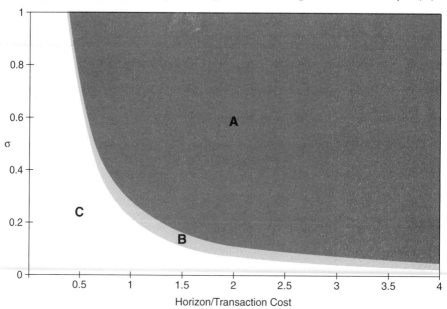

Figure 5.6 Stability portrait in σ vs. H/T phase space for a system with resource pay-offs $G_1 = 4 + 7f - 5.333f^2$ and $G_2 = 4 + 3f$, $\alpha = 1, \tau = 6$, $\sigma = 0.5$ and $T = 1$. System is always unstable in region A and always stable in region C. In region B, the system either relaxes to a fixed point or is pulled into a noisy limit cycle, depending upon the initial conditions.

Fortunately, a theorem in the theory of neutral differential–difference equations states that the roots of Equation 5.23 fall asymptotically on a line parallel to the imaginary axis, as $|S_2| \to \infty$, simplifying the task.

For the same resource pay-offs and parameters as earlier, the resulting stability diagram (for fixed transaction cost) is shown in Figure 5.6. As can be seen, it is very similar to that of Figure 5.1, the phase space diagram for the case of flat expectations. Notice, however, that the unstable regime is much larger for the system with trendy expectations. In region A all fixed points are unstable, while in region C the system is always stable. The upper boundary to region A extends to even larger values of uncertainty ($\sigma > 4.5$). Again, for small values of σ, only very large horizon lengths destabilize the system. In region B, equilibrium behaviour depends on the initial conditions. For some initial conditions, the system relaxes to a fixed point; for others, the system is pulled into a limit cycle.

Trends are misleading

Closer examination shows that, while the phase diagrams for the two types of expectations are qualitatively similar, a system of trend-followers always becomes unstable at smaller horizon lengths than a collection of agents with flat expectations. This can be understood intuitively as follows. Linear extrapolation is an accurate prediction method only for short times following the arrival of information. Consequently, for systems with non-negligible delays in obtaining information, the accuracy of the extrapolation from the past state of the system to the present is already compromised, not to speak of extrapolation to the future. The expectations of trend-followers are thus often very far off, especially considering that for large gradients the expectations rapidly saturate to $f = 0$ or $f = 1$, both rather unlikely states of the system. Agents react to a large slope by flocking to the less popular resource, creating a large gradient in the opposite direction, and in such a way, trend-followers needlessly cause large fluctuations.

Figure 5.7a exemplifies this type of behaviour. The choice of parameters $H = 0.5$, $T = 1$, $\alpha = 1$, $\tau = 6$, and $\sigma = 1.0$ places a collection of trend followers in region A of Figure 5.6, but in the stable regime (region C) of the $\sigma - H/T$ phase space portrait for the system made up of agents with flat expectations. Thus, a flat expectation system damps down to the fixed point, while the trendy system continues to oscillate.

An important point remains to be raised about the way in which we modelled agents which follow trends. Our computational representation of such agents detects gradients up to the numerical precision specified by our experiments, which are limited by the precision of the computer. Real-life agents probably wouldn't notice trends with slopes flatter than about 1 per cent over a few delay periods, as such gradients would not be judged significant. Since small gradients are magnified due to the compensating mechanism described above, slopes that might be ignored in a real system contribute to the instability of the simulated system when the system is near a fixed point.

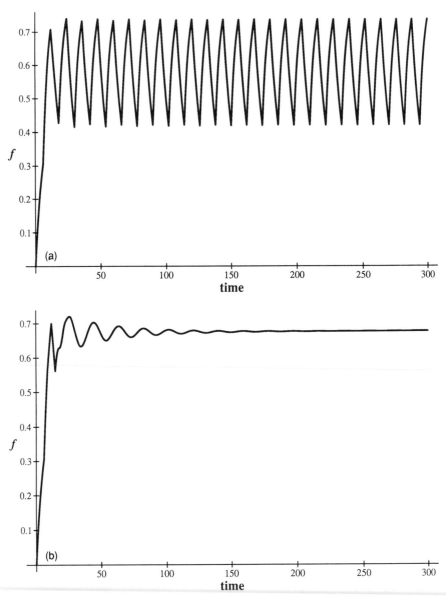

Figure 5.7 Resource pay-offs of Figure 5.6 with $H = 0.5$, $T = 1$, $\alpha = 1$, $\tau = 6$ and $\sigma = 1$. System is in region A of Figure 5.6. Initially, $f = 0$ (a) Demonstrates destabilizing effect of following short-term trends in a system of agents which base their decisions on expectations of the future. For the same choice of parameters, a system of agents with flat expectations damps out to the fixed point after about 200 time-steps. (b) If agents are oblivious to gradients of less than 0.05 change in fractional density per time-step, the system converges to the fixed point at $f = 0.674$ after about 150 time-steps.

Indeed, increasing the threshold at which agents observe slopes above the numerical precision (for example slopes less than 0.01 are truncated to zero) also increases the stability of the system. Figure 5.7b shows the eventual relaxation to the fixed point of a system of trend-followers blind to gradients in the fractional density of agents larger than 0.05 per time-step for the same parameters as in Figure 5.7a.

Thus, while following trends may superficially seem like a more intelligent way of formulating expectations, it is inherently destabilizing. In reality, it is often a very unintelligent prediction mechanism, since in a world with finite resources, trends tend to top-off or bottom-off, a fact of which smart agents should be aware.

Diversity and competition

In the previous sections we assumed that all agents have identical methods of forming expectations about the future, a first attempt to gauge the effect of expectations on overall system behaviour. In a real system, however, different agents might have different types of expectations. We now incorporate the diversity of expectations by allowing several types of agents with differing expectations to coexist within a system. Specifically, we consider agents with flat expectations, but allow the horizon length to vary among types of agents. As a concrete example, we postulate an inverse relationship between an agent's level of uncertainty and its horizon length. The smaller the agent's uncertainty, the greater its confidence in its ability to extrapolate into a future, and thus the longer its horizon length. The different types of agents are then characterized by their uncertainty and horizon length, where the relation $H\sigma$ = constant is taken to hold across all agent types.

In a closed world with a finite amount of resources, these different strategies are in competition with each other. In order to model the effect of competition, we now introduce a reward mechanism which encourages the spread of high-performing strategies at the expense of the worse ones. The reward can be thought of in an economic sense as corresponding to monetary benefits, for example, or in a biological sense to reproductive success. The implementation of rewards presented here generalizes the treatment given in Hogg and Huberman (1991, pp. 6–10) to include the effect of transaction costs.

While agents base their decisions on perceived accumulated future pay-offs, the system rewards them in proportion to their actual performance or net income; i.e., the agents' instantaneous pay-offs diminished by transaction costs incurred. The computational ecosystem can now be described by specifying the fraction of agents, f_{rs} of a given type s using a given resource r at a particular time t. The fraction of agents using a resource r is then

$$f_r^{res} = \sum_s f_{rs}$$

and the fraction of agents of type s is

$$f_s^{type} = \sum_r f_{rs}$$

As mentioned previously, the net effect of rewarding performance is to increase the fraction of highly performing agents. If κ is the rate at which performance is rewarded, then Equation 5.13 is enhanced with an extra term which corresponds to this reward mechanism, giving

$$\frac{df_{rs}}{dt} = \alpha[f_{1s}\rho_{1\to1,s}(f_1^{res}(t-\tau))+f_{2s}\rho_{2\to1,s}(f_1^{res}(t-\tau)-f_{rs}] + \kappa(f_r^{res}\eta_s-f_{rs}) \quad (5.25)$$

The second term now incorporates the effect of rewards on the population. In this equation

$$\rho_{1\to2,s}(f_1^{res}(t-\tau)) = \frac{1}{2}\left\{1 + \exp\left[\frac{H_s[G_2(f_1^{res}(t-\tau) - G_1(f_1^{res}(t-\tau))] - T}{2H_s\sigma_s}\right]\right\}$$

is the probability that an agent using resource 1 of type s with horizon length H_s will prefer resource 2 (taking into account transaction costs) and

$$\rho_{1\to1,s}(f_1^{res}(t-\tau)) = \frac{1}{2}\left\{1 + \exp\left[\frac{H_s[G_2(f_1^{res}(t-\tau) - G_1(f_1^{res}(t-\tau))] - T}{2H_s\sigma_s}\right]\right\} \quad (5.26)$$

is the probability that it will prefer to stay with resource 1. The function η_s is the probability that agents will be of type s, which we take to be proportional to the earnings achieved by agents of type s. Specifically, we choose

$$\eta_s = \frac{A - \alpha TB}{A - \alpha T \Sigma B} \quad (5.27)$$

where

$$A = f_{1s}G_1(f_1^{res}(t)) + f_{2s}G_2(f_1^{res}(t))$$

and

$$B = f_{1s}\rho_{1\to2,s}(f_1^{res}(t-\tau)) + f_{2s}\rho_{2\to1,s}(f_1^{res}(t-\tau))$$

so that an agent's earnings are linearly proportional to its net earnings.[4]

The question we now ask is how a diverse system of agents with different horizon lengths evolves when good performance is rewarded at the expense of bad performance. In some cases, competition serves to stabilize behaviour to a large extent. For many different populations of agent types, the behaviour of the system is stable most of the time with comparatively brief bouts of instability. Consider, for example, a population of agents with horizons ranging from 0 to 2. Initially, 9.1 per cent of the agents are of each different type. The transaction cost is set at $T = 1.5$, $\alpha = 1$, $\tau = 6$, and $H_s\sigma_s = 0.5$. Without the reward mechanism, this mix of agents oscillates between the two resources at a fixed frequency and with large amplitude, due to the influence of the agents with longer horizons. Once the agents are permitted to

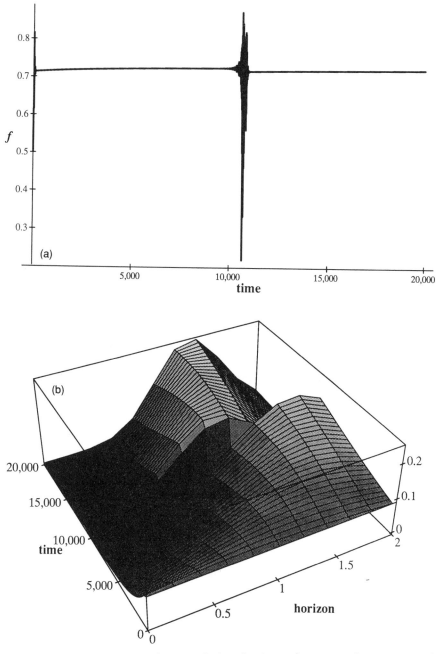

Figure 5.8 (a) Time evolution of the fraction of agents using resource 1. Competition for rewards among agents with different horizon lengths dumps out oscillations, but remains latently unstable. Resource pay-offs are $G_1(f_1^{res}) = 4 + 7f_1^{res} -5\,333(f_1^{res})^2$ and $G_2(f_1^{res}) = 4 + 3\,f_1^{res}$, $\alpha = 1$, $\tau = 6$, $H_s\sigma_s = 0.5$, $T = 1.5$, $\kappa = 1$. Horizon lengths of the eleven different types range uniformly between 0 and 2. Initially, the population of agents is evenly split among the different types. (b) Time evolution of the percentages of agents of different types. Note the abrupt decrease of agents with long horizons after the onset of oscillations with the complementary increase in agents with shorter horizons.

compete for payment among themselves, the system rapidly stabilizes after about 200 time-steps. Subsequently, the system drifts very slowly, as shown in Figure 5.8a. As the system drifts, the population of agents gradually re-distributes itself among the different types, the ones with longer horizon times garnering a greater share of the system's earnings and consequently attracting more and more of the agents.

This behaviour is not surprising, since when the system changes little over time, expectations about the future are significantly more accurate. An agent with a long horizon length correlated to its low level of uncertainty then has a big advantage: the agent can look out far ahead with great accuracy. As a result, agents with the longer horizon times distribute themselves among the two resources more optimally, have a greater instantaneous pay-off, and a larger share of the system's earnings.

Earlier, we observed that a stable system of agents with identical levels of uncertainty can support a sub-population with longer horizons as long as that sub-population remains small. Again, we see here that once a large enough majority of the agents have long expectations, the system goes unstable. This instability is dramatically depicted in Figure 5.8b where the distribution of agents among different types is seen to change abruptly after the onset of instability. The proportion of agents with long horizons falls abruptly, with types at shorter horizons taking up the slack. The large oscillations of the system render the agents' flat expectations completely inaccurate, despite their smaller uncertainty; however, agents with shorter horizons switch between resources less often, incur less transaction costs and thus receive a greater proportion of the system's earnings. Once again, the reward mechanism serves to damp out the oscillations, and as time passes agents with long hori-zons regain their advantage. This crash–stabilize cycle repeats itself over and over, every 12,000 time-steps or so. It is an open question whether or not the system ever achieves fixed point behaviour by eliminating diversity. If this occurs, however, it is on a time-scale so large that is inconceivable that a real system would not have meanwhile suffered some destabilizing perturbation.

Analytical results corroborate the experimental finding that no stable mix of agents with different horizon lengths is possible. Fixed point behaviour occurs only when one type of agent prevails completely. The following three conditions can be shown to be sufficient for fixed point behaviour for a system with uncertainty: (1) factorization of the fixed point, i.e., $f_{rs} = f_r^{res} f_s^{type}$; (2) the different types of agents share a common fixed point in the absence of interactions, that is $f_1^{res} \rho_{1 \to 1,s} + f_2^{res} \rho_{2 \to 1,s} - f_1^{res} = 0$ for all s; and (3) the number of transactions per type of agent (again in the absence of interactions) is also independent of type: $\alpha(f_1^{res} \rho_{1 \to 2,s} + f_2^{res} \rho_{2 \to 1,s}) = $ const. Combining (2) and (3) implies that $\rho_{1 \to 2,s}$ is independent of s at a fixed point. This is a contradiction, since $\rho_{1 \to 2,s}$ depends on s through H_s. Consequently, no stable mix (of two or more types) exists, although the system can still achieve stability by evolving into a system with only one type of agent.[5]

Discussion

We have shown how the global behaviour of a system of locally acting intentional agents can be analysed by allowing them to form expectations about the future and act upon them, and how agents' expectations of the future have a strong effect on the group dynamics. In this spirit, we extended the Huberman–Hogg theory of computational ecosystems to incorporate the effect of individuals' expectations about the future. Specifically, we considered two different types of expectations, both of which reflect different beliefs of how systems evolve in time. The first type of agent believes that systems change very little in time. The second type follows short-term trends, trusting that they will continue. All agents discount the future to some extent, at a rate inversely proportional to the horizon length of their expectations. Lastly, we also penalized agents for switching between resources by charging transaction costs.

Our results show that, to a large extent, the effect of transaction costs is to stabilize behaviour. We demonstrated that transaction costs can also trap the system in suboptimal states for extremely long periods of time, since near a fixed point or an almost fixed point the transition rate between resources drops by a factor exponentially small in the transaction cost. We saw that at small uncertainty, the horizon length of expectations at which the system goes unstable approaches infinity given fixed transaction costs. In addition, for small ratios of the horizon length to transaction costs, the fixed point is stable at all uncertainty levels, and for any choice of horizon length and transaction it is possible to stabilize the system by increasing the uncertainty. From our computer experiments we also discovered that in some regimes the equilibrium dynamics of the system depends on its initial state: for some initial configurations the system relaxes to fixed point behaviour; for others it is pulled into a limit cycle. These results hold for agents with either flat or trendy expectations, although the former always do better in the sense that their behaviour remains stable for longer horizon lengths.

More significantly, we found that agents with flat expectations attempting to optimize their horizon length face a trade-off between the goals of maximizing performance within a set response time and maintaining stability. Increased horizon length improves the response of the system while jeopardizing stability. Greedy agents hoping to maximize profit might gradually increase their horizon lengths at times when the system appears to be stable, unaware of incipient instabilities caused by non-zero uncertainty.

In the last section, we studied the effect of competition among a diverse group of agents with flat expectations but different horizon lengths correlated to different levels of uncertainty. Agents were rewarded in proportion to their share of the system's earnings, so that agents which performed well prospered at the expense of those which performed poorly. As expected, agents with long horizons do better when the system changes little over time, while agents with short horizons are more successful when there are fluctuations as they rack up less transaction costs. Consequently, rewards can stabilize the behaviour of a mixture of agents with different horizon lengths by encouraging the growth of the number of agents with short horizon lengths.

Once the behaviour is stabilized to the extent that it changes little as time progresses, agents with long horizons take advantage of this transient stability and multiply. However, the system can only support a certain sub-population of agents with long horizons before instability sets in. Thus, a mixture of agents with different horizon lengths can repeatedly undergo this crash–stabilize cycle without ever settling into an equilibrium. One cannot avoid making an association between this phenomenon and the observed dynamics of human societies and constructs, with their long periods of stasis followed by sudden discontinuous changes.

In light of these results, we feel confident that the approach that we have taken will be useful for studying even more complex interactions among social and economic agents with expectations.

Notes

1   In practice, of course, there may be a limit on the longest allowable horizon length (due to lifetime or finite patience of the agent/resource, for example).
2   The state $f = 0$ is suboptimal since the value of the instantaneous pay-off is far from its maximum value.
3   We have showed elsewhere that oscillations are not necessarily inferior when the environment itself changes with time (Glance *et al.* 1991).
4   It is possible for the total net earnings of the system to be negative. In this case the dynamical equation describing the evolution of f becomes:

$$\frac{df_{rs}}{dt} = \alpha[f_{1,s}\rho - {}_{1,s}(f_1^{res}(t - \tau)) + f_{2,s}\rho - {}_{1,s}(f_1^{res}(t - \tau) - f_{rs}] + \kappa f_{rs} - f_1^{res}\eta_s)$$

5   While we have not been able to prove rigorously that in general these three conditions are necessary as well as sufficent, the exceptions are at most rare and eccentric.

References

Axelrod, R. 1984. *The Evolution of Cooperation.* New York: Basic Books.
Bellman, R., and K.L. Cooke 1963. *Differential-Difference Equations.* New York: Academic Press.
Bendor, J. and D. Mookherjee 1987. Institutional structure and the logic of ongoing collective action. *American Political Science Review* 81, 129–54.
Ceccato, H.A. and B.A. Huberrman 1989. Persistence of non-optimal strategies. *Proceedings of the National Academy of Sciences USA* 86, 3443.
Day, R.H. and W.H. Huang 1990. Bulls, bears and market sheep. *Journal of Economic Behavior and Organization* 14, 299–329.
Glance, N., T. Hogg, and B.A. Huberman 1991. Computational ecosystems in a changing environment. *International Journal of Modern Physics C* 2, 735–53.

Hogg, T., and B.A. Huberman 1991. Controlling chaos in distributed systems. IEEE transactions on systems. *Men and Cybernetics* 21, 1325.

Huberman, B.A. and T. Hogg, 1988. The behavior of computational ecologies. In *The Ecology of Computation,* B. A. Huberman (ed.), 77–115. Amsterdam: North-Holland.

Kephart, J.O., B.A. Huberman and T. Hogg 1990. Can predictive agents prevent chaos? In *Proceedings of CECOIA 2, Second International Conference on Economics and Artificial Intelligence.*

Part II

MODELS FOR ARCHAEOLOGY

This section presents a range of case studies of modelling on different topics directly related to archaeology, ranging from learning through mammoth hunting to early historic epidemiology. Most of these topics, and the contribution of the models to the issues discussed, speak for themselves. We would like to introduce this section, however, with a discussion of some of the differences between the modelling techniques used, as such a discussion may shed some light on their utility.

Each of these models is of course the result of a variety of different trajectories. The authors come from different backgrounds, began modelling at different points in time (and thus under the impact of different opinions), and have different aims. It is therefore not possible to categorize them in any simple way, but roughly, Francfort's PALAMEDE model mixes AI with elements of the expert systems approach and Mithen's uses a Leslie matrix, while King and Lindh, as well as Zubrow, use cellular automata to approach the phenomena they are investigating. Doran and Reynolds, both computer scientists who have long worked with archaeologists, prefer to draw upon Artificial Intelligence, whereas McGlade and van der Leeuw, finally, use systems of differential equations.

But the approach to modelling is in each case also designed to deal with a particular problem. Indeed, the success or failure of the model depends on the match between the problem and the approach chosen. We have therefore chosen that match as the thread through this introduction and the organization of the subsequent chapters.

Francfort's chapter models an extremely reduced indicator of 'complexity', the size of the flow of energy and information through a society. It therefore deals with the simplest dynamics of all the models here presented. Mithen and Zubrow are essentially concerned with demography – the demography of mammoths on the one hand, and the demographies of people and microbes on the other. In both cases, known dynamics are studied under a range of circumstances which constrain them, *but which do not directly change as a function of them.* The same relative independence between the internal dynamics of the processes studied and the external circumstances under which they occur is valid for the model which King and Lindh propose: *they study different 'learning' dynamics under changing external circumstances, but the dynamics which rule these circumstances do not change as a result of the learning.*

That is not the case with the following set of models. Reynolds constructs, again, two structurally different 'learning' automata, *but the behaviour of one can, and does, structurally change that of the other, and vice versa.* Doran studies not learning but the behaviour which is based upon it, and therefore has a model in which *individual units adapt their behaviour to that of other such individual units* – adding yet again to the complexity required of the model.

The kinds of problem with which McGlade and van der Leeuw deal are of a very different degree of complexity – the dynamics are self-organizing (i.e., they have many feedback loops which may change the structure of the dynamics) so that they choose not to approach them from the side of the individual occurrences, by means of automata, but *to simulate global behaviour of the dynamics with the help of sets of differential equations.*

Now let us look at each of the models in some detail. An immediate difference, then, between Francfort's chapter and the others, is that the former proposes an extremely reductionist perspective on the nature of complex societies. That perspective is grounded in a conception of society as a 'flow structure' generated by the transmission of matter, energy and information between individuals. Based on that assumption, Francfort argues that the variety and complexity of material remains of human occupation reflect the relative amount of energy input per unit of volume in archaeological remains and the relative amount of information processing per unit of matter/energy in ancient societies. He concludes that variety and complexity of material remains can thus be used as a measure of the degree of socio-economic complexity.

Firstly, one needs to ask the question whether such extreme reductionism makes sense. It needs to be seen against the background of Gardin's analyses of archaeological reasoning, which point to an extreme underdetermination of theories by observations. In fact, Gardin, Francfort and others argue that most of archaeology's theoretical superstructure bears no relation to observations made in the field or the laboratory, and that we must therefore limit and simplify the domain and nature of our interpretations to remain within the realm of the demonstrable (i.e., 'Science'), or admit that we are unscientific (i.e., 'Artists').

The strength of his approach resides in the modesty of its aims: to build an expert system which can measure this volume of information in different ways (range of artefacts, standardization of types, complexity of manufacturing process, role of imports, etc.), as reflected in a standardized volume of excavated remains, and which gives indications, on this basis, concerning local temporal and spatial differences in socio-economic complexity within and between sites (e.g. relative indications of 'intensity' and 'sophistication' of craft production, but also decisions assigning 'prestige', 'crafts' and 'domestic' roles to units of space, and 'urban' and 'rural' epithets to settlements, etc.).

On the other hand, the model shows the inherent limitations of expert systems which do not signal anything 'new' or 'unknown' but merely operationalize standardized systems of description, measurement and inference. Applying it does generate counter-intuitive conclusions, but these are of a local nature – at best discovering the applicability of extant knowledge to unknown situations. Moreover, it operates only at one level, averaging out all variation between categories of remains, between results of individual behaviour, etc., in order to arrive at a 'global' conclusion. It is thus a 'top-down' model which ignores a large amount of information present in the data which are fed into it. In that sense it contrasts with all other models in this section – they all attempt to arrive at detailed descriptions of (sometimes unpredictable) behaviour at the group level by studying the interaction between individuals.

Matrix algebra has been used for some time in dealing with population dynamics in biology, and Mithen's modelling of the dynamics of mammoth populations under different external constraints (environments, hunting strategies, etc.) is what one could call a 'classic' application of this approach in archaeology. Here, the individuals in a population are assigned certain characteristics, notably concerning age, sex, life-span, fecundity, etc., and the model tracks the life trajectories of the individuals through a series of discrete time-steps in order to enable the researcher to predict overall demographic behaviour of the group. The approach is essentially positivist, in the sense that the dynamics assumed to determine the outcome reflect a mixture of 'law-like' and probabilistic hypotheses, and that the individuals within the age and sex classes are treated as essentially the same. By perturbing the dynamics in various ways, the effect of different external conditions can be investigated but these external drivers do not in any way change the nature of the internal dynamics qualitatively. The model is thus a very effective one in situations (such as in demography) where the internal dynamics are well known, where they can be approached adequately by models which are not too complex, and where the external variables have not too direct an effect on the structure of the internal dynamics.

Much the same is true of the dynamics of epidemics which Zubrow models by applying a cellular automata technique to a GIS-based mapping of terrain, communication routes and population densities. Although people move, and the spatial dimension is thus subject to external change, the dynamics of contagion, illness and death which are internal to the spread of the epidemic remain the same. Such phenomena are effectively modelled by according a spatial configuration to a set of cellular automata, cells which represent the dynamics of epidemic spread as a sequence of discrete event rules. In Zubrow's case, experimenting with the location and number of 'ill' cells results in a degree of understanding of the way in which the spatial variables influence the spatio-temporal configuration of the epidemic.

King and Lindh's main criticism against many models of species-environment relationships is that such models assume either abrupt or gradual change; i.e., change occurring at a single time-scale. Under circumstances in which changes in the environment are multi-scalar (or in their terms 'fractal') and thus much less predictable, they argue, it is the existence of a 'trans-generational memory' which makes the difference between a species' demise or survival, as it permits the species to carry a 'baggage' of (dormant) alternative strategies which allows it to adapt efficiently to a much wider range of changing circumstances than would be possible on the basis of 'activated' strategies alone.

The model investigates the behaviour of two different trans-generational information transmission strategies ('clonal' (Lamarckian) and 'non-clonal' (Darwinian) respectively) under a given range of environmental circumstances, characterized by a mix of time-scales at which change occurs. But these transmission strategies are not subject to structural change; rather, certain assumptions concerning the environment serve to generate an 'environmental evolution' as 'test condition' for a comparison between two transmission structures. This permits the authors to investigate them by constructing an automaton – a cyclical routine which transforms its inputs each time by applying the same, or one of a limited set of, transformation(s) to them, depending on the values of those inputs. The outputs it thus generates serve as inputs for the next cycle.

The automaton they construct sets values for the minimum amount of information which, at any time-step, the species and each individual must have to survive changes occurring in the environment over, respectively, the long-term and the individual's lifetime. Then they introduce in this environment 'organisms' which transfer to their offspring either (1) only 'active' information (which interacts with the environment in the lifetime of the organism) or (2) a mix of 'active' and 'dormant' information which the organism cannot 'use' during its lifetime, but can pass on to its offspring. The critical parameter in comparing these two kinds of individuals is the relative probability of viable mutation, and its evolution seems to show that non-clonal (i.e., multi-temporal) transmission favours survival, although the size of the surviving population fluctuates heavily. Moreover, the simulations seem to show that there is a relationship between the chances of survival and the temporal mix of changes occurring in the environment: if the latter fluctuates too much too quickly, neither kind of transmission permits populations to survive.

An important implication upon which the authors briefly touch is that if on the one hand multi-temporal transmission enhances a population's chances of survival, while on the other increasing the size of short-timescale environmental fluctuations threatens survival, then the introduction of cultural transmission (which is multi-temporal and covers the short end of the time-scales) would have had considerable survival value. Their remarks encourage us to reflect on the nature of human learning as a mixture of 'active' and 'dormant' cultural transmission and on the ways in which such a mixture could be transmitted non-genetically across more than two generations.

It seems to us that the description of cultural transmission which the authors propose could profitably be enhanced by investigating the nature of cognition and learning. Some of the things which distinguish human learning from the 'clonal' learning King and Lindh attribute to most animal species are the (genetically determined?) capacities to abstract, to hierarchize, to construct and reverse sequences, to communicate complex information and to transform objects into artefacts. It is not our role here to demonstrate at length how these capacities are in all probability necessary and sufficient to establish under all but the most extreme demographic circumstances the kind of cultural transmission the authors refer to. We would argue that the multidimensionality of artefacts and abstract concepts go a long way towards creating a mixture of short-term and long-term information which would transmit generic (wide-range) adaptations on the back of specific (short-range) ones. And that the presence in a group of up to four generations would seem to allow sufficient trans-generational contact to guarantee transmission of wide-ranging information.

It is no accident, therefore, that the models which follow distinguish themselves from the last four in that they attempt in one way or other to deal with human learning and human interaction. Clearly, the assumption that external change does not unduly induce changes in the nature and structure of the internal dynamics is not valid with respect to such models. The essence of human nature is that external circumstances have a structural impact on individual behaviour and the interaction dynamics of society. Hence, these models are rather different. They fall into two categories, those which deal with the trajectory of the group by simulating the interactions between individuals, such as Doran's Distributed Artificial Intelligence model, and Reynolds's Autonomous Learning Systems. Of these, the latter most closely investigates the question posed by King and Lindh; i.e., whether the combination of genetic and cultural information transmission systems enhances the performance over that of a system which disposes only of one of these mechanisms.

To do so, Reynolds constructs two automata, the Experience Generator (EG) and the Knowledge Base Integrator (IG) which represent, respectively, neo-Darwinian and cultural ways of dealing with information. The former, based on Holland's genetic algorithm, 'learns to find example instances that represent hypotheses currently being investigated by the system'. It represents a group of individuals as a set of values. Each individual is evaluated in terms of its interaction with the environment, according to a pay-off function. Individuals reproduce at a rate proportional to their fitness (as expressed in the pay-off function). Additional functions representing mutation and crossover guarantee the production of new combinations of traits.

The Knowledge Base Integrator (IG) 'learns to identify relationships that pertain to the high performance examples', and stores them as a knowledge representation. It is constructed as a hierarchically structured lattice in which each hypothesis 'corresponds to a category or collection of objects or relations'. The automaton executes a search for the most general category associated with a given level of performance in a chunk of the total hypothesis space. It begins with the individual leaves of the tree and moves a level upward (to a parent node) once all nodes springing from that parent have been found effective, thus representing the hierarchical nature of information storage in the human mind.

The two systems are coupled by a routine (VIP) which assesses the performance of each individual (set of chromosomes) not only against the environment, but also relative to the set of chunked hypotheses which represent 'culture', and which decides on the reproduction rate of that individual following both these comparisons. Finally, both the collective and the individual lattices representing 'cultural knowledge' are updated to take the result of the comparisons into account.

The most important innovations in this model are thus, on the one hand, that changes in the environment actually change the internal structure of the systems, and on the other hand, that two different learning structures are used which impact on one another as well as on the environment. By running the genetic module alone, it is established that the rate of 'genetic learning' is reduced as 'genetic knowledge' increases, probably because the length (and the order) of the relevant 'knowledge schemata' increases, and therefore the risk that they get broken by the genetic operators. By combining the two automata it becomes clear that chunking reduces this effect, so that the introduction of 'cultural learning' allows the combined system to continue at a high rate of learning for much longer than would be the case if only 'genetic learning' occurred.

The model Doran proposes is not so much concerned with the impact of cultural learning on evolutionary efficiency (or 'survival value'), but rather with the interaction between deliberative (i.e., active as well as reactive) individuals in a social and natural environment, and notably with the emergence of new forms of such interaction ('social complexity'). His investigation is concerned with the range of precise conditions under which the emergence trajectory (of social stratification) is not followed, and notably with the role of the relationship between the internal representations of the agents and their actions in such a system.

As it had not yet been fully implemented at the time this chapter was written, we will briefly focus on some of the structural elements of the model rather than on what it might teach us about the development of complex social systems. Some of the interesting features of the testbed developed for the modelling are:

1   Each agent is associated with its own database concerning its possible actions and their properties, as well as about the other agents. These databases contain, for example, the perception of groups (which has no 'objective' existence).

2 Each agent has operators which become active when the conditions for their activity are matched in the agent's database.

3 The interaction between the agents is governed by a communication system in which actions performed by one agent send messages to other agents to signal this fact to them.

4 There is a unified hierarchical planning and plan execution system.

5 The environment is shared by the agents, but does change (if not differentially).

It is interesting to compare this model with the one presented by Glance and Huberman (Chapter 5). Doran's model proposes a social development from an unstructured community, via crowding and growing awareness of the other agents, to the building of representations about the other actors, then to implementing their own actions with a view to the acquired knowledge concerning the community, and finally culminating in various trajectories towards the emergence of co-ordination and leadership. Probably because Doran is interested in the conditions which would inhibit emergence of these various steps, it seems that the structure of the progression itself is written into the programme. If that is so, his approach contrasts with that of Glance and Huberman and with the last two models, where self-emergence plays an essential role.

Much of the philosophy behind Chapters 12 and 13 has been outlined in Chapter 1. Here, we would like to draw attention to two important aspects. Firstly, neither of these chapters tries to model a reality. Ultimately, all the authors discussed thus far are aware of the degree of reductionism involved in the kind of modelling that they are doing. But this awareness leads them to argue that, nevertheless, the model represents reality sufficiently well to be able to draw conclusions from the model. These last two chapters do not do so – they argue that the purpose of the modelling is to elaborate hypotheses about different kinds of dynamics, in order to look at their implications, and eventually to measure the latter against the archaeological data.

McGlade's chapter deals with a much later period in the development of complex social systems – his model was written to investigate the later prehistoric period of Southern Britain, rather than the Palaeolithic in the Périgord. Using sets of coupled differential equations (as opposed to the rule-based systems of the others in this section) he sets out to account for the production and transactional dynamics resident in so-called 'prestige goods' economies. The model structures presented by McGlade are designed to reveal the non-linear dynamics which are embedded in trade/exchange processes, and which are intrinsically unstable. The qualitative transformations to which such systems are prone are demonstrated by means of phase space reconstructions which track system behaviour through a sequence of period doubling bifurcations *en route* to chaos.

McGlade shows two separate scenarios which induce complex behavioural dynamics: the first is represented by self-organizing structuration as an *endogenous* process, and the second is the result of the action of periodic *exogenous* (seasonal) fluctuations in generating complex bifurcation sequences. Finally, the implications of complex metastable dynamics and the possible role of chaotic trajectories in the maintenance of social control are speculated on.

The last chapter in this section, by van der Leeuw and McGlade, continues these latter explorations and anticipates Rosen's point (Chapter 14) about the need to explore a wider set of model formalizations in our representation of complex systems. One of the primary objectives of this chapter is the need for multiple modelling scenarios as a way out of the reductionist trap produced by models that purport to describe complexity through a single analytical lens. The chapter deals with the well-known archaeological phenomena of the emergence of urban centres and seeks to unravel a number of non-linear structuring processes which are implicated in urban/rural evolution as sets of self-organizing dependencies. While conventionally urban studies have been viewed from an exclusively hierarchical perspective, van der Leeuw and McGlade argue forcibly for the existence of networks in which heterarchical organisation coexists with hierarchical forms so as to constitute 'information processing landscapes' which foster the emergence of urban centres. These self-organizing dynamics are represented in a series of model scenarios which attempt to capture the qualitative dynamics at different temporal and spatial scales of resolution, thus underlining the importance of a multiple modelling perspective for a more rigorous understanding of the complex social and economic interdependencies which articulate urban dynamics.

6   Archaeological interpretation and non-linear dynamic modelling: between metaphor and simulation

Henri-Paul Francfort

Introduction: the nature of archaeological data, archaeological theory and dynamic modelling

In order to clarify the purpose of this chapter, we will first pay some attention to the way in which we have arrived at the particular position we see as our own among the various contemporary conceptions of the modelling of past human systems, and in particular among archaeologists. Firstly, we would like to make explicit that our quest is to investigate the limits of the applicability of science to archaeology or, in other words, to clarify the limits of those archaeological interpretations which can be validated with the present state of the art. Our approach in doing so draws upon the French 'logiciste' school of thought. Various logicist reconstructions of examples of interpretative reasoning in natural languages have seen the light. Since the 1980s they use the techniques of AI (Francfort 1987, 1990; Francfort *et al.* 1989; Gardin *et al.* 1987, 1988; Lagrange and Renaud 1987). Logicist analyses in terms of facts and rules demonstrate the malleability of constructs in the humanities; they invite us to 'see more clearly where the frontier lies between that part of our inter-pretive constructs which follows the principles of scientific reasoning and another part which ignores or rejects them' (Gardin 1990, p. 26).

All such analyses share the general perspective that we have to choose either Science or Art (Literature) and that a 'third way' (i.e., a hermeneutic approach) is unacceptable. Briefly, the argument, as exposed by Gardin (1990, pp. 27–30), runs as follows:

> It is very difficult to differentiate 'other than in social terms, between the knowledge of laymen and the science of professional hermeneuticians'; the 'third way' leaves us without criteria to eval-uate the credibility and acceptability of interpretations, or to choose between schools of thought, research programmes and professional interpreters.
>
> (Gardin 1990, pp. 27–30)

This facilitates the imposition (by the use of authority, coercion, or vote, etc.) of a judgement by a group, band, nation, caste, order, class, race or gender, which in turn is simply not acceptable. Faced with the stark alternative between 'Science' and 'Art', after excluding hermeneutics, we have deliberately chosen to try the 'first way' (i.e., scientific analysis). Why? Our choice is rooted in three main criteria: the nature of archaeological data, the nature of archaeological theory, and the nature of dynamic modelling.

Following Gardin (1990, pp. 24, 34–5) we have, in the process of developing any interpretative construct in the humanities, 'considerable freedom' to:

1. select a set of *objectives*,
2. select a *corpus* of empirical phenomena,
3. select a language or system of *description*,
4. select an *argumentation* leading from the descriptive basis to the conclusion,
5. select ways to *validate* the latter.[1]

But this freedom has to be exercised in a way which is compatible with the nature of data, theories and models, and we must thus for a moment focus on each of these three components of any archaeological argument.

The nature of archaeological data is material

Archaeological data are differentiated from their environment by their form and physical state and/or by their spatial position. Both notions (form/state and position) are physical and spatial and the whole process of archaeological interpretation rests upon this.

The difficulties begin when we take into consideration that humanity is the agent responsible for these physical and spatial transformations of matter. From fairy tales to the concept of dictatorship of the proletariat, the socio-cultural (not to be confused with computational, see pp. 170–1) symbolic dimension of humanity transcends and obscures the process of physical transformation of the world, which itself results in phenomena ranging from chopping tools to the largest cities, full of both masterpieces of art and waste.

This socio-cultural symbolic dimension and its importance are not negated, but the scientific approach has to be restricted to what it can really do. Thus, at least temporarily and tactically (*pace*: the historical questions are there!), the approach proposed here is strictly materialist and only symbolic in the computational sense. It leaves aside the socio-cultural and psycho-spiritual side of the human agent. These aspects of humanity remain to be re-introduced into the picture at a later time, either in a literary, or in a scientific way (which does not yet exist).

Archaeological theory is of a more evanescent nature

There is no archaeological theory as such. There are either local explanatory theories, advocated by Gardin and Binford (1989) for instance, or general socio-political preconceptions depicting humans and their interests. It is unanimously admitted that:

> our [archaeological] interpretive constructs are obviously influenced by our 'interests' as well as by 'ideological and cultural determinisms', but the same applies to 'hard' sciences, and physicists and biologists do not conclude that it is consequently impossible to distinguish a good piece of work from a bad one in physics or in biology, except at a very elementary level.
>
> (Gardin 1990, p. 29)

To explain our position, we would like to follow Changeux and Connes (1989) in making a clear distinction between the (first) level of (computational) consistency-validity, the (second) level of ('symbolic') efficiency-validation and the (third) level of creativity. They argue cogently that verification is an essential part of the scientific procedure:

> comme le seul moyen que nous avons de transmettre un résultat est une chaîne logique de raisonnements, il faut bien revenir rapidement du troisième niveau au premier. Il est nécessaire de procéder à une vérification pédestre de la démonstration que l'illumination a permis d'entrevoir.
>
> (Changeux and Connes 1989, p. 195)

This is contrary to the general conception of '*reading*' the past. That approach wishes to encompass the whole process of discovery and interpretation and all its human context (Hodder 1986, 1989; Shanks and Tilley 1987a, 1987b; Tilley 1989). It implies explaining the 'third level' of Changeux and Connes, and ultimately leads to as many interpretations as readers or 'states of minds' of readers. This is another game altogether, ultimately implying the activation of different areas of the brain and the 'equivalidity' of all states of the minds of every reader or group of readers, regardless of their origin.

Shennan (1990, pp. 90 ff.) advocates that we take socio-cultural or socio-political presuppositions (theories) into consideration in archaeological interpretation, but he leaves the question of validation to be answered at some unspecified point in the future. This position reduces us *volens nolens* to the hermeneutic approach and brings us, again, face to face with the problem of multiple equivalent interpretations between which we cannot decide.

Our conception also differs to some extent from the mere interpretation of argument (Shennan 1990, pp. 94–6; Stutt 1987) since it covers less. As a student of history, I found that a lot of boring, uninteresting and quickly forgotten literature in the social sciences used the concepts of Darwinian, Marxist and/or Freudian 'theories'. In local limited cases, though, it has been possible (and elementary) to model the interpretation of the origin of the state in urban oriental civilizations along Marxist lines (but without modelling *Das Kapital*, Althusser's exegesis, etc.; that is, without the second and third levels of Changeux and Connes).[2]

The position chosen here is closer to that of Gallay (1986, pp. 280, 288–95), who proposes 'multi-interpretation', which is taken to be a 'fan-shaped' architecture of various possible internally valid testable interpretations to be validated. This implies an exploration of the field of possible interpretations, at an interpretive level where validation is possible. In our opinion, the existence of presuppositions is not to be ignored, but *in the writing of interpretative constructions* the argument is, as far as possible, to be built at the computational level and with testable material and verifiable relations.

To conclude, we have chosen to forgo borrowing socio-cultural explanatory theories, and instead to build our ideas on the fundamental conception of the transformation of matter. There is a continuous chain of human actions which eventually transforms natural raw material into published archaeological material, via the manufacture, contextual use, depositional and post-depositional processing of various substances, their collection and subsequent recording. These operations are here conceived of as successive stages of technical operations actually performed.

We admit that the technological systems (of the past) and their transformations reflect a more or less distorted subset of the economic, societal and ideological systems and of their transformations. The degree and nature of this distortion are a matter of thought for us, but we assume that the remains of past technical systems are the direct and admirable products of the kinetic and cognitive abilities of the human brain, individual as well as social (Francfort 1990, pp. 120–4). What we need to do next is to prepare the archaeological data to give evidence concerning their relations with the economic and/or socio-cultural 'variables' of the dead system.

The nature of dynamic modelling

Dynamic modelling is here considered from the point of view of its use in archaeology. It will not surprise the reader that from the perspective which has just been outlined, serious limitations in the use of such modelling have to be acknowledged by anybody who wants to try it, let alone test it. Of the following remarks, six are cautionary and one positive, but the conclusion is optimistic:

1 Non-linear dynamic modelling is developing in fields of application where the systems, if not simple, are at least clearly defined. This is not the case with ancient societies: what sort of 'system' is the 'culture' or the 'civilization' of a place and/or a time in the past? Is it not the target of the research rather than a given?

2 The fuzziness of societal, socio-cultural, and socio-political entities makes the identification of the variables and parameters involved in the

dynamic of past societies difficult, if not arbitrary and unnecessary. In archaeology, moreover, there immediately arise problems about the measurement of 'parameters'.

3 The selection of a model, of the variables and parameters to be considered, and finally of the past society to be targeted, are so 'unconstrained' that we suspect that no attempt at modelling will really fail, but that in most cases no real discoveries will be made either. This is obvious in the case of qualitative modelling: a growth in complexity or a collapse of a given society can be 'modelled' more or less painstakingly (depending upon the formalization selected), but this brings no new insights when the same list of socio-economic or cultural factors and of archaeological variables and parameters is repeatedly used (albeit with some permutations) in order to arrive at the expected results. If, with the parameters, we introduce (implicitly or explicitly) a model which works nicely in contemporary societies or economics, then we are back to borrowing a metaphor without rules for transfer or application.

4 The explanatory or enlightening power of qualitative modelling is questionable since it is often simply another way of expressing old interpretations; moreover, since there is no other validation than a subjective feeling of satisfaction (perfectly admissible), we are back to hermeneutics.

5 The transfer and use of concepts from non-linear dynamic modelling can be dangerous if it is done without rules: chaos and order are simply meaningless when we look at concrete archaeological remains. If we imagine past societies or cultures in general, difficulties arise in the application of such concepts. The political history of France in the nineteenth century, after the collapse of the *ancien régime*, is rather chaotic, for example, though industrial production and the physical sciences are in constant progress towards some kind of order. Such differences are not anomalous and can be modelled when sufficient relevant data are available; to do this without misuse or abuse of the concepts and/or without imposing an incorrect interpretation seems very difficult in, for example, the Central Asian or Indus civilizations of the Bronze Age. (The only safe criterion to assume collapse, for example, is the total disappearance of the material culture of a civilization, but we often take 'collapse' in the wider, and archaeologically untenable, sense of political transformation.)

6 Suppose that initial conditions can be defined at all, how do we elicit the 'initial conditions' of past human systems when our chronologies and our knowledge of the remains *and* of the environment are uncertain? What, moreover, is 'equilibrium' in a socio-cultural system? Does it makes sense at all?

7 However, dynamic modelling, even non-linear, can be used when we deal with the actual dynamics of any sort of real population (neurons, cells, individuals, etc.), as populations can be calculated. As can be

seen from the literature, the modelling of the dynamics of biological populations, for example, can be imposed upon the past with a good chance of generating plausible schematic representations of transformations and evolutions. But even then, the modelling raises some fundamental issues.

We conclude that from our perspective the modelling of social, economic or cultural phenomena is fraught with difficulties and of limited, if any, value as long as such modelling implies the 'dynamicized' introduction of preconceived and inherited ideas about human behaviour, society, and the like. Rather, we would suggest that more attention be paid to understanding the dynamics of artefact populations.

In general, whilst it is happily accepted that scientific metaphor and the transfer of concepts can provide insights and can help archaeologists move towards interpretations, they must not prevent those who want to play a scientific game to respect the exigencies of internal consistency and empirical validation, and it is with that purpose in mind that we will now turn to the expert system 'PALAMEDE', which has been developed with such an aim in mind.

PALAMEDE: an application of AI to the interpretation of some proto–historic pre–literate 'civilizations'

In 1977, when we were facing some strange and attractive problems of interpretation, we became aware that the site of Shortughaï could be considered an open system exchanging matter and energy with the environment, a 'dissipative structure'. Shortughaï is a small (<1 ha) proto-historic (c. 2200–1700 BC) site located in NE Afghanistan, in a small plain near the Tadjik border. The particularity of Shortughaï is cultural: during the first phase of occupation (phase A, periods I and II) it was a pure Mature Indus settlement and in the second phase (B, periods III–IV), it exhibits, along with strong continuous elements of the Indus tradition, the appearance of a typical local Bactrian Central Asiatic civilization.[3]

The site raised the following historical problem. During the second half of the third millennium BC, an urban civilization flourished on the Iranian Plateau, in Central Asia and in the Indus Valley. It was characterized by large concentrations of population in cities occupied for centuries, except in Bactria and Margiana, where no cities in the form of huge mounds (tepas) exist. Where present, this urban phase ended more or less simultaneously in all the cited regions, apparently c. 1800 BC.

How to characterize an urban civilization in the absence of large cities and of all the traditional correlates listed by Childe (and since refined by various scholars)? The question was crucial at Shortughaï, a small site where the first phase (A) could be called urban by immediate reference to the Indus 'metropoles' but where no reference (in terms of urban/non-urban civilization) was available for phase B.

In the archaeological context, the term urban may be slightly misleading, but we should all bear in mind its considerable implications, summarized in the widely used equation:

$$\textit{urban civilization} \iff \textit{class society} \iff \textit{state}$$

We found, among others, that this equation is unfortunate and that the dichotomy urban/non-urban hides a continuum of various situations. The total absence of ordinary 'proto-state' criteria at Shortughaï (plus the fact that many of the listed criteria have no archaeological correlates) induced us to focus first on an evaluation of the differences in the complexity of the production economy between the two phases, leaving other aspects for later. Intuitively, phase A was richer in craft products, luxury (prestige) goods and items of remote origin than phase B, but was that enough to recognize a transition from a 'urban' type to a 'rural' type of economy? It is this we set out to test. To do so, PALAMEDE was created in three phases:

1 Conception at Shortughaï and elaboration by hand.
2 AI modelling and simulation.
3 Extension.

1 Conception and manual elaboration

On one hand, the following discussion will show how a change in complexity of an archaeological system has been brought to light in unfavourable conditions. But a brief description of this first phase (cf. Francfort 1988; Francfort *et al.* 1989, pp. 285–338) is also important because it shows the interest and the limitations of the AI modelling which followed it.

All application of modelling to populations of artefacts necessitates conceptual preparation, in order to define a system which can be modelled at the computational level and which stands in an acceptable relation to the socio-cultural or economic world of the past such as we can imagine it (at the third level). From the start of our work onwards, we have attempted to take this into account by trying to:

- clearly define a system, purely archaeological and material;
- determine measurable parameters, actual populations;
- define meta-notions, constructed in acceptable relation to proto-historic statehood;
- select a mode of computation, in the broad sense;
- restrict the application to the domain of production economy;
- restrict the modelling to relative change;
- validate the modelling by matching the results with those arrived at by ordinary archaeological means and by simulation and extension. Empirical validation awaits the reopening of the field in Afghanistan.

To answer the question whether our intuitive observations concerning arte-facts in the different phases at Shortughaï were sufficient to warrant theories about the decay of urbanization at the site, we decided to assess the quan-tity of all and any sort of remains, artefacts and wastes (to be weighed on the site and in Kabul), but also to quantify the sequences of technological operations (*chaîne opératoire*) necessary to obtain the artefacts and the wastes. Such sequences are more or less long and complicated; i.e., more or less 'costly' in terms of time, energy and information.

The calculation was made as follows. The natural soil, before settlement, is considered the system at time T_o, when anything can still happen. The excavation of the site, after the life and ruin of the settlement, brings to light quantities of things that were imported by human agents. The history of the system would have been different without the intervention of these human agents. At the time of the archaeological activities, the system has reached state T_x.

The transformation $T_o \rightarrow T_x$ results from imports and transformations of matter (M) by energy (E). M and E stand in direct relation to the environ-mental resources. We can thus conceive of functions describing the 'production of remains' (artefacts and wastes). At state T_o, the energy expen-diture was E_o (at a non-geological scale of observation); the final state T_x corresponds to an energy expenditure E_x.

During the transformation $T_o \rightarrow T_x$, the system's energy expenditure was:

$$E_x - E_o' = E_x$$

But as E_x is the sum of an infinity of micro-states of the system E_1, E_2, E_3, we can apply the thermodynamic law of finite transformation of internal energy in an open system at constant volume (this condition will be speci-fied):

$$E = E_2 - E_1$$

We have then to define the system. It is conventionally defined as a cubic metre of archaeological layers. This cubic metre will be the 'box' in which transformations of matter and energy occur. Like biological organisms, this system is open to the environment. Now, how to measure?

We have to determine a measure of energy, conventionally defined but linked to actual remains. The relation elaborated is of the type:

$$E_i = M_i \star I_i$$

in which I (information) $= v.t$

$$E_i \text{ (conventional)} = \mathbf{M}_i \left[\sum v_i \star t_i \right]$$

where M_i = mass of matter i by cubic metre of layer (density, quantity of discovered remains);

  v_i = number of types (categories) of artefacts in matter i (indi-cating the degree of differentiation of remains);

t_i = number of technological operations of the technological chain producing v (indicating the degree of complexity of the production technologies).

In this equation, v and t stand therefore in relation to the information handling technology of the period. It is then easy to obtain E_i by comparing different levels, periods, phases by techniques, by forms, by materials, etc. To do so, we:

- segment the matter in i_1, i_2, ... i_n, material categories (usual in archaeo-logy);
- segment each material in v_1, v_2, .. v_n, artefact types (usual in archaeo-logy);
- determine the sequences of operations (*chaînes opératoires*) t_1, t_2, ... t_n applied (to be reconstructed, depending upon our knowledge of the ancient technologies concerned, by means of scientific analysis, ethnography, and experimentation; this is no more arbitrary than any taxonomy and has the advantage that it must be coherent).

Thus defined, the product $v*t$ is a measure of the quantity of technical information I brought to bear on a standard amount of matter.

It must be noted that the E obtained is strictly relative because the remains reach us as results of the impact of 'functions of remains production' which are themselves derivatives $f'(x)$ of the 'functions of artefact production' $f(x)$. It follows that we cannot ever hope to extend our investigation beyond consideration of families of 'artefact production functions'. All we can do is accept, depending on the sign (+ or −) of the derivative, that they increase or decrease, though there can be fluctuations between E_o and E_x.

We shall here summarize briefly the results obtained at Shortughaï, comparing phase A and B in the following tables. First the weight of arte-facts per cubic metre is indicated in Table 6.1.

Table 6.1   Weight of different objects per phase (gm/m^3)

Phase	Pottery	Artefacts and wastes	Pebbles	M	M without pebbles
A	2,174.10	0.9764	4,832.5	7,124.24	2,291.74
B	1,186.66	0.9828	525.3	1,811.30	3,576.68

Next the complexity of the artefacts. The simplified technological *chaînes opératoires* for the ceramics number from three to five operations; the typology differentiates twenty six types types. The simplified technological *chaînes opéra-toires* of the other artefacts and wastes include from two to six operations; their typology differentiates fourteen types. The artefact comparisons between phases A and B are presented in Tables 6.2 and 6.3.

Table 6.2 Technological comparison of artefacts per phase

Phase	With beads	Without beads
A	45	39
B	36	33

Table 6.3 Number of technological operations per phase (value of the chain multiplied by the number of chains of this value)

Phase	Ceramics	Artefacts	Total
A	104	81	185
B	83	60	143

The calculation of the variation of E (conventional energy) can be done according to three formulae:

1 By taxonomical class, multiplying the mass m of each class by the value of the v technological chain and adding the $m \star t$ products for the v categories.
2 By technological chain, multiplying the value of chain t by the number of taxonomical classes v on which chains of similar values apply and multiplying the total obtained by the mass m.
3 By calculating the product of the total mass M by the sum of the $v \star t$ products.

The results are indicated in Table 6.4.

Table 6.4 Different calculations of conventional energy per phase

Phase		Computation 1	Computation 2	Computation 3
A		14,214.37	101,049.13	1,317,984.4
B		5,658.85	41,463.4	259,015.0
Factor of variation (decrease)	with pebbles	2.5	2.4	5.0
Factor of variation (decrease)	without pebbles	1.79	0.68	2.3

The results indicate a decrease in the mass of matter processed (M), of the technological information applied (I) and of the conventional energy used ($E = M \star i$). In detail, we can see that categories of ceramics disappear with the transition of phase A to phase B, or that they decrease or increase: the decrease of I is: 1.48 per cent and the decrease of M: 1.8 per cent. With the objects the decrease of I is: 1.72 per cent and M increases slightly: 1.02 times.

The major historical conclusion is that from A (Indus) to B (Bactrian) the crafts production economy of Shortughaï declines, indicating that the economy becomes a more rural type. *This does not mean the decline of the civilization.*

Such a result would not have been attainable and certainly not measurable with only intuitive evaluation in natural language. If we apply the usual conclusions about the evolution of organisms to this result, we would have had to admit a decrease in economic complexity, in socio-economic organization, in 'negentropy' (i.e., a decrease in the flux of matter-energy extracted from the environment and processed through information and energy). The entropy of the system increased from A to B.

2 AI modelling and simulation

Next, the AI model and simulation were implemented between 1985 and 1989, in the form of an Expert System (ES), using the inference engine SNARK (Francfort 1987; Lagrange and Renaud 1987; Francfort *et al.* 1989). SNARK gives information on each step of reasoning: 'from facts *a* and *b* ... and with rules *x* and *y*, I infer fact *c* ...' . The aim of this model was to widen the scope of the above approach, and to provide a tool which could be used for future investigations and simulations. PALAMEDE is local and relativist but the system can easily be adapted.[4] As we will see, PALAMEDE can give unexpected results, adding information to the intuitively hand-written versions of the studies (Francfort *et al.* 1989).

A first part of PALAMEDE , the **CIV** module, is dedicated to the Indus Civilization (a limited case of state-formation). It simulates various kinds of interpretive reasoning about the origins of the state (Francfort 1990) and shows the gap in the chain of argument between archaeological data on the one hand and interpretive theories on the other. In particular, it shows that the quantity and the quality of archaeological data have no bearing upon the proposed interpretation. This is done by simulating archaeological reasoning and applying it to considerably enlarged, enriched and detailed sets of facts. It is clear from this simulation that the accumulation of facts is useless, since, beyond a certain interpretative level, all the explanations appear to be ready-made, repetitive and extracted without any rules from the general socio-cultural thesaurus of imagery used in the humanities.

The same thing has recently been noted by Stoczkowski (1994) in a logicist analysis of the conceptions underlying the description of the process of hominization: all efforts at collecting data have, until now, changed nothing in the explanatory theory used, which stems from the 'naïve anthropology' which can be traced back to the Enlightenment and to Antiquity. Here, as in the case of the proto-historic period in the Middle East, there are few variations on the theme of 'growing societal/cultural complexity'.

The fault is with the interpretive 'theories', which are too vague to actually operate; with the archaeological data, which have not been collected and treated in such a way that they can serve as proper correlates to be evaluated and measured; and with the chains of arguments linking excellent but hardly relevant data to borrowed socio-cultural theories by means of big conceptual jumps. In fact, only three kinds of archaeological data, i.e., large urban concentrations (± 100 ha), very large territories, and the presence of writing, indicate the existence of a state, and they are ambiguous and/or tautological at that!

Having come this far, The second part of PALAMEDE (Francfort *et al.* 1989, pp. 89–211) tries to elaborate some meta-notions from the archaeological data. Notions which are strictly defined and limited in sense, but which stand in acceptable relation to the current socio-cultural interpretive schemes. The question of the definition of the 'State' is left aside; rather, the focus is on constructing meta-notions which are less general than 'cultural complexity' and semantically more powerful than the notions of today's general and social sciences contexts (such as 'craft specialization').

PALAMEDE has a module **TOP** ('topography of activities'; Francfort *et al.* 1989, pp. 91–124), the aim of which is to evaluate the differentiation of topographical units by periods in terms of the Prestige, Craft and Domestic functions of space.[5]

The database lists in *c.* 600 lines all the data organized according to the three functions (open to discussion), with or without a threshold beyond which the representative nature of these data is accepted (open to discussion), and by place and stratigraphical unit. The index **P** cumulates the indications for each kind of archaeological remains in its context. It does so with respect to one of the three functions, and at a scale which is open to discussion. The (*c.* 100) rules of the rule-base decide the increments of the scale.

The evaluation of some data can be conditioned by the availability of certain kinds or levels of function indicator, such as fireplaces, for example, which could be pluri-functional structures. The evaluations are conventional, but not arbitrary, and we chose deliberately to open up the possibility for discussion at this modest level, and at each step, rather than leaving all discussion until one reaches the high level socio-cultural interpretations.

TOP calculates the relative value of the three functions for each topo-stratigraphical unit and cumulates the results, at Shortughaï, for each of the two phases A and B. Then there are rules which allow evaluation of the *relative variation* of the values of the three functions between A and B. Thirteen kinds of variations are possible, with each function increasing, decreasing, stable or indefinite (Francfort *et al.* 1989, pp. 108–10).

Another set of rules interprets the variations in function and allows conclusions (open to discussion) about the value of the variation of specialization of the areas, the amplitude of the variation on a conventional scale (open to discussion) and the direction of the variation (±).

The next rules of the **TOP** module deal with long distance 'exchange' at the site, quantified with respect to imports such as lapis lazuli etc. They give a value to the exchange, a measure of the amplitude and direction of the variation. All the evaluations are open to discussion. The results at Shortughaï are printed by **TOP** in the following format:

From phase A to phase B, the domestic indicator increases, the crafts indicator is stable, the prestige indicator decreases; conclusion: in the site of Shortughaï, from phase A to phase B, the specialisation of the areas diminishes somewhat (−2), the long distance trade diminishes enormously (−4).

(Francfort *et al.* 1989, p. 116)

This is consistent with what we knew; the unexpected result is the stability of craftsmanship, which we can comment upon as a shift in the domain of application of the crafts involved.

An attempt to deal with the Shahr-i Sokhta site, in proto-historic Iran, was not very successful since the data (taken from a publication) were too biased towards the topographical concentration of crafts (equated with power), but were not quantified enough and were chronologically ambiguous; the results of **TOP** are opposite to the author's conclusions.

The second module of PALAMEDE (Francfort *et al.* 1989, pp. 125–53), **TEC** ('technology of objects') models the techno-informational aspects of the data as described above. We shall abbreviate the description of this part of the model. The database has 250 lines and the rule-base works with forty-four rules. The data consist of the artefact typology, the mass of finds, the technological *chaînes opératoires*. The indicators allow the module to proceed from data to the measurement of types, total mass per unit and complexity of *chaînes opératoires* to the conventional E (***M.I***, see p. 160), and to construct notions like ELA-MOY ('mean elaboration of products': number of technological operations divided by number of types) or TECH-PON ('weighted technicity': the sum of the ***M.I*** coefficient divided by the artefact mass), giving more information about the system. Altogether there are six indicators.

Further rules indicate the change occurring between the phases and necessitate the definition of internal criteria of validity (open to discussion) for the comparison (Francfort *et al.* 1989, pp. 135–7). The comparisons of indicators by phase give 0, −1 or +1 values for the change between phases. Further rules construct the meta–notions of intensity (INTENS) and of sophistication (SOPHI) of the production, compare the direction and the importance of the variation on a scale ranging from −4 to +4 and finally translate the result into linguistic equivalents.

The results at Shortughaï are:

From phase A to phase B, the volume of production diminishes greatly (4) when the sophistication of production diminishes little (1) [or 'is stable' if the huge quantity of pebbles is taken into account].

(Francfort *et al.* 1989, p. 142)

This is consistent with **TOP** and with the new result on the stability of crafts. We have less mass and prestige production and a shift in the production towards rural life and metallurgy.

Attempts with the Indian sites of Mitathal (Indus and Late Indus), Kalibangan (Early Indus and Mature Indus) and Shahr-i Sokhta in Iran, gave only partial results because of the non-availability of artefact and waste weights (replaced by quantities for Mitathal, by nothing for the other sites). At Mitathal, contrary to the perception of the excavator, no decline is visible, but rather stability and/or increase.

At Kalibangan, the only attainable result concerns the 'sophistication of the production', which is growing as expected. At Shahr-i Sokhta, again, the results are not consistent with the conclusions of the author for the development of an urban culture.

In sum, **TEC** of PALAMEDE generates propositions which confirm (Kalibangan), modify (Shortughaï) or contradict (Mitathal, Shahr-i Sokhta) the conclusions of the excavators. But only for Shortughaï did the system have the complete quantitative measures at its disposal.

The next module of PALAMEDE (Francfort *et al.* 1989, pp. 155–97), **ARCHI**, ('architecture'), evaluates all the architectural and urban features excavated, using indicators (open to discussion as always), and constructing meta-notions. It would be too long to describe **ARCHI** in detail here. We can however explain that **ARCHI** evaluates any identified structure (for example wall, platform, fortification, stove, street, brick, etc.), respecting the hierarchy of inclusions (the walls make rooms, then houses, etc.), but evaluating also the confidence in the function of the structures (fire place/altar, etc.), and in the dimensions attributed (supposed width of a street etc.). This evaluation of confidence is combined with the conventional, but not arbitrary, value attributed to the structures with respect to the following meta-notions: PLANURB ('urban planification'), PLANURBMETRO ('metrology applied to urban planification'), ARCHI-SOPH ('architectural sophistication'), ARCHI-MONU ('monumentality of architecture'), ARCHI-METRO ('metrology applied to architecture'), URB-CONFORT ('urban comfort'), ARCH-CONFORT ('architectural elements of comfort', i.e., 'private comfort') DEFENCE, IDEOLO-COM ('common ideology'), TRAVAIL ('work').

The **ARCHI** module cumulates and combines the values of the first-level meta-notions to construct second-level meta-notions in acceptable relation with socio-cultural theories: TECH-ARCHI ('architectural technicity'), GENIE-URB ('urbanism'), CAP-CALCUL ('capacity for calculation'), QUANT-W ('quantity of work'), ORGANIS-W ('organization of work'), CONTROL-COL ('collective control'), DEFENCE-TER ('defence of territory'), IDEOLO ('ideology').

The values of the eight indicators of meta-notions are compared by phase. This gives the direction and intensity of change on a scale of −4 to +4, and generates linguistic equivalents.

The results for Shortughaï, Kalibangan, Banawali (Early, Mature and Late Indus) and Mitathal (Early, Mature and Late Indus), are globally consistent with the conclusions of the excavators. It would require too much space to present and comment on them here.

But the great interest of **ARCHI** of PALAMEDE is to give many more interpretive possibilities, explicitly formulated, than any of the comments we read in the natural language of the social sciences. For Shortughaï, for example, the stability of GENI-URB and CAP-CALCUL was unexpected whilst all the other parameters decreased; we read it as a transfer of technologies towards new kinds of planning and the appearance of structures like silos for grain-storage. We relate this to the stability of crafts (**TOP**) and to the stability of the sophistication of production (**TEC**).

Altogether, these indications seriously moderate and/or modify the initial idea that there was a process of decline or de-urbanization going on. Application of the ES to other sites confirms a variety of scenarios for a de-urbanization process.

The last module of PALAMEDE, **SYN** ('Synthesis of conclusions'; Francfort *et al.* 1989, pp. 199–211) uses twelve indices obtained from the previous modules and cumulates them in three indicators on a scale from −4 to +4. The three indicators are the following meta-notions:

- INFO ('technology of information'): deals with the complexity or sophistication of the techniques utilized in architecture, urbanism, craft production and the degree of elaboration of the writing system plus the importance of long-distance trade by cumulating TECH-ARCHI, GENIE-URB, CAP-CALCUL, SOPH-PROD, IDEO-SYMB, COMM-LONG; it considers information independently of its sense.
- TEC-ENER ('energetic technology'): deals with quantitative information on architecture, crafts, considered as systems producing more or less objects by cumulating QUANT-W, CONTR-COL, INTENS-PROD; it evaluates quantities in relation with production and therefore with energy, but it is not a measure of actual production or energy.
- TECH-SOCI ('social technology'): deals with organizational capacities of the social groups by cumulating ORGANIS-W, SPEC-AIRES, DEFENCE.

Each indicator can take nine values (with the zero value) and be combined with the others, giving a range of 729 possible solutions. The results are expressed on a conventional scale (between −0.5 and +0.5) after a decision of internal validity depending on the number of occurrences of indices. At present, we do not yet know which solutions are real and uninterpretable and which have no relation to any historical reality.

To conclude, **SYN** of PALAMEDE gives linguistic conclusions:

- If the indeterminacy of the relative evolution of the system of one of the three indicators has no value (x value), it considers that 'data insufficient to conclude'.
- It shows the contradictory case of opposite evolution of the three indicators, not generally studied in our interpretive schemes: 'attention! the indicators do not vary all in the same direction'.

- It outlines the tendency of variations, NETTE in the case of three variations of the same sign and FAIBLE in the case of at least one indicator is stable (value < 0.5).
- It qualifies the type of socio-economic system towards which the site evolved: URBAIN or RURAL.
- It writes a verbal paraphrase on the evolutions as CONCLUSION; the system may become 'much', 'more', or 'less', 'technical', (INFO) 'produce' (ENER), and 'organized' (SOCI).

The results obtained, when data were available, are consistent with the broad conclusions of the authors at Banawali, Kalibangan, Shortughaï, Mitathal (from Early to Mature Indus but not for the supposed 'decline': contradiction in the evolution of indicators). For Shahr-i Sokhta, data are not sufficient.

Historical comments about these results may observe that the global conclusions obtained at the end of **SYN** cover various sorts of evolutions, even local contradictions, and nuances that are revealed by the various lower-level indicators and meta-notions of PALAMEDE. For the Indus Civilization, PALAMEDE suggests that the Mature phase has to be seen more like a phenomenon of intensification of craft production coupled with social reorganization, rather than a technical 'urban' revolution; most of the techno-informational system was, it seems, created during the Chalcolithic phase. Concerning the 'decline', Late and Post-Indus, various local situations are described. PALAMEDE describes step by step, in a relative manner, the growth or decrease in various domains, more precisely than any other approach. The link with models and theories will be examined below.

3 Extension

The PALAMEDE system has been built especially for the Shortughaï data and those data were specially prepared for analysis with the system (notably by weighing the materials). Extension of the research to other sites was possible but limited, due to the fact that properly prepared data were not available.

It must be stressed that PALAMEDE does not provide any assessment in absolute terms; it is only meant for intra-site analysis and gives relative results. It does not allow comparison of inter-site or regional evolutions in ways other than the traditional approach (comparison of evolutions) but adds the results of spatial analysis to such comparisons. Using PALAMEDE never prevented anyone from also using more familiar interpretive ways. Moreover, the extension of conceptualization to include notions of a higher rank, at the socio-cultural and the cultural-symbolic levels, has not been applied to modelling.

However, the techno-informational approach of the kind which PALAMEDE uses forms the core of a re-interpretation proposed (in natural language) for all the material of proto-historic Central Asia (Francfort *et al.*

1989, pp. 339–456). It allows one to discriminate conventionally between an 'urban' and a 'post-urban' phase, particularly in Bactria and Margiana where all the Bronze Age artefacts were generally considered as 'non-urban' and of a later date than the comparable ones in north-east Iran, Turkmenia and the Indus Valley, for example. The recent results from the Franco-Soviet excavations at Sarazm in Tajikistan (since 1984) and from the Americano-Soviet research in Margiana (since 1989) support the views expressed here, and demonstrate the fecundity of the PALAMEDE kind of approach.

Nine simulations were made with the module **TEC** in order to test the model's sensitivity. Once a number of changes had been made (the manner in which we calculated E was changed to $E = 1/2M.i^2$, the weights taken into account in B were doubled, the weights calculated in A and B were equalized, the *chaînes opératoires* were diversified, and the number of types was varied) these tests revealed that the model was effectively stable: only the two most improbable hypotheses can invert both the sign (+ or −) of variation of the volume and the sophistication of production at the same time.

On the other hand, if we compare the twelve 'meta-notions' of the four modules of the model part of PALAMEDE with the 140 'real' socio-cultural notions inventoried in the module USE, we are happy to admit that PALAMEDE is less ambitious than all the interpretive models in use today.

The role of matter/energy, information, time and concepts

Efficient though limited as it is, PALAMEDE relies upon some theoretical concepts. Notably, the model presented here, with AI or not, utilizes the concepts of matter/energy, information and time in a way reminiscent of physics, but not so rigorously.

Like most archaeologists, we are mainly concerned with the concept time in the context of chrono-stratigraphy. We have to make the assumption that we are considering the same system at different times, simply because it is located in the same place (though Paris is not *Lutetia Parisiiorum*). It is only on that basis that we can recalculate our conventional cubic metre units on the basis of measurements taken of the actual volume excavated per spatio-temporal unit.

We consider the quantity of material remains from a certain period as representative for the flow of matter/energy through the system at that period. In this, our approach is different from those which try to calculate the energy actually consumed by the system, from those which deal with energy at a very general level (Francfort 1988, pp. 28–30) and from the voluntarist-strategic approach (Torrence 1989).

Ideally, it would have been nice to be able to measure the entropy (and/or negentropy) of the system, and the way in which it might change, because that would permit us to consider the improbability of the more complex states of the system's remains in probabilistic terms with the occurrence of the natural soil without any artefacts as null hypothesis. A formula of the Boltzmann, Shannon, or Brillouin type could then have been used, and a choice would have had to be made between the various conceptions of self-organization, order through noise or fluctuation, and of complexity, in order to comment on our results. We tested such formulae in 1977, but found that they added little to simple observation of the data (see Francfort 1988, pp. 28–9).

The work of the Brussels school was more promising, since this approach would allow us to express entropy in terms of affinities and speeds (Prigogine 1947, p. 43 ff.; Prigogine and Stengers 1979, p. 148 ff.).[6] In this perspective, the open system is traversed by a permanent flow of matter and energy: this is how we imagined the role of Shortughaï with respect to the surrounding area. One could then argue that spatial organization appeared after fluctuations and bifurcations, and the degree of complexity and organization in such open systems could be considered proportional to the flow of matter/energy. Looking at it like this would allow us to structure at least the technical and production economy (but not the whole socio-cultural system, of course!).

From an epistemological point of view, order by fluctuation, as well as order by noise, have been criticized by Thom (1980) and Scheurer (1979, pp. 302–8). Those criticisms, however, could be met in our case, as we had the value of the aggregate function of the functions of production at our disposal (in the form of the material remains from each period). We considered information as stored in the object, following Leroi-Gourhan (1965, pp. 188 ff.) and Scheurer (1979, 52; 310), rather than attempting to measure it in the usual probabilistic method.

Our measure of information is in the tradition of the 'mechanical alphabets' of Leibnitz, Diderot, Beckmann, Reuleaux (Sigaut 1987; Gille 1978, pp. 1417–53). The diversity of the material and of its transformations is assumed to reflect the quantity of information which past humans had about their environment: 'a stone → a decorative dark green stone → a piece of copper ore'. The measurement is carried out on the basis of sequences of *chaînes opératoires*. But we do not in any way evaluate the technological information with reference to 'sense'; sense needs other approaches. We are purely dealing with the quantification of a chain of events leading from raw materials to artefacts, remains, interpreted remains. Apprenticeship, experiment and language, though they allow these traditions and innovations, are not measured in any way. The combination of Time, Energy (Matter) and Information we propose $(M.I)$ is thus a conventional, approximate or attenuated evaluation of the entropy variation occurring in extinct systems.

The site at Shortughaï functioned as an attractor of matter and energy, organizing and consuming it through information; its 'capacity' and organization decreased from phase A to phase B and finally the site ended. However, the anthropological question whether complex societies exist without considerable flows of matter/energy and/or (?) without flows of information remains open.

Such are the ideas at the heart of PALAMEDE, the dispositions and evaluations in the **TOP**, **TEC**, **ARCHI** and **SYN** modules. But are they, here, more than metaphorical?

An evaluation of the results

What is the possible place of AI-oriented approaches in connection with historical-anthropological models and physico-mathematical modelling of human systems? After the preceding pages, it should be clear that in the case we dealt with, the historical – anthropological models of interpretation were not effective. Experience has shown that some empirical support can always be found for such models by the appropriate selection of archaeological data from an enormous body of material. Even without new data or without archaeological data at all, they look plausible.

Such is the lesson to be learned from operating the first part of PALAMEDE, the AI simulation of interpretive reasonings. But there is more. We think that in the present state of the art, AI (not only ES) is a powerful tool to be used when exploring areas of knowledge by means of modelling and simulation. Logicist analysis of models indicates the gaps in chains of argument, highlights the malleability of interpretation in the humanities, and points out the groups of notions which are at the core of the models. We applied such analysis to the emergence of the state in the East, albeit less completely than could be desired.

The next area we hope to explore is the interpretation of burial practices. Are we going to find, again, that most of the models – at best – lack explicit links with data or – at worst – float high above the facts they claim to explain?

The outlook in the direction of physico-mathematical modelling of human systems is sunnier. In that area, at least, there is no need for logicist analyses or the simulation of reasoning to point to the foibles of argument, since the models were written in a scientific language (mathematics) which supposes total internal consistency. In general, they are also validated in their original field of application (Bergé et al. 1988). But the transfer of such models to the social sciences is not so simple, and in that area some practical questions arise (see above, and Tolstoy 1989), as well as a number of philosophical ones (Dumouchel and Dupuy 1983; Brans et al. 1988; Thom 1988).

Either we must master rigorous rules of transfer, so as to escape arbitrary and simplistic metaphorical borrowing of concepts (or even bare diagrams), or there must be some aspect of the data concerning the social (in my case archaeological) system, which provides an overriding reason for choosing to apply a particular model rather than another one in order to explain the phenomena properly. Unfortunately, however, I have not encountered any explicit application of rules for the transfer of concepts in the archaeological literature I usually read, and neither do I know of a proper demonstration of the *necessity* of selecting a particular model (see above, and Trigger 1990). Studies of the evolution in space and time of populations (of any kind) are an exception: epidemiological and other models generally 'work' correctly. Connectionist approaches, neural networks, etc., *will* also contribute to the modelling of emerging structures in the brain as well as in human populations. Though other phenomena are easily described by almost any model, any transfer of concepts from science, knowledge about them does not progress from one model to the next.

As with any application of mathematics to archaeology, the question is to formulate the problem correctly, and to get the right kind of data correctly prepared, before one chooses any particular formalization (see, for example, Hodder 1978; Renfrew and Cooke 1979; Renfrew *et al.* 1982; Sabloff 1981; Stickel 1982; van der Leeuw 1981).

We chose to work with a metaphorical (but operational) and attenuated version of the dissipative structure approach (the physico-mathematical model) and to construct the meta-notions (the socio-cultural model) using specifically prepared (measured) data; the model was programmed as an ES. Rewriting ideas in an ES format, such as was done with PALAMEDE, is a great help in explicitly bridging the gap which occurs at the level of computational symbolism between the facts and the two kinds of models. Object-oriented languages are even more adaptable to archaeological modelling. The manipulation of symbols in AI, such as was brilliantly defined at the level of computational symbols by Fodor and Pylyshyn (1983, pp. 64–97) cannot be circumvented if we want to build real social sciences (scientific archaeological interpretations).

What we see in archaeology today is a juxtaposition of languages: the Maya collapse, for example, is described and explained in detail and by using natural language concepts (Lowe 1985); the spatio-temporal propagation of that collapse (in a sense the collapse itself), is however explained and described by using two formulae and a software package; where is the explanation? Ultimately all such constructions, like many of the growth–decay constructions, rely upon good old demographic causality. The modelling is a very small part of a historical argument which is much broader in scope; the model itself was designed to model collapse (of the Club of Rome type) so it is not surprising that it works.

Ultimately, there are interesting methodological problems concerning the use of non-linear models, concepts from 'deterministic chaos' and connectionist models in AI (see discussion in Thom 1982 and in Memmi 1990). These include the following:

1   A small number of parameters can be used to model the behaviour of complex systems in *cases where the elements are few and clearly isolated*. In modelling human systems, this poses the problem what to do with the holistic aspects of human behaviour (which entail infinite values for certain parameters) if one uses such modelling techniques.

2 For human systems, the initial conditions (of the natural environment and the socio-cultural 'milieu', notably) evolve permanently, adding to the basic unpredictability of the system which is inherent in its sensitivity to initial conditions.

3 Although it is possible to model transitional (ephemeral) states of the 'brain', (i.e., emerging structures at the sub-symbolic level), we cannot at present implement the necessary links with the level of (computational) symbols. Unfortunately, the functioning of such models throws no light on the processes occurring. We do not know how and why things happen.

4 Similarly, at the macroscopic 'supra-symbolic' level, the unpredictable appearance of structures and/or chaos means that the models have little predictive value on the time-scales which interest archaeologists. At best, we can point to short-term predictions in economics and meteorology which are based on a huge amount of data, and have been arrived at with enormous computational power. This means that the game of 'predicting the past' will either give us, at best, any kind of *ad hoc* results (delivered by *ad hoc* miniature models of any kind) or, at worst, uncontrolled, unattested, uninterpretable results, whatever the number and quality of data available about past human motivations, evaluations, 'strategies', behaviour', etc. These are some of the reasons why the level of computational symbolism, which we can master, should be explored more thoroughly and systematically so as to, at least, provide useful material for future, more elaborate models. It follows that we propose to build knowledge bases.

In short, AI techniques provide good tools for large-scale conceptual modelling, helping us to make all steps explicit and to rigorously conceptualize the limits of our applications of science to human systems (e.g. Doran 1988). The rest must be left to literature, politics, etc. That is why we concentrate upon the construction of a field-related knowledge-base.

Conclusion: about the feasibility and utility of a 'cognitive archaeology'

It is the philosophy of the team responsible for the building of PALAMEDE that work must be directed towards building field-related knowledge-bases at the computational-symbolic level. Since we cannot assume that the cognitive abilities of *Homo sapiens sapiens* have changed since its origins, we consider humanity as a social body. As such all the actions performed by individuals, whilst moving, shaping, or transforming matter, display cognitive capacities and the organization of cognitive capacities at various hierarchical levels. All the sequences of decisions and actions which were implemented while shaping artefacts, or configurations of artefacts in an area, or the configurations of configurations of artefacts in a site, etc., can be investigated and often established (see also Schiffer 1987). Leroi-Gourhan (1965) and some others recognized that these sequences reflect important computational capacities and knowledge about the environment, linked to functional rhythms and to memory.[7]

Here we are handicapped by the nature of archaeological data in much the same way as those who intended to elaborate the notion of 'cognitive maps' (developed in ethology to describe aspects of animal behaviour) for use in describing human behaviour. The 'social maps' they proposed (Vauclair 1990), encompassed places, associated events and paths connecting them; but lacked the possibility to incorporate the linguistic visuo-spatial and gestural abilities of humankind.

In human systems, traditional and innovative *chaînes opératoires* were transmitted and transformed through the ages, resisting all sorts of political oppression and all sorts of social chaos (Francfort 1985; Masson 1981, 1990). The recording and the modelling of actual decisions made by humankind (in terms of techno-structures) will open new perspectives. In *The Modularity of Mind*, Fodor (Fodor and Pylyshyn 1983) distinguished x kinds of intelligence. We could add technical intelligence to this list, which we could define as an aptitude for computation combined with a capacity for body-kinetics. Some of us may prefer discourse and argue about societal and political reconstructions of past groups of humans, but I feel on the side of the *techné*, closer to the construction of language (Goody 1977; Levy 1987; Shunchiu 1989; Francfort 1990, pp. 122–4; Weiskrantz 1988). The techno-structures and the factual taxonomies of the past are not out of reach (Vogel 1988). Moreover, any symbolic interpretation of art has to be based on a thorough reconstruction of the steps involved in creating the work of art concerned, as students of Prehistoric Art know.

A 'cognitive archaeology' which is initially conceived narrowly, as the description of techno-informational systems will, with the help of archaeometry, ethnoarchaeology and experimentation, provide us with data which are exactly suitable for AI modelling of a considerable part of the activities of the human mind and the related socio-economic systems.[8]

> computability is a priori no more foreign to human sciences than creativity is to scientists. Work from the perspective of artificial intelligence at least has the merit of obliging us to take sides on this point, on empirical grounds which are more interesting than prejudice.
>
> (Ennals and Gardin 1990, p. 350)

The field-oriented knowledge-bases which we have in mind may explore a field, a problem, a site or a category of data. They will provide the relevant data and an inventory of the kinds of interpretive argument performed on them, properly modelled at the computational symbolic level. They will also propose simulations and build meta-notions in order to model the transformations of past techno-structures. Such notions are devoid of any kind of technological determinism, and will enrich the interpretive field by auto-matically generating testable multi-interpretations.

The proper place of AI-oriented approaches in archaeology is, at present, between metaphor and simulation. This will allow us to prepare archaeo-logical data for future ('real') quantitative modelling of past human systems.

Notes

1   Logicist analysis (Gardin 1980, pp. 135–44, 170–5; 1990, p. 24) deals with all of the above steps but concentrates mainly on points 3 and 4.
2   See PALAMEDE, module USE, implemented with rules from Childe, Diakonoff, Tosi (Francfort *et al.* 1989, pp. 19–54; Francfort 1990, pp. 102–3).
3   The archaeological bibliography is not detailed in the present chapter; interested readers may consult the PALAMEDE and Shortughaî volumes which appeared in 1989. See Francfort *et al.* 1989, refs.
4   There are colleagues interested in employing it for some Latin-American data.
5   The latter is neglected in most of the studies on urban societies.
6   Applications outside chemistry have been proposed, notably in the biological sciences (Prigogine & Stengers 1979, pp. 142, 178 ff.).
7   Thresholds in memory can now be measured (Kosse 1990) as well as similar notions such as 'standard of living' in history (Baulant 1989).
8   See the papers by S. van der Leeuw, N. Schlanger, C. Karlin and M. Julien in: Renfrew & Zubrow (eds), 1994, part V: *The Material Basis of Cognitive Inference*: technology; and papers by C. Chippindale, V. Roux, H.-P. Francfort, J. Doran, M.-S. Lagrange, C. Peebles in: Gardin & Peebles (eds), 1992, part IV: *Formal Analysis, Artificial Intelligence, and Cognitive Perspectives*.

The author wishes to express his warmest thanks to Sander van der Leeuw for his help with corrections and editing.

References

Baulant, M. 1989. L'appréciation du niveau de vie. Un problème, une solution. *Histoire & Mesure* IV, 267–302.

Bergé, P., Y. Pomeau and C. Vidal 1988. *L'ordre dans le chaos. Vers une approche déter-ministe de la turbulence.* Paris: Hermann.

Binford, L.R. 1989. *Debating Archaeology.* New York: Academic Press.

Brans, J.-P., I. Stengers and P.H. Vincke (eds) 1988. *Temps et devenir. A partir de l'oeuvre d'Ilya Prigogine. Colloque de Cerisy.* Genève: Patino.

Changeux, J.-P. and A. Connes 1989. *Matière à pensée.* Paris: Editions Odile Jacob.

Doran, J.E. 1988. Expert systems and archaeology: what lies ahead? In *Computer and Quantitative Methods in Archaeology*, C.L.N. Ruggles and S.P.Q. Rahtz (eds.), pp. 237–41. Oxford: British Archaeological Reports International Series 393.

Dumouchel, P. and J.-P. Dupuy (eds) 1983. *L'auto-organisation de la physique au politique* (Colloque de Cerisy). Paris: Seuil.

Ennals, R. and J.-C. Gardin (eds) 1990. *Interpretation in the Humanities: perspectives from artificial intelligence* (Library and Information Research Report 71). London: The British Library.

Fodor, J.A. and Z.W. Pylyshyn 1983. *The Modularity of Mind*. Cambridge, Mass.: MIT Press.

Francfort, H.-P. 1985. Tradition harappéenne et innovation bactrienne à Shortughaï. In: *L'archéologie de la Bactriane ancienne*, J.-C. Gardin (ed.), 95–104. Paris: CNRS.

Francfort, H.-P. 1987. Un système expert pour l'analyse archéologique des sociétés proto-urbaines, première étape: le cas de Shortughaï, *Informatique et Sciences Humaines*, 7, 71–91.

Francfort, H.-P. 1988. A propos de l'urbanisation du site de Shortughaï (Afghanistan). Une approche archéologique des transformations de l'économie de production. *Bulletin du Centre Genevois d'Anthropologie* 1, 15–34.

Francfort, H.-P. 1990. Modelling interpretative reasoning in archaeology with the aid of expert systems: consequences of a critique of the foundations of inferences. In *Interpretation in the humanities : perspectives from artificial intelligence*, R. Ennals and J.-C. Gardin (eds), 101–29. London: The British Library (Library and Information Research Report 71).

Francfort, H.-P., M.-S. Lagrange and M. Renaud 1989. PALAMEDE. *Application des systèmes experts à l'archéologie de civilisations urbaines*. Paris: CNRS (LISH/UPR 315, Document de travail no. 9).

Gallay, A. 1986. *L'archéologie demain*. Paris: Belfond.

Gardin, J.-C. 1980. *Archaeological Constructs: an aspect of archaeological theory*. Cambridge: Cambridge University Press.

Gardin, J.-C. 1990. Interpretation in the humanities: some thoughts on the third way. In *Interpretation in the Humanities: perspectives from artificial intelligence*, R. Ennals and J.-C. Gardin (eds), 22–59. London: The British Library (LIR Report 71).

Gardin, J.-C., M.-S. Lagrange, J.-M. Martin, J. Molino and J. Natali-Smith 1987. *La logique du plausible: essais d'épistémologie pratique en sciences humaines* (2nd edn). Paris: Maison des Sciences de l'Homme.

Gardin, J.-C., O. Guillaume, P. Herman, A. Hesnard, M.-S. Lagrange, M. Renaud and E. Zadora-Rio 1988. *Artificial Intelligence and Expert Systems: case studies in the knowledge domain of archaeology*. San Francisco: Ellis Horwood.

Gille, B. 1978. *Histoire des techniques*. Paris: Gallimard.

Goody, J. 1977. *The Domestication of the Savage Mind*. Cambridge: Cambridge University Press.

Hodder, I. (ed.) 1978. *Simulation Studies in Archaeology*. Cambridge: Cambridge University Press.

Hodder, I. 1986. *Reading the Past*. Cambridge: Cambridge University Press.

Hodder, I. 1989. Writing archaeology: site reports in context. *Antiquity* 63, 268–74.

Kosse, K. 1990. Group size and societal complexity: thresholds in long-term memory. *Journal of Anthropological Archaeology* 9, 275–303.

Lagrange, M.-S. and M. Renaud 1987. Description de SNARK, un système déclaratif de représentation et d'acquisition de la connaissance. *Informatique et Sciences Humaines* 74, 19–29.

Leroi-Gourhan, A. 1965. *Le geste et la parole*, Paris: Albin Michel.

Lestienne, R. 1990. *Les fils du temps. Causalité, entropie, devenir*. Paris: Presses du CNRS.

Levy, P. 1987. *La machine univers*. Création, cognition et culture informatique. Paris: Editions La Découverte.

Lowe, J.W.G. 1985. *The Dynamics of Apocalypse. A systems simulation of the classic Maya collapse*. Albuquerque, N. M.: University of New Mexico Press.

Masson, V.M.(ed.) 1981. *Tradicii i innovacii v razvitii drevnikh kultur*. Leningrad.

Masson, V.M. 1990. *Istoricheskie rekonstrukcii v arkheologii*. Frunze.

Memmi, D., 1990, Connectionism and artificial intelligence as cognitive models, *AI & Society* 4, 115–36.

Prigogine, I. 1947. *Etude thermodynamique des phénomènes irréversibles*. Liège: Desoer.

Prigogine, I. and I. Stengers. 1979. *La nouvelle alliance*. Paris: Gallimard.

Renfrew, A.C. and K.L. Cooke (eds) 1979. *Transformations. Mathematical approaches to culture change*. New York: Academic Press.

Renfrew, A.C., M.J. Rowlands and B.A. Segraves (eds) 1982. *Theory and Explanation in Archaeology: the Southampton conference*. London: Academic Press.

Sabloff, J.A. (ed.) 1981. *Simulations in Archaeology*. Albuquerque, N. M.: University of New Mexico Press (School of American Research Advanced Seminar Series).

Scheurer, P. 1979. *Révolutions de la science et permanence du réel*. Paris: Plon.

Schiffer, M.B. 1987. *Formation Processes of the Archaeological Record*. Albuquerque, N. M.: University of New Mexico Press.

Shanks, M. and C. Tilley 1987a. *Re-constructing Archaeology. Theory and practice*. Cambridge: Cambridge University Press.

Shanks, M. and C. Tilley 1987b. *Social Theory and Archaeology*. Cambridge: Polity Press.

Shennan, S. 1990. Why should we believe archaeological interpretations? In *Interpretation in the Humanities: perspectives from artificial intelligence*, R. Ennals and J.-C. Gardin, (eds), 80–100. London: The British Library (LIR Report 71).

Shunchiu, Y. 1989. Moulded gestures and guided syntax: scenario of a linguistic breakthrough. In *Studies in Language Origins*, J. Wind, E.G. Pulleyblank, E. De Grolier and B. Bichakjian (eds), Amsterdam/Philadelphia: John Benjamins Publishing Company.

Sigaut, F. 1987. Préface. In *La technologie, science humaine*, H.G. Haudricourt (ed.), 9–36. Paris: Maison des Sciences de l'Homme.

Stickel, E.G. (ed.) 1982. *New Uses of Systems Theory in Archaeology*. Los Altos: Ballena Press (Anthropological Papers no. 24).

Stoczkowski, V. 1994. Anthropologie naive, Anthropologie savante. De l'origine de l'Homme, de l'imagination et des idées reçues, Paris: CNRS Editions.

Stutt, A. 1987. *Second Generation Experts Systems, Explanations, Arguments and Archaeology*. Milton Keynes: The Open University (Human Cognition Research Laboratory, Technical Report No. 25).

Thom, R. 1980. Halte au hasard, silence au bruit. *Le débat* 3, 119–32.

Thom, R. 1982. Mathématique et théorisation scientifique. In *Penser les mathématiques*, R. Apery (ed.), 252–73. Paris: Seuil.

Thom, R. 1988. *Esquisse d'une sémiophysique. Physique aristotélicienne et théorie des catastrophes*. Paris: Interéditions.

Tilley, C. 1989. Excavation as theatre. *Antiquity* 63, 275–80.

Tolstoy, P. 1989. Chiefdoms, states and scales of analysis. *The Review of Archaeology* 10, 72–8.

Torrence, R. (ed.) 1989. *Time, Energy and Stone Tools*. Cambridge: Cambridge University Press.

Trigger, B. 1990. Monumental architecture: a thermodynamic explanation of symbolic behaviour. *World Archaeology* 22, 119–32.

Van der Leeuw, S.E. 1981. Information flows, flow structures and the explanation of change in human institutions. In *Archaeological Approaches to the Study of Complexity*, S.E. van der Leeuw (ed.), 230–329. Amsterdam: Instituut voor Pre- en Protohistorie (Cingula VI).

Vauclair, J. 1990. Les images mentales chez l'animal. *La Recherche*. 224, 1006–14.

Vogel, C. 1988. *Génie cognitif*. Paris: Masson.

Weiskrantz, L. (ed.) 1988. *Thought Without Language*. Oxford: Oxford Science Publications.

7   *Simulating mammoth hunting and extinctions: implications for North America*

STEVEN J. MITHEN

Introduction

The question why mammoths became extinct has been debated for many years. Explanation is often polarized between either over-hunting or climatic change. Considerable progress has occurred from recent analyses of mammoth bone assemblages (e.g. Haynes 1985, 1986, 1989, 1991), improved understanding of mammoth palaeo-ecology (e.g. Guthrie 1984; Vereshchagin and Baryshnikov 1984) and an increase in the number and quality of absolute dates on mammoth remains (Lister 1991; Stuart 1991). This problem of mammoth extinction is one in which mathematical models may be able to make a significant contribution for several reasons. First there is a well-defined problem to be addressed – what is the critical level of hunting intensity on mammoths to threaten their survival. Second, it is widely acknowledged that modern elephants provide an appropriate analogy for Pleistocene mammoths (Haynes 1986, p. 661) and there has been a considerable amount of work and discussion on elephant population dynamics – including modelling – which further studies can build upon. Third, while the archaeological data concerning mammoth hunting is relatively poor compared to that of modern elephant hunting/poaching, the recent work on mammoth assemblages, such as by Haynes (1985, 1986, 1991) and Soffer (1985, 1991) provides a sound base for developing mathematical models for mammoth exploitation and extinction.

I have previously attempted to use Leslie matrix models in archaeology for studying prehistoric red deer and reindeer exploitation (Mithen 1990). In this chapter I wish to continue this exploration of Leslie matrix models by turning to the issue of mega-fauna extinction at the end of the Pleistocene, and in particular mammoth extinction, in the hope that the chapter can contribute both to the specific issue of mammoth extinction and to the more general issue of how we can improve the use of mathematical models in archaeology.

My intention is to construct a mathematical model for mammoth population dynamics based on a Leslie matrix, and then use computer simulation to examine the relationship between the character and intensity of human predation on mammoth population decline and extinction. As such, it inevitably requires certain assumptions to be made about mammoth population dynamics and prehistoric hunting strategies. The aim is to derive a general understanding of the sensitivity of mammoth populations and then to reflect, with this knowledge, upon the archaeological data, notably those from the Central Russian Plain (Soffer 1985). In the latter part of this chapter I will develop a model that specifically concerns mammoth extinction in North America, building upon the simulation studies of Mosimann and Martin (1975) and Whittingdon and Dyke (1984). Simulation modelling will not in itself provide any answers as to what caused mammoth extinction, but it will provide a sounder base from which to interpret the available data. The first step, however, is to briefly review the archaeological data for mammoth extinction and exploitation.

Mammoth exploitation and extinction

The recovery of frozen mammoth carcasses, complete with gut contents, have provided us with considerable information about mammoth palaeo-ecology. Certain critical gaps in our knowledge remain, such as mammoth migratory behaviour and population densities. The dates we are acquiring from mammoth bones and ivory will allow us to monitor the variation in the timing of extinction throughout the world and search for correlations with hunting pressure and climatic change. At present it appears that mammoths became extinct throughout Europe by 12,000 BP, in North America slightly later at c. 11,000 BP and in Siberia as late as 10,000 BP (Stuart 1991).[1] Soffer (1991) describes the pattern of mammoth extinction as time transgressive from the south-west to the north-east of the Old World. As a large terrestrial mammal, mammoths exemplify the types of species that became extinct at the end of the Pleistocene.

Mammoth populations would certainly have suffered from the environmental changes at the end of the Pleistocene. Guthrie (1984, p. 269) argues that the increase in seasonality and consequent zonation of vegetation was critical in having a detrimental effect on the viability of large mammal populations. In regions such as Siberia, the small size of mammoths and the evidence for naturally induced mass deaths suggest that the populations were suffering from environmental stress (Soffer 1991). It is likely that mammoths were pushed into refugia (Lister 1991) making the populations more vulnerable to local extinction due to short-term environmental fluctuations. But a problem with the primacy of climatic change as the causal factor in mammoth extinction is that mammoths had survived numerous earlier glacial/interglacial cycles.[2] At present we know of just one critical difference between the last and earlier glacials: the presence of *Homo sapiens sapiens* hunter-gatherer populations over large areas of the Old World and rapidly spreading into the New.

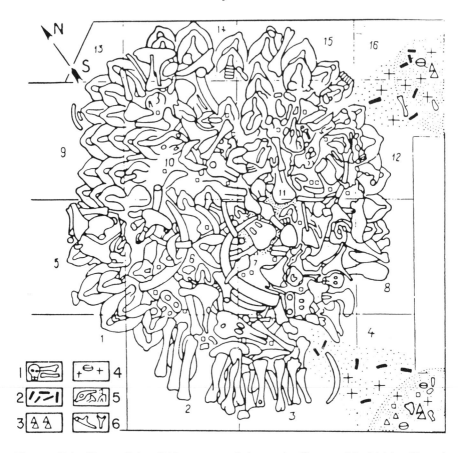

Figure 7.1 Upper Palaeolithic mammoth-bone dwelling at Mezhirich, Central Russian Plain. Dwelling 1: 1, mammoth bones; 2, hearths and ash layer; 3, bone charcoal; 4, worked bone; 5, marine shells; 6, reindeer antlers. Excavation grid = 2 × 2 m (after Soffer 1985, Figure 2.63).

Various types of archaeological evidence indicate that Upper Palaeolithic hunters exploited mammoths and had a keen interest in their distribution and behaviour. Most notable are the settlements on the Russian Plain with mammoth-bone dwellings (Figure 7.1) (Soffer 1985). As many as 149 and 116 individual mammoths are represented in the faunal remains from Mezhirich and Mezin respectively. Mammoths feature significantly in Palaeolithic art (Bahn and Vertut 1988, pp. 128–9), particularly on the engraved plaquettes from Gönnersdorf (Figure 7.2) (Bosinski 1984), and indicate that the artists were knowledgeable about mammoth anatomy and keen to produce naturalistic images. We also have many carved objects made of mammoth ivory, including utilitarian and decorative items. These include spear-throwers, figurines, and bracelets. Some sites, such as Paviland cave in

Figure 7.2 Mammoth depicted in Upper Palaeolithic art. Plaquette no. 98 from Gönnersdorf. The engraved mammoth is *c.* 15 cm from head to tail (after Bosinski 1984, Figure 1).

south Wales, appear to have been specialist ivory procurement and processing locations (Jacobi 1980, p. 35 ff.). Mammoth bones are frequently recorded within Lower/Middle and Upper Palaeolithic assemblages, and mammoths may have constituted an important source of food. As Soffer (1991, p. 39) describes, the presence of large numbers of mammoths is a ubiquitous feature of Central and Eastern European Upper Palaeolithic sites.

The extent to which this evidence indicates that mammoths were actively hunted is controversial (cf. Diamond 1984, 1986, 1989; Frison 1990; Haynes 1985, 1986, 1989, 1991; Agenbroad 1984; O'Connell *et al.* 1991; Musil 1968; Saunders 1980; Soffer 1985, 1991). But even if Upper Palaeolithic hunters regularly hunted mammoths, there remain important arguments against the view that humans pushed mammoths into extinction. On cost–benefit grounds, it might be doubted if mammoths were ever a preferred prey of Upper Palaeolithic hunters, particularly in light of the wide range of resources in the late Pleistocene environments. Webster and Webster (1984) argue that once mammoth populations had been depleted, human hunters are likely to have switched to more profitable game which may have allowed mammoth populations time to replenish. In addition there may have been constraints on the intensity of mammoth hunting due to technical and organizational factors: mammoth hunting is likely to have been an activity requiring the co-operation of a large group which may have only been feasible at certain times of the year, or indeed in certain years.

Before proceeding we need to distinguish between the local extinction of a population and the total extinction of the species. The local disappearance of a mammoth/elephant population may have been a not uncommon occurrence throughout the Pleistocene due to short-term environmental events. As Haynes (1989) describes, a series of 'die-offs' could lead to the local disappearance of a population, a situation he refers to as a (local) 'die-out', due to a variety of causes. Mammoths may have survived in a series of dispersed refugia across the world from which they expanded at more favourable times. For instance, mammoths appear absent from North and Central Europe between 20,000–15,000 BP, the period of the last glacial maximum, although they survived in the Russian Plain. Species extinction will simply occur when all local populations have become extinct. Between the two extremes of local and species extinction, it is also useful to think of regional extinction as the loss of mammoths from a large land mass, such as North America, while they may have remained present elsewhere in the world. Soffer (1991) has characterized the species extinction of mammoths as being a mosaic of successive local and regional extinctions.

Our archaeological questions can be focused at the level of either local, regional or species extinction. For local extinction we are more concerned with the detailed interactions between hunters and mammoths and must be concerned with issues such as hunting strategies and prey-switching as Webster and Webster (1984, *passim*) suggest. Our appropriate time-scales are in single, tens or hundreds of years. When we are concerned with regional or species extinction, and believe that human predation may have been significant, a major interest is with the growth rate of the human population and the character of climatic deterioration over time-scales of thousands of years. Ultimately, however, we will need to explain species extinction in terms of multiple local and regional extinctions.

To develop our hypotheses concerning the role of human hunting in mammoth extinction we need to acquire further information concerning the effect of predation on mammoth populations for both small scale local populations and those covering continental areas. How many animals can be taken on an annual basis before populations begin to decline? How many can be taken before the population is pushed into extinction? Are these numbers feasible levels for humans to take with a Palaeolithic technology? How might climatic variables affect the level of hunting intensity required to push a mammoth population into extinction? While simulation cannot provide answers to these for a Pleistocene mammoth population, it can certainly provide some reasonable bounds for these values which may considerably improve our discussion of the role of human predation as a factor in mammoth extinction.

A simulation model

In this simulation, the mammoth population is modelled by using a Leslie matrix (Leslie 1945), which is a means to model the population dynamics of a species with respect to the age/sex structure of the population. Using Leslie matrices we can explore the effect of different types of hunting strategies and environmental events, which are age/sex specific in their effects, on the short- and long-term viability of the total population (cf. Mithen 1990). For this simulation both female and male portions of the population are modelled and sixty age classes are used. Birth and death parameter values are based on those of African elephants. There have been several recent models for elephant population dynamics, some using Leslie matrices (e.g., Hanks and McIntosh 1973; Croze et al. 1981; Pilgrim and Western 1986). I draw on parameter values used in these models and on more general discussion of elephant popu- lation dynamics (e.g., Laws et al. 1975). Elephants have been frequently drawn upon as an analogy for mammoths (e.g., Haynes 1991; Soffer 1991). My principal rationale is their equivalence in body size to mammoths, since body size is one of the main determinants of life history characteristics.

A density-dependent model in a constant environment

Survival

The annual natural survival of non-juvenile elephants (>5 yrs) is in the order of 97–98 per cent, which decreases rapidly after the age of 50. Males appear to suffer higher non-juvenile mortality than females (Laws et al. 1975, passim). In this model I will use values of 97.5 per cent for female animals aged 5–49 yrs, 95 per cent for those between 50 and 59 yrs and 50 per cent for those 60 yrs or older. For males the values 95 per cent, 90 per cent and 25 per cent are used for the same age classes. If density dependence is a factor controlling population size, then this is likely to operate on the survival of juvenile animals, i.e. those less than five years old. Here I will use a linear function of the form $S_t = a - bP_t/P_k$, where S_t is the probability of survival at time t, a and b are constants (b defining the fall in survival rate with popu- lation size), P_t the population at time t and P_k the population level at carrying capacity. This is initially set at the arbitrary value of 1,000 to model rela- tively small populations in order to explore the process of local extinction. The value of a is kept constant. Values for b are explored, 0.05, 0.2, and 0.35. These give progressively stronger density dependence on juvenile survival.

Fecundity

Following Pilgrim and Western (1986) the fecundity of animals aged 50 or over is set at zero. Annual fecundity itself is a function of interbirth interval and age at sexual maturity, both of which are variable in living populations

Table 7.1 Twenty-seven runs of the mammoth simulation model, in a constant enviroment with varying population parameters and summary statistics on resulting population dynamics.

Run no.	Parameter values			Age at reproduction			Juvenile suvival			Growth rate		Time to equilibrium	Equilibrium population size
	b	e	f	max.	min.	mean	max.	min.	mean	max.	mean		
1	0.05	0.05	0.15	10	10	10	0.93	0.89	0.91	1.02	0.22	510	1111.91
2	0.20	0.05	0.15	10	10	10	0.90	0.88	0.90	0.34	−0.09	278	277.97
3	0.35	0.05	0.15	10	10	10	0.89	0.82	0.89	−0.01	−0.27	292	161.05
4	0.05	4.00	0.15	12	11	12	0.94	0.91	0.92	0.88	0.10	–	749.70
5	0.20	4.00	0.15	11	10	11	0.98	0.88	0.90	0.34	−0.36	99	250.55
6	0.35	4.00	0.15	11	10	10	0.89	0.82	0.89	0.00	−0.28	288	161.04
7	0.05	7.50	0.15	14	12	13	0.94	0.92	0.93	0.74	0.14	279	536.62
8	0.20	7.50	0.15	12	11	11	0.90	0.88	0.90	0.24	−0.18	219	242.41
9	0.35	7.50	0.15	12	11	11	0.90	0.82	0.89	−0.01	−0.26	357	148.88
10	0.05	0.05	0.25	10	10	10	0.93	0.81	0.85	2.93	0.90	231	2852.39
11	0.20	0.05	0.25	10	10	10	0.88	0.81	0.83	2.48	0.38	183	713.00
12	0.35	0.05	0.25	10	10	10	0.84	0.81	0.82	2.03	0.08	160	407.47
13	0.05	4.00	0.25	17	11	15	0.93	0.86	0.88	2.72	0.58	286	1885.70
14	0.20	4.00	0.25	12	11	12	0.88	0.82	0.84	2.27	0.30	200	648.18
15	0.35	4.00	0.25	11	11	11	0.84	0.81	0.82	1.82	0.05	170	389.14
16	0.05	7.50	0.25	20	12	18	0.93	0.88	0.89	2.52	0.44	315	1413.85
17	0.20	7.50	0.25	14	12	13	0.88	0.83	0.85	2.07	0.23	204	588.07
18	0.35	7.50	0.25	12	12	12	0.85	0.82	0.83	1.62	0.02	179	370.36
19	0.05	0.05	0.35	10	10	10	0.93	0.75	0.82	6.35	1.53	158	3907.77
20	0.20	0.05	0.35	10	10	10	0.88	0.75	0.79	5.90	0.78	129	976.97
21	0.35	0.05	0.35	10	10	10	0.82	0.75	0.78	5.45	0.39	113	558.16
22	0.05	4.00	0.35	20	11	17	0.93	0.82	0.86	6.06	1.13	175	2555.55
23	0.20	4.00	0.35	13	11	12	0.88	0.77	0.80	5.61	0.62	146	884.23
24	0.35	4.00	0.35	12	11	11	0.82	0.77	0.79	5.16	0.31	120	523.55
25	0.05	7.50	0.35	24	12	20	0.93	0.86	0.88	5.77	0.95	177	1897.81
26	0.20	7.50	0.35	16	12	15	0.88	0.79	0.80	5.32	0.16	500	799.68
27	0.35	7.50	0.35	13	12	13	0.82	0.77	0.79	4.87	0.25	136	505.31

Note: Parameters b and e relate to the degree of density dependence on juvenile survival and age of female sexual maturity respectively; parameter f is the percentage of sexually mature females reproducing in any one year.

and may be density dependent (Pilgrim and Western 1986). In this model I will treat age at sexual maturity as density dependent by using the linear function, $F_t = d + eP_t/P_k$, where d and e are constants, the latter defining the rate of increase in age of sexual maturity with population size. An animal of age class i at time t is defined as sexually mature if $i > F_t$. The value of d is kept constant at 9.0 (the age at which pregnancy becomes physiologically possible) and three different values for e are explored, 0.05, 4.0, and 7.5, giving a progressively stronger density dependent relationship. For animals between the age of sexual maturity and 50 three different values for fecundity, f, are used, 0.15, 0.25 and 0.35.

The simulation

With three values for each of the parameters b, e and f, twenty-seven different models are possible. Some of these may be unrealistic for elephants and/or mammoths. To examine the pattern of population growth and the demographic characteristics of the equilibrium population, the growth of the population under each combination of parameter values was simulated. The population began with an arbitrary age/sex structure and size (three in each age/sex class, making a starting population of 360 individuals). Growth was simulated until equilibrium was reached, defined as an absolute rate of

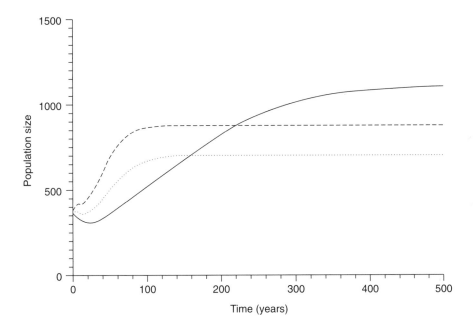

Figure 7.3 Simulated growth of mammoth populations in stable environment and with density dependence on juvenile survival and age of female sexual maturity. Run 1 (solid), Run 11 (closed dash) and Run 23 (open dash); see Table 7.1 for parameter values.

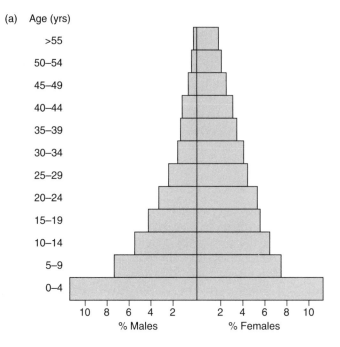

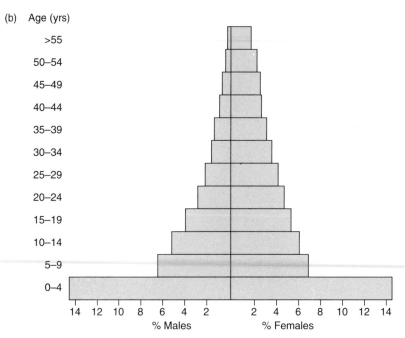

Figure 7.4 Age/sex structures for simulated mammoth populations at equilibrium, (a) = Run 1, (b) = Run 11.

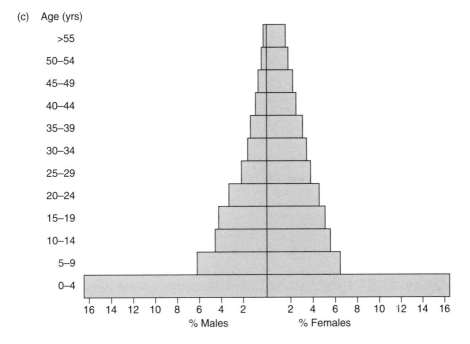

Figure 7.4 (continued) (c) = Run 23; see Table 7.1 for parameter values.

growth of less than 0.0001 per cent for ten successive years. On each of the twenty-seven runs the following data were recorded:

- Time taken to reach equilibrium.
- Maximum, minimum and average survival rates for juveniles.
- Maximum, minimum and average ages of sexual maturity.
- Maximum rate of growth, average rate of growth.
- Total population at equilibrium.
- Age/sex structure of the equilibrium population.

The results for these twenty-seven runs are given in Table 7.1. Figure 7.3 shows the growth of the population to equilibrium in three of these runs (nos. 1, 11, 23), and Figure 7.4(a)–(c) their equilibrium age/sex structure. I will use these three runs throughout the chapter to cover the range of feasible mammoth population models. Run 23 models a vigorous population – one that can grow rapidly but is also sensitive to density dependent controls on population size; run 1 is a much less vigorous population with a slow growth rate; and run 11 falls between these extremes.

A density independent model in a fluctuating environment

In many, if not all, contemporary elephant populations density independent factors may play a more significant role in both constraining population size and allowing periods of rapid growth than the density of the population. For African elephants, rainfall is the main density independent factor; dry years reduce juvenile survival and fecundity rates from their average while wet years increase these (Lee and Moss 1986; Barnes 1982). A sequence of dry years can have substantial cumulative effects on a population, particularly on the male portion since juvenile males are particularly sensitive to drought (Lee and Moss 1986). The approximate effects of good (wet) and bad (dry) years on survival and fecundity in Ambroseli are given in Table 7.2. There is no a priori reason to suppose that Pleistocene mammoth populations did not also suffer from such environmental events, causing density independent factors to be the main control on population size. While in low latitudes a good year may be one with high precipitation, in higher latitudes a good year may be one that is dry, since high precipitation would have been in the form of snow which would have made foraging more difficult.

To explore the effect of such density independent effects I define each year of the simulation as either good, average or bad on a random basis. Initially these are defined so that any type of year may follow any other type by using a Markov matrix in which all elements are equal (Figure 7.5(a)). To model the density independent effects I introduce a further parameter, g and use this to define the effect of a good year on female fecundity in terms of the percentage increase of the average rate; in Table 7.2 this would have the value of 20.0. Now, all other DI effects are defined as multiples of g. For instance fecundity in the second of two consecutive bad years will have the value of $-4g$, while male survival in a good year will have the value of $0.625g$. By this means I can introduce just one single new parameter and maintain the variation of DI effects across different population parameters.

Table 7.2 The effect of good (wet), bad (dry) and consecutive bad years on the fecundity and juvenile survival of elephants in Ambroseli Park.

		Juvenile survival	
Year type	Fecundity (%)	Female (%)	Male (%)
Average	25	80	80
Good year	30 (+20)	90 (+12.5)	90 (−12.5)
Bad year	15 (−40)	65 (−18.75)	55 (−31.25)
Consecutive bad years	5 (−80)	65 (−18.75)	40 (−50)

Source: Lee and Moss 1986; Lee, pers. comm.

Note: The figues in parentheses denote the percentage change from the 'average' figures in the first row.

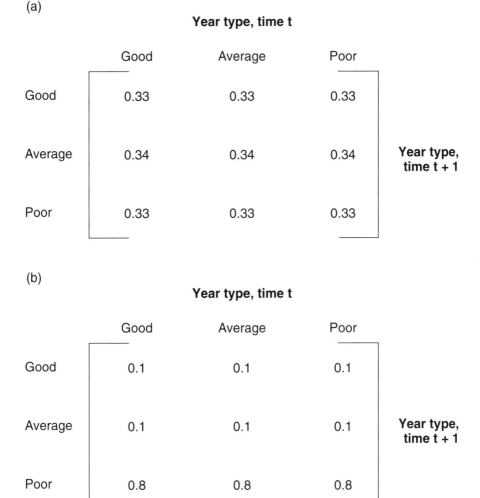

Figure 7.5 Markov matrices for simulating pseudo-random sequences of good, average and bad years. (a) = matrix with equal year type probabilities, (b) = matrix for simulating an environment with higher frequency of poor years. When climatic deterioration is modelled the elements of the matrices are treated as functions of time.

To demonstrate the effects of the value of g, Table 7.3 shows three runs of the simulation (nos. 1, 11, 23, Table 7.1), each made with three different values of $g - 5$, 15, 25. As equilibrium is no longer reached in such a fluctuating environment, the values in Table 7.3 are for the final year of the simulation. Simulation runs with g values of 5 and 15 applied to run 11, are illustrated in Figure 7.6.

Table 7.3 The effect of random environmental fluctuations on the population dynamics from three runs (1, 11, 23) of the mammoth simulation model.

Run no.	Parameter values				Age at first reproduction			Juvenile survival			growth rate	
	b	e	f	g	max.	min.	mean	max.	min.	mean	max.	min.
1	0.05	0.05	0.15	5.00	10	10	10	0.94	0.90	0.92	2.27	0.20
	0.05	0.05	0.15	15.00	10	10	10	0.94	0.93	0.94	5.00	0.08
	0.05	0.05	0.15	15.00	10	10	10	0.95	0.93	0.95	6.93	−0.50
11	0.20	0.05	0.25	5.00	10	10	10	0.88	0.81	0.83	3.63	0.15
	0.20	0.05	0.25	15.00	10	10	10	0.91	0.81	0.85	9.28	0.25
	0.20	0.05	0.25	25.00	10	10	10	0.92	0.81	0.87	14.31	0.45
23	0.20	4.00	0.35	5.00	13	11	13	0.88	0.77	0.79	4.92	0.20
	0.20	4.00	0.35	15.00	13	11	12	0.89	0.76	0.81	12.64	0.35
	0.20	4.00	0.35	25.00	13	10	12	0.91	0.76	0.83	21.34	0.67

Note: Parameter g denotes to the sensitivity of the population parameters to either good or bad years.

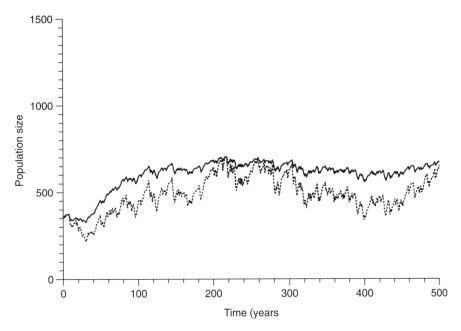

Figure 7.6 Simulated mammoth populations in fluctuating environments. Run 11 with $g = 5.0$ (solid), and $g = 15$ (dash); see Table 7.1 for parameter values for Run 11.

Using a Markov matrix to produce a pseudo-random sequence of good/average/bad years allows us to model climatic deterioration, as occurred for the mammoth at the end of the last glacial. We can do this by beginning the simulation with a matrix as in Figure 7.5(a) with an equal occurrence of good, average and poor years. We can then gradually increase the probabilities for transitions to poor years (elements of the third row) and accordingly decrease those for transition to good or average years. Figure 7.5(b), for instance, shows a matrix that models an environment with a high frequency of poor years. To do this we make the elements of the matrix linear functions of time. If the final probability for a transition to a poor year is denoted by h, and the initial value at $t = 1$ is 0.33, then at time t, the probability for a bad year, P_{bt}, will equal $0.33 + ((h - 0.33)/t_{max})t)$, in which t_{max} denotes the period over which climatic deterioration is occurring (i.e., the time taken to move from the matrix in Figure 7.5(a) to that in 7.5(b)). The values for the transition to good or average years, $P_{g/a,t}$ are set equal at $(1 - P_{b,t})/2$. Such a model will simulate an increasing frequency of die-offs, which may create a die-out irrespective of hunting pressure. Figure 7.7 illustrates run 11 for $t_{max} = 750$, $g = 15$ and $h = 0.8$. In this example the population approaches extinction due to climatic deterioration alone.

How appropriate are these models for modern elephants and Pleistocene mammoths?

Now we must briefly consider whether these simulated populations are viable models for modern elephants and Pleistocene mammoths, by comparing aspects of the simulated populations with those of the real world, using data independent from those employed in constructing the models. We have two points of contact: maximum rates of population growth and age structure.

Observed rates of population growth among elephants in Uganda have been between 3–4 per cent p.a. (Hanks and McIntosh 1973). In Hwange National Park, Zimbabwe they have been 5 per cent p.a. since the 1930s (Haynes 1985). A population in the Addo National Park, South Africa, has maintained an annual growth rate of *c.* 7 per cent for twenty-seven years between 1953–79 (Calef 1988). Calef suggests that 7 per cent is likely to be the maximum possible annual rate of growth for elephant populations.

In the light of these data the maximum growth rates of the simulated populations in constant environments, with density dependence the only control on population size, appear to be rather low (Table 7.1). Only when fecundity reaches the relatively high value of 0.35 per cent do maximum growth rates rise above 3 per cent, and the maximum recorded is only 6.35

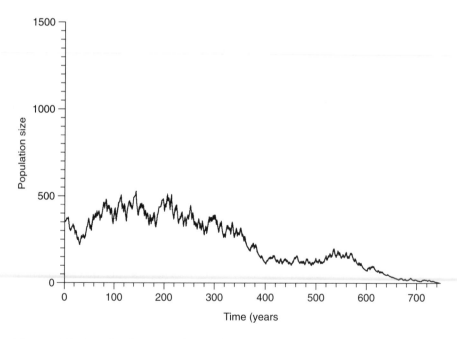

Figure 7.7 Simulated mammoth population in a deteriorating environment. Run 11 with $g = 15$, $h = 0.8$, $t_{max} = 750$. In this example the mammoth population becomes effectively extinct after *c.* 750 years; see Table 7.1 for parameter values for Run 11.

per cent. Once the environmental fluctuations are added, however, and density independent factors play a significant role in controlling the population, we find a much wider, and generally higher, range of maximum growth rates (Table 7.3). When $g = 15$, maximum growth rates of 5.0, 9.28 and 12.64 are recorded for runs 1, 11 and 23 respectively. The character of the population fluctuations represented in Figure 7.6, when $g = 15$, appears to be a good model for those of real elephant populations in historic times, although long-term sequences of elephant numbers are very difficult to reconstruct.

A comparison between observed and simulated age structures also indicates that the simulation model is realistic, particularly when environmental fluctuations are added. Figure 7.8 compares the frequency of animals aged between 0 and 10 years (inclusive) in a set of ten real populations and twenty-three

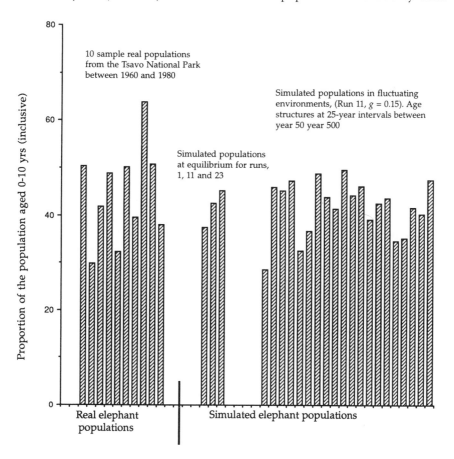

Figure 7.8 Age structure (proportion of population between 0–10 yrs) in real and simulated elephant populations. Real samples from Tsavo National Park, between 1960 and 1980, after Ottichilo (1986). Simulated populations from Runs 1, 11 and 23 in constant environment, and Run 11 in fluctuating environment, $g = 15$; see Table 7.1 for parameter values for Runs 1, 11 and 23.

simulated populations. The real data are from Ottichilo's (1986) study of age structure of elephants in the Tsavo National Park between 1966 and 1980, a period during which drought and poaching led to fluctuations in the population sizes and structure. The proportion of 0–10-year-olds varies between 29.9 per cent and 63.82 per cent, with most in the range 38–50 per cent. The simulated age structures also fall in this range, both for the three equilibrium populations (runs 1, 11, 23) and for a sample of twenty annual populations taken from a simulation run in a fluctuating environment (run 11, $g = 15$). These data suggest that the simulated mammoth population dynamics are similar to those of real elephant populations. The small sample size and variability within the data detracts from the value of this comparison. Nevertheless, if elephants are accepted as an analogy for mammoths, then the current model will be an effective tool for exploring the effect of human predation and climatic change on the decline and extinction of mammoths at the end of the Pleistocene.

Simulating Palaeolithic hunting

All the simulations I describe involve a random/catastrophic killing pattern rather than the selection of specific age/sex classes. Human hunting can be modelled in different ways relating to different types of exploitation pattern. First, hunting can be modelled in terms of a 'fixed percentage'. In this a fixed percentage of each age/sex class of the population is killed each year. This creates a catastrophic mortality profile in the archaeological record (varying the percentage across age/sex classes would create an attritional age/sex profile). If the percentage killed is large enough to cause the population to fall, the number of animals taken each year, as a fixed percentage, will also fall. In this scenario, human hunters are being modelled as responsive to the size/density of the mammoth populations – a constant 'effort' is being modelled. If we assume that the human population size remains constant, then hunters are assumed to be switching to other prey as the size of the mammoth population/number killed declines (or switching from other prey as the size increases should environmental factors cause population growth that outweighs the decline due to hunting). There is a second hunting pattern – 'reduced percentage' – in which declining animal populations lead to a reduced level of exploitation in the percentage of the population take. This is used by game managers and may also be inferred from ethnographic accounts of North American hunters (Rick, pers. comm.).

The third strategy is a 'fixed number' kill of mammoths. This takes the same number of animals each year irrespective of the size of the mammoth population. This number is distributed across age/sex categories in proportion to their frequencies, and therefore it also creates catastrophic mortality profiles and cannot easily be distinguished from a 'fixed percentage' kill. For instance, if the fixed number kill was set at ten animals, and male animals aged 0–1 yr represented 5 per cent of the population, then their numbers would be reduced by 0.5 animals. Hence this models the killing of a male calf every other year. With a fixed number kill, the percentage of the population which is taken annually increases, as the population declines. Consequently, hunting effort is increased as the population declines (or decreased as the population increases) to maintain the same size kill.

Which of these strategies is more appropriate for Palaeolithic hunters is debatable. It is likely to depend upon the role of mammoth in the economy. If mammoths were exploited as just another large mammal resource, along with reindeer, horse and bison, then a fixed percentage cull is probably the most appropriate. If however, it had a slightly different role due to its size, perhaps a specialized exploitation for ivory or a single organized mass hunt once a year, then a fixed number kill might be more appropriate.

The simulations I will initially describe are concerned with the exploitation, and extinction, of a local population – I use $P_k = 1,000$. However, the qualitative results (i.e., the sensitivity of the populations to extinction) are directly applicable to much larger populations and total extinction. Later I will develop a model with a mammoth population size appropriate for the continent of North America It should be noted here that by these simulations I am exploring the consequences of the killing of animals which would have otherwise survived until the following year. Hunters may have been killing animals which were dying, or about to die, of natural causes, as Haynes (1991, *passim*) has proposed for the Clovis hunters. I will explore this issue in the latter part of this chapter when I simulate mammoth extinction in North America.

Results

Table 7.4 and Figure 7.9 present the results from exploring fixed percentage hunting of mammoths for three runs, nos. 1, 11 and 23, showing that hunting intensities of 2, 4 and 5 per cent are sufficient to push each of these into extinction (i.e., the equilibrium population size is zero). Figure 7.10 illustrates the exploitation of population no. 11 at three hunting intensities. Table 7.5, Figures 7.11 and 7.12 present similar results from fixed number hunting.

Both of these show mammoth populations to be very sensitive to increased mortality through hunting pressure. They are only able to sustain low fixed percentage and number killing. Comparison with large (rather than mega-) herbivores is striking. In Figure 7.13 I compare fixed percentage hunting of mammoth (run 11) and reindeer, with both populations having an equilibrium, unexploited level of *c.* 4,000 individuals (in the present model this is achieved by manipulating the value of P_k). (The reindeer population is also simulated by a Leslie matrix and described in Mithen 1990.) Red deer are able to sustain an annual fixed percentage random kill of 17 per cent (Mithen 1990, p. 219).

Table 7.4 Fixed percentage hunting on three runs (1, 11, 23) of the mammoth simulation model.

Run no.	Parameter values				Size of kill		Equilibrium/ extinction time	Population size at equilibrium
	b	e	f	$K\%$	year 1	equilibrium		
1	0.05	0.05	0.15	1.0	11.16	1.79	–	177.53
	0.05	0.05	0.15	2.0	22.31	0.00	466	0.00
	0.05	0.05	0.15	3.0	33.47	0.00	236	0.00
11	0.20	0.05	0.25	1.0	7.14	5.05	175	500.13
	0.20	0.05	0.25	2.0	14.28	5.77	329	282.87
	0.20	0.05	0.25	3.0	21.42	1.97	1146	63.65
	0.20	0.05	0.25	4.0	28.56	0.00	358	0.00
23	0.20	4.00	0.35	1.0	8.85	7.09	106	701.50
	0.20	4.00	0.35	2.0	17.70	10.21	–	500.14
	0.20	4.00	0.35	3.0	26.55	9.70	300	313.47
	0.20	4.00	0.35	4.0	35.40	6.74	501	161.70
	0.20	4.00	0.35	5.0	44.24	0.00	703	0.00

Note: Parameter K denotes the percentage of each age/sex class killed each year.

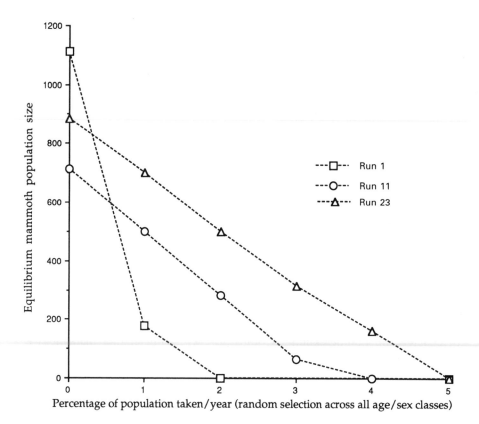

Figure 7.9 Equilibrium mammoth population sizes in constant environments and under varying intensities of fixed percentage culling. None of the three models for mammoth population dynamics (Runs 1, 11 and 23) can sustain more than a 4 per cent annual cull.

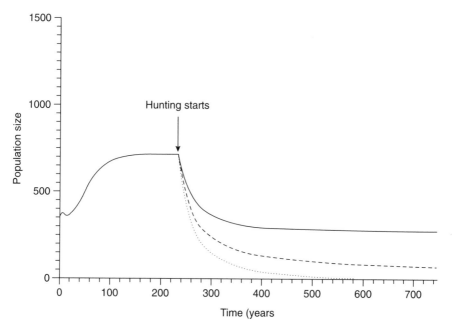

Figure 7.10 Fixed percentage culling of mammoth population (Run 11) under three hunting intensities, 2 per cent (solid), 3 per cent (spaced dash), 4 per cent (dotted line). The population is allowed to reach equilibrium in a constant environment, free from predation, before hunting starts.

Fixed number hunting also shows mammoths to be very sensitive to predation. For Run no. 1, the kill size of four which is sufficient to extinguish the population, is only 0.35 per cent of an unexploited population size at equilibrium. Similarly for Run 11, the critical figure of seven animals represents 0.84 per cent and, for Run 23, eleven animals represents 2.7 per cent. It must be emphasized however, that these fixed number kills are distributed across the population according to the frequency of each age/sex class within the population. If the fixed number kill targets specific age/sex classes then either higher, or lower, annual culls may be possible. Such selective culling awaits further modelling.

If we introduce random environmental fluctuations to let DI factors play the most significant role in controlling population growth and decline, we find that the sensitivity of the mammoth populations to hunting is increased (Table 7.6). This is in terms of both the size of the annual kill required to cause extinction and of the rate at which populations become extinct. Run 1 is unable to sustain any exploitation, run 11 becomes extinct with either a 3 per cent fixed percentage cull or a fixed number of three animals per annum, and run 23 with a percentage cull of 3 per cent or a fixed one of eight animals.

Table 7.5 Fixed number hunting on three runs (1, 11, 23) of the mammoth simulation model.

Run no.	Parameter values				Size of kill		Equilibrium/ extinction time	Population size at equilibrium
	b	e	f	K%	year 1	equilibrium		
1	0.05	0.05	0.15	1	1	1	214	1036.07
	0.05	0.05	0.15	2	2	2	346	922.53
	0.05	0.05	0.15	3	3	3	624	749.25
	0.05	0.05	0.15	4	4	0	838	0.00
	0.05	0.05	0.15	5	5	0	449	0.00
	0.05	0.05	0.15	10	10	0	153	0.00
	0.05	0.05	0.15	20	20	0	73	0.00
11	0.20	0.05	0.25	1	1	1	87	683.78
	0.20	0.05	0.25	3	3	3	142	610.34
	0.20	0.05	0.25	5	5	5	247	504.26
	0.20	0.05	0.25	6	6	6	678	382.09
	0.20	0.05	0.25	7	7	7	338	0.00
	0.20	0.05	0.25	9	9	9	164	0.00
	0.20	0.05	0.25	20	20	20	55	0.00
23	0.20	4.00	0.35	5	5	5	–	749.14
	0.20	4.00	0.35	8	8	8	179	657.83
	0.20	4.00	0.35	9	9	9	254	594.28
	0.20	4.00	0.35	10	10	10	–	500.53
	0.20	4.00	0.35	11	11	0	946	0.00
	0.20	4.00	0.35	12	12	0	286	0.00
	0.20	4.00	0.35	15	15	0	134	0.00
	0.20	4.00	0.35	20	20	0	81	0.00

Note: Parameter K denotes total number of animals taken each year from the population; this figure is equally divided between all age/sex classes according to their frequency in the population.

The introduction of climatic deterioration will further increase the sensitivity of the mammoth populations to extinction. Table 7.7 shows three simulated populations suffering either a fixed percentage or fixed number cull in deteriorating environments (t_{max} = 500, h = 0.5, 0.6 and 0.7). Not surprisingly, there is a substantial reduction in extinction time from the non-deteriorating fluctuating environment. Figure 7.14 illustrates the effect of a fixed 2 per cent cull on population modelled by run 11 in fluctuating (g = 15) and deteriorating (g = 15, h = 0.8, t_{max} = 500) environments.

Discussion

The simulations I have so far conducted demonstrate that local mammoth populations are very sensitive to predation, which confirms previous suggestions made without quantitative support (e.g. Haynes 1991). The dramatic population collapses that we have seen following a slight increase in hunting intensity agree with the patterns observed among modern elephants. In the

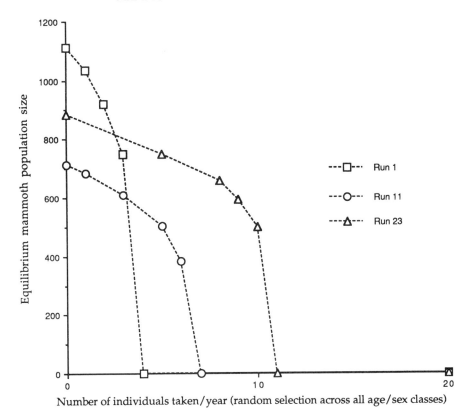

Figure 7.11 Equilibrium mammoth population sizes in constant environments and under varying intensities of fixed number culling. None of the three models for mammoth population dynamics (Runs 1, 11 and 23) can sustain an annual cull of more than eleven animals distributed across all age/sex classes according to their frequency in the population.

very recent past the intensity of elephant hunting may have increased dramatically. For instance, in the Kabalega Falls National Park, Uganda, poaching led to a fall in elephant numbers from 14,337 in 1973 to 2,448 in 1976 (Eltringham and Malpas 1980). In Kenya, numbers of elephants are thought to have fallen from 75,300 in 1977, to 51,200 in 1980/1 (Ottichilo 1986). Our simulations indicate that such population falls are not only due to the specific ecological/economic/political conditions of the elephant populations and poaching in Africa today, but partly due to the inherent sensitivity of elephants (and mammoths) to predation.

In view of these results, three issues posited by the archaeological data can profitably be discussed here: the relevance of prey-switching, the extent of bone collection (rather than hunting) on the Central Russian Plain, and regional extinction in North America.

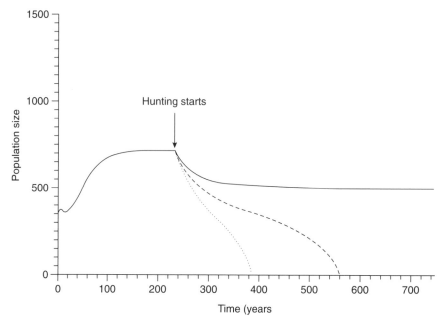

Figure 7.12   Fixed number culling of mammoth population (Run 11) under three hunting intensities, 5 (solid), 7 (spaced dash), 9 (dotted line). The population is allowed to reach equilibrium in a constant environment, free from predation, before hunting starts.

Prey-switching

By prey-switching I mean the phenomenon that foragers change hunting behaviour to avoid the exploitation of depleted resources. This is often efficient behaviour for hunters since an increase in search time may make it expensive to exploit a depleted resource. Prey-switching may enable the resource to replenish itself, although there is no necessary assumption that hunters deliberately avoid the resource to allow this to occur (i.e., resource management). This type of foraging behaviour has been well documented among many hunter-gatherers and has a rigorous theoretical basis in optimal foraging theory. It has been used to counter the arguments that human hunters pushed mammoths into extinction (Webster and Webster 1984) by suggesting that hunters would have switched away from mammoths if their populations became particularly low.

The above simulation results, the ecological data on which the model was built and the archaeological data concerning mammoth exploitation suggest, however, that the phenomenon of prey-switching is probably not applicable to mammoth hunting. Three arguments can be made to explain the probable absence of prey-switching. First, I suspect that when mammoths were hunted this was done for reasons other than those for large (as opposed to

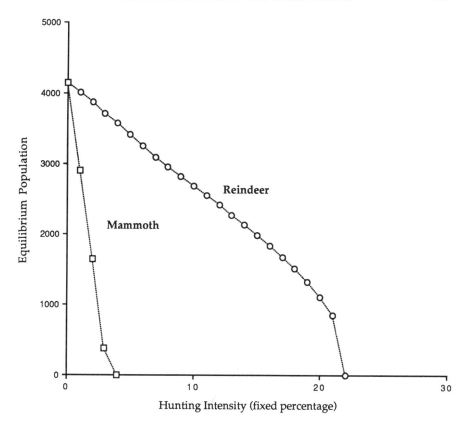

Figure 7.13 Comparison of mammoth (Run 11) and reindeer equilibrium population sizes in constant environments under increasing intensities of fixed percentage hunting. Reindeer model from Mithen (1990).

mega-) herbivores such as reindeer; i.e., not for general sustenance but to acquire prestige materials (ivory), or for the prestige from the actual activity of hunting mammoths themselves. If this was the case, then rather than a decrease in mammoth hunting as mammoths become rare, we may in fact have an increase as demand for ivory and building materials increased since there were fewer carcasses available for scavenging arising from animals dying due to natural processes. In this respect, therefore, I find that fixed number hunting was most likely and the issue of prey-switching non-applicable.

Even if Palaeolithic hunters would have wished to switch away from mammoths if mammoth populations became low, the difficulties of estimating population densities may have prevented them from doing this. As demonstrated by attempts to make census counts of modern elephant numbers (which have the advantages of modern technology) it appears inherently difficult to gain accurate figures on the size of an elephant/mammoth population (Haynes

Table 7.6 The effect of random enviromental fluctuations (g = 15) on the time to extinction in three runs of the mammoth simulation model, for both fixed percentage and fixed number hunting with varying degrees of hunting intensities.

Run no.	Parameter values			Kill	Time to extinction
	b	e	f		
1	0.05	0.05	0.15	1	330
	0.05	0.05	0.15	2	129
	0.05	0.05	0.15	3	82
	0.05	0.05	0.15	4	65
	0.05	0.05	0.15	1%	462
	0.05	0.05	0.15	2%	214
	0.05	0.05	0.15	3%	129
11	0.20	0.05	0.25	2	Sustainable
	0.20	0.05	0.25	3	932
	0.20	0.05	0.25	2%	Sustainable
	0.20	0.05	0.25	3%	323
	0.20	0.05	0.25	4%	218
23	0.20	4.00	0.35	7	Sustainable
	0.20	4.00	0.35	8	356
	0.20	4.00	0.35	9	302
	0.20	4.00	0.35	10	212
	0.20	4.00	0.35	11	149
	0.20	4.00	0.35	12	114
	0.20	4.00	0.35	3%	Sustainable
	0.20	4.00	0.35	4%	650
	0.20	4.00	0.35	5%	269

Table 7.7 The effect of climatic deterioration in a randomly fluctuating environment on the time to extinction for three runs of the mammoth simulation model (t_{max} = 500).

Run no.	Parameter values				Kill	Time to extinction
	b	e	f	h		
1	0.005	0.005	0.15	0.7	1	170
				0.6		219
				0.5		253
11	0.20	0.005	0.25	0.7	3%	227
				0.6		270
				0.5		295
23	0.20	4.00	0.35	0.7	9	150
				0.6		196
				0.5		221

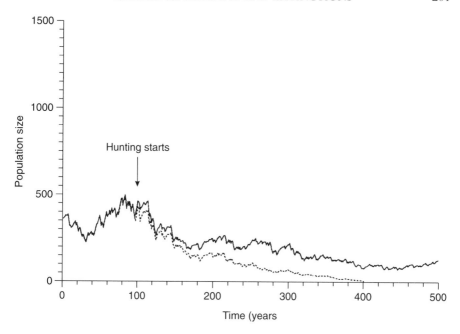

Figure 7.14 Two per cent fixed percentage culling of mammoth population (Run 11) in a fluctuating environment ($g = 15$) (solid), and in a deteriorating environment ($g = 15$, h = 0.8, t_{max} = 500) (dashed). In both cases the hunting begins at year 100. When the environment is deteriorating extinction occurs.

1985; Eltringham and Malpas 1980; Ottichilo 1986). This problem is confounded by population fluctuation and the longevity of elephants/mammoths, so that the effects of one or more die-offs on the size of the adult population, or the consequences of a mammoth hunt, may not be apparent for several years. Factors such as 'bad years' for mammoths, and sequences of bad years, are inherently unpredictable. These cause problems for modern game managers devoted to estimating elephant population numbers and trends (Croze *et al.* 1981). It is indeed only with models such as developed in this chapter that elephant ecologists will become able to make accurate predications for future elephant numbers (e.g. Pilgrim and Western 1986). I find it difficult to imagine how a Palaeolithic hunter could make decisions concerning prey-switching from mammoths which serve to maintain the population, even granted the extensive and detailed information hunter-gatherers can gather from their natural environments and the understanding they have of animal physiology and ecology (see Mithen 1990, Chapter 3).

Third, as we have seen, if mammoth hunting is substantial even for a short number of years, the population may be unable to recover and local extinction will occur very rapidly. I suspect that the rapid speed at which populations can collapse is a further factor preventing the applicability of prey-switching to mammoth populations.

Bone collecting and hunting on the Central Russian Plain

The results of these simulations suggest bone collecting, rather than active hunting, as the source of the large mammoth bone assemblages. Settlements on the Central Russian Plain which have substantial mammoth bone assemblages range over a period of *c.* 7,000 years, from *c.* 20,000 to *c.* 12,000 years BP (Soffer 1986). If there was a significant level of active mammoth hunting it becomes very difficult to understand how the mammoth population could have survived for such a long period given their sensitivity to predation. An implication of these simulation results is that the relative longevity of the mammoth population on the Central Russian Plain during a period with relatively high human population densities would only have been possible if a substantial component of the mammoth bones on settlements came from collecting. Active mammoth hunting must have been very light.

We can explore this proposition by making some speculations concerning mammoth and human population densities in the Central Russian Plain. Soffer (1985) used estimates of Pleistocene biomass to propose that the number of mammoths in her study area of 180,000 sq. km is likely to have been between 14,000–42,000 if the distribution was linearized along river valleys, or 7,000–21,000 if linearized and seasonal migration occurred. Let us slightly widen these bounds to between 5,000–50,000, or densities between 0.028 and 0.28 mammoths/sq. km. These are densities which are at the lower end of the range recorded among modern African elephants by Croze *et al.* (1981) of 0.4–8.0 sq. km (with an outlier of 24). The simulations with the fixed cull models indicated that for a vigorous population (run 23) extinction will occur if the cull is greater than 2.7 per cent of the equilibrium population. For a less vigorous population (run 1) this proportion is as low as 0.35 per cent. These imply that fixed number cull levels of 135–1,350 for a vigorous population, and 1.4–140 for a less vigorous, would have caused extinction. As we have seen in the models, such extinction would have been rapid.

Ethnographic estimates of human population levels in high latitude areas vary between 0.01 and 0.178 people/sq. km (Burch 1972; David 1973). Soffer argues that human population densities would have been at the higher end of this range, if not beyond it. On the basis of these figures the required hunting intensity to push mammoths into extinction in all possible combinations of mammoth/human population densities and population characteristics is only 0.75 mammoths/person/year. If we use the lower estimates for the number of mammoths, or the higher estimates for the human population density, this figure becomes markedly lower. There are two points that we must note. First this estimate is based on simulations involving constant environments. As I have described, when we move to more realistic models involving environmental fluctuations, mammoths become even more sensitive to predation. Second, these hunting intensities relate to the killing of animals that would have otherwise survived until the following year. Hunters may have been killing mammoths which may have been fated to die from natural causes and hence not affecting the population dynamics of the mammoth population. I will explore the consequences of this possibility below. Even if such hunting was occurring, the figure 0.75 mammoths/person/year as the maximum required hunting intensity for mammoth extinction certainly does not support the contention that we are dealing with specialized mammoth economies. For mammoths to have survived in this region for over 7,000 years, hunting intensities must have been very low.[3]

Colonization, subsistence and mammoth extinction in North America

The size of the populations modelled so far is appropriate for dealing with local populations of mammoths. But the sensitivity to hunting pressure is generally applicable. To demonstrate this I will use the model to explore the regional extinction of mammoths throughout the continent of North America at *c.* 11,000 BP. Here I will simply examine the relationship between the rate of growth of a human population, the intensity of mammoth hunting and the time between human colonization and mammoth extinction.

This model has both similarities and differences to that of Mosimann and Martin (1975) which was further explored by Whittingdon and Dyke (1984). The aim is essentially the same: to investigate the number of human hunters necessary to cause extinction and the time required for extinction to occur. Like Mosimann and Martin I start with a colonizing human population of 100 individuals, let them experience exponential growth and then record how long it takes for the mammoth population to become extinct. Mosimann and Martin used a very simple and unrealistic model for the large herbivore population, employing some gross assumptions about rates of replacement. Here I examine just one specific species, mammoths, and use a realistic model for their population dynamics. I also dispense with the notion of a 'front' – the wave of advance of human hunters leaving behind a seriously depleted environment upon which their model was based (Figure 7.15). I believe a more realistic model involves a rapid colonization of the continent, as suggested by recent dates on the last mammoths and the earliest settlements in South America (Gowlett 1986; Agenbroad 1984). Consequently the simulation model is rather simpler in structure, but probably more realistic, than that of Mosimann and Martin. It is notably more sophisticated in its treatment of the mega-faunal population. In essence I aim to place some numerical estimates on to the qualitative diagram of Agenbroad (1984), Figure 7.16, describing the demise of mammoths and the rise of humans in North America.

I start this simulation with a population of *c.* 50 million mammoths, which for the area of late Pleistocene North America given by Mosimann and Martin (3 million sq. miles) gives a population density of 0.65 mammoths/sq. km. This is at the lower range of observed elephant populations (see above), and

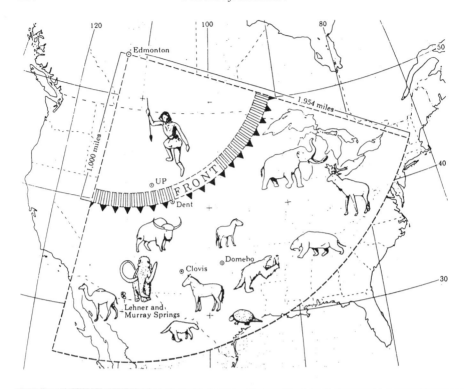

Figure 7.15 Mosimann and Martin's (1975) model for overkill of the mega-fauna in North America. They introduced a group of hunters at, what is now, Edmonton, who then increased in number and spread southwards once the area immediately in front of them had become depleted in game.

provides a population level of the appropriate order of magnitude taking into account the very diverse mega-fauna present in Late Pleistocene North America. Inevitably, this figure of 50 million is arbitrary. Below, I will explore starting populations of 25 and 100 million. This mammoth population is assumed to include both *M. columbi* and *M. primigenius* and is modelled using the parameter values of run 23. The simulation model allows the mammoth population to reach equilibrium; it then introduces a population of 100 humans which then grow at a predefined rate. Five rates of growth were explored between 0.0025 and 0.0125. Each year the number of mammoths killed is in direct ratio to the size of the human population. I explore four hunting intensities: 0.01, 0.1, 1.0 and 10.0 mammoths/person/year (the last value of 10 mammoths/hunter/year is very probably outside the range of feasible hunting intensities, given the danger involved in hunting mammoths, and I have included it for comparative purposes). The simulation is initially run with a constant environment and continues until the mammoth population becomes extinct. The general pattern is to have an almost stationary

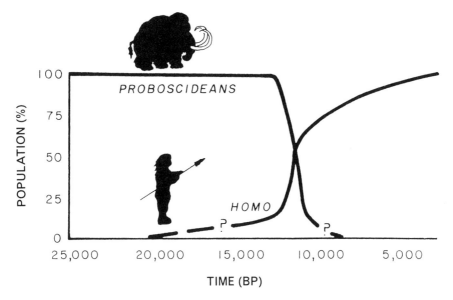

Figure 7.16 Agenbroad's model for population and temporal relationships of mammoth and men in the later Pleistocene of the New World (after Agenbroad 1984, Figure 3.8).

population which then experiences a very rapid collapse to extinction, as illustrated in Figure 7.17. Table 7.8(a) and Figure 7.18 summarize the results from twenty simulation runs. These provide an elapsed time between initial colonization and extinction between 590 and 5,487 years. Table 7.8(b) and Figure 7.19 provide simulation results for starting populations of 25 and 100 million mammoths.

As we have seen, such extinction times will be reduced by introducing fluctuating and deteriorating environments. Of course, when dealing with a mammoth population covering a whole continent it is unlikely that all parts of the population will be suffering good, average and poor years simultaneously, due to spatial variation in weather and climate. Consequently the fluctuations that are now entered into the model are assumed to be the average effect across the whole continent.

Haynes (1985, 1991) suggests that the Clovis hunters may have been principally concerned with exploiting those animals which were dying, or had died, due to natural factors. To model this we can simply calculate the number of mammoths that would be killed each year, as in the current simulation, and then subtract from this a proportion of those naturally dying in that year, assuming that the hunters either made a *coup de grâce* killing or scavenged upon their carcasses. The remainder will constitute the animals actually killed and can be spread across the age/sex classes as before. Table 7.9 documents the effect of these factors on the extinction time for

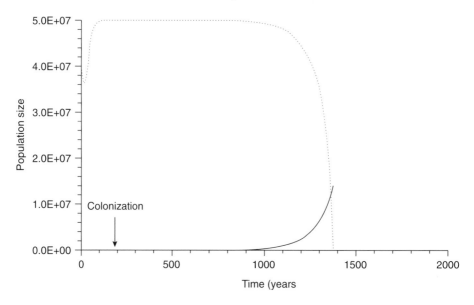

Figure 7.17 Simulated mammoth extinction in North America. In this run the initial mammoth population (dashed) is set at *c*. 50 million prior to human colonisation of 100 people. These (solid line) grow at a rate of 0.01 per cent year and hunt mammoths with the frequency of 0.1 mammoths/persons/year. Extinction occurs after 1,380 years by which time the human population has reached *c*. 13.8 million.

mammoths when human population growth is 0.005 and hunting intensities 1.0 mammoth/person/year. The first row ($h = 0.33$) represents a fluctuating, but not deteriorating, environment which reduces the time between human colonization and mammoth extinction by 82 years (4.4 per cent) from that when the environment is constant. Introducing climatic deterioration ($t_{max} = 2,500$) at a rate of $h = 0.7$ (row 3), further reduces this by 167 years. Substantial use of the naturally dying mammoths, e.g., 75 per cent (row 7), can then extend the time between colonization and extinction by 305 years.

Figures 7.20(a) and 7.20(b) illustrate the interaction between humans, mammoths and climate for the final 200 years before mammoth extinction in a deteriorating environment ($g = 15$, $h = 0.7$, 75 per cent naturally dying mammoths used; human growth rate 0.05; 1 mammoth/person/year, $t_{max} = 2,500$). In Figure 7.20(a) the mammoth and human populations are illustrated, the former fluctuating due to the random sequence of good, average and bad years and the latter growing at a smooth, exponential rate (note the different scales). Figure 7.20(b) illustrates the actual sequence of good, average and bad years during this period and the number of mammoths killed by the human populations that would have otherwise survived to the following year. The first time such hunting occurs is 1,751 years after human colonization – prior to this all the needs of the human population were satisfied by

Table 7.8 The time between human colonization and mammoth extinction for twenty-six runs of the mammoth simulation model under different conditions of human population growth and mammoth-hunting intensity.

Initial mammoth population	Human population growth rate	Mammoths killed per person per year	Time to mammoth extinction	Human population density at mammoth extinction (person/km²)
(a) 50,000,000	0.0025	0.01	5487	1.1605
		0.1	4565	0.1161
		1.0	3642	0.0116
		10.0	2721	0.0012
	0.005	0.01	2784	1.3962
		0.1	2322	0.1394
		1.0	1861	0.014
		10.0	1399	0.0014
	0.0075	0.01	1877	1.6055
		0.1	1569	0.1607
		1.0	1261	0.0161
		10.0	953	0.0016
	0.01	0.01	1421	1.8002
		0.1	1190	0.1807
		1.0	958	0.018
		10.0	727	0.0018
	0.0125	0.01	1146	1.9831
		0.1	961	0.1992
		1.0	776	0.02
		10.0	590	0.0020
(b) 25,000,000	0.005	1.0	1722	0.007
	0.0075	10.0	860	0.0008
	0.0125	0.1	905	0.0993
100,000,000	0.005	1.0	1999	0.0279
	0.0075	10.1	1044	0.0032
	0.0125	0.1	1046	0.3994

exploiting animals which had died, or were going to die, of natural causes. We should note that this hunting first occurs in a 'good' year, since this is one in which there would have been a relatively low level of mammoth mortality. All of the next thirteen instances of the killing of mammoths which would have otherwise survived in the population also occur in 'good' years, except in year 1784 which is an 'average' year. Hunting appears to have occurred in that year since it followed a sequence of four consecutive bad years which pushed the mammoth population to the local minimum of *c.* 17 million. After year 1843, hunting of 'healthy' animals regularly occurs in both average and good years, and after a further forty-seven years, in years of all types. The human population had by then passed 12 million and the mammoth population collapses to become extinct 1,917 years after human colonization. With the resulting population of 12 million people in North America at

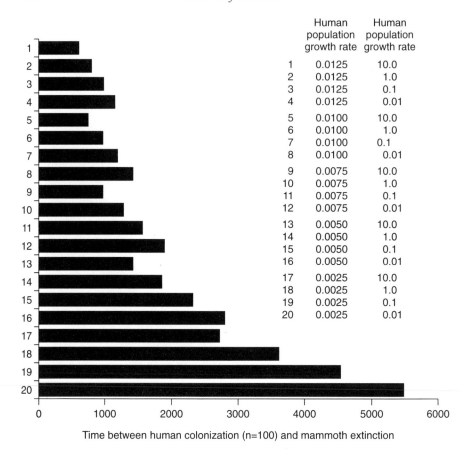

	Human population growth rate	Human population growth rate
1	0.0125	10.0
2	0.0125	1.0
3	0.0125	0.1
4	0.0125	0.01
5	0.0100	10.0
6	0.0100	1.0
7	0.0100	0.1
8	0.0100	0.01
9	0.0075	10.0
10	0.0075	1.0
11	0.0075	0.1
12	0.0075	0.01
13	0.0050	10.0
14	0.0050	1.0
15	0.0050	0.1
16	0.0050	0.01
17	0.0025	10.0
18	0.0025	1.0
19	0.0025	0.1
20	0.0025	0.01

Time between human colonization (n=100) and mammoth extinction

Figure 7.18 Extinction times for 20 different scenarios of human population growth rates and mammoth hunting intensities, applied to an initial population of *c*. 50 million mammoths and with an initial human population of 100 individuals.

c. 11,000 BP, this particular model would seem unrealistic, in either its basic structure or initial parameter values.

The results of this simulation model agree with those from Mosimann and Martin's in that low degrees of mammoth exploitation and low numbers of human hunters may have been sufficient to push mammoths into extinction in North America by 11,000 BP. Relative to their model, I have examined human populations with low growth rates – Whittingdon and Dyke used a base line value of 0.0443 which I believe to be markedly too high to be sustained over a long period of time. When they used a rate in line with one in my simulation – 0.0043 comparable to my 0.005 – the timing of mammoth extinction is similar – 2,798 years compared to my figures of between 1,399 and 2,784.

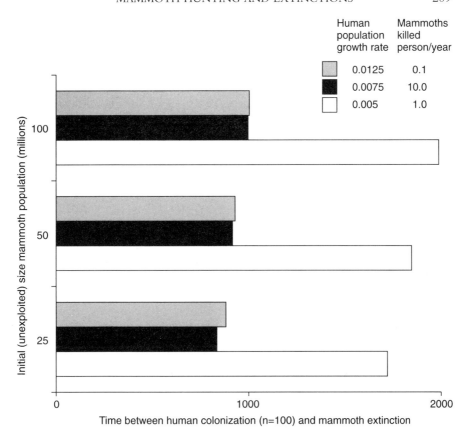

Figure 7.19 Comparison between initial mammoth population size and timing of extinction, for three human growth rate/hunting intensity scenarios.

Of the three variables I have examined – human population growth rate, intensity of mammoth hunting and the mammoth starting population – it is the first that is of most significance for the time of extinction. Changing the size of the mammoth population to either half of the 50 million, or doubling it, had little effect on the timing of extinction (Figure 7.19). This is simply because when human populations are of a sufficient magnitude to affect a mammoth population level of the order of 25 million, they are growing very quickly and within a short time can similarly affect populations twice and four times as large. We should note, however, that in all of the simulation runs except those in which mammoth hunting intensity is 0.01 mammoths/person/year, the human population densities at which extinction occurs appear to be feasible. These range from 0.1992 to 0.0012 persons/sq. km. Modern Eskimo hunters range between 0.178 (Tikiraqmiut) to 0.01 (Asiaqmiut) (Mithen 1990).

Table 7.9 The time between human colonization and mammoth extinction under varying conditions of climatic deterioration and carcass use.

Human population growth rate	Mammoths killed per person per year	Degree of climatic deterioration (h)	Percentage use of naturally dying mammoths (?)	Time to mammoth extinction	Human population density at mammoth extinction (person/km²)
0.005	1.0	0.33	0.0	1779	0.0093
		0.5	0.0	1737	0.0075
		0.7	0.0	1612	0.0040
		0.9	0.0	1481	0.0021
		0.7	0.25	1795	0.0010
		0.7	0.5	1867	0.0144
		0.7	0.75	1917	0.0185

Note: All runs with an initial mammoth population of *c.* 50 million and t_{max} = 2,500; the first row (h = 0.33) denotes a fluctuating, but not deteriorating, enviroment.

One of the implications of this study concerns the timing of colonization and the subsistence practices of the first hunters in North America. As we have seen, even with very low rates of population growth and human hunting intensity (0.0025 and 0.01 mammoths/hunter/year), mammoth extinction will still occur *c.* 5,500 years following colonization of 100 hunters. This case creates what are probably unfeasibly high human population densities (1.1605 persons/sq. km). Increasing the hunting intensity to 0.1 mammoths/hunter/year – still a very low hunting intensity – decreases extinction time to 4,565 and creates a feasible human population density at the time of extinction. We should note here that the archaeological record suggests that mammoth hunting may have been rather more intensive than these figures suggest – Clovis points are more regularly associated with mammoths than with any other large game, and mammoths are present on the majority of early settlements. In conclusion, colonization by mammoth hunters either occurred relatively late, *c.* 15,000 BP, or it occurred earlier but mammoth hunting was not a major element of the colonist's subsistence practices.

Figure 7.20 Final 200 years of a simulation run for mammoth population in a fluctuating and deteriorating environment (*g* = 15, *h* = 0.7, t_{max} = 2,000), 0.75 per cent of the naturally dying animals available for exploitation by humans. Human population growth rate of 0.01 and hunting intensity of 0.1 mammoth/hunter/year. (a) Mammoth and human population levels, note the different scales. The mammoth population collapses and extinction occurs rapidly after human population levels have passed *c.* 1.2 million. (b) The fluctuation of year types and the number of animals killed by humans which would have otherwise survived in the mammoth population.

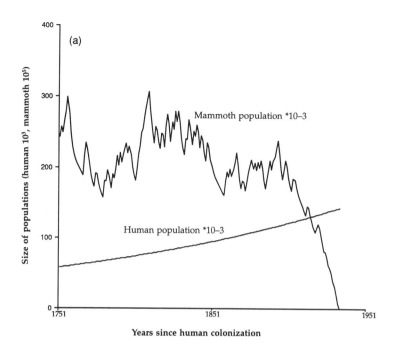

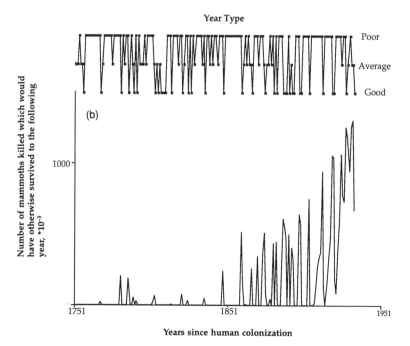

Summary

The models described in this chapter face the problems of any simulation model in archaeology (and in many other disciplines) – limited and fuzzy data, a necessary set of assumptions, the need to find a balance between generality/realism and simplicity/complexity. It is precisely because of, not in spite of, the limited and fuzzy archaeological data that we need simulation models to improve our interpretations. The most uncontroversial and important result of this study has simply been to demonstrate that mammoth populations were extremely sensitive to predation. This increases the probability that human hunters played a significant role in the timing of mammoth extinction in the Old and New Worlds. Using the simulation results, and the information about modern elephant ecology on which they were based, I have suggested that prey-switching is unlikely to be a phenomenon that may have prevented or delayed humans pushing mammoths into extinction.

While deterministic models have remained at the core of this chapter I have tried to attain greater realism by exploring those which include stochastic environmental variability. By simulating pseudo-random sequences of good, average and bad year types I have attempted to develop models which can combine the effects of human hunting and climatic deterioration in mammoth extinction. One of the main problems facing this work is that it may not have been the simple fact that environments were fluctuating or deteriorating that was critical to mammoths, but the specific sequence of bad years in relation to human hunting activity. Unfortunately, we cannot reconstruct palaeo-environments in sufficient detail to identify climatic fluctuations at the scale of resolution that our theoretical models require. However, it is hoped that the models here will improve our understanding of how human predation and climatic deterioration may interact to create the variability in the timing and cause of mammoth extinction at the end of the Pleistocene.

I have used the simulation results to reflect upon the archaeological records in Russia and North America. For the first of these I suggested that since this archaeological record documents a substantial use of mammoth bones and ivory over c. 7,000 years, it is more probable that the principal quantity of bones/ivory derived from carcass scavenging rather than direct hunting, as Soffer (1985, 1991) has argued. For the North America record, I have shown that the clustering of mammoth kill sites at c. 11–11,500 BP, rather than a more even spread across a longer time period, is not surprising since if mammoth hunting is sufficiently intense to enter the archaeological record as a number of kill sites, extinction is probably rapid. If there were human populations in North America prior to 15,000 BP, it is unlikely that they were actively hunting mammoths.

The significance of the results from this simulation requires further discussion and critical evaluation of the model. Simply by generating this discussion, the modelling approach developed here may be considered to have played some role in tackling this 'mammoth' archaeological problem. Hopefully the chapter has made a more general contribution by describing the nature of a Leslie Matrix model, and constructing one to tackle a well defined archaeological problem.

Notes

1 This chapter was prepared before the sensational discovery of mammoths on Wrangel Island in the Arctic Ocean, 200 km north-east of the Siberian coast, which date from between 7,000 and 4,000 years ago.

2 As Soffer (1991) has described, a reduction in body size and evidence for mass deaths occurred at ca. 45,000 BP but this was followed by a return to healthy populations, unlike at the end of the Pleistocene. While interglacials certainly varied in their climatic characteristics, it remains to be demonstrated that the last glacial had features which were particularly detrimental to mega-herbivores and which were absent from earlier cold periods. Climate-related explanations for mega-faunal extinction fail to account for the selectivity in terms of geography, time, taxa and size of these species becoming extinct at the end of the Pleistocene (Diamond 1989).

3 Of course, the simulation may be inappropriate for the Central Russian Plain at the height, and end, of the last glacial. We may have been dealing with mammoth populations which were 'open' and continuous over large geographic areas so that predation was always compensated for by immigration of animals. But such open populations seem unlikely due to the spatial patchiness of the landscapes in the Russian Plain and by analogy with the social organization of elephants among which relatively closed populations are found (Laws *et al.* 1975).

References

Agenbroad, L. 1984. New World mammoth distribution. In *Quaternary Extinctions: a prehistoric revolution,* P.S. Martin and R.G.Klein (eds), 90–108. Tucson: University of Arizona Press.

Bahn, P. and J. Vertut 1988. *Images of the Ice Age.* London: Windward.

Barnes, R. 1982. A note on elephant mortality in Ruaka National Park, Tanzania. *African Journal of Ecology* 20, 137–40.

Bosinski, G. 1984. The mammoth engravings of the Magdalenian site Gönnersdorf, Rhineland, Germany. In *La Contribution de la Zoologie et de l'éthologie a l'interprétation de l'Art des Peuples Chasseurs Prehistoriques,* H.-G. Bandi, W. Huber, M.-R. Sauer and B. Sitter (eds), 295–322. Fribourg: Editions Universitaires.

Burch, E. 1972. The caribou/wild reindeer as a human resource. *American Antiquity* 37, 339–68.

Calef, G.W. 1988 Maximum rate of increase in the African elephant. *African Journal of Ecology* 26, 323–7.

Croze, H., A.K.K. Hillman and E.M. Lang 1981. Elephants and their habitats: how do they tolerate each other. In *Dynamics of Large Mammal Populations,* C.W. Fowler and T.D. Smith (eds), 297–316. New York: John Wiley and Sons.

David, N.C. 1973. On Upper Palaeolithic society, ecology and technological change: the noallian case. In *The Explanation of Culture Change,* A.C. Renfrew (ed.), 277–303. London: Duckworth.

Diamond, J.M. 1984. Historic extinction: a Rosetta stone for understanding pleistocene extinctions. In *Quaternary Extinction: a prehistoric revolution,* P.S. Martin and R.G. Klein (eds), 824–62. Tucson: University of Arizona Press.

Diamond, J.M. 1986. The mammoths' last migration. *Nature* 319, 205–6.

Diamond, J.M. 1989. Quaternary megafaunal extinctions: variations on a theme by Paganini. *Journal of Archaeological Science* 16, 167–75.

Eltingham, S.K. and R.C. Malpas 1980. The decline in elephant numbers in Rwenzori and Kabalega Falls National Park, Uganda. *African Journal of Archaeology* 18, 73–86.

Frison, G. 1990. Experimental use of Clovis weaponry and tools on African elephants. *American Antiquity* 54, 766–82.

Gowlett, J.A.J. 1986. Problems in dating the early human settlement of the Americas. In *Archaeological Results from Accelerator Dating*, J.A.J. Gowlett and R.E.M. Hedges (eds), 51–9. Oxford: Oxford University Committee for Archaeology (Monograph No. 11).

Guthrie, R.D. 1984. Mosaics, allelochemicals and nutrients: an ecological theory of Late Pleistocene extinctions. In *Quaternary Extinctions: a prehistoric revolution,* P.S. Martin and R.G. Klein (eds), 259–98. Tucson: University of Arizona Press.

Hanks, J. and J.E.A. McIntosh 1973. Population dynamics of the African elephant (Loxodonta africana). *Journal Zoological Society of London* 169, 29–38.

Haynes, G. 1985. Age profiles in elephant and mammoth bone assemblages. *Quaternary Research* 24, 333–45.

Haynes, G. 1986. Proboscidean die-offs and die-outs: age profiles in fossil collections. *Journal of Archaeological Science* 14, 659–88.

Haynes, G. 1989. Late Pleistocene mammoth utilization in northern Eurasia and North America. *Archaeozoologia* 3, 81–108.

Haynes, G. 1991. *Mammoths, Mastodons and Elephants: biology, behaviour and the fossil record*. Cambridge: Cambridge University Press.

Jacobi, R.M. 1980. The Upper Palaeolithic in Britain, with special reference to Wales. In *Culture and Environment in Prehistoric Wales*, J.A. Taylor (ed.), 15–99. Oxford: British Archaeological Reports 76.

Laws, R.M., I.S.C. Parker and R.C.B. Johnstone 1975. *Elephants and their Habitats.* Oxford: Clarendon Press.

Lee, P.C. and C.J. Moss 1986. Early maternal investment in male and female African elephant calves. *Behavioural Ecology and Sociobiology* 18, 353–61.

Leslie, P.H. 1945. On the use of matrices in certain population mathematics. *Biometrika* 33, 183–212.

Lister, A. 1991. Late glacial mammoths in Britain. In *The Late Glacial in Europe,* R.N.E. Barton, A.J. Roberts and D.A. Roe (eds), 51–9. London: Council for British Archaeology (CBA Research Report 77).

Mithen, S. 1990. *Thoughtful Foragers: a study of prehistoric decision making*. Cambridge: Cambridge University Press.

Mosimann, J.E. and P.S. Martin 1975. Simulating overkill by palaeoindians. *American Scientist* 63, 305–13.

Musil, R. 1968. Die Mammutmolaren von Predmosti (CSSR). *Palaeontologische Abhandlungen* A. III, Berlin.

O'Connell, J.F., K. Hawkes and N.B. Jones 1991. What do Clovis kill sites really represent? Sceptical comments from the Hadza perspective. Paper presented at the 56th annual meeting of the Society for American Archaeology, 14–28 April, 1991, New Orleans.

Ottichilo, W.K. 1986. Age structure of elephants in Tsavo National Park, Kenya. *African Journal of Ecology* 26, 323–37.

Pilgrim, I. and D. Western 1986. Inferring hunting patterns on African elephants from tusks in the international ivory trade. *Journal of Applied Ecology* 23, 503–14.

Saunders, J.J. 1980. A model for man–mammoth relationships in Late Pleistocene North America *Canadian Journal of Anthropology* 1, 87–98.

Soffer, O. 1985. *The Upper Palaeolithic Settlement of the Russian Plain*. London: Academic Press.

Soffer, O. 1991. Upper Palaeolithic adaptations in central and eastern Europe and man/mammoth interactions. In *From Kostenki to Clovis: upper palaeolithic-palaeoindian adaptations*, O. Soffer and N.D. Praslov (eds), 31–50. New York: Plenum Press.

Stuart, A.J. 1991. Mammalian extinctions in the Late Pleistocene of northern Eurasia and North America. *Biological Reviews* 66, 453–62.

Vereshchagin, N.K. and G.F. Baryshnikov 1984. Quaternary mammalian extinctions in Northern Eurasia. In *Quaternary Extinctions: a prehistoric revolution,* P.S. Martin, and R.G. Klein (eds), 483–516. Tucson: University of Arizona Press.

Webster, D. and G. Webster 1984. Optimal hunting and Pleistocene extinction. *Human Ecology* 12, 275–89.

Whittington, S.L. and B.Dyke 1984. Simulating overkill: experiments with the Mosimann and Martin model. In *Quaternary Extinctions: a prehistoric revolution,* P.S. Martin and R.G. Klein (eds), 451–65. Tucson: University of Arizona Press.

8   Clusters of death, pockets of survival: dynamic modelling and GIS

EZRA ZUBROW

The *danse macabre*

In the pale moonlight, one sees figures dancing. They spin, gavotte across the stage, and fall – never to rise again. Each dancer commands the scene for only a brief moment. Then they are replaced by one of the many 'wallflowers' waiting in the wings. There is a seemingly endless progression of would-be dancers. Our fascination with the *danse macabre* is not accidental. It speaks to one of the central events of our actuality – the anticipation of our ultimate lack of existence.

Sometimes, the *danse* has intensified to wild flings for considerable portions of the human dance card and sometimes it has slowed to a stately waltz. Individual dancers have performed acts of the greatest heroism ministering to their partners before collapsing on the floor. Others have been universally condemned for dispersing the dance to new floors. They have plundered the abandoned homes of the fallen dancers and even the tumbling bodies of the dancers themselves.

This chapter is concerned with the spread of major epidemic diseases such as smallpox and typhus into large unprotected populations. For the duration of such events, the *danse* turned from a chaotic and somewhat accidental tango associated with age or bad luck into a highly patterned *passacaglia*, a promenade which inexorably crushed entire cultures on a continental scale. The depopulation of the Americas, for example, appears to be one of the largest demographic catastrophes of all time. Population was reduced in many areas of the New World up to 90 per cent, which makes it a calamity three or four times the size of the Black Death of the 1300s in Europe.

Poignantly, the music was very quiet – very little is known about this episode. The *danse* moved on small, microscopic feet and there were few survivors to write of its passing. One of the few contemporary commentators was Holbein, who depicted the association of exploration and commerce with the *danse* in his portrait of a merchant (Figure 8.1).

Figure 8.1 Holbein's merchant. Death, trade, and transportation are combined in a single image.

Figure 8.2 Le Moyne's 'How they treat their sick' is one of the earliest known illustrations from the New World, dating to the 1560s.

The close juxtaposition of the ship, the trade goods, the merchant and death is what this chapter is about. It dynamically models the interaction of these figures, tracing the routes of the disease as the explorers and merchant companies contacted the New World. To do so, the chapter combines prehistoric data from the New World with navigational and content analysis of historic ships' logs, dynamic modelling and GIS systems.

The unadorned argument is modest. The large corpus of prehistoric and historic data, as well as the topographic and hydrological reality of the New World, presents one with the broad outlines of the distribution of native populations at the time of contact as well as with native trade routes. Ships' logs were examined to determine when and where contact with the New World was made. Furthermore, one may note the recorded incidents of disease aboard ship as well as the comments recorded in the logs regarding diseases among the natives on shore (Figure 8.2). Lastly, dynamic modelling and GIS systems were used to simulate the expected spread of disease from these points of contact through the given population distributions along the trade routes.

Once it was thee, now it is we: Population replacement

The replacement of native American populations by immigrants in the centuries after 1492 is one of the great demographic shifts in the history of the modern world. It embodied two interrelated and complementary components: the depopulation of the native New World, and the replacement of this 'native' population by immigrants from the Old World. The latter has long been an area of fruitful study, but only recently has there been serious study of the depopulation of native America. During the last decade, new and significant research into the prehistoric and historic demography of the New World has set a firm stage upon which the whirling dervishes of social and scientific theory act. The issues have been broadened, reaching a wider audience, becoming more relevant to our own lives, and extending far beyond archaeology. New publications have appeared such as Thomas's volumes in the Columbian Consequences series (1989–91).

In 'The Depopulation of Native America' (Zubrow 1990), the author has examined the general characteristics of the depopulation of native America, focusing on weaknesses in the case for depopulation, on different estimates of aboriginal population at the time of contact, on the type and quality of the prehistoric data from several case areas, and finally on the scale of depopulation and the mechanisms behind it. He provided results from several simulation models. The study led him to draw two conclusions: first, that epidemic disease effected social disorder and collapse and that the depopulation of the New World by disease affected the chiefdoms far more significantly than the tribes. Indeed, it may have been the rise of the large-scale chiefdoms which made depopulation such a significant factor in the destruction of the social fabric of the New World. Second, a very simplified simulation using GIS to model the spread of disease showed that the distribution of death was not even. Indeed, there were clusters of death and pockets of survival. This chapter is a first step in the process of grounding the simulation model in historic and archaeological reality and of making it more accurate.

Voyages into the unknown

For almost three centuries after Columbus's landing in the West Indies, voyage after voyage was sent into the unknown 'Western Sea'. These voyages originated in Spain, England, Portugal, France, Holland, as well as the other European countries. They landed in what were to become Hispaniola, Cuba, Mexico, Canada, Costa Rica, Venezuela, Brazil, Peru, Colombia and the United States, to name only a few countries. Table 8.1 represents the major voyages of exploration prior to 1650 which landed in the New World. There are some fifty-two listed for North America (counting five prior to 1492) and twenty-five for South America.

Table 8.1 The voyages to the New World.

Names	Dates	Landings
North America:		
Bjarni Herjolfsson	986	NE Coast
Leif Ericsson	1000	Labrador
Thorvold Ericsson	1004	Labrador, Newfoundland
Thorfinn Karlsefni	1020	Newfoundland
Freydis	1020	
Christopher Columbus (1)	1492	Bahamas, Hispaniola, Honduras to Isthmus of Panama
John Cabot (2)	1497, 1498	Cape Breton Island, Newfoundland
Amerigo Vespucci (3)	1497–1503	South and south-east Seaboard
Gaspar Corte Real (4)	1501	Labrador, Newfoundland, Belle Isle Str.
Vincente Yanez Pinson, Juan Diaz de Solis (5)	1506	Yucatan Peninsula, Honduras
Hernandes de Cordova	1517	Yucatan Peninsula
Hernando Cortes (6)	1515–22	Yucatan,Vera Cruz
	1535–6	G. of California
Pedro de Alvarado (7)	1523	Guatemala
Giovanni de Verrazano (8)	1524	Carolina to Newfoundland
Alvaro de Saavedra	1527	Mexico
Panfilo de Narvaez	1528	Florida, G. of Mexico, Texas
Hernando de Soto (9)	1528	Guatemala, Yucatan
Alvar Nonez Cabeza de Vaca (10)	1528–36	Texas, Mexico, G. of California
Jacques Cartier (11)	1534	Belle Isle, Cabot Str., P. Edward Island
	1535–36	St Lawrence to Montreal
M. Hore	1536	Newfoundland, Cape Breton
Marcos de Niza (12)	1539	New Mexico, Arizona
Hemando de Soto (13)	1539–42	Florida, Mississippi River, Ozarks
Francisco de Ulloa (14)	1539, 1540	G. of Mexico, Coast of Califonia
Francisco Vasquez de Coronado, Pedro de Alascon (15)	1540–2	Colorado River, Rio Grande, Oklahoma to Kansas
Luis de Moscoso de Alvaro	1542	Arkansas and Mississippi Rivers, Mexico
John Hawkins (16)	1565, 1567–8	West Indies
Martin Frobisher (17)	1576	Resolution Is., Frobisher Bay
	1578	Hudson Str.
Francis Drake (18)	1578	Coast of S. California
Sir Humphrey Gilbert (19)	1583	Florida coast and northwards
Captain Arthur Barlowe (20)	1583	Canaries, Mexico, Florida, Havana, Virginia
Walter Raleigh (21)	1584	Virginia, Roanoke Is.
	1585	N. Carolina
John Davis	1585–6	Davis Str., C. Dyer, Cumberland Sound, C. Chidley
Bartholomew Gosnold (22)	1602	Mass. Bay, C. Cod
Martin Pring (23)	1603	Coasts of N. Hampshire, Mass., Martha's Vineyard
Sebastian Vizacalno	1603	W. Coast to C. Blanco
Samuel de Champlain (24)	1603	St Lawrence
	1604–5	Bay of Fundy
	1608–11	Ottawa R., Richelieu R.

Table 8.1 (continued)

Names	Dates	Landings
North America (continued)		
John Smith (25)	1607	Chickahominy R., Chesapeake Bay, Potomac R.
Etienne Brule	1608–11	L. Huron, Georgian Bay
	1615	Susquehanna R.,
	1621	L. Huron to Duluth
Henry Hudson (26)	1609–10	Hudson R., Hudson Str., Hudson Bay
Thomas Button (27)	1612	Nelson R., R. Ross, Welcome Sound
Samuel de Champlain, Etienne Brule (28)	1615	L. Nippising, French R., Georgian Bay, L. Ontario, L. Oneida
South America		
Amerigo Vespucci (29)	1497, 1499	Campeche Bay
	1501–2	Amazon R., Coast of Brazil, Rio de Janeiro, Patagonia
Christopher Columbus (30)	1498	Venezuelan Coast
Alonzo de Ojeda (31)	1499	G. of Uraba, Parria, Cumana
Pedro Alvares Cabral (32)	1500	Coast of Brazil
Vincente Yanez Pinson (33)	1500	Coast of Brazil
Vasco Nunez de Balboa, Martin Fernandez de Encisco (34)	1510	Panama
Juan Diaz de Solis	1515	Rio de la Plata
Hernando de Soto	1519	Darien (?)
Ferdinand Magellan (35)	1520	Straits of Magellan
Sebastian Cabot (36)	1526, 1527–8	Rio De Plata, Parana R.
Francisco Pizarro (37), Diego De Almagro	1527, 1533	Tumbes
	1535	Lima, Cuzco
Diego Garcia (38), Sebastian Cabot	1528	Pilcomayo
Sebastian de Balalcazar	1536	Cauca R., Popayn, Cali, Magdalena R.
Gonzalo Jimenez de Quesada (39)	1536–7	Magdalena R.
	1569–71	Guaviare R., Orinoco R.
Diego de Almagro (40)	1537	Cuzco, Andes, Concepcion
Francisco de Orellana, Gonzalo Pizarro (41)	1541–2	Napo R., Amazon R. to Belem, Paraguay
Pedro de Valdivia (42)	1541	Santiago de Chile
Alvaro Nunez Cabeza de Vaca (43)	1542	Igucu R., Parana R., Asuncion
Francis Drake (44)	1577–78	Coast of Brazil, Magellan Str., Chile and Peru
Walter Raleigh (45)	1595	Caroni R.
Willem Cornelisz Schouten (46), Jacob Le Maire (47)	1616	Le Maire Strait and Desolation Island
Pedro Teixeira	1637–8	Amazon R., Napo R., Quito
Matias Abad	1648	Columbia

Note: Figures in parentheses refer to the logs or maps listed in the References at the end of the chapter. Thus, for example, 'Sebastian Cabot (36)' is cross-referenced to the Arber, Beazley, Columbus and Tytler entries – all of which contain documents relating to Cabot's voyages which were examined for routes and disease references.

Fortunately, contemporary accounts and logs were often made and soon they were recognized as valuable documents. In 1600, Richard Hakluyt began to systematically collect the logs and contemporary accounts of the early voyages of exploration and published them in three large folio volumes. Since then there has been an active group of scholars trying to collect and to publish as many of the original documents from the voyages of exploration as possible. The Hakluyt Society, which has dedicated itself to this task since the late nineteenth century, has now published more than 200 volumes of original documents and logs in two series. In addition, there are numerous other sources.

I examined the available logs and the contemporary documents for each of these voyages, searching for the routes and for references to disease either aboard ship or on land. In one or two cases no firsthand accounts could be found but there were contemporary secondary sources which described the voyages in question (see note to Table 8.1, p. 221). These accounts provided information about the routes of voyages and the location of landings. Frequently, they recorded information about the natural world which was encountered as well as descriptions of natives and native customs. As incidents of illness increased, these were noted by explorers, colonists, and Native Americans. Sometimes the evidence was textual and sometimes illustrative. The following quote, from Cartier's log of his second voyage (in 1535, some four decades after Columbus's initial voyages), gives an example of the kind of information which is available:

> In the month of December, we understood that the pestilence was come among the people of Stadacona, in such sort, that before we know of it, according to their confession, there were dead above 50; whereupon we charged them neither to come neere our Fort, nor about our ships, our us. And albeit we had driven them from us, the said unknowen sicknese began to spread itselfe amongst us after the strangest sort thatever was eyther heard of or seene, insomuch as some did lose all their strength, and could not stand on their feete, then did their legges swel, their sinnowes shrinke as blacke as any cole. Others also had all their skins spotted with spots of blood of a purple colour: then did it ascend up to their ankels, knees, stincking, their gummes so rotten, that all the flesh did fall off, even to the rootes of the teeth, which did also almost all fall out. With such infection did this sickness spread itselfe in our three ships that about the middle of February, of a hundreth and tenne persons that we were, there were not ten whole, so that one could not help the other ... There were alreadie eight dead, and more than fifty sicke, and as we thought, past all hope of recovery ... [description of prayers] ... That day Philip Rougemont, borne in Amboise, died, being 22 yeeres olde, and because the sickness was to us unknowen, our Captaine caused

him to be ripped to see if by any meanes possible we might know what it was, and so seeke meanes to save and preserve the rest of the company: he was found to have his heart white, but rotten, and more then a quart of red water about it: his liver was indifferent faire, but his lungs blacke and mortified, his blood was altogither shrunke about the heart so that when he was opened great quantitie of rotten blood issued out from about his heart: his milt toward the backe was somewhat perished, rough as it had bene rubbed against a stone. Moreover, because one of his thighs was very blacke without, it was opened, but within it was whole and sound: that done, as well as we could he was buried. In such sort did the sicknesse continue and increase, that there were not three sound men in the ships . . . Sometimes we were constrained to bury some of the dead under the snow, because we were not able to digge any graves for them the ground was so hard frozen, and we so weake.

(Burrage 1906, pp. 72–3)

Systematically reading the logs and accounts provides one with a distinctly different conception of these voyages into the unknown than is generally presented in modern literature. The wonder of exploration and the joy of discovery may be found, but the feeling of freedom which is connected to the great unknown is far stronger. One realizes that after Columbus the fear of the unknown is greatly diminished. The logs indicate that the members of the expedition have a general knowledge of what they will discover but are not familiar with the specifics. They expect to find new islands, rivers, bays, tribes, but do not know their specific shape, form or friendship.

The toughness of the voyages and the sailors also becomes apparent. They sailed in northern waters surrounded by icebergs in unheated boats. They frequently are fighting the Indians and each other, with little respect for life. For example, a captain orders his seamen to refuse wine to a dying sailor and when disobeyed hangs the wine-giving mariner for mutiny.

Third, it is surprising how frequently the various expeditions are interacting. In the earlier expeditions, many of the voyages find Europeans from previous voyages. These are sailors who were marooned as punishment; sailors who had been lost wandering away from shore parties; and sailors who jumped ship believing a 'savage world' cannot be worse than the hellish conditions of a seaman's life. Later, there is a tradition of stopping at colonies when arriving in the New World and stopping again prior to returning to Europe.

Finally, there is a sense of information overload. The logs are full of information. There is almost an indiscriminate recording of impressions and descriptions. There are descriptions of plants and people and shores and weather and minerals. It is as if the writer knew the information was valuable but did not have the categories by which to organize and distinguish it.

Table 8.2   Examples of disease descriptions (quoted by Burrage).

Letter to Lorenzo di Pier Francesco de Medici 1502 (48)★ 'As to the nature of the land, I declare it to be the most agreeable, temperate, and healthful, for in all the time that we were in it, which was ten months, none of us died and only a few fell ill. As I have already said, the inhabitants live a long time and do not suffer from infirmity or pestilence or from any unhealthy atmosphere.'

Cartier's Second Voyage 1535 (48) 'After he had with certaine signes saluted our captaine and all his companie, and by manifest tokens bid all welcome, he shewed his legges and armes to our Captaine, and with signes desired him to touch them, and so he did, rubbing them with his owne hands: then did Agouhanna take the wreath or crowne he had about his head, and gave it unto our Captaine: that done they brought befor him divers diseased men, some blinde, some criple, some lame and impotent, and covered their cheekes, and layd them all along before our Captaine, to the end they might of him be touched: for it seemed unto them that God was descended and come downe from heaven to heale them. Our Captaine seeing the misery and devotion of this poore people, recited the Gospel of Saint John, that is to say, In the Beginning was the Word; touching every one that were diseased.' (Burrage 1906, p. 62).

Hore's Voyage to Newfoundland 1536 (48) 'but the famine increasing, and the reliefe of herbes being to little purpose to satisfie their insatiable hunger, in the fieldes and deserts here and there, the fellowe killed his mate while he stooped to takeup a roote for his reliefe, and cutting out pieces of his bodie whom he had murthered, broyed the same on the coles, [not a disease statement but a statement of famine which caused disease] (Burrage 1906, p. 100).

Hawkins Voyage of 1568 (48) 'and out of the chanell and gulfe of Bahama, which is betweene the Cape of Florida, and the Ilandes of Lucayo. After this growing neere to the colde countrey, our men being oppressed with famine, died continually, and they that were left, grew into such weaknesse that we were scantly able to manage our shippe . . . in a place neere unto Vigo called Ponte Vedra (in Spain) our men with excesse of fresh meate grew into miserable disseases, and died a great part of them'. By Hawkins himself (Burrage 1906, p. 147).

Francis Drake 1579 (48) 'we came into 42 deg of North latitude, where in the night following we found such alteration of heate, into extreame and nipping cold, that our men in generall did grievously complaine thereof, some of them feeling their healths much impaired thereby . . . [in California probably Drake's Bay]. . . they presently enclosing them about offred their sacrifices unto them, crying out with lamentable shreekes and moanes, weeping and scratching and tearing their very flesh off their faces with their nailes; . . . After that time had a little qualified their madnes, they then began to shew and make knowne unto us their griefs and diseases which they carried about them; some of them having old aches, some shruncke sinews, some old soares and canchred ulcers, some wounds more lately received, and the like; in most lamentable manner craving helpe and cure thereof from us; making signes, that if we did but blowe upon thier griefes, or but toched the diseased places, they would be whole' (Burrage 1906, p. 153, 169).

Table 8.2 Examples of disease descriptions (quoted by Burrage).

Humphrey Gilbert's voyage to Florida (48) 'Thursday following, when we hailed one another in the evening (according to the order before specified) they signified unto us out of the Vizadmirall, that both the Captaine, and very many of the men were fallen sicke. And about midnight the Vizeadmirall forsooke us, not withstanding we had the winde East, faire and good. But it was after credibly reported, that they were infected with a contagious sicknesse, and arrived greatly distressed at Plimmoth . . .'

Even so, amongst very many difficulties, discontentments, mutinies, conspiracies, sicknesses, mortalitie, spoylings, and wracks by sea, which were afflictions, more then in so small a Fleete, or so short a time may be supposed, albeit true in every particularitie, as partly by the former relation may be collected, and some I suppressed with silence for their sakes living, it pleased God to support this company, (of which only one man died of a maladie inveterate, and long infested): the rest kept together in reasonable contentment and concord, beginning, continuing, and ending the voyage, which none else did accomplish either not pleased with the action, or impatient of wants or prevented by death' (Burrage 1906, 193, 220).

At which Islands we found the ayre very unwholesome, and our men grew for the most part ill disposed: so that having refreshed our selves with sweet water and fresh victuall, we departed' (Burrage 1906, p. 193).

From White's log of Raleigh's expedition of 1587 (48) 'The 22 (of June) we came to an anker at an Island called Santa Cruz, where all the planters were set on land, staying there till the 25 of the same month. At our first landing on this Island, some of our women, and men, by eating a small fruit like greene Apples, were fearefully troubled with a sudden burning in their mouthes, and swelling of their tongues so bigge, that some of them could not speake. Also a child by sucking one of those womens breasts, had at that instant his mouth set on such a burning, that it was strange to see how the infant was tormented for the time: but after 24 houres, it ware away of it selfe . . .'

'The eighteenth, (of September) perceiving that of all our fifteene men in the Flyboad there remained but five, which by meanes of the former mischance, were able to stand to their labour . . . which for six dayes ceased not to blowe so exceeding, that we were driven further in those sixe then we could recover in thirteene daies: in which time others of our saylers began to fall very sicke and two of them dyed' (Burrage 1906, pp., 283, 296).

'On Whitsunday Even at Cape Tyburon, one of our boyes ranne away from us, and at tenne dayes end returned to our ships almost starved for want of food. In sundry places about this part of Cape Tyburon we found the bones and carkases of divers men, who had perished (as wee thought) by famine in those woods, being either strangled from their company, or landed there by some men of warre.' (Burrage 1906, p. 153).

Note: ★For the significance of numbers in parentheses, see the note to Table 8.1 (p. 221).

Table 8.2 renders a selection of contemporary descriptions of diseases, which exemplifies the relative detail as well as the lack of frameworks within which to fit such detail.

Previous work

For the last few years, the author has been using theoretical models, GIS algorithms and data model structures for the testing, handling and representation of space–time data derived from proto-historic and historic epidemics. The research design consisted of several steps. First, I constructed algorithms for epidemic spread and growth and then simulated the results by the application of the model on the theoretical and the actual spatial distribution of

Table 8.3 Changing the temporal dimension of the disease spread.

Changing the rate of spread and the amount of time that the disease takes to spread makes no difference to the ultimate spatial distribution of the disease and to the ultimate number of deaths if the disease originates in one place (i.e. node 1957) and follows one route. Neither does it make a difference to when the deaths occur.

Node	Limit	Capacity	Delay	Spread
1957	10,000	10,000	0	139
1957	10,000	10,000	10	139
1957	10,000	10,000	20	139
1957	10,000	10,000	100	139

Table 8.4 Changing the amount of pathogens or the number of migrating infected individuals given one route and one point of disease origin.

Node	Limit	Capacity	Delay	Spread	Descr.
1957	10,000	10,000	0	139	(1)
1957	100,000	100,000	0	295	(2)
1957	1,000,000	1,000,000	0	2077	(3)

The resulting areas infected are described for each case above:

1 For the Old World the infected area includes Spain, along the French coast and north to the Gulf of Finland, as well as along the coastal areas of the northern Mediterreanean. In the New World, it went to Mexico, south along the eastern coast to Panama and north along the east coast to Florida.

2 In this case, the infection spread in the Old World through all of Europe and into the Middle East as far as Saudia Arabia while in the New World it covered central Mexico and went up both the eastern and western coasts to southern Canada creating a 'W' shape infected area. The two long sides of the 'W' are along the coasts and the central point covers central Mexico.

3 In this case the spread of the disease for the Old World covers Europe entirely (and Asia up to India), while in the New World all of North and Central America are infected but not South America.

the populations prior to the epidemic. The second step was to run the simulation and analyse the resulting predicted spread pattern of the disease and the resulting predicted distribution of the surviving populations.

The first simulation was a simulation in which the disease spreads from Europe to the New World along one route. The question asked was 'do the rate of spread and the size of the temporal delay of the disease in reaching different villages make a difference to the ultimate spatial distribution of the epidemic'. The answer was that as long as there was only one centre or one route by which the disease was continuing to be brought into the New World neither rate nor delay mattered. The time the disease took to spread through the population varied, but the ultimate size of the spread and the size of the population killed did not change (see Table 8.3)

The third stage was to increase the amount of capacity for disease spread that the routeing system could sustain. In other words, if the amount of pathogens moving through the routeing system or the number of people moving between infected villages increased, did the distribution of the disease change? The change in the pattern of disease spread was considerable. One should note that by increasing the amount of pathogens, the spread of the disease increased significantly. In addition, according to the simulation, the spread of the disease in Europe and its spread in the New World increased equivalently. Obviously, this was not the case as far as the documentary evidence is concerned. Thus, one has to adjust for this in the simulation. In order to protect the Old World population one may set up disease barriers or define the Old World population as immunized. The spread of disease never moves along the single Caribbean route into South America. It moves rapidly up the coasts of Mexico and the United States as well as up the Mississippi valley. The leading edge forms almost a 'W' shape (see Table 8.4)

The fourth stage allowed for the possibility of disease spreading from the Old World to the New World by two routes. In this case one changes the structure of the model but not the algorithms. The results are very interesting. As one dynamically increases the amount of pathogens in the system, the area infected (by two routes rather than one) did not significantly increase (see Table 8.5). In other words, the amount of pathogens is more important than the number of routes. Furthermore, the infected areas were actually slightly more restricted to the Mexican and Central American interiors with less infection on the coast. The spread index is 139, 295, 2,077 for one point of origin and one route and 96, 256, 840 for two points of origin and two routes, respectively, under similarly changing conditions of increasing pathogens.

On the other hand, there is a pivotal change in the system if one increases the number of disease routes between the Old World and the New World to four. The result is a significant difference among the speed, the location, and the distribution of the disease spread. If one examines the dynamic visualization of the model, one watches the disease refluxing back to Europe. The initial barriers and natural immunizations do not hold and Europe is

Table 8.5 Changing the number of routes by which disease enters the New World to two routes from two different points of origin.

Node	Limit	Capacity	Delay	Spread
1946	10,000	10,000	0	96
1840	10,000	10,000	0	
1946	100,000	100,000	0	256
1840	100,000	100,000	0	
1946	1,000,000	1,000,000	0	840
1840	1,000,000	1,000,000	0	

Table 8.6 Changing the number of routes by which disease enters the New World to four routes from four different points of origin.

Node	Limit	Capacity	Delay	Spread	Descr.
1482	10,000	10,000	0	188	1
1571	10,000	10,000	0		
1842	10,000	10,000	0		
1948	10,000	10,000	0		
1482	100,000	100,000	0	568	2
1571	100,000	100,000	0		
1842	100,000	100,000	0		
1948	100,000	100,000	0		
1482	1,000,000	1,000,000	0	2080	3
1571	1,000,000	1,000,000	0		
1842	1,000,000	1,000,000	0		
1948	1,000,000	1,000,000	0		

1 Spain, France, England, and area c on Figure 8.8(c)
2 Europe excluding Scandinavia, and area d on Figure 8.9(c)
3 All of western Europe, all of western Asia, all of North America, but none of South America or Africa.

rapidly covered with this 'returned disease' and it is not until there is a significant pool of the 'returned disease carriers' in Europe that the diseases take hold in the New World. Once this happens, the spread of disease in the New World is very fast and far more complete than in the previous scenario. All of North America is infected. It is worth noting that in none of the cases, even with four Caribbean routes, does the disease spread to South America (see Table 8.6).

New work

The new research changes other parameters and makes use of the actual logs and the plotted voyages. The routes of the fifty-seven historic voyages are plotted. Pools of 'original infected individuals', the carriers, are located

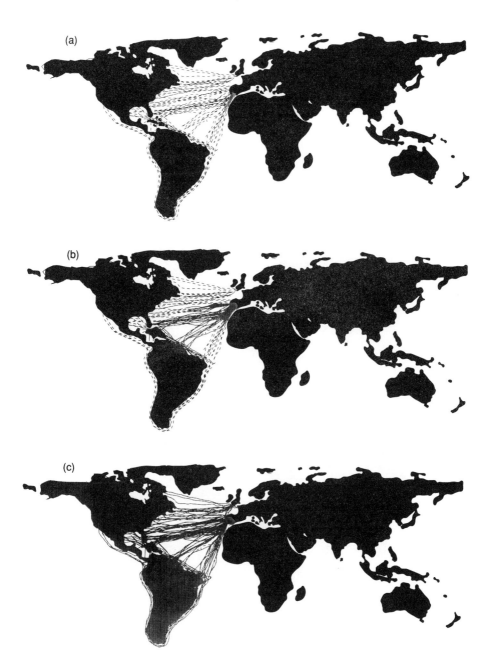

Figure 8.3 The simulated spread of disease into the New World if recipient community sizes are 50, 1,000, or 5,000 people or population densities 0.017, 0.34, or 1.7 per square kilometre. (a) shows the area infected if the population is 0.017; (b) shows the area infected if the population is 0.34; (c) shows the area infected if the population is 1.7.

in Europe in large port cities. The diseases then cross the Atlantic and the Pacific on the appropriate historic voyages. The simulator may determine which pools are infected, the number of pools infected contemporaneously, and a variety of characteristics of the New World populations.

Population distribution

This work begins by changing the density distribution for the recipient population in the New World. It is directed towards answering the question as to whether, all other things being equal, the size of the native American villages affected the spread of the disease. The population indices for the villages of are 50, 1,000, and 5,000 which are translated as population densities of 0.017, 0.34, and 1.7 per square kilometre. The disease resides originally in populations in Portugal and leaves on any actual voyage which these Portuguese populations contact. Figure 8.3 shows the spread of the disease

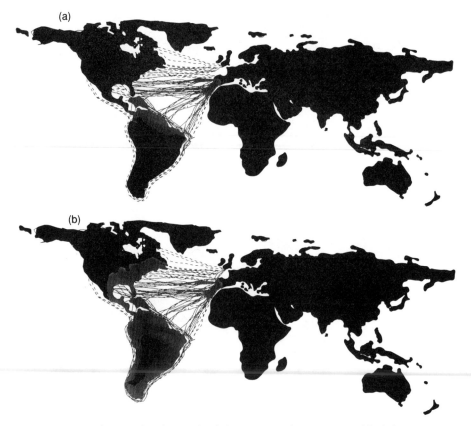

Figure 8.4 The simulated spread of disease into the New World if the recipient population densities vary spatially. (a) shows the area infected if the population increases systematically from the south to the north; (b) shows the area infected if the population increases systematically from the north to the south. Increasing density north to south is more conducive to the spread of disease.

into the New World in which density of the recipient population is constant in the three cases and varies between 0.017, 0.34 and 1.7. As one can see, density is important: at 0.017 (Figure 8.3a) there is no disease spread in the New World while at 0.34 (Figure 8.3b) the epidemic spread is limited to the north eastern coast of South America into Columbia, Venezuela, Guyana, Surinam, French Guyana, and Brazil. At a density of 1.7 per square kilometre (Figure 8.3c), disease spreads throughout the New World. (In all the figures disease is indicated by lighter shading.)

Two inferences may be drawn. First, *the density of the recipient population partially determines the spread of the epidemic.* Second, *that in order for the disease to spread there must be approximate densities of more than two people per 100 square kilometres and when the densities reach two people per square kilometre the disease moves completely through the areas.*

One knows that the population density is neither spatially nor numerically evenly distributed. The next simulation analysed the spread of disease assuming that the population density increased from south to north (1 per sq. km to 45,000 per sq. km) and then if it decreased from south to north (45,000 per sq. km to 1 per sq. km). Figure 8.4 shows the difference between a spatially increasing and decreasing south to north population density. Having high southern densities is more conducive to the spread of disease than having high northern densities. Unfortunately for the native Americans, the archaeological and historical evidence clearly indicates that denser populations were in Mesoamerica, Central America, and parts of South America. One of the interesting spatial characteristics is the inland 'island' of non-infected populations which appears in this and other simulations.

The *Danse* Masters: Spain, Portugal, and England

There is no clear evidence upon which voyage and from which country the dancers came to the New World. However, it is possible to simulate and analyse where and how the disease would have spread if it emanated from each of these countries.

Spain

If the epidemic diseases began in Spain, then what would have happened to the native American populations is shown in Figures 8.5 and 8.6. Figures 8.5(a), 8.5(b) and 8.5(c) show the increasing distribution of the disease as the limit index (an index of the amount of pathogens) increases from 0.5 to 1 and 2. In Figures 8.6(a) and 8.6(b) this limit increases to 5 and 7.5. The disease spreads towards the north-eastern coast of South America and towards the Caribbean (Figure 8.5(a)). Taking hold in both areas, it spreads more rapidly along the South American coast than into Central or North America (Figure 8.5(b)). The *danse* extends south along the coast of Brazil reaching Rio de Janeiro. It moves west through Panama along the most narrow part

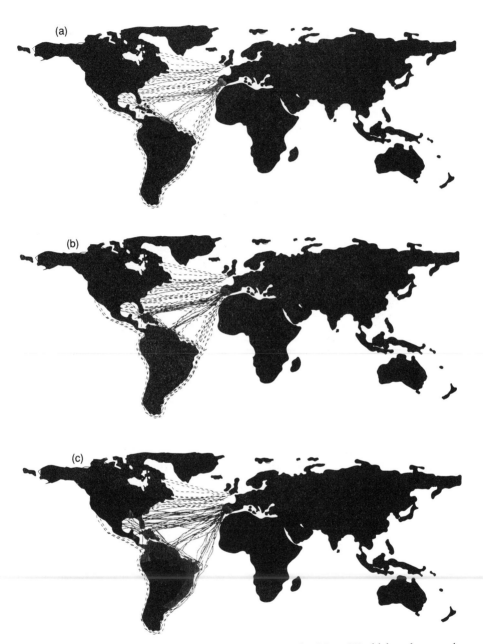

Figure 8.5 The simulated spread of disease into the New World based upon the disease beginning in Spain and moving along known routes of Spanish voyages with increasing amounts of pathogens: (a) has a pathogen index of 0.5: (b) has a pathogen index of 1; (c) has a pathogen index of 2.

of South America and simultaneously shifts inland, reaching the Rio Orinoco. Spreading north through Central America almost to Yucatan, it reaches the Gulf of Mexico and enters the United States through Louisiana and Texas as well as on the Eastern coast, infecting areas which will become the Carolinas (Figure 8.5(c)).

In Figure 8.6(a) the epidemics have spread throughout South America, except for small islands in the most central part of the continent. Moving through all of Central America they cover all but the most north-westerly parts of Mexico. Stretching west and north from the Carolinas, the entire eastern seaboard of the United States and Canada is covered and the disease moves westward incorporating the south-eastern and north-eastern states completely and trailing off as one moves to the mid-west and the Rocky Mountains. Parts of this area, and the west coast, remain uninfected. Finally, as shown in Figure 8.6(b), the entire New World has been decimated except for a small northern area in Canada and the Aleutian islands. *In summary, if*

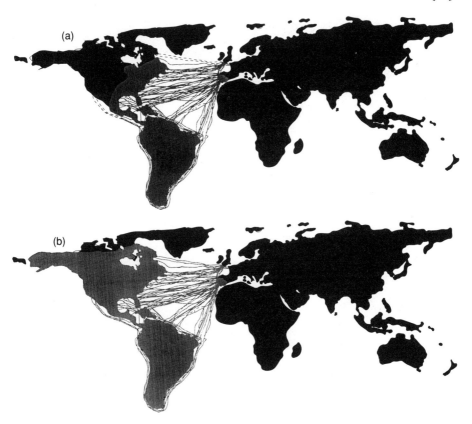

Figure 8.6 The simulated spread of disease into the New World based upon the disease beginning in Spain and moving along known routes of Spanish voyages with increasing amounts of pathogens: (a) has a pathogen index of 5: (b) has a pathogen index of 7.5. Spanish diseases moved more rapidly to the south than to the north.

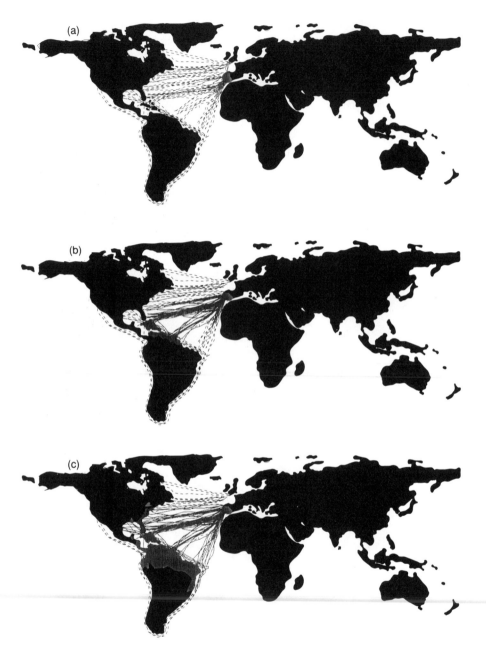

Figure 8.7 The simulated spread of disease into the New World based upon the disease beginning in Portugal and moving along known routes of Portuguese voyages with increasing amounts of pathogens: (a) has a pathogen index of 0.5: (b) has a pathogen index of 1; (c) has a pathogen index of 2. The Portuguese and Spanish epidemics are similar. However, the Portuguese epidemics have a larger northern impact.

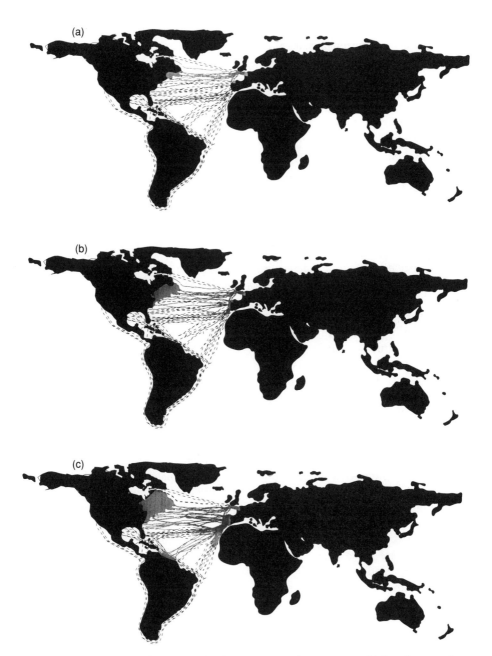

Figure 8.8 The simulated spread of disease into the New World based upon the disease beginning in England and moving along known routes of English voyages with increasing amounts of pathogens: (a) has a pathogen index of 0.5: (b) has a pathogen index of 1; (c) has a pathogen index of 2.

the dancers were brought by the Spanish, the danse began in South America, rapidly expanding south while moving at a more stately pace north. The slow northern expansion met a later expansion from Spaniards and native Americans infected along the Eastern seaboard of the United States and then rapidly expanded westward.

Portugal

Figures 8.7(a), 8.7(b) and 8.7(c) show the spread of disease from Portugal. The limits are set at 0.5, 1, 2. In other words analogous to Figures 8.5(a), 8.5(b) and 8.5(c). The pattern of spread is almost identical to the analogous expansion from Spain. The major difference occurs when the limits are set at 2. At this level (Figures 8.5(c) and 8.7(c)) the Portuguese disease pattern does not extend as far south along the Brazilian coast as does the Spanish pattern. Instead, the Portuguese epidemic wreaks more destruction in the north. While the Spanish epidemic does not affect the north-eastern US and south-eastern Canadian coastline, the Portuguese epidemic not only affects the coastline but moves considerably inland in two distinct areas. It would be fair to conclude, that *the Spanish and Portuguese epidemics were essentially very similar except the Portuguese could have had a wider northern impact.*

England

The English population may also have been the locus for the epidemic expansion. The limits are again set at 0.5, 1, and 2 in Figures 8.8(a), 8.8(b) and 8.8(c). The routeing of the disease to the New World is very different, as is its spread. The disease begins at Newfoundland, Nova Scotia, and New Brunswick, sweeping through the Gulf of St Lawrence and westward up the St Lawrence river and then into Quebec (Figure 8.8(a)). It extends south, moving through New York, Massachusetts, Maryland, and reaches into the Carolinas. It migrates west simultaneously, reaching Pennsylvania and creating a thumb into Ohio (Figure 8.8(b)). It continues to spread west into central Canada and the mid-western United States, but remains south of the Hudson Bay and reaches over to the Mississippi. However, there are no indications pointing to the epidemic in Florida, and the expansion into the south-eastern states is very limited.

Figures 8.9(a) and 8.9(b) show the continuation of this 'English epidemic'. The limits are set at 5 and 7.5. The disease spreads throughout Canada and the United States, except the north-western parts of Canada and Alaska. It drives south through eastern Mexico, the Caribbean and infects all of Central America, a broad band around all of eastern South America and then a narrower band around western South America. In fact, South America is ringed by disease (Figure 8.9(a)). Finally, the English epidemic infects the entire New World with the exception of the very northern parts of Canada such as Melville and Bathurst islands (Figure 8.9(b)). *In short, unlike the Spanish or Portuguese epidemics, the English epidemic expands from north to south rather than from a central point to both the north and the south. In addition, it tended to penetrate inland more rapidly than did the Spanish and Portuguese simulations.* If one returns

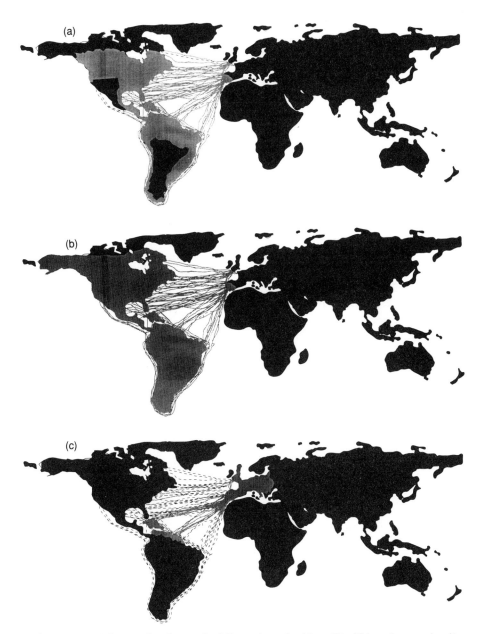

Figure 8.9 The simulated spread of disease into the New World based upon the disease beginning in England and moving along known routes of English voyages with increasing amounts of pathogens: (a) has a pathogen index of 5: (b) has a pathogen index of 7.5. English diseases spread from north to south and penetrated inland more rapidly than the Spanish and Portuguese diseases. Figure 9(c) shows the possibility of 'refluxed' infection. The disease spreads not only to the New World but back to the Old World impacting European populations which are not re-immunized.

the limit to 2, and simultaneously assumes that the European population is not re-immunized against the possibility of 'refluxed' disease, a very different picture of the expansion of infection appears as in Figure 8.9(c). The disease moves to the Caribbean and the northern shores of South America and never reaches Central or North America. Instead it spreads throughout the UK missing Ireland, through Western and Central Europe into the western parts of Russia but excluding Scandinavia and part of the Balkans. The disease also campaigns into Africa infecting Morocco, Western Sahara, Mauritania, Senegal and inland into Mali (not shown in this run).

The *danse* steps: focusing on small feet in a small area

One wishes to examine the distribution of disease in far more detail. As an experiment, one might consider an area corresponding roughly to archaeo-logical Mesoamerica. The routeing pattern is based on the correlation between 3,587 prehistoric sites and their nearest historical equivalents. These settle-ments were plotted (Figure 8.10) and several assumptions made. The first assumption is that the population actually existing at the time of disease contact was located more or less in the areas of prehistoric settlement and historic settlement. In other words, the settlement data conflate time by making late prehistoric and early historic sites contemporary. Second, in order to be conservative one creates the most conservative disease routing pattern. If disease is density dependent then the routing pattern should try to maximize the distance from each settlement. This pattern is similar to Thiessen polygons in which the disease moves along the edges of the polygons.

Three issues were examined. First, whether it makes a difference if the disease enters into an area in multiple simultaneous infections in different locations or as the result of a single entrance at a single location. Second, what effect there is on the ultimate distribution of the infection if the epidemic enters through an area of high or low settlement density. (This spatial density need not correspond to demographic density.) Third, what difference there is in disease distribution at the more local level when the locus of disease origin is Spain, Portugal, or England and to what extent is it limit-dependent.

Although the graphic evidence cannot be easily presented here, the con-clusions are reasonable. *If one compares multiple simultaneous entries in widespread coastal towns to either a single entry in a highly dense area or to a single entry in a widespread area, the spread of disease is considerably less for the simultaneous entries.* The reason appears to be that for the disease to spread widely it must go through one or more high density areas. With the simultaneous entries the probabilities are higher that the disease will die out prior to reaching a high density area. One needs to remember that the disease is not an infinitely renewable resource.

Figure 8.10 The location of contact communities in Mesoamerica based upon 3,587 prehistoric sites and their nearest historical equivalents.

(a)

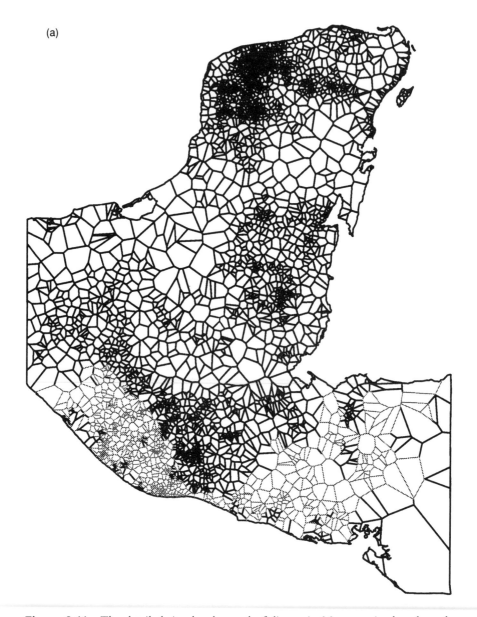

Figure 8.11 The detailed simulated spread of disease in Mesoamerica based on the actual routeing of Spanish and Portuguese voyages and the location of 3,587 communities: (a) shows the disease entering on the north-eastern shores of Honduras with a pathogen index of 0.5.

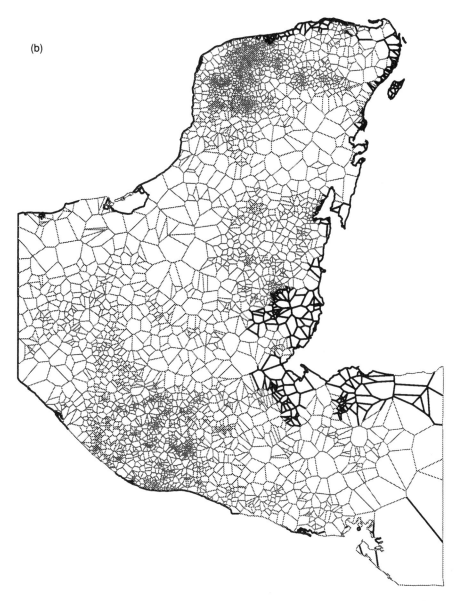

Figure 8.11 (continued) (b) shows the disease entering on the north–eastern shores of Honduras with a pathogen index of 1. Pacific coastal routes are very important to the simulated epidemic.

(a)

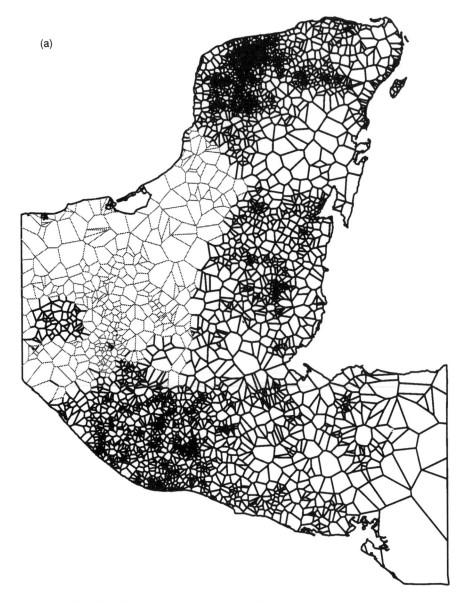

Figure 8.12 The detailed simulated spread of disease in Mesoamerica based on the actual routeing of English voyages and the location of 3,587 communities: (a) shows the disease entering on the Atlantic shores of the Isthmus of Tehuantepec with a pathogen index of 0.5.

(b)

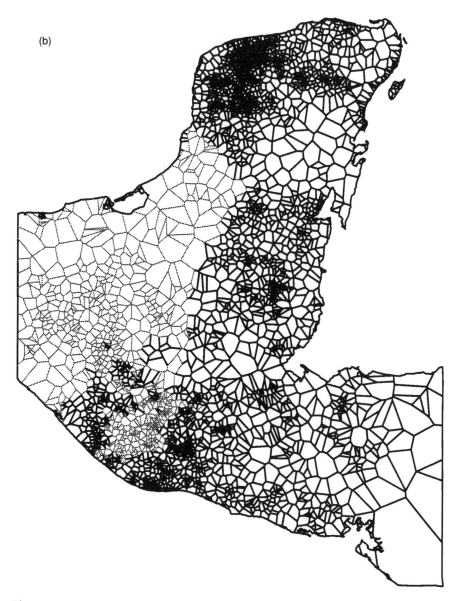

Figure 8.12 (continued) (b) shows the disease entering on the Atlantic shores of the Isthmus of Tehuantepec with a pathogen index of 1.

(c)

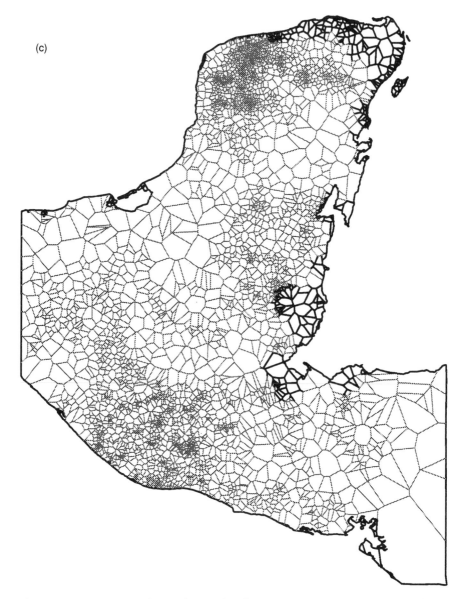

Figure 8.12 (continued) (c) shows the disease entering on the Atlantic shores of the Isthmus of Tehuantepec with a pathogen index of 2. More pathogens are necessary for the disease to infect all of Mesoamerica in a southern expansion than a northern expansion.

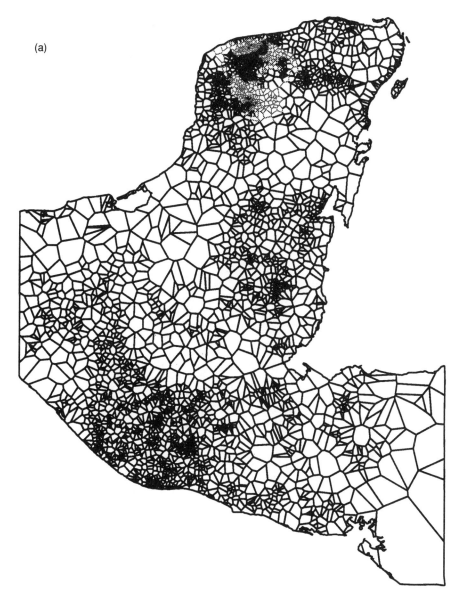

Figure 8.13 The detailed simulated spread of disease in Mesoamerica based on the disease entering on the northern tip of the Yucatan Peninsula and the location of 3,587 communities: (a) shows the pathogen index of 0.5.

(b)

Figure 8.13 (continued) (b) shows the pathogen index of 1.

(c)

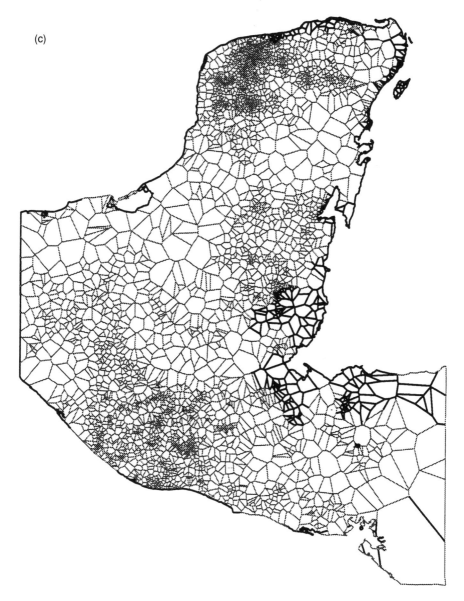

Figure 8.13 (continued) (c) shows the pathogen index of 2. Higher pathogen indices are necessary for the disease to infect all of Mesoamerica with this routeing.

The Spanish and the Portuguese epidemics reached Mesoamerica from the south and the east. Figure 8.11(a) shows the Mesoamerican routeing pattern. Continuing the Spanish and Portuguese examples, the disease enters on the south-eastern Atlantic side of the map – more specifically on the north-eastern shores of Honduras near the town of La Ceiba. With a limit of 0.5 it spreads south and west reaching the Pacific side in El Salvador and spreading north along the Pacific coast into the more densely settled southern Guatemala and Chiapas. If one increases the limit index to 1, the disease spreads throughout all of Mesoamerica, leaving only a few areas uninfected (Figure 8.11(b)). These are essentially parts of the northern coast of Honduras and the south-eastern coast of Yucatan. A small sliver of uninfected area is on the very northern and north-eastern coast of the Yucatan peninsula but it is very small. *The importance of the Pacific coast routes to infection is very clear from this simulation.*

The English epidemics would have reached Mesoamerica from the north-east. Thus Figures 8.12(a), 8.12(b) and 8.12(c) simulate this spread with limits of 0.5, 1, and 2. In Figure 8.12(a) the disease, beginning near the Atlantic shores of the Isthmus of Tehuantepec, spreads north and east along the western edge of the Yucatan Peninsula as well as South towards Chiapas and the Pacific ocean. It leaves the entire eastern half of the Yucatan Peninsula, most of Chiapas, all of Guatemala, El Salvador and Honduras, as well as a small western 'island' uninfected. When the limit increases to 1 the disease spreads through the dense settlements of Chiapas and Southern Guatemala ending at a north–south line connecting Campeche to Sonsonata. The western 'island' is infected. The northern part of Yucatan and the eastern areas including Honduras are not infected (Figure 8.12(b)). It is not until the limit reaches 2 that most of Mesoamerica is infected (Figure 8.12(c)). The only areas not infected are a slight sliver of the north-eastern part of the Yucatan Peninsula and a few slivers of land along the eastern shore of Yucatan and the northern shores of Honduras. *It takes a higher limit for the disease to infect the entire Mesoamerican area if it is moving from north to south rather than from south to north.*

Finally, it is possible to examine the expansion of the disease if the point of entrance is on the northern tip of the peninsula near the present city of Merida. With the same limits, a very different scenario occurs. First, the disease begins with a much more spatially limited pattern – remaining in the highly dense settlements of the north Figure 8.13(a)). Second (Figure 8.13(b)), with limit 1 the disease spreads southward but never reaches the Pacific coast nor the eastern side of the peninsula and seems to falter in Chiapas. In fact there is a relatively wide band of uninfected areas in the southern part of the map. Finally, at limit 2 the entire area is almost completely infected except for a few coastal areas particularly in Honduras and Belize (Figure 8.13(c)). In this simulation, two inferences are important. *The longer time and higher index of system limit is necessary for the entire area to be infected and the same southern routes which acted as a conduit for the Spanish and Portuguese infections are a barrier to this peninsular infection.*

Conclusions

This chapter has used GIS, epidemic models, and the logs and routes of the voyages to the New World between 1492–1650 to begin to understand the depopulation of the New World. Together with previous work, there are several points worth noting. They are:

1 If the epidemics originated from one point of origin and travelled a single route to the New World then changing the rate or parameters made no difference: it changes the scheduling of the depopulation but not its character. The number and location of the infected population did not change.

2 If the amount of pathogens increases, the spatial distribution of the disease increases and systematically changes demographic distribution in a predictable manner. This increase in capacity corresponds to the number of infected people moving through the system.

3 If the disease followed a single 'Caribbean route' structure, it never reached South America. It moved into North America in a 'W' pattern with the leading edges of the three prongs being the West coast, the Mississippi, and the East coast.

4 Changing the structure of the model to two Caribbean routes makes no significant difference. On the other hand changing it to four routes does, with rapid spread of disease in Europe as well as the New World as a result of increased routeing possibilities and refluxing disease from the New World.

5 Changing the structure of the model to correspond to the actual voyages between 1492 and 1650, providing one point of disease origin in Portugal and then varying the population density of the native New World shows that a minimum of approximately two people per 100 square kilometres is necessary for the epidemic to infect large portions of the New World. Furthermore, if population density increases from south to north in the New World, the impact of epidemics is less than vice versa.

6 Given the actual voyages, if the epidemics originated in Spain or Portugal, then South America is decimated more rapidly as the disease spreads quickly south and expands more slowly north.

7 The English epidemic expands from northern North America to the south and penetrates far more rapidly inland.

8 The worst type of epidemic would have been one which simultaneously entered the New World through a number of dense local populations. The least-wide infection would have taken place if there had been simultaneous entries in smaller, more widely spaced coastal villages.

9 The western coast of Mesoamerica is a very important conduit for disease.

10   In Mesoamerica it is more difficult for disease to move from north
     to south than from south to north.

This work, and indeed all simulation work, should be considered preliminary and tentative. Its value is primarily heuristic in that it creates detail
and shows relationships that might not have been otherwise recognized. It is
clear that the demographic catastrophe which occurred in the New World was
very complicated and that the true *danse* steps are yet to be discovered. In all
my scenarios, the distribution of death is patterned and it is fortunate that in
reality there were clustered areas of infection and pockets of survival. Without
those pockets, the native American population might not have survived.

References

Aguero, Jose de la. [1962] *Obras completas de Jose de la Riva-Aguero* [microform]. Lima:
   Pontificia Universidad Catolica del Peru.[39]
Alvarado, Pedro de. [1525] 1924. *An Account of the Conquest of Guatemala in 1524
   by Pedro de Alvarado.* Sedley J. Mackie (ed.) with a facsim. of Spanish original.
   New York: Cortes Society. [New York: Kraus Reprint, 1969.][7]
Andrews, K.R. (ed.) 1972. *The last Voyage of Drake & Hawkins*, Cambridge: published
   for the Hakluyt Society at the University Press.[16]
Arber, E. (ed.) 1885. *The First Three English Books on America (?1511)–1555 A.D.*
   [microform]. – Birmingham: [s.n.], Edinburgh: Turnbull & Spears.[36]
Bandelier, A.F.A. 1981. *Decouverte du Nouveau-Mexique, par le moine franciscain frere
   Marcos, de Nice en 1539.* Translated from the French and edited by Madeleine
   Turrell Rodack. Tuscon: University of Arizona Press.[12]
Barbour, P.L. (ed.) 1969. *The Jamestown Voyages under the First Charter, 1606–1609:
   documents relating to the foundation of Jamestown and the history of the Jamestown colony
   up to the departure of Captain John Smith, last president of the council of Virginia under
   the first charter, early in October 1609.* London: published for the Hakluyt Society
   by Cambridge University Press.[25]
Baxter, J.P. 1906. *A Memoir of Jacques Cartier, Sieur de Limoilou* [microform]. New
   York: Dodd, Mead & Company.[11]
Beazley, C.R., Sir. 1898. *John and Sebastian Cabot: the discovery of North America.*
   London: T. Fisher Unwin. Microfiche – Chicago: Library Resources, Inc., 1970.[36]
Best, G. [1867] 1963? *The three voyages of Martin Frobisher, in Search of a Passage to
   Cathaia and India by the North-west, A.D. 1576–8 with Selections from the Manuscript
   Documents in the British Museum and State Paper Office, by Richard Collinson.* New
   York: B. Franklin.[17]
Brereton, J. 1602. *A briefe and true relation of the discouerie of the north part of Virginia;
   being a most pleasant, fruitfull and commodius soile: made this present yeere 1602, by
   Captaine Bartholowmew Gosnold, Captaine Bartholowmew Gilbert, and diuers other
   gentlemen their associats.* London George: Bishop. Microfilm: Ann Arbor, Mich.,
   University Microfilms (American Culture series, Reel 3.19.[22]
Burrage, H.S. (Henry Sweetser) 1906. *Early English and French Voyages, Chiefly from
   Hakluyt, 1534–1608* [microform]. New York: C. Scribner's Sons.[11][16][20][23][44][48]
Cabral, Pedro. 1938. *The Voyage of Pedro Cabral to Brazil and India: from contemporary
   documents and narratives.* Translated by William Brooks Greenlee. London: Hakluyt
   Society.[32]
Carmack, R.M., J. Early and C. Lutz (eds). 1982. *The Historical Demography of Highland*

Guatemala. Albany, N.Y.: Institute for Mesoamerican Studies, State University of New York.

Champlain, Samuel de. 1971. *The Works of Samuel de Champlain*. 6 vols. Toronto: Champlain, Samuel de 1567–1635.: [*Brief discours des choses plus remarquables. English*] *Narrative of a voyage to the West Indies and Mexico in the years 1599–1602*. Translated by Alice Wilmere. Edited by Norton Shaw. New York: B. Franklin [1964].[24]

Champlain, Samuel de. 1907. *Voyages of Samuel de Champlain, 1604–1618*. W.L. Grant (ed.). New York: C. Scribner's Sons.[28]

Christy, M. (ed.) 1894. *The Voyages of Captains Luke Foxe of Hull & Thomas James of Bristol, in Search of a Northwest Passage in 1631–32 with Narratives of the Earlier Voyages of Frobisher, Davis, Weymouth, Hall, Knight, Hudson, Button, Gibbons, Bylot, Baffin, Hawkridge, and others*. 2 vols. London.[26][27]

Cieza de Leon, Pedro de. 1913. *The War of Quito, by Pedro de Cieza de Leon, and Inca Documents*. Translated and edited by Sir Clements R. Markham. London: Hakluyt Society.[37][41]

Columbus, Christopher. 1988. *The Four Voyages of Columbus: a history in eight documents including five by Christopher Columbus*. Translated and edited by Cecil Jane. New York: Dover Publications.[1][4][30]

Columbus, Christopher. [1893] 1971. *The Journal of Christopher Columbus (during his first voyage, 1492–93), and Documents Relating to the Voyages of John Cabot and Gaspar Corte Real*. Translated by Clements R. Markham. New York: B. Franklin.[1][36]

Cook, James. 1955. *The Journals of Captain James Cook on his Voyages of Discovery*. Edited by R.A. Skelton. Cambridge: published for the Hakluyt Society at the University Press.[45]

Cortes, Hernan. [1868] c. 1963. *The Fifth Letter of Hernan Cortes to the Emperor Charles V*. Translated by Don Pascual de Gayangos. New York: B. Franklin.[6]

De Soto, Ferdinando. [1851] 1966. *The Discovery and Conquest of Terra Florida by Don Ferdinando de Soto and Six Hundred Spaniards, his Followers, Written by a Gentleman of Elvas, Employed in all the Action and Translated out of Portuguese by Richard Hakluyt*. Edited by William B. Rye. New York: B. Franklin.[9][13]

De Vaca, Alvar Nunez Cabeza. 1972. *The Narrative of Alvar Nunez Cabeza de Vaca*. Translated by Fanny Bandelier. Barre, Mass.: Imprint Society.[10][43]

De Vaca, Dominguez, Luis L. (ed.) *The Conqest of the River Plate (1535–1555)*. Translated for the Hakluyt Society by Luis L. Dominguez. New York: B. Franklin.[10]

Dobyns, H. 1983. *Their Numbers Become Thinned*. The University of Tennessee Press. Knoxville.

Drake, Francis, Sir. 1981. *Sir Francis Drake's West Indian Voyage, 1585–86*. Edited by Mary Frear Keeler. London: Hakluyt Society.[18][44]

Drake, Francis, Sir. [1628] 1970. *The World Encompassed by Sir Francis Drake* [microform]. Edited by Sir Richard Carnac Temple. [London: Hakluyt Society 1854.] Microfiche. Chicago: Library Resourses, Inc.[18][44]

Fernandez de Enciso, Martin. 1932. *A Brief Summe of Geographie*. Translated by Roger Barlow. Edited E.G.R. Taylor. London: Hakluyt Society.[34]

Friede, Juan (ed.) 1960. *Gonzalo Jimenez de Quesada a traves de documentos historicos; estudio biografico*. Bogota: Editorial ABC.[39]

Garcia de Palacio, Diego. 1983. *Carta relacion de Diego Garcia de Palacio a Felipe II sobre la provincia de Guatemala, 8 de marzo de 1576*. Mexico: Universidad Nacional Automona de Mexico.[38]

Garcia de Palacio, Diego. 1985. *Letter to the King of Spain: being a description of the ancient provinces of Guazacapan, Izalco, Cuscatlan, and Chiquimula, in the Audiencia of Guatemala, with an account of the languages, customs, and religion of the aboriginal inhabitants, and a description of the ruins of Copan*. translated by Ephraim G. Squier. Culver City, Calif.: Labyrinthos.[38]

Giovio, Paolo. *Historiarum sui temporis*. Illescas, Gonzalo de, fl. 1565. Historia pontificaly catolica.[39]

Hakluyt, Richard. 1589. *The principall navigations, voiages and discoveries of the English nation, made by sea of ouer land, to the most remote and farthest distant quarters of the earth at any time within the compasse of these 1500 yeeres: deuided into three seuerall parts, according to the positions of the regions whereunto they were directed . . . Whereunto is added the last most renowmed English nauigation, round about the whole globe of the earth*. Microform by Richard Hakluyt. London: Bishop and R. Newberie. Microfilm. Ann Arbor, Mich., University Microfilms (n.d.) (American Culture Series, Reel 3. 16).

Hammond, George Peter. 1940. *Narratives of the Coronado Expedition, 1540–1542*. Edited and translated by George P. Hammond and Agapito Rey. Albuquerque: The University of New Mexico Press.[15]

Heidenreich, C.E. 1976. *Explorations and Mapping of Samuel Champlain, 1603–1632*. Toronto: B.V. Gutsell.[24]

Holbein, Hans. 1856. *Dance of Death*. Paris: E. Tross.

Hudson, Henry. 1964. *Henry Hudson the Navigator: the original documents in which his career is recorded, collected, partly translated, and annotated*. New York: B.Franklin.[26]

Jimenez de Quesada, Gonzalo. 1952. *El antijovio. Edicion dirigida por Rafael Torres Quintero; estudio prelimin arpor Manuel Ballesteros Gaibrois*. Bogota.[39]

Kelly, J.E. [1932] 1971. *Pedro de Alvarado, Conquistador*. Port Washington, N.Y.: Kennikat Press.[7]

Lopez, Pero. 1953. *Narrative of the Closing Events of the Conquest of Peru and the Warfare between Gonzalo Pizarro and Diego de Almagor* (microform). Buffalo, N.Y.: Biel's Microfilm Corp.[40]

Magellan, *First Voyage Round the World* [1874] 1963. Translated by Lord Stanley of Alderley. New York: B. Franklin.[35]

Markham, C.R., Sir (ed.) 1967. *Early Spanish Voyages to the Strait of Magellan*. Translated by Sir Clements Markham. Nendeln, Liechtenstein: Kraus Reprint.[34][46][47]

Markham, C.R., Sir (ed.) [1878] 1970. *The Hawkins' Voyages During the Reigns of Henry VIII, Queen Elizabeth, and James I*. New York: B. Franklin.[16]

Markham, C.R., Sir. 1970. *Reports on the Discovery of Peru*. Translated and edited by Clements R. Markham. New York: B. Franklin.[37][41]

Markham, C.R., Sir [1859] 1963. *Expeditions into the Valley of the Amazons, 1539, 1540, 1639*. Translated and edited by Clements R. Markham. New York: B. Franklin.[41]

Medina, J.T. 1888–1902. *Coleccion de documentos ineditos para la historia de Chile, desde el viajede Magallanes hasta la batalla de Maipo, 1518–1818*. Santiago: Ercilla.[43]

Morrison, S.E. 1972. *Samuel de Champlain, Father of New France*. Boston, Mass.: Little, Brown.[24]

Pizarro y Orellana, Fernando. 1639. *Varones ilustres del Nuevo Mundo: descrubridores, conquistadores y pacificadores del opulento, dilatado y poderoso imperio de las Indias Occidentales: sus vidas, virtud, valor, hazanas y claros blasones . . . con un discurso legal de la obligacion que tienen los reyes a premiar los servicios de sus vassallos . . .* Madrid: D. Diaz de la Carrera.[31]

Pocock, H.R.S. 1967. *The Conquest of Chile*. New York: Stein & Day.[41]

Pohl, F.J. 1944. *Amerigo Vespucci: pilot major*. New York: Columbia University Press.[48]

Quesne, Abraham. 1696. *A new voyage to the East-Indies in the years 1690 and 1691* [microfiche]: *being a full description of the isles of Maldives, Cicos, Andamants, and the Isle of Ascension. . .*[Original French edn published as *Journal du voyage de Duquesne aux Indes Orientales, par un garde-marine servant sur son escadre*. Brussels, 1692].[48]

Quinn, D.B. 1955. *The Roanoke Voyages*. 2 vols. London: Hakluyt Society. [Microfiche – Chicago: Library Resources].[21]

Quinn, D.B. 1940. *Voyages and Colonising Enterprises of Sir Humphrey Gilbert*. London: Hakluyt Society.[19]

Raleigh, Walter, Sir. [1848] 1970. *The discovery of the rich and beautiful empire of Guiana, with a relation of the great and golden city of Manoa (which the Spaniards call el Dorado) etc. performed in the year 1595, by Sir W. Ralegh. Reprinted from the ed. of 1596 with some unpublished documents relative to that country.* Edited by Sir Robert H. Schomburgk. New York: B. Franklin.[21][45]

Ramenofsky, A.F. 1987. *Vectors of Death: the archaeology of European contact.* Albuquerque: University of New Mexico Press.

Rodriguez Villa, A. (ed.) 1908. *Cronicas del Gran Capitan, por Antonio Rodriguez Villa.* Madrid: Bailly.[38]

Schouten, Willem Corneliszoon. [1619] 1968. *A wonderful voiage round about the world.* New York: Da Capo Press.[46]

Smith, M.T. 1987. *Archaeology of Aboriginal Culture Change in the Interior Southeast: depopulation during the early historic period.* Gainsville: University Presses of Florida: University of Florida Press Florida State Museum.

Thomas, D.H. 1989–91. *Columbian Consequences.* 3 vols Washington, DC: Smithsonian Institution Press.

Tytler, Patrick Fraser. 1832. *Historical view of the progress of discovery on the more northern coasts of America, from the early period to the present time.* Edinburgh: Oliver & Boyd.[36]

Ulloa, Antonio de. [1748] 1978. *A voyage to South America, describing at large, the Spanish cities, towns, provinces, &c. on that extensive continent: interspersed throughout with reflexions on whatever is peculiar in the religion and civil policy in the genius, customs, manners, dress, &c. &c. of the several inhabitants; whether natives, Spaniards, creoles, Indians, mulattoes, or negroes undertaken by command of the King of Spain, by Don George Juan, and Don Antonio de Ulloa;* Boston: Longwood Press.[14]

Valdivia, Pedro de. c. 1970. *Cartas de relacion de la Conquista de Chile.* Santiago: Editorial Universitaria.

Vespucci, Amerigo. [1894] 1964. *The Letters of Amerigo Vespucci and other Documents Illustrative of his Career.* Translated by Clements R. Markham. New York: B. Franklin.[3][5][33]

Vernon, I.S.W. 1946. *Pedro de Valdivia, Conquistador of Chile.* Austin: University of Texas Press.[42]

Williamson, J.A. 1962. *The Cabot Voyages and Bristol Discovery under Henry VII.* Cambridge: published for the Hakluyt Society at the University Press.[2]

Winship, G.P. 1966. *The Journey of Coronado* [by Pedro Castaneda]. Edited and translated by George Parker Winship. Ann Arbor, Mich: University Microfilms.[15]

Winship, G.P. (ed.) [1905] 1968. *Sailors' Narratives of Voyages Along the New England Coast, 1524–1624* New York: B. Franklin. [8][23]

Zubrow, E. 1990. The depopulation of Native America. *Antiquity* 245, 754–65.

Note: For the significance of superior numbers in parentheses see note to Table 8.1 (p. 221).

9   *Fractal environmental changes and the evolution of culture*

Geoffrey C.P. King and Allan G. Lindh

It is a clear, though lamentably common, error to assume that the current utility of a feature permits an inference about the reasons for its evolutionary origin. Current utility and historical origin are different subjects. Any feature, regardless of how or why it first evolved, becomes available for co-option to other roles, often strikingly different.

Stephen Gould

Tradition, tradition . . .

Topol

Introduction

This chapter describes an automaton which simulates features of the transfer of information between generations of a species. It illustrates that strategies of information transfer which involve sexual transfer of information in recessive genes (strategies which we term Darwinian) are more effective than Lamarckian strategies when coping with a fractally varying environment. It is suggested that humans have incorporated Darwinian features into the inherently Lamarckian process of transmitting learned behaviour. An ability to transmit 'unused' behaviour patterns over several generations is a key to acquiring this facility and carries corrollaries such as the tendency for individuals or groups to retain apparently non–utilitarian belief systems. Features such as these can be seen to be identical to those which are associated with the appearance of culture.

We start by discussing features of the genetic transfer of information which have existed for much longer. This is because we will argue that, for humans, learned behaviour simulates aspects of genetic information transfer. The reader should not at this stage imagine that we propose to rehash old ideas of selection processes acting on cultural values to ensure their efficiency. On the contrary, we explain why such selective pressure can apparently have so little effect. None the less, we explain the origin of culture within an evolutionary framework (see also Boyd and Richerson 1985).

Biological models, and the social models that derive from them, either assume a static environment or one that changes abruptly or gradually. In the former case, biologists examine how optimal adaptation arises and they have been surprised to find how genetically ill-adapted a successful species can be (e.g., Ho and Saunders 1984). Abrupt environmental change is seen as creating an abrupt population change, such as the extinction of the dinosaurs at the Cretaceous–Tertiary boundary (Glen 1980), while gradual changes such as the change of tree-trunk colour in industrial England created a stress that turned moth populations from white to black.

There is ample evidence that the environment varies in ways that do not approximate such simple functions but are better described as a fractal process. In other words, change occurs at all time-scales and not as single steps or ramps. A survival response to a fractal function can be very different from responses optimized for surviving simpler changes. We shall argue that the genetic techniques pioneered by simple organisms in the Pre-Cambrian have evolved because they are very effective in this respect. These techniques include, sexual or quasi-sexual exchange of information, recessive genes and mutation. While most organisms fail to optimize for a given environment, these genetic techniques confer on a group or species an ability to survive change that arrives in an unpredictable way. Critical to this capacity is the role of unexpressed genes which can carry either 'memory' of an earlier successful strategy or a mutation that might be useful. This 'baggage' of alternative strategies is very important (e.g., Dobzhansky *et al.* 1977).

The Lamarckian transmission of learned behaviour acquired by some verte-brates, however, does not possess this property. For example, tits in the British Isles have learnt to open milk bottle tops delivered to door-steps. The absence of milk bottles with tops for one generation of tits would eliminate their ability to open them. Offspring learn only what the parent teaches directly. Only human culture transmits 'un-used' behaviour over many generations and has this parallel with genetic information transfer. We suggest that under-standing the conditions that lead to the evolution of such trans-generational transmission of learned behaviour will be a critical step in understanding human evolution.

Environmental variation

Mandelbrot describes his experience of modelling changes in the levels of the river Nile as leading to his appreciation of fractional dimension; he named the fractal behaviour of the Nile levels the 'Joseph Effect' (Mandelbrot 1983). It serves to remind us that apparent patterns, such as seven years of plenty

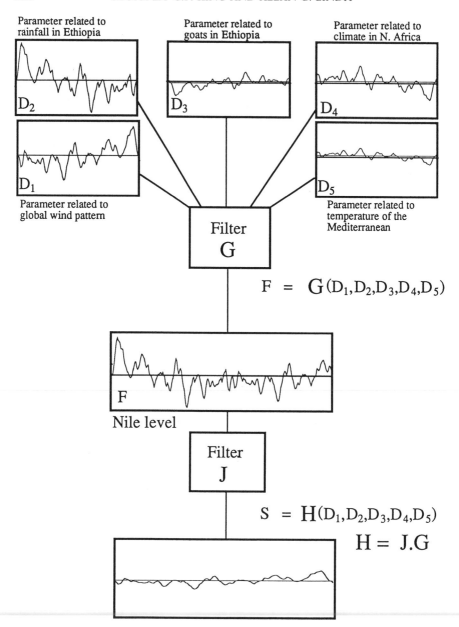

Figure 9.1 Schematic diagram to show the relation between different fractal inputs (causes) and their outputs (effects).

followed by seven years of famine need not result from a 'divine intervention' or other simple change of 'cause'.

Numerous advocates and opponents of fractals have further noted that measuring the fractal dimension is much easier than determining the underlying cause of fractal behaviour. A brief examination of why this should be will serve later discussions where we examine the relations between different fractal behaviours. It also serves to introduce the concept of filters that is used later. In Figure 9.1, a possible set of causes of Nile level changes are shown and include: rainfall in Ethiopia, temperature change in the Mediterranean, global wind patterns, climate in North Africa and goats in the Ethiopian uplands. This does not form a complete set, but, if it did, and if linear or moderately non-linear conditions prevail, then a filter with these functions as input could be constructed to predict Nile levels.

In the example, provided any of the inputs to the filter are fractal, the output will also be fractal under a wide range of conditions. Fractal behaviour in one part of a system causes fractal response in another and the origin of that fractal behaviour can be hard or impossible to locate when a process has numerous causes.

In a coupled system, such as that outlined, where some parts fluctuate in a fractal fashion, not all fluctuate to the same degree. For example, a water-retentive soil can retain fertility despite climatic variations and hence exhibit insensitivity to climatic variations (see King and Bailey 1985 for an archaeological example of the role of climatic insensitivity). The lower part of Figure 9.1 shows a filter that reduces variations in this way. The next section points out that such environments are favourable to life and discusses the evolutionary implications of exploiting environments with greater variation.

Stable environments, unstable environments and the evolution of complexity

No organism is capable of coping with all environmental possibilities. Broadly speaking, the simpler the organism the more stable the conditions that it requires in order to survive. In evolution, stable environments were populated before the less stable ones (the oceans before the continents, for example, and more stable land environments before less stable ones). That is not to say that stability is the only criterion. To take extreme examples, the base of the Antarctic icecap or the magmas of mid-ocean ridge volcanoes have stable thermal and chemical conditions but do not support life. None the less, the generalization that environmental stability is favoured by life, is reasonable.

The evolution of complexity in organisms can be seen in the context of stability of environments. A simple organism can cope with a stable environment but suffers competition. The evolution of a more complex strategy to deal with a less stable environment opens new unexploited niches to the first organisms with the ability to enter them (Lindh 1985, p. 218). Thus, under

Table 9.1 Evolutionary responses to environmental insensitivity.

Innovation	Insensitive to	New opportunity
Cell walls	Insensitivity to other chemicals	Localization of enzymes to permit digestion of large items.
Mitochondria	Insensitivity to oxidization	Exploitation of oxygen
Multi-celled hydraulically supported membranes	Insensitivity to famine by burrowing for old food	Exploitation of food left from previous systems
Differentiated multi-celled organisms	Rapidly changing environments	Primitive nervous systems as a new way of acquiring information about the environment
Egg shells	Insensitivity to dehydration	Exploitation of the land
Warm bloodedness	Insensitivity to wide temperature changes	Activity in otherwise inaccessible (cold) conditions, such as night-time hunting

appropriate circumstances, complexity is selected for. Table 9.1 shows examples of evolving strategies, the environmental insensitivity conferred and the new niche opened. The result of the progressive expansion of niches which complexity permits, means that evolution is not a 'zero-sum' competition for the same territory, and that survival of the fittest need not involve expansion at the expense of others; indeed, important innovations in life, such as those shown in the examples, were not primarily at the expense of other organisms.

The overall effect of complexity is to provide the individual or species with the ability to survive conditions where the environment does not naturally filter out variations.

Organism or species flexibility versus environmental stability

Concepts in the foregoing sections can be made numerical in the following way. Let $E(t)$ represent the environment at time t. (For later convenience we will define E as being in the same units of information as those required to survive an environment.) Over a period of time t, this function fluctuates over a set of values E which is related (linearly) to the variance of E. This is the minimum amount of information that must be possessed by a species to survive for a time that extends for many generations of its individuals.

Table 9.2 Steps in the chemical evolution of genes.

	Error rate
Non-enzymic replication	$1/10 - 1/100$
RNA replication	$10^3 - 10^4$
DNA replication	$10^9 - 10^{10}$

The survival information E_s of the species, in other words the information that all the individuals collectively transmit to successive generations, must exceed **E**. If this is not true, at some time the environment exceeds the range of the species and the latter becomes extinct. In a truly fractal environment, with no fractal limits, **E** increases with time and no species can survive. In the extreme, this is saying that life cannot survive eternally or, on a smaller scale, that even the successful cockroach will not survive the explosion of the sun or even lesser future variations.

The ability of an individual, as opposed to a species, to survive depends on it possessing the information to survive the range of conditions during its life which we can define as E_i. In general, the range of environmental conditions that an individual can survive, E_i, is less than the range the species as a whole can survive E_s. The chemical evolution of the gene has been concerned with increasing E_i. Steps in this evolution, together with the error rate in transmitted bases is shown in Table 9.2. The value of about $10^9 - 10^{10}$ achieved by proof reading DNA appears to be a limit that chemical evolution has not exceeded and explains why the RNA of higher organisms never exceeds 10^9 bases (Maynard Smith 1989).

For early organisms and many bacteria or viruses E_s and E_i are virtually the same. (It has to be assumed that quasi-sexual behaviour appears to be widespread now and probably was in the past, and that exception must be made for genetically isolated populations.) Except for mutation resulting from transcription error, clonal reproduction by fission produces offspring with E_i identical to their parent. We note now that Lamarckian information transfer has clonal properties. The body form of the parent expresses all of the information that it will transmit to the next generation. The environment can shape the organism during its life but only if it has the necessary incipient body form (phenotype) to respond to the environment in that way, or if a mutation occurs at its conception which is consistent with modifying the organism to suit the new environment. A mutation that might happen to confer survival advantage on a great-grandchild but is deadly to intervening generations is not transmitted.

The introduction of sex and recessive genes greatly changes the process of information transfer between generations. Only a part of the genetic code is used to describe the actual body morphology of an individual and a great part is given over to transmitting survival strategies that the individual cannot exploit but can pass on to offspring. We shall refer to all of these non-clonal strategies as Darwinian strategies. In practice, strategies lie on a clonal–non-clonal continuum of which we have described end members. Species that reserve all the genetic code to describe the individual are at the clonal extreme, while species for which only a small part codes for the individual and most of the information is recessive, are at the non-clonal extreme.

A model for evolution in a varying environment

The foregoing concepts can be incorporated into an evolutionary automaton which allows us to compare clonal and non-clonal strategies. The operation of the automaton can be explained with reference to a typical output shown in Figure 9.2. The upper part of the figure shows the state of the environment as a function of time and corresponds to $E(t)$. The units are arbitrary

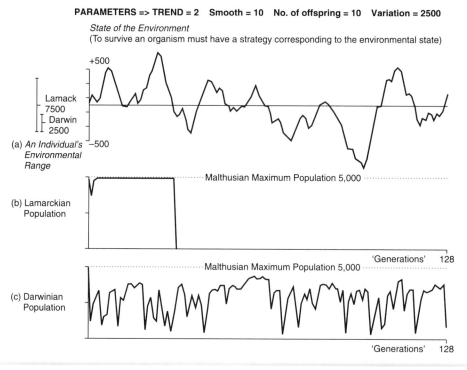

Figure 9.2   The response of Lamarckian (clonal) and Darwinian (non-clonal) populations to an environment that varies in an approximately fractal fashion. The number of offspring for each surviving individual is ten. The parameters Trend and Smooth determine the dimension of the fractal which is created by integrating and then detrending and smoothing a sequence of random numbers. Identical conditions are maintained for Figure 9.3. The environments are only the same in a statistical sense so that different 'runs' give different results. The figures are chosen to be representative. Other features of the figure are explained in the text.

Table 9.3 Breeding table.

Just from parent

Primary (1) from self (2)	Self (3) from self (1)
Self (2) from self (2)	Primary (1) from self (3)
Self (3) from self (3)	Self (2) from self (1)
Primary (1) from self (3)	Self (3) from self (2)
Self (2) from self (2)	

Sexual exchange and rearrange

Primary (1) from partner (3)	Self (3) from self (1)
Self (2) from self (2)	Primary (1) from partner (2)
Self (3) from self (1)	Self (2) from self (3)
Primary (1) from partner (3)	Self (3) from partner (2)
Self (2) from partner (1)	Primary (1) from partner (3)
Self (3) from self (2)	Self (2) from self (2)
Primary (1) from partner (3)	Self (3) from partner (3)
Self (2) from partner (2)	

Mutant

Primary (1) from self (1)	Primary (1) mutant
Self (2) mutant	Self (2) mutant
Self (3) mutant	Self (3) mutant

Note: Primary is the expressed strategy, and self (2) and self (3) are reserve (recessive) strategies. The partner is chosen at random from the population. The breeding possibilities are chosen at random.

but correspond, as explained earlier, to some measure of information. To the left of the figure are two ranges. One is for a clonal individual and the second for a non-clonal individual. The exploitable range of the clonal individual is *three* times that of the non-clonal. For the non-clonal individual, however, the difference is taken up by two recessive strategies so that organisms transmit identical amounts of information from one generation to the next. We have chosen the number three arbitrarily. However, much less than *three* would not illustrate the difference between clonal and non-clonal strategies well, while larger differences would greatly increase computing time since larger populations would be needed to make non-clonal strategies viable.

When the automaton starts, each individual has the centre of its range (E_i) chosen at random between ±10,000. At each time-step or generation, if the environment does not fall within the range of the individual, the individual dies. Those that do not die are permitted to breed by producing a specified number of offspring per individual. Breeding stops at a maximum of 5,000 individuals which we refer to as the Malthusian population limit.

The breeding strategy of the clonal individual is very simple. Except for mutation, which will be discussed below, the offspring are identical to the parent. The breeding strategy of the non-clonal individuals is much more complex and is shown in Table 9.3. Ten different types of offspring can be created each time an individual reproduces, and are chosen at random. The information that they receive falls into three categories:

1   One or more of the individual's three strategies, primary or one of the two secondary, may come from any of the parents' strategies.
2   One or more of the individual's three strategies, primary or one of the two secondary, may come from any of another individual's strategies. The individual is selected at random from the population. This is quasi-sexual behaviour.
3   One or more of an individual's strategies is a random mutation.

The way in which mutation is arranged is important to the way in which the automaton operates. A mutated strategy is simply one whose centre point is chosen at random from the $\pm 10,000$ range. The method of calculating the relative probability of mutation occurrence for clonal and non-clonal individuals, however, is critical.

Every point in an individual's range, in principal, can alter at random. However, the vast majority of these are totally unviable. To start, we consider only those mutations where all points that correspond to an individual's range mutate to another continuous range (i.e., they can still be represented by the range and a single centre point). It is not obvious that the conditions placed on real organisms are really the same as requiring a continuous range for the model. However, some similar conditions must prevail so that it is reasonable to suppose that continuity of range imposed on the automaton is at least analogous to real life conditions. We shall discuss relaxing these conditions below and we will see that real life would have to behave in a dramatically different way in order to affect the assumptions underlying our model.

Any one consecutive arrangement of points can be expressed as a permutation nPr, where n is the total number of possibilities (i.e., $\pm 10,000$) and r is the individual range.

$$nPr = n(n-1)(n-2) \ldots (n-r+1)$$

The probability nGr of any one permutation occurring is $1/nPr$. If $r \ll n$ then the expression can be approximated as:

$$nGr = n^{-r}$$

For our model we do not need to know absolute mutation probability. The critical parameter in comparing the behaviour of clonal and non-clonal individuals is the relative probability of viable mutations. This relative probability is nG_{r1}^{r2}, where an organism of range r_1 is compared with one of range r_2.

$$nG_{r1}^{r2} = \frac{nG_{r2}}{nG_{r1}} = \frac{n^{-r2}}{n^{-r1}} = n^{r1-r2}$$

If n is 20,000 and $(r_1 - r_2)$ is 5,000 (the values for the model in Figure 9.2 with $r_1 = 7,500$ for clonal and $r_2 = 2,500$ for non-clonal) the relative probability of mutation in the clonal organism is minute (10^{-5000}) compared with that in the non-clonal one.

As we pointed out, the requirement of continuity of a range, defined above, may not represent the condition in real organisms. For example, blocks of information may mutate together or other processes might increase the probability of viable mutations being favoured. The result will be to reduce both r and n. However, any such process can apply equally to clonal and non-clonal individuals and provided that n remains large and r is much smaller than n, the relative probabilities remain very large. It is difficult to imagine any conditions under which nG_n^{r2} will not be a very large number. To allow for the difference in mutation probabilities in the automaton, the non-clonal reproduction is permitted a relatively large mutation probability of 5 in 30 for each of the 128 generations of each run. Even if we assume nG_n^{r2} vastly increased from 10^{-5000}, no viable clonal mutations may be expected in each automaton run of 128 generations.

Figures 9.2(b) and 9.2(c) show the evolution of the clonal and non-clonal populations respectively. Both initially dip in population as the totally unviable individuals of the random initial distribution are eliminated. The clonal population then rapidly climbs to the Malthusian limit where it remains until an environment occurs outside the range of any remaining individual at which point the population becomes extinct. The non-clonal population, on the other hand, never approaches much more than 80 per cent of the Malthusian limit and frequently drops to 5 or 10 per cent of the possible maximum. It is however very robust and can survive fluctuations of environment that far exceed the capability of any individual.

Changing model parameters

The model shown in Figure 9.2 was run for particular parameters, many of which can be varied. It is beyond the scope of this chapter to show samples of all categories of change, and the main purpose is only to illustrate the broad differences between clonal and non-clonal strategies. Some remarks, however, will serve to give the reader some reason to accept later generalizations:

1   Changing the fractal dimension of the environment alters response. If the fractal dimension is increased, the amplitude of rapid change is increased relative to gradual change. Offspring are likely to confront an environment very different from their parents. Tests suggest that clonal and non-clonal strategies appear to converge on being equally ineffective for large fractal dimensions.

2   Changing the size of the range of individuals increases the length of time that the species will survive, whether by clonal or non-clonal strategies. The non-clonal population, however, always appears to do better.

3   Changing the relative range of clonal and non-clonal organisms is diffi-
    cult to experiment with, as pointed out earlier, and it was always kept
    at three.

4   Figure 9.3 shows a run with the number of offspring changed from
    ten per individual to two. Changing the number of offspring scarcely
    affects Lamarckian populations provided the number of offspring per
    individual exceeds unity by a small amount. However, for the non-
    clonal population, the behaviour changes, and two features are evident.
    First, the non-clonal population takes longer to rebuild after a collapse.
    Second, after an initial collapse, a further decline often follows. This
    appears to be associated with re-establishing a diversity of secondary
    strategies (a gene pool).

Non-clonal response as a filter

Earlier (pp. 255–7) we described filters that convert parameters of climate to
river levels or river levels to soil conditions. In the latter we noted that the

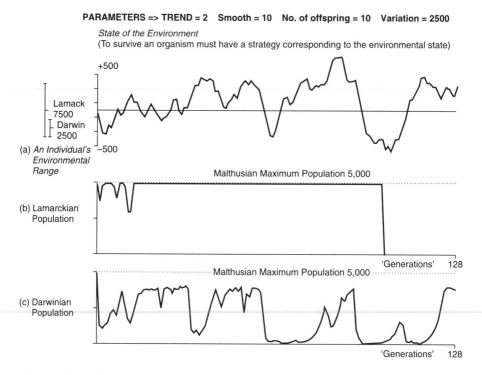

Figure 9.3   The response of Lamarckian (clonal) and Darwinian (non-clonal) populations to an environment that varies in the same fashion as Figure 9.2. The number
of offspring for each surviving individual is changed to 2. Other features are described
in the text or the caption to Figure 9.2.

effect of such a filter is to reduce the effects of environmental variation. As we also pointed out, such climatically insensitive environments have always been favoured as habitats.

The non-clonal response of the automaton can be seen as another filter. It is highly non-linear and is therefore not amenable to approximation by classical filter theory; indeed this is why the automaton approach in this chapter is needed. If we simply regard the output population as either 'there' or 'not there', the filter produces a constant output (population exists) over a wide range of inputs. In other words it is a filter that avoids going to zero. Hence a species following this strategy survives. The size of the population however, is far from stable and the ability to survive comes at the expense of an ability to optimize for any particular set of conditions.

It is also interesting to note that population and environments do not correlate in a simple way. Large drops in population are not necessarily associated with large swings in environmental conditions. A series of smaller swings can have a much greater effect. For this reason, looking at simple variations of climate (abrupt changes or steady shifts) as the cause of changes of animal or plant populations may be misleading.

In addition, catastrophic drops in population numbers or species diversity may depend on the coincidental impact of several unrelated effects. For instance, the decline in the population of the dinosaurs during the Late Cretaceous has been cited as evidence against the Cretaceous extinction being due to an extra-terrestrial event (Glen 1990). However, the models presented here suggest that mass extinctions following a comet's impact might only have occurred because the range of unexpressed strategies of some populations had been reduced by other unrelated events. This class of models might explain why some apparent impacts produce no mass extinctions. The basic point is that the 'environment' of a population will have many 'inputs' most of which will have some fractal character, and the most effective strategy to respond to this is highly non-linear. Thus, a simple cause and effect relationship between one input and its effects will not hold.

We noted earlier that fractal variations of environment can have many causes. One of these can result from chaotic variations in the population of another species due to non-linearities in its reproductive habits. It is evident that one species can use this ability to affect the environment to its advantage. For example, the periodic population explosions in locusts provide them with a means of controlling the populations of competing vertebrate herbivores by introducing time-scales of variation to which the latter are ill-suited to respond.

Implications for the evolution of human intelligence and culture

Information transfer in life started as a chemical process which finally resulted in proofreading DNA; a spectacular result that took 10^9 years to achieve.

None the less, even error rates of 10^{-9}–10^{-10} limited the effective complexity of strategies to cope with different environments and about Cretaceous times or possibly before, vertebrates developed a neurocortex which allowed the transmission of learned behaviour from parent to child (Bonner 1980). This expanded the amount of information that can be transmitted between generations. The learning process is often considerably assisted by genetic predisposition, but many vertebrates, particularly mammals and birds, fail to become viable adults in natural environments if separated from their parents. This process of transmitted behaviour, that can be modified within the range of predisposition of the animal itself, has commonly been described as Lamarckian.

It is evident, by comparison with the automaton models, that a Lamarckian strategy is far from being the most efficient in terms of conferring an ability to survive. A non-clonal strategy is much more effective. However, whereas the transmission of unexpressed strategies can be developed in a straightforward way chemically, they are much less easy to implement for learned behaviour. In effect, what is required is a genetic disposition to transmit apparently useless information to children and grandchildren plus a tenacity in doing so. We suggest that much that is referred to as 'culture' is a by-product of a mechanism that originally came into existence to do this.

Most people would agree that cultural or religious attitudes expressed by individuals or groups are not based on obvious utility in all respects. Schools of thought which attempt to find simple meaning for ritual have been mocked and similar fates have been visited on those that look for deeper psychological or structural meaning. It is recursive, however, to seek a consensus on what is useful and useless. A genetic disposition that prevents consensus is among the very properties required to transmit unexpressed information across generations. In this view, a large part of our cultural 'baggage' will be useless and there is no reason for it to be self-consistent, either superficially or to carry a consistent deeper meaning. However, meaning and utility is conveyed within the *mélange* at both superficial and more profound levels and thus attempts at explanation are not meaningless. Except in obvious cases, however, their significance is untestable. We can observe such simultaneous success and failure in grand systems of interpretation of which two obvious examples are those of Sigmund Freud dealing mainly with individuals, and Claude Lévi-Strauss dealing mainly with groups.

As an aside, it is interesting to note that the tenacity with which humans cling to systems of ideas is repeatedly illustrated by history. In complete contrast, there is little concern for genetic purity, despite political philosophies that urge their followers otherwise. Were this not true, the strong would indulge in 'pillage' alone and never indulge in 'rape'. Chemistry protects the diversity of genetic information, only human stubbornness protects similar features of culture.

Conclusions

The processes that transmit genetic and learned information between generations are very different. The Darwinian character of genetic processes has often been contrasted with the Lamarckian nature of learned behaviour. Some authors (e.g. Maynard Smith) have suggested that the non-Lamarckian nature of genetic transfer is rooted in the nature of the chemical or molecular processes involved.

In this chapter we suggest, with the aid of automaton models, that this may not be true. What we call Darwinian (non-clonal) processes of information transfer, with their paraphernalia of sex and recessive genes, are strongly selected for in a species subject to an environment that varies in a fractal fashion. When a Lamarckian (clonal) genetic strategy is simulated it is much less effective in coping with random change than a Darwinian (non-clonal) one. Darwinian processes have evolved because they confer survival advantage, not because they happen to suit chemistry (Conrad 1983).

This observation leads us to ask whether Darwinian processes have been incorporated into learned information transfer on the grounds that the versatility conferred would have a survival advantage. With the exception of humans, transmitted learning appears to be entirely Lamarckian (clonal) in character. Human culture, however, does incorporate the ability to transmit unexploited survival strategies across several generations and thus incorporates a vital element of the Darwinian (non-clonal) process.

How did this arise? The automaton modelling provides clues. Darwinian strategies are most effective at times when the environment fluctuates over times long compared to the life-span of individuals. A series of small changes with this character (or mini-catastrophes) will select for trans-generational information transfer whereas major catastrophes or gradual changes will not.

We can consequently outline, in principle, what the archaeological record might show. Art or burial ritual are examples of an outward manifestation of the transmission of information free from direct utility, and provide evidence of continuity existing beyond the individual life-span. The birth of these characteristics should accompany, or immediately follow, evidence for variations in environment that would have favoured groups of individuals that could pass successful, but unused strategies, to their great grandchildren or beyond. We may ask, for example, whether the last glacial maximum was important because conditions were extreme or because they were unstable in a fashion that favoured memory of reserve strategies.

Modern techniques of environmental reconstruction based on indicators of palaeo-climate and palaeo-vegetation permit reasoned speculation about how resources in a region were exploited. Such techniques could readily be adapted to considering the comparative stability of resources in differing geographical regions and noting their association or otherwise with the relative appearance or lack of appearance of the 'early- or pre-cultural' effects we have discussed here. For example, did conditions in higher latitudes require more complex exploitation techniques to be developed than in lower ones and hence create the conditions for culture first?

References

Bonner, J.T. 1980. *The Evolution of Culture in Animals*. New Haven: Princeton University Press.

Boyd, R. and P.J. Richerson 1985. *Culture and the Evolutionary Process*. Chicago: University of Chicago Press.

Conrad, M. 1983. *Adaptability: the significance of variability from molecule to ecosystem*. New York: Plenum Press.

Dobzhansky, T., F.J. Ayala, G.L. Stebbins and J.W. Valentine 1977. *Evolution*. San Francisco: W.H. Freeman.

Glen, W. 1990. What killed the dinosaurs? *American Scientist* 78, 354–70.

Ho, M.-W. and P.T. Saunders 1984. *Beyond Neo-Darwinism*. London: Academic Press.

King, G.C.P. and G.N. Bailey 1985. The palaeo-environment of some archaeological sites in Greece: the influence of accumulated uplift in a seismically active region. *Proceedings of the Prehistory Society* 51, 273–82.

Lindh, A.G. 1985. On the evolution of hierarchical ordered systems. *Evolutionary Theory* 7, 218–32.

Mandelbrot, B.B. 1983, *The Fractal Geometry of Nature*. San Francisco: W.H. Freeman.

Maynard Smith, J. 1989. *Evolutionary Genetics*. Oxford: Oxford University Press.

10 Why does cultural evolution proceed at a faster rate than biological evolution?

ROBERT G. REYNOLDS

Introduction

Renfrew (1981) argues that the significant steps in cultural evolution, at least subsequent to the development *of Homo sapiens sapiens*, while always operating within the framework determined by the genes, are not elucidated by considerations of the genetic code, by roles of genetic inheritance or even, to any great extent, by analysis in terms of natural selection. He suggests that cultural evolution can be described in terms of individual/group models. In this model each individual possesses a mental map, or *mappa*, that includes a memory of past events and the potential for inferring future events. These individuals *mappae* can be merged to form a collective *mappa* for the group as a whole.

Doran has investigated the evolution of social complexity using related concepts from Distributed Artificial Intelligence (1989).

The question of interest here is whether these two evolutionary activities, biological and cultural, act independently or whether there exists the possibility of some combination of influences. For instance, is it possible that the rate of cultural evolution can be enhanced by the presence of a neo-Darwinian process operating on the individuals that participate in the cultural component.

In this chapter, it is argued that the combined operation of evolutionary processes at both the genetic and cultural levels can produce a synergy that will enhance the performance of the hybrid system over that of a system in which only one of the processes is operative. In other words, the power of cultural evolutionary processes based upon symbol manipulation can potentially be enhanced or amplified if performed in concert with neo-Darwinian adaptive processes. Therefore, it is expected that cultural evolution can proceed at an accelerated rate over biological evolution due to the combination of both evolutionary processes.

In order to accomplish this goal, it is necessary to express these processes in a formal framework. The approach taken here is to view each process as a learning activity. First, the concept of autonomous learning systems is introduced. Second, the various evolutionary processes under consideration are mapped into an ALE framework. Specifically, processes associated with biological individual and group adaptations will be considered. Each of these processes is represented procedurally in the form of a machine learning algorithm. Finally, it is demonstrated theoretically that the rate of learning associated with the specific ALE will exceed that of the neo-Darwinian learning component by itself.

Autonomous learning system

An autonomous learning system (ALE) is a hybrid learning system consisting of two components. The first component, the experience generator (EG), learns to find example instances that represent hypotheses currently being investigated by the system. The second component, the knowledge base integrator (IG), learns to identify relationships that pertain to the high performance examples. These relations are stored in terms of a given knowledge representation. The two components are linked by a protocol composed of three basic phases or relations. This protocol is termed the VIP or Vote–Inherit–Promote cycle. It is through this protocol that the two learning systems interact.

At any point in time the experience generator contains a finite subset of possible examples. Each example in this subset is said to be active. The knowledge base of the integrator sub-system also contains a subset of hypothesized relationships that are currently being considered. Each relation in the subset is said to be active. At the onset of the VIP cycle the performance of each of the active examples is evaluated relative to a given performance environment. Next, the voting phase associates each active example in the EG with a subset of active relations in the IG which it represents. Metaphorically, each example is considered to be a potential vote for or against a set of active relations in the IG.

Each active hypothesis inherits the performance associated with those example instances that represent it. This can result in a modification of the overall performance of each hypothesis. The adjusted overall performance of each active hypothesis can then be used to promote the status or performance of those example instances currently supporting it.

After the VIP protocol is completed each component learning system is able to adjust its contents based upon the new information. For the EG, this corresponds to the generation of a new set of instances that will exhibit improved performance. For the IG, this corresponds to the modification of its set of active hypotheses. This process can result in the removal or modification of less productive hypotheses and the addition of new ones.

Describing cultural evolution in terms of autonomous learning systems

In order to demonstrate the symbiotic relationship that can exist between biological and cultural evolutionary processes, both processes are expressed as parts of an autonomous learning system. Biological evolution based upon neo-Darwinian principles is associated with the Experience Generator (EG) in the ALE system. It is this process that will generate individuals whose performances in a given environment can be assessed. These individuals can represent relations present in the cultural component. The cultural component is associated with the knowledge base integrator (IG) in the ALE system. The structure of the cultural component will support the individual/group model suggested by Renfrew.

In the ALE each component is viewed as a learning element in its own right. It is therefore necessary to ensure that learning can take place in both the EG and the IG component. Here, the evolutionary activities taking place in each model component are expressed in terms of machine learning algorithms that support the assumptions of that component.

Holland's Genetic Algorithm, an evolutionary learning procedure based upon neo-Darwinian principles, is used as the basis for the experience generator. In this algorithm a population of individuals is represented as a set of values. Each individual is evaluated in terms of its interaction with a given environment. The environment interaction is expressed in terms of a payoff function. Individuals in the basic model reproduce at a rate proportional to their fitness based upon the pay-off function. The genetic operators of mutation and crossover function to produce new combinations of traits in the resultant offspring. The basic algorithm is given below:

> *Procedure GA:*
> begin
> initialize population POP(0);
> evaluate POP(0):
> $t = 1$
> repeat
>   select POP(t) from POP($t - 1$);
>   recombine POP(t);
>   evaluate POP(t);
> $t = t + 1$
> until (termination condition);
> end.

A population of chromosomes are initially generated, where each chromosome is viewed as a sequence of genes. Each gene encodes a trait or traits that can be used to solve problems posed by the environment. The chromosomes are 'unfolded' to produce individuals who operate in a given performance environment. The initial population is given as POP(0), where the number in parentheses indexes the generation. Next, the initial population, POP(0), is evaluated given the performance function for a specific environment. The generation index, t, is then incremented by one. The process in the body of the 'repeat ... until' loop is iterated until particular termination conditions are met.

The iterated part consists of 'selecting' a new population of individuals for the next time-step, POP(t), based upon the performance of individuals in the previous generation. Here, individuals reproduce at a rate proportional to their fitness relative to the average for the population. Copies of each individual are made and then 'recombined' by applying the mutation and crossover transformation operators. Mutation can be applied to one or more sites on a chromosome. The result of mutation is to change the value at each site. In crossover, each of two selected chromosomes is sliced in two. The subsequences are exchanged so that the left portion of one chromosome is matched with the right portion of the other and vice versa.

The power of genetic algorithms lies in their ability to implicitly allocate an increasing number of trials to equivalence classes of structures exhibiting above average performance (Holland 1975). These equivalence classes are called schemata (Grefenstette 1987) and for structures over a binary alphabet they are expressed as a sequence of binary digits interspersed with don't care symbols, #. An example is 1101###1. Such a schema can be described in terms of its order and defining length (Grefenstette 1987). The order of a schema is the number of positions that are fixed by a 0 or a 1. In this case the order is five. The defining length of a schema, dlen, is calculated by subtracting the position indices for the left and rightmost fixed positions. Here the defining length is (8 − 1) or 7.

These properties can be used to describe the likelihood that a schema will contribute to the population in the time-step in terms of the Schema Theorem given below (Holland 1975):

$$m(H, t+1) \geq m(H, t) \; \frac{f(H)}{f} \left[1 - p_c \frac{\text{dlen}(H)}{\text{len} - 1} - p_m o(H) \right]$$

For a given schema H, the number of instances of it in the next population, $m(H, t + 1)$, will be a function of the current number of instances, its fitness relative to the average fitness of the current population, and the likelihood that its structure will be disrupted by the actions of the two genetic operators. This assumes a selection function that employs fitness proportional reproduction in conjunction with the operations of crossover and mutation.

Goldberg's (1989) summary of Holland's (1975) schema theorem stated that above-average, short, low-order schemata are the ones given increased trials in successive generations. However, during the localization phase of the search process the number of relevant schemata can be drastically reduced, and it is likely that the most relevant schemata are ones of high order and long defining length. These will certainly be the ones that have not been well sampled up to this point according to the schema theorem. This will result in a noticeable degradation of the power of genetic algorithms in this situation since, in order to keep these schemata around, the mutation and crossover probabilities may have to be reduced.

This problem results from the fact that the pool of chromosomes perform a dual function. They record not only the new candidates for search but also the system's past history for a finite population. Increasing the frequency of the genetic operators increases the number of new chromosomes in the population at the cost of modifying older, successful ones. The presence of a cultural component allows the experience of individuals to be recorded and preserved for time periods well beyond the life-span of an individual. This allows the genetic operators to remain at relatively high frequencies in the biological realm, and at the same time allows the range of knowledge and experience to extend beyond that of any given individual.

However, the burden is now placed upon the cultural system to associate the experience of individuals with hypotheses concerning the behaviour of collections or sets of individuals. Whether the various perspectives of individuals may be aggregated into a single perspective for the group remains undecided (Renfrew 1981). But if we assume that it may, then the question is how to represent and organize the knowledge associated with the group in such a way that the contributions of individual experience can be easily encoded within it. The representation selected here is supported by cognitive behaviours which seem common to all human groups. Specifically, he states that all of those cognitive behaviours unique to human groups serve to support the formation of categories based upon the properties of objects and relationships between them. For example, the use of symbols by humans allows the labelling of objects, their properties and relationships. These labellings can also be used to describe categories produced by grouping objects with similar properties. It therefore seems appropriate that the knowledge encoded in the *mappa* for an individual concerns the description of categories and their relationships.

One can view the space of possible hypotheses or categories to be considered in a search activity as a hierarchically structured lattice, where each hypothesis corresponds to a category or collection of objects or relations. The root node is the category of all objects and the leaf nodes are the individual objects. The goal of the search is to find the most general category that is associated with some given level of performance. For example, in the search space it will be assumed that leaf nodes represent singleton categories of individual objects or relations. The intermediate nodes represent potentially acceptable relations between two of the three objects. The root node is the most general category and includes all of the objects in the current range (Figure 10.1).

It is assumed that a performance function can be applied to evaluate any of the hypotheses in the graph. However, since the size of the space is the

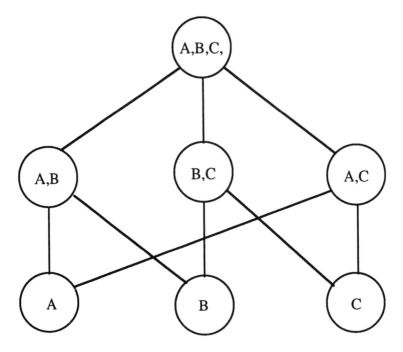

Figure 10.1 Search space. Each leaf node represents a singleton category of individual objects or relations. The intermediate nodes represent potentially acceptable
relations between two of the three objects, while the root node is the most general
category and includes all of the objects in the current range.

set of all possible combinations of objects, the power set, it is not feasible in
many cases to examine the performance of all nodes.

Because the basic performance information is easiest to come by for individual leaf nodes, it is reasonable to consider first those more general categories
that can be produced by combining successful categories at this lowest level.
In general, a parent node will be investigated if all of its constituents perform
acceptably. If, in Figure 10.1, all of the individuals associated with categories
A and B perform satisfactorily then the parent hypothesis will be investigated.
Let us assume that the parent is successful as well. In the future when two
individuals from categories A and B appear, then it can be presumed the
joint relation between them will apply. That is, a 'chunk' of the hypothesis
space (shown below) can now be stored in memory and retrieved when
needed. The storage of a collection of structures for future use as described
here is termed 'chunking' (Miller 1956) (Figure 10.2).

Ample evidence for the ubiquity of chunking as an intrinsic learning mechanism is present in the cognitive science literature. Rosenbloom and Newell
propose that chunking is the basic way by which individuals learn.

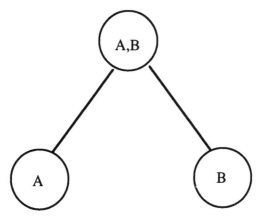

Figure 10.2 A chunk of a hypothesis space which can be stored in memory and retrieved as needed.

> The chunking hypothesis: A human acquires an organized knowledge of the environment by forming and storing expressions called chunks, that are structured collection of the chunks existing at the time of learning.
>
> (Rosenbloom and Newell 1986, p. 253)

The existence of chunks implies that memory is hierarchically structured as a lattice rooted in a set of pre-existing primitives. Work by Perlin suggests that the caching of various chunks in a hierarchical structure can be performed quite efficiently (Perlin 1991).

Since the space of possible hypotheses is large, it may be that different individuals chunk different portions of the space. In our example suppose that the experience of one individual produces the chunk (Figure 10.3(a)), the experience of another produces (Figure 10.3(b)), while that of a third individual produces (Figure 10.3(c)). These individual chunks can be merged to form the following (Figure 10.3(d)) which can be stored by each. Note that the merging of individual experience can, at times, reduce the complexity of the stored structure. This is particularly likely when the experiences are complementary in nature.

The chunking procedure as described above can be formalized as follows:

    Procedure Chunk:
    begin
      Initialize active population of chunks CPOP(0)
      $C_1(0), \ldots, CN(0)$
      Evaluate CPOP(0)
      $t = 1$
    repeat

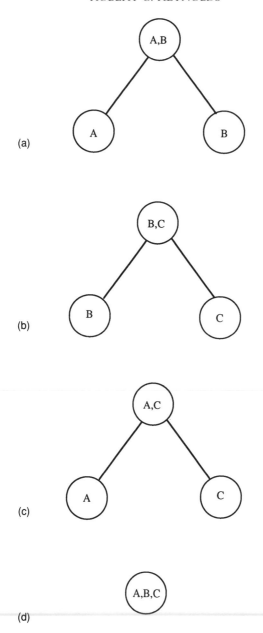

Figure 10.3 When the hypothesis space is large, it is possible that different individuals chunk different portions of it. This may lead to the following chunks (a, b, c) being held by different individuals. However, these chunks can be merged to form the chunk (d) which can be stored by each. The merging of individual experience can thus reduce the complexity of the stored structure.

Associate each active chunk in CPOP($t - 1$) with its parent chunk to produce set of parent hypotheses, CPAR($t - 1$). Evaluate ability of each unique parent in CPAR($t - 1$) to replace its children.
Generate CPOP(t) by replacing each selected child hypotheses with its parent hypothesis.
Evaluate CPOP(t)
$t = t + 1$
until (termination condition is met or root node is reached).
end

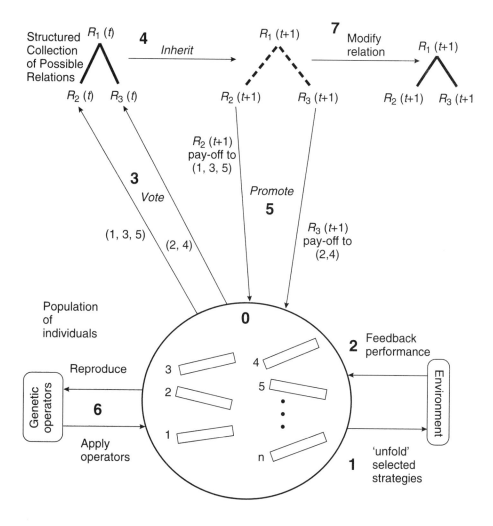

Figure 10.4 A model of cultural evolution based on chunking. For an explanation, see the text (pp. 278–9).

The process described above does not include backtracking – that is, the retraction of active hypotheses. This can occur when not all of the children for a hypothesis are examined before it is proposed, or not enough observations of each child hypothesis has been made to ensure that it meets acceptable performance standards. While such complicating scenarios can be added to this model when a specific situation warrants it, the current model is adequate for the purposes of this chapter (Figure 10.4).

This model of cultural evolution based upon chunking comprises the knowledge-base integration sub-system in the ALE here. The two sub-systems are then interconnected using the VIP protocol as shown in Figure 10.4. Each indexed step in the overall activity of the ALE will now be described.

STEP 0:   This stage corresponds to the identification of the currently active chromosomes in the population.

STEP 1:   These chromosomes are each unfolded. That is, the particular physical attributes associated with the chromosomes are identified and used to solve problems presented to the organism in its environment. This corresponds, in part, to the evaluation phase in the GA.

STEP 2:   Next, the performance information for each individual is fed back to the population. In the GA procedure given earlier, the next step would be to generate copies of individual chromosomes based upon their performance. However, in this model the performance of an individual must also be assessed in cultural terms relative to the current set of chunked hypotheses. That assessment is mediated by the VIP performance of the individuals in the cultural sphere and is then used to augment their original performance within the problem-solving environment. The number of copies of each individual will be a function of the combined pay-off from both activities.

STEP 3:   In this phase each individual in the population is associated with relations in the chunked hypothesis space for the population that they represent. The current set of active relations at time t are $R_2(t)$, and $R_3(t)$. The dashed areas are used to denote the parent, or more general, relation $R_1(t)$ that is currently not active. The cached set of relations can be stored in many forms. This collective *mappa* can be written down symbolically. Individuals can memorize portions of the collective *mappa* as part of their individual *mappa*. In practice, when an individual observes the performance of others relative to the relations currently present in that individual's portion of the collective *mappa*, the performance relative to those relations can be noted. Next, the annotated individual *mappae* are pooled to form the updated collective *mappa*. In the figure, the behaviour of individuals 1, 3 and 5 supported R_2 at time t, and the behaviour of individuals 2 and 4 supported R_3 at time t. It is possible that individuals 1 and 3 were observed by one individual relative to their portion of the collective *mappa*, and individual 5 was observed by another. The figure shown here represents the collective *mappa* produced by pooling the constituent observations.

STEP 4: In this step the observed performance for the population is associated with the relations in the collective *mappa* that they support. It is possible that there are several relational structures that comprise the collective *mappa* instead of just the one shown here.

STEP 5: The updated performance for each of the relations at the cultural level is then fed back to those individuals that support it. A given individual in the population may support several relations, and therefore get feedback for each. This is termed the 'promote' phase.

STEP 6: The reproduction phase of the genetic algorithm now commences. However, the number of copies for each individual is a function of the combined performance of that individual from the perspective of the problem-solving environment and the cultural environment. The standard genetic operators are then applied to produce a new population for the next cycle.

STEP 7: Just as the population of individuals was adjusted based upon experience, so are the collective and individual *mappae*. In this example, it is assumed that the performance of R_2 and R_3 are sufficient to allow the more general hypothesis, R_1 to become active at time $t + 1$. The new set of active hypotheses can then be chunked by individuals who comprise the group. If the set was small, then each can retain a copy. If the set was large, then individuals can each store a portion.

In the framework described above, evolutionary change is modelled explicitly at both the biological and the cultural levels. The biological model of change supports the basic neo-Darwinian view of evolution while the cultural model supports Renfrew's 'think' approach. Both approaches are operationalized in terms of specific learning paradigms. These learning paradigms are used as the basis for generating formal results about the relative and combined rates of evolution for biological and cultural processes in the next section.

How cultural evolution accelerates the evolutionary process

Van der Leeuw and McGlade stated at the symposium that:

> The ability to learn, to introduce abstractions (symbols) and to communicate distinguishes humans from other species, at least quantitatively. Humans need to operate in groups in order to survive, and their capacity to do so is contingent on symboling behaviour. Symboling allows them to co-ordinate the behaviour of groups of individuals, and it permits them to adapt quickly to changing circumstances through learning. The hierarchical nesting of symbols moreover facilitates extremely economic and flexible use of memory, as well as allowing humans to learn, and thus to accelerate learning.

In this section it is demonstrated in terms of the ALE model that, indeed, the hierarchical structuring of hypotheses serves to speed up the rate of learning relative to that associated with biological evolution alone.

It was pointed out earlier that the rate of learning associated with the genetic algorithm was reduced as search knowledge was accumulated and stored in the chromosomes. This was due to the fact that at this stage the most relevant schemata will be those of higher order and longer defining length. These are most likely to become broken up or lost as a result of applying the genetic operators. The chunking of active hypotheses in the cultural component reduces this problem in several ways:

1   The symbolic representations in the *mappa* that correspond to schema of high order and defining length are not directly accessible to modification by the genetic operators. These hypotheses are active as long as their performance remains at acceptable levels.

2   If one assumes that the criteria for acceptable performance imply use above average performance, then new parent hypotheses that are added to the active set inherit the averaged performance properties of all their above-average children. In other words, the hierarchical structure of the lattice allows the performance achievements of the child's schemata to carry over to the parent. Since, at the GA level the number of copies of a chromosome is a function of performance, and its performance is explicitly that of the active schema that it supports, this will guarantee that any new parent will initially get an above-average number of trials.

3   Also, since the hypothesis space is a directed acyclic graph, as the cultural evolutionary process proceeds and the set of active hypotheses ascends the hierarchy, the number of active hypotheses will, by definition, get smaller. This factor will also be influential in assuring that new schemata inherit an above-average number of individuals in the GA population that support it initially.

Therefore, certain hierarchical structures such as the lattice assumed here can guarantee, at least initially, that any new hypothesis will receive an above-average number of trials since it is derived from the combination of more than one above-average schema in the first place. A hypothesis space structured as a lattice in conjunction with a process for generating instances based upon neo-Darwinian principles can continually allocate an above-average number of trials to new schema. To illustrate, recall the schema theorem of Holland for individual schema given below:

$$m(H, t+1) \geq m(H, t) \frac{f(H)}{f} \left[1 - p_c \frac{\text{dlen}(H)}{\text{len} - 1} - p_m o(H) \right]$$

Any new schema, H', that derives from the combination of its children is called a hyperschema. The support for a hyperschema is the number of children from which it derived. In the case of a hypothesis that does not yield a new one in the next time-step, it will be considered as a hyperschema with a support of one – itself. Therefore, the schema theorem above can be re-expressed as a hyperschema theorem. In this case, the number of copies of a new hyperschema, H', at time $t + 1$ will be a function of those schema from which it derives. Note that in the special case where the support for a hyperschema is itself, the schema theorem results.

$$m(H', t+1) \geq \text{ave}(m(\text{support}(H', t))) \star \text{ave}(f(\text{support}(H', t))) \star 1/f \star$$

$$[1 - pc \star \text{ave}(\text{DLEN}(\text{support}(H', t))) - pm \star \text{ave}(0(\text{support}(H', t)))].$$

$$m(H', t+1) \geq \text{ave}(mS) \star \frac{\text{ave } fS}{f} [1 - pc \star \text{ave}(\text{DLEN } S) - pm \star \text{ave}(0 S)]$$

where

$$S = (\text{support}(H', t)$$

The expected number of instances in the GA population for the new hyperschema is now a function of the average number of instances of its supporting schema, their average performance, their average length, and average order. The cultural component allows the schema theorem to be extended to sets of individuals. As a result, the performance of new hyperschema will be less sensitive in general to issues of defining length and order. This will allow more complex schema to be carried along.

Conclusion

In this chapter a model of evolution consisting of both a biological component based upon neo-Darwinian principles and a cultural component based upon Renfrew's 'think' model was presented. These two theories were expressed in terms of an ALE framework and operationalized as specific learning procedures. The 'think' model was expressed in terms of the chunking approach to learning. The neo-Darwinian model was expressed in terms of genetic algorithm.

It was then demonstrated that the cultural component was able to modify the learning rate for the neo-Darwinian component as expressed in terms of the hyperschema theorem. This new rate now depended upon collections of hypotheses and their properties. As a result, the learning rate of the combined system is less sensitive to the structure of individual schema. This will allow the system to continue a high rate of learning at later stages in the evolutionary search process.

References

Doran, J.E. 1989. Distributed AI Based Modelling of the Emergence of Social Complexity. *Science and Archaeology* 31, 3–11.

Doran, J.E. 1990. A Distributed Artificial Intelligence Reading of Todorov's 'The Conquest of America'. In *Interpretation in the Humanities: perspectives from artificial intelligence*, R. Ennals and J.-C. Gardin (eds), 143–68. London: The British Library (LIR Report 71)

Goldberg, D. 1989. *Genetic Algorithms in Search, Optimization and Machine Learning.* Reading, Mass.: Addison-Wesley Inc.

Grefenstette, J. 1987. Incorporating problem specific knowledge into genetic algorithms. In *Genetic Algorithms and Simulated Annealing*, L. Davis (ed.), 42–60. Los Altos, CA: Morgan Kaufmann Publishers Inc.

Holland, J. 1975. *Adaptation in Natural and Artificial Systems.* Ann Arbor, Michigan: University of Michigan Press.

Miller, G.A. 1956. The magic number seven plus or minus two: some limits on our capacity for producing information. *Psychological Review* 63, 81–97.

Perlin, M. 1991. *Transforming Conjunctive Match into RETE: a call-graph caching approach,* Washington D.C.: Carnegie-Mellon University (Research Report, CMU-CS-91–142).

Renfrew, A.C. 1981. *Towards an Archaeology of Mind.* Cambridge: Cambridge University Press.

Renfrew, A.C. 1990. Unpublished address to the Conference

Rosenbloom, P. and A. Newell 1986. The chunking of goal hierarchies: a generalized model of practice. In *Machine Learning,* R. Michalski, J. Carbonell and T. Mitchell (eds), 2 vols., vol 2, 247–88. Los Altos, CA: Morgan Kaufmann Press.

11   *Distributed artificial intelligence and emergent social complexity*

JIM DORAN

Introduction

Several years ago (Doran 1982), I suggested that multiple agent systems (MAS) theory could form the basis of models of socio-cultural dynamics including the growth of social complexity. Since then MAS theory and distributed artificial intelligence (DAI) generally have developed substantially (Bond and Gasser 1988; Gasser and Huhns 1989; Demazeau and Muller 1990) and now the idea of studying 'societies' on computers is becoming not just tenable but fashionable – although the emphasis is as yet largely on studying the properties of systems of abstract rather than realistic agents. In spite of this limitation, it now looks possible to develop my original suggestion in a more serious way, and briefly to compare it with the more prominent alternatives.

The discussion which follows divides naturally into two parts: a discussion of (my version of) the DAI approach to socio-cultural modelling, the assumptions it makes, some of its key concepts and a typical DAI software tool; and then a description of the ongoing EOS project and the associated 'Aztec' problem, both concerned with emergent social complexity.

Objective and basic assumptions

I take the basic objective to be to understand and to explain the changes that took place in human society and culture in prehistory, especially the emergence of different types of social complexity. To help attain this objective I make the following three fundamental, and certainly controversial, assumptions:

> *Assumption 1*: Scientific modelling is appropriate. By 'scientific' I imply a serious commitment to objective, repeatable derivation of new knowledge (e.g., by formal symbolic proof or systematic experimentation). 'Modelling' implies an assumption that there really are general abstract

essentials of human societies which may objectively and usefully be identified. It also implies addressing a hard problem: to determine what levels of abstraction in the models are both tractable and sufficient to yield valuable new knowledge (Doran 1986, 1989a). It may be that simple models which ignore the particularities of belief, say, are not sufficient.

Assumption 2: Human society is influenced by distinctively human characteristics. So effective models must embody the essentials of those characteristics and be used to explore their consequences (compare Renfrew 1987, pp. 184–5, and other chapters in this book). Seemingly distinctive characteristics include cognition (internal symbolic representations, plans, structured communication, etc.), as well as emotions and their relationship to reasoning.

Assumption 3: A partly reductionist model is appropriate, where the reduction is to individuals and the interactions between them, and especially to cognition within individuals. Put another way, the assumption is that the 'driving force' behind social dynamics is located in the struggle for survival at the individual level. There are two very different reasons for taking this stance. First, the aim is to study the increase in complexity of societies which are initially at the small group level (including families and bands). So to design models in terms of higher level social concepts (for example, warfare, culture, organization) seems self-defeating. Second, models must not embody assumptions about cognition or society which are merely part of our own local culture – or we shall only 'discover' what we already believe (and what is very likely wrong). Working in terms of a small set of basic elements and their combinations is some protection against this hazard – at worst we may hope to uncover pure (as contrasted with applied) theory.

Why DAI?

DAI is about the study, in computational terms, of systems of agents and their properties. There is no agreed DAI definition of an agent as such, but a typical view is that an agent is an active entity able to perceive, reason and act. Agents programmed or programmable on a computer are typically able (albeit in very limited ways) to detect and react to their context, to communicate with one another, to accept and set themselves goals, to generate, reason about and execute plans of action in pursuit of their goals, and to maintain and update individual belief sets. Within DAI there are different approaches, notably an experimental approach using 'software testbeds' such as MCS (see pp. 288–9), MACE (Gasser *et al.* 1987), MAGES (Bouron *et al.* 1990), and CADDIE (Farhoodi *et al.* 1991), and a more formal logic-oriented approach. Here I shall only be concerned with the former.

One of the DAI concepts most relevant here is that of emergent functionality (Steels 1990). The idea is that in addition to the behaviour explicitly programmed into an agent or some system of agents, further significantly different and useful types of behaviour may arise, perhaps quite unexpectedly, as a result of interactions between the behaviours explicitly specified. This concept of 'emergent functionality' is perhaps commonplace in itself, but it is a current focus of attention in DAI research.

The DAI repertoire of concepts and techniques seems the best toolkit available to meet the socio-cultural modelling requirements set out above. It makes it possible to perform precise and repeatable computer-based experimental studies of the essentials of the relationship between structure and change at the group/society level, and the internal characteristics of individuals within the group/society. In particular it provides a way to meet the apparently conflicting requirements of Assumptions 1 and 2 above, since it is possible to combine details of individual cognition and group interactions and behaviour within the same experimental framework.

There are, however, problems in using the DAI repertoire. First, some may question whether models expressed only in the computational domain are indeed acceptable as 'scientific models' of social systems by comparison with explicitly mathematical models. However, this does not raise too many difficulties, provided that the old and long outmoded view of computers as 'number crunchers', with all its negative connotations, is firmly rejected.

Much more serious is that there is still very little in the way of established 'pure' DAI theory to be used by modellers. DAI is at the initial exploration stage with systematization still to come. The task of programming a group of agents to interact on a computer system is not easy but nor is it impossible. It is clear that there are very many possible agent designs and multiple agent combinations of which only a very few of the simplest and least powerful have as yet been worked out and tested. The regularities of interaction between agent design, task environment and macro-behaviour remain to be established.

Another difficulty with the use of DAI-based models is that most DAI practitioners are interested in gaining new theoretical insights, or in designing effective practical systems, rather than in modelling human systems with their inefficiencies and peculiarities. This is an important difference in emphasis, and can and does cause confusion. It is a problem that will, however, recede with time.

DAI in context

It is important to see the DAI approach to socio-cultural modelling in perspective, especially as it seems to cut across some established theoretical categories. For example, the ability of DAI experimental scenarios to combine representations of individual agent cognition (including individual and specific beliefs) with processes of memory and knowledge transfer, and with group interactions in a specified environment, seems to defy many of the distinctions commonly made by theorists, for example that between *Homo sociologicus* and *Homo oeconomicus* discussed by Shennan (1991).

Further, typical DAI work concerns the design and implementation of explicit processes of cognition, of communication and of (symbolically represented) knowledge manipulation, including learning. No assumptions of linearity or of optimality are made. Thus DAI systems may straightforwardly be interpreted as non-linear systems operating far from optimality. But in DAI work the focus of attention is not at all on that interpretation. Rather it is on particular behavioural trajectories at a less abstract level. The work of Huberman and his colleagues (*e.g.*, Kephart *et al.* 1989; Glance and Huberman, Chapter 5, this volume) is particularly interesting as it has a foot in both the DAI and the non-linear systems camps.

Key concepts on the DAI–social science interface

There are a number of concepts that have emerged naturally in DAI work and which seem to have important social science resonance.

In DAI there is growing recognition that agents and agent systems must be analysed by reference to the task environments to which they relate, not merely by comparison with the human example. The behaviour of agents and systems of agents is bound up with the properties of the environments in which they exist and with the problems that those environments pose. An aspect of this is the concept of the potential technology of a physical environment; that is, the repertoire of actions and action combinations beneficial (to agents) which is available in an environment. There will be an interaction between any particular process of technological discovery used by agents and the 'structure' of the potential technology itself. This interaction will, one may reasonably hypothesize, play an important role in the system dynamics.

As regards the architecture of agents, that part of an agent's internal world model (variously 'world-view', 'belief-system', 'cognized model', or 'mental map' in human terms) which is concerned with other agents in the multi-agent system may be called its social model. The design of social models is a key issue in DAI since, in an obvious way, it is the basis of an agent's reasoning as it relates to communication with and manipulation of other agents. Further, an agent's social model may embody a view of the agent system (as regards, say, groupings and sub-groupings) which may be both a simplification and a distortion of the 'reality', with major implications both for the individual agent's behaviour and for the behaviour of the system.

The origin of the simplification and possible distortion in agents' social models lies not just in an agent's possibly limited access to information (depending upon the circumstances of the particular multi-agent system), but also in straightforward computational limitations. Each agent can only do so much processing in a given time and has only so much 'memory' space. There is cognitive limitation or, in Simon's famous phrase, 'bounded rationality' (Simon 1957, pp. 198–9). In consequence there is a need for cognitive economy (Lenat *et al.* 1979) – heuristic strategies which reduce processing and memory storage requirements without too great a cost in accuracy and effectiveness. Important examples are the use of focusing techniques, aggregation and the storage of knowledge in terms of object prototypes, and the reuse of suitably generalized successful plans of action. In any substantial system (including the human system) strategies of cognitive economy are obligatory. Yet the impact of the distortions and inflexibility that they clearly imply is poorly understood. However, both Johnson (1982) and Cohen (1985) provide insightful anthropological discussions of aspects of cognitive economy.

Also important in DAI work are the notions of a contract and, more recently, commitment (Gasser 1991). In the influential CNET system of Davis and Smith (1983) a contract is an automatically negotiated agreement between two programmed agents whereby one performs a task for another. The contract net protocol is a basis for (sub)task delegation. There are a number of later developments of this basic idea. In Doran (1982) I suggested a rather different concept: 'a recurring piece of behaviour, standardised by schemata in the agents participating in it' (p. 383). Contracts in this latter sense derive partly from cognitive economy, since the schemata mentioned are executable representations of past successful behaviour and thus the product of one of the basic strategies of cognitive economy. A commitment is something a little more general and fundamental than a contract. From a DAI perspective, a commitment is something which is binding or constraining in the social world, and which, further, is integrated into the world producing a change of world-view.

A collection of commitments within a community of agents yields a type of organization. However, there are differing DAI conceptions of what organizations essentially are. A typical interpretation is that an organization is a stable pattern of relationships between agents such that the actions of the agents achieve some discernible collective goal – though this leaves open the question of just what constitutes a collective goal. It is important that an organization persists even with change of agents. Thus the relationships are really between roles, where a role is a restricted piece of behaviour which is a fixed part of the collective goal-oriented behaviour of the whole organization. Assumption 3 (above) implies that organizations and roles should emerge within socio-cultural models, not be explicitly built into them.

It is useful to distinguish between agents, and hence organizations, which are deliberative and non-deliberative. Non-deliberative agents are purely reactive without the ability to manipulate internal representations of their fellow agents and the organization of which they are a part. An insect community is a non-deliberative organization in this sense. Recent DAI work has begun to look in detail at the properties of systems of reactive agents (e.g. Steels

1990), sometimes referring to 'eco-agents' which comprise 'ecosystems'. By contrast, deliberative agents build complex representations of their social environment, and engage in cognitive activities such as predictive planning. It seems a plausible conjecture that organizations whose agents are deliberative are inherently the more flexible and adaptive.

An example of DAI software: the MCS testbed

The MCS multiple agent software testbed (Doran *et al.* 1991) has been developed as a research tool in the University of Essex Department of Computer Science. It enables an experimenter to specify and run a system of agents which seek to achieve their individual goals by (re-)acting and (multi-)planning, and by communicating with one another. Although the testbed runs on single processor machines, concurrency between the agents is simulated by a 'round robin' scheduler which gives each agent in turn a basic 'chunk' of computation.

With each agent is associated:

- its own database of 'beliefs' about its possible actions and their properties, and about other agents;
- 'demons' whose action parts execute when their condition part is matched in the agent's database;
- a unified hierarchical planning and plan execution system (IPEM – Ambros-Ingerson and Steel 1988).

A simple inter-agent interface is provided whereby actions executed by one agent, in effect, send messages to one or more other agents enabling acts of communication to be modelled.

Commonly one (or more) of the agents will be set up by the experimenter to simulate some kind of shared physical environment within which the remainder are notionally located.

The testbed provides a graphical interface which makes it possible for the experimenter to monitor and to vary the multi-agent community.

MCS runs in CProlog, NIP and Quintus Prolog on Sun-3 and Sun-4 workstations.

Using the MCS testbed

Carvajal-Sanchez-Yarza (1990) has recently enhanced MCS by structuring each agent's belief base as a dynamic frame system – SOMS. The frame system implemented allows the usual slot assignment and access operations, implements attribute inheritance, and makes the usual distinction between generic and instance frames. With slots are associated defaults, and constraints on the nature and number of possible slot fillers. The primary motivation for implementing SOMS was to study the properties and behavioural impact of agents' social models. Accordingly, in MCS-SOMS an agent possesses generic frames for agents, groups, roles and organizations, and may therefore represent information about one or more instances of any of these. This may include representation of itself, and of any groups or organizations of which it may be a part.

Working within MCS-SOMS, Carvajal-Sanchez-Yarza posed for a system of agents an abstract spatially distributed collection, production and redistribution task. He then studied the impact of cognitive limitation and cognitive economy in the agents' social models on the effectiveness with which the agents performed the collective task. Specifically, he assumed that the agents' social models contained mutually consistent representations of non-existent groupings in the agent community. Thus viewed from outside the system the agents existed 'objectively' but *not* the groups, which existed only within the agents' social models. The underlying idea was that the demands of cognitive economy commonly require agents to 'view' the set of individual agents of which they are aware in terms of a small number of groups of agents, because a few groups and their properties are much 'easier' to remember and work with than a multitude of individuals and their properties.

The further experimental assumption was made that perceived group boundaries do act as barriers in the production and distribution process. Specifically, an agent would unconditionally try to meet a simple request from (what it believed to be) a fellow member of a group, but would require a 'fair' exchange for a request coming from an 'outsider' – and this would quite possibly impede meeting the request. Thus the impact of cognitive economy was linked via a kind of 'group loyalty' to the extent to which the distributed task would be performed.

The results obtained supported (with qualification) the expectation that simplified representations of external groups save cognitive effort, but that the resulting 'perceived' boundaries impede effective co-operation (for details of these and other experiments see Carvajal-Sanchez-Yarza 1990). The anthropological significance of experiments such as these should be clear. The linkage between group performance, group boundaries and the conceptualizations of group members is a critical one – as discussed by, for example, Cohen (1985, p. 110).

The EOS project

The EOS project (*eos*, Greek 'dawn') is a collaboration between the universities of Cambridge, Essex and Surrey. In it, DAI techniques are being used to examine a model of the emergence of social complexity in the Upper Palaeolithic period in South-western France.

Mellars (1985, pp. 284–6) has put forward an outline model for the flowering of a seemingly simple hunter-gatherer society into enhanced social complexity and culture, most famous for its cave and rockshelter art, which took place during the Upper Palaeolithic period in south-western France. He suggests that particularly favourable ecological factors led to patterns of economic resources characterized by wealth and diversity of food resources, the concentration of these resources in space and at particular times of year, and long-term stability and predictability. These features in turn yielded, he suggests, a high local density of human population with large co-residential units and relatively stable patterns of settlement involving at least some degree of sedentism. In these circumstances, crowding stresses, including cognitive stress and the need for greater inter-agent co-ordination (discussed in persuasive detail by Cohen 1985, pp. 109 ff.), might well prompt the emergence of more elaborate social organization including the emergence of incipient social hierarchies or ranking systems. The trend to social elaboration would have been reinforced if the socio-cultural system were subjected to economic stress by, for example, food resources beginning to decline – as appears to have happened in this instance.

Unfortunately, although well grounded in archaeological evidence, the Mellars model is relatively imprecise when viewed from a computational perspective. There is insufficient detail for its internal consistency to be checked, nor can the effects of variations in its constituent processes be determined. Accordingly, the goals of the EOS project are (a) to give a precise computational DAI interpretation to the model and to demonstrate its feasibility and coherence at the computational DAI level, (b) to study its properties experimentally using a suitable software testbed, and (c) to relate experimental conclusions back to the processes by which social complexity emerged in the Upper Palaeolithic.

Building a DAI interpretation of the Mellars model

Translating the Mellars model into computational form is far from straightforward. Difficult decisions must be made as to which features of a human community explicitly or implicitly mentioned in the original model are to be abstracted and expressed in a computational form and exactly how this is to be done. There have been three main strands to our approach:

1   We have formulated our task as that of finding possible trajectories between complex start and end structures (within the machine) representing the corresponding forms of society. This formulation usefully invokes standard AI problem-solving techniques, but, amongst other things, requires a decision as to just what in computational terms is the end state (i.e., the 'complex' society). This is not as easy to decide as might at first appear, if only because we have cognitive processes to consider, and the same 'external' social formation may involve different 'internal' cognitive processes (Li 1991). For example, one computationally oriented

definition of (social) hierarchy is a relatively permanent arrangement of agents into successively 'higher' levels, such that the highest level has just one agent, the leader, and every agent at a lower level is 'subordinate' to some one agent in the next higher level, where agent X is 'subordinate' to agent Y if Y successfully allocates tasks to X, but not vice versa, and where an agent Y successfully allocates a task to agent X if Y passes a command or goal to X which X then attempts to execute or to achieve – which operations may involve further allocation of tasks. Task allocation may or may not involve multi-agent planning. This definition is arguably inadequate since it makes no mention of 'roles'.

2   We have simplified and abstracted structures and processes to the bare essentials (including cognitive essentials) needed to demonstrate an emergence process. Thus, we have not tried to incorporate explicit representations of birth–death processes and hence to open the possibility of expressing abstractions of the nuclear family and of kin relationships and of their place both in the behaviour of the community and in agents' social models. Such representations would make the anthropological significance of the model much more apparent and would enable us to address emergence trajectories where, as has often been suggested, the generalization by agents of kin relationships is an important factor. We have not (yet) done so because it is not clear that these representations are needed for a core emergence process to be captured.

3   We have necessarily tried to identify and make commitments to certain key processes. Our starting point has been that at the heart of the Mellars model is crowding stress, which has two aspects. First, in crowded circumstances more difficult co-operative problem-solving is required of people if they are to acquire and distribute resources effectively. Second, people must make cognitive adjustments because of the more complex social environment they experience. From a DAI point of view, then, the key feature of the Mellars model is the interaction between these two aspects of crowding stress as an emergence trajectory is followed. Our hypothesis is that the right conceptual response to crowding stress is necessary for the development of the hierarchical social formation needed to handle the resource handling problems which arise in crowded situations.

Hence, our current computational model of the emergence of a (social) hierarchy may be stated as:

1   In an initially unstructured community, 'crowding' occurs, which is interpreted to mean that (a) agents become more aware of one another, and (b) more intricate problem solving is required to meet the subsistence requirements.

2   Agents heuristically build representations of neighbouring agents and their observable interrelationships, and seek to achieve their individual goals in the light of this 'social' knowledge.

3   The positive individual pay-off associated with effective complex co-ordination leads to (a) individual agents seeking to persuade others to follow a particular co-ordination pattern, (b) conflict between particular attempts at co-ordination and (c) the emergence of repeatedly successful persuaders/co-ordinators, (i.e., 'leaders'), necessarily using 'sound' conceptualizations in their social models.

4   The process of leader emergence (steps 2 and 3) operates recursively amongst the leaders themselves as they become aware of and distinguish one another. In consequence a decision hierarchy emerges.

It is a central hypothesis that where a hierarchical organization of the agents will indeed pay off, and where the agents embody social models correctly structured in response to the cognitive stress imposed by crowding, then the multiple heuristic choices distributed over the individual agents can be so tuned that the agents and the relationships between them converge to that organization.

If we can establish and demonstrate (a range of) precise conditions under which this emergence trajectory is followed, then we shall feel that we have contributed to understanding the substance of the Mellars model. If these conditions can then be related to the archaeological evidence, then we may have something to say about the actual archaeological significance of the model.

The EOS experimental scenario

To advance with our translation of the Mellars model, and our hypothetical emergence trajectory into DAI terms, more detailed experimental scenarios are needed and some kind of software testbed in which to explore them. Again, this requires a careful choice of the essentials to be captured and the non-essentials to be omitted.

Our proposed initial experimental scenario is a system of agents in which the following are being given a precise, if abstract, computational interpretations:

1   A resource exploitation problem which requires sustained co-operation amongst the community of agents. This is relatively easy to specify by way of: a range of distinct 'spatial' localities (upon which is defined an adjacency relation), agents moving amongst these localities, and the repeated 'spontaneous' generation (by the 'environment') of resources at localities. Some resources may be 'harvested' by single agents and some only by groups. For full details of such a formulation see Doran (1989b).

2   Agent population density. Key variables are the number of agents of which each agent is aware and the degree of imposed competition between agents for the resources provided. For a fixed sensing

range and density of resources over the defined set of localities, then the more agents in the community, the greater the agent population density.

3 Agents' cognitive response to population density. As the agent population density changes so does the degree of difficulty of the collective task of acquiring and distributing resources. Further, each agent will have its own social model, structured as a class hierarchy. As population density increases and the limit of complexity (an experimental variable) for such models is approached, the agent concerned will (reactively) apply simplifying meta-actions to its model by, for example, replacing a set of descriptions of individual agents by a single class description.

4 The ability of an agent to generate and to seek to execute plans for the achievement of its own subsistence goals. In general, such a plan will rely upon the co-ordinated behaviour of neighbouring agents (as represented in the agent's social model). Implicit is the existence of some kind of contract or commitment mechanism (cf. Davis and Smith, 1983; Doran and Corcoran 1985). Also implicit is the possibility of one agent being offered several different contracts and being able to choose between them.

Key independent variables in this scenario are (a) the precise nature of the resource exploitation problem (for example, how much wide-area co-ordination is needed for optimal exploitation, and how far does the co-ordination problem lend itself to simplified representation by the agents), (b) the precise structural form of the agents' social models and the complexity limits imposed upon them (see pp. 290–2), and (c) the nature and complexity of the multi-agent plans generated by agents and their relationship to the commitments between agents.

The EOS testbed

The main features of the specialized software testbed currently being developed for the EOS project are:

• a layered object-oriented architecture embedded in the Prolog programming language;
• simulated agent concurrency;
• a standard agent architecture embodying, amongst other things, rules and procedures organized by subsumption architecture principles (see e.g. Steels 1990), implementing contract negotiation, plan manipulation, social model update, etc. as well as 'physical' actions;
• a dynamic social model implemented as a simple frame system (cf. MCS/SOMS described pp. 288–9);
• a representation of the physical environment of the agents, including agent locations and resource availability;
• a graphical interface to support experimentation.

The testbed is intended to support a variety of experiments along the lines indicated earlier (see pp. 292–3). Parts of it will be easily varied on an experimental basis, including the rules, procedures and social models embodied in agents.

Obstacles to emergence – the 'Aztec' problem

As described, the research focus of the EOS project is to elaborate emergence trajectories for social complexity relevant to the social changes that took place in the Upper Palaeolithic. The 'Aztec' problem (I shall explain the name shortly) is to identify and understand the obstacles which may impede progress along an emergence trajectory.

There are important reasons for looking at these obstacles. It is apparent even at this stage in the EOS project that the kind of emergence trajectory sketched earlier will be highly sensitive to variations in its contextual parameters. It is easy to see ways in which things may 'go wrong'. For example:

1   agents may be unable to achieve the required cognitive reorganization and elaboration of their social models as crowding develops, or
2   the specific case may be such that conflict dominates co-ordination, or
3   there may simply be failure of the environment to provide such benefits (e.g., a limit to, or some kind of plateau in, the potential technology).

Each of these possibilities will elaborate into a range of specific possible failures at the level of the detailed computational processes. An explanation of an instance of social complexity emergence may, therefore, be more a matter of explaining why the potential obstacles were avoided on this particular occasion than merely describing the actual trajectory followed.

Another, and more dramatic, failure possibility is that agents develop and transmit amongst themselves false beliefs about one another (and their shared environment) which impede the emergence trajectory. This possibility arises at stages 1 and 2 of the trajectory suggested earlier when agents are expected to acquire beliefs about other agents and their characteristics and relationships for later use in co-ordinated resource handling. Algorithms required to detect other agents and establish their properties and abilities will be heuristic and able to get things badly wrong. A sufficient degree of error must render co-ordination impossible. Systematic, hindering, but not disabling patterns of error are also possible.

The 'Aztec' problem is named for this last possibility and one seeming human instance of it. It is a commonplace that cultures (other than our own) and people (other than ourselves) systematically believe, or appear to believe, things we regard as false. For example, the Aztecs had 'the intimate conviction that time repeats itself' (Todorov 1985, p. 84; and see Doran 1990, pp. 163–4). This had practical implications. For the Aztecs, 'since time repeats itself, knowledge of the past leads to that of the future – or rather, is the same thing' (Todorov 1985, p. 84). All was determined. So the Aztecs neither sought nor found a developed theory of action in the world, rather they struggled to interpret their own records of the past and a multiplicity of perceived omens. Their characteristic question was not: 'What is to be done?' but rather: 'How are we to know?' (Todorov 1985, p. 69).

Another example, rather nearer home, is the world-view of classical and medieval scholars. In its various forms it was elaborate, coherent, persuasive, elegant and, judged from here and now, largely untrue (Lewis 1964). It also had practical impact. To take just one example, Cicero wrote that the Earth was spherical and habitable in the southern hemisphere, but that crossing the equator, the torrid zone, was quite impossible because of the deadly heat. To try, therefore, was futile – and few did. As late as 1578 the sea captain George Best found it necessary to write against the doctrine of the five Zones (Lewis 1964, p. 28) and its practical implications.

This ubiquity of 'false' social belief-systems provokes questions to which, I think, we have as yet no answers. For example, in what circumstances will a false (as distinct from incomplete) social belief-system impede or halt an emergence trajectory? In what circumstances can false (again as distinct from incomplete) belief-systems be *beneficial* either as regards the performance of resource exploitation tasks or in following an emergence trajectory? Clearly the answers to such questions as these have potential significance for the EOS project.

DAI can give a computational interpretation to such questions and potentially find some answers to them. Given a system of agents there can be a precise concept of the total set of beliefs possessed by the agents. It is therefore possible to ask and (in principle) to answer the question: what will the behaviour of the agent system be (and how effective) for each possible total set of beliefs, and what is the structure of the set of behaviours corresponding to the set of possible total sets of beliefs?

Concluding remarks

The importance of DAI computer-based socio-cultural modelling for prehistoric archaeologists is as a source of new general theory about alternative socio-cultural trajectories and the constraints and conditions which apply to them, and hence as a source of insights into specific cases. The EOS project is intended to contribute to our understanding of socio-cultural change in the Upper Palaeolithic. But, as indicated earlier, lack of developed DAI theory means that the creation of relevant theory must precede its application to this specific instance. So at this stage in the project the emphasis is on the computational structure and detail of possible emergence trajectories and of the obstacles to them – even while remaining within the bounds set by the Mellars model.

There is, I believe, no real alternative to unravelling the complexities of the possible emergence processes in full *computational* detail. Informal debate may (or may not) clarify, but proves nothing. Mathematical analysis provides general insights, and meets the need for precise incontrovertible demonstration, but is commonly at too high a level of abstraction to yield case-specific insights of the type we really need.

Acknowledgements

I gratefully acknowledge discussions with my EOS project collaborators Mike Palmer, Nigel Gilbert, and Paul Mellars. They are, however, in no way responsible for any omissions, inaccuracies or other infelicities that this chapter may contain. The EOS project is funded by the UK Joint Council Initiative in Cognitive Science/HCI by grant no. SPG8930879.

References

Ambros-Ingerson, J.A. and S. Steel 1988. Integrating planning, execution and monitoring. In *Proceedings of the 1988 Conference of the American Association for Artificial Intelligence*, St Paul, Minnesota, 83–8.

Bond, A.H. and L. Gasser 1988. *Readings in Distributed Artificial Intelligence*. San Mateo, Calif.: Morgan Kaufmann.

Bouron, T., J. Ferber and F. Samuel 1990. MAGES: a multi-agent testbed for heterogeneous agents. In *Proceedings of the Second European Workshop on Modellizing Autonomous Agents and Multi-Agent Worlds, Saint-Quentin en Yvelines, France, August 1990*, Y. Demazeau and J.-P. Muller (eds), 219–39. Amsterdam: Elsevier.

Carvajal-Sanchez-Yarza, H. 1990. A computational implementation of actors' social models using the MCS-IPEM software testbed. M. Phil. dissertation, Department of Computer Science, University of Essex.

Cohen, M.N. 1985. Prehistoric hunter-gatherers: the meaning of social complexity. In *Prehistoric Hunter-Gatherers: the emergence of cultural complexity*, T.D. Price and J.A. Brown (eds), 99–119. New York: Academic Press.

Davis, R. and R.G. Smith 1983. Negotiation as a metaphor for distributed problem-solving. *AI Journal* 20, 63–109.

Demazeau, Y. and J.-P. Muller (eds) 1990. *Decentralized Artificial Intelligence*. Amsterdam: Elsevier Science Publishers.

Doran, J.E. 1982. A computational model of socio-cultural systems and their dynamics. In *Theory and Explanation in Archaeology: the Southampton conference*, A.C. Renfrew, M.J. Rowlands and B.A. Segraves (eds), 375–88. New York: Academic Press.

Doran, J.E. 1986. A contract-structure model of socio-cultural change. In *Computer Applications in Archaeology 1986*, S. Laflin (ed.), 171–8. Birmingham: University of Birmingham Computer Centre.

Doran, J.E. 1988. Expert systems and archaeology: what lies ahead? In *Computer and Quantitative Methods in Archaeology*, C.L.N. Ruggles and S.P.Q. Rahtz (eds), 237–41. Oxford: British Archaeological Reports International Series 393.

Doran, J.E. 1989a. Distributed artificial intelligence and the modelling of socio-cultural systems. In *Intelligent Systems in a Human Context*, L. Murray and J. Richardson (eds), 71–91. Oxford: Oxford University Press.

Doran, J.E. 1989b. Distributed AI based modelling of the emergence of social complexity. *Science and Archaeology* 31, 3–11.

Doran, J.E. 1990. A distributed artificial intelligence reading of Todorov's 'The Conquest of America'. In *Interpretation in the Humanities: perspectives from artificial intelligence*, R. Ennals and J.-C. Gardin (eds), 143–68. London: The British Library (LIR Report 71).

Doran, J.E. and G. Corcoran 1985. A computational model of production exchange and trade. In *To Pattern the Past*, A. Voorrips and S. Loving (eds). *PACT* (Journal of the European Study Group on Physical, Chemical and Mathematical Techniques Applied to Archaeology, Special Issue) 11, 349–59.

Doran, J.E., H. Carvajal-Sanchez-Yarza, Y.J. Choo and Y. Li 1991. The MCS multi-agent testbed: developments and experiments. In *Co-operating Knowledge Based Systems 1990: Proceedings of the International Working Conference on Co-operating Knowledge Based Systems, University of Keele, October 1990*, S.M. Deen (ed.), 240–51. Berlin: Springer-Verlag.

Farhoodi, F., J. Proffitt, P. Woodman and A. Tunnicliffe 1991. An approach to the modelling of functional organization. In *Proceedings of the 10th UK Planning SIG Workshop*, Cambridge, April 1991. Cambridge: Logica Cambridge.

Gasser, L. 1991. Social conceptions of knowledge and action. *Artificial Intelligence Journal* 47, 107–38

Gasser, L. and M.N. Huhns 1989. *Distributed Artificial Intelligence*, Vol. 2. London: Morgan Kaufmann and Pitman.

Gasser, L., C. Braganza and N. Herman 1987. MACE: a flexible testbed for distributed AI research. In *Distributed Artificial Intelligence*, L. Gasser and M.N. Huhns (eds), Vol. 1, 119–52. London: Pitman and Morgan Kaufmann.

Johnson, G.A. 1982. Organizational structure and scalar stress. In *Theory and Explanation in Archaeology: the Southampton conference*, A.C. Renfrew, M.J. Rowlands and B.A. Segraves (eds), 389–421. New York: Academic Press.

Kephart, J.O., T. Hogg and B.A. Huberman 1989. Dynamics of computational ecosystems: implications for DAI. In *Distributed Artificial Intelligence,* Vol. 2, L. Gasser and M. N. Huhns (eds), 210–21. London: Morgan Kaufmann and Pitman.

Lenat, D.B., F. Hayes-Roth and P. Klahr 1979. Cognitive economy. In *Proceedings of the Sixth International Joint Conference on Artificial Intelligence, Tokyo*, 531–6. New York: William Kaufmann.

Lewis, C.S. 1964. *The Discarded Image*. Cambridge: Cambridge University Press.

Li, Y. 1991. M.Sc. Dissertation, Department of Computer Science, University of Essex, Colchester, UK.

Mellars, P.A. 1985. The ecological basis of social complexity in the Upper Palaeolithic of south-western France. In *Prehistoric Hunter-Gatherers: the emergence of cultural complexity*, T.D. Price and J.A. Brown (eds), 271–97. New York: Academic Press.

Renfrew, A.C. 1987. Problems in the modelling of socio-cultural systems. *European Journal of Operational Research* 30, 179–92.

Shennan, S.J. 1991. Tradition, rationality and cultural transmission. In *Processual and Postprocessual Archaeologies: multiple ways of knowing the past,* R.W. Preucel (ed.), 193–210. Carbondale: Centre for Archaeological Investigation, University of Southern Illinois.

Simon, H.A. 1957. *Models of Man*. New York: John Wiley.

Steels, L. 1990. Co-operation between distributed agents through self-organization. In *Decentralized Artificial Intelligence*, Y. Demazeau and J.-P. Muller (eds), 41–56. Amsterdam: Elsevier Science Publishers.

Todorov, T. 1985. *The Conquest of America* (trans.: Richard Howard). New York: Harper and Row.

12 The limits of social control: coherence and chaos in a prestige-goods economy

JAMES MCGLADE

> A form of reproduction is one in which social institutional properties are imprinted on the production–distribution cycle in a way that necessarily defines a dynamic system, i.e. one whose properties can only be expressed as a function of time.
>
> (Friedman and Rowlands 1977, p. 267)

Introduction

In recent years, what has come to be known as the archaeology of power has assumed a high profile in the construction of theories of socio-cultural change (e.g. Miller and Tilley 1984; Bradley 1984). Largely a consequence of the adoption of structural-Marxist approaches, it has promoted a renewed interest in the role of ideology as a legitimating instrument in the promotion and enforcement of social control. Not surprisingly, the asymmetrical dimensions of power and the way in which it promotes unequal access to goods and resources have been primary concerns.

Benton's (1981, p. 176) definitional distinction separating *'power over'* from *'power to'*, provides us with a distinction conforming to the *enabling* and *constraining* factors in social relations. Here, 'power to' denotes a capacity to alter and affect the social conditions within which people operate, and 'power over' represents the means by which social control is exercized (Miller and Tilley 1984, p. 7).

For the purposes of the present discussion, we are interested in the dynamics which articulate the essence of 'power over', and are manifest in prestige goods exchange systems. Since there is provocative archaeological evidence from the Bronze Age in Wessex which is suggestive of a degree of authoritarian control, we shall consider Wessex as a case study — certainly the Early Bronze Age provides abundant evidence of unequal access to prestige items and indicates their possession by a relatively small proportion of the population. Nevertheless, we shall not dwell on the finer details of the archaeological record – our point is a more general one. It will be argued here that the structures upon which social control is founded and the circumstances within which it is exercised, comprise a dynamic that is at once highly contextual and yet possesses attributes which, at a larger scale, can be seen to have generic properties.

This stress on the general aspects of the argument finds its justification in the fact that the dominant theoretical discourse within the discipline assiduously avoids discussion on the possible contribution of 'supra-individual' structures operating within societal systems (e.g. Shanks and Tilley 1987). In effect a new voluntarism has crept in; the new critical awakening ushered in by the post-modern agenda, while generating important insights, may yet be responsible for creating something of a theoretical cul-de-sac as it has been pursued at the expense of *generality* – some of the variability resident in human social systems may conceal underlying structural similarities.

The possibility of the emergence of structural coherence over the long-term, and hence its reinsertion into theoretical discourse, is thus the principal concern of our discussion, more especially in its relationship to the processes of exchange. We will try to develop a formal analytical approach to questions such as:

1   Are exchange systems stable?
2   Are the non-linearities resident in such systems amenable to formal modelling procedures?
3   How are the dynamics of exchange related to the larger issues of social control?

Prehistoric exchange systems

Studies of prehistoric exchange have proliferated over the past two decades (e.g. Earle and Ericson 1977; Ericson and Earle 1982). Much of this discussion has been carried out under an economic rationale, within which the processes of trade and exchange are seen as manifestations of a distinct sub-system within society. A prominent orientation of this research has been concerned with the classification of exchange mechanisms such that they may be reduced to one of two theoretical approaches – Formalist or Substantivist. These approximate respectively a rational, analytical explanatory paradigm in contradistinction to a contextual one in which the economy is seen to be embedded in social relations. This is by now a rather well-worn debate, in which the weakness of both positions lies in their inability to treat the symbolic and ideological dimensions of exchange (cf. van der Leeuw 1994).

An exception to these limitations is Frankenstein and Rowlands' (1978) analysis of Bronze Age European society in which exchange relations are placed within a structured set of social and political relations, and within which the symbolism of artefacts is used in the legitimation of authority.

This seems to be a more apposite approach to the rise of hierarchical societies, where exchange systems assumed an asymmetrical form, being focused around powerful individuals who emerged as the controlling forces in the accumulation and exchange of scarce and/or luxury commodities. Renfrew (1973, 1979) has argued that just such a process characterizes the situation in EBA Wessex with the emergence of territorial chiefdoms. While it may be premature to describe the flows of tribute and exchange in Wessex as being controlled by distinct chiefdoms, it is reasonable to assume that a great deal of this type of pre-market exchange was co-ordinated by predominant individuals or those who for various reasons had assumed the function of 'tribal banker' – either as a short-term, opportunist measure or on a more permanent basis.

Clearly, once a system of control by a few individuals is established it effectively undermines the principles of reciprocity which had, we shall assume, previously dominated the process of gift exchange; it introduced an entirely new set of asymmetries in social relations as powerful individuals could manipulate exchange, not to achieve any reciprocal balance, but for purely personal advantage. The role of 'tribal banker' was henceforth transformed so as to assume a position of superiority. What was gathered in from kinsmen became tribute, and thus came to signify higher status. Additionally, once this shift was embedded within the regional economy, it became prone to the increasing consumptive demands of ambitious individuals seeking the ultimate prestigious office of clan or tribal chief. In discussing the structure of the highland clan systems of Scotland, Dodgshon captures something of a process whose generic properties may shed light on the situation in later prehistoric Wessex:

> What kinsmen gave up as tribute was used to maintain the ceremonial feasting of the tribe, feasting in which the chief played a central role: to support a tribal reserve of food under the chief's direct control, and to support the production of 'prestige' goods for the chief's own use or distribution.
>
> (Dodgshon 1987, p. 27)

But there is yet another dimension missing from this discussion of exchange. These ideas can usefully be cast within a dynamical systems context, in which exchange processes are seen to *possess evolutionary potential*. In the introduction to this volume it has been argued that intrinsic self-reinforcing strategies, which often contain unstable dynamics, are present in most social processes. As a consequence, we might legitimately ask:

1 Are complex dynamics an intrinsic part of the production and distribution of prestige goods economies?
2 Are these dynamics in this case structurally stable or not?

These issues require more rigorous study and much of the remainder of this chapter is geared towards contributing to their understanding.

Prestige-goods economies

Archaeological research in Wessex over the past two decades has suggested that the groups of people who inhabited the Late Bronze Age and Iron Age landscape were united by kin (and other) ties which found expression in the circulation and exchange of highly prized commodities. Some authors (e.g. Friedman and Rowlands 1977, pp. 224 ff.) have gone further, arguing that the political advantage to be accrued by controlling the flow of such resources could be converted into control over labour and production. Further, the central importance of these prestige exchange networks in maintaining elite groups was paramount; their decline (e.g. Wessex II) is coeval with the disruption of the long-distance trading arteries between southern Britain and continental Europe.

By the Late Bronze Age the focus of wealth had shifted from the Wessex downland to the Thames valley. Thus social change is said to be a consequence of the disruption of trade links which had sustained the pre-eminence of Wessex. The conventional argument is that not even the reorganization of the subsistence economy – manifest in the massive landscape alterations demonstrated by elaborate field-systems and linear ditches – could stem the tide of decline. Bradley (1980, p. 72; 1984, pp. 114–27) has speculated on two alternative explanations. One, suggesting that the superior agricultural potential of the Thames valley attracted upland populations, particularly as there is evidence of soil exhaustion on the Wessex chalk; and two, arguing that there existed a vigorous bronze industry which ensured the survival of certain groups as long as there was a demand for their products. But whatever the ultimate cause or causes of the later prehistoric transformations within Wessex, clearly a major element of its temporary pre-eminence involved the operation of a prestige-goods economy.

From the dynamical systems perspective which we have chosen for the purposes of this chapter, the behaviour of a prestige-goods system presents an interesting analytical problem since it comprises a number of non-linear connections linking the supply of goods to both a perceived demand and a created demand – i.e., one stimulated by those controlling the flow of products or weapons.

The distinction between two modes of exchange, i.e., a local domestic sphere and a regional or long-distance prestige sphere, is a first prerequisite in understanding exchange dynamics. The importance of the latter sphere in questions of social dynamics has been discussed at length by Ekholm (1972), Friedman and Rowlands (1977) and Frankenstein and Rowlands (1978). These studies are essentially based on Marcel Mauss's work (1954), which focused on the relationship that exists between the material transfer of objects and social hierarchy.

Anthropologists such as Meillassoux (1972) have been very influential in showing how in lineage societies, where no privileged group has control over land or the means of production, the elders exercise their control by supplying the prestige goods needed by their juniors on critical occasions such as initiation, marriage or other social or cultural rites of passage. Ekholm's work in central Africa, for example (1972, 1977), demonstrates that power relationships are established, consolidated and maintained through the control of prestige articles – products not necessary for survival in everyday life, but essential in the maintenance of social relations. All individuals need prestige articles at a number of critical junctures in life, otherwise their access to social and political advancement is severely impeded.

One of the inherent dangers in such a 'prestige-goods' system is that the number of special purpose items in circulation may increase until they threaten to spread into the general economy; they thus forfeit their exclusivity (Meillassoux 1972, p. 92). Should this occur, they need to be taken out of circulation, for example by hoarding, offering to the gods, destruction or burial. As Bradley (1984, p. 103) has pointed out, this places a great deal of emphasis on the social dimensions of different artefacts within different exchange modes.

The main thrust of these ideas has been picked up by Frankenstein and Rowlands (1978) in their model of Late Bronze Age European society. Based on the reconstruction of alliance systems as suggested by Indo-European kinship terms, they propose that the movement of fine metalwork, cattle, women and other items, was linked to a wider European system in which exchange was an intrinsic element in a process of social competition:

> relations of dominance and hierarchy depend directly on the manipulation of relations of circulation and exchange and not on control of production per se. But circulation and exchange cannot be separated from the production of surpluses needed for such transactions and hence the resources required to produce them ... Since alliances are established through exchange involving material goods, women and symbolic knowledge, success depends on maintaining the flows of these resources.
>
> (Frankenstein and Rowlands 1978, pp. 76–7)

Modelling exchange processes

There is some consensus on the fact that, generally speaking, since the majority of prehistoric non-market exchange systems are based on status as opposed to wealth, they tend to be regulated by reciprocity – i.e., by forms of altruistic gift-giving and balanced exchange (Sahlins 1972, p. 206). Breakdown in these systems is argued to be the result of individual failure to meet primary obligations. While a plethora of ethnographic examples can be amassed to support these contentions, it is argued here that they tend to ignore a fundamental property which characterizes exchange economics; that is their inherent instability.

Exchange systems can generate a dynamic which in many ways is unperturbed by, and often independent of, the vagaries of individual transactions; moreover, the non-linearities which form the core of the transactional processes structuring exchange systems can induce complex and potentially chaotic behaviours. Importantly, the chaotic behaviour of these transactional processes may ultimately have a deterministic origin, as opposed to being the result of exogenous stochastic influence or fluctuation. In order to demonstrate this, the remainder of this chapter will concern itself with a number of modelling experiments, designed to uncover the less obvious, fugitive proccesses at work in the dynamical behaviour of exchange systems.

For our present purposes, clearly we cannot hope to conceptualize the totality of a prestige goods economy – particularly a prehistoric one – nor are we concerned with debates relating to the 'meaning' of exchange or the relationship between exchange and concepts of social distance. Critically important though they are, they belong to another level of analysis which must logically succeed the primary investigations advocated here. What we are involved with is a search for the underlying qualitative dynamics – in essence the intrinsic structural properties which are involved both in the structuring of social relations and the flow of goods. In effect, since these non-linear relationships are not only complex, but are largely inaccessible and/or imperceptible by conventional descriptive means, they present themselves as appropriate subjects for formal mathematical treatment. It is here that formal description comes into its own since it provides a useful language with which to explore a variety of temporal scales. It promotes, not reductionism, but a process of disaggregation which in turn facilitates new levels of description.

In effect, we will initiate a series of interactive scenarios from which we might usefully focus on the internal dynamics of exchange; thus our task becomes one of isolating a number of generic behaviours which individually and in concert act to co-ordinate transactional processes. Since these exist on a continuous trajectory, obviously we must be content with analytical snapshots. However, it is possible to collapse a sequence of these and map them onto a dynamical phase space, so that microscopic behavioural events may be studied in some detail.

On the basis of a set of idealized behaviours generated by our models, we can then return to the data and pose new questions relating to the kinds of asymmetries, contradictions or distortions affecting the flow of transactions. Essentially we can set up exploratory models, not in any attempt to trap a single 'correct' set of relationships – there are none – but to encounter as many degrees of variability as can be extracted from the qualitative dynamics driving the system.

Production dynamics

Our first investigation is into some aspects of the production of bronze metalwork, which constitutes one of the key processes at work in Late Bronze

Age Wessex. Rowlands (1980, p. 35) has postulated that long-distance trade was co-ordinated by coastal and riverine settlements, and that these sites held pre-eminence over their downland counterparts. In dealing with metalwork production, he asserts that the relative uniformity of the weapon types supports the notion of control of production being in the hands of elites who co-ordinated and manipulated extensive socio-political groups and large-scale alliance networks. In that context, we can think of the downland and riverine settlements as being involved in a symbiotic relationship, such that the lowland area's ability to foster industrial activities and to take part in long-distance exchange was facilitated by the provision of cattle, sheep and other commodities from the chalklands.

It is worth reiterating that we must not fall into the trap of characterizing such a system as a purely 'economic' phenomenon, for the emphasis here on the production and exchange of weaponry must be set within a wider compass, in which the 'weapon complex' is characteristically associated with the negotiation and formation of political alliances. Irrespective of the particular contextual attributes which operate at a 'local' level in such systems of exchange, there is yet the possibility of uncovering macroscopic properties encoded in the 'global' behaviour of the system.

In order to elucidate the global properties of just such a 'weapon complex', our model examines the expansions and contractions in the production sector of a generic prestige goods system, as it adjusts to fluctuations in the desire for a particular artefact. This may, for example be the result of changing value systems, or the competition produced by the presence of alternative status-enhancing goods. Figure 12.1 shows a flow diagram outlining a reduced description of the fundamental dynamical relationships. The existence of a self-reinforcing mechanism in the prestige goods sector, i.e., the positive feedback associated with the dependence of the prestige goods system on its own output for an expansion of its production capacity, causes the model to be unstable. Additionally the model is, under far from equilibrium conditions, confined by non-linearities. For example, one such non-linearity arises from an assumed saturation of the status value as the production of prestige items reaches an excessive level, thereby destroying their 'value'.

The structural properties of our model are based on work by Sterman (1985) and Rasmussen et al. (1985) on the Kondratieff long-wave cycle. Our starting point involves the interaction and interdependence of two state variables:

1 PRESTIGE GOODS: representing the accumulation process – for reasons of simplicity we have no interest in the means of accumulation;
2 DEMAND: that is, realized demand as opposed to potential demand, which is dealt with as a separate parameter.

The more important linkages articulating model dynamics can be summarized. For example, PRESTIGE GOODS, *PG*, divided by the prestige goods

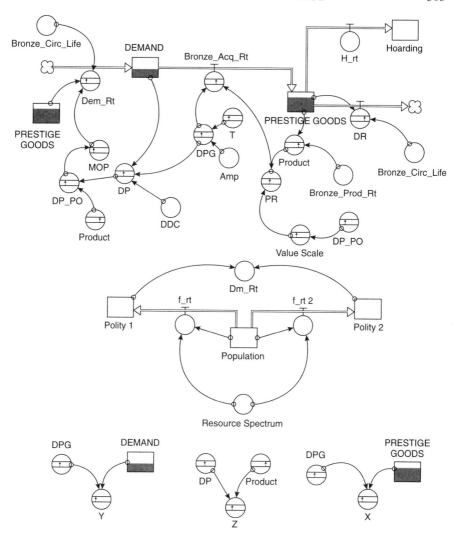

Figure 12.1 Flow diagram of the basic model relationships that induce self-reinforcing (positive feedback) mechanisms in a prestige production economy.

output ratio, *POR*, gives us the potential output, *PO*, and along with a non-linear function representing a prestige 'value' scale, *PVS*, we can calculate the actual production rate of luxury goods, *PR*. If *DPG* equals *PO* then we assume that the prestige value (*PVS*) reaches a maximum value of 1. For the purpose of analytical simplicity, we shall initially consider the desired production of goods, *DPG*, to be constant. By subtracting *DPG* from the total production rate *PR*, we obtain the rate of bronze production which is equal to the bronze acquisition rate *BAR*.

The flow of new status-enhancing commodities or gifts automatically reduces the demand for existing items in the current prestige sphere. For simplicity, the prestige goods are accorded an average circulation lifetime, *ACL*, approximately equal to one human generation – this can of course be modified later to account for the fact that many status objects are 'curated' for future kin members, or are alternatively removed from circulation as hoards. Additionally, the model includes a demand rate, *DR*, which is calculated as a function of discarded or hoarded weaponry, modified by a multiplier factor from desired production, *MDP*. The multiplier assumes that the rate of demand for prestige items equals the depreciation rate of the prestige items when desired production corresponds to the potential output of bronze goods. In the event that the desired production exceeds potential output, then *MDP* increases rapidly to a saturation threshold. The final part of this feedback process involves the determination of desired production, *DP*, as comprising the desired production of bronze artefacts, *DPG*, plus the desired production of raw material for metalworking. This 'production capital' is calculated as the demand for prestige goods divided by a factor *AD*, to account for an acquisition delay in the procurement of prestige items.

The above relationships can now be collapsed into two non-linear coupled first order differential equations which account for the interaction and dynamical evolution of our two state variables, PRESTIGE GOODS and DEMAND. We have,

$$\frac{dPG}{dt} = \frac{PG}{POR.PVS}\left\{\frac{DP}{PO}\right\}DPG - \frac{PG}{ACL} \tag{12.1}$$

$$\frac{dD}{dt} = \frac{PG}{ACL.MDP}\left\{\frac{DP}{PO}\right\} - \frac{PG}{POR.PVS}\left\{\frac{DP}{PO}\right\} + DPG \tag{12.2}$$

The statements $PVS\{DP/PO\}$ and $MDP\{DP/PO\}$, are graphical functions in which the independent variable can be expressed as

$$\frac{DP}{PO} = \frac{D/AD + DPG}{PG/POR} \tag{12.3}$$

For mathematical simplicity we can now substitute, thus:

$$\frac{dX}{dt} = \frac{X}{-\lambda - X/r} \tag{12.1a}$$

$$\frac{dY}{dt} = \frac{X}{r\omega(\mu/\nu)\,X/\alpha\beta(\mu/\nu) + \lambda} \tag{12.2a}$$

where, X = prestige goods;
$\quad\quad\quad Y$ = demand;
$\quad\quad\quad \alpha$ = prestige goods production ratio;
$\quad\quad\quad \beta$ = prestige value scale;
$\quad\quad\quad \mu$ = desired production;
$\quad\quad\quad \nu$ = potential output;
$\quad\quad\quad \lambda$ = desired production of prestige items;

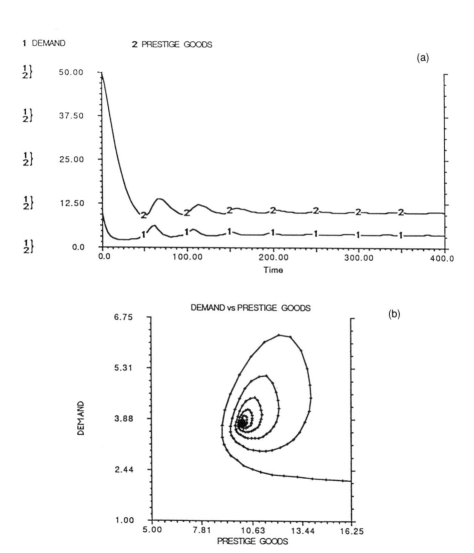

Figure 12.2 Simulation results for base parameters of the basic model showing, in (a), damped oscillations. The point attractor to which the system converges is clearly seen in the accompanying phase plot (b).

r = intrinsic rate of depreciation;
$\bar{\omega}$ = multiplier function;
ρ = acquisition delay.

The simulation of the above system reveals a number of interesting properties. Figure 12.2(a) shows the time evolution of the two state variables prestige goods and demand, and reveals the effects of self-reinforcing or

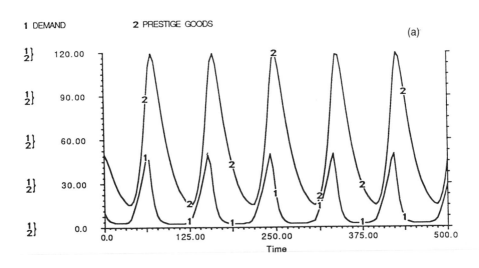

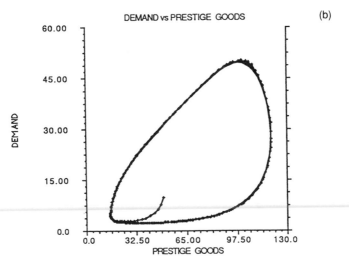

Figure 12.3 Simulation results showing (a) the time evolution of our production system as conforming to a stable limit cycle, and (b) a phase plot of the same initial conditions showing the co-evolution of the two main state variables, PRESTIGE GOODS and DEMAND.

positive feedback properties. For the base parameters chosen, the model exhibits the damped oscillations we see in Figures 12.2(a) and 12.2(b); that is, after initial periodic behaviour the system settles down to converge on a *point attractor*. Within these conditions the exchange system can be referred to as structurally stable. However, if the prestige goods output ratio (*POR*) is increased, it produces the stable limit cycle behaviour we see in Figures 12.3(a) and 12.3(b). This stable oscillatory or periodic behaviour defines an attracting set to which the exchange system is driven and within which it retains a measure of predictability. This attractor may be thought of as a region in a multi-dimensional phase space to which the system is driven.

We can visualize this more clearly by looking at a phase portrait of our system as is represented in Figure 12.3(b). This plot, which shows the co-evolution of Prestige Goods and Demand, can be thought of as representing a series of points – each one containing the complete history of the system at that time-step. Thus the evolutionary trajectory of the system can be mapped, its orbit through phase space being captured by a geometric representation. What we see from the figure is that after an initial 'start up' transient, the behaviour settles down so as to conform to a periodic cyclical motion.

However, given the complexity of the interactions operating in our prestige goods economy, this idealized state has a low probability of occurrence. It is quite clear, for example, that factors controlling the desired production of goods are highly variable, since they must reflect both socio-political dynamics as well as changes in the supply of raw materials for artefact production. For these reasons, *DPG* is more accurately expressed as a fluctuating parameter.

To incorporate these ideas, we shall introduce a sinusoidal variation in *DPG* thus:

$$DPG = 1 + \delta \star \cos(2\pi \star \text{TIME} / \phi) \qquad (12.4)$$

where ϕ is the time-span during which the fluctuation occurs and δ is the strength of the disturbance.

Thus we can consider, for example, the effects of variability in the desire to possess particular bronze items; the type of periodic disturbance in the rate of acquisition, for whatever reason, is clearly an important factor in understanding the structure of any prestige exchange economy. Since the long-term effects of fluctuations in desired production are inherently non-linear, we might reasonably expect complex behaviours to manifest themselves.

This is precisely what is apparent from Figures 12.4 and 12.5, as they demonstrate the results of periodic perturbations in the desired production of goods. Significantly, we see that the attractor to which the system is drawn is no longer that of the simple periodic motion described by a limit cycle. Figure 12.6 presents us with a complex situation which at first seems to possess the characteristics of a chaotic trajectory. In fact it is not a chaotic attractor, but another type of attractor known as a 'torus'. This type of

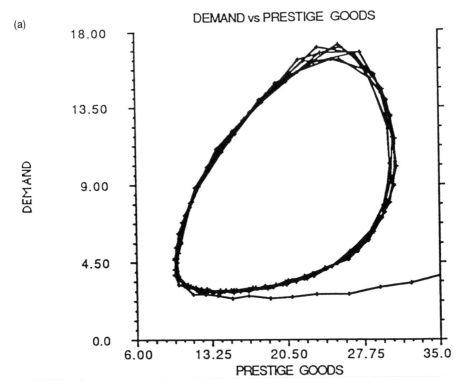

(a)

Figure 12.4 Simulation results showing 'noisy' limit cycle behaviour as a result of a sinusoidal variation in *DPG*, for increasing values of the parameter δ, which accounts for the strength of the disturbance.

attractor generally evolves in systems which are quasi-periodic, often possessing time-series which seem to mimic chaos. A close inspection of the time-series in Figure 12.5 reveals that we have a periodic motion modulated by a second motion, itself periodic, but operating at another frequency. Collectively, these conspire to produce a system which, though extremely complex, yet retains a high degree of *predictability*. We shall now examine ways in which the irregularity and unpredictability characteristic of chaotic motion can arise.

Delayed regulation and chaos

The non-linear attributes of our simple production system imply that, as well as being susceptible to qualitative change generated by self-reinforcing mechanisms, it is also prey to complexities which arise as a consequence of the existence of delays; that is, situations in which the flow of goods is subject to production delays or the delay involved when demand for prestige bronze artefacts exceeds their immediate availability. Such situations are common in

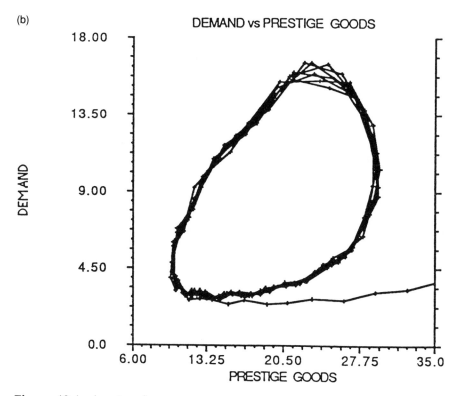

Figure 12.4 (continued)

modern economic systems and it is clear that delayed regulation is respon-sible for the 'boom and bust cycles' which characterize the structure of modern market economies. A convenient method of studying these processes is by means of differential delay equations, the most common of which is the 'time delayed logistic' model,

$$\frac{dN}{dt} = rN(t) \left[1 - \frac{N(t-T)}{K} \right] \tag{12.5}$$

This equation and its variants (e.g., Mackey and Glass 1977; May 1980) have been extensively studied within the realms of population dynamics and have contributed enormously to our understanding of the behaviour of eco-systems generally (Maynard Smith 1974; May 1974).

More recently, Chen (1988) has extended this work, constructing a delayed feedback model of economic growth, which is worth discussing in our present context since it presents a situation that is sufficiently generic to contribute to our understanding of patterns of growth in the types of

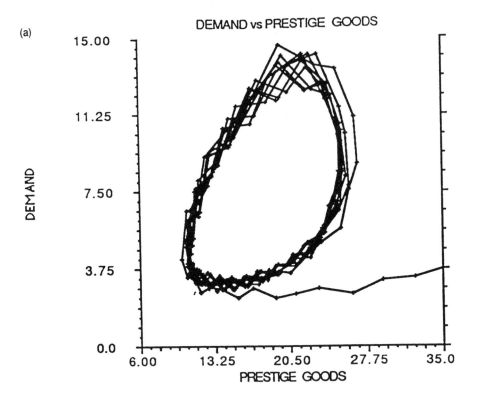

(a) DEMAND vs PRESTIGE GOODS

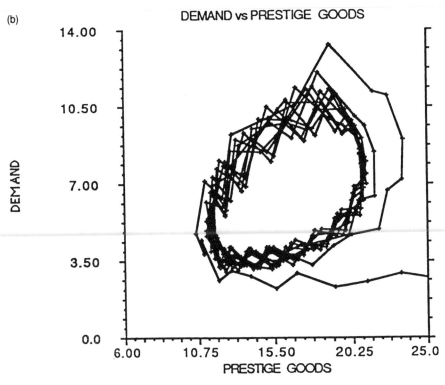

(b) DEMAND vs PRESTIGE GOODS

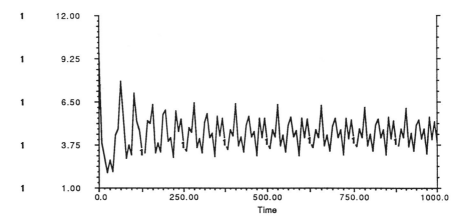

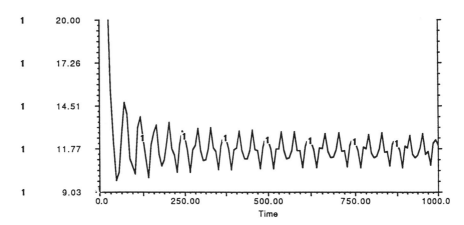

Figure 12.5 (a), (b) Simulation results showing 'noisy' limit cycle behaviour as a result of a sinusoidal variation in *DPG*, for increasing values of the parameter δ, which accounts for the strength of the disturbance. These figures represent a transition from limit cycle behaviour (a) to a more complex type of periodicity (b). (c), (d) Time-series plots of Figure 12.5(a) and (b), showing the complex periodicity structuring the economic system.

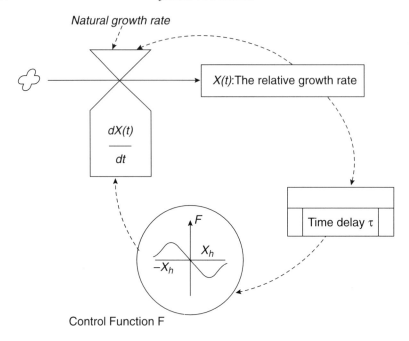

Natural growth rate

X(t):The relative growth rate

$\dfrac{dX(t)}{dt}$

Time delay τ

Control Function F

Figure 12.6 Flow diagram illustrating the dynamics of the simple time-delay structure appropriate to our prestige production model.

non-market economies operating in Late Bronze Age Wessex. Thus, the following equations may be profitably added to the growth sector in our Prestige Production model:

$$\frac{dX}{dt} = aX(t) + F(X(t - T)) \tag{12.6}$$

$$F(X) = X.G(X) \tag{12.7}$$

where X can be thought of as a relative growth function; T is the time delay; a is the rate of expansion; F is the control function; and G is the feedback function. The first term on the right-hand side of Equation 12.6 represents an exponential growth function acting as a response to demand for prestige items. The second term, F, acts as a controlling mechanism, and accounts for system feedback; that is $X(t - T)$ is the feedback signal and G is the feedback function. The precise form that G takes is essentially exponential:

$$G(X) = -\beta \exp(-X^2 \phi^2) \tag{12.8}$$

where β is the control parameter and ϕ is the scaling parameter. Finally, the presence of the time delay, T, in the loop is able to deal with information lags and their effect on the production cycle. These relationships can be more readily understood from the flow diagram presented in Figure 12.6.

We can now substitute Equations 12.7 and 12.8 into Equation 12.6, so as to arrive at the differential delay equation;

$$\frac{dX(t)}{dt} = \alpha X(t) - \beta X(t - T) \exp\left(\frac{-X(t-T)}{\phi^2}\right) \tag{12.9}$$

If we change the scale by $X = X'\phi$ and $t = t'T$, and next drop the prime terms for convenience, we have;

$$\frac{dX(t)}{dt} = \alpha T X(t) - \beta T X(t - 1) \exp(-X(t - 1)^2) \tag{12.10}$$

The delayed regulation in this model provides it with a degree of endogenous instability which induces a series of period doubling bifurcations in the manner described by Feigenbaum (1978) as representing one of the classic routes to chaos. We can observe the stages in such a route by examining the phase portraits of Figures 12.7(a)–(d). The sequence begins in Figure 12.7(a) with a period-1 orbit, the limit cycle we have seen elsewhere, and is followed in 12.7(b) by a period doubling. Chaos is encountered in Figure 12.7(c) with the evolution of a 'strange' attractor, as the bifurcation parameter, $\beta = 6.0$. Further increases in this parameter to 6.3, however, cause the system to revert back to a complex, non-chaotic, period-3 orbit as can be seen from Figure 12.7(d). What this demonstrates, apart from the role of time-delayed regulation in inducing chaos, is that the 'window' of chaos exists in a very small area of parameter space.

Transactional dynamics

The above excursion into the qualitative behaviour of a generic production cycle has presented us with some pertinent observations on the macroscopic structuring properties which can reasonably be imputed to pre-market economic systems. In order to further demonstrate the utility of the present analytical framework we shall investigate a second model with the express purpose of generating another level of description.

An obvious follow-on from a concern with production dynamics is to move to the next stage represented by the flow of prestige goods through a regional landscape. While this is essentially a spatial phenomenon, and the subject of current research (McGlade, in prep.), for the moment we shall restrict ourselves to a species of non-spatial model building aimed at identifying the long run dynamics.

The context of our study may again be said to be the Late Bronze Age in Wessex, where we are dealing with a series of competing local lineage structures operating with a great deal of autonomy, and not subject to central political control. Following Rowlands (1980, p. 23) we shall assume that the principal luxury items involved in social transactions were women, cattle and metalwork. While each of these items is clearly the product of complex ritual and symbolic assignations, it is not the *meaning* of such transactions which

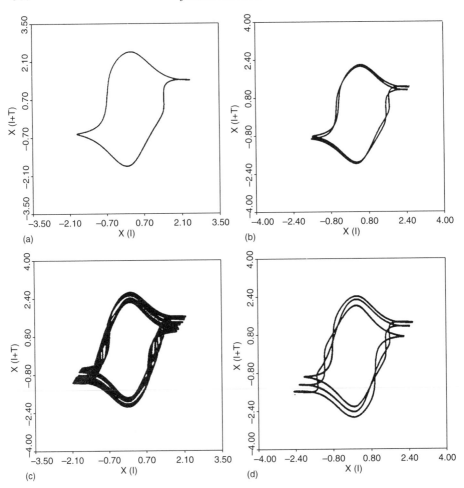

Figure 12.7 Period doubling route to chaos for the differential delay equation 12.8. The sequence begins in (a) with a period-1 orbit, followed in (b) by a period doubling, and in (c) we encounter chaos with the evolution of a strange attractor as the bifurcation parameter; $\beta = 6.0$. Increasing β causes the system to revert to a complex, period-1 orbit, as in plot (d).

concerns us here, but the potential global properties which govern their dynamic description. For the purpose of analytical simplicity, initially we shall collapse the various categories into a single prestige goods entity.

Mathematical models of transactional dynamics form a useful starting point for this study, especially those designed to simulate epidemiological processes. The acquisition, transaction and spread of prestige artefacts can thus be seen as being analogous to the transmission dynamics of some endemic and epidemic disease patterns – particularly those constrained by social and

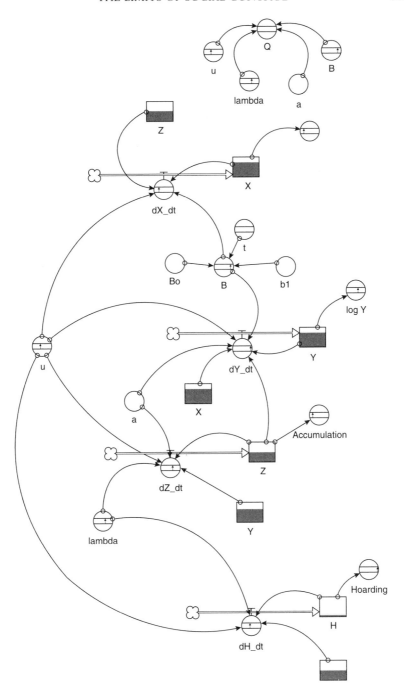

Figure 12.8 Flow diagram illustrating the dynamics of the exchange transaction model.

physical boundaries (Figure 12.8). Within this convention, we can represent the regional population as being divided into four groups or states:

X Those individuals who have privileged access to prestige goods, either by their elite status, or their membership of a pre-eminent lineage or clan.

Y Those who have acquired prestige items, but have yet to initiate transactions.

Z Those individuals who accumulate the goods and organize or control their circulation; those with transactional power or acumen, (e.g., those who used to be called 'big men').

H Those who upon gaining access, remove the goods from circulation by hoarding. Thus H is effectively a removal process, functioning in a similar manner to a recovered or immune sector in conventional epidemiology.

In the manner of Dietz (1976) we assume that,

1 X, Y, Z, H are smooth functions of time such that $X+Y+Z+H = 1$.
2 Prestige goods are introduced and exit from the region at a constant rate, μ.
3 The transaction rate β defines the average number of successful transactions per unit time.
4 The probability of those who have acquired prestige items (Y) passing them on in a specified time interval is logically independent of time after initial acquisition; hence the probability of still remaining in class Y at time T after initial acquisition is $e^{-\alpha T}$, where we can consider $1/\alpha$ as the mean delay period.
5 The probability of an unsuccessful transaction or when an individual decides to remove the goods from circulation by hoarding, is given by $e^{-\lambda T}$, where $1/\lambda$ is the mean period during which goods are in circulation and 1 represents the rate at which goods are removed from circulation.
6 Once prestige items are hoarded, they are not reintroduced into the transactional process.

The above assumptions form the basis of our initial exploration, and can now be expressed as a series of coupled differential equations, thus:

$$\frac{dX}{dt} = \mu - \beta(t)\,X(t)\,Z(t) - \mu X(t)$$

$$\frac{dY}{dt} = \beta(t)\,X(t)\,Z(t) - (\mu + \alpha)\,Y(t) \qquad (12.11)$$

$$\frac{dZ}{dt} = \alpha Y(t) - (\mu + \lambda)\,Z(t)$$

$$\frac{dH}{dt} = \lambda Z - \mu H$$

When β is given a constant value, there are two known steady states for such a system: $(X, Y, Z, H) = (1, 0, 0, 0)$ and $(X, Y, Z, H) = (X_0, Y_0, Z_0, H_0)$ where,

$$X_0 = (\mu + \alpha)(\mu + \lambda)/\beta$$

$$Y_0 = (\mu + \lambda/\alpha)(Z_0) \tag{12.12}$$

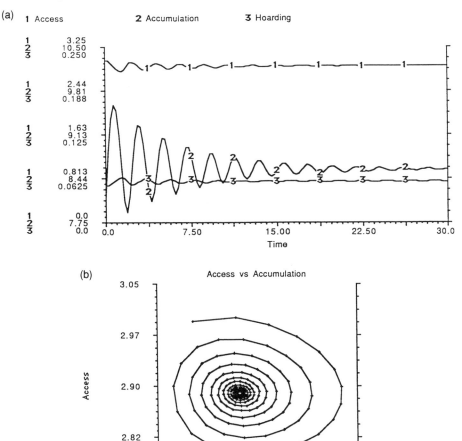

Figure 12.9 Simulation results for the exchange system showing (a) its evolution as a damped oscillation for $\beta = 1800^{-1}$; the phase plot in (b) shows the equilibrium solution, as convergence on a point attractor.

$$Z_0 = \mu(Q- 1)/\beta$$

This latter equilibrium condition, usually referred to as the 'endemic steady state', for our purposes describes a constant level of transactional interaction throughout the region. This process is governed by the value of Q, here regarded as a basic rate of flow of prestige goods, where

$$Q = \beta\mu/[(\mu + \alpha)(\mu + \lambda)] > 1 \qquad (12.13)$$

If $Q < 1$, then the flow of goods is insufficient to sustain the growth of the exchange system. Simulation results for this system show that when the transaction rate, β, is given a fixed value, then all solutions typically exhibit damped oscillations which converge as t approaches infinity (Figures 12.9(a) and 12.9(b)). One way in which this trading system can perpetuate itself however, is by the addition of fluctuations around the mean delay period α, which controls the flow of goods through the regional population. The effect of extremely small perturbations around this parameter can be seen from Figure 12.10 which, after an initial transient phase, demonstrates a sustained pattern of oscillation. Similarly, if we change, μ, the rate of introduction and exit of artefacts to that of a variable factor, so as to account for interruptions in supply – or changes in the rate at which artefacts are hoarded – then we have a situation described in Figures 12.11(a) and 12.11(b) where fluctuations in μ generate noisy limit cycles, orbits which are nevertheless stable.

These assumptions can be more realistically extended if we attempt to account for the fact that in primitive exchange systems the processes which control the exchange of goods are poorly described by constant flow dynamics; that is, the ritual nature of transactions meant that they were generally tied to specific times in the reproductive or farming year. Thus we must account

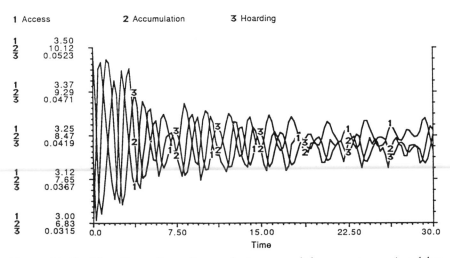

Figure 12.10 The effects of a small perturbation around the mean transaction delay period, α, which controls the flow of exchange goods through the population.

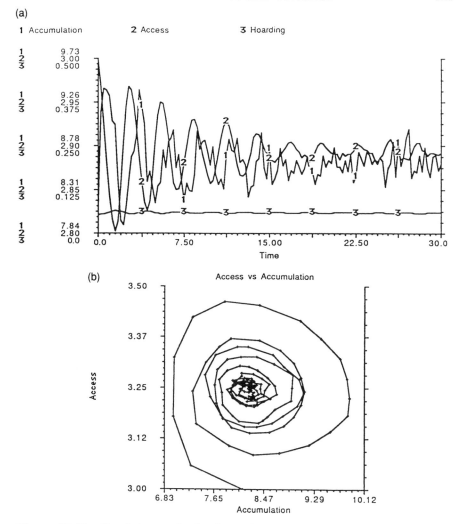

Figure 12.11 Simulation results for the exchange system showing the evolution of noisy limit cycles when the parameter controlling the introduction and exit rate of artefacts, μ, is given a variable value.

for seasonality as another structuring aspect in exchange dynamics. To implement this, we can replace the transaction rate β in Equation 12.11 with a periodic function,

$$\beta(t) = B_0(1 + \delta \cos^2 \pi t) \tag{12.14}$$

What we shall assume is that the volume of prestige goods flowing into the system peaks at biannual intervals, thus representing the way in which social and material culture transactions are co-ordinated with periods of ingathering, such as, for example, calendrical events such as the spring equinox

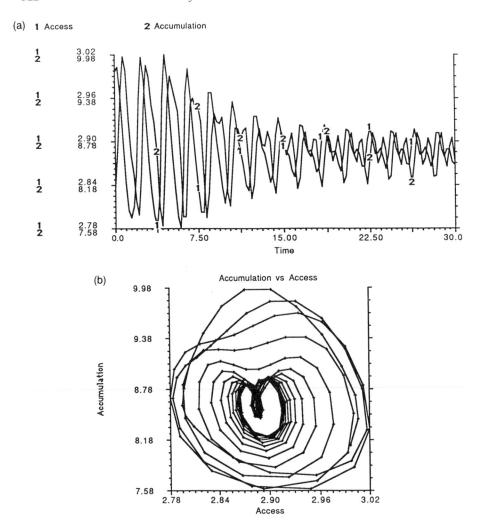

Figure 12.12 Simulation results for the exchange system showing the results of seasonal variations in the volume of exchange transactions; what we see is that after initial large-amplitude oscillations, the system settles down to converge on a limit cycle with complex periodicity ($\beta_0 = 0.05$).

or summer solstice – dates with traditional significance in the structuring of the yearly farming cycle and in the negotiation of alliances. In order to simulate these dynamics, we are interested in the effects on the system for different values of B_0, the parameter which describes variations in the density of interaction, or in the volume of trading.

The following series of figures represents a range of stable periodic solutions as a result of seasonal variations in the volume of exchange transactions.

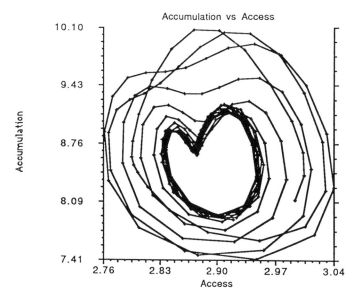

Figure 12.13 Simulation results for the exchange system showing the results of seasonal variations in the volume of exchange transactions; what we see is that after initial large-amplitude oscillations the system settles down to converge on a limit cycle with complex periodicity ($\beta_0 = 0.065$).

Each of the plots calculates the negative of the logarithm of that section of the population accumulating prestige items and controlling transactions ($-\log Z$) as a function of the negative of the logarithm of those with potential access to these goods ($-\log X$). For $B_0 = 0.05$, Figure 12.12(b) shows that after an initial phase of large amplitude oscillations, the system settles down to converge on a limit cycle with a complex periodicity. The structure of this periodicity can be more easily identified from the accompanying time-series plot in Figure 12.12(a). For a slightly larger seasonal variation ($B_0 = 0.065$), the system settles to a similar attractor, though with a less complex orbit (Figure 12.13). For $B_0 = 0.075$, this simplification continues as we can see from Figures 12.14(a) and 12.14(b)). For values of $1 < B_0 < 1.5$ the system structure becomes more erratic, as can be seen from the phase plot in Figure 12.15(b); however, the time-series plot (Figure 12.15(a)) shows a distinct periodicity in the long-term behaviour of the system. This only breaks down when $B_0 > 1.5$, when we encounter a chaotic regime.

What we are seeing here, is that relatively small periodic solutions emanating from a seasonally forced exchange model produce a series of period-doubling bifurcations. Whether or not our system becomes chaotic is a moot point; what is important is that it possesses the potential to do so. In addition, what we see is that our exchange system is behaving in a self-structuring, or

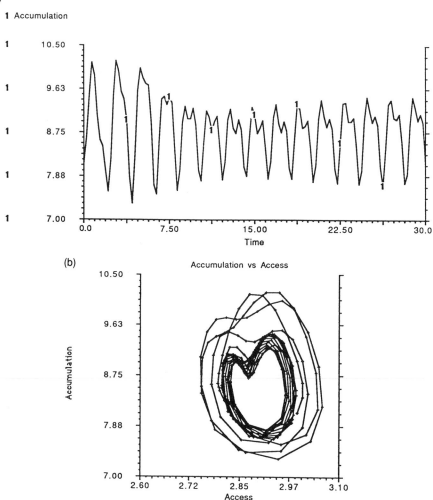

Figure 12.14 Simulation results for the exchange system showing the results of seasonal variations in the volume of exchange transactions; what we see is that after initial large-amplitude oscillations the system settles down to converge on a limit cycle with complex periodicity ($\beta_0 = 0.075$).

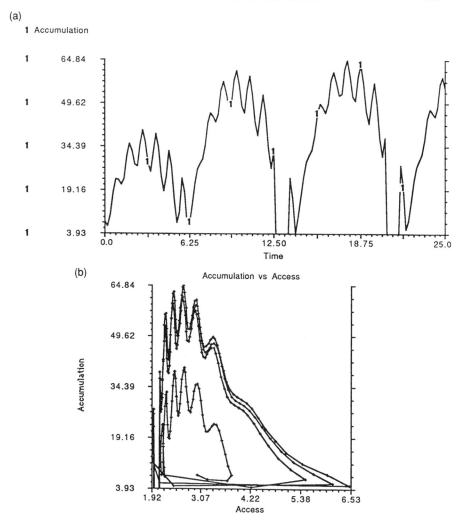

Figure 12.15 Simulation results for the exchange system showing the results of seasonal variations in the volume of exchange transactions; what we see is that after initial large-amplitude oscillations the system settles down to converge on a limit cycle with complex periodicity ($1 < \beta_0 < 1.5$).

self-organizing manner. The seasonal variations in the flow of artefacts are ultimately responsible for the qualitative restructuring of the system and the emergence of a self-organizing dynamic; i.e., periodic forcing in the rate of transactions at specific intervals in the year results in the emergence of a prestige-goods exchange system which, to all intents and purposes, is 'stable'. This suggests that the system is relatively robust, in the sense that short-term perturbations or time delays do not radically affect its structural dynamics.

Obviously, while the preceding analysis operates at a fairly 'coarse grained' level, it does demonstrate a number of *generic* features which may characterize exchange processes, even though these are represented by widely divergent contextual properties.

Predictability and social control

The primary message from the foregoing excursion into the qualitative dynamics of change is that when we are dealing with a highly non-linear system – and one driven by a predictable degree of human acquisitiveness – the intrinsic transactional relationships are capable of generating extremely complex behaviours which can threaten the coherence of the system, and in some cases promote chaotic outcomes. This is all the more significant when we consider that such qualitative transformations can be induced without the conventional archaeological invocation of external influence or disruptions in long-distance trade connections. Complexity thus becomes the outcome of simple *deterministic* forces, which display a strong sensitivity to initial conditions.

The implications of these observations for an understanding of social control and the maintenance of power networks cannot be underestimated. It is here that the conceptual platform provided by a dynamical systems perspective is most useful; the geometrical behaviour traced out by our exchange system in phase space (i.e., the representation of its possible states) can readily be conceived as the 'possibility space' of any societal system (cf. Garfinkel 1981).

Thus, what is worrying about systems whose evolutionary history is traced out on a 'strange' attractor is, as we have already alluded to, the impossibility of making meaningful long-term predictions. This is precisely analogous to Lorenz's discoveries about long-term weather patterns – the state of the system at time t need bear no relationship to that at time $t + 1$. The ability to wield control by organizational or elite bodies is predicated on a relatively high level of predictability in the operation and maintenance of exchange networks, such that any threat to the coherence of such a system induces a degree of uncertainty that severely compromises the ability of an elite to exercise effective political control. It is this inability to predict the future behaviour of, for example, the mechanisms of production and circulation in a prestige economy which acts as a fundamental constraint, especially over the long term.

The practical consequences of such circumstances mean that given the existence of individual agents and their opportunistic pursuit of self-interest, we can expect interruptions in the circulation of goods; the orderly flow of transactions in time and across a region becomes subject to discontinuity. It is the magnification or reinforcement of such processes which can induce the kinds of structured irregularities we associate with chaos. Based on our previous analyses, if we assume that this state is reached through a series of period doubling bifurcations, then we must examine the archaeological record for manifestations of such a process; i.e., a social order whose relations of power have evolved towards a bifurcation point – a threshold pregnant with alternative choices. Just such a situation is to be seen in Wessex during the Early Bronze Age/Late Bronze Age transition.

Prior to this juncture, there is arguably a relative degree of cohesion defining the Early Bronze Age exchange systems in Wessex, principally since there is evidence of control at the hands of an elite group. We might go further and suggest that the relative homogeneity of Wessex II can be represented geometrically as being governed by a fixed point attractor, or some form of stable trajectory about such a point. We envisage here a high degree of structural stability – a top-down model of exchange, controlled by a single dominant group or lineage. Over time this system was in fact operating in an increasingly restricted area of 'phase space'. It was increasingly becoming prey to the destabilizing effects of excessive food production on gradually eroding soils. The maintenance of an agricultural surplus, crucial to the smooth functioning of a prestige goods system, was severely threatened. The uncertainty attendant on such a process, when coupled with the inherent unpredictability of exchange transactions, can reasonably be assumed to generate stress, which itself begets instability.

Power structures and the institutional frameworks by which social control is maintained respond to instability in a number of predictable ways. An elite whose continuing credibility is threatened will almost certainly engage in visible public displays of authority; the reassertion of its continued access to prestigious status is critical to its survival. The situation in Wessex provides us with a particularly compelling example, where we see a dramatic demonstration of a social system in the throes of dissolution or transformation, as the landscape is witness to a vigorous display of barrow construction. Significantly this activity took place within a relatively restricted time-frame, between about 1300 and 1000 BC (Barrett 1980, p. 82), and is given added importance when we note that the date of the final building phase at Stonehenge is 1240 ± 150 BC.

Taken together, these events present useful evidence of the kinds of posturing which often characterizes unstable thresholds – a flurry of conspicuous flag waving by a social order threatened with eclipse. Thus the construction of Stonehenge IIIc under such circumstances is not to be seen as the flowering of greatness, but rather as a self-conscious display of insecurity and uncertainty; a last desperate attempt to shore up a redundant and increasingly impotent system. As Bradley (1980, p. 63) has pointed out, it is worth noting Cherry's (1978, p. 427) observation that the building of peak sanctuaries in Mycenaean Greece took place in two distinct phases: the first relating to an initial stage in social organization and the second to a crisis period prefiguring system collapse. Dramatic displays of wealth and status thus often stand as indicators of a terminal condition; the death throes of a fossilized order. In examining the meaning of pathological relationships at particular times and places in history, Boulding reminds us that it is often the most successful world views or images that become the most dangerous: 'The image becomes institutionalised in the ceremonial and coercive institutions of society. It acquires thereby a spurious stability. As the world moves on, the image does not' (Boulding 1956, p. 79).

It is in this sense that we can see the monumental excesses of Stonehenge IIIc as an evolutionary cul-de-sac. Seen from the morphogenetic perspective presented here, Wessex II underwent a process of restructuring – a phase change – as the inevitable consequence of an over-specialized and increasingly rigid system. The growing conceptual and structural insularity of this system inevitably led to a complete breakdown in the authoritarian power base: thus the elitist core contracted and gradually eliminated diversity. It effectively became a closed system, reliant upon the perpetuation of traditional power structures and maintained by the control of prestige goods. More seriously, the knowledge structures which co-ordinate the symbolic and structural 'rule sets' became constrained since the system was resistant to innovative behaviours. Such resistance to creativity in the form of new information can have only one outcome – atrophy. It is in this sense that we can understand the ensuing structural changes which saw the subordination of the exchange systems of the Wessex downland to those operating in the Thames Valley.

Instability and disorder thus form the necessary basis for a new order. Within this conception, change is articulated by a process of structural elaboration, rather than conforming to a more conventional progressive evolutionary trajectory. It is this fact alone which conspires to subvert a large measure of the necessary predictability by which social control is maintained.

Conclusion

From the foregoing it is clear that if we are to contribute to the debate on the means by which social control is exercised, then we must adopt a long-term perspective that is able to situate transactional behaviour within a larger scale of reference – one able to account for the important contribution played by non-linear dynamics in the structuring process. What we need to consider is the way in which the individual events which give rise to this structuring, i.e., the simple, localized contextual rules, can also give rise to the emergence of pattern at more global scales.

Finally, we might note that the suggestion that chaotic dynamics might be prevalent in human societal systems – or at least in the natural and physical systems to which they are coupled – has significant implications for the modelling of social processes. For archaeology, the lessons provided by the theory of dynamical systems, in particular the impossibility of meaningful prediction over the long term, has an important, if as yet unacknowledged, contribution to make to a more sophisticated understanding of the time evolution of human/environmental interaction.

References

Barrett, J.C. 1980. The evolution of Later Bronze Age settlement. In *Settlement and Society in the British Later Bronze Age*, J.C. Barrett and R. Bradley (eds), 71–100. Oxford: British Archaeological Reports British Series 83.

Benton 1981, M. 1981. 'Objective' interests and the sociology of power. *Sociology* 15, 161–84.

Boulding, K. 1956. *The Image*. Ann Arbor: University of Michigan Press.

Bradley, R.J. 1980. Subsistence, exchange and technology: a social framework for the Bronze Age in southern England c. 1400–700 BC. In *Settlement and Society in the British Later Bronze Age*, J.C. Barrett and R.J. Bradley (eds), 57–75. Oxford: British Archaeological Reports, British Series 83.

Bradley, R.J. 1984. *The Social Foundations of Prehistoric Britain*. London: Longman.

Chen, P. 1988. Empirical and theoretical evidence of economic chaos. *System Dynamics Review* 4, 81–108.

Cherry, J.F. 1978. Generalization and the archaeology of the state. In *Social Organization and Settlement*, D. Green, C. Haselgrove and M. Spriggs (eds), 411–37. Oxford: British Archaeological Reports, International Series 47.

Dietz, K. 1976. The incidence of infectious diseases under the influence of seasonal fluctuations. (*Lecture Notes in Biomathematics* Vol. 11.), pp. 1–15. Berlin: Springer-Verlag.

Dodgshon, R.A. 1987. *The European Past: social evolution and spatial order*. London: Macmillan.

Earle, T.K. and J. Ericson (eds) 1977. *Exchange Systems in Prehistory*. New York: Academic Press.

Ekholm, K. 1972. *Power and Prestige: the rise and fall of the Congo kingdom*. Uppsala: Skriv Service.

Ekholm, K. 1977. External exchange and the transformation of Central African social systems. In *The Evolution of Social Systems*, J. Friedman and M.J. Rowlands (eds), 115–36. London: Duckworth.

Ericson, J. and T.K. Earle (eds) 1982. *Contexts for Prehistoric Exchange*. New York: Academic Press.

Feigenbaum, M.J. 1978. Quantitative universality for a class of non-linear transformations. *Journal of Statistical Physics* 19, 25–52.

Frankenstein, S. and M.J. Rowlands 1978. The internal structure and regional context of Early Iron Age society in southwest Germany. *Bulletin of the Institute of Archaeology* 15, 73–112.

Friedman, J. and M.J. Rowlands 1977. Notes towards an epigenetic model of the evolution of civilization. In *The Evolution of Social Systems*, J. Friedman and M.J. Rowlands (eds), 201–76. London: Duckworth.

Garfinkel, A. 1981. *Forms of Explanation*. New Haven: Yale University Press.

McGlade, J., in prep., Transactional dynamics and prehistoric exchange: spatial outcomes.

Mackey, M.C. and L. Glass, L. 1977. Oscillations and chaos in physiological control systems. *Science* 197, 287–89.

Mauss, M. 1954. *The Gift: forms and functions of exchange in archaic societies*. London: Cohen and West.

May, R.M. 1974. Biological populations with non-overlapping generations: stable points, stable cycles and chaos. *Science* 186, 645–47.

May, R.M. 1980. Non-linear phenomena in ecology and epidemiology. *Annals of the New York Academy of Sciences* 357, 267–81.

Maynard Smith, J. 1974. *Models in Ecology*. Cambridge: Cambridge University Press.

Meillassoux, C. 1972. From reproduction to production. *Economy and Society* 1, 92–105.

Miller, D. and C. Tilley (eds) 1984. *Ideology, Power and Prehistory*. Cambridge: Cambridge University Press.

Rasmussen, S., E. Mosekilde and J.D. Sterman 1985. Bifurcations and chaotic behaviour in a simple model of the economic long wave. *System Dynamics Review* 1, 92–110.

Renfrew, A.C. 1973. Monuments, mobilization and social organization in Neolithic Wessex. In *The Explanation of Culture Change*, A.C. Renfrew (ed.), 539–58. London, Duckworth.

Renfrew, A.C. 1979. Wessex as a social question. In *Problems in European Prehistory*, A.C. Renfrew (ed.), 304–9. Edinburgh: Edinburgh University Press.

Rowlands, M.J. 1980. Kinship, alliance and exchange in the European Bronze Age. In *Settlement and Society in the British Later Bronze Age*, J.C. Barrett and R.J. Bradley (eds), 15–55. Oxford: British Archaeological Reports, British Series 83.

Sahlins, M.D. 1972: *Stone Age Economics*. New York: Aldine.

Shanks, M. and C. Tilley 1987. *Social Theory and Archaeology*. Cambridge: Polity Press.

Sterman, J.D. 1985. A behavioural model of the economic long wave. *Journal of Economic Behaviour and Organization* 6, 17–53.

Van der Leeuw, S.E. 1994. Whispers from the context of real life: towards pluriformity in archaeology. *Archaeological Dialogues* 1, 133–64.

13 Structural change and bifurcation in urban evolution: a non-linear dynamical perspective

SANDER E. VAN DER LEEUW
AND JAMES MCGLADE

Introduction

The emergence of what we refer to as civilization is synonymous with the rise of urban centres, and the study of these, along with writing, markets and craft specialization has conventionally been regarded by archaeologists as a key element in the evolution of 'complex societies' (cf. Childe 1956). Yet there seems to be no commonly accepted explanation why, at some point in their history, people in such vastly different areas and with such very different cultures and subsistence economies 'chose' to settle in spatial config-urations which are so strikingly similar. Similar not only because people are living in densely built-up 'special-purpose' areas, but also because the way in which these areas are spread over the landscape is highly regular, and usually conforms to one of five or six known patterns – even allowing for distor-tions due to accidents of physical geography and other social and historical phenomena.

Questions such as why people distribute themselves in precisely these configurations and not in any of a myriad other conceivable ones, as well as issues of causality, have preoccupied archaeologists, geographers and social scientists alike. But, notwithstanding a considerable research effort, we still have an imperfect understanding of urban dynamics, especially those of incip-ient urbanism. In addressing this issue, the present chapter will consider the origins of urbanism as any other qualitative transformation in the social and spatial organization of human interaction. As a point of departure we will summarize what, in our opinion, are some of the main problems with our present perspective on incipient urbanism.[1] Next, we will present an alter-native perspective,[2] and third, we shall discuss some preliminary dynamic models on the genesis of urbanization, which may serve as an aid to future research.

It is important to stress, finally, that the models which we present in this chapter are in no way 'models of how urbanisms actually came about'. In keeping with the philosophy of this book, all they aspire to be are tools to help us think about the genesis of urban systems, and some of the problems involved in that process. Natural scientists, and many others, could reproach us that we have not calibrated these models against 'real data'. From their perspective that would be entirely justified, and we are well aware of it. In doing so they would, however, demonstrate their imperfect knowledge of the problems facing archaeology. It is our opinion that within that discipline we do need to combine the kind of rigour shown by Francfort in Chapter 6, which leads him to be very reductionist indeed in his theories, and an approach which *experimentally* transforms the bare bones we find into human beings. This both serves to remind us of what we are sifting through the sand for, and allows us to generate the 'understanding' which is needed before we could even hope to begin to generate 'knowledge' about the past. What follows is in many ways an attempt at sculpting processes in order to better understand the *kind* of dynamics which may have underlain them.

Town, territory, and urban systems

Broadly speaking, definition of the spatial agglomerations which we classify as towns has been approached in two ways: (a) *intrinsically*, by trying to find shared characteristics of towns and/or their populations and making enumerative lists of such characteristics, and (b) *extrinsically*, by imposing a defining characteristic on those agglomerations which are to be accepted as 'urban'. In both cases the approach has been 'bottom up'; the research has proceeded by comparing individual cases in order to arrive at general ideas.

This chapter argues that such a 'bottom up' approach is not sufficient because it separates towns from their context. It defines a perspective (either 'what is urban' or 'what is rural') and anything that does not fit that perspective is therefore considered a non-phenomenon or at best a different phenomenon ('non-urban' or 'non-rural'), to be studied from a different perspective, with a different conceptual toolkit. That such an approach has not been a successful basis for the study of urbanism is not surprising in view of the fact that a city is in essence a locus of interaction, among other things between itself and its non-urban environment. The conceptual tools necessary to understand it must therefore include relational ones which apply to both the town and its rural context. In other words, we must develop a concept of a town as an *open* system in full interaction with its natural and cultural environment, including both rural areas and other towns, and focus our efforts on understanding the *dynamics* of that system.

The dominance of a simple cultural-evolutionist paradigm within archaeology and history has tended to cast the beginnings (or evolution) of urbanism as something of a non-problem − or has at least avoided confronting its real complexity. From this perspective, the rise of urban agglomerations constitutes a necessary step to accommodate the social, political and organizational requirements of an expanding population, eventually moving along an inevitable trajectory towards statehood. Urban agglomerations evolve to meet economic exigencies, and are predicated on supply and demand criteria.

Moreover, most extant models of urbanism summarize the observable variation in normative, average or probabilistic terms. This implies that similarity between towns is deliberately over-stressed, and differences undervalued, which in turn leads to the description of change as a sequence of static situations at the macroscopic level. The study of settlement systems thus deals with the *result* rather than the *dynamics* of long-term developments, or with time-slice *stills* taken during a development (i.e., 'results so far').

All efforts at explanation are limited to interpretation of observations at the macroscopic level, ignoring the fact that most information is available at the microscopic level, and thus curtailing our ability to come up with a wide range of adequate hypotheses. Depending on which 'average' was retained, one or another 'cause' for the appearance of, or changes in, an urban system is observed and subsequently generalized, leading to unacceptable over-simplification of the causality involved. As a result, the vast literature on urban geography and related disciplines generally interprets variations in settlement patterning in terms of variables such as topographic location and access to trade and transportation networks. Its key feature is the 'irrelevance of history' in the locational process.

This empiricist–positivist tradition has succeeded in reducing the settlement landscape to sequences of morphological and topographic detail. These are 'de-peopled' locational landscapes; Cartesian containers that somehow disregard the sense in which space is a socially constructed phenomenon, articulated by communication and learning structures.

It seems to us that any alternative approach to understanding urban systems needs to develop new approaches to at least two aspects of the above.

First, the fact that human communities *themselves* structure learning and the communication flows across the landscape – not in response to optimal, least cost solutions to perceived problems, but within a nexus of relationships that are structured according to the shifting and conflicting needs of specific interpersonal and intergroup relationships. Locational decisions, for example, are often affected by prior concentrations of settlement and industry; such 'agglomeration economies' rely on location by competitive emulation and spin-off, as well as by chance elements dictated for example by political and/or ideological circumstances (cf. Arthur 1988, 1990). The essentially 'open' nature of this process is of fundamental significance for any successful attempt at understanding it, for it contains an underlying non-linear dynamic which is both unstable and discontinuous, and hence rapidly promotes structural transformation. Human societal organization comprises a dynamical set of social relationships, the autocatalytic aspects of which can generate 'emergent structures', often wholly unintended by the actors themselves (McGlade 1987, 1990, 1994).

Towns as open, dissipative structures

The second major problem, that of accounting for structural change posed by some of these issues, has yet to penetrate archaeological theory. In geography, however, the situation is somewhat different, and a number of recent contributions have sought to account for the role of stochastic events – particularly their relationship with deterministic event histories – in generating spatial evolutionary models of urban systems (e.g. Allen and Sanglier 1978, 1979; Pumain *et al.* 1989; Haag and Weidlich 1984; Wilson 1984). Generally speaking, these view urban aggregations as self-organizing systems (cf. also Pumain, Chapter 4) which are thermodynamically open and dissipative like all other living systems, and are thus subject to similar operational and evolutionary principles. The models involved move from the micro to the macro level, and show how initially non-structuring decision-making becomes at once structured and structuring (for a critical review see Pumain *et al.* (1989) and Sanders (1992).

The structural similarity between urban systems in widely differing regions, periods and circumstances can only be explained if we assume that it is due to a remarkable convergence in the ways in which different people have dealt with very different environments. It is that convergence which needs explaining, rather than the fact that in each particular instance of urbanization encountered, the exact trajectory followed was different. Hence, we have to do with phenomena which are inherent in human organization at a level above that of the individual culture. That fact has prompted us to investigate whether aspects of the organization and dynamics of human information processing might be responsible for such a remarkable convergence.

The prima facie case rests on two observations. Structural similarity in human reaction under widely different circumstances seems to point to underdetermination of human ideas by facts, and a critically important role for the nature of our cognitive systems in determining the solutions we choose (cf. Atlan 1992). Moreover, recent work in anthropology and sociology has demonstrated that all material phenomena resulting from human activity are as much constrained by mental, social and in general cognitive constraints as by material and energetic ones (cf., for example, Lemonnier 1986; Latour 1988; van der Leeuw 1989, 1990). We conclude that towns have to be understood in a double perspective as the result of a coincidence of two 'windows of opportunity', one in the world of ideas and one in the world of matter and energy. Only where such a coincidence exists, it seems to us, can ideas (such as towns) be realized.

It is the thesis of this chapter that, in the most general of terms, urban systems can profitably be viewed as self-organizing human communications structures, and that as such they are not qualitatively different from other forms of human social organization, such as small band societies or hierarchical tribes. The differences are merely due to the need to deal with larger amounts of information flow as human problem-solving generates more knowledge, and involves more people.[3]

Dynamics of urban systems

Spatial agglomeration of settlement as a problem-solving solution

Following Mayhew and Levinger (1976, 1977) and Johnson (1978, 1982, 1983), we have argued (van der Leeuw and McGlade 1993) for the existence of three distinct classes of human communication structures; i.e., (1) processing under universal control (egalitarian systems), (2) processing under partial control (hierarchical systems), and (3) processing without central control (heterarchical systems).

In this context, we viewed towns as complex systems in which all three of the above communications structures occur, and their emergence a manifestation of the fact that in the societies concerned, the nexus in the development has shifted from the realm of energy and matter to that of information and communication. The 'classical' argument has always been that the emergence of towns introduces economies of scale in the procurement, by any individual, of a variety of products. The degree to which geography, economy, ecology and other disciplines had a fixation with flows of matter and energy seems to have blinded us to the fact that it is the *limited availability of the knowledge needed for, and represented by the transformation from raw material to specialized product* which made such products scarce, and their production and/or assembly at certain points necessary. Sufficient energy and matter to sustain human life is locally available, in one form or another, in most places on earth. As long as they are the nexus in the society's survival, there is therefore no need for any population to aggregate into urban centres.

Maintaining urban populations is very expensive in terms of energy, as considerable costs are incurred in the transportation of matter. The fact that groups of towns always emerge together is therefore a prime indication that their function as nodes in a communication network is more important than any other one,[4] indicating that the flow of information became crucial to the survival of society. The fact that in different areas of the world, writing, craft specialization, and professional bureaucracies emerge at the same time as towns (and, as far as writing is concerned, in different, independently invented forms) seems again to point in the same direction, as does the fact that at present there is increasing dispersal of human settlement precisely in those areas of the world where non-human energy has been harnessed for purposes of individual communication by the invention of the car and various forms of information technology.[5]

The 'information-processing landscape': interaction between communications structures

The origin and development of towns can thus be conceived of as occurring under particular conditions in an 'information-processing landscape' at the interface of the physical and social geographies of a region; such regions can in turn be seen as a dynamical set of relationships in which the autocatalytic aspects of society can generate emergent spatial structures (*sensu* Allen

1982, p. 370). It follows that the location of population nodes in such a land-scape could be considered the result of self-structuring interaction between long-distance and shorter-distance, more frequent communication flows.[6] The interaction between different communications structures such as egalitarian, hierarchical and heterarchical ones could then be viewed as the structuring dynamic. In the case of complex societies, egalitarian structures only play a minor part, as they integrate only relatively small groups of people (cf. Johnson 1981, 1982). We will therefore focus on the relationship between hierarchies and heterarchies.

Simon (1981, *passim*) defines heterarchical structures as those which emerge, in the absence of hierarchy and overall control, from the interaction of indi-vidual and generally independent elements, each involved in the pursuit of separate goals, and with equal access to information; competition for resources characterizes such an organization. The best-known example is the 'classical' free economic market. An important feature of market systems is their inherent non-optimizing behaviour. There are two basic reasons for this. Optimality in such structures would require that each actor has perfect information; but this is impossible since we inhabit a world of incomplete and erroneous infor-mation. Consequently, our mode of operation is best defined as satisficing rather than optimizing. On the other hand, the non-linear structuring which underwrites market systems acts to constrain optimal behaviours. The strength of existing structures can act to prevent the emergence of competing struc-tures in the nearby environment even though the new structure may be more obviously efficient.[7]

Hierarchies, on the other hand, operate on the basis of a central control-ling authority; decision-making is thus not democratic. Simon (1973) showed that most complex systems[8] throughout the (natural and) social world conform to multilevel hierarchical structures, in which each level is characterized by units or assemblies possessing a degree of autonomy and internal coherence. As the number of hierarchical levels increases linearly, the number of elements increases non-linearly. Under idealized conditions, hierarchical structures are governed by goal-seeking strategies, as they attempt to maximize or optimize given resources. They have the ability to harness and process greater quan-tities of material, energy and information than market organizations.

It is thus clear that whatever advantages hierarchies and market systems display individually, they both have inherent limitations. We argue here that structural coherence in urban systems is due to a (hybrid) combination of hierarchical and heterarchical structures which presents a more resilient form of organization for complex systems. As large heterarchical systems are more adaptable, but less stable and less efficient than large hierarchical ones, most of the arguments in favour of hybrid systems centre around adaptability, effi-ciency and stability.

Urban systems are dependent for their existence on continued innovation, which in turn presumes continuous adaptability.[9] Huberman and Hogg (1988) have shown that with time, the complexity of hierarchical self-organizing systems is reduced, as are their rate of evolution and their adaptability; in addition, it seems that very large distributed systems also have difficulty adapting due to the persistence of non-optimal strategies (Ceccato and Huberman 1988). However, the introduction of globally controlled (hierarchical) communications in market systems causes them to lose their penchant for retaining non-optimal strategies, whereas the existence of untied (heterarchical) connections in a hierarchical system increases its adaptability. Thus, when a new strategy has been adopted which is at that moment optimal, the system would ideally need the optimum efficiency afforded by a hierarchical system and the optimum adaptability inherent in a heterarchical one. Inevitably, a hybrid structure will develop which is a 'best fit' in the particular context involved. As it develops solutions to the problems which face it, its hierarchically organized pathways will become simpler, reducing overall adaptability and possibly reducing efficiency. On the other hand, its heterarchical actions may become better informed and/or improve their decision-making efficiency without reducing their adaptability.

Innovation also introduces new resources into a system, reducing competition, and increasing the efficiency of the distributed actors, which in turn will prompt more and more of them to co-operate, further increasing efficiency gains for a limited time, until competition for resources becomes dominant again. This inherent fluctuation of the market aspect of the system is reduced by the much more stable efficiency of the hierarchy. Similarly, in market systems both the time-delays and their oscillations increase rapidly with increasing numbers of actors, whereas in hierarchical systems time-delays proportionately decrease with each increase in the number of participants, and oscillations are virtually non-existent.

Process rates and organization

The evolution of hierarchies can be viewed as the product of feedback mechanisms similar to those observed in other dissipative systems. Their structural differentiation is a function of the propensity of processes at higher levels to occur at slower rates, in contrast to those at lower organizational levels, which exhibit more rapid expansion. Their overall organization is thus nearly decomposable since each level in a hierarchical system can be segregated on the basis of response times – a fact which ultimately has a bearing on how a complex system responds to fluctuations. Thus, for complex ecosystems and social organizations where fluctuations may be periodic (e.g. daily or seasonal):

> the characteristic rates of a level determine the frequency of fluctuations that can be attenuated i.e., the frequencies over which responses can to some extent be controlled.
>
> (O'Neil *et al.* 1986, p. 78)

Equally important in hierarchical organizations is the role of horizontal structuring, where we see the existence of similar differential rate processes: within each level, we can encounter components that interact frequently (strongly) with each other, but only infrequently (weakly) with other components. Thus, interaction rates occurring within levels are usually rapid and rather uniform, whereas rates between levels are typically slower and less frequent. These differential rate gradients are referred to as 'loose horizontal coupling'.

Stability, resilience and switching between organizational forms

Any discussion on the structural attributes of hierarchies naturally brings us to the question of stability. Highly non-linear dissipative systems such as the ones we are discussing, for which change is an essential aspect of survival, are inherently unstable. Their survival is, rather, due to their 'resilience' (*sensu* Holling 1973, p. 7) i.e., the system's capacity to maintain a degree of structural continuity in the face of perturbation, its ability to 'renew' itself by means of innovative strategies in the face of environmental or social change. Thus, societal systems operate within a domain of resilience in which there potentially exist multiple steady states, such as hierarchical, heterarchical and hybrid organization, between which switching occurs. Such switching increases the 'possibility space' which a social organization can effectively explore (McGlade 1990, p. 65).

A key point is that the switching thresholds represent critical boundaries at which local organizational capacities are either overconnected or redundant. There occurs a reduction in diversity within both the physical and the cognitive landscape (e.g. alternative, equally viable, settlement locations or new technological or ideological solutions are ignored). Indeed, much of the creative, innovative 'stochastic' input is selected against. This leads to what we might call information knots, such that an inflexible 'lock-on' results.

Evolution thus only becomes possible through a 'jump' to a new basin of attraction. It may be that this process defines the way in which societal organization either enhances the robustness of the system – increasing the degrees of freedom within which it can operate – or induces potentially pathological outcomes such as catastrophic decline. The particular attractor to which the system jumps will be a function of the information processing efficiency at a particular moment in time and space.

Elements of a model on the origins of urbanism

Hierarchical versus heterarchical dynamics

In postulating an appropriate modelling framework within which to view urban structuring, we will first identify and describe the qualitative dynamics underlying system evolution; this entails identifying the attractors to which the system converges, and the feedback mechanisms governing its macroscopic behaviour.[10]

For the purposes of discussion, we shall assume that the pre-existing dynamic is a rural one, in which a human component and an environmental component are interlocked in a mutually reinforcing way. Of these two, the former consists of relatively few superimposed rhythms and can potentially be accelerated with relative ease (people can learn), whereas the latter is a very complex composite of myriad different embedded biological and ecological rhythms. As a consequence, one might say that in the rural situation the (faster) human dynamic has locked on to the (slower) environmental one. The latter dominates the overall dynamic, and its diversity is what stabilizes the symbiosis between people and their environment.

If we move forward in time, to our present urban–industrial society, we see that all processes have accelerated; the human dynamic increasingly sets the pace for, and thus dominates, the environmental dynamic. This reversal is a fundamental constituent of our present world. In order to achieve it, humans have reduced the environmental dynamic in many places to a much simpler set of rhythms. As a result, the symbiotic system has become less stable in the classical ecological sense (diversity has been reduced), but it has gained in resilience and now survives through more rapid adaptation.

In the period around the beginnings of urbanism, there are few major changes to be observed in the environmental dynamic, while those in the human dynamic of communication are striking. In the initial pre-urban situation small, widespread village-level communities are connected by the hierarchical communications networks we usually term 'tribal' or 'chiefly'. These are very efficient in their use of (mostly local) energy and information (news spreads quickly), but relatively slow to adapt as a consequence of the fact that the decision-makers are few, and of limited diversity. Thus, after a certain time they are no longer so well adapted to their environment.[11] The non-linear coupling of a relatively structured, slow environmental dynamic and a more rapid and stochastic human one generates bifurcation behaviour. In the accelerating/structuring phase the system is more deterministic, and in the catastrophic phase more stochastic. These dynamics are precisely analogous to the behaviour of non-linear oscillators studied by physicists.

We have seen that small-scale distributed systems display a relatively high degree of adaptive flexibility – much more so than hierarchical systems. On relatively small scales, one bifurcation that we might impute is a physical separation between hierarchical (more linear) and heterarchical (more stochastic) communications modes. Such a bifurcation might be triggered by the (highly probable) situation that in some places a more rapid adaptation is required of the total human/environment system than in others, which is equivalent to stating that in some places the total dynamic is more dependent on the human component of the symbiosis than in others. That would, for example, be the case in those areas which have a less diverse ecology. Examples of such poorer environments could be drier climates, or areas of poorer soils. By thus allowing distributed communications systems to become spatially separate, communities organized on heterarchical principles (their dynamic being the more adaptable) would spread and would create spatial connectivity over relatively long distances, through specific heterarchical 'corridors'. By implication, the rest of the society would conform to a slower rate of adaptation through its hierarchical communications system. Prime candidates for such corridors or channels would be long valleys, coastal waters around inaccessible islands, etc.

Once heterarchical systems grow in size, as long as there is no partial separation within them and formation of dominant effective sub-systems, they become much less adaptable. In effect, as they grow they have the choice between splitting into sub-systems or hierarchizing. Probably both occur, but the degrees to which may be crucial in the dynamics. We might thus conceive of towns as nodes which accumulate in such heterarchical communications corridors. This would imply that the encompassing long-distance distributed processing network differentiates to some extent, creating room for a degree of local independence between towns. For a while at least, such uncoupling might have allowed sufficient localized dynamics within the network to maintain adaptability of the total system.

We have thus been able to identify two attractors which act to keep the total urban and rural system in oscillation, and which drive it towards increased spatial differentiation. In effect, what we are describing is a model encoding of what in physico-chemical systems is known as a reaction-diffusion process.

Increasing adaptability within the heterarchical component of the system would reduce the efficiency of that component – the occurrence of 'energy crises' (misharvests, famines or other natural disasters which affect the foodweb on which the existence of a part of the network is predicated) would therefore exert pressure to optimize efficiency once the different nodes had become sufficiently independent. Such pressure would probably translate into reliance on local hierarchies ('leaders' would come out of the woodwork), which would in turn enhance adaptability of the urban networks as a whole because we have seen that partial hierarchizing of very large heterarchical systems has such an effect. We thus see another bifurcation within that part of the system which is driven by a market dynamic, where a hierarchy is prone to develop at a lower level. A number of local hierarchies are in all probability connected through heterarchical connections.

We have also seen that heterarchical systems are much less stable unless they differentiate (cf. Glance and Huberman, Chapter 5) – the need to differentiate may therefore be a contributing positive feedback to acceleration of the growth of the cognitive sphere and the process of disembedding at the cognitive and social levels, driving the separation between hierarchical and heterarchical systems even further.

The transition towards urbanism is the point at which being more adaptable has won out over optimizing communications and resources: the system's coherence now comes from its rapid change rather than from its optimization. After all, optimization in the use of any resource demands time (hierarchies have to shed some of their branches/nodes), and at the rate of change occurring, it must be assumed, the hierarchies do not have the time to adapt any more.

Thus, immediately preceding any initial urbanization we can expect to see the spatial spread of a simplified system of energy procurement which makes the environment dependent on humans and which reduces the complex periodicities of that part of the environment which was exploited to much simpler ones. A crucial aspect of non-linear dynamics is of course the spatial component; the incidence and spread of such in principle isolated patches of simplified ecosystem must have crossed a density threshold like the ones known from epidemiology or the study of the spread of forest fires, in which a localized, smouldering epidemic suddenly spreads like wildfire.[12]

From the spatial perspective one could thus see the beginnings of urbanization as consisting of an oscillation between closed rural systems with mainly local interaction, such as existed over large areas of Europe, and open systems. What interests us is the spatial distribution of the different intermediate states in this transition.

Bifurcation sequences and the route to urbanism

The first bifurcation could be characterized by a limit cycle attractor (cf. Chapter 1), i.e., a situation in which the system diverges from its steady state behaviour around a fixed point attractor and follows an oscillating trajectory with a defined periodic rhythm. It can be thought of as a situation in which a dispersed, small settlement-based group of people, functioning in a traditional hierarchical communications structure, responds to fluctuations in the (social or natural) environment by temporarily reducing communications distances by means of periodic meetings. Such get-togethers would facilitate extra-hierarchical communication on a face-to-face basis and act to re-homogenize the group's 'information pool'. One could even hypothesize that, as the symbiotic system's oscillations increase as a result of the growing maladaptation of the material expressions of the cognitive structure (as exemplified in subsistence technology and the organization of subsistence activities), they become periodic, requiring periodic 'powwows', probably in fixed locations. Johnson (1982, p. 405) has called this the need for 'feather-waving'.

A second bifurcation could initiate more permanent and spatially widerspread heterarchical corridors between separating hierarchical islands. An interesting non-linear model for such spatial structuring is proposed by Chernikov et al.(1987, p. 561), who see such 'stochastic webs' developing wherever structured and unstructured oscillations form a pattern of interferences. Qualitatively, such webs would in our opinion consist of a more or less independent group of 'information brokers', among them tradesmen, priests and other kinds of marginals. One could, for example, consider the liminally placed sanctuaries in early urban Greece as the remains of such a stochastic web (cf. Morgan 1988).

The third bifurcation could be called 'pre-urban smouldering' – a situation in which, at a regional level, short-term structuring occurs here and there, petering out, only to rekindle elsewhere. The existence of long-distance heterarchical corridors would act to permit certain groups of hierarchically organized societies to integrate into a larger system. This has a locally destabilizing effect because the symbiotic system's connectivity is enhanced through spatial extension. Dealing with this consequently requires increased reliance on distributed information processing and energy obtained from elsewhere. This would be one way to look at the 'prestige-goods economy' which is in some places contemporaneous with 'hillforts' and locally generates a size hierarchy among the latter. Physically, this would require close integration of the heterarchical communications network with the hierarchical one. It would seem probable that the apex of the local hierarchy would move to the centres of long-distance communication, as we do indeed observe in temperate Europe north of the Alps.

Contemporaneously, we observe on some of the peninsulas of southern Europe the first real towns, notably in Greece and Etruria. In these cases, a number of small, more or less equivalent city-states spring up in an area in what has been called 'peer-polity interaction', a kind of bootstrapping each other (Renfrew and Cherry 1987). This phenomenon resembles in many ways that of convection and might be modelled as an example of a Bénard-like instability (see Nicolis and Prigogine 1977; Prigogine and Stengers 1984). The peer-polity/convection cell model is essentially one of increasing information flow in a local circuit, which has a differentiating and structuring effect on the inhabitants of the cell itself: centre–periphery, town–hinterland. What regional and supra-regional exchange there was, was initially effectively stochastic (down-the-line).

As these cells grow, the cores get to interact more closely, and boundary phenomena take over: neighbouring cores begin to exchange information on a regular basis; i.e., no longer in a stochastic manner, but directional. In that intermediate phase, long-distance exchange becomes 'hybrid'; i.e., between cells it moves stochastically, but once it hits the periphery of a unit it cannot but go to its centre. This entails a major reduction in stochasticity of communication as well as the beginnings of opening up the cells. Once the flows are directional, the cells can become dependent on them; the time delays in communication are drastically reduced, and this enables them to play into each other's needs.

As more and more individuals participate in the heterarchical channels, long-distance communication becomes more and more directional, meets more and more needs, and eventually connects very large spaces to such a degree that the centres become dependent on their trade networks. Importantly, the way the individual centres develop is highly dependent on minimal differences in initial conditions and on the path they take. Guérin-Pace (1993) has sketched the highly variable dynamic at the regional level within a full-grown urban structure. The crucial variable in the transition seems to be the degree of long-distance complementarity.

Eventually, the growth of large heterarchical systems threatens stability and increases sluggishness in adapting to change. Some degree of separation of interactive spheres may have been a response (city-states?) as well as hierarchization (for example in the early development of Greek city-states in which oscillations take place between tyranny and democracy). The towns eventually become permanent hybrid systems.

Modelling metastability in rural–urban interaction

In this vein, we shall first consider the intrinsic qualitative dynamics which can generate evolutionary structuring. Perhaps the best way to understand the concept of qualitative dynamics is to examine a simple form of instability to which non-linear systems are prone. To do so, we shall present an example of a generic urban/rural system coupled to human resource exploitation, and demonstrate the concept of metastability as a function of the non-linearities inherent in open systems. This model could refer to the first bifurcation in the last section, or alternatively and on another level of complexity, to what has been called 'pre-urban smouldering'.

For the purposes of clarity, and bearing in mind the fact that the first principle of a good model is parsimony, we shall select a reduced description of the phenomena of interest. The first stage in our representation is to conceive of the rural environment as a self-organizing system (Gallopin 1980, p. 240), described by a modified sigmoid growth process:

$$\frac{dR}{dt} = B(R - T)\ (K - R);\ R > 0 \tag{13.1}$$

where R = rural environment production; T = lower threshold; K = upper asymptote; B = a positive growth function.

From Equation (13.1) it can readily be seen that the rural sphere has two equilibria, at $dR/dt = 0$, $R = T$ (lower equilibrium) and $R = K$ (upper equilibrium). In addition, a third equilibrium appears at $R = 0$ because of the constraint $R > 0$.

It can also be shown that for $K > T$, $R = T$ is an unstable equilibrium, and $R = K$ is stable. Also, $R = 0$ is stable because all negative values are excluded from the form of Equation (13.1). A general picture of the behaviour of this model can be seen from Figure 13.1, and its more important properties can be summarized thus:

1 Whenever R is above the upper asymptote K, it tends to decrease and move towards it.
2 Whenever R is below K (but above the extinction threshold T), it converges on K in a sigmoid or logistic way.
3 Whenever R is below T, it decreases to zero [R stops at zero because Equation (13.1) is restricted to positive values of R].

We shall next introduce the effects of urban development (U) and its rate of growth (dU/dt or U^*). Either, or both, may influence the rural subsistence

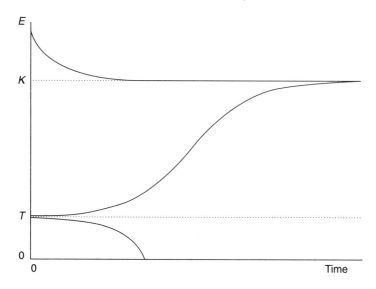

Figure 13.1   Generic time-behaviour of the model.

sphere in a number of possible ways. Initially, we shall exclude the effect of the rural sphere on urban development, and instead assume that the urban sector grows at its own pace, independently of rural effects. We then have:

$$\frac{dR}{dt} = B\,(R - T)\,(K - R) + mU + ndU/dt;\ R > 0 \qquad (13.2)$$

Here, both U and $U^\star$ are exogenous to the rural sector, and the relationship between U and $U^\star$ is not taken into account at this stage. The coefficients m and n indicate the sign and the strength of the unitary effect of urban development and its rate of growth on the rural environment. We can now distinguish a number of effects of urbanism upon the rural sector, thus:

1 m and/or $n = 0$. This implies the absence of a net effect of U and/or $U^\star$ upon R.
2 m and/or $n < 0$. This implies that the net effect of urbanism (and/or its growth) is harmful, or exerts a negative effect on the rural environment.
3 m and/or $n > 0$. This implies that the net effect of urban development (and/or its growth) is beneficial to the rural sector.

The coefficients m and n can be considered as being composed of two factors, one accounting for negative, constraining effects, while the other accounts for positive, enhancing effects. Their sum gives the net effect: thus, $m = (y - g)$, $n = (e - v)$. What is of interest, here, is that Equation (13.2)

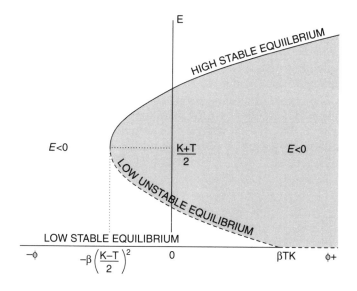

Figure 13.2 Rural environment equilibria as a function of urban development.

has equilibrium values which are no longer constant, but depend on the values of $\phi = mU + nU^\star$. For different constant values of ϕ, the equilibria can be displaced (see Figure 13.2), where ϕ^+ and ϕ^- indicate positive and negative values of ϕ respectively. Additionally, when $\phi^+ > \beta TK$, the zero equilibrium becomes unstable ($dR/dt > 0$, and thus R begins to grow).

For both ϕ^+ and ϕ^-, the upper equilibrium is stable, and the lower is unstable, if the equilibrium value of R ($R^\star$) is greater than $(K + T)/2$. For $\phi^- = - [(K - T)/2]^2 \beta$, both equilibria collapse into one, such that R tends to move towards $R^\star$, if $R > R^\star$, but it tends to move away from $R^\star$ when $R < R^\star$. Thus, for all practical purposes, this point is unstable. To the left of $\beta[(K + T)/2]^2$ there is no equilibrium, and the rate of change of R is always negative (R tends to go to zero for all values of ϕ^- lower than this). The behaviour of this system, particularly when the effect of urbanization (ϕ) can be assumed to change relatively slowly with respect to change in the rural sector (R), can be regarded as an example of Thom's (1975) first elementary catastrophe: the fold catastrophe. This catastrophe exhibits three basic properties – bimodality (because of the double stable equilibria), discontinuity (catastrophic jump) and hysteresis (the path differs according to the direction of change).

Our analysis has, so far, assumed that the only effect of urban development on the rural environment was a negative one ('extraction') on rural subsistence production. It is represented in the model by the fact that the upper equilibrium value of the rural sector is significantly higher in the absence of urban development. But the influence of the urban sector need not necessarily be deleterious; as we shall later, the two sectors are largely symbiotic, particularly within the later prehistoric context.

First, we might examine the potential effects of urban development on T, the lower unstable threshold of the rural system. As we have noted earlier, T is the value of R such that if $R > T$, R tends to go to the upper stable equilibrium, and if $R < T$, R tends to go to zero. If T is very high, it means that rural production must be maintained at a high level, so as to avoid collapse (the highest possible value for T is when $T = K$, in which case the system collapses). A value of $T = 0$ implies that rural subsistence production will tend to regenerate, even if R is pushed around zero values. Finally, increasing negative values of T affect the initial speed of growth of R when $R = 0$.

Within the terms of our present interest in societal evolution in the Iron Age, it is reasonable to infer that different rural settlement systems might be characterized by different values of T. Those rural systems with an ability to recover rapidly from perturbation, such as relatively fast growing settlements in the initial stages of colonization, should have a low value of T. By contrast, systems with a high T, such as systems whose persistence depends on management (agriculture), are probably characterized by a high degree of complexity and are relatively fragile and prone to collapse.

Another way in which urbanism can affect the persistence of the rural sector is by changing K, the upper stable equilibrium. When K is at its maximum, the rural production system is maintained at a peak of sustainability with a high rate of growth that is able to sustain major interaction with towns. Measures that are likely to modify K affect the maximum capacity of the rural environment, such as genetic improvement of crops (increases K) or agricultural soil degradation through overuse (decreases K).

Finally, urban development can alter the rural environmental system by affecting β, the growth parameter controlling rural production. Increasing β, induces faster growth (or collapse) at all levels of urban development. The systems with higher β can support greater levels of extraction or exploitation.

We have thus far treated urban development as a single parameter, ϕ; however, remembering that $\phi = (\gamma - g) U + (e - v) U^\star$, then the distinction between urban development, U, and its rate of growth, $U^\star$, becomes important with respect to the viability of responses to rural over-exploitation or potential collapse.

Modelling rural/urban interaction in a regional system

We shall now introduce a related model illustrating how the dynamics of bifurcation can be used to describe regional interaction. The role of sudden and discontinuous evolution in regional phenomena has assumed increasing importance in the literature of regional development (e.g., Wilson 1981; Andersson and Batten 1988). An important earlier work by Mees (1975) used Pirenne's (1925) hypothesis for the revival of European cities in the Late

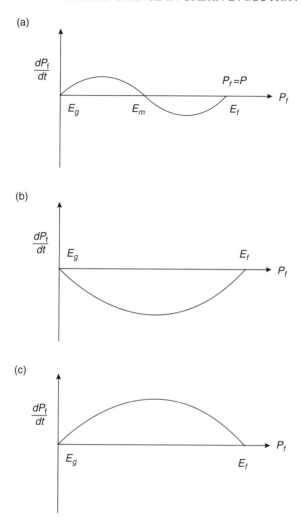

Figure 13.3 (a) Oppida/rural equilibrium in the absence of long-distance trade; (b) Oppidum specializing in long-distance trade; (c) Long-distance trade in a rural area.

Middle Ages, as the basis for an analysis of sudden changes in the patterns of regional trade. The key element was seen to be the fact that slow, gradual improvements in transportation networks, ultimately had a *discontinuous effect* which became manifest in the emergence of urbanization. The generic properties of this model make it particularly interesting in our present context of the rise of oppida-dominated landscapes in the later prehistory of north-western Europe.

We shall establish as the initial condition, open, small rural settlements in a localized valley landscape. For a given territory or region, a population, *P*, is initially assumed to be constant and divided between farming, p_f, and oppida, p_o. U_f and U_o are considered as rural and oppida utility levels and t is the long-distance transportation cost of traded goods. Above a certain threshold of t, there is no long-distance trade, but as t declines below that level, trading opportunities grow and expand.

The demographic dynamics are represented by a utility maximizing migration function, given by:

$$\frac{dp_f}{dt} = p_f\, p_o\, (U_f - U_o) = \frac{-dp_o}{dt} \tag{13.3}$$

When t is high and long-distance trade falls to zero, the dynamics are illustrated by Figure 13.3(a). Here, the only stable equilibrium is E_m, representing a mixture of oppidum–rural area interaction. As t declines further, the curve takes one of the two forms shown in Figure 13.3(b) or 13.3(c), depending on a combination of three factors; (a) the overall population density, (b) the average productivity of the territory, and (c) the oppidum–rural area productivity difference. For example, in Figure 13.3(b), a territory with a high population density and a high oppidum–rural area productivity difference has E_g as its only stable equilibrium and has completely specialized in oppidum production for long-distance trade. Figure 13.3(c), on the other hand, demonstrates the opposite scenario, because E_f is the only stable equilibrium and the region is defined as dominated by rural production for long-distance trade.

These results are consistent with a catastrophe surface (*sensu* Thom), and define a butterfly catastrophe whose four control variables form a four-dimensional bifurcation set. Figure 13.4 shows a projection of this set on to a two-dimensional t and C space (where C is the population density), along with the possible equilibria, f, m, g, depicted for each zone of the space. It is the average productivity factor, q, which produces the butterfly effect in which the triple equilibria occurs, while the sector productivity difference, δq, is the bias factor that determines the tilt of the butterfly zone one way or another. By implication, when t is high, the equilibrium will be m, but as t declines it can move to f or o, depending on C. We might note that any external population movement, by changing c, could potentially trigger such shifts.

In summary, this qualitative analysis shows that discontinuous, sudden shifts from either oppida-dominated or rural-dominated landscapes to mixed settlement structures are a function of t. Thus we see the importance of long-distance trade as a factor in producing unstable morphogenetic transitions.

More recently, Andersson (1986) has claimed that fundamental qualitative changes (in production, location, trade, culture and institutions) in the world economy over the last millennium, can be explained by slow steady changes in the structure of the associated *logistical networks*. Logistical networks are those systems in space which can be used for the movement of commodities, information, people and money in association with the production and consumption of commodities.

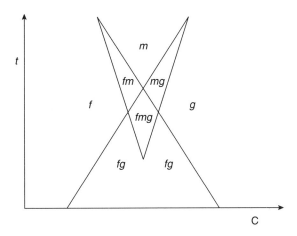

Figure 13.4 Butterfly bifurcation set for long-distance trade model.

His model presents us with a useful analytical tool for understanding the dynamics of archaeological phenomena such as the rise of proto-urban oppida. The basic assumption is that the observed fluctuations (such as occur in oppida development) can be captured – or approximated in qualitative terms – by a third order system of differential equations consisting of a 'fast equation'

$$\frac{dY}{dt} = -T\,(Y^3/3 - rY - X) \tag{13.4}$$

and a 'slow equation'

$$\frac{dX}{dt} = -T^{-1}\,Y \tag{13.5}$$

in which r is a control parameter, and T an adjustment speed coefficient. Y can be interpreted as an oppidum's capacity for producing commodities, and X, as its accessibility to networks of transportation and communication. In effect this system is a reformulation of the celebrated van der Pol equation, such that discontinuous changes in the value of Y (oppidum production) can be produced as the value of X (access to transportation) moves into a critical parametric domain. Figure 13.5 illustrates a generic cycle in which changes take place repetitively. Abrupt rises and falls in the dominance of oppida are clearly to be expected, given their often fragile and unstable socio-political power structures. Gradual changes in local resource accessibility, for example, can give rise to rapid discontinuity. What this model shows is that while the influence of the 'slow' variable is generally dominant, the 'fast' phase, nevertheless, has the capacity to 'flip' the whole system into a fundamentally different regime.

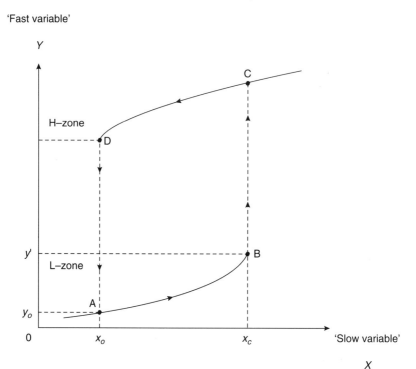

Figure 13.5   A generic cycle of fast and slow variables.

For the Late La Tène in north-western Europe, we might reasonably hypothesize that a form of network expansion through trade, alliance and even domination generated a slowly expanding system controlled from key locations occupied by the oppida. From Figure 13.5 we can see that as this network infrastructure and, consequently, the system's knowledge base (X) gradually grows, it follows the trajectory located in the L-zone of the figure. The system's initial conditions are given by A; as X changes, ultimately, a point B is reached – a threshold beyond which the productive capacity of the oppida system changes markedly. At this bifurcation point, the equilibrium loses its stability and a 'phase transition' takes place. In this far-from-equilibrium phase, the speed of change is determined by constraints on environment (natural resources), production and population (labour force). It should be noted here, that a prominent feature of this type of non-linear analysis is its cyclical nature; if, for example, the trade/transportation network linking the oppida is disrupted by other external competitive alliances or by warfare, once the H-zone is reached, unstable alliance structures are produced, and the system may follow the trajectory depicted on the H-zone until it converges on the initial state at D, and finally returns to the L-zone.

The role assumed by the critical points B and D needs to be further elaborated, so as to make the model dynamics easier to grasp. The essential underlying process is one of divergence, since a smooth but minor change in the network infrastructure can cause abrupt and unexpectedly large fluctuations in the equilibrium value of the production sphere. This (relatively sudden) phase transition takes place no matter how slowly the network capacity increases. By implication, the expansion of the oppida may simply be triggered by the addition of one small but important link in the network. Slight differences in transportation conditions, for example as a result of changes in alliance structures, may eventuate major differences in the production capacity if the oppidum growth parameter finds itself at a critical point.

Instabilities in inter-regional trade

This latter question has a major bearing on our understanding of inter-regional settlement dynamics, as the inherent instability in the trading patterns of the proto-urban oppida of temperate Europe is largely a consequence of it. We shall next attempt to demonstrate the qualitative dynamics at work, and suggest some of the implications for socio-political organization.

The model is an expansion of an original model of a reaction-diffusion equation due to Glanzdorff and Prigogine (1971), recently developed within the context of oppida expansion and contraction in Gaul as a consequence of long-distance trade (McGlade 1990, p. 158). It provides a useful set of descriptors for systems whose evolution is a process of 'order through fluctuations' governed by diffusion-driven instabilities.

The model assumes implicitly the existence of a 'prestige goods' economy as elaborated in Chapter 12. First we shall define two regional systems involved in the export and import of specific high status or prestige commodities, and denoted by X and Y. These may be taken to represent Mediterranean Europe and Gaul respectively. At this level of aggregation, we are not concerned with the fate of individual oppida but rather with a global regional dynamic. Their encoding as a dynamical system can be written in the following way:

$$\frac{dX}{dt} = F(X) - H(X) - X \tag{13.6}$$

$$\frac{dY}{dt} = F(Y) + H(X) \tag{13.7}$$

where

$$F(X) = rX(1 - X/N) + X^2Y \tag{13.8}$$

$$F(Y) = -X^2Y \tag{13.9}$$

$$H(X) = Q(K, L) - mK - C = Q_oK^mL^n \tag{13.10}$$

thus we have

$$\frac{dX}{dt} = rX\ (1 - X/N) + X^2Y - X\ [Q_oK^mL^n - mK - C] - X \qquad (13.11)$$

$$\frac{dY}{dt} = -X^2Y + X\ [Q_oK^mL^n - mK - C] \qquad (13.12)$$

where r is the intrinsic rate of growth in commodity production; N is a production saturation level; Q is a measure of economic output; with Q_o as the initial value of Q; K is commodity stock; L is labour; m is the rate of commodity stock depreciation; C is consumption. The production function $H(X)$ is modelled as a non-linear Cobb–Douglas function, with m as an exponential capital growth rate and n as an exponential accounting for the growth rate of labour. $H(X)$ is a major contributory factor to model dynamics, since it functions as an autocatalytic element in the system, effectively establishing the reaction-diffusion structure of the model. Initially, Y (northern Europe or Gaul) is seen as a major importer of prestige goods, with relatively little control of the trade routes. The $(+X^2Y)$ term is essentially the status income accrued and exhibits strong self-reinforcing properties due to the growing monopoly of the Mediterranean region in controlling trading transactions. The $(-X^2Y)$ term represents constraints acting to prevent a total monopoly; it accounts for the loss of revenue as a result of the ability of Gaul to take part in alternative exchange systems. Additionally, we shall assume that the wealth of the Mediterranean region – due to its pre-eminence in trade – will grow as a logistic function over time, so long as the *status quo* is maintained, but will be reduced by any competing flow from Gaul.

The steady state of this system, i.e., the state for which $dX/dt = dY/dt = 0$, corresponds to critical states X_o and $Y_o = F(X)/H(X) = (Q_oK^mL^n - mK - C)/rX(1 - X/N)$. The critical transition point at which the system becomes unstable, is given by

$$H(X) > (1 + F(X)^2) = (Q_oK^mL^n - mK - C) >$$

$$(1 + rX(i - X/N)^2 \qquad (13.13)$$

For example, when $F(X) = 1$, the critical point is unstable for $H(X) > 2$; as $H(X)$ is increased, a Hopf bifurcation[13] occurs with the result that the system is attracted towards a limit cycle trajectory. Figures 13.6(a)–(d) show this behaviour for increasing values of $H(X)$, since it is this function which controls the action/reaction nature of our trading system.

What we see here is instability generated by purely endogenous factors; i.e., due to the non-linearities in the system and their amplification by positive feedback mechanisms embedded in trade/exchange dynamics. Trading systems are also subject to external fluctuations, for example due to periodic increases in the volume of trade/exchange at particular times of the year. This we shall simulate by introducing a sinusoidal forcing term of amplitude a and frequency f (cf. Tomita and Kai 1978). Thus, Equation (13.13) becomes

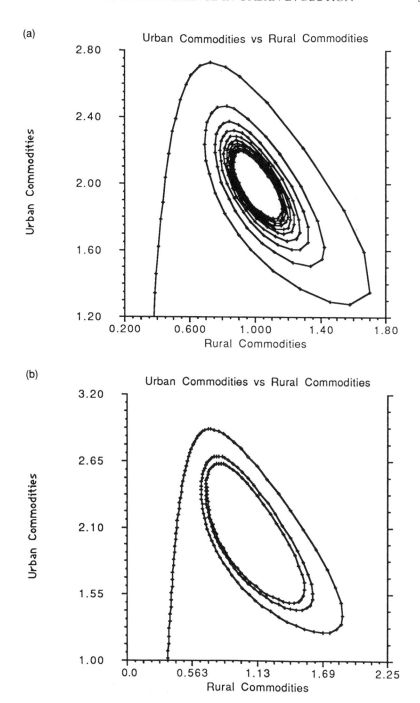

Figure 13.6 Simulation results of the oppida–rural environment interaction model, showing (a) (b) (c) (d).

(c)

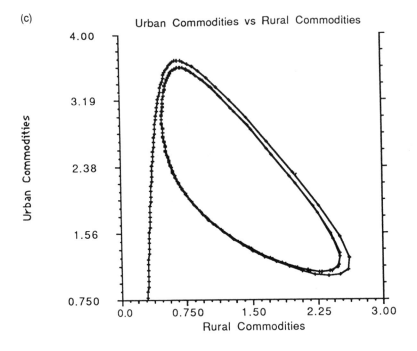

(d)

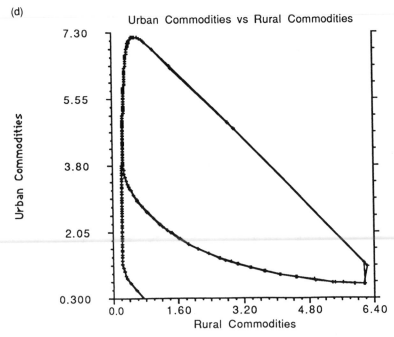

Figure 13.6 (Continued)

$$\frac{dX}{dt} = rX(1 - X/N) + X^2Y - X[Q_oK^mL^n - mK - C] - X + a\cos(ft) \quad (13.14)$$

Figures 13.7(a)–(d) show the results of such a perturbation, pushing the system progressively towards unstable orbits through a sequence of period-doubling bifurcations on the route to chaos.

Short-run dynamics: inter-regional chaos

To further illustrate the potential for chaos in open, dynamical systems and its possible role in understanding oppida/hinterland interaction, we shall focus on the useful insights of the Lorenz (1963) system. The richness of the Lorenz equations is still being investigated, and it has been shown that a number of questions can be addressed by recourse to this model (e.g. Haken 1977; Yorke and Yorke 1979; Sparrow 1982; Zhang 1989). As an illustration of the qualitative insights that it provides, we shall adapt the work of Zhang (1989) to the question of settlement/regional dynamics. Notably, we shall consider a Late La Tène agricultural system consisting of a group of interconnected sites, and its relationship to the wider regional system; we assume also the operation of a settlement hierarchy maintained by a system of tribute, and an incipient market economy.

Our production system is a relatively small (kin-based) one, set within a much larger region. For the sake of analytical simplicity, we assume that changes in the operation of the agricultural settlement system have little impact on the operation of the region which is structurally stable. What we are addressing here, then, is a short-run dynamic. The locational dynamics of this system are controlled by three principal variables, X = the output of the agricultural system, Y = the residential population, Z = the income diverted (e.g. as tribute exacted, etc.). Agricultural and animal husbandry products can be consumed locally, or exchanged beyond the region. Joining the above concepts, we can now present a possible dynamical description of the agricultural system, thus:

$$\frac{dX}{dt} = a_1 (a_2Y - a_3X) \qquad (13.15)$$

$$\frac{dY}{dt} = c_1 (c_2X - c_3Y) - c_4X \qquad (13.16)$$

$$\frac{dZ}{dt} = d_1XY - d_2Z \qquad (13.17)$$

where a_1, c_1 and d_1 are positive parameters; a_2 is the per capita demand of agricultural productivity; a_3 is the rate of consumption of goods by the local population. The term a_2Y is therefore the total demand of the population for its local product and a_3X is the total supply of goods to the marketplace. From this we can see that Equation (13.16) relates the rate of change in productivity to excess demand; thus, if demand outstrips supply, productivity tends to increase. Here, a_1 acts as an adjustment speed coefficient.

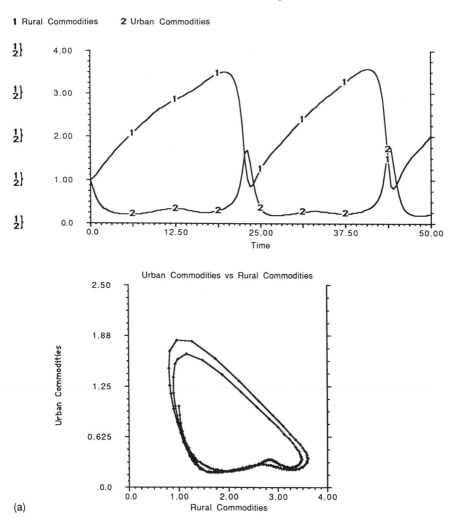

Figure 13.7 Simulation results of the oppida–rural environment interaction model, showing (a) (b) (c) (d).

Next we assume that population changes in the settlement system are represented by two terms, c_1 $(c_2X - c_3Y)$ and $-c_4XZ$, where c_2 is the labour demand for production. Thus, c_2X is the total demand of labour from the market, and c_3Y represents the total supply of labour to the marketplace. From this it follows that the term $(c_2X - c_3Y)$ is the excess demand for labour. Finally, population movement is controlled to a large extent by the level of tribute; i.e., people will tend to cluster in areas where the level of tribute (or tax) extracted is low, also, the term d_1XY accounts for the fact that the rate of change of tribute is positively related to X and Y.

1 Rural Commodities   **2** Urban Commodities

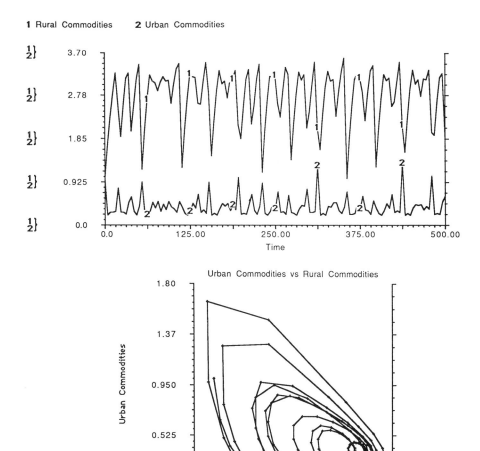

(b)

Figure 13.7   (Continued)

The structural equivalence of this model to the Lorenz system can be demonstrated by making the following transformation

$$a = a_1 a_3 / c_1 c_3, \qquad\qquad x = (c_4/d_1)1/2 d_1 X / c_1 c_3,$$

$$r = a_2 c_2 / a_3 c_3, \qquad\qquad y = (c_4/d_1)1/2 d_1 a_2 Y / a_3 c_1 c_3, \qquad (13.18)$$

$$b = d_2 / c_1 c_3, \qquad\qquad z = c_4 a_2 Z / a_3 c_1 c_3$$

Thus (13.18) transforms (13.15)–(13.17) into the Lorenz equations

(c)

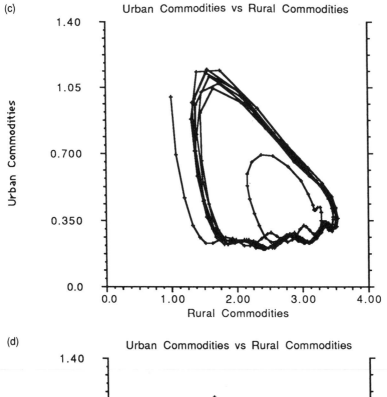

(d)

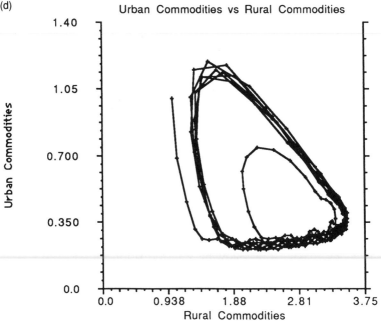

Figure 13.7   (Continued)

$$dx/dt = -ax + ay$$

$$dy/dt = -xz + rx - y \qquad\qquad (13.19)$$

$$dz/dt = xy - bz$$

and we have a model structure which is able to account for the embedded non-linearities in an intra-regional settlement system. For example, the global relationship linking agricultural productivity (X) and the tribute or taxation levied can give rise to unstable and unpredictable evolutions since they are coupled in a non-linear way to population dynamics – especially to factors controlling labour supply and demand. Examples of the kinds of complex aperiodicities can be seen from the sequence of attractors we see in Figures 13.8(a), 13.8(b) and 13.8(c); Figures 13.9(a) and 13.9(b) show the chaotic region to which this system can be driven, on account of its extreme sensitivity to initial conditions and its strong positive feedback mechanisms.

None the less, at a generic level, we can see that behaviours accounting for the precise relationships between productivity, population, and tribute, though they may be said to be *locally unstable*, at a collective level possess a *global stability*. The system thus possesses an intrinsic coherence that is described by the strange attractor in Figure 13.9(d). The paradox of chaos can be seen in the fact that that the dynamics of the time-series in Figure 13.9(c) appears to be completely irregular, but, as the phase space portrait described by the attractor in Figure 13.9(d) shows, is entirely deterministic. It is important to point out here that this is quite different from external stochastic effects such as 'white noise', which allows the dynamics to explore the entire phase space (i.e., to become ergodic).

From a social perspective, chaotic evolution and strange attractors allow us to see the evolution of structures as broadly cumulative and stable at a macroscopic level of description, but characterized by erratic and idiosyncratic properties at lower, more local levels. By implication, no complex system can be described by recourse to either micro or macro levels; it is a subtle confluence of both and as such is fundamentally irreducible. It is in the impossibility of reductionist explanation for natural phenomena that resides one of the fundamental lessons of chaos.

Spatial interaction

This section shall propose an explanation in terms of self-organizing evolutionary processes for the way in which a relatively homogeneous settlement pattern may change into complex hierarchical and heterarchical structures. Regional settlement dynamics involving proto-urban organization have recently been discussed within the later prehistoric context of northern Gaul (McGlade 1993). It was argued that these settlement systems display a number of generic characteristics allowing their description in terms of 'classic' spatial

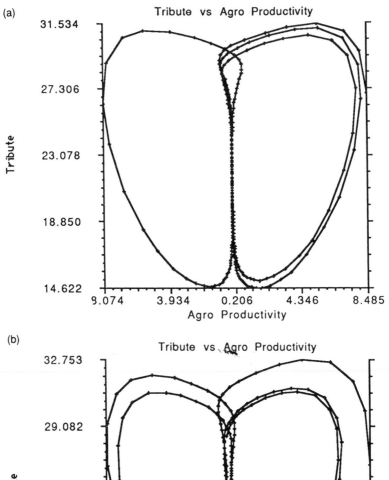

Figure 13.8   Simulation results of the oppida–rural environment interaction model, showing (a) (b) (c).

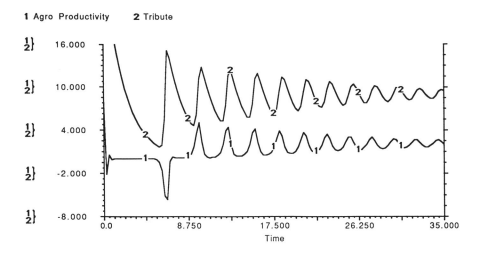

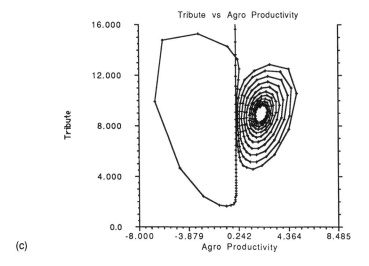

(c)

Figure 13.8   (Continued)

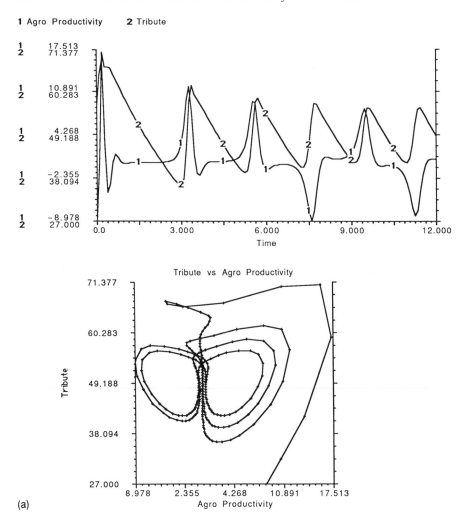

Figure 13.9 Simulation results of the oppida–rural environment interaction model, showing (a) (b) (c) (d).

interaction models developed in locational geography and regional science.[14] The linear assumptions of these models have more recently been extended to a more realistic scenario, involving non-linear transportation costs (Beckmann and Puu 1985). Importantly, in these analyses, the role of non-linearities induced by transportation effects results in quadrangular market areas, rather than the hexagonal lattices of the linear Christaller–Lösch models. To illustrate this, we might consider a generic model for the flow of a single economic commodity in our Late La Tène landscape.

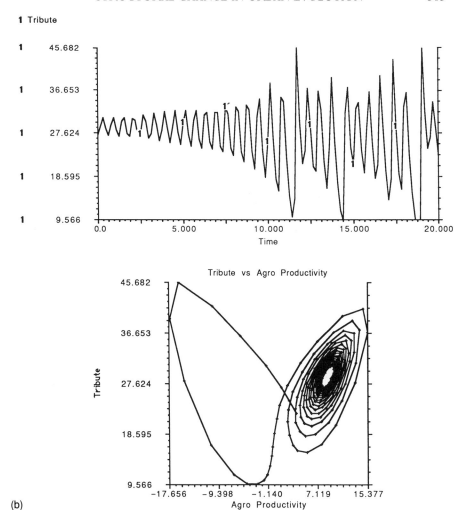

Figure 13.9 (Continued)

Let x_1 and x_2 refer to co-ordinates along the north–south and east–west axes, respectively, thus specifying locations. Within such a space, trade/exchange flow vectors and tribute patterns can be represented by two flow equations determined by a 'divergence law' and a 'gradient law'. Thus, excess demand according to location is given by

$$q = q \ (x_1, \ x_2) \tag{13.20}$$

Here, maxima will be sinks that represent the market nodes, and minima will be the sources representing oppidum production. Spatial equilibrium is first given by:

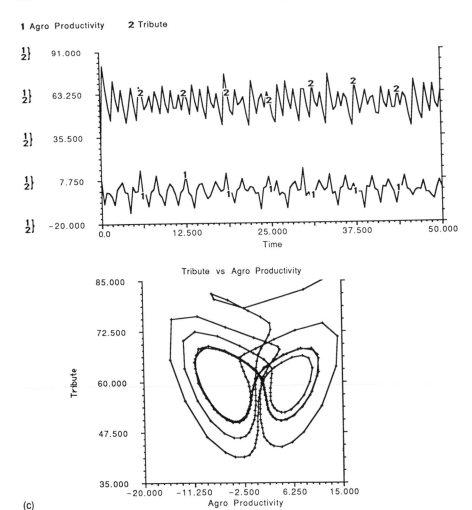

Figure 13.9   (Continued)

$$q = q\,(x_1,\ x_2)\ dx_1\ dx_2 = 0 \tag{13.21}$$

According to the divergence law, the local flow vector, $\mu\,(x_1, x_2)$ of commodity movements will be given by

$$-q\,(x_1,\ x_2) = d\mu_1/dx_1 + d\mu_2/dx_2 \tag{13.22}$$

with

$$\mu_n = 0 \tag{13.23}$$

accounting for a trade-limited outer boundary. If the expression $k(x_1,\ x_2)$ represents the unit transportation cost expressed as tribute, and $\pi(x_1,\ x_2)$ is

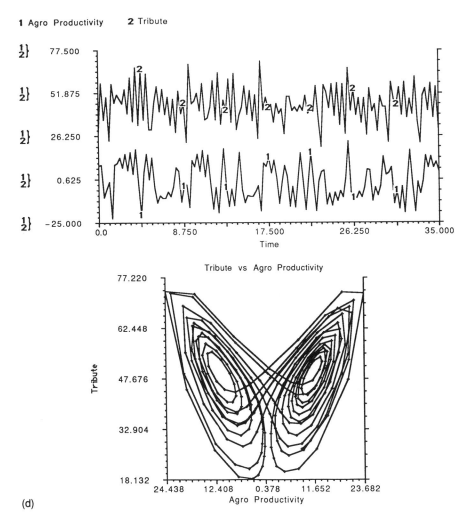

1 Agro Productivity   **2** Tribute

(d)

Figure 13.9 (Continued)

the 'value' at location (x_1, x_2), then locational optimization is given as a potential function

$$m\mu \ k/\mu/dx_1 \ dx_2 = k \tag{13.24}$$

This is solved by the gradient law solution,

$$k\mu/ \ / \ \mu \ / = \text{grad} \ \pi \tag{13.25}$$

which implies that flows move in the direction of the most powerful node or oppidum. The Christaller–Lösch hexagonal pattern will occur when k is constant for all locations. However, in the more general non-linear case,

Beckman and Puu (1985, p. 85) note that the hexagonal spatial structure is structurally unstable, and should disappear under perturbation to be superseded by a more stable quadrilateral pattern. In this way, a finite number of sinks and sources will alternate with a finite number of saddle points. Most important of all, by way of contrast to the Christaller–Lösch model, trade and exchange flows will occur along boundary lines. This is shown in Figure 13.10. While such flow patterns are structurally stable, it has been shown that sudden structural changes can occur in response to continuous changes in the efficiency of the transportation network – something highly likely in pre-Roman and early Roman Gaul which was prey to the fluctuating 'value' of exchange items.

Conclusion

Given the relatively unstable social and political power structures operating in the Late La Tène, where, for example, exchange systems could all too readily break down, with interruptions in long-distance trading either as a consequence of inter-regional rivalry over access and control of exchange networks, or of warfare, then there is every reason to suspect that the political, social and economic jurisdiction enjoyed by a particular oppidum was short lived. The fragility of such settlement systems means that the spatial dynamic defining the Late La Tène landscape is not easy to define.

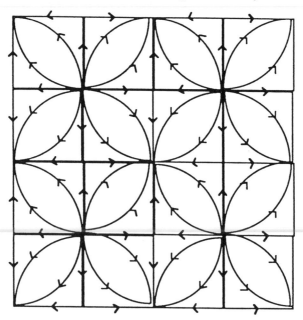

Figure 13.10 Beckmann–Puu quadrangular grid with non-linear transportation costs.

What we can say, first, is that such a fluid and essentially discontinuous process of structuring and restructuring is imperfectly captured by any single spatial, all encompassing, geometric structure as an explanation of societal organization. For example, under the type of dynamic evolution postulated here, territoriality and the social boundedness of society must have been subject to constant redefinition; a political tug-of-war between competing adjacent polities for control and supremacy in exchange relations, both within the transportation network itself, and outside. Under such circumstances, pre-eminent social control by any single social group is thus unlikely for other than short periods; indeed, Caesar's stress on the importance of the Suessiones as the most powerful tribe, may best be treated, not so much as any fixed factual entity, but as a temporally bounded 'snapshot' that may have limited resemblance to the long-term history of the region.

Such an observation is highlighted simply to make the point that many potential evolutionary pathways were open to such a system, given our stress on the twin concepts of non-linearity and metastability, and their role in generating discontinuous evolution – particularly in logistical networks. Perhaps, in this respect, too much work on oppidum-dominated landscapes has been content to focus on a Cartesian conception of events, in which point distributions are studied as abstract interactions on a homogeneous, fixed plane.

It is hoped that some of the above modelling approaches based on open dissipative systems can now be integrated into a new programme of spatio-temporal dynamics that will demonstrate structural morphogenesis within urban and proto-urban settlement systems. More generally, what we have tried to demonstrate in this chapter is that archaeological approaches to questions of urban evolution have much to gain from an alignment with dynamical systems concepts – an alignment that is much more than metaphorical. Indeed, it is clear that the open, dissipative nature of urban/rural dynamics and their propensity to evolve through discontinuous transitions, cannot be adequately understood by recourse to normative models; they require the combination of creative insight and experimental qualitative methods which is the unique contribution of non-linear dynamics.

Finally, we would like to stress, again, that none of these ideas has the pretence to represent 'reality'. Even if such a representation were theoretically possible (and we do not think so), it is much too early to adopt one. For the moment we are in that delightful phase of 'playing with hypotheses', and have tried to show that there are different kinds of games out there, which are fun because they bring us some glimpses of insight which add to our understanding.

Notes

1 We have chosen to forgo the usual summary of earlier opinions, not out of dis-respect, but due to inevitable limitations of space. For a more encompassing discussion we refer the reader, for example, to Smith (1976), Pumain (1982) or Guérin-Pace (1993).

2 Developed at some length in van der Leeuw and McGlade (1993).

3 For a more detailed treatment, see van der Leeuw and McGlade (1993).

4 To our knowledge the first people to stress this in the literature were H.T. Wright (1969) and G.A. Johnson (1972, 1975, 1977).

5 There are many other aspects of urban development which intuitively seem to tie in with this perspective, such as the social instability of early towns, but elaborating on them is impossible in the context of this chapter. For the moment we would only like to put forward the hypothesis that, contrary to general belief among those studying urban systems, it seems that the critical variables which govern the emergence of towns, and in all probability their long-term dynamic, lie in the realm of their communications structure rather than elsewhere, and that the 'classical' variables held responsible for the structuring of urban systems should be re-examined in that light. To give just one example, it might just be worth while to measure the diversity of the goods flowing from one centre in a hierarchical settlement system to the next, rather than the volume of such flows.

6 By implication one way to study both urban and non-urban aspects of human settlement from one and the same spatial perspective is to monitor the transformations by mapping the 'communication landscape' at each stage. That landscape is evidently constrained by the geomorphological and environmental features of the landscape, but is not at all isomorphous with them. Rather, it takes into account the relative densities and efficiencies of 'grey matter', i.e., the aggregation pattern of the population and some of its consequences for the capacity of the average individual in each location to communicate with others. A map of such a landscape would therefore be based on a physiographic map, but would in addition take into account the flows of matter, energy and information in the landscape, maybe as a series of isochrestic 'overlays' of each. Such a map evidently changes continuously due to population dynamics (and notable age distribution), migration, etc. Moreover, this dynamic map of the information-processing land-scape would have a number of 'sources' of organization (cf. Rosen 1979, p. 99 who also speaks of 'pumps' on p. 101) which create potentials in information-processing capacity across space, and the concomitant flows of organization which emanate from these sources and spread to areas with lower information-processing capacity values – areas which are less likely to create new forms of organization, but which may adopt them once they have been developed elsewhere. The average information-processing capacity of the total landscape will therefore increase as a result of the innovations introduced at the sources, but only after a certain time-lag which varies from point to point.

The first steps in the derivation of such a map from a physiographical map would include some of the following transformations:

First, the physiographic landscape would have to be transformed into a physical communication landscape, by calculating the appropriate communication distances between all the points, for the different kinds of flows. Recently a very inter-esting method for spatially mapping the connectivity of points on such a landscape was presented in an archaeological context by Gorenflo and Gale (1990). It is based on a geographical technique developed by Tobler (1978) which calculates the 'field of displacement vectors' that results from the transformation of geographic space into travel time by space by a simple trilateration algorithm.

Second, one would have to map on this communication landscape the population densities involved, in cells which are sufficiently fine in relation to the map as to show enough local variability.

Third, combining the population aggregation map with the physical communication map generated earlier in this sequence would show the number of potential interactions of an average individual in any location, representing the fact that aggregation of the population reduces the energy cost of communication and thus non-linearly increases the potential interactiveness or connectability, up to a certain threshold.

Evidently, the exact nature of other non-linearities to be taken into account depends on the specifics of the system state to be mapped, and is the aim of further research into the specific circumstances of urban origins in different parts of the world and at different periods.

7   A useful example is to be seen in the American motor industry which remained 'locked in' to the production of large, energy-inefficient cars, long after it was apparent that smaller cars were more efficient and advantageous.

8   That is, systems composed of a great number of elements in complex interaction.

9   What follows are some examples; this topic has been discussed at length in van der Leeuw and McGlade (1993).

10 The size limitations of this chapter, however, do not permit us to give the full argument, which will have to wait for a book form publication which is in preparation.

11 Elsewhere van der Leeuw (1987) has sketched the dialectic which is responsible for this maladaption in terms comparable with the present perspective.

12 Such processes are, again, well-known examples of the effect of non-linear dynamics, and can be modelled (cf. Grassberger (1991) and, for an archaeological example, Zubrow, Chapter 8, this volume).

13 As parameters are changed in a dynamical system, the stability of the equilibrium points can change. The study of these changes in non-linear problems is the subject of *bifurcation theory*. Values of these parameters at which the qualitative or topological nature of motion changes are referred to as critical bifurcation values.

14 The analysis of dynamic spatial patterns has advanced in recent years to include work on multiple equilibria and discontinuous transitions in migration analysis, transportation networks and labour economics (see Beckmann and Puu 1985 for a review).

References

Allen, P.M. 1982. The genesis of structure in social systems: the paradigm of self-organisation. In *Theory and Explanation in Archaeology: the Southampton conference*, A.C. Renfrew, M.J. Rowlands and B.A. Segraves (eds) 347–74. London: Academic Press.

Allen, P.M., and M. Sanglier 1978. Dynamic models of urban growth. *Journal of Social and Biological Structures* 1, 265–80.

Allen, P.M., and M. Sanglier 1979. Dynamic models of urban growth. *Journal of Social and Biological Structures* 2, 269–78.

Andersson, A.E. 1986. The four logistical revolutions. *Papers of the Regional Science Association* 59, 1–12.

Andersson, A.E. and D.F. Batten 1988. Creative nodes, logistical networks and the future of the metropolis. *Transportation* 14, 281–93.

Arthur, W.B. 1988. Self-reinforcing mechanisms in economics. In *The Economy as an Evolving Complex System*, K.J. Arrow, P.W. Anderson and D. Pines (eds), 9–31. New York: Addison-Wesley.

Arthur, W.B. 1990. Positive feedbacks in the economy. *Scientific American* 263, 94–9.

Atlan, H. 1992. Self-organizing networks: weak, strong and intentional. The role of their underdetermination. *La Nuova Critica N.S.* 19–20, 51–70.

Beckmann, M.J. and T. Puu 1985. *Spatial Economics: density, potential and flow.* Amsterdam: North-Holland.

Ceccato, H.A. and B.A. Huberman 1988. Persistence of non-optimal strategies. *Physica Scripta* 37, 145–50.

Chernikov, A.A., R.Z. Sagdeev, D.A. Usikov, M.Y. Zakharov and G.M. Zaslavsky 1987. Minimal chaos and stochastic webs. *Nature* 326, 559–63.

Childe, V.G. 1956. *Piecing together the Past: the interpretation of archaeological data.* London: Routledge and Kegan Paul.

Gallopin, G. 1980. Development and environment: an illustrative model. *Journal of Policy Modelling* 2, 239–54.

Glanzdorff, P. and I. Prigogine 1971. *Structure, stability and fluctuations.* London: Wiley Interscience.

Gorenflo, L.J. and N. Gale 1990. Mapping regional settlement in information space. *Journal of Anthropological Archaeology* 9, 240–74.

Grassberger, P. 1991. La percolation ou la géométrie de la contagion. *La Recherche* 232, 640–6.

Guérin-Pace, F. 1993. *Deux siècles de croissance urbaine.* Paris: Anthropos

Haag, G. and W. Weidlich 1984. A stochastic theory of interregional migration. *Geographical Analysis* 16, 331–57.

Haken, H. 1977. *Synergetics – an introduction.* Berlin: Springer-Verlag.

Holling, C.S. 1973. Resilience and stability of ecological systems. *Annual Review of Ecology and Systemstics* 4, 1–23.

Huberman, B. A. and T. Hogg 1988. Behaviour of computational ecologies. In *The Ecology of Computation,* B.A. Huberman (ed.), 77–115. Amsterdam: North-Holland.

Johnson, G.A. 1972. A test of the utility of central place theory in archaeology. *Man, Settlement and Urbanism,* P. Ucko, R. Tringham and G. Dimbleby (eds), 769–86. London: Duckworth.

Johnson, G.A. 1975. Locational analysis and the investigation of Uruk local exchange systems. In *Ancient Civilization and Trade,* J.A. Sabloff and C.C. Lamberg-Karlovsky (eds), 285–334. Albuquerque: University of New Mexico Press.

Johnson, G.A. 1977. Aspects of regional analysis in archaeology. *Annual Review of Anthropology* 6, 479–508.

Johnson, G.A. 1978. Information sources and the development of decision-making organizations. In *Social Archaeology: beyond subsistence and dating,* C.L. Redman, M.J. Berman, E.V. Curtin, W.T. Langhorne Jr., N.M. Versaggi and J.C. Wander (eds), 87–112. New York: Academic Press.

Johnson, G.A. 1981. Monitoring complex system integration and boundary phenomena with settlement size data. In *Archaeological Approaches to the Study of Complexity,* S.E. van der Leeuw (ed.), 144–88. Amsterdam: University of Amsterdam.

Johnson, G.A. 1982. Organizational structure and scalar stress. In *Theory and Explanation in Archaeology: the Southampton conference,* A.C. Renfrew, M.J. Rowlands and B.A. Segraves (eds), 389–421. New York: Academic Press.

Johnson, G.A. 1983. Decision-making organizations and pastoral nomad camp size. *Human Ecology* 11, 175–200.

Latour, B. 1988. Mixing humans with non-humans: sociology of a door-closer. *Social Problems* 35, 298–310.

Lemonnier, P. 1986. The study of material culture today: towards an anthropology of technical systems. *Journal of Anthropological Archaeology* 5, 147–86.

Lorenz, E.N. 1963. Deterministic nonperiodic flow. *Journal of Atmospheric Science* 20, 130–41.

McGlade, J. 1987. Chronos and the oracle: some thoughts on time, time-scales and simulation. *Archaeological Review from Cambridge* 6, 21–31.

McGlade, J. 1990. The emergence of structure: social transformation in later prehistoric Wessex. Unpublished Ph.D. dissertation, University of Cambridge.

McGlade, J. 1993. Modelling structural change in the later prehistory of the Aisne Valley: evolutionary dynamics and human/environmental interaction. Unpublished MS, ERA 12, CNRS, ATP Grands Projets Regionaux, Paris.

McGlade, J. 1994. The dynamics of change in the human modified environments of the Vera Basin. In *The ARCHAEOMEDES Project*, S.E. van der Leeuw (ed.), Vol. 2, 143–321. Cambridge (Report to DG XII of the European Union).

✓ Mayhew, B.H. and R.L. Levinger 1976. On the emergence of oligarchy in human interaction. *American Journal of Sociology* 81, 1017–49.

✓ Mayhew, B.H. and R.L. Levinger 1977. Size and density of interaction in human aggregates. *American Journal of Sociology* 82, 86–110.

✓ Mees, A.I. 1975. The revival of cities in medieval Europe. *Regional Science and Urban Economics* 5, 403–25

Morgan, C.M. 1988. Ethne, ethnicity and state formation in the early Greek world. Unpublished paper, Department of Classics, Cambridge University.

Nicolis, G. and I. Prigogine 1977. *Self-Organization in Non-Equilibrium Systems*. New York: Wiley Interscience.

O'Neill, R.V., D.L. De Angelis, J.B. Waide and T.F.H. Allen 1986. *A Hierarchical Concept of the Ecosystem*. Princeton, N.J.: Princeton University Press.

Pirenne, H. 1925. *Medieval Cities* (English translation by F.D. Halsey). Princeton, N.J.: Princeton University Press.

Prigogine, I. and I. Stengers 1984. *Order out of Chaos*. New York: Bantam Books.

Pumain, D. 1982. *La dynamique des villes*. Paris: Economica.

Pumain, D., L. Sanders and T. Saint-Julien 1989. *Villes et auto-organisation*. Paris: Economica.

Renfrew, A.C. and J. Cherry (eds) 1987. *Peer-polity Interaction*. Cambridge: Cambridge University Press.

Rosen, R. 1979. Morphogenesis in biological and social systems. In *Transformations: Mathematical approaches to culture change*, A.C. Renfrew and K.L. Cooke (eds), 91–111. New York: Academic Press.

Sanders, L. 1992. Modèles de la dynamique urbaine: une approche critique. In *Temporalités Urbaines,* B. Lepetit and D. Pumain (eds), 3–41. Paris: Anthropos.

Simon, H.A. 1973. The organization of complex systems. In *Hierarchy Theory: the challenge of complex systems*, H.H. Pattee (ed.), 3–27. New York: George Braziller.

Simon, H.A. 1981. *The Sciences of the Artificial* (2nd ed.). Cambridge, Mass.: MIT Press.

✓ Smith, C.A. 1976. Regional economic systems: linking geographic models and socio-economic problems. In *Regional Analysis*, C.A. Smith (ed.), 3–63. New York: Academic Press.

Sparrow, C. 1982. *The Lorenz Equations, Bifurcations, Chaos and Strange Attractors*. Berlin: Springer-Verlag.

Thom, R. 1975. *Structural Stability and Morphogenesis*. Reading, Mass.: W.A. Benjamin.

Tobler, W. 1978. Comparison of plane forms. *Geographical Analysis* 10, 154–62.

Tomita, K. and T. Kai 1978. Stroboscopic phase portrait and strange attractors. *Physics Letters* 66A, 91–3.

Van der Leeuw, S.E. 1987. Revolutions revisited. In *Revolutions Revisited,* L. Manzanilla (ed.), 215–41. Oxford: British Archaeological Reports, International Series 349.

Van der Leeuw, S.E. 1989. Risk, perception, innovation. In *What's New? A closer look at the process of innovation*, S.E. van der Leeuw and R. Torrence (eds), 300–29. London: Unwin and Hyman.

Van der Leeuw, S.E. 1990. Rythmes temporels, espaces naturels et espaces vécus. In *Archéologie et Espaces,* J.L. Fiches and S.E. van der Leeuw (eds), 299–346. Antibes: A.P.D.C.A.

Van der Leeuw, S.E. and J. McGlade 1993. Information, cohérence et dynamiques urbaines. In *Temporalités Urbaines*, D. Pumain and B. Lepetit (eds), 195–245. Paris: Economica.

Wilson, A.G. 1981. Catastrophe theory and bifurcations. *Applications to Urban Regional Systems.* London: Croom Helm.

Wilson, A.G. 1984. Making urban models more realistic: some strategies for future research. *Environment and Planning* A 16, 1419–32.

Wright, H.T. 1969. *The Administration of Rural Production in an Early Mesopotamian Town.* Ann Arbor: University of Michigan Museum of Anthropology (Anthropological Papers 38).

Yorke, E.D. and A. Yorke 1979. Metastable chaos: transition to sustained chaotic behaviour in the Lorenz model. *Journal of Statistical Physics* 31, 263–77.

Zhang, W.-B. 1989. *Synergetic Economics,* CERUM Working Paper CWP-1989: 8.

Part III

ISSUES IN MODELLING

This last section serves to raise explicitly some of the problems which are, to an extent at least, inherent in the use of dynamical models. Some such problems have been mentioned in Chapter 1, for example dynamical models' sensitivity to initial conditions, the limits which this sensitivity implicitly sets to our capacity to reason in terms of 'cause-and-effect' (i.e., to the predictability of system behaviour), and the difficulties one inherently encounters in calibrating dynamical systems models on the basis of archaeological data. Others will have become clear to the reader in perusing the last section. But what distinguishes such problems from those to be dealt with here is in our opinion that the latter are of a different order of magnitude altogether, as they question the very basis of modelling on the one hand, and the very basis of archaeology on the other.

By their nature, some such problems are inevitable and insoluble. So limited are our human means to perceive, to cognize and to reason that any approach we take is fraught, any 'mind's eye' image we form is distorted. The spirit of this section is that such inherent difficulties should not prevent us from exploring any path towards understanding, but that we should proceed down such a path with our eyes open. Over the last thirty years, archaeologists have generally not been very good at placing their own discipline in an epistemological perspective. Indeed, they have suffered from a sense of inferiority in this respect, which in our opinion is due to insufficient knowledge of the foibles of other disciplines rather than to the fact that interpreting the data is so much more difficult in archaeology than in a range of other disciplines.

It is thus appropriate that this section begins with the perspective of a philosopher who stems from the life sciences and whose work has been dedicated to elaborating and testing non-linear models in biology. Rosen (Chapter 14) asks the fundamental question whether it is not so that any and all models we make are always of the (few) exceptional situations rather than of the (generally observed) messier ones. His elegant argument is based on the observation that even in the exceedingly formal discipline of mathematics,

which is the basis of the kinds of models we are talking about, formalizability of systems is very rare indeed. It follows in Rosen's eyes that that
property, formalizability, must be even more exceptional in the non-
mathematical disciplines, and that mathematical models of non-mathematical
phenomena must therefore be limited to very exceptional examples. But
rather than give up modelling altogether as an unattainable ideal, he concludes
that we have to widen our conception of what models are, and maybe the
way in which we use formalizations in furthering our understanding of
complex systems.

Clearly, this is an issue which lies at the heart of the role of mathematics
in archaeology. All too often, whatever the nature of their models, archaeologists have been tempted by the elegance of mathematics to assume that the
model in question, or its results, were the best possible approximation of the
dynamics they were studying. Yes, such models permitted a kind of clarity,
a neatness, which is unusual in our muddy discipline, and they therefore
reinforced the feeling that there is order in the universe after all. But, according
to others, by ignoring the muddles, the models lost touch with 'reality' (whatever that may have been)!

Let us therefore explore Rosen's argument in some detail to make it somewhat more accessible to archaeologists. In archaeology, at least since the
famous discussion in 1952/3 between Ford, Steward and Brew on the one
hand, Spaulding and Gifford on the other, we have been asking: 'what is a
type?', and we have not been able to give a good answer. Rosen, too, asks:
'what is typical?' and points to the circularity of categorizing something as
'typical' in order to define the type for which it is typical. His point of
departure is thus one which we know all too well. Clarke (1968, p. 522)
mentions the same circularity in our archaeological definitions of 'type', but
does not manage to circumvent the problem (van der Leeuw 1976, p. 55).
Rosen concludes that being typical, i.e., having no special properties, is itself
a property: genericity.

In order to evaluate the congruence of models of change with the changes
they model, we need to decide whether in such models either the processes
or the perturbations (or neither, or both) are generic or not. Were we to
conclude that our models are generally non-generic, but that the changes
they model are generic, this would severely limit the uses of such models.

The first step is to distinguish between the mere perturbation of, and
change in, a process. Which perturbations allow a process to remain essentially the same (or stable), and which do transform the nature of that process
(or engender a bifurcation)? There are two issues involved, the first ontological, the second epistemological. Drawing, in part, on earlier work, Rosen
argues that ontologically speaking, stability will generally be neither generic
nor exceptional, and that with the appropriate perturbation every point is in
fact a bifurcation point. This is an important issue, as it questions the prevailing
view in archaeology that stability is generic and change the exception. Rosen
argues that such a view is due to an inherent bias in favour of reductionism,

similar to the tendency in number theory to focus on the rational numbers which make up only an infinitely small part of the total set of numbers (the others are called irrational!).

But the epistemological point is equally important. Stability is defined as the case in which every sufficiently good approximation of a point or a process is also similar to it, while in the case of non-stable points (bifurcation points), no approximation, however close, guarantees similarity. Our capacity to model is thus of equal importance in deciding between stability and instability.

Rosen considers that:

> An arbitrary (i.e., a generic) perturbation of what is generic yields something again generic; an arbitrary perturbation of what is non-generic destroys the special properties (e.g., breaks the symmetries, or lifts the degeneracies) on which non-genericity depends . . . We need to characterize what a generic [i.e., typical] perturbation is before we can decide, by this criterion, whether what we perturb is generic or not.
>
> (Rosen, Chapter 14)

For example, if our modelling were to restrict the perturbations we apply to a point – as it often will, even inadvertently, especially in the case of complex systems – we can no longer be sure whether or not an (observed) bifurcation is due to a (hidden) restriction in the perturbations applied or not; i.e., whether it is due to our modelling or inherent in the system modelled. Rosen goes on to prove in mathematical terms that, indeed, what looks like *an arbitrary (generic) perturbation of one member of a (parametrized) family of functions is equivalent to a very special perturbation of (the arguments of) the fixed function which represents the whole family.* Our fears have become true, genericity of perturbations is only apparent.

Rosen presents examples of theories which have generally been accepted as generic, but which turn out to be generated by fixed functions in the sense in which that term was used above. René Thom's 'Catastrophe Theory' is a typical example. It presents us with a number of phenomena which may happen 'generically' around a set of functions which turn out to be very special (i.e., non-generic) functions, generated by his 'Classification Theorem'.

According to Rosen, it is the condition of possessing a 'largest model' (the non-generic 'fixed function') which allows simulation; i.e., expression of the system in such a way that it can be expressed as 'software' on an extraneous symbol processor. He defines any such system as an essentially 'simple' system. Lifting this condition, i.e., making every perturbation generic, inherently decouples all the parts of the system, thus transforming it into a (non-simulable) complex one. It follows that complexity is thus generic (and not simplicity – archaeologists should finally accept that Occam's Razor is not for them!): perturbing a complex system gives another complex system, but perturbing a simple one does not generate another simple system.

Rosen's conclusions concern us no less. He sees modelling as the creation of a congruence between a system of inferential entailment (the model) and a system of causal entailment (the real-world system being modelled). The implications of the chapter for such modelling are primarily that simulability heavily impoverishes the range of causal entailments which can be taken into account: 'Almost everything about such a (simple) system is unentailed from within the system, and must accordingly be externally posited; all that remains is the entailment of 'next state' from 'present state'. Complex systems, on the other hand, have more entailment than can be accommodated in the system. They are infinitely open (and simple systems at best finitely open), so that they manifest non-mechanistic or counter-intuitive behaviour.

We should of course include most of our mental models among the simple systems, hence the term 'counter-intuitive'. As Atlan argues in a paper which was presented at the symposium, but which has been published elsewhere (1992, pp. 59–60), most of our theories are underdetermined by our obser- vations (because all the observations could not be accommodated in the model, we would argue) and hence over-determined by our pre-conceptions and simplifications!

Finally, all this does not mean that it is not useful to make dynamical models, as long as we keep in mind that the models are local in time and space, and that we thus have to shift from model to model, considering complex models as limits of sets of simple ones, modelling theories instead of modelling the 'real world', modelling what something entails rather than what entails it (i.e., modelling consequences rather than causes, another funda- mental divergence from present-day archaeological doctrine; cf. van der Leeuw 1990a, 1990b).

Chapman's (Chapter 15) argument is not dissimilar from Rosen's. On the basis of a diagrammatic sketch of the differences between the domains of a number of disciplines within the physical, life and social sciences, Chapman distinguishes between *complication* (quantitative escalation of phenomena which are theoretically reducible), *complification* (artefacts, which are theoretically reducible but won't work in their reduced state: cars, watches, etc.), *complexity* (phenomena for which we are no longer sure that reductionist explanations work) and *complexification* (non-reducible, consciously reflexive phenomena which can purposefully change their own state).

He then asks whether the same modelling procedures can be used for all four of these kinds of phenomena. Traditional modelling ('order modelling' in Chapman's terms) depends on the expectation that (1) the processes would converge on a final equilibrium state (or stable periodic/quasi-periodic behav- iour), and (2) the number of variables and functions involved was so limited as to permit the derivation of analytical solutions. Such modelling is effec- tive for both the domain of *complication* and that of *complification*.

Recent developments in non-linear theory have shown that all dynamic systems of two dimensions will show equilibrium or periodic behaviour, but that this is not true at higher dimensionalities, where they are governed by strange attractors, and can only be calculated if the initial conditions were observed with infinite precision. As such, dynamical models seem therefore to have a major potential in the realm of *complexity*, and notably in the study of living non-human systems. They lead us to reconsider equilibrium-based approaches, and maybe the concept of equilibrium itself, at least for the life sciences. In turn, this could undermine aspects of existing evolutionary theory, notably ideas concerning mutation. The main problem with the applicability of such models to human systems, however, resides in the fact that these belong to the realm of *complexification*, which incorporates ideas of reflexivity. For this reason, Chapman argues, it is difficult to see how dynamical systems modelling can have an impact on the social sciences.

He then points out that there are also consequences for the realm of experiment, and for the experimental role which modelling has often been given in the human sciences. Under the 'order modelling' approach, experiment is based on the idea of keeping out extraneous variables, thought to affect the result in undesirable ways, and on the requirement that experiments are replicable. Non-linear approaches seem, however, to suggest that even the tiniest fluctuation is significant (so that nothing can be left out as 'extraneous'), and that very few things are replicable. In both these conclusions, then, Chapman is, again, on the same line as Rosen although he comes at it from a very different angle (fieldwork on the relationship between western and indigenous technologies).

The last two chapters in this section voice complementary criticisms of the use of dynamical modelling in archaeology. The authors are archaeologists and the criticisms are hence formulated in a different language, which requires less of an introduction to the audience at which this book is aimed. Wobst (Chapter 16) focuses on an area which in our opinion has been undervalued for a considerable time, since well before dynamical models befell us. The attention devoted to such models, however, only makes the task more urgent: designing adequate systems of measurement for the kinds of phenomena which we pronounce judgement upon in archaeology.

In essence, his argument is that, throughout a period in which we have seen at least two major shifts in the theoretical superstructure of archaeological interpretation, there has been little or no assessment of the most basic of methodological tools, such as our ways to analyse artefacts. Hence, the phenomena we observe and attempt to quantify in the archaeological record are still those which seemed initially compatible with the 'culture-historical' paradigm of the 1950s and before.

In a detailed argument, Wobst goes through what he calls the 'research flow' of the early New Archaeology and the early post-processual archaeology, comparing practice observed in the applied literature of these schools of thought with theoretical statements by their protagonists on how the research flow should go. In both cases, the discrepancies are considerable.

His argument raises a number of issues. First, has our 'metrology' ('all of the measurements taken in the service of a paradigm') ever really been theorized at all? There are many indications to the contrary – most measurements are entirely untheorized and survive from a period in the history of archaeology in which the approach was predominantly intuitive – simple grouping for 'similarities' and 'differences' which remained in part implicit (van der Leeuw 1976, pp. 53–5). Here, Wobst's argument implicitly touches upon the question of 'what is typical?' also raised by Rosen.

In many ways, we have never moved beyond 'propositions [which] had been intuited and were then selected for further testing because they looked reasonable within the given data structure: [the] data had not been produced to be particularly sensitive for measuring the implications of hypotheses for change and variation'. Looking at the impact of both the New Archaeology and the post-processualist school, it is clear that, little by little, we have become aware of many more areas of potential variability in the process of generating the archaeological record in the past, as well as in the processes which have destroyed it to the point at which we discover it in the present. In that sense, both the above paradigms have made major contributions (and, we believe, so will the modelling paradigm proposed in this volume).

But it is also remarkable that the rethinking of our archaeological categorizations has predominantly occurred outside the communities which promoted these paradigms (Leroi-Gourhan and his students using the concept of *chaîne opératoire*, for example), or even outside the discipline (by borrowing from ethnography or anthropology). We have failed to make the necessary adjustments to our descriptive and analytical toolkit so that it can deal with processes (transformations) rather than stable categories. But whereas Wobst raises the question and impresses us with the need to do something about it, Rosen actually gives a very cogent argument as to how we might, at least to some extent, deal with the problem. That is a challenge which we will need to meet, and to which the approach proposed here can contribute because it allows us, and forces us, to model theories rather than realities.

Wobst also relates some of these points explicitly to the present, the structure of archaeology as a discipline and the way in which that may have contributed to the absence of change in archaeological metrology. There seem to us to be at least two underlying issues here.

We may need to ask the question whether there is a relationship between the maximum density of data available in archaeology and the kinds of metrologies and/or theories we proffer. As archaeologists, we are traditionally in a different position than most scientists. We have relatively few remains from the operation of (very) complex systems, whereas most natural (and to some extent, life) scientists have many observations on (presumably) much simpler systems. Thus, we touch again on the problems Rosen (Chapter 14) and Chapman (Chapter 15) bring up concerning mathematical modelling, but in a somewhat different way. Is formal modelling a sensible strategy in a fundamentally data-poor archaeology? We find ourselves in a quandary: though archaeology is fundamentally data-poor in relation to the complexity of the systems it studies, it nevertheless often has, as Wobst points out, too many data to make interpretation easy. Indeed, his argument that data-overload has contributed to maintaining metrology in its unsophisticated state seems entirely reasonable.

But then, the argument on an underlying poverty of data is only valid if we keep separating the past from the present, and studying the former for its own sake. Were we to accept for all aspects of archaeology, and not only environmental archaeology, artefact technology etc., that data from the present are admissible, then this constraint would be mitigated. The success of these areas of archaeology shows the strength which such an assumption can give to our reasoning. What is the value of keeping past and present separate in this sense? There seem to be three reasons: (1) 'our interpretations should not be ethnocentric' (or centred on our own culture); (2) 'The past may be a foreign country' (and there is much in social anthropology that points that way); (3) only if the past is separate, is archaeology a coherent discipline. Although the first of these is on the surface quite valid, it is based on a confusion between 'the same' and 'of the same value'. As any anthropologist knows, the dual purpose of research on other cultures is to understand and to respect that other culture. Such understanding must pass through translation of observations into, or extension of, one's own culture's 'world-view'. In that sense the purpose of the work is to create a link between the two cultures. Only such a link can guarantee the respect due to that other culture. Similarly, the purpose of archaeology is in our eyes to create a link between past and present, present and past – not to keep them separate. If the link is a sufficiently subtle and respectful one, all that is foreign about the past should theoretically be acknowledged and respected, and the foreignness is no longer a reason to keep past and present apart. If we were better listeners, we would be able to distinguish between words we recognize in the stone's speech, and those we don't recognize. But we don't solve the problem either by taking their words at face value or by declaring them mute and speaking at them in our own way. And that brings us to the third point: is archaeology archaeology and nothing but archaeology, or is it the interaction between palaeoecologists, palaeoanthropologists, palaeodemographers, etc.? It follows from the above that we would choose for the latter conception of archaeology, while acknowledging that there are theoretical, methodological and substantive aspects to the study of the past which are particular to our work.

This brings us to Murray's contribution (Chapter 17). Both Murray and Wobst are archaeologists of the Pleistocene, and that is not a trivial detail in this context. Indeed, the distinctions between archaeologists of the Palaeolithic and those studying much more recent periods (such as the two editors of this volume) may well be more fundamental than many other distinctions in archaeology. Palaeolithic archaeologists work with the weakest signals of the past, the largest spatio-temporal scales, potentially the greatest differences between the subjects of their studies and ourselves, the poorest resolution, etc. They therefore have a different focus, different approaches, different needs above all.

It is in that context that Murray's three fundamental points about non-linear modelling should be seen:

1   Non-linear modelling allows us to learn more about the scale and resolving power of our archaeological models of the past – it may show us whether our minimum scales of measurement (of the order of thousands of years) are simply too gross to observe the difference between order and chaos? What is the role of averaging-out in hiding past processes from us?

2   How much would the use of non-linear models drive us towards imposing modern models of society on the past?

3   Would the short-termism of non-linear models not push us to understand that such short-term interpretations of the archaeological record are without sense or merit?

If we were to summarize our opinion in this respect, it would be a subdued and qualified 'yes' to most of the problems these questions raise, at least for Palaeolithic studies. The application of non-linear approaches as presented in this volume was directly motivated by the suspicion, even for much later periods which we know in much more detail, that averaging-out hides most of the dynamics of the processes which we wish to study. Certainly, what we seem to be doing is applying a variety of modern models on the past, *but the aim of that is to see where they are deficient, and to develop different models accordingly – hence the stress on the fact that we attempt to model theories, not reality.* Finally, it seems to us that short-term interpretations are applicable to all those issues for which we also have short-term data, whether these date from the Palaeolithic or not. Applying non-linear models to aspects of the past as known through very detailed excavations with high temporal resolutions such as Pincevent seems entirely reasonable, as Murray is the first to agree. Moreover, non-linear modelling need not be confined to modelling the short-term, as is shown by the (implicit) use of non-linear models for palaeontology by Gould throughout much of his work (1990, for example).

One very important underlying issue which all the present chapters raise is that of the ontological distinctiveness and homogeneity of the Pleistocene archaeological record. Here, Murray claims a realist position, arguing that the Palaeolithic record is ontologically different, not because Palaeolithic human behaviour is necessarily different from more recent human behaviour, but because the reduced power of resolution for that period forces us to look at different phenomena, and thus to abandon the short time-frame, high-resolution kinds of explanations which are based on social theory and which are applicable to more recent periods. Hence Murray's fear that non-linear modelling, with its stress on explaining the long term by means of the dynamics of the shorter time-scales, might add to an unrealistic perspective on the past.

A related issue is the nature of the fact that according to Murray 'it is the palimpsest of behaviours on Pleistocene sites which delivers the primary element of ontological distinctiveness', requiring a rethink of the extent to which such a palimpsest can be reduced to its component 'texts', which in turn touches on issues of scale, for example.

Finally, taking this position (and Wobst does so too albeit in more subdued terms) places the sociology and history of archaeology in a different light as methods of approaching the 'epistemological/ontological muddle' (the difficulty of distinguishing in how far 'the stones speak'). In that context, it is notably the fact that scientific investigations also have unexpected results, and that therefore the stories we tell need not entirely be dictated by the history of research, which brings us back to the core issue in all this: how can we safeguard that we do our research with enough subtlety that we keep our balance in this field of tension, that we are not swayed too far to the ethnographically known interpretation or, on the contrary, to the past as a 'foreign country' (Lowenthal 1988).

And therein lies the Art . . .

References

Atlan, H. 1992. Self-organising networks: weak, strong and intentional. The role of their underdetermination. *La Nuova Critica N.S.* 19–20, 51–70.

Clarke, D.L. 1968. *Analytical Archaeology*. London: Methuen.

Gould, S.J. 1990. *Wonderful Life*. Harmondsworth: Penguin.

Lowenthal, D. 1990. *The Past is a Foreign Country*. London: Heinemann.

Van der Leeuw, S.E. 1976. *Studies in the Technology of Ancient Pottery* (2 vols). Amsterdam: University of Amsterdam.

Van der Leeuw, S.E. 1990a. Archaeology, material culture and innovation. *SubStance* 62/63, 92–109.

Van der Leeuw, S.E. 1990b. Rythmes temporels, espaces naturels et espaces vécus. In *Archéologie et Espaces,* J.L. Fiches and S.E. van der Leeuw (eds), 299–346. Antibes: APDCA.

14 Are our modelling paradigms non-generic?

ROBERT ROSEN

Introduction

It is appropriate to begin with a few words of explanation for what is to follow. I have been, and remain, entirely dedicated to the idea that modelling is the essence of science, and the habitat of all epistemology. Although I have concentrated my efforts on biology, and the nature of organisms, I have also asserted for a long time that human systems and organisms are very much alike; i.e., share or realize many common models. I was a pioneer in the wide deployment of mathematical ideas for purposes of modelling, particularly in the area of stability theory; indeed, I wrote perhaps the first modern text devoted to this purpose (Rosen 1970).

I regard what follows as a natural extension and continuation of these efforts. What I will claim, however, is that the tactics of modelling which, in a small way, I helped pioneer, and the mathematical machinery currently regarded as the only way to implement these tactics, are much too narrow for our scientific purposes. In a nutshell, I will claim that this mathematical machinery, and hence what it allows us to capture about the world around us, necessarily misses most of what is really going on.

Let me be a little more specific. Any mathematical structure, any mathematical system, whether it be an explicit model of something in the material world or not, may possess the property of being formalizable. There are many ways of describing this property, but they all amount to being able to describe the entire system as software to a mathematical machine (Turing machine), in such a way that the machine can simulate the system. Everything about a formalizable system can be expressed as pure syntax; every inferential process in such a system can be thought of as rote symbol manipulation or word processing.

Concern with formalizability arose historically from the need to eliminate paradoxes and inconsistencies in mathematical operations which had been presumed safely free from them. Hilbert and others argued that every mathematical system was thus formalizable, and hence that mathematics itself can and must be expressed as a game of pattern generation on a set of symbols, devoid of any semantic component. However, Hilbert's program was destroyed by the celebrated Gödel Incompleteness Theorem. This showed that the property of being formalizable was exceedingly special, excessively special among mathematical systems; i.e., that one cannot capture very much of conventional mathematics in purely formalistic, syntactic terms.

What I am going to argue is that the special character of computability or simulability spills over into the sciences, through the intervention of mathematical models to characterize material phenomena. The idea that every model of a material system must be simulable or computable is at least tacitly regarded in most quarters as synonymous with science itself; as I have argued elsewhere (e.g. Rosen 1962, 1988), it is a material version of Church's Thesis (i.e., 'effective' means computable).

I have called a material system with only computable models a simple system, or mechanism. A system which is not simple in this sense I call complex. A complex system must thus have non-computable models.

To say that material systems may be complex in this sense, and in particular to assert that organisms or human systems are thus complex, is a radical thing to do. For one thing, it says that differential equations, and systems of differential equations (i.e., dynamical systems), which are inherently simulable, miss most of the reality of a complex system, just as any attempt to formalize (e.g. Number Theory) misses most of its theorems. It does not say that we learn nothing about complex systems from simple models; it merely says we should widen our concept of what models are.

We shall proceed with a discussion of the concept of genericity, culminating in an argument that simple systems are non-generic (rare). We will then discuss the related concept of stability, and the testing for stability by applying generic perturbations. We will conclude by showing that dynamical systems, systems of differential equations, become complex when generically perturbed, and briefly discuss what this means for the scientific enterprise.

Genericity

In an intuitive mathematical context, genericity means roughly that which is typical; that which is devoid of special qualifications or properties superimposed on the typicality in question. The best way to introduce this concept is through some familiar examples.

1 It is generic for a real number to be irrational; it is non-generic for a number to be rational, or even to be computable in the usual sense.
2 It is generic for two lines in a plane to intersect; it is non-generic for them to coincide or be parallel.

3   It is generic for a square matrix to be invertible, and hence generic for its determinant not to vanish. It is accordingly generic for a set of ≤ N vectors in an N-dimensional space to be linearly independent. Linear dependencies, vanishing of determinants, and non-invertibility of matrices are thus non-generic.

4   It is generic for a differential form to be non-exact or non-integrable.

5   It is generic for sets to be infinite.

Generic properties are thus what we expect to see when we approach something in an objective, unbiased way. We are very strongly biased, for instance, in the direction of rational numbers; this is why 'irrationalities' were so named in the first place. Nevertheless, by any objective criterion, it is the rational numbers which are the rare and special ones, and our predilection for them tells more about us than about numbers.

Indeed, recall that rational numbers are those represented by terminating or periodic decimal expansions. This illustrates the proposition that non-genericities are encumbered with special properties, degeneracies, symmetries, which in fact characterize or separate the generic from the special.

Ironically, in mathematics, it is often the non-generic that yields the theorems, precisely because of all the special conditions which define them. This very fact is what thrusts non-genericity into the spotlight when modelling material reality. Even though we know that Hamiltonian or conservative systems, for example, are non-generic, that is where we have come to think the theorems are.

Yet the property of being typical, of having no special properties, is itself a property. Arguing from the typical is, for instance, what underlies the Thom Classification Theorem (Thom 1975), or, in quite a different area, behind the notion of 'forcing' by means of which Paul Cohen could prove the independence of the Continuum Hypothesis (and the Axiom of Choice) from the rest of Set Theory (Cohen 1966, *passim*). It expresses the 'robustness', so often invoked to justify conclusions drawn from a model or metaphor.

What is the diagnostic of genericity? What is the difference between being typical and being special? One way to formulate it is the following. An arbitrary (i.e., a generic), perturbation of what is generic yields something again generic; an arbitrary perturbation of what is non-generic destroys the special properties (e.g. breaks the symmetries, or lifts the degeneracies) on which non-genericity depends.

The reader may perceive a little circularity in this intuitive treatment: namely, we need to characterize what a generic perturbation is before we can decide, by this criterion, whether what we perturb is generic or not. If we do not address this properly, and tacitly mandate perturbations which are themselves non-generic, we will get wrong answers. This, as we shall see, is the crux when trying to decide whether computability or simulability of something is non-generic.

The diagnostic of comparing a perturbed and an unperturbed situation relates genericity to ideas of stability and bifurcation. But they are not the same, and it is important to distinguish the province of stability from that of genericity. Thus, we must turn now to a discussion of what they have in common, and what they do not.

Stability

Stability also requires us to compare a perturbed with an unperturbed situation. But central to stability questions is the requirement that our perturbations be in some sense small (or small enough); i.e., it implies an idea of metric approximation. Roughly, we must determine whether a first-order change in some system characteristic produces a higher-order change in another (stability), or a lower-order change (instability) or neither.

As I have developed elsewhere, the prototypic situation for stability studies involves playing off an equivalence relation (i.e., a notion of similarity) against a metric. The equivalence relation partitions the metric space into a family of disjoint equivalence classes. A point is stable if it lies in the interior of its equivalence class; there is thus a whole neighbourhood, a sphere of some finite radius, about a stable point which lies entirely in the class. Thus, a point is stable if every sufficiently good approximation to it is also similar to it.

A point which is not stable is called a bifurcation point. Any neighbourhood of a bifurcation point must intersect more than one equivalence class; i.e., no matter how closely we metrically approximate to such a point, that does not guarantee similarity.

We can ask a question like the following: is it generic for a point to be stable (i.e., are bifurcation points non-generic)? We might be tempted to answer yes, arguing that bifurcation points must lie on lower dimensional boundaries separating open equivalence classes. But why should there be any open equivalence classes at all? To presume that in advance, is itself a bias like the one we have for rational numbers, and a non-generic bias at that. And if there are none, then every point is in fact a bifurcation point. Indeed, in general, stability will be neither generic nor non-generic.

We will be concerned below with one particular aspect of bifurcation. Namely, with the question of what happens when we restrict the perturbations we apply to a point, so that we no longer have generic perturbations available to us. In this case, we clearly cannot reach every point in an open neighbourhood, so we cannot be sure we can sample every nearby equivalence class. In more formal terms, no longer can we be sure that an unfolding of a bifurcation point is a versal or universal restriction on perturbations which has been concealed by complexity.

Some basic terminology

In what follows, we will direct ideas of genericity towards dynamical systems (e.g., systems of differential equations) and their perturbation, with an eye to their ultimate role as models of real-world phenomena. To that end, we pause here to introduce some basic concepts and the terminology which describes them.

Let X be a manifold; something which looks like a chunk of a Euclidean space of some finite dimension. In particular, X is thus a metric space. Moreover, we can differentiate certain functions defined on X; it suffices to consider real-valued functions. We will think of X as a prototypic *state space*. However, our main area of interest for the moment is not X itself, but functions defined *on* X. Let us denote these functions by $H(X, Y)$, where Y is another set. Since we are considering real-valued functions on X, we can fix the range Y of our functions as the real numbers $\mathcal{R}$.

Now $H(X, \mathcal{R})$ is not in general a manifold; it does not look like a piece of Euclidean space. However, it can be turned into a metric space in many ways; any such metric allows us to discuss *approximations* of a function f in $H(X, \mathcal{R})$ by others.

We usually write such a function from X to $\mathcal{R}$ in the notation

$$f(x_1, \ldots, x_n),$$

which we can do because X is a manifold; thus it must have (local) co-ordinate systems. In this notation, the arguments x_i, the co-ordinates of a point in the manifold, are interpreted as *state variables* of any material system which X models.

But this notation is incomplete. It omits or conceals tacit arguments of f, which are usually called *parameters*. Roughly, these can be thought of as numbers whose values must be specified before we can evaluate f at a state. Hence, in some way, these numbers determine or specify f itself. If there are r such numbers, say $a_1, \ldots, a_r$, then the value of a function f at a state is really determined by $n + r$ arguments, which can be somewhat redundantly expressed as

$$f(x_1, \ldots, x_n, a_1, \ldots, a_r).$$

In this notation, there is no mathematical distinction between the state values and the parameters; they are all equally arguments of the function f. However, a slight change in notation will completely change this. Let us write

$$f(x_1, \ldots, x_n, a_1, \ldots, a_n) = f_{a_1} \ldots a_r (x_1, \ldots, x_n)$$

The effect of this is to change a single function of $n + r$ arguments into a parametrized family of functions of only n arguments. Thus the parameters now appear as local co-ordinates *in the function space* $H(X, \mathcal{R})$. We can ask what happens in this parametrized family as (a) we vary the state variables

$x_1, \ldots, x_n$, or (b) we change the co-ordinates or parameters $a_1, \ldots, a_r$. And most importantly: we can ask whether either (a) or (b) is a *generic* way of exploring a whole neighbourhood of a given function f in $H(X, \mathfrak{R})$.

We have just seen that we can turn a fixed function of $n + r$ arguments into an r-parameter *family* of functions of n arguments. It is clear that this procedure works the other way: *an r-parameter family of functions of n arguments can be turned into a single fixed function of n + r arguments*. This is the result we shall need.

In the light of these ideas, let us consider the following particular way of introducing parameters. Suppose we have a function of n arguments, say $f(x_1, \ldots, x_n)$. Let us take N more functions of these same arguments; say

$$g_i(x_1, \ldots, x_n), \ i = 1, \ldots, N$$

and use these to generate new functions of the form

$$f + \sum_{i=1}^{N} \in_i g_i \qquad (14.1)$$

Clearly, if the numbers $\in_1$ are small, then (1) can be regarded as a perturbation of f, or an approximation to f. The totality of these constitute what is called an unfolding of f, for reasons we shall come to in a moment.

On the other hand, by the above, there is a fixed function

$$F = F(x_1, \ldots, x_n, \in_1, \ldots, \in_n)$$

of $n + N$ arguments, such that

$$F = f + \sum_{i=1}^{N} \in_i g_i \qquad (14.2)$$

Clearly $F = f$ when the parameter values $\in_i$ are put equal to zero. Moreover, a variation of the *function* f via the above unfolding is equivalent to a variation of the *arguments* of the fixed function F.

If we think of a function as constituting *hardware*, and its arguments as *software*, then the very concept of unfolding says that there exists hardware (the function F) which can only be varied through manipulations of its arguments (i.e., its software). What looks like an *arbitrary* perturbation of the original function f, via the unfolding, becomes *equivalent to a very special perturbation of the function F*. And conversely: a truly arbitrary (generic) perturbation of F does something quite drastic around f.

The existence of fixed hardware, which only communicates with its ambient environment via its software, is one of the essential features of computability or simulability; the essence of a Turing machine, and hence of pure syntax. The direct action of an environment on the hardware itself is strictly, if tacitly, forbidden. And this in turn is the essence of a simple system; that we be able to reach a function like F, completely closed off from its environment (and hence from its neighbours) except through variations of its arguments.

Dynamics

So far, we have only talked about metric aspects; i.e., about perturbations or approximations of functions on a manifold X, and about parametrized families of such functions (e.g., unfoldings). To talk about stability, and in particular, about stable parametrized families, we need an equivalence relation on $H(X, \mathcal{R})$. We can get one by turning our functions, and their parametrized families, into dynamical systems.

We can go from functions to dynamical systems by the deceptively simple formal device of identifying the value of a function at a point χ of our manifold with a tangent vector at χ; i.e., by putting

$$d\chi/dt = f(\chi) \tag{14.3}$$

Remembering that f contains parameters, which in fact determine what its values will be, we can see that the space of these parameter values maps thereby into the tangent spaces at each state χ; that is why parameters are often called *controls*.

Call two dynamical systems *equivalent* if there is a co-ordinate transformation on the manifold χ which maps the trajectories of the first on to the trajectories of the second. If one of these dynamical systems is obtained by changing the parameter values of the other, then their equivalence means that we can wipe out the effect of that parameter variation by means of a compensating co-ordinate transformation in χ alone. It is easy to see that this is a true equivalence relation on dynamical systems on χ (reflexive, symmetric and transitive), and hence on the functions on χ which define them via (14.3) above. It is with respect to this relation that we can talk about stability; about the interplay between this equivalence relation and the metric on $H(X, \mathcal{R})$.

More specifically, let us look at a parametrized family $f_\alpha(\chi)$ of such functions. This of course gives a parametrized family of dynamical systems

$$d\chi/dt = f_\alpha(\chi) \tag{14.4}$$

We can now ask whether this is a stable family, i.e., lying within a single equivalence class. In turn, this means that we can go from the trajectories of any system in the family to any other by a change of co-ordinates in X, which depends only on the parameter values which specify the two systems in the family.

A parameter vector $\alpha^\star$ is thus called *stable* if it has a neighbourhood U such that all the systems f_α, $\alpha \in U$, constitute a stable family. Otherwise, we call $\alpha^\star$ a *bifurcation point*. Clearly, if $\alpha^\star$ is a bifurcation point, then no matter how small we choose the neighbourhood U, there will be a parameter vector $\alpha \in U$ such that f_α and $f_{\alpha^\star}$ are dissimilar; their trajectories are not inter-transformable by a mere co-ordinate transformation of X. Bifurcation here thus means that there are perturbations $\alpha^\star \rightarrow \alpha$, metrically as small as you please, which cannot be undone by just a change of co-ordinates. Any such U thus intersects several similarity classes.

Next, let us suppose that the parametrized family (14.4) comes from an unfolding; something of the form (14.2). Thus, the parameter vector we have called α should now be called $\in$. The question is now: if $\in^\star$ is a bifurcation point, and if U is a 'small' neighbourhood of $\in^\star$, how many of the similarity classes near $f_\in^\star$ can actually be reached by perturbing $\in^\star$? This is a highly non-trivial question, because these similarity classes are independent of any parametrizations and any unfoldings; they depend only on the metric in $H(X, \mathfrak{R})$, and on the equivalence relation or similarity.

An unfolding is called *versal* if a neighbourhood U of a parameter vector $\in^\star$ in (14.3), which is only an N-dimensional thing, is nevertheless big enough to touch every equivalence class near $f_\in^\star$. The unfolding is called *universal* if the dimension N of U is as small as possible; i.e., any lower-dimensional U will miss some of the similarity classes near $f_\in^\star$.

The habitat of catastrophe theory constitutes such unfoldings for those very special functions f which admit versal and universal parametrized families. The famous Thom Classification Theorem proceeds by examining what happens 'generically' in the neighbourhood of these very special functions and their unfoldings. We shall not be concerned with this, but rather with the non-genericity of the concept of unfolding itself. The root of this resides in the idea that there is ultimately a single fixed function F which generates the unfolding, and which can only be varied through variation of its arguments.

As we have said, non-genericity seems to generate the theorems, and the Classification Theorem is a case in point. Where its hypotheses hold, we can learn many deep and important things. But those hypotheses already restrict us to the realm of *simple systems*, and to those perturbations which keep us restricted to this realm.

Dynamics and 'information': AI networks

Given a dynamical system

$$d\chi/dt = f(\chi) \text{ or } dx_i/dt = f_i(\chi) \tag{14.5}$$

where we have for the moment omitted writing any explicit parameters, we can associate with it a variety of other quantities which express important aspects of its local behaviour.

For instance, following Higgins (1967, pp. 50–1), we can introduce the quantities

$$
\begin{aligned}
u_{ij}(\chi) &= \delta/\delta x_j \, (dx_i/dt) \\
&= \delta f_i/\delta x_j
\end{aligned}
$$

These state functions u_{ij} have the significance that their signs at a state χ tell how a change in a state variable x_j is translated by the dynamics into a corresponding effect on the rate of change of another, x_i, in that state χ.

More specifically, let us call x_j an activator of x_i at a state χ if

$$u_{ij}(\chi) > 0$$

Intuitively, an increase in x_j at χ will be reflected in an increase in the rate of production dx_i/dt of x_i; likewise, a decrease in x_j will decrease that rate of production. On the other hand, if

$$u_{ij}(\chi) < 0.$$

then we can call x_j an *inhibitor* of x_i in that state. The matrix of functions u_{ij} constitutes what we have called (cf. Rosen 1979 p. 238) an *activation–inhibition* network.

The original interest in these networks resides in the fact that 'activation' and 'inhibition' are informational terms, pertaining to semantic aspects of the dynamical behaviour. There are many situations (e.g. in brain theory; or in ecology) where it seems more natural to consider the AI network as primary. So we have the question: given such a network, can we always go back to a generating dynamics, a set of rate equations like (14.5) which generate them?

Writing such rate equations means in effect producing the functions f_i. The above argument produces not the f_i themselves, but rather a set of relations which the *differentials df_i* must satisfy; namely

$$df_i = \sum_{j=1}^{n} u_{ij} \, dx_j \tag{14.6}$$

If there is to be a set of rate equations which produce a given network $(u_{ij}(\chi))$, then, *the differential forms (14.6) must all be exact.*

But it gets worse. We can iterate the ideas which led to the AI patterns as follows. Let us introduce the quantities

$$u_{ijk}(\chi) = \delta u_{ij}/\delta x_k \tag{14.7}$$

The signs of *these* quantities reflect the effects of a change in a state variable x_k on the activation or inhibition which x_j imposes on x_i. Thus, if

$$u_{ijk}(\chi) > 0$$

in a state, we may call x_k an *agonist* of the activation (or inhibition) of x_i by x_j; otherwise, an *antagonist*. These are again semantic, informational terms, which are defined whenever we start from a set of rate equations, but which seem independently meaningful.

In any case, we must superimpose the pattern of agonism/antagonism, embodied in the functions u_{ijk}, on the AI pattern obtained previously. And of course, we can iterate this process indefinitely.

Clearly, at each step of this process, we obtain another collection of differential forms like (14.6). Again, if we start from a system of rate equations like (14.5), they are all exact. Moreover, we can pass from any informational level to any other, and from any of them to the generating rate equations, just by differentiating and/or integrating. Thus, in this case, all these layers of 'informational' or semantic interactions are inter-transformable and equivalent; just another way of talking about rate equations.

But surely, if we generically perturb a non-generic thing like an exact differential form, we will get a non-exact (generic) form. So suppose we try to unfold the functions f_i in (14.5) above; i.e., replace (14.5) by a system of the form

$$dx_i/dt = f_i + \sum_{R=1}^{n} \in_k g_k \qquad (14.8)$$

where the $\in_k$ are small parameters, and the g_k are arbitrary but fixed functions. What happens to the u_{ij}, and, in particular, to the differential forms (14.6) which they define?

It can be immediately verified that the new AI pattern $(u'_{ij}(x))$, coming from (14.8), *still gives us an exact differential form*. That is: what we thought of *as a generic* perturbation of the rate equations translates into a highly non-generic perturbation of the associated AI pattern (and also, of course, of the agonist–antagonist pattern, and all of the iterates of this process).

Conversely, a *generic* perturbation of the AI pattern, which necessarily will typically make the differential form (14.6) *inexact*, translates into something very peculiar in the vicinity of the original rate functions f_i.

In what follows, we will touch on some ramifications of the above, especially in the modelling of material systems.

Complex systems

As we have just seen, what looks like a generic perturbation of a system of rate equations (i.e., a dynamical system) necessarily gives rise to a highly non-generic perturbation of the infinite networks of differential forms which coincide with the dynamics (e.g., the AI pattern, the agonist–antagonist pattern, etc.). On the other hand, a generic perturbation of the AI pattern, or any of the others, renders all these patterns independent, and wipes out the concept of rate equations entirely. It thus looks like there is something very special, very degenerate, about systems of rate equations, and about the ways we have been perturbing them.

In a nutshell, what is special is precisely what we drew attention to above; the tacit presupposition that everything can be described in terms of one overarching function (we called it F above) which can only be varied through variation of its arguments; i.e., variations in states and parameters. When we know this F, we know everything about the system there is to know; in particular, every *model* of the system can be obtained from it, through restrictions on its arguments alone. Indeed, F itself thus appears as the *largest* model.

This property of possessing a largest model is a hallmark of simple systems or mechanisms. It is basically what allows a whole system to be expressible as software (i.e., as program and data) to an extraneous symbol-processor or mathematical machine, and hence to make the system simulable.

The restriction that a function F cannot be varied except through variation of its arguments, which we may express formally by mandating that

$$(\delta F)(\chi) = F(\delta \chi)$$

places a terribly strong restriction on what can be in a *neighbourhood* of F. Conversely, if we try to vary F only through variations $\delta \chi$ of its arguments, we cannot thereby see what is typical (generic) in such a neighbourhood, because we are trying to explore that neighbourhood through means which are themselves highly non-generic.

In the preceding section, we sketched a way to lift this non-genericity. Namely, instead of trying to perturb a system of rate equations in the usual way, we apply a perturbation to one or more of the systems of exact differential forms which are ordinarily completely equivalent to the system itself, and to each other. That decouples everything, very much like the splitting of a degenerate spectral line when a perturbing magnetic field is applied (Zeeman Effect).

It should be intuitively clear that such a decoupling renders the system *complex*. It is no longer possible to express what happens in it in the form of a finite program to a syntactic simulator. It is further clear that complexity is thus *generic* in the usual sense; perturbing a complex system as we have done gives us another complex system, while perturbing a simple one does not preserve simplicity.

Some implications for modelling

There are many deep ramifications of the ideas sketched above, which we can only hint at in this short space. Let us, however, touch on a few.

I would characterize the modelling relation as a kind of congruence between two systems of entailment. The mathematical model is a system of inferential entailment put into such a congruence with a real-world system of causal entailment. The property of simulability in a model of something turns out to impose very strong limitations on causality in what it models. In fact, simulability mandates an extreme degree of causal impoverishment. Almost everything about such a system is unentailed from within the system, and must accordingly be externally *posited*; all that remains is the entailment of 'next state' from 'present state'. It is precisely this paucity of entailment in simple systems or mechanisms which allows them to be expressible as software.

Complex systems may be thought of, on the other hand, as manifesting more entailment (more causality) than can be accommodated by a mechanism.

Things like organisms, for example, sit at the other end of the entailment spectrum than mechanisms do; almost everything about them is in some sense entailed from something else about them.

On the other hand, in a complex system, there is no meaningful intrinsic distinction into 'hardware' and 'software'; no single overarching function which stays fixed while only its arguments can vary. In material terms, a system of this type is literally infinitely open, whereas a mechanism or simple system can be at best finitely open. The upshot of this is that if we try to replace a complex system by a simple one, we necessarily miss most of the interactions of which it is capable. Herein lies the primary basis for the 'counter-intuitive' characteristics or 'non-mechanistic' behaviour so often manifested by organisms; the causal entailments on which they depend are simply not encoded into the simulable models we are using.

No superposition of simple models will yield a complex system; we cannot leave the realm of computability in this fashion, any more than we can build an infinite set by means of finite operations on finite sets. Thus, in general, it is not a good tactic to try to study open systems by opening closed ones; it usually turns out that closure, in the material sense, is so degenerate (i.e., so non-generic) that the behaviour of a perturbed closed system will depend much more on how it was perturbed than on its behaviour when closed.

It must be emphasized that we can still make dynamical models of complex systems, just as we can formalize fragments of Number Theory. We can approximate, but only locally and temporarily, to inexact differential forms with exact ones under certain conditions. But we will have to keep shifting from model to model, as the causal structure in the complex system outstrips what is coded into any particular dynamics. The situation is analogous to trying to use pieces of planar maps to navigate on the surface of a sphere.

Indeed, just as a sphere is in some sense the limits of its approximating planar maps, a complex system can be regarded as a *limit* of simple ones. Pursuit of this analogy, however, would take us far beyond the scope of this chapter.

We will conclude with the remark that concepts like activation/inhibition, agonism/antagonism, etc., which as we noted earlier are informational (semantic) terms, may be used to introduce a language of 'function' into the study of (complex) systems. Here, we use the word 'function' in the biological rather than the mathematical sense; e.g. the 'function' of X is to do Y. For instance, in the dynamical example described above (see pp. 390–2), we could identify the 'function' of a state variable x_i in a state c with what it activates and inhibits in that state. We thus inch towards a legitimation of the Aristotelian category of Final Causation, bound up with what something entails rather than with what entails it. In complex systems, it is not only completely legitimate to use such a language, it is absolutely necessary to do so. Indeed, this is another fundamental way in which complexity differs from mechanism. Using this kind of language leads us in the direction of *relational models* (cf. Rosen 1978, 1985), which have proved most appropriate for biological purposes (and, by implication, for any kind of human or social system). But that is another story.

References

Cohen, P.J. 1966. *Set Theory and the Continuum Hypothesis.* Reading, Mass.: W.A. Benjamin Inc.

Higgins, J. 1967. The theory of oscillating reactions. *Industrial and Engineering Chemistry* 59, 18–62.

Rosen, R. 1962. Church's thesis and its relation to the concept of realizability in biology and physics. *Bulletin of Mathematical Biophysics* 24, 375–93.

Rosen, R. 1970. *Dynamical System Theory in Biology* (2 vols). New York: Wiley-Interscience.

Rosen, R. 1978. *Fundamentals of Measurement and Representation of Natural Systems.* New York: American Elsevier.

Rosen, R. 1979. Some comments on activation and inhibition. *Bulletin of Mathematical Biophysics* 41, 427–45.

Rosen, R. 1985. *Anticipatory Systems.* Oxford: Pergamon Press.

Rosen, R. 1988. How universal is a universal unfolding? *Applied Mathematics Letters* 1, 105–7.

Thom, R. 1975. *Structural Stability and Morphogenesis.* Reading, Mass.: W.A. Benjamin.

15 On wholeness, reflexive complexity, hierarchies, structures and system dynamics

GRAHAM P. CHAPMAN

Part I: Introduction – A paradigm shift?

There is a major shift occurring at the moment in our understanding of the behaviour of complex dynamical systems. This understanding usually goes under the unfortunately chosen term 'Chaos Theory'. I say unfortunate because the basic thrust is to understand the processes and mechanisms behind the occurrence of apparently chaotic phenomena (such as the patterns of convection in boiling water, the tumbling behaviour of unstable objects, unsystematic and unrepeated fluctuations of animal numbers in ecosystems) by showing that there are parameters governing such behaviour, and that we can make plots of those parameters.

In many ways one may think of these parameter plots in a loose analogical way as structures: they help to give us some sort of idea of both dynamics and the supporting structure. This means that the dynamics, although un-repeating and in a sense unpredictable (but not uncalculable), are constrained. The analogy is not a strong one, yet it has resulted in some extravagant claims. Prigogine (1985, p. 115) has 'discovered' that the fractal dimension of the weather system governing temperature over the last 700,000 years is 3.3, leading to the conclusion that 'this enormous complex system, which has given rise to the particular succession of temperatures observed over this period, can be understood as the outcome of a non-linear deterministic system of four variables'. But what are these four variables? He does not say, yet if he could he would solve half the current argument about global environmental change. The best one could imagine is that they are some sort of orthogonal composites, à la factor analysis, in which case they are simply reconstituting the original data.

In the social sciences we also deal with dynamics and structure. We are concerned with the (chaotic?) performance of stockmarkets against a back-drop of international politics and national regulatory measures. We know that a Saddam Hussein is not unrelated to his back-cloth – in his case the discord-ance in the patterns of world wealth production and consumption. Expressed like this we seem to be dealing with structure and dynamics in a similar way to the physical sciences – but there are certain additional features that we need to take into account in the biological and social sciences. One is holism, the idea that there are features of the biological worlds that only have dynamics if they have minimal wholeness; the other is reflexivity, or consciousness. One result of consciousness is both the recognition and creation of phenomena of partial wholeness, and of multiple and over-lapping (cover-set) hierarchies. If the subject matter of the social sciences is different, compared to the physical sciences, in terms of wholeness and reflexivity, and in terms of complexity (discussed on pp. 401–2) does this mean that dynamics and structure have different meanings too?

I believe the paradigm shift (as I think it will turn out to be) is profound and of great significance for many sciences, particularly non-experimental environmental science. But this does not mean that it will necessarily be significant for social sciences. Although I am aware it is such a hoary old chestnut, I feel compelled to start this chapter by spelling out what I see as differences between the domains of the physical and social sciences, in order to assess whether what I have just said is true.

Gradients of existence and observation

I start with a schematic diagram of the subject matter and a few related disciplines (Figure 15.1). This diagram has no objective value, it is merely a personal view which should be treated as more or less useful, but neither right nor wrong. A distinction is drawn, following Popper and Eccles between three Worlds. These are: (a) the World of physical objects – World 1; (b) the World of thought within any one individual's head – World 2; and (c) the collectivity of human thought (more than just the sum of all the Worlds 2) which is World 3. But my knowledge of all these three Worlds rests in my own World 2 – hence Figure 15.1 contains itself, and hence World-2 is written both outside the biggest box, and also inside it where I conceive it to be. It is like the painting of an inn, whose inn-sign depicts a painting of the inn, whose inn-sign depicts a painting of the inn.

The majority of the detail in Figure 15.1 is in the three left-hand columns, which cover the domain of World 1, the world of physical things. It is about this world that science has made most 'Progress'. But if I were to redraw Figure 15.1 to discuss the intellectual history of mankind including all art, music and literature, World 3 would be greatly expanded.

The divisions between the four columns are important. On the left we stay firmly within the domain of physics and chemistry, and the realm of reductionist explanation. This is true even to the extreme, where at the largest scale astrophysics is tied intimately to the smallest scale, of particle physics. The next column is the world of artifice – the machines of mankind that obey the laws of physics and chemistry, but which have not been observed

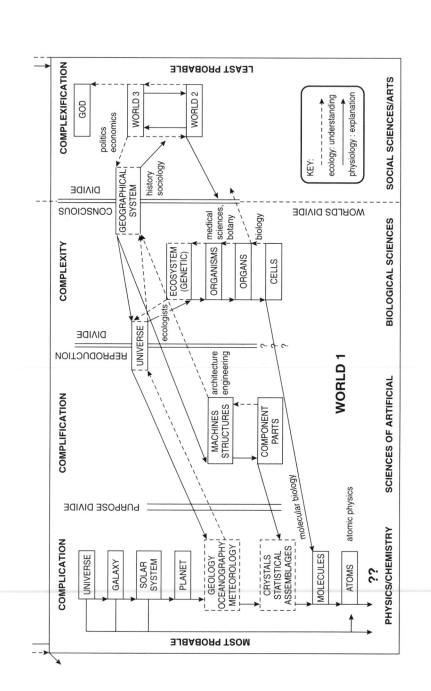

Figure 15.1 Hierarchies, Worlds 1, 2 and 3 and levels of complexity (source: Chapman 1983).

to occur spontaneously. Although all these machines and buildings perform, in so far as they do, according to non-teleological explanation, their existence is understood in teleological and ecological terms – they are invented and built by humanity for man's own purposes. They are therefore split from the 'natural' world of the inanimate by the 'purpose' divide. They have an exterior teleology.

The divisions between the inanimate world and the world of biology can be made on several grounds. The most immediate one is self-reproduction – perhaps one definition of life itself.

The next division is accordingly between the real world of physical existence – World-1 – and the worlds of conscious and reflexive thought – Worlds 2 and 3. Note that the brain therefore simultaneously exists as an organ in World 1, and as thinking in World 2. The relationship between physical substance and mind is of course the subject of some of the greatest debates ever, which need not concern us here, except to point out that there are only very tentative links of understanding and explanation across the division, if any.

The last general point to be made about the diagram is that many academic disciplines can be loosely tied to certain objects of study – cell biology to cells, medical sciences to organisms, chemistry to atoms and molecules. But at the level of the geographical system what we see is not so much objects of study, as merely the administrative structure of knowledge itself. Hence we see Economics and Sociology, whereas in reality there is no Economy separate from Society, no Economy separate from Ecology.

The nature of the problems for analysis and the modes of analysis change over a gradient that stretches from the bottom left of the diagram to the top right. Many of these gradients may be approximately summarized in terms of oppositions:

1   Thing, object (noun), at the bottom left: process, becoming (verb), transformation at the top right.
2   Universality and generality at the bottom left, or immanence (as in the laws of physics): uniqueness, or contingency, at the top right (as with human individuality).
3   Experiment at the bottom left with isolated causes and effects: non-experiment multiple-cause multiple-effect at the top right (as in humanity in the biosphere).
4   Replication, risk and probability at the bottom left: idiosyncracy, uncertainty and creativity at the top right. (What then belongs at the bottom left and what at the top right often depends on the observer's viewpoint. People can be treated statistically, as objects, as by army commanders, or as beings and individuals.) In (2) replication is related to immanence, and contingency to uniqueness.
5   Externality at the bottom left: reflexivity at the top right. This needs some elaboration. At the bottom left, we observe phenomena (subject ultimately to Heisenberg's Uncertainty Principle) as if the observation

did not affect the phenomena, and as if the facts were independent of theory and in some sense can pre-exist theory. Philosophers of science of course adopt a variety of postures around this problem. In extreme versions of deductivism, the theory–observation dichotomy is taken to imply that truth and falsity are properties only of observation statements, while theories are not propositional and do not purport to describe the real, but are only instruments for correlation and the prediction of observations. Others adopt less extreme views, and consider observation and theory to be part of an iterative process, and consider that though the facts are 'out there', which facts we observe and the manner in which we measure them are very much based on the evolution of conjectural theory. Measurement can also be seen to be both the measurement of an immanent property of a thing (no matter whether we weigh something by a fulcrum balance or by a spring scale, it is supposed to weigh the same) or as a process of interaction between observer and observed. Any social scientist who has used a questionnaire would understand that view. What happens when we get to Worlds 2 and 3? If we observe ourselves, then we observe ourselves observing ourselves. Human contemplation of the realm of the human changes it. In these circumstances the notion of objectivity becomes problematical, and so in particular does the notion of prediction (Hesse 1976, p. 14).

6   Computers at the left: brains at the right. Both computers and brains-as-organs belong to World 1, but to different hierarchies, one in the inanimate, the other the animate. More importantly, the thoughts of the brain are World 2. Any output of any program of any computer can always be explained by reductionist argument back to the binary operations that generated it. No emergent effects can be spontaneously created. Neither do computers create their own self-intervention, unless programmed to do so, in which case it is not self-intervention. To this extent all the dynamics are reducible and are what I call pseudo-dynamics. Computers as mere artefacts also only have exterior teleology.

7   The next gradient is in terms of wholeness. According to Feibleman (1954), and Rowe (1961, cited in Chapman 1977, p. 17), there are three basic kinds of objects, which I shall elaborate in not quite the same order as they lie on the axes in the diagram. The 'highest' is a structurally integrated volumetric whole, known as a First Order object – such as a plant, an organism, even a motor car. Arrangement is usually highly significant. Next there are areal aggregates, in which the co-ordination of the parts is not so important – for example a collection of trees known as a wood. Last there are aggregates known as intellectual classes, for which the restriction of contiguity is relaxed. We may thus talk about 'poor people' in this way. Quite clearly a good descriptive process ought to be able to capture the essence of the First Order object, but in fact, as with the human body, there are

many ways in which partial description is made and none which are 'total'(which is probably an impossibility anyway). At the left, in the inanimate world phenomena above the scale of molecules and crystals are essentially aggregates only, although perhaps exhibiting statistical co-operation in some degree. In the middle of the diagram wholeness is a pre-requisite for life-forms. These are, in Angyal's terms, first order objects of study – volumetric wholes that exhibit arrangement. The principles of arrangement can only exist by virtue of being enshrined in physical form. At the top right of the diagram we have both intellectual class, the result of perception, and non-volumetric wholeness-with-arrangement as in completed works of art (in literature and music), in which the principles of arrangement can exist independently of specific physical enshrinement.

8   Structure and dynamics. This is the most difficult of the gradients to discuss, and the one in which my ideas are most confused. At the left-hand side of the diagram structure is created by dynamics: suns are outcomes of gravitational attraction, rivers are outcomes of energetic throughput resulting from gravitational forces acting on water. In the middle, with artefacts and with life-forms, the structure captures or directs the energetic throughput, and the structure dominates the kinds of dynamics observed. At the extreme right, it seems that structures are necessary to the dynamics, to support and control them, but also the structures can be changed by the dynamics. A language that is deficient in expressing certain ideas may often evolve new words to support new concepts. The questions that emerge from this are: what exactly is structure? in what ways may it be defined? and how does it control the dynamics?

The four faces of complexity

Much of the above can be summarized for the four columns of Figure 15.1, in terms of the different meanings that I attribute to complexity.[1]

Complication
Complication is a quantitative escalation of that which is theoretically reducible. We may observe phenomena at particular scales (planets, continents, estuaries) as a shorthand, but all are explicable in terms of their component molecules and attendant physical and chemical laws. This does not preclude co-operative phenomena where particles in proximity to each other in close assemblies influence each other's state.

Complification
In this category it remains true that explanation is still reductionist and that therefore complexity is still merely a quantitative escalation. But I make it a

separate category because this is the world of the artificial, the artefact, that we make for a purpose which is usually attained only with parts working in co-operation. They have exterior teleology. This is true for a watch, for a car, for the Space Shuttle. In other words, whereas the outcome of complication is just an outcome (an estuary, a beach, a planet) the outcome of complification is a higher hierarchical goal to which the behaviour of the parts is subordinated – the exterior teleology referred to above. (The fact that the outcome of complication can be self-reinforcing does not break the distinction; e.g. the fact that a river erodes its bed and initiates an increase in basin area, that reinforces the river, does not mean that there was ever a purpose to the river in the first place to which the parts are subordinated.) The whole, showing arrangement, is structured to achieve the behavioural goals.

Complexity

Complexity is that stage where we find that we are no longer sure that reductionist explanation by physics or chemistry will suffice. Living organisms describe themselves and reproduce themselves as totalities. If we remove some part of an organism and see how it behaves, we have no proof that that is how it behaves when not removed. But although we may be dealing with holistic properties, these are not reflexive. It is at this stage that concepts of multiple cause and effect first become prominent. Structure is important in constraining and permitting the dynamics, but structure itself can evolve, and partly in response to the dynamics.

Complexification

Complexification I reserve for those phenomena which are not reducible, which are consciously reflexive, which have an autonomous force (creative will) which can change purposefully their own state. Here many would accept that teleology is internal. This is the world of individuals and of society. This is the world where we contemplate the meaning of meaning. It is the world where undoubtedly thought is a kind of dynamic, and based on structures, be they conceptual, linguistic or whatever, and also where dynamics create structures.

Modelling and the implications of Chaos Theory

If I wish to model the four different kinds of complexity, will the same modelling procedures work for all four? Let me approach this by looking at the dominant modelling paradigm in many parts of social science till the recent advances in Chaos Theory. The best single word to describe it is, not surprisingly, its opposite – Order.

Order produces good lines, good graphs, and error is dismissed as noise, fuzziness, around some clearly modelled relationship. The geometry is simple

ON WHOLENESS, REFLEXIVE COMPLEXITY, ETC. 403

and (of the physical world and time) limited to three or four dimensions. It may appear that science can also cope with dynamics – but it has been of a simple kind, for example considering a very limited number of bodies at a time, such as an Earth in orbit around a Sun. One of the reasons for this state of affairs is that our understanding has depended on being able to make mathematical analytical statements about such behaviour from the initial relationships modelled. Such statements could only be made if:

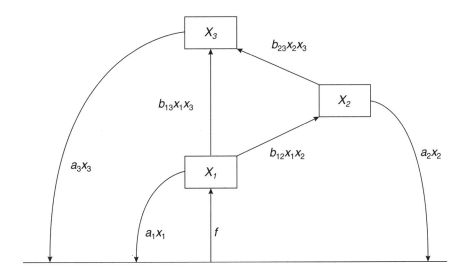

Sensitivities of the forced three-compartment system as a closed network			
Independent variable	Dependent variable		
	δx_2	δx_2	δx_2
δf	+	−	+
δb_{12}	−	+	?
δb_{13}	+	−	+
δb_{23}	?	?	?
δa_1	−	+	−
δa_2	+	−	?
δa_3	−	+	−

Figure 15.2 A forced three-compartment model of an ecosystem; (a) the network; (b) system sensitivities. Note that for some pairs of variables there is no algebraic solution to the sensitivity (source: Williams (1972), cited in Chapman (1977)).

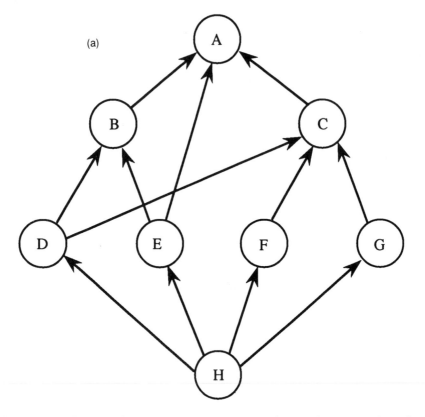

Figure 15.3 (a) An eight-compartment ecosystem. There is also a return loop from A to H. (b), (c), (d) and (e) are three runs of 400, and one of 1,000 iterations. In each, some of the numerical coefficients have been changed. The left axis shows the number of the species in $\log_{10}$ (source: Chapman 1977).

1   there was some expectation that there would be a final equilibrial state (or stable periodic behaviour,[2] indicated by repeating states);
2   the number of variables and the functions relating them permitted a reasonable chance of the derivation of analytical solutions.

With the advent of computers we have been able to model the behaviour of systems of several parts. By this means we can avoid the difficulty of trying to find a solution to the behaviour patterns with the aid of pencil, paper and analytical reasoning. Instead we simply calculate the result at any point in time of our assumptions.

The initial expectation was that our multi-part dynamic systems would of course settle down at some equilibrial state, or show periodic behaviour. But when the powerful new tools were used to flood the darker corners of the existing paradigm with new light, expecting comfortably to see close cousins of the familiar, what happened of course was that the dark corners turned

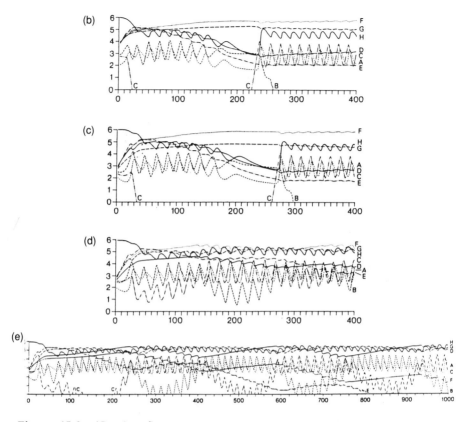

Figure 15.3 (Continued)

out to have some rather ugly-looking gremlins in them. Ugly, that is, until in the eye of the beholder a new concept of beauty grew.

The date when the old paradigm began cracking up can be pin-pointed to a few years. In the early 1970s systems simulation in ecology was trying to maintain the marriage between the greater number of components and more complex functional relationships that could be included in a model, and traditional analytical explanations. The rather extensive Figure 15.2 here exemplifies the approach. Sensitivity analysis shows analytically the way in which change in one component in a system would change others. But as can be seen in Figure 15.2(b), there are many occasions when there is no analytical solution to the sensitivities – it depends on numerical values and computation. Worse, with small increases in the number of parts, it seems that it is impossible to find if these systems have any steady-state equilibria, or, if they do, it may be only if they are started at such a position.

The obvious answer is to abandon the pursuit of the Order, just build models instead, and see what happens. In 1974/5 I was doing just that, and produced some graphs of the behaviour of an 'ecosystem' that seemed to me to be fascinating (see Figure 15.3, taken from Chapman (1977, p. 192)), but although I tried to find if there might be some region in the phase space that contained the trajectory of these systems, I did not have the technical competence to follow the issue properly. Modellers such as Jay Forrester (1971) and his *World Dynamics*, and Meadows *et al.* (1972) and their *Limits to Growth*, produced interesting patterns, and believed the results of their simulations were actually in some prophetic sense 'true' possibilities.

We now know from Chaos Theory that all dynamic systems of two-dimensionality will show some equilibrial or periodic behaviour, but *at higher dimensionality this is not necessarily true*. The result is that as well as systems going into stable or periodic states, they can produce non-repeating behaviour, which is constrained in the phase space – the constraint being revealed by the patterns that the trajectory traces. These patterns are of course the strange attractors (discussed in Chapter 1). These unrepeating trajectories are in a colloquial sense random – in that it is not possible to predict them, only to calculate them. And it is only possible to calculate exactly where the trajectory will go if one can observe the initial starting point with infinite precision – something which is of course impractical.

What implications, if any, do these findings have for the environmental, and/or human sciences? It is easy to see the extent to which analogy with the sciences has been important in the past, and to that extent to see that there are aspects of these new theories that can change our pattern of thinking. The idea of equilibrium in ecosystems has to be looked at again very carefully. If ecosystems do indeed go to equilibrium, what has been the driving force of evolution? Would all internal change, i.e., deriving from Darwinian mutation, not end up by selecting the *status quo*? To be sure there could always be external stress – from orbital wobbles that induce climatic change – but that is not the point. Perhaps mutation causes change that is not selected out: but that cannot be true for any species on its own. The dynamics of the system as a whole can move, but then we are saying essentially the same thing; namely, that if the ecosystem dynamics are chaotic (as indeed technically they are) then that can provide the 'stress' in which some mutations do have a marginal advantage. We are aware that from time to time sudden species blooms take place. In the 1970s an explosion of the crown of thorns starfish was, apparently, going to wipe out the Great Barrier reef of north-east Australia. There was also a presumption that humankind must have done something wrong, that the balance of nature had been disturbed, and the equilibrium destroyed. Seeing simulations such as I produced in 1975 (Figure 15.3) and now realizing the theory behind it, it seems much more likely that we have to abandon the whole idea of equilibrium. What does this say for concepts such as sustainable yields? Who is going to be brave enough to work out the natural balance of species in the North Sea?

Modelling the parts of different complexity

So far modelling – in the sense of good explanatory theory – has been strongest in the world of complication. It is also relevant to note for what follows below that within this world there is universal agreement that there is a significant level of existence from which we can build both up and down – namely the atomic level. The fact that there is disagreement and debate at various sub-atomic or astronomic levels does not change this.

Modelling complification is no problem at all, by definition. We do, after all, actually speak of different *models* of cars, washing machines, aircraft, cameras. Most of these models share the characteristics that they are built on the paradigm of 'order'. We make sure they have stable or periodic stable states, and to that end if they have very many components, we put components in sub-assemblies and limit the degrees of freedom of their connections. If we did not, then parts would begin communicating with parts all over, inducing unpredictable chaotic behaviour, inducing vibrations etc., which might ultimately destroy the model.

With complexity we are on very interesting ground. No one has yet come out with a grand unified theory of biological humans – whatever that would mean. There are of course a myriad of theories about the circulation of blood, the operation of the digestive system, the behaviour of the nervous system. Clearly there are hierarchies within the whole, and there are some degrees of freedom such that limited independent behaviour is possible for some of these sub-systems. It is also interesting that there are several ways in which we can talk of sub-systems – demonstrating that the body in a sense is constructed from a cover-set hierarchy, not a partition. We can for example talk of the blood circulation system, the nervous system, but from my own point of view I prefer to think of my left and right arm, which have limited degrees of freedom with respect to each other. Given the complexity of all this and the numerous interacting parts – why do we not behave chaotically? Or do we? What aspects of our growing, being, becoming, could be described as equilibrial, periodic, or quasi-periodic? (The normal expectation is that the heart will show periodic behaviour, but cardiac fibrillation has indeed been explained in terms of chaotic behaviour.)

What of complexification? Our understanding of physical dynamical systems may have seen a paradigm change and a major advance. But it has said nothing about reflection, and enquiry. Actually, I have discovered that I can 'model' this level of complexification, but only in a very particular way which others might not see as a model at all. This is through the gaming simulation of national economies, in which people are given resources (unevenly), and the non-linear functions that relate inputs to outputs in productive purposes, but the participants are otherwise free to interact in any way they like – to construct societies with whatever rules they like, the politics of co-operation or envy, deceit, dishonesty, inspiration, lethargy, etc. These societies are also manifestly reflexive. There is no finite set of full information in a game which they may discover, or perhaps not discover. The potential information which could be solicited about the state of all players and all resources at any one time is infinite: the players choose for whatever reason to collect certain information – much of it which is of course contingent on what they have done before, which is contingent on what information they previously sought. In other words, looking at their society, they change it.

The end of experimental science

I am not suggesting for a moment that experimental science is about to cease, that laboratories are about to shut up. There has been too much invested in experimental science for that to happen; besides which, it has been invested partly in order to and has succeeded in making money – new technologies, new products. Why that is the case, I will return to shortly. Just for the moment I wish to look at two basic requirements of experimental science. The first is that the experiment is controlled by keeping out unwanted or extraneous variables, and the second is that it is repeatable or replicable. If an experiment such as cold-fusion in a test-tube cannot be replicated, it has not 'passed'.

Part of the philosophy of modelling in human sciences has been that models are a kind of surrogate experiment. But any model, apart from the fact that it is an abstract representation of reality, has to leave something out (in fact nearly everything – see pp. 415–18). This 'leaving out' is somewhat analogous to the procedure of isolating an experiment from extraneous variables. According to the old paradigm this did not necessarily matter much, because what was left out would result in 'noise' or 'deviation' from the trend. But according to the new paradigm, anything, even the beat of a butterfly's wings, is significant.

There is a relationship between this and the tensions between what is known as Modern Scientific Knowledge (MSK) and the opposing Indigenous Technical Knowledge (ITK) (see Chapman 1983, p. 945). MSK has proceeded to date on the basis of the paradigm of Order. To use the products of that knowledge, the operating environment is also similarly ordered – cars require particular kinds of roads. In agriculture, the circumstances in which fertilizer were shown to have dramatic effects in experiment, are reproduced on farms, with controlled water supplies, and chemical control of pests and fungi. The subtle combinatorial nature of local environments is to a large extent ignored. The contrast between the two approaches was aptly summarized for me by an Indian farmer, who said 'Traditional farming methods co-operated with nature, modern methods compete'. In trying to tease out the sense of this remark, one has to admit of course that all farming competes with nature, so the secret of his meaning has to be something slightly more subtle. It is that in Traditional Farming, pursuit of the major aim (producing food) does not cause additional side-effects which have to be additionally controlled. But modern farming with fewer varieties and predominant monoculture produces the side-effects which require further use of agro-chemicals. We are beginning to understand through our own environmental crises the extent to which we apply the products of 'order' only at a high cost. We are beginning to find that one cannot isolate the applications of this or that technology. Everything is related to everything else, and the 'success' of Experimental Science (almost all within the realms of complification) in cutting through this Gordian knot is looking increasingly problematical.

SUMMARY OF PART I

The discovery of our ability to model chaotic behaviour has stimulated the imagination, because it provides intuitively satisfactory images of the kind of complex (*sensu stricto*) behaviour seen in the 'real world' rather than the artificially constrained world. At one level it seems to exclude the possibility of any meaningful prediction. At another level it does provide parameter boundaries for behaviour, through the derivation of strange attractors. These are however derived from observation of the behaviour of the system. The tantalizing question that remains is, is it possible to define what are the structures of the systems, such that one is likely to be able to define the likely kinds of attractors the systems will demonstrate? To even begin to answer that kind of question one has to know what structures are, and how they relate to dynamics. It is quite clear from the above that there are many complicating factors that would make such modelling more difficult in the world of complexity and complexification. Yet, perhaps the structures become more and better defined so the relationship with the dynamics is closer.

Part II: Introduction

This part of the chapter simply points at a way I have tried (not very successfully) to get at the relationship between one way of defining structure, and the system's dynamics.

Much of the thinking on this topic reported here is derived from Gould *et al.* (1984), itself heavily drawing on the work of Atkin (1974). I wish to emphasize at the beginning that there are obvious deficiencies of the approach, in the light of what I have just said. A set theoretic approach is used, which is applicable to intellectual classes and areal aggregates. It can also deal with combination as well as aggregation, thereby to a degree encompassing wholeness, but it is wholeness without arrangement. The approach therefore fails to incorporate very significant aspects of First-Order objects. Nevertheless the approach has proved valuable and stimulating. It helps clear the confusion over a diagram such as the 'systems' diagram (Figure 15.4).

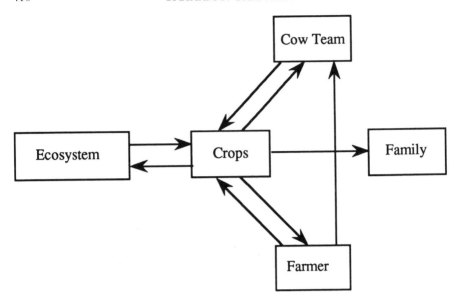

Figure 15.4   A 'systems' model of a farm.

I distrust such models profoundly. Why are the boxes labelled at such arbitrary hierarchical levels? Why is the box labelled 'crops' not broken down into the actual crops? Why are the cows not shown individually? Why is the ecosystem shown as a box rather than a whole complex of arrows relating components? For another attempt, again without a rigorous theory, consider Figure 15.5.

This, too, looks like it has some kind of meaning. But, what do the arrows mean? Are they subordination − but are crops 'subordinate' to farmers? − are they location (crops are in fields)? − are they control (but do animals 'control' rather than 'provide' work)? And are not farmers and labourers both humans, of the same hierarchical importance?

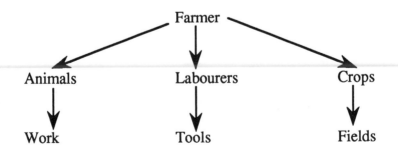

Figure 15.5   A '?' model of a farm?

Hierarchies

The approach we have adopted is to be rigorous in identifying sets, hierarchies of sets (both partitional and coverset), and the relations (well-defined) between sets. To improve the systems model above I start with the hierarchies CROPS, FIELDS, IMPLEMENTS, PEOPLE, ANIMALS (Table 15.1).

We can define any appropriate number of levels we wish – here we have three levels. Having identified the sets, we can record and analyse the relations of interest between them: the *sowing* relation between fields and crops, the

Table 15.1 Hierarchies of sets of farm descriptors

			Hierarchy name
C^N	C^{N+1}	C^{N+2}	CROPS
Variety 1			
Variety 2	Rice		
Variety 3		Crops	
Variety 4	Wheat		
Variety 5	Rabi		
Variety 6	Kharif		
Variety 7			
Variety 8			
F^N	F^{N+1}	F^{N+2}	FIELDS
Field 1			
Field 2	Wet		
Field 3		Fields	
Field 4			
Field 5	Dry		
Field 6			
Field 7			
I^N	I^{N+1}	I^{N+2}	IMPLEMENTS
Plough			
Hoe	Field		
Ladder		Implements	
Thresher	Farmstead		
Stove			
P^N	P^{N+1}	P^{N+2}	PEOPLE
Male 1			
Male 2	Labourers		
Male 3			
Male 4	Family	People	
Female 1			
Female 2	Kitchen		
Female 3			
A^N	A^{N+1}	A^{N+2}	ANIMALS
Cow	Domestic		
Bullock	Wild	Animals	
Hen	Draught		
Duck	Milch		

working relation between labour and fields, the *employing* relation between farmer and labourers, the *using* relation between labourers and implements, the *eating* relation between people and crops, etc. It is also possible of course to aggregate the sets of animals, implements, etc., at a particular hierarchical level into one larger set, called EVERYTHING. (This is a local everything, defined for the farm only and by hierarchical levels and the chosen constituent sets.) Again we can form a matrix with the members of EVERYTHING on both sides, and in that matrix we can record all the relations we have just considered between the constituent sets. So in the matrix of EVERYTHING by EVERYTHING there will be a small area of cells in which the relation 'labourers *using* implement' is recorded, and another in which the 'crops *being sown* in field' is recorded, and another in which the 'people *eating crops*' is recorded.

This much larger matrix has many empty cells in it. But by powering it, blank cells become filled by product relations, that is to say two–step, three–step, etc., relations. Suppose that 'people *eating* crops' is compounded with 'crops *being sown* in fields'. The result is that at the second power we find which particular 'people *eat* (the crops which are grown in which) fields', i.e., which 'people *eat* which fields'.

Defining the hierarchies is not intrinsically difficult, but can be confusing. For many purposes there is no God-given natural level. In the social sciences we are not as fortunate as having the atomic level as baseline. Rather, we use hierarchies of things, because to us they 'make sense': letters, of interest to calligraphers, make up words; words of interest to authors make up sentences; sentences make up paragraphs of interest to readers; paragraphs make up chapters of interest to editors; chapters make up books of interest to publishers and librarians.

We can use two different kinds of set operations to put things into higher ranking boxes, or pigeon-holes. The first defines WHOLES, totalities made of the sum of their parts, using *combinations* of elements. A HOUSE is a combination of (walls AND floor AND roof AND door AND windows), i.e., a HOUSE is defined as a member of the power-set of architectural elements. In this case if we say a WALL is part of a HOUSE and a HOUSE is part of a FARM (at the next level), we cannot say A WALL is a FARM. This contrasts with what happens with aggregation.

Suppose, for the sake of argument, that all the trees are: pear, apple, chestnut, birch, sycamore. Then we can say that the set FRUIT TREES is the aggregation, (pear OR apple), the set TIMBER TREES, (chestnut OR birch OR sycamore). The set TREES can be defined as the union of FRUIT TREES and TIMBER TREES, and gives us (pear OR apple OR chestnut OR birch OR sycamore).

In this case, if pear is an element of FRUIT TREES, and FRUIT TREES an element of TREES, then pear *is* a TREE. The distinction between the Combinatorial and Aggregative Hierarchy is therefore significant.

The two kinds of hierarchy have different information properties. Suppose there are sheets of glass, door frames, and door panels in a locality. These

Table 15.2 Information gain in a combinational classification. The columns are all to be read as members of the power set of the rows. The last column is, therefore, 'Glass pane, Door panel, Frame' – i.e., what would realistically be recognized as a door

	Glass pane	Frame	Door panel	Door panel Frame	Glass pane Door panel Frame
Glass pane	0.2				0.1
Frame		0.1		0.1	0.1
Door panel			0.2	0.1	0.1

The information gain $T = H(J) + H(I) - H(IJ)$ is $0.621 = 1.556 + 1.089 - 2.024$

could either be separate and loose, or put together as complete doors-with-windows-in-frames, or some partial assembly. In Table 15.2 I have calculated the information terms of a one-to-many mapping between some assumed frequencies of the lower elements and the occurrence of members of the power set. The output has a higher Average Expected Information value than the input, because of the Information Gained. If we merely class all door materials as Door Materials, we find there is zero information in the output, because no information was introduced.[3] The original information contained in differentiating between components is lost.

The human mind instinctively works with a conflation of both types of hierarchy. Thus what is real to us is a massively filtered and magnified version of 'the facts', created by simultaneous information loss and information gain. Consider the idea of diet, to be selected from chawal (cooked rice), lentils, chapati and fish, and the difference between a rich person's and a poor person's diet. A rich person might afford rice and/or chapati with fish and/or lentils at every meal. The poor person might eat only rice or chapati. The set defining the POOR DIET is thus (rice OR chapati). The concept of RICH DIET is ((rice AND/OR chapati) AND (fish AND/OR lentil)), in which both AND and OR work together (Chapman 1984, p. 218).

Partitions vs. coversets

Traditional scientific thought has conditioned conscious humankind to think in terms of distinct partitioning: that things belong in one and only one box. I give here (Table 15.3) an example of some crop types, each known by a combination of properties relating to genetic family, breeding history, and season of use.

Using a partitional approach, we can class the crops by any of six possible hierarchies, two of which are shown in Figure 15.6.

Table 15.3 Eight plant types classified in three dimesions. The third dimension is the distinction between wheat (type 'e') and the others, which are all varieties of rice.

Genetic type	Season		
	Aus	*Aman*	*Rabi*
High-yielding variety	a	bc	e
Improved variety		g	
Local variety	df	h	

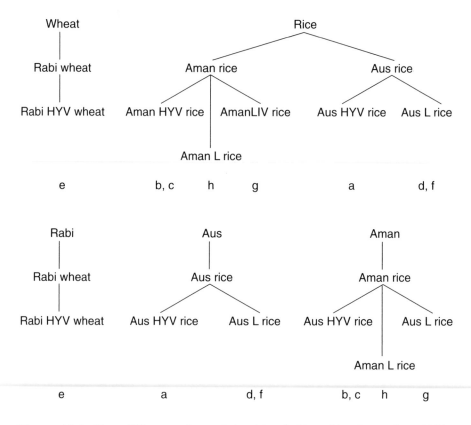

Figure 15.6 Two different orthogonal (partitional) hierarchies drawn from Table 15.3.

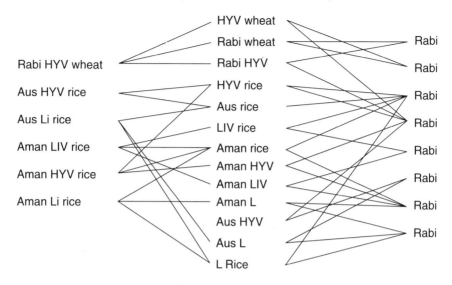

Figure 15.7   The simultaneous cover-set hierarchy derived from Table 15.3.

The distinction between these hierarchies is however false. They are arbitrary subsets of a single overall hierarchy, known as a Galois Lattice (Ho 1982, p. 397; McGill 1985, p. 1089), from which they have been extracted by the rigid constraint that hierarchies must be partitional (see Figure 15.7). From this we realize that for many purposes in the social sciences *wholeness is not exclusive*.

The complete picture

Much of what we have considered so far can be summarized by Figure 15.8. Here we see the different sets of the farm, and the different levels of the aggregations. Mostly (but not always), vertical classifications are matters of definition, so these vertical relations are *defining* ones. Mostly the horizontal relations are *observing* ones and therefore constitute basic data.

The diagonal relations 'upwards' can be found by calculating the product relations of the horizontal observation with the vertical definition. As an example, suppose we observe a relation between crops and fields at the lowest level (horizontal): and define (or observe) different fields to be members of different farms (vertical). Then the product relation will say which crops are grown on which farms. This can of course be checked by observation, or by a questionnaire instead of a field survey. The diagonal relation found by calculation should be consistent with the diagonal relation found by survey. (If it is not, either the observation or the definition is clearly askew for some reason.) Can one calculate diagonal relations downwards? It is possible, if the

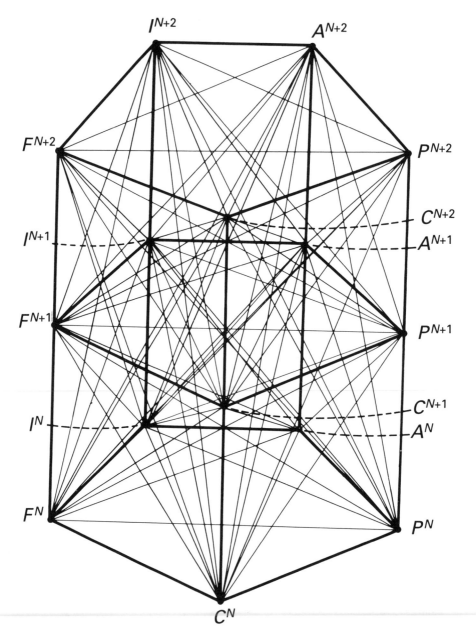

Figure 15.8   Three levels of each of the five farm hierarchies, and relations between the sets so defined.

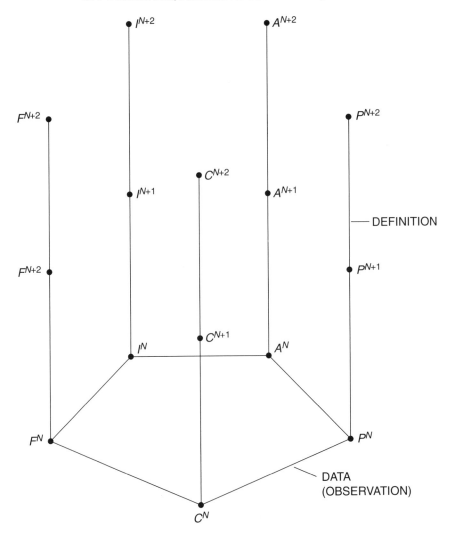

Figure 15.9 A minimal feasible representation from which Figure 15.11 could be reconstructed.

hierarchy is a combinatorial one with an information gain, but it is *not* if the hierarchy is by aggregation and there is information loss in it. If a person has eaten a Lemon Meringue Pie, we know s/he has eaten lemon, and egg, and pastry. If s/he has eaten Food, we do not know whether it was egg, or lemon, or pastry, or anything else.[4]

If all data are observed at the lowest level, then all diagonal relations can be found by calculation, and the basic structure of the data looks like Figure 15.9. In this case, we have observation at one horizontal level only, and classification upwards by definition.

The vertical definitions[5] are classifications by either aggregation or combination or both. They therefore can impose some restrictions on the way diagonal relations are calculated. Suppose we have at the bottom of the hierarchy a blackbird in one set, and a worker in another, and trees in another, and architectural features in the last. Suppose the trees are classed hierarchically by aggregation, and the architectural features by combination. Then, from the relation 'the blackbird pecks the pear tree' we can derive the diagonal relation 'the blackbird pecks a tree'. We cannot, however, go from 'the worker paints the wall' to 'the worker paints the farm'. This is an issue on which further developments are necessary, and about which the reader is cautioned here.

Backcloth and traffic: structure and dynamics

Quite often we find we can make a distinction between what Atkin (1974, p. 26) termed Backcloth and Traffic. This pairing often turns up in other contexts but with different names.

The idea of backcloth is that it supports an activity – the traffic. We can talk of basic physical geography that supports a traffic of human settlement, or of a backcloth of roads that supports vehicular traffic, or of a backcloth of law that underpins the legal cases that are heard each day in court. The idea of support and greater permanence relative to traffic is important, but of course the backcloth can change, and often does if the support can no longer bear the traffic trying to move on it. (Witness the changes in political structure in East Europe in 1989/90.) In the same way that the lowest level of description is arbitrary, and defined only by a concept of practicality, so the particular nature of backcloth and traffic is dependent on the observers' interests. For example, crop types may be a traffic on the backcloth of the structure of land ownership. On the other hand particular pests and diseases are traffic on the backcloth of particular crops. A television play may depict a love story, traffic on a backcloth of real historical characters in the Second World War. The historical characters may be seen as traffic on the events of the war itself; and the war, as Freud saw it, as traffic on the deeper backcloth of the psychology of humanity.

Work on relating traffic dynamics to structural properties is an exciting and important new research frontier. As an example of its possibilities, consider the notion of trade in economics. Trade in prehistoric times was limited by barter exchanges – and could therefore occur slowly in limited chains of complex bilateral negotiation, chains which exhibited high dimensional structure of the kind defined by Atkin (1974, p. 173) (see below). The invention of money frees trade and requires only multilateral balances to be observed. Money essentially defines a very low dimension, almost structure-free, backcloth on which goods can flow. However, politicians and bankers do not like structure-free flows: so a myriad of structural complications are introduced to induce the traffic to flow in supposedly more desirable ways: national currencies, exchange rate mechanisms, tax differentials between earned and unearned income, between capital goods and consumption goods; long-term and short-term interest rates, etc.

None of this tells us, however, in rigorous terms, what is meant by structure – an elusive concept although much invoked by everyone from Marxist Theoreticians of the Hard Left to Organization Men/Women of the Corporate Hard Right. Atkin (1974, p. 32) has suggested one definition of structure, based on the set-theoretic approach outlined above and the associated relations between sets. The definition of structure is rigorous, but obviously suffers from the fact that at best the approach can only handle wholeness without arrangement. The idea is that a relation (such as we have used for data-relations or hierarchical relations above) is described by a simplicial complex. The simplices exist in as many dimensions (–1) as they have vertices – so the maximal dimension of the space required to display such a complex is at least as large as $n - 1$, where n is the number of vertices of the largest simplex, and often larger if many simplices do not share vertices in common. Because this is difficult to comprehend, and because the shapes and connectivities of the simplices are important in his view to the patterns of permissible traffic, he has proposed an analysis of these connectivities. The multi-dimensional connectivity pattern defines his structure vector.

A highly simplified example may help. Suppose we have a relation between a set of four people, p1, p2, p3 and p4, and a set of four academic subjects A, B, C and D. The relation is 'this person is an expert in' (never mind the precise details of 'expert'!). Suppose the relation is as in Figure 15.10(a). Clearly, p1 and p2 can have interesting conversations in which they can combine knowledge of A. Such discussions constitute traffic, or dynamics. Remembering that two points define a line of one dimension, this represents one-dimensional level traffic. There is therefore a single piece of the structure which links p1, p2 and p3 in one-dimension via connectivities.

Each person is represented by a simplex – her/his combination of Knowledge. Figure 15.10(b) shows a diagram of the simplices together, showing how the maximum dimension of p1 is 2 (represented by a triangle of three points), so is the maximum dimension of p4. p2 exists as a one-dimensional side of p4's two-dimensional triangle. p3 exists as a single point – zero dimensional. In Figure 15.10(c) the people have been listed according to their dimensionality and connectivity, but without showing which subjects they know. The single link at one-dimensional level can be seen between p1, p4 and p2, as well as the zero-dimensional connectivity which unites all of them. Note that p1 and p4 cannot talk to each other using their full range of knowledge, since there are vertices B and D which are not in common. This is reflected by the spiky tops to the columns for p1 and p4 in Figure 15.10(c). The diagram is the basis for Atkin's structure vector, which defines the number of pieces into which the structure breaks at each successive dimensional level. In this case it is given in Figure 15.10(d). At the two-dimensional level there

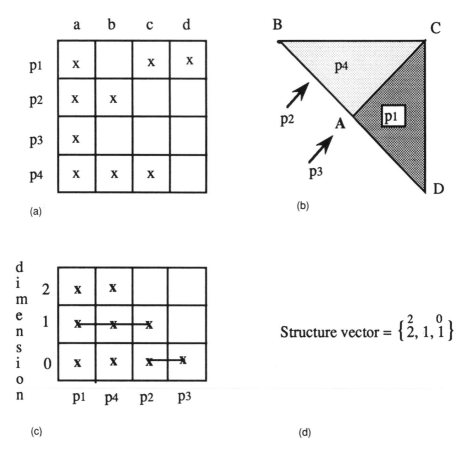

Figure 15.10 (a) The 'knows' relation between four people and four subjects; (b) how the simplices of the four people show different dimensionality, and how they 'stick' together; (c) the dimensionality and connectivity of (b); (d) the structure vector of (c), and therefore of (a). The small numbers above indicate maximum and minimum dimensions in the structure, the larger numbers show the number of components at each dimensional level.

are two pieces, because p1 and p4 cannot talk to each other with their full combinations, whereas at the one-dimensional and zero-dimensional levels there is a single structure. It can be appreciated intuitively how these structures would say what traffic is not possible. They do not say what kind of traffic is necessary.

To go back to the beginning of this chapter, I have been wondering for a long time over the kind of network I constructed for the animal ecosystem shown in Figure 15.3 and its relation to the patterns of behaviour. In Atkin's scheme of things, clearly this relation of A eats B has a representation as a simplicial complex. Is there a kind of hyper-state-space in which this particular network exists? The answer is, of course, that we can construct one by defining an axis for each animal which comprizes the power set of the set of animals. If we have four animals, such an axis will have 2^4 categories on each axis, and there will be four such axes. There are therefore $2^{16} = 65,536$ cells to this space, and by marking any one of them we have specified a unique configuration for the relation. Within this cell we can think of the four dimensions of its sides as being the four axes of a phase space within which we will plot the behavioural pattern of the simulation of that relation. Quite clearly the behaviour pattern within any one cell could be varied by changing coefficients in the model, but would this change the gross behaviour pattern? How similar would behaviour patterns be in different collections of cells in the hyperspace. At some point we know that behaviour would be trivially simple – for example those networks that consisted of each animal eating just one other in a loop with the ground as one element in the loop. But for the others I do not know.

There are two possibilities that intrigue me. One is that there may be patterns of behaviour that can be related to these different cells, and this behaviour could be chaotic, but around different attractors. The second is that a measure of structure has been provided by Atkin, which can be applied to these cells. We would then have the possibility of making a relationship between structure and a range of behaviour. To that extent the dynamics would no longer be around 'black holes'.

We need to return to Atkin's (1974) concept of structure for a moment. The simplicial complex can be represented by a solid shape in multi-dimensional space. Since there can be arbitrarily any relation on the product of two sets, this shape also is of any arbitrary form. Indeed it is the distinctiveness and individuality of these forms that makes them intuitively interesting. But several of the cells in the hyper-state-space conceived of above would map on to the same structure vector – so the structure vector represents a way of typing or grouping the individual structures. It therefore becomes even more intriguing to wonder whether there are types of behaviour which relate to the types of structure vectors.

Because the combinatorial terms become difficult very rapidly, for the sake of exposition I shall assume a 3×3 matrix. In this case there are $2^9 = 512$ possible different relations on the matrix. Let us look at those matrices which contain two blanks. These constitute $9 \times 8/2 = 36$ of the 512 possible matrices.

If we still stick to Atkin's definition, then it is permissible to permute the rows and the columns of these matrices to see which ones of the thirty-six are equivalent to each other *because they give rise to the same structure vector*. In this sense there are only three different types of matrices with two blanks, as shown in Figure 15.11. These three are:

1 matrices in which the blanks do not occur in either the same row or the same column;

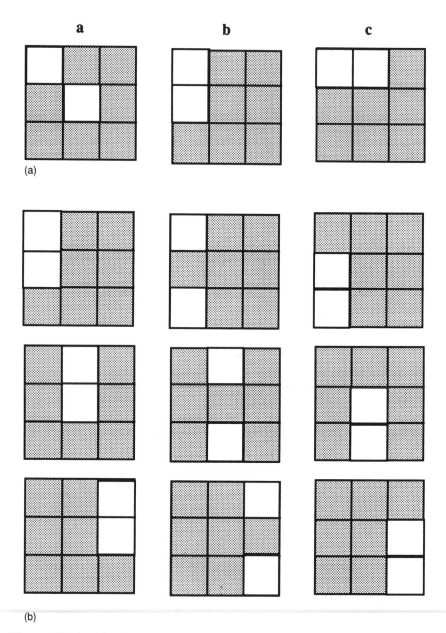

(a)

(b)

Figure 15.11 (a) Three structures defined by two blanks in a 3 × 3 relation; (b) The nine individual matrices which all give rise to the same structure as Figure 15.10(b).

2 matrices in which both blanks occur in the same column;
3 matrices in which both blanks occur in the same row.

(An analysis performed on the last two and their conjugates would actually in each case give the same two structure vectors, but in reverse order.) Of the thirty-six distinct matrices, there are eighteen distinct matrices of the first type, and nine each of the other two.

Let us arbitrarily go to a 4×4 matrix with three blanks. Already this becomes a difficult combinatorial problem. There are 560 such possible matrices – a subset of the 65,536 noted above. For these 560 how many structure vectors are there, and what is the 'probability' of each? It turns out that there are six distinct structure vectors, with frequencies (found by permuting all rows and columns) of 16, 16, 96, 144, 144, and 144.

For four blanks in a four by four matrix there are 1,820 possible relations. I have calculated that these are reduced to eleven distinguishable structures (though I have not calculated their frequencies).[6] In other words, what Atkin's structure vector does do is produce a classification of structural types, which groups together many cells of my hyper-state-space to a vastly reduced number of regions. Is there any relationship between the structure vectors and the type of behaviour on them? It may of course be a complete blind alley, but at present I find it intriguing, at least intuitively.

SUMMARY AND CONCLUSIONS OF PART II

So far, many of the new models examining complexity and chaos may have shown us much more about the nature of apparently complex and unpredictable, yet deterministic dynamics. But these models assume a world made up of interacting simple parts all of one hierarchical level. The real world is arranged in complex hierarchies, which contain and are contained hierarchically, and which also overlap in complex ways. The containing and the overlapping create complex structures; in the human world these are more complex than in the physical. The structure is clearly permissively important to dynamics – particular structures do not necessarily generate particular dynamics, but in any one case they certainly do prohibit much that is impossible. Classifying structures is therefore an important way to understanding dynamics. Clearly, to pursue this line, we need good definitions of structure – and ones that are sensitive to coverset hierarchies. This is not a well-developed field – but there is at least one line of enquiry that can be followed, which has been described in this part of the chapter. In detail it may not turn out to be a good definition of structure and a good line of enquiry, but the general strategy of such an approach should nevertheless be very fruitful. It may in the first instance divert attention away from dynamics – the subject of this volume – but only because I see structures as a first step towards a better understanding of dynamics in the future.

Notes

1 Let me be very clear that I am *not* using 'complexity' in the technical sense of Complexity Theory in computing, which has to do with the theoretical computation time required for different classes of algorithms, even though there may be some connections between what I am saying and such theory at some points.

2 I include quasi-periodic behaviour with periodic. In periodic behaviour a pattern repeats itself exactly. In quasi-periodic behaviour each component of a pattern may repeat itself, but the whole never repeats itself exactly. So, for example, an orbiting astronaut may swing her/his cat with a period which is not a rational fraction of the period of orbit. The result is that the cat's path defines a torus in which the trajectory never repeats itself, although it is continually in the same region of phase-space.

3 I have not thought adequately about the issue yet, but it is quite obvious that although there could be considerable information gain in combination (i.e., wholeness without arrangement) it is probably trivial compared with the much greater information gain in the case of wholeness-with-volumetric-arrangement.

4 This second case illustrates a problem with field research which is very common in geography and I suspect many other social sciences, namely that the researcher collects all sorts of different information from respondents without having worked out beforehand a realistic evaluation of the hierarchical levels and relations between sets, so that much data is collected that neither will nor can be used later. We find that local labourers are given two free meals a day, that meals are constituted of food, and that the local foods are rice, fish and dal. But we find to our cost that from this information we cannot calculate whether the food in kind to labourers is dietarily satisfactory or not. The problem here is in a sense analogous to forming the product of two numbers, one with four significant numbers, the other with two – e.g., 4.356×1.13. The product is only given to two places, and the first of the two numbers was unnecessarily 'accurate', and if such accuracy was achieved at a cost, it is a cost wasted.

5 One further observation needs stressing here too. The vertical dimension of this diagram in nearly all circumstances depends upon classification, a human perceptual process. There are therefore as many diagrams as there are classifications – – and that of course is limitless. Since some of these classifications may appear arbitrary to some observers, and since we know that the same basic phenomena are seen differently by different observers, it is important that in any database, as far as possible, only bottom level data are entered (more is said later on this later – see pp. 417–18).

6 The 'easiest' solution to finding these numbers is to envisage the matrices so that all the occurrences of blanks for a given structure vector type occur in the smallest subset of cells possible, say in the top left of the matrix. Then the number of arrangements of this type of structure vector in that subset is determined, and multiplied by the number of ways we can draw such a subset of cells from the whole matrix. For large matrices the determination of the number of distinct structure vectors becomes increasingly complicated.

References

Atkin, R.H. 1974. *Mathematical Structure in Human Affairs*. London: Heinemann.
Chapman, G.P. 1977. *Human and Environmental Systems*. London: Academic Press.
Chapman, G.P. 1983. The folklore of the perceived environment in Bihar. *Environment and Planning* A 15, 945–68.

Chapman, G.P. 1984. A structural analysis of two farms in Bangladesh. In *Understanding Green Revolutions*, T.Bayliss-Smith and S. Wanmali (eds.), 212–52. Cambridge: Cambridge University Press.

Feibleman, J.K. 1954. The theory of integrative levels. *British Journal for the Philosophy of Science* 5, 59–90.

Forrester, J. W. 1971. *World Dynamics*. Cambridge, Mass.: MIT Press.

Gould, P.M., J. Johnson and G.P. Chapman 1984. *The Structure of Television*. London: Pion.

Hesse, M. 1976. Models versus paradigms in the natural sciences. In *The use of Models in the Social Sciences,* L. Collins (ed.), 75–89. Tavistock, London,

Ho, Y.-S. 1982. The planning process: structure of verbal descriptions. *Environment and Planning* B 9, 397–420.

McGill, S. 1985. Structural analysis of social data. *Environment and Planning* A 17, 1089–1109.

Meadows, D.H., D.L. Meadows, J. Randers and W.W. Behrens 1972. *The Limits to Growth*. New York: Universe Books.

Prigogine, I. 1985. New perspectives on complexity. In *The Science and Praxis of Complexity*, S. Aida, P.M. Allen and H. Atlan *et al.* (eds), 107–18. Tokyo: The United Nations University.

16 Towards an 'appropriate metrology' of human action in archaeology

H. MARTIN WOBST

Introduction

My aim in this chapter is to help in theorizing the lowly measurement phase of archaeological research, on our way to 'make sense' of change and variation in material culture – the material precedents and products of human behaviour. If mensuration is not thoroughly embedded within one's agenda, it can torpedo one's research through the back door. The most convincing hypothetical argument or the most massive interpretive *tour de force* must ultimately fail if the points where measurements enter the research stream, and the measurements themselves, are not carefully theorized. The argument is presented here in support of those paradigms interested in human agency, in the priority of the social, and in understanding and explaining change and variation in humans and in the material products and precedents of their behaviour.

Let us for simplicity's and my argument's sake divide research designs into two component parts: theory and metrology. Theory then encompasses such steps as problem definition, trial problem solution, hypothesis theory or law statements, interpretations, and inferences. The term 'metrology' may then circumscribe all of the measurements taken in the service of a given paradigm (and their theoretical justification). Of course, this division arbitrarily separates theory from mensuration, while both parts are, of course, inseparably theoretical (see, for example, Wylie 1989, p. 19), and what is being measured, of course, does not exist independent of theory and mensuration (cf. Binford and Sabloff 1982). As a matter of fact, given the paradigm, one would expect theory to rigorously instruct, and reverberate across, metrology. One would also expect to see the latter justified in terms of the former.

It is my sense, however, that little attention has been paid to the evaluation and theoretical justification of metrology in archaeology. As a trite example of this, traditional, processual and post-processual archaeologists utilize similar-size excavation units, make shovel testpits of the same size, and work with Marshalltown trowels of similar shape, hardness and acuity. Of course, shovel tests, Marshalltown trowels and excavation units are relatively non-sexy aspects of the archaeological enterprise. Yet, they are bound to structure our social information in important ways, if only by reducing, suppressing, or deflecting from, the observation of change and variation at certain scales of variability, and by drawing attention to other scales. To stay with the examples: behavioural remains larger than earthworm tracks will be under-recorded if shovel tests are our only windows; behavioural deposition contexts larger than 5-foot or 10-foot squares will be under-observed if that is the size of our excavation units. So far, the theorization of these aspects of metrology simply has not been much on the agenda.

Frequently, even in well exposed papers, there are tensions if not outright contradictions between the paradigm and the metrology utilized to illustrate that the paradigm is working. It is rare for such contradictions to become the focus of critique and resolution (for exceptions see, for example, some of the papers in Moore and Keene 1983, or Wobst and Keene 1983; these critiques themselves, however, do not seem to attract much attention). Instead, the theory parts of the research receive the bulk of the attention, critique and modification. The metrology, meanwhile – seemingly viewed as being dull compared to the pizazz of theory formation – remains as untheorized as it ever was. Also, quite probably, it serves up the same data that previous metrologies utilized to make their point, in the same way.

This raises the possibility that our archaeological knowledge of the 1990s is not grounded in the most forceful way, embedded in a web of sensitive measures and observations. Instead, we may simply be pairing up our new ideas with the same kinds of stale measures that we had been taking fifty to one hundred years ago – measures insensitive to change and dynamism, actors and agency.

If our measurements are not (re-)theorized in terms of our present paradigms, what does a smooth fit among questions, trial answers, and metrology mean? How much can we learn about the world preceding or surrounding us if our observations and measurements have not been changing in logic, despite massive changes from traditionalist to modernist to post-modernist paradigms? Most kinds of measurements we are presently using have been habitual in the discipline from the time when a very different archaeology from that of today was practised. If we uncritically continue to utilize such measures – are we not adjusting our modern world to fit a model of variation introduced into the discipline as early as the later nineteenth and early twentieth century?

As indicated, for example, by this book, there is increasing interest in dynamically changing systems and multifarious trajectories of change. In many of our minds the locus of change has changed from 'the system personified' (or an environment similarly personified) to actors and their relations, tensions, contradictions, and mismatches within and between systems. This should encourage us to (re)evaluate metrology in archaeology. Changed concerns call for an 'appropriate' metrology, much as we need an 'appropriate technology': a metrology that theorizes our measurements in the context of our theoretical goals. Such an 'appropriate metrology' does not deflect from the changes we need to observe and understand. It measures what is necessary and provides us with live ammunition to illustrate, evaluate and modify our new hunches and ideas about change.

In the following, the metrologies of the early stages of New Archaeology and post-processual archaeology are critically evaluated in their dealings with change and variation: how they dealt with change and dynamics, and their description and measurement in human systems; how well they theorized what they measured; and what can be learned from their shortcomings about (in)appropriate metrology.

Metrology in the early New Archaeology

The early papers by Lewis and Sally Binford (Binford and Binford 1966; Binford and Binford 1969) and Lewis Binford (for example, 1967) on variability and change in archaeological data, like the Ph.D. theses of their early students, such as Freeman (1964; cf. 1966), Hill (1965; cf. 1970) and Longacre (1963; cf. 1970), are often used to illustrate the workings of an explicitly scientific, modernist archaeology. Many readers walk away from these publications convinced that they epitomize a 'Hempelian' (Hempel 1965, 1966) deductivist, positivist paradigm of scientific logic, in which change and variation in the archaeological realm are treated with relative elegance, sensitivity and internal consistency, if the paradigm and the early publication dates within it are conceded. How does the metrology of these early papers measure up to that expectation?

Expected research flow in early New Archaeology
Several New Archaeologists caricatured the flow chart of pre-New Archaeologists to emphasize the mainly inductive nature of traditional archaeology and to bring out that the inferential parts of the research of their predecessors tended to remain unevaluated. For example, Fritz and Plog (1970, pp. 409–10) see the following sequence of steps in the traditionalist (i.e., pre-new) research design (Figure 16.1).

In this sequence, research starts with the data and ends with hypotheses that are not contradicted by the data. Aside from establishing the fact that the hypotheses fit the given case (not a big deal since they were intuited to do that), they otherwise remain unevaluated. The important feature of these research designs for our purposes here is that their metrology (in stages 2 and 3) is untheorized by the hypotheses that originate in stages 4 to 7, since it precedes these stages. Hypotheses about change and variation are advanced *post hoc*, in order to fit data that are not explicitly selected to be particularly sensitive to those kinds of hypotheses. Thus, the image of change and variation captured in these measurements is bound to be less sharply focused,

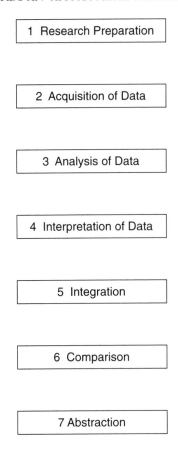

Figure 16.1   Model of a traditionalist research design as seen by New Archaeologists.

less captivating of what the hypotheses address, and more spurious, than if one had been able to approach the measuring process with the foresight of the given hypothesis or interpretation.

The model research design that many modernist archaeologists considered ideal looked quite different (cf. Figure 16.2). It tended to start with a theoretical puzzle, addressed trial solutions to that puzzle, derived implications for archaeological measurements from those hypotheses, took the anticipated measurements on the archaeological data, and thus, allowed the archaeologist to evaluate whether or not the trial hypotheses were working.

Several early New Archaeologists published virtually identical versions of this model (see, for example, Binford 1968, pp. 19–20; Fritz and Plog 1970, pp. 410–11; Plog 1969, 1974, Ch. 2; Watson *et al.* 1971, Ch. 1). In theory, in this model research design, the measurements about change and variation were directly guided and implied by, and thus logically consistent with and

1 Theoretical Problem

2 Trial Hypotheses

3 Implications for Measurements

4 Measurements on Data

5 Hypothesis OK?

Figure 16.2   Model New Archaeology research design.

– one assumes – sensitive to, the given hypothesis about change and variation. Certainly, the paradigm in its model version should have forced people
to look for change and variation, and to do so with appropriate measurements; i.e., measurements that did not destroy the information on change or
variation before the research started.

Observed research flow in early archaeology
As far as metrology is concerned, the flow chart of many early New Archaeology papers is often more complex or convoluted than this model would have
one suspect. In practice, that research sequence (cf. Figure 16.3) usually starts
with a similar boiler-plate: a disclaimer of traditional approaches, a systemic
basic assumption, a strong claim of adherence to deductivist logic, and a statement of procedure implying a hypothesis-testing, instead of a hypothesis-
generating, procedure. Initially no hypotheses are presented for evaluation
except paradigmatic claims about goals (social theory, process, etc.) and doubts
about previous approaches, hypotheses, and paradigms (Figure 16.3, Step 1).

The paradigm and some of its more explicit early cook-books would have
led one to expect the next research steps to consist of intuiting theory, or
deducing hypotheses from ulterior theory for subsequent test and validation
(as in Figure 16.2, Step 2). Yet, the next step in many of the early papers
was metrological itself (Figure 16.3, Step 2): quite often a massive measurement or remeasurement phase preceded the presentation of any hypotheses.[1]

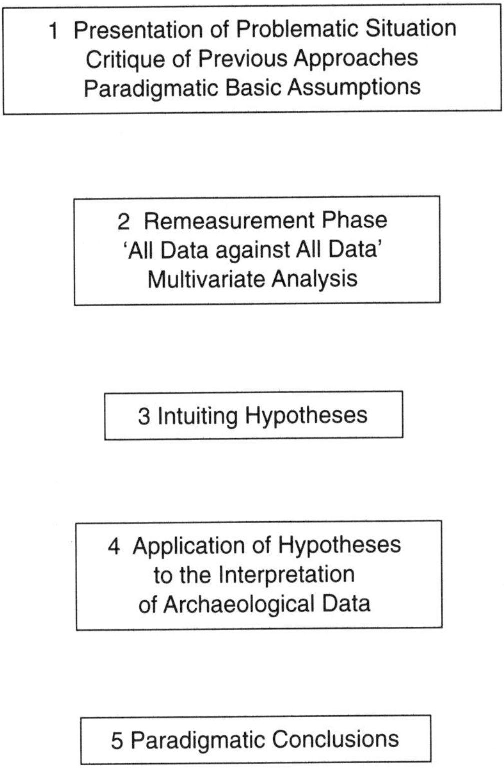

> **1** Presentation of Problematic Situation
> Critique of Previous Approaches
> Paradigmatic Basic Assumptions

> **2** Remeasurement Phase
> 'All Data against All Data'
> Multivariate Analysis

> **3** Intuiting Hypotheses

> **4** Application of Hypotheses
> to the Interpretation
> of Archaeological Data

> **5** Paradigmatic Conclusions

Figure 16.3 Research design of many early New Archaeology projects in practice.

For example, for Longacre (1970, p. 2), it was 'essential to measure the mutual covariation among all classes and types of archaeological data' at an early point in his research so that explicit hypotheses might be developed. In Hill's (1968, p. 106) case, 'much of the data was quantified and manipulated statistically', *before* explicit propositions were presented. For Freeman (1966, pp. 232–3), the first step consisted of carrying out a correlation analysis between *all* of the variables before hypothesis tests are attempted.

In other words, hypotheses about change and variation are presented (Figure 16.3, Step 3) only *after* all artefacts have been measured. Thus, in these cases, hypothetical information on change and variation is *also post hoc*, post measurement – measurements are not specifically gathered so as to maximize their sensitivity to the processes that are later hypothesized about.

Some of the early archaeology publications then go on to systematically evaluate their propositions against their (other) implications for archaeological data (see, for example, Hill 1968).[2] Early on, this raised some hackles about potential circularity as a logical threat to the formal evaluation of the given propositions (for example LeBlanc 1973, pp. 199–200). In our context, it is more important that these propositions had been intuited and were then selected for further testing because they looked reasonable within the *given* data structure: these data had not been produced to be particularly sensitive for measuring the implications of hypotheses for change and variation. If we cannot reject hypotheses about change and variation in this process, they may not tell us about change and variation as much as about the initial data structure and its relative insensitivity to change and variation (because no explicit aforethought had been given to that in its initial selection).

New Archaeology factor analyses and other multivariate analyses

A research structure even less self-critical about the role of metrology was common to many early New Archaeology papers, in which multivariate analysis preceded the presentation of any specific hypotheses, and where that multivariate analysis remained the only interaction with the data, short of their interpretation. The factor analysis papers of many early New Archaeologists may serve as example here. The Binfords' Mousterian research (L.R. Binford and S.R. Binford 1966; S.R. Binford and L.R. Binford 1969) provides a particularly well-known model of that research structure.

The Binfords' papers on the Middle Palaeolithic open with a discussion of the data and of previous hypotheses that failed to account for the observed variation (see Figure 16.3, Step 1). In contrast, the Binfords view the archaeological record as structured by 'a large number of possible 'causes' in various combinations' which puts a premium on 'groups of artefacts that vary together' (Binford and Binford 1966, p. 241). These groups are thought to represent activities. Thus, techniques are needed 'to isolate artefact groups reflecting activities within assemblages' (*ibid.*).

Judging from the paradigm, the next step should consist of deducing implications from that set of hypothetical statements[3] for the structure and distribution of measurements in Middle Palaeolithic archaeological data. But the paper deviates from the paradigmatic model flow chart of the time: at this point, metrology in the form of factor analysis is introduced and carried out.

In this case, again, the metrological section does not evaluate any hypotheses or theory (whether the implications of theories or hypotheses are reflected in measurements on the data). On the contrary, factor analysis takes for granted that the data (here, the archaeological record) are structured by multiple causes in complex ways. The method generates its measurements as if they were structured in that way, whether or not they are, and it always generates those measurements, even if the data are completely random. It simply requires new observations on the old counts per unit (e.g., correlation coefficients of all variables against all variables), and it produces new observations upon these correlation coefficients (e.g. factor loadings, commonalities, etc.).

The observations generated by Factor Analysis serve to intuit hypotheses, such as 'the variables for a factor represent a functionally related set of tools'

(Binford and Binford 1966, p. 249); or 'factor II represents the implements used for hunting and butchering' (*ibid.*, p. 252). These hypotheses, in turn, serve to *interpret* variation in the old data (frequency distributions and Mousterian variants). Neither (1) the original hypothetical statements about multiple causes complexly structuring the Middle Palaeolithic archaeological record, nor (2) the hypotheses intuited to interpret the results of factor analysis, nor (3) the hypothetical interpretations of the original data and of assemblage types with the interpretations generated in (2) are logically evaluated in this procedure. Rather, the interpretations in (1), (2), and (3) remain unevaluated in terms of the paradigm.

In these examples, the 'new' paradigm of deductivism and falsificationism is implicitly combined with an 'old' metrology (see Figure 16.1 vs. Figure 16.3). That metrology does not straightforwardly (or deductively) originate from the strictures of the modernist paradigm. Instead, the metrology serves up untheorized measurements, with little logical bridge building. There is little guidance that explains why that metrology should follow upon the statement of the given problematic. The metrology essentially shuffles and recombines pre-existing measurements into new structures in order to stimulate the archaeologist to intuit new hypotheses (a doubtful procedure in terms of the philosophy of science). In practice, a deductivist boiler-plate has been combined with a very traditional and *very* inductivist metrology. Sensitivity to change and variation, since not theorized in the original measurements, is compromised.

In the processual paradigm, such factor-analytic metrologies have been repeated on many other constellations of data, including, among others, Lower Palaeolithic assemblages of East Africa (Binford 1972), the Lower and Middle Palaeolithic sites of Spain (Freeman 1973), the Upper Palaeolithic of France (Montet-White 1973) and Italy (Pollnac and Ammerman 1973), the Corded Ware culture of Bohemia (Neustupny 1973), and the La Téne societies of France (Rowlett and Pollnac 1971).

Factor analyses themselves are, of course, only the tip of a metrological iceberg of multivariate analysis carried out in the service of New Archaeology (see Shennan 1988, Chs 11–13). In most of these analyses, it would have been more consistent with the paradigm to have anticipated, from pre-existing theory or other sources, the pervasiveness or the content of the factors (or other multivariate data structures), the number of significant ones, or their distribution and recombination across space, time or assemblage type. Then, metrology could have evaluated the implications and thus the theory, as in the paradigmatic model (as, for example, Binford 1968, pp. 19–20, himself had proposed).

Despite such internal contradictions, several of the seminal papers are still held up as prime examples of an internally consistent deductive modernist scientific paradigm, that links theory and data with appropriate metrology, and some continue to be reprinted in readers because they supposedly illustrate the paradigm so well.

Other metrological problems in early processual archaeology

The New Archaeology appeared on the scene (and was aided in its appearance) when computers had entered social science for good. Computers made possible the massive introduction of probability, sampling, rapid seriation, systematic survey, and statistics (for early references, see, for example, Binford 1964; Gelfand 1971; Gumerman 1971; Ragir 1967; Redman and Watson 1970; Sterud 1967; Whallon 1963), the numeric processing and evaluation of vast amounts of data (Cowgill 1968), the modelling, fine tuning, and evaluation of complex archaeological ideas through computer simulation of complex phenomena (see, for example, Thomas 1971; Wobst 1971; Zubrow 1971), and various other advances and improvements.

But the excitement about the facility with which numbers in the field and laboratory could be generated, cumulated, shuffled and regurgitated for publication, and the relative ease with which canned programs like Factor Analysis could generate new numbers from the field and laboratory ones, created a new problem: numerical overload. So many numbers were generated that the individual measurement or observation had to lose in value. Even if it did not lose in value in the mind of the investigator, there was no easy way to keep it in view in one's publication. It is probably here that another serious paradigmatic conflict arises.

Where there is metrological overload, the indigestible mass of measurements needs to be reduced, simplified, sifted and shuffled until it can be digested by the reading public or bureaucracies. Observation overload compels retreat into summary measures of variation: where a given variable is indeed variable, that variation will be reported as central tendency (e.g., mean, mode, or median). Where that variation has interesting shapes (as in a histogram), those shapes will be reduced to standard deviations or ranges around the mean. Where two variables may co-vary, covariation is reduced to *linear* regression and *linear* correlation. And where there is change, that change will be dissected into internally non-changing, self-replicating modules, much like the stills of a movie.

The publications of processualists (as well as those of their predecessors) abound with untheorized means, modes, and medians, and with central tendencies and clusters, with unjustified parametric statistics, and with linear regressions and correlations. In total metrological innocence, behaviour is measured and reported as if it took place in reference to norms. Frequently such measurements are published as if the universe had forced all observable behaviour, particularly that materially fossilized, under bell-shaped khaki helmets. As if behaviour had no other options but to approximate the means of distributions or to err in standard deviations relative to means. As if behaviour had no other alternative but to be part of a measurement cluster on the way to a central tendency, and to be separated by metrological vacua from the next such measurement cluster (cf. Wobst 1978; Wobst and Keene 1983).

Remember the bogey person of the early New Archaeologist – the normative archaeologist? (see, for example, Binford 1965; Watson *et al.* 1971, Ch 3). S/he:

> sees his [or her] field of study the ideational basis . . . of human life – culture. Information is obtained by studying cultural products as the objectifications of *normative* ideas about the proper ways of life executed by now extinct people. The archaeologist's task lies in abstracting from cultural products the *normative* concepts extant in the minds of men [and women] now dead.
>
> (Binford 1965, p. 203)

One wonders if that is not actually and in all innocence measured or published for posterity by the majority of the processualists! In three-dimensional image, the metrics of a single variable in processual archaeology are assumed to look like the mountain top of the normal curve, surrounded symmetrically by slopes of error, and separated by deserts (of no measurements at all) from the next such topological phenomenon. At least that is the image one gets if all that is recorded for the reader's edification is the mean and the standard deviation for the metrical distribution of given variables.

The same model underlies the linear correlation that has served as input for much of the multivariate analysis of the New Archaeology (cf. above and Speth and Johnson 1976). At a given frequency for one variable, there is only one theoretically 'right' or 'proper' frequency for the other variable: the remainder is error obscuring that 'proper' behaviour.

In the nomothetic context of processual archaeology: how many people have ever systematically recorded (or thought about and theorized) the shape of the metric distribution of a single variable, as the sole outcome of functional exigency (holding everything else constant)? How should that shape differ if raw material constraint was at work on the variable? Or, post-depositional wear and tear? Or, the pull of fashion or avant-garde? Or revolution?

What even, in this context, is the behavioural rationale for the stereotypic normal curve in *biology*? Even in the simplest possible case, where a single metric variable is taken into a vice of selection, with the largest and smallest measures discriminated against, what is there in theory to guarantee a bi-variate normal curve? Even if the normal curve is biologically derived from a very strong selectionist or functionalist argument (where options other than the region of the mode would be absolutely precluded), the expectation of a bell-shaped curve shape would still need to be justified. Even in that case, a bimodal curve (with peaks just inside the first loss of fitness in either direction) would be as compelling as a normal curve. In terms of selection, *any* curve shape would be as good as any other, as long as the mode(s) stayed on the inside of the areas where fitness is lost.

Modernist archaeologists might very well believe they are not trying to build a normative model of culture and society (and of the world for that matter). If their metrology implicitly continues to be normative, as it was inherited from their predecessors, they will continue to produce a normative world through the back door: with entities that are tightly bounded, in which the behaviour is strongly patterned, and in which people try to be each other's clones (with some error).

That kind of society can be personified like the ecosystem is personified. Within a given category there is virtually no contradiction, tension, rebellion, and revolution – only error. Between social variables, there is determination (with error) of one variable by the other, not social practice with a multitude of right and appropriate metrical stances per two-variable combination along both axes.

The solution here lies in breaking out of a normative metrology in the direction of embracing variation on its own terms – a metrology that admits of the sanity, rightness and intelligence of alternative variable states and understands them in context, as an exemplification of sentient actors.

Metrology in early post-processual work

Beginning in the early 1980s, a post-modernist, 'post-processual' (Hodder 1985) paradigm has aggressively taken on processual, modernist archaeology. The attack has been carried forward by Ian Hodder in his own publications (e.g., Hodder 1982a, 1985, 1986), in a number of volumes edited by him (1982b, 1987a, 1987b), or published or edited by his students (e.g., Miller and Tilley 1984; Moore 1986; Shanks and Tilley 1987a, 1987b). Of course, post-modernist archaeology is not restricted to the 'Cambridge School' of post-processual archaeology nor is the 'Cambridge School' particularly homogeneous. I focus on the publications of the first wave of post-processual archaeology from Cambridge here because they are programmatic and 'exemplary'. They had been written to generate a paradigm clash. Thus, they tend to be more sharply explicit than other papers.

How is metrology integrated into this series of post-processual publications? How well is it theoretically justified? How consistent is post-processual metrology with the theoretical claims of the paradigm? How did post-processual archaeology handle change and variation, and the description of its dynamism?

Symbols in Action

Let us take a look at *Symbols in Action* (Hodder 1982a) – the counterpoint to the Hatchery West of the New Archaeology (Binford *et al.* 1970) – the earliest monograph of the anti-new, post-processual forces.

The surface structure of this book is straightforward enough. Its point of departure is material culture and its relation to social variables. An introductory chapter chronicles the gradual disenchantment of pre-New Archaeologists with normative approaches; their loss of faith in 'archaeological cultures'; and their gradual shift from holistic notions about the material culture–society interface to more processual but specific relationships and to the New Archaeology. Hodder attributes this shift in part to the increasing pre-eminence of functional, adaptive paradigms in all of science.

In the next seven chapters, specific hypotheses from the processual litera-ture are introduced in the realms of production, style, burial, refuse, settlement and exchange, and evaluated against ethnoarchaeological fieldwork in Africa. This fieldwork demonstrates to Hodder, step by step, that the processual sciencing is logically flawed, can be falsified, if not altogether insufficient. Negotiation of the 'new' hypotheses allows the author to introduce his alter-native paradigm piecemeal, chapter by chapter. In Ch. 9, Hodder presents the morals of his ethnographic work for the future of archaeology, which are then partially put to work in an archaeological test case, the Late Neolithic of the Orkney Islands, in a concluding chapter.

As the argument develops, a couple of strands recur relative to change, variation and metrology. The first is an assumption which Hodder blames on the practitioners of processual archaeology – that material culture 'reflects' behaviour (e.g., Hodder 1982a, pp. 11–12; 1982c, p. 4; 1986, p. 6). Even though that verb 'reflect' is reiterated in all chapters as a red flag to mark modernist archaeology, it is not clearly defined here. Hodder uses the term to caricature what may well be an implicit assumption in much pro-cessual archaeology – that behaviour is so tightly constrained by functional and adaptive exigencies that material culture would have to be as tightly constrained. Thus, material culture would merely and rather passively *reflect* behaviour.

If that were so, then artefacts, their form and distribution, could be treated as the direct and unavoidable output and dead-end by-product of a given behaviour. In a given case, if the one (material culture) were known, the other (behaviour) could be inferred safely, semi-automatically, through a process of canned inference. A similar red flag is that of 'material correlates' (*cf.*, for example, Hodder 1982a, p. 11). 'Simplistically put, one could corre-late material culture patterning with human patterning, and "read off" the latter from the former' (Hodder 1986, p. 4).

Another strand remains implicit in *Symbols in Action*, though it explains Hodder's dislike with 'reflection' and 'material correlates' and constitutes the book's agenda: the dichotomy between 'action' and 'behaviour'. This did not become explicit in Hodder's writing until the publication of *Symbolic and Structural Archaeology* (Hodder 1982b). Giddens (e.g., 1976, 1979) from whom the Cambridge group derives its notions of agency, structure, and enstruc-turation, is cited only in passing in *Symbols in Action* (Hodder 1982a). He becomes a stereotypic citation only in later works, in a place of honour similar to that of Carl Hempel (1965, 1966) in the early New Archaeology. In Hodder's Giddensian scheme, 'behaviour' is viewed as that which animals have and do, activity which is so constrained by variables of the environ-ment and instinct that no choice is possible.

> Even in Binford's studies, ['behaving'] individuals appear bound
> by universal rules concerned with what individuals will [have to]
> do 'if other things are equal' . . . the ability of individuals to create
> change and to create their culture as an active social process is
> minimized.
>
> (Hodder 1986, p. 148)

Humans 'act'; they are sentient actors, with 'action' or agency rather than behaviour. While constraints around human actions might be acknowledged, humans think about these constraints. They choose a course of action with considerable latitude. The chosen action has meaning to them within the world of meanings that surrounds them. Humans choose actions in reference to their concepts, norms, meanings and beliefs. Social action, in turn, continually constitutes and reconstitutes the structure of meanings for other actors and for themselves, in the process of 'enstructuration' (cf. Tilley 1984, pp. 26–7). 'Material symbols' also 'actively justify the actions and intentions of human groups' (Hodder 1982a, p. 36). 'Symbol sets are negotiated and manipulated in social action' (*ibid.*, p. 214).

In this view, measurables such as constraints, social and natural environments, actors, actions, and material culture, among others, are linked and linkable only through enstructuration and the structure of meanings in which they are embedded. The world of symbols connects the observables and ultimately makes them understandable. Observables are seen as a mere surface phonology. If one wants to unravel what goes on and why it goes on as observed, one needs to get to semantics, grammar, and to the structures in which the phonology is embedded and continually modified, and without which one is thought to hear only hollow, vacuous sound (cf. Hodder 1982a, pp. 186, 210–11, 215–16).

The programmatic papers written later (Hodder 1985, 1986) lead one to expect a need for rich and varied measurements to provide context and history, on the one hand, and variation through time and place, on the other. Measurements and observations need to be taken to illustrate, track, and chronicle the 'structure in process'. Context and history are necessary to expose meanings and their negotiation in the enstructuration process. Contextual variation is important because the evocative effect of a symbol depends on it (Hodder 1985, p. 14). Observation of 'the history of a particular trait is fundamentally important in the interpretation of its position and use' (Hodder 1982a, p. 217). Measurements that chronicle variability, variation, and change are needed to visualize actors, agency, and action, and to get a sense of the room for action as it varies through time, space and class or other socio-cultural position or role.

The goal of *Symbols in Action* is not the systematic interpretation of the ethnoarchaeological cases, according to the new post-processual paradigm, with a metrology designed to accomplish that goal. Instead, the paradigm is put to work indirectly. It is used to interpret those data which are not fully

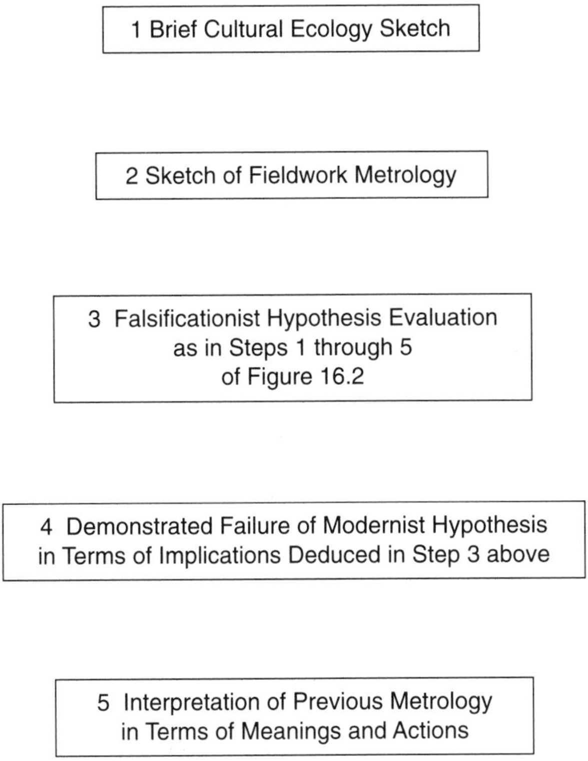

1 Brief Cultural Ecology Sketch

2 Sketch of Fieldwork Metrology

3 Falsificationist Hypothesis Evaluation
as in Steps 1 through 5
of Figure 16.2

4 Demonstrated Failure of Modernist Hypothesis
in Terms of Implications Deduced in Step 3 above

5 Interpretation of Previous Metrology
in Terms of Meanings and Actions

Figure 16.4   Model of early post-processual ethnoarchaeology.

explained by the processual logic, or on which processual hypotheses have failed altogether. Chapter by chapter, the structure of the argument is roughly as follows (see Figure 16.4).

The ethnographic test case is introduced in a brief sketch, with passing references to cultural ecology, geography, and history. Because the selection of the individual cases is not justified, one may safely assume that the author considered the choice of cases to have no bearing on his conclusions (Figure 16.4, Step 1).

A very brief sketch of what was actually done in the field follows. The variables selected for observation are introduced and the kinds and numbers of observations actually obtained are briefly and superficially hinted at (Figure 16.4, Step 2).

In the next step (Figure 16.4, Step 3), selected variables are exposed to processual hypotheses. In the different chapters of this book (and in some other ethnoarchaeological illustrations of the paradigm, *cf.*, for example, Parker Pearson 1982 on style in burials, or Miller 1984 on modernist architecture), this step presents some of the most elegant attempts to falsify hypotheses about change and variation with the tools of processual archaeology (i.e., deducing implications from general hypotheses about change and variation for one's data, as in Steps 3 and 4 of the model New Archaeology paradigm in Figure 16.2).

The modernist hypotheses of New Archaeology are usually found wanting (the anticipated measurements are shown not to have materialized). The observed measures either fail to fully explain the observed form and distribution of the given category of material culture, or are completely at odds with the expected constellation of observations.

These shortcomings usually foreshadow the conclusion that modernist explanations of change and variation have to fail because the latter are 'reflexive' and because they assume 'behaviour' but find themselves exposed to 'action'. As the only feasible alternative, they need to be replaced by action interpretations of the historic context in all of its sketched ethnographic depth.

For example, in Hodder (1982a, Ch. 2) (in the numeric sequence of Figure 16.4):

1   The Baringo area of north-central Kenya is briefly introduced (*ibid.*, pp. 13–17).

2   The data are sketched: an attempt was made to study 'all' artefact categories within the main categories of objects (*ibid.*, pp. 17–18), in up to 50 per cènt of the compounds.

3   Dress, ear decoration, basket drinking cups, and shield types are exposed to the 'interaction hypothesis' ('the greater the degree of interaction, the greater the material cultural similarity' (*ibid.,* p. 21).

4   Even though these traits are distinct by tribe, (the processual hypothesis would say: 'because there is lots of interaction *within* the tribes'), lots of social and economic intercourse *links* the tribes, such as migration, movement, exchange, and marriage. Thus, the interaction hypothesis *per se* does not predict the (degree and kind of) differentiation.

5   Instead, it is the *kind* of interaction which explains the observed distribution (read: the meaning of the interaction or the context for action behind the interaction). Where relations between tribes are particularly competitive (as illustrated through space and time), clear boundaries are marked by material culture. Material culture thus is not a passive by-product of interaction, but actively provides the context for competitive interaction. Material culture is not different because, reflectively, there are different tribes; rather, the differences between the tribes reside in the way actors construct contrastive material worlds. Mundane items such as dress and ear-spools are symbols in action on the part of individuals. They compose, in part, the social structure within which individuals act and which such actions maintain, modify, or comment on.

In *Symbols in Action*, metrology is primarily used to falsify the implications of modernist hypotheses, in a mode very nearly identical to the falsificationist strategy of New Archaeology (as, for example, in Binford 1967, p. 11). As these hypotheses fail (which of course is the goal of the case studies), the alternative paradigm is called in to fill out what was left unexplained, and to replace the failed processual hypotheses with the sketch of a richer interpretation that links aspects of context, history, and form with meanings.

Since the processual hypotheses in these examples did in fact fail, the job for the new paradigm is not all that difficult. The author can briefly hint at more satisfying alternative readings of the situation and sketch what these might look like. No well-defended, independently argued case study is logically called for or provided. That, certainly, does not make it easier for readers to chew over and evaluate the particular reading of the case independently in their own minds.

Interestingly, in terms of metrology helpful for describing and understanding change and variation, what *Symbols in Action* has to offer resides in those sections that knock down New Archaeology hypotheses. There, some very interesting information on variation is presented, and appropriately sensitive methodologies are utilized to bring out relevant variation in the data: for example, scattergrams of the metrics of a given type as utilized by different groups (e.g., Hodder 1982a, Figure 26) or as produced by different makers (e.g., *ibid.*, Figure 27); spatial autocorrelation measures of stylistic attributes (e.g., *ibid.*, Figures 28 and 29); and linkage analysis of design elements (*ibid.*, pp. 172–3). Measures such as these help bring out the fine details of change and variation, and the distribution thereof, while retaining much of the individual contributions to the summary statements in that illustration or table.

What is the structure of the alternative, the '*Symbols-in-Action*' interpretation? The starting points here are either the same measurements that foiled the processual expectations, or the residuals of these measurements, with some *post hoc* measures introduced to complete a richer interpretation. Relative to this ultimate interpretation, the author does not explicitly justify why the given measurements and observations should be particularly telling of, or sensitive to, his interpretative linkages and if he has explored potential alternative readings. Since, in the order of his research, these measures were taken originally to trip up a different paradigm in its own logic, we should not expect the same data to be particularly convincing as examples for the new paradigm's metrology.

The paradigmatic concern with agency and structuration in meaning and symbols leads one to expect considerable sensitivity to change and variation writ small, in context, in historical, spatial, and intra-societal variation and variability, with considerable open(minded)ness and receptiveness to the complexities of the given cases. Yet, little guidance is provided on how agency and structuration are exemplified in the given cases by the given measurements, or where they enter the enriched or alternative description of the given contexts.

In this book, structure is stressed at the expense of structuration, and agency remains largely decontextualized. Where change or variation are the point of departure of the interpretation, they are chronicled in changed (material) structure, not in changed interfaces among agents, structure, context, history, meanings and their vehicles. The meaning of structure, in turn, is not embedded in, nor linked with, agency, but imposed from the pan-human outside, in terms of what are assumed to be pan-human symbolic or structural principles, primarily structural oppositions such male vs. female, old vs. young, left vs. right, clean vs. dirty, life vs. death, and pan-human 'models and analogies concerning the way man [and woman] gives meaning to his [and her] actions' (see Hodder 1982a, p. 215; basing himself on Douglas 1966, 1970).

The same themes are investigated in a number of other early ethnoarchaeological and archaeological applications of the paradigm. For example, Henrietta Moore (1982), while very sensitive to the charge of ethnocentrism in observing and recording the ethnoarchaeology of others (*ibid.*, pp. 75–7), recommends as solution exactly the same kind of structural and organizational translation that was championed by Hodder above (*ibid.*, p. 78), with the help of the conceptual oppositions of the accomplished structuralist.

There is a heavy reliance on those kinds of structure that (some) members of our own system consider to be human universals. It is dangerous to accept this metrology at face value, without *self-critical* evaluation of the role of the archaeologist or ethnographer in our society and without a *critical* evaluation of the context and history of the given cases. Otherwise, the metrology raises the spectre of a pan-human 'normative' archaeology.

That kind of interpretation could approach some of the more extreme pre-new and New Archaeologists in its cheerful determinism. The pre-new archaeologist saw people following norms like irrelevant automata, at least in the eyes of the New Archaeologists. The New Archaeology believed in determinism almost as tight, by functional exigency and opportunism in context, at least as caricatured by the post-processualists, with quite a bit of the old 'normativism' re-entering their research via pre-new metrology through the back door. If such 'structuralist structuration', in evidence in this monograph, would be let loose upon our entire ethnographic and archaeological record, the entire sample of ethnographic, historic and archaeological cases would be reduced to, and regenerated as, a given normative 'scheme', replaying and recombining *ad infinitum* (those largely) binary oppositions and general models in which our own system seems to particularly abound and rejoice.

Of course, in terms of agency and meaning, any histogram *can* be expressed as one of binary opposition (big vs. small), and any continuum of measurements *can* be dissected into two contrastive parts. Whether or not that kind of subdivision, in the absence of the investigator, has any meaning in the historical, structural, contextual terms of the specific case, is a research question that needs to be approached with utmost care. Particularly because that kind of scheme is so 'black' and 'white', we have to take care that we do not unthinkingly 'naturalize' something that is not at all 'natural', pan-human, or even widely shared in our own society. Precisely, because of its stark simplicity and because of its distasteful connotations in our own society, we should be doubly certain that the application of what we consider a natural opposition 'makes sense' in cases very remote from us.

It is well established how our ways of asking questions force the information we receive in the ethnographic context (e.g. Briggs 1986). That problem is encountered with material culture in the same way as with any other ethnographic observation. If we now re-construct our archaeological cases as never ending replays of the ways in which we are accustomed to think of variation in our own society, the archaeological record becomes nothing else but a tool for naturalizing a *certain way of conceiving of variation and change*.

This critique should not be misread as an attempt to impugn the ability of post-processual paradigms to deal with change and variation and their description in human societies. Quite to the contrary. The comments are delivered because I view agency and structuration as the only presently feasible ways in which to conceive of, describe, understand, and explain variation and change among humans.

On the other hand, just as in the case of the early New Archaeology, a post-processual archaeology needs to be theorized in terms of its paradigmatic goals and central concepts. The very image of human history (and evolution) as a never ending replay and recombination of a limited number of structural rules and 'natural models' (all of which we experience in our own society) is antithetical to the very paradigm it is supposed to make visible in archaeological data, and strangely self-fulfilling if it were to be accepted uncritically. One cannot combine a paradigm that has structure eternally in process, in practice, with a metrology in which agency is merely a set of distances to preconceived 'universals' and their negations. Either agency is an active ingredient in the process of structuration, or structure is merely a mindless recombinant automaton like DNA, with humans residing in the chemicals.

Variation and change in our society and in prehistory

The metrology in the later new and post-New Archaeology has turned considerably more sophisticated relative to their respective original metrologies, and there are several fine archaeological examples that track change and variation in archaeological data with a considerably more theoretically sophisticated metrology than the seminal papers (see, for example, Shanks and Tilley 1987a, Chs 7 and 8). But examples were not chosen from the early new and early post-New Archaeology because they are the only practitioners of these paradigms that have metrological problems. The metrological problems of the earlier paradigm papers are simply much more on the surface. It would have called for a considerably more complicated argument to make paradigm-inherent metrological problems visible with examples from the more mature paradigmatic literature. The more mature in, and secure with, the paradigm that literature is, the more implicit, 'natural', tacit and boilerplate the metrology – it has become an integral and implicit part of 'normal science' (cf. Kuhn 1970).

In the discussion of post-processual metrology above, the assumption that our own ways of subdividing variation and change (e.g., structural or conceptual oppositions) work, is one example of many in which we can unthinkingly turn our prehistoric data into a mirror image of our own society. We do not know enough yet even in our society to resolve, under what circumstances we ourselves (are forced to or choose to) utilize binary oppositions, instead of ternary or more complex subdivisions and who, on social, age, gender, or economic scales, gains in our society by one or the other ways of splitting variation in those ways. In what contexts, under what conditions, within what temporal, spatial or social scales, are we allowed to roam freely over the range of variability of a given variable? When do we (have to or choose to) choose between two, three, or an infinite number of variable states?

On the other hand, if standard deviations and means as well as normal curves have graced the publications of pre-new, new, and professional archaeologists alike, this should indicate something important about change and variation: archaeological science might not have remained normal during the past thirty years, but its metrology well might have. The question arises again: are we still adjusting our present understanding with the help of a metrology (and the data in its image) that made sense more than thirty years ago, when archaeologists on the whole did have a normative view of culture? Are our interpretations of human societies more normative than need be simply because our metrology has remained a normative one (regardless of ideas that we play against it).

Or is the problem broader? Is our social niche one in which we are enstructurated to think normatively, in which we make tiny motions of agency to pretend we are acting non-normatively, as agents with few important constraints, yet in which that powerful structure keeps us measuring normatively regardless of how we act in the boilerplates of our publications?

Archaeological publications are material culture in their own right, like the artefacts that archaeologists study. As material culture they constitute part of the structure in which we live and they are simultaneously instances of agency in which our publication recreates or modifies that structure, in a never-ending process of enstructuration. In unselfconsciously producing artefacts (publications) that foist certain untheorized metrologies upon an unsuspecting world (ourselves, other archaeologists, other scientists, and the unsuspecting public), we contribute to the naturalization of certain kinds of blinders in our society.

The archaeological record (beyond the publications of archaeologists) is also bound to contain some alternatives to our present senses of structure, and to the variation and variability allowed for agents. Our metrology should never be let lie untheorized lest it become another way in which we contribute unknowingly to our own jail in the form of an ever-hardening material shell that generates certain kinds of measures solely (and unthinkingly so). Instead, we should always probe, weigh, question, test, and evaluate the 'preconceived' ways of sorting variation, which is a significant part of the structure which surrounds us. That action goal is particularly important because material culture in our own society, including that produced by archaeologists, is considered a sleeper, of research interest essentially only to archaeologists. That observation alone should make us redouble our efforts to find out why a theorized metrology for change and variation in the social sphere has been and continues to be of so little interest in the present and in the past.

Acknowledgements

This chapter is dedicated to Jude, Natalia and Gregory, to Carbost and to Lerags. Some of this argument goes back to 1982 when Ian Hodder invited me to review *Symbols in Action* for a seminar at Cambridge. Incipient trial balloons and modules of this chapter were presented: to a seminar at the Department of Anthropology, University of Tennessee, at the invitation of Fred Smith; in our department, to a bunch of friends at Art Keene's house; to the seminar 'Biocultural Processes of Change'; and to a graduate seminar on Theory in Typology. I thank all of the above for their hospitality and for their patience in listening to me. Yet, despite very cogent criticisms then and since then, my ideas have got the better of me. I cannot blame anybody but myself for the flaws of this chapter.

Notes

1 This was so, even though data shuffling at that point in the research sequence transpired at exactly the same point as in the despised traditionalist research design! See Figure 16.1, Steps 1 to 3.
2 Though this must be tempered by the criticism that all that is being formally evaluated here are inductive generalizations and the adequacy of definitions (Binford 1977, pp. 3–4).
3 That is that multiple causes structure the archaeological record in complex ways, that groups of artefacts that vary together represent activities, etc.

References

Binford, L.R. 1964. A consideration of archaeological research design. *American Antiquity* 29, 424–41.
Binford, L.R. 1965. Archaeological systematics and the study of culture process. *American Antiquity* 31, 203–10.

Binford, L.R. 1967. Smudge pits and hide smoking: the use of analogy in archaeological reasoning. *American Antiquity* 32, 1–12.

Binford, L.R. 1968. Archaeological perspectives. In *New Perspectives in Archaeology*, S.R. Binford and L.R. Binford (eds), 5–32. Chicago: Aldine.

Binford, L.R. 1972. Contemporary model building: paradigms and the current state of palaeolithic research. In *Models in Archaeology*, D.L. Clarke (ed.), 109–66. London: Methuen.

Binford, L.R. 1977. General introduction. In *For Theory Building in Archaeology*, L.R. Binford (ed.), 1–10. New York: Academic Press.

Binford, L.R. and S.R. Binford 1966. A preliminary analysis of functional variability in the Mousterian of Levallois facies. *American Anthropologist* 68, 238–95.

Binford, S.R., and L.R. Binford 1969. Stone tools and human behaviour. *Scientific American* 220, 70–84.

Binford, L.R., S.R. Binford, R. Whallon and M.A. Hardin (eds) 1970. *Archaeology at Hatchery West* (Memoir 24). Washington, DC: Society for American Archaeology.

Binford, L.R. and J.A. Sabloff 1982. Paradigms, systematics and archaeology. *Journal of Anthropological Research* 38, 137–53.

Briggs, C.L. 1986. *Learning How To Ask: a socio-linguistic appraisal of the role of the interview in social science research*. Cambridge: Cambridge University Press.

Cowgill, G.L. 1968. Computer analysis of archaeological data from Teotihuacan, Mexico. In *New Perspectives in Archaeology*, S.R. Binford and L.R. Binford (eds), 143–50. Chicago: Aldine.

Douglas, M.1966. *Purity and Danger*. London: Routledge and Kegan Paul.

Douglas, M.1970. *Natural Symbols*. London: Barrie and Rockliff.

Flannery, K.V. (ed.) 1976. *The Early Mesoamerican Village*. New York: Academic Press.

Freeman, L.G. 1964 *Mousterian Developments in Cantabrian Spain*. Unpublished PhD dissertation. Department of Anthropology, University of Chicago.

Freeman, L.G. 1966 The nature of Mousterian facies in Cantabrian Spain. *American Anthropologist* 68, 230–237.

Freeman, L. G. 1973. The analysis of some occupation floor distributions from earlier and middle Paleolithic sites in Spain. Paper presented at the IXth International Congress of Anthropological and Ethnological Sciences, Chicago, USA.

Fritz, J.M. and F.T. Plog 1970. The nature of archaeological explanation. *American Antiquity* 35, 405–12.

Gelfand, A.E. 1971. Rapid seriation methods with archaeological applications. In *Mathematics in the Archaeological and Historical Sciences*, F.R. Hodson, D.G. Kendall and P. Tautu (eds), 186–201. Edinburgh: Edinburgh University Press.

Giddens, A. 1976. *New Rules of Sociological Method*. London: Hutchinson.

Giddens, A. 1979. *Central Problems in Social Theory*. London: Macmillan Press.

Gumerman, G.J. (ed.) 1971. *The Distribution of Prehistoric Population Aggregates*. Prescott, Ariz.: Prescott College Anthropological Reports 1.

Hempel, C.G. 1965. *Aspects of Scientific Explanation*. New York: Free Press.

Hempel, C.G. 1966. *Philosophy of Natural Science*. Englewood Cliffs, N.J.: Prentice-Hall.

Hill, J.N. 1965. Broken K Pueblo: a prehistoric society in eastern Arizona. Unpublished PhD dissertation. Department of Anthropology, University of Chicago.

Hill, J.N. 1968. Broken K Pueblo: patterns of form and function. In *New Perspectives in Archaeology*, S.R. Binford and L.R. Binford (eds), 103–42. Chicago: Aldine.

Hill, J.N. 1970. *Broken K Pueblo: prehistoric social organization in the American Southwest*. Tucson: University of Arizona Press.

Hodder, I. 1982a. *Symbols in Action*. Cambridge: Cambridge University Press.

Hodder, I. (ed.) 1982b. *Symbolic and Structural Archaeology*. Cambridge: Cambridge University Press.

Hodder, I. 1982c. Theoretical archaeology: a reactionary view. In *Symbolic and Structural Archaeology*, I. Hodder (ed.), 1–16. Cambridge: Cambridge University Press.

Hodder, I. 1985. Post-processual archaeology. *Advances in Archaeological Method and Theory* 8, 1–26

Hodder, I. 1986. *Reading the Past*. Cambridge: Cambridge University Press.

Hodder, I. (ed.) 1987a. *Archaeology as Long-term History*. Cambridge: Cambridge University Press.

Hodder, I. (ed.) 1987b. *The Archaeology of Contextual Meanings*. Cambridge: Cambridge University Press.

Kuhn, T.S. 1970. *The Structure of Scientific Revolutions*. Chicago: University of Chicago Press.

LeBlanc, S.A. 1973. Two points of logic concerning data, hypotheses, general laws, and systems. In *Research and Theory in Current Archaeology*, C. R. Redman (ed.), 199–214. New York: John Wiley.

Longacre, W.A. 1963. Archaeology as anthropology: a case study. Unpublished Ph.D. dissertation, Department of Anthropology. University of Chicago.

Longacre, W.A. 1970. *Archaeology as Anthropology: a case study*. Tucson: University of Arizona Press.

Miller, D. 1984. Modernism and suburbia as material ideology. In *Ideology, Power and Prehistory*, D. Miller and C. Tilley (eds), 37–49. Cambridge: Cambridge University Press.

Miller, D. and C. Tilley (eds) 1984. *Ideology, Power and Prehistory*. Cambridge: Cambridge University Press.

Montet-White, A. 1973. *Le Malpas rockshelter*. Lawrence: University of Kansas (Publications in Anthropology No. 4).

Moore, H.L. 1982. The interpretation of spatial patterning in settlement residues. In *Symbolic and Structural Archaeology*, I. Hodder (ed.), 74–79. Cambridge: Cambridge University Press.

Moore, H.L. 1986. *Space, Text and Gender*. Cambridge: Cambridge University Press.

Moore, J.A. and A.S. Keene (eds) 1983. *Archaeological Hammers and Theories*. New York: Academic Press.

Neustupny, E. 1973. Factors determining the variability of the Corded Ware culture. In *The Explanation of Culture Change*, A.C. Renfrew (ed.), 725–30. London: Duckworth.

Parker Pearson, M. 1982. Mortuary practices, society and ideology: an ethnoarchaeological study. In *Symbolic and Structural Archaeology*, I. Hodder (ed.), 99–113. Cambridge: Cambridge University Press.

Plog, F.T. 1969. An approach to the study of prehistoric change. Ph.D. dissertation, Department of Anthropology, University of Chicago.

Plog, F.T. 1974. *The Study of Prehistoric Change*. New York: Academic Press.

Pollnac, R. and A.J. Ammerman 1973. A multivariate analysis of late palaeolithic assemblages in Italy. In *The Explanation of Culture Change*, A.C. Renfrew (ed.), 161–65. London: Duckworth.

Ragir, S. 1967. A review of techniques for archaeological sampling. In *A Guide to Field Methods in Archaeology*, R.F. Heizer and J.A. Graham (eds), pp 181–98. Palo Alto: National Press.

Redman, C.L. and P.J. Watson 1970. Systematic intensive surface collection. *American Antiquity* 35, 279–91.

Rowlett, R.M. and R.B. Pollnac 1971. Multivariate analysis of Marnian La Tène cultural groups. In *Mathematics in the Archaeological and Historical Sciences*, F.R. Hodson, D.G. Kendall and P. Tautu (eds), 46–58. Edinburgh: Edinburgh University Press.

Shanks, M. and C. Tilley 1987a. *Re-constructing Archaeology. Theory and practice.* Cambridge: Cambridge University Press.

Shanks, M. and C. Tilley 1987b. *Social Theory and Archaeology*. Cambridge: Polity Press.

Shennan, S. 1988. *Quantifying Archaeology*. Edinburgh: Edinburgh University Press.

Speth, J.D. and G.A. Johnson 1976. Problems in the use of correlation for the investigation of tool kits and activity areas. In *Cultural Change and Continuity. Essays in honour of James Bennett Griffin*, C. E. Cleland (ed.), 35–57. New York: Academic Press.

Sterud, E. 1967. Seriation techniques in archaeology. Unpublished Master's thesis, Department of Anthropology, University of California, Los Angeles.

Thomas, D.H. Jr. 1971. Prehistoric subsistence-settlement patterns of the Reese River valley, central Nevada. Unpublished Ph.D. dissertation, Department of Anthropology, University of California, Davis.

Tilley, C. 1984. Social formation, social structures and social change. In *Symbolic and Structural Archaeology*, I. Hodder (ed.), 26–38. Cambridge: Cambridge University Press.

Watson, P.J., S.A. LeBlanc and C.L. Redman 1971. *Explanation in Archaeology. An explicitly scientific approach*. New York: Columbia University Press.

Whallon, R. 1963. A statistical analysis of some Aurignacian I assemblages from southwestern France. Unpublished Master's thesis, Department of Anthropology, University of Chicago.

Wobst, H.M. 1971. Boundary conditions for paleolithic cultural systems: a simulation approach. Unpublished PhD thesis, Department of Anthropology, University of Michigan, Ann Arbor.

Wobst, H.M. 1978. The archaeo-ethnology of hunter-gatherers, or the tyranny of the ethnographic record in archaeology. *American Antiquity* 43, 303–9.

Wobst, H.M. and A.S. Keene 1983. Archaeological explanation as political economy. In *The Socio-politics of Archaeology*, J. M. Gero, D. M. Lacy, and M. L. Blakey (eds), 79–88. Amherst, Mass.: University of Massachusetts (Anthropological Research Report no. 23).

Wylie, A. 1989. The interpretative dilemma. In *Critical Traditions in Contemporary Archaeology*, V. Pinsky and A. Wylie (eds), 18–27. Cambridge: Cambridge University Press.

Zubrow, E. 1971. A south-western test of an anthropological model of population dynamics. Unpublished Ph.D. dissertation, Department of Anthropology, University of Arizona, Tucson.

Dynamic modelling and new social theory of the mid- to long term

TIM MURRAY

Introduction

This chapter is about theoretical innovation, the usefulness of borrowing theories and frameworks from other disciplines, the consequences of inertia in the cultural traditions of archaeology, and the role of the imagination. The primary focus of the chapter will be an exploration of some of the implications of the widespread application of radiometric dating systems to archaeology and of the results of the first decade or so of studies of site formation process. As I will be mostly concerned with time-scales in the 10,000 to 1,000,000 year range, the chapter concludes with a brief exploration of alternative pathways for the building of social theory relevant to Pleistocene archaeological records. My interest here, apart from conveying my hope rather than my expectation that non-linear modelling will be a valuable tool in the armoury of the archaeologist, will be to assess the ways in which non-linear modelling can contribute to the expansion of theoretical options for the Pleistocene archaeologist, and to argue that the successful application of such modelling strategies will depend on what is being modelled and why.

This focus on building social theory for the mid- to long term stems from several factors. First, what passes for theory in these parts of prehistoric archaeology is usually a crude pastiche of social and cultural evolutionary theory given some focus by ethnographic analogy. It is important to determine whether we can do better. Second, leading from the spirit of the first, there are fundamental questions about the nature of archaeological knowledge – particularly about what archaeologists want to know about the past and what security they wish these knowledge claims to have. Finally, while there has recently been some retreat from extreme relativist archaeological epistemologies (an acceptance that the structure of archaeological records can constrain interpretation), the implications of such constraints have not been worked through.

Notwithstanding the 'trendiness' of realist epistemologies (there are a variety on offer), archaeologists are still deeply troubled about how one squares the cognitive plausibility of the theoretical instruments currently in use with what we understand to be the empirical structural properties of (Pleistocene) archaeological records. Are these structural properties simply an artefact of theory or is there something more significant lurking there? Do we need to worry about the fact that archaeologists are adept at borrowing theory but curiously shy about building it?

These questions are familiar enough to most archaeologists after twenty-five years of disciplinary soul-searching and aggravation. Indeed, sometimes it seems that one of the things archaeologists are best at is promoting new ways of conceptualizing the past, novel visions which have, more often than not, been borrowed because they seem to have the potential to improve our ability to either describe or explain (or sometimes both) the archaeological past. Naturally archaeologists are not the only people who borrow; the recent career of 'chaos theory' in any number of disciplines is a case in point. Yet archaeologists tend to be worried about the nature and extent of such borrowing, primarily because it tends to loom so large in our practice, and because there is a feeling that such borrowings literally structure our perception of the possibilities of the archaeological record. Consequently there has been a brisk trade in cautionary tales and admonitions to the archaeologist that what is borrowed must first be adapted to specific archaeological circumstances (Schiffer 1987). But, at a time when practitioners are still nervous about courting the charge of empiricism, working out how archaeological circumstances differ from anthropological or historical ones has proved to be something of a problem.

These sorts of fears are a fundamental impetus to the continuing debate about analogical reasoning and the use of inference in both describing and explaining the archaeological record. Are our cultural preconceptions about what it is meaningful and valuable to know about the past so unconstrained by the archaeological record that we may as well not even bother to collect archaeological data? Or again, does the archaeological record, if our concepts, categories and theories were developed to seriously engage with it, have the power to offer us a unique perspective on human behaviour that might allow us to reformulate the goals and approaches of the human sciences?

If one actively works with Pleistocene archaeological records then these fears take on a special kind of force. On the one hand archaeologists are attempting to account for the very faint signals of societies for which there might be no ethnographic parallels. On the other those archaeologists are working with accounts of human action which have been developed for ethnographic and ethnohistoric scales. This difficulty of matching empirical structure with the terms of plausible explanation has begun to refocus our attention away from evermore precise chronological determinations towards an exploration of the value of current archaeological theory and practice.

Surely there must be something else archaeologists can do apart from making up stories with the texture of individual action taking place against a backdrop of vast impersonal forces of climate and population? Despite some hard searching, nothing has come through to capture the imaginations of practitioners, because it has proved difficult to conceive of goals and approaches other than those currently in place. The discourse of (Pleistocene) archaeology, unsatisfying though it may be, sometimes seems (wrongly) to be an artefact of nature rather than of history.

But all is far from lost when we consider a more abstract fascination with the potential power of such archaeological records to disorder our imaginations, thereby posing real challenges to human ingenuity and giving us a vantage point from which to begin a deconstruction of the terms of human self-perception. Here I refer to ontological matters – time-scale and spatial scale, issues of entropy, problems of causality, and (most significant) the vexing task of developing a conceptual framework for Pleistocene archaeology which is both meaningful and scientifically defensible. Lying behind the superficial appreciation that the business of archaeology seems to have become a great deal more complicated than either Worsäae or Lubbock could have envisaged, is a growing fear that we may, once again, be about to lose our chance to create this kind of conceptual framework for prehistoric archaeology.

I fear this loss of opportunity for several reasons, all of which stem from the traditions of Pleistocene archaeology: that this part of the archaeological record is widely thought of as being especially impoverished; that change and variability have traditionally had meaning only through the teleology of social evolution; that ethnography has always provided the exemplar of what constitutes the goal of any reconstruction or account of prehistoric human action; that archaeologists, to convincingly explain change and/or variability in the prehistoric record, have generally attempted to reconstruct precise causal links between beginning and end states. Any failure has generally been put down to poor data or, indeed, to the improbability of there ever being clear links between behaviour and material consequences; that the archaeologist places the weight of conviction and/or plausibility on statements which are primarily generated from contemporary social theory. Problems with application thus become the fault of the data (or of the archaeologist) rather than the theory.

These reasons also reflect a constant theme in the history of our discipline – that of the 'normalization' or 'humanization' of Pleistocene archaeological information – the process whereby the ontological and epistemological distinctiveness of the Pleistocene archaeological record (as a record of human action) is lost in favour of intelligibility in terms of the conventions of short-scale social theory. The link between this theme and the notion of an impoverished (and theoretically impotent) record can be seen to produce a client relationship between Pleistocene archaeology and contemporary social theory, with archaeology eternally the supplicant, never able to produce images of social life in the Pleistocene past which would be acceptable to the social theorist, and having to live with the fact that it all really doesn't matter because prehistoric archaeology has only a small role in the grand sweep of the human sciences.

Even with this level of disciplinary inertia optimism is still possible, indeed in Australia at least there is a growing sense of excitement and possibility. In my view this change of fortunes can be explained by reference to three core principles or processes within the history of Pleistocene archaeology. The first is the developing significance of the Pleistocene archaeological record. Allied with a growing army of recruits to the realist cause, it is now more widely understood that this record itself has structure, coherence and (most important of all) *a distinctiveness* that is theoretically consequential. Many archaeologists now accept that the empirical character of the archaeological record should play an active role in the development of interpretation and explanation. The fact that we still have the task of building the theory which would make that constraint effective only makes the game more attractive.

The second principle is the impact of radiometric dating systems. The real impact of radiometric dating systems is only now being appreciated, and it has less to do with matters of chronology and much more to do with characterizing the structural properties of the Pleistocene record. I shall expand on this aspect in the next section by sketching elements such as the minimum chronological unit and long/short time-spans.

The third principle is the impact of site formation process studies. We can no longer simply translate an archaeological record into evidence of human action – there is no simple reading-off possible. Again, I will expand on this in the next section by briefly exploring elements such as palimpsest and the 'Pompeii premise'.

These are the big principles, but we should also be mindful of powerful causes which act in a secondary or integrative role: the exponential increase in the amount of data to hand on a world-wide frame of reference, and the upgrading of data recovery and manipulation technologies are only a few. It now seems clear that 'normalizing' Pleistocene archaeological knowledge within the conventions of social theory is a no-win situation for both partners. We now need to ask whether social archaeology can (or should) be done on Pleistocene records. We also need to ask whether the archaeologist can build theories about human action at the short to medium term (or even the long term) and still call them social theory. I think they can and I think we should. That piece of rhetoric aside, I doubt whether social theorists of the short term will be especially taken by Pleistocene archaeologists redefining the basic concepts and categories of the human sciences in attempt to approach the past in a new way.

Over the last decade, hunter-gatherer archaeology has experienced another of its periodic realignments of goal and perspective. While vestiges remain of the 1960s 'Man the Hunter' conceptualization of the field, the bulk of practitioners now at least think more often about issues of social process, and of cognition. Social archaeology, exemplified in studies of prehistoric art, has generally implied a more thoroughgoing discussion of boundedness, information flow, and evidence of intensified social activity. It is significant that such developments in the social archaeology of the Pleistocene direct the attention of practitioners to later prehistory, particularly to the Holocene, where change of this kind is considered to be either more observable or, indeed, *present*. Little attention has been paid to the vast bulk of the Pleistocene record where things seem (wrongly as it turns out) to chug along without much variability.

As a result of the expansion in the amount and variety of archaeological data of Pleistocene age, and the associated ontological issues dealt with in greater detail below, it now seems mandatory for archaeologists to reconsider the competing interpretations of the Pleistocene, and to reassess the agenda of Pleistocene archaeology itself. What are the core questions of the field? What are the appropriate theoretical frameworks for interpretation and explanation? How are knowledge claims to be assessed? How are archaeologists to justify practice to a non-professional (and occasionally hostile) audience? How does Pleistocene archaeology articulate with the rest of the discipline, and with other disciplines concerned with understanding human nature?

Scales, resolving powers and ontology

I stress the need for a liberation of the Pleistocene in the context of this book because I think we need to be clear that meaningful units of observation and well-thought-through interpretations of the behavioural significance of those observations are crucial for non-linear modelling to make a contribution to Pleistocene archaeology. The recent changes in our comprehension of the Pleistocene records are tailor-made for supporting the notion that there is nothing natural about those units, and for clarifying the related point that there is nothing natural about the interpretations either. Issues of scale, resolving power and ontology are of crucial importance when we re-examine goals and standards.

I also want to simply raise three gut responses (apart from the jaundiced reaction of 'here we go again') to non-linear modelling on Pleistocene records, if only to wonder aloud about the possibility of learning something new about human behaviour, and to ask again – how do we innovate, or indeed, even build theory?

The first response is probably predictable. The possibility of chaos (of non-linearity) gives us the chance to learn more about scale and resolving power. Is the Pleistocene archaeological record coherent? Does the presence of palimpsest and minimum chronological units of 1,000 years and more mean that we may simply be unable to tell the difference between order and chaos in the Pleistocene archaeological record? By extension, are order and chaos smoothed out in time-averaged archaeological deposits?

The second response concerns traditional relationships between archaeology and other human sciences. Because we note that non-linear models are useful in describing what can actually happen when people make decisions and track the implications of those decisions, archaeologists, to maintain their goal of producing meaningful (and hopefully accurate) interpretations of past human actions, move towards an active consideration of non-linear modelling. But are we modelling human systems in the same sense as the economist or management analyst? Furthermore, we can understand that systems go to chaos at different rates and conform to different trajectories. Can we determine the presence of chaos in Pleistocene records *post facto*?

The third response is that by taking non-linear modelling on board in a serious fashion we might detect that our desire to couch interpretation and explanation in terms of short-term social science has now reached the level of self-parody, and this might prompt some useful reflection about previous taken-for-granteds in the archaeologist's project.

I hold the view that the establishment of radiometric chronologies (e.g., Bailey 1981, 1983, 1987; Isaac 1972, 1981) and an improved comprehension of the nature of archaeological site formation processes (Binford 1981, 1983; Schiffer 1985, 1987) must lead us to recognize that the archaeological record is not the subject of common-sense understandings – and raise the real possibility that the contours of its ontology might require some serious reconsideration. The possibility of a remade archaeological ontology raises a whole host of epistemic issues foremost among which must be the significance we are to attach to the empirical character (structural properties) of the archaeological record.

Indeed, I think that archaeological records of the Pleistocene *are* ontologically distinctive records of human action – i.e., that their comprehension now requires the development of a new scientific ontology other than that utilized in the human sciences. Significantly, the argument for ontological distinctiveness does not claim that prehistoric human behaviour was ontologically different from that manifest in historic periods. What it does contend is that in the bulk of cases such prehistoric behaviours cannot be comprehended in anything other than circular terms if we apply social theories derived from the ontology of the contemporary human sciences. Furthermore it implies that there is no reason beyond disciplinary tradition to commit the Pleistocene archaeologist to the short time-span, low-scale accounts of humanity.

Let me be clear that I am not referring to Pompeiis or archaeological records for which there is a time resolution better than 10,000 years. I strongly suspect that a similar case for ontological distinctiveness can be extended into still shorter time-frames (perhaps even to the century level), but the argument involved in making the case is too underdeveloped to survive much interrogation at this point! Let me also be clear that I am not here advocating the wholesale rejection of contemporary social theory for the analysis of the kinds of archaeological records under review. Rather, my point is that such theories should be used even more intensively, but with a changed psychology of research.

Let me also be clear that the essence of this ontological distinctiveness does not rest only on the fact of long time-spans for Pleistocene archaeology.

Much more important is the notion of the minimum chronological unit over which action (or at least the results of action) can actually be observed. In many cases this minimum chronological unit is in the order of some thousands of years, which obviously places some strong constraints of the *kinds* of stories Pleistocene archaeologists should be able to tell.

Perhaps the most important constraint is the notion of palimpsest when linked with the idea that archaeological sites are also geomorphological events. Are there 'behaviours' to be analysed, and how are we to make sense of the analyses which flow from the notion that if resolving powers are low, the appropriate strategy is to go macroscale? It is the palimpsest of behaviours on Pleistocene sites which delivers the primary element of ontological distinctiveness, and it goes a great deal of the way towards an argument for epistemological singularity as well. Consequently we may decide for the bulk of Pleistocene records that concepts like microscale and macroscale (or even long and short time-spans) may require some difficult rethinking.

These are tough problems with some interesting implications for that great raft of social archaeology done on Middle and Upper Palaeolithic records. One of the most interesting implications for me is the strong sense of history repeating itself, of archaeological records throwing out strong challenges of understanding. In the next section I will re-examine the history of the discovery of high human antiquity in the 1860s in the light of our present difficulties.

Although Shanks and Tilley (1987a) and others may argue the post-positivist line that it is the actions of archaeologists which establish the nature of the archaeological record, an argument which has been supported by Lewis Binford (1987) among others, the fact remains that actions by archaeologists also have unintended consequences. The discovery of material culture more 'primitive' than any previously noted was just one of the unintended consequences of the discovery of a high human antiquity. In more recent years the application of radiometric chronologies have radically reshaped our ideas of what archaeologists need to explain.

A realist epistemology (see Murray 1987; Wylie 1982a, 1982b, 1985), in contrast to the various post-positivist epistemologies advanced by Hodder (1986), Miller and Tilley (1984) and others, recognizes the significance of the sociology of knowledge but also stresses the fact that materials recovered by archaeologists can possess identities different to those ascribed to them by practitioners. The issues raised by a high human antiquity time-scale, and the relevance of contemporary social theory for the explanation of prehistoric human behaviour, provide a significant example of this idea of difference.

The history of archaeology has a great deal to offer proponents of a realist epistemology for the discipline, because it allows us to see that the plausibility of archaeological representations has long been the product of cultural factors such as the long-standing dominance of social theoretical representations of 'humanness'. It also confirms that our current relationship with social theory is not a 'natural' one − it is the product of history.

That relationship has had far-reaching consequences for the practice of archaeology. The one which most concerns us here is the response by archaeologists to the differences between archaeological and ethnographic data. There is no need to rehash old debates about the validity of ethnographic analogy or the differing views archaeologists hold about the reliability of empirical over theoretical knowledge, but we should be aware that they are the subject of constant debate precisely because they are important.

Archaeologists have long understood that information about human behaviour is 'lost' when material culture leaves what Schiffer (1976) calls the systemic context and enters the archaeological context. This perception has attracted a variety of responses. The most common response (and the one used by Lubbock, Tylor *et al.*) is to replace 'lost' information by means of structured comparison between archaeological record and ethnographic observation – the structure being provided by what passes for social theory at any point in time. The significant thing here is that such replacement ensures that the prehistoric past is not beyond the bounds of our understanding, a possibility which would severely damage the credibility of the structures through which we make sense of contemporary experience.

However, even the advocates of this common-sense view in the nineteenth century recognized two worrying potential outcomes. First, that the archaeological record might well lose its power to actively critique contemporary representations of 'humanness' (it would be disenfranchised by being overly determined by theory). Second, which links to the first, that the lack of significance accorded the empirical character of the record may reduce the reliability of archaeological knowledge claims. These fears were uppermost in Hawkes's (1954) mind when he developed the notion of the ladder of inference, a notion which attained great popularity in the decade or so prior to the advent of Lewis Binford's (1962) spirited (though positivist) defence of theoretical knowledge.

A lot of water has since passed under the theoretical bridge – with Binford (supposedly) recanting his positivism and with post-structuralist archaeologists finding different epistemological justifications for the significance of theoretical knowledge. None the less practitioners generally still adhere to the notion that meaningful explanation or interpretation of prehistoric human behaviour should mirror the forms found in contemporary social theory. But there are many varieties of social theory. How are archaeologists to judge between them, or indeed assess their overall worth for archaeology? A historical reflection might help with the problem.

Time stories and some history of archaeology

> A first [hu]man who existed 100,000 years ago escapes altogether from the grasp of popular thought (Anonymous 1863).

Grayson (1983) has done an excellent job in characterizing the intellectual climate in which the claims for a high human antiquity were first accepted.

Clearly the link between archaeology, geology and natural history was absolutely crucial in conferring reliability on the claims made for material recovered at Brixham Cave and on the Somme. Yet it is worth noting that barely twenty years after those heady events the vast sense of time had been lost. Why?

Between the years 1858 and 1870 the science of prehistoric archaeology was firmly established through a combination of problem, database, theory, methodology and disciplinary institutions. Furthermore, the archaeological demonstration of social and cultural evolution was crucial to the successful foundation of anthropology.

Two aspects of the events of those years generally receive little attention in the histories. First, the fact that the practice of this new prehistoric archaeology systematically violated the scientific canons laid down by its practitioners (without any significant reduction in the plausibility of their statements). Clearly the linking of palaeontology and geology to archaeology allowed practitioners to claim a scientific reliability for their reconstructions of human life during the Palaeolithic. None the less, a careful analysis of this passage of the history of archaeology reveals a structure of assumption about the nature and significance of archaeological knowledge which established that archaeological representations of human action should mirror those of contemporary social theory. Significantly, these a priori assumptions violated the inductivist epistemology of the practitioners. This failure of induction, caused by the theory-dependence of observation, was more pronounced for the explanation of these new data than for those synthesized by Nilsson and Worsäae precisely because such data were unfamiliar, unusual. Moreover, this disjunction between rhetoric and practice went, for the most part, unremarked either by practitioners or by consumers of archaeological knowledge. In effect, Lubbock's and Evans's characterization of the 'people of the Palaeolithic' allowed contemporary social theory to dominate natural history as the conceptual core of archaeology, creating a prehistoric archaeology that, while having considerable cognitive plausibility, ultimately depended on the systematic disenfranchizement of the archaeological record for the continuing meaningfulness of archaeological knowledge. In essence, the discovery of high human antiquity did not make prehistoric archaeology more scientific, it simply allowed ethnology and later, anthropology, to extend its coverage back to the dawn of human history.[1]

Aiding and abetting this is a second factor, the great uncertainty surrounding the quantification of the new time-scale until the advent of radiometric chronologies in the 1950s and 1960s (a century later). The disagreements among geologists, fired by the work of Lord Kelvin and by unresolved problems in quaternary geology, only increased uncertainty about the truth (or the probability of truth) of inductions from supposedly value-free observations. In practice the new time-scale was broken up into sub-classifications of the Stone Age by Lartet, Lubbock, and de Mortillet, as practitioners sought a means of gaining relative measurements of chronology.

These sub-classifications provided an important part of the empirical reality of stage theories of human socio-cultural evolution produced by Lubbock (1882), Tylor (1865, 1870) and Morgan (1871, 1877). For both the practitioners of prehistoric archaeology and of ethnology or anthropology, observation statements were not free from the a priori. The new data were incorporated into theories of socio-cultural evolution which had their roots in the eighteenth century, and which owed much to the structures supporting the universal histories of that time. These theories, despite protests by Lubbock, Morgan and Spencer, had a marked teleological flavour. They assumed the reality of human progress, as noted by opponents such as the Duke of Argyll (1869; see also Gillespie 1977). This dictated that ethnographic analogy be used as the primary basis for explaining socio-cultural change and variation during the course of human history. The net result of this was that contemporary 'savages' and 'barbarians' were effectively denied a history (again despite the protests of Lubbock and Tylor). Instead, their peculiarity was explained as being the product of a complex process which might include elements of stasis, regression and progress.

This denial of history to the 'savage' and 'barbarian' (and a lack of interest in its investigation) was itself a response to the daunting prospect of human action in the deep prehistoric past being unintelligible to contemporary observers armed with contemporary structures of knowing about human beings. The only way to preserve the universality of those structures was to demonstrate their general applicability to the explanation of other contemporary cultures, and then to argue that these contemporary societies could be ordered as modern representatives of prehistoric human socio-cultural types.

The final factor, which cannot be developed here, was the time lag between the discovery of material culture in unimpeachably old strata, and the general acceptance that there were pre-Sapient hominid fossils to go with them. This acted to further squeeze the time-scale and to support the validity of theories of socio-cultural evolution guaranteed by ethnographic analogy. Despite the predictions of Darwin and Huxley that fossils intermediate between apes and humans would be found, it was not until near the end of the nineteenth century, with the discovery of *Homo erectus*, that a fossil hominid markedly different from contemporary human beings and closer to the apes was unearthed.

Thus, for much of the nineteenth century hard evidence for human physical evolution, hence evidence for an evolutionary time-scale similar to other contemporary animals, was simply lacking. Flowing from this, despite the attempts by philologists such as Max Müller to conceptualize the origins of language and the development of the human mind (a task shared with anthropologists such as Tylor), a lack of pre-Sapient fossils meant that such theorizing was generally applied to contemporary 'savages' and 'barbarians' and to languages reconstructed by philologists.

This 'squeezing' of human prehistory and the value of uniformitarian models of human behaviour remains a significant issue in contemporary archaeology where we now (for the most part unsuccessfully) deal with time-spans of some millions of years.

Concluding remarks

I may seem to be drawing a longbow by arguing that some of the intellectual context of the discovery of high human antiquity back in the middle of the nineteenth century has a lesson for contemporary archaeologists. However, I regard the process of humanizing the Palaeolithic as simply being a more glaring example of the process of normalization which is a constant feature of archaeological practice. The fate of high human antiquity indicates, to me at least, how the maintenance of conventional relationships between archaeological knowledge and other types of knowledge about human beings overcomes the daunting prospect of an unintelligible deeper human past. This is a crucial aspect of the culture of archaeology, and it operates as effectively today as it did back in the 1860s. We still interrogate the deeper past with essentially the same theoretical instruments which we use to make sense of the present.

Thus, while archaeologists may seek model-building strategies which more effectively encompass the data under review they do so within a disciplinary environment which expresses clear preconceptions about the objects of analysis and the terms under which plausible explanation of past human action is developed. It seems to me that the real lesson of Brixham is that we should evaluate why we select particular units of analysis and why plausibility resides where it does. Adopting new modelling strategies without a clearer reflection on *what* is being modelled and *why* will not advantage the archaeologist. I am afraid that the early history of non-linear modelling in archaeology has demonstrated an enthusiasm not tempered by the need for reflection, even reflection about the likelihood of scepticism among archaeologists deeply suspicious of miracle cures and the like.

The picture I have been endeavouring to paint has been one of challenge and of the need for theoretical innovation against a background of disciplinary inertia and limited expectations. Can this deadlock be broken, or is it inevitable that the Pleistocene archaeological record will be normalized and stripped of any chance to destabilize the theoretical structures through which we make sense of contemporary experience? But how do we begin to conceive of the inconceivable, how can we generate concepts and categories which more accurately address the structural properties of the Pleistocene archaeological record as a record of human action? Furthermore, what is the role of theory in generating these new instruments of enquiry – is the whole enterprise falling headlong into the empiricist trap?

By way of a conclusion I want to briefly describe four strategies which, if followed concurrently, may well help us to develop social theory for the mid- to long term, free us from the tyranny of the short term and (this one is a real long-shot) use this new social theory to actively critique contemporary social theory. Here I am looking for more than a strategy which says that the concepts and categories of contemporary social theory require redefinition in archaeological terms before they can be meaningfully applied to Pleistocene archaeological records.

The first strategy focuses on the search for anomalies, those events or patterns which destabilize extant theory by posing puzzles which cannot be solved using it. This strategy can be implemented by the application of pattern generation statistics in a framework which recognizes the theory dependence of observation but also recognizes that anomalies can tend to have an interesting life of their own if one is sceptical about the theoretical instruments which begin the process. This strategy is therefore a mixture of a changed psychology of research and a playful attitude to the rift between patterns in search of a process and process in search of empirical characterization. Note that there is a large measure of inductivism in this strategy and that this factor alone should ensure that archaeologists refrain from pursuing only this strategy. Needless to say there is also a real sense of liberation flowing from an almost whimsical excursion through pattern and structure. I feel that non-linear modelling has a real role to play here.

The second strategy seeks to develop, change or discard extant theory by 'working through' its implications. This strategy also reflects a changed psychology of research in the sense that extant theory will have clearer performance measures, and that Pleistocene archaeologists recognize their responsibility to develop those theories so they more directly engage the empirical. This strategy also has elements of liberation which flow from the notion that non-correspondences between theory and the empirical are now something which can lead to a re-examination of theory rather than the traditional response, which was to protect the theory and discard the empirical anomaly because of the 'intransigence' of the Pleistocene archaeological record.

Clearly there are limitations on the extent to which we can expect theories born of accounting for highly detailed contemporary behaviours, and using complex concepts such as culture, society, ethnicity or class, to have direct empirical referents in the Pleistocene. I am not here advocating a rule stating that unless we can specify the material culture correlates of behaviours then the plausibility of the theories involved will be diminished. Rather I seek to establish the point at which these theories begin to experience difficulties, and the terms under which archaeological redefinition might assist them in overcoming those difficulties. Furthermore, it is still useful for Pleistocene archaeologists to explore approaches which might give some empirical dimension to the instruments of social theory, and to reflect on whether these instruments really provide a practical exemplar for Pleistocene archaeology.

The third strategy is to continue the process of borrowing, of multiplying perspectives and of increasing theoretical and methodological options. For archaeologists the links with geomorphology and the foundation of studies like taphonomy have had profound implications for the comprehension of Pleistocene archaeological records. At the heart of this strategy is an attempt to explore the distinctiveness of Pleistocene records (distinctive, that is, in terms of short-scale records of the 1,000-year range or less) as records of action, and to reflect on the appropriateness of our theoretical inheritance. Here again there is a search for the interesting anomaly or the body of theory which more directly speaks to problems of palimpsest and scale than does contemporary social theory.

The fourth strategy is to consider the ways in which archaeological knowledge is formulated and disseminated to a wider community. Science fiction, for example, is one way in which we can free our imaginations from the inertia of disciplinary tradition by listening to how non-practitioners comprehend matters of scale, resolving power, and ontology. There is another, deeper benefit flowing from fiction – the creation of a region of the mind where we can examine our implicit social and ideological assumptions, concepts and categories.

This freedom exists because such assumptions are more easily revealed in fictional contexts which stress the differences between our societies and those of other worlds and times. The fact that they remain as familiar markers in a context striving for unfamiliarity makes them more visible, but it also argues for their implicitness and for their necessity. Without such markers works of fiction would be meaningless, literally uninterpretable. In this account science fiction is not about creating uninterpretable contexts but rather to enable an understanding of ourselves in the present by placing that understanding in unfamiliar situations. Explorations of this kind are notoriously difficult to undertake in the same surroundings that generate those understandings.

The implicit concepts and categories underlying the archaeologist's project are my particular interest because they are tangible representations of the metaphysical background of unexamined (some would say unexaminable) contextual assumptions which guide our work. Significantly, the character of these assumptions is not unchanging although, as Foucault (1981) has discovered, it is extraordinarily resistant to change. Why and how assumptions change, and why and how they manage to resist change for long periods are questions which historians and philosophers find compelling. One obvious explanation is that they are extremely difficult to describe in such a way that empirical tests can be developed which place them at risk.

Change, when it does occur, usually results from the incorporation of whole new fields of phenomena which give us reason to doubt the efficacy of old assumptions or restrict their universal applicability. In my view the structure of Pleistocene archaeological records as manifestations of human action provides ample cause for change. Thus our basic task is to understand how implicit assumptions provide the context of archaeological practice and often remain unaffected by the discovery of anomalous data. The vehicle for the exploration of disciplinary identity is the process of critical self-reflection and it is fundamental to the successful pursuit of all four strategies. Clearly this process of critical self-reflection is never-ending.

Note

1   What interests me is why these practitioners sought meaning in terms of contemporary 'savages', why others found their accounts plausible, and the consequences of this framework of interpretation for the future of prehistoric archaeology. Space prohibits an extended discussion of these issues, which have been more fully dealt with elsewhere (Murray 1987, Ch 4).

References

Argyll, Duke of (George Douglas Campbell) 1869. *Primeval Man: an examination of some recent speculations.* London: Strahan.

Bailey, G.N. 1981. Concepts, time-scales and explanations in economic prehistory. In *Economic Archaeology: towards an integration of ecological and social approaches*, A. Sheridan and G.N. Bailey (eds), 97–117. Oxford: British Archaeological Reports International Series 96.

Bailey, G.N. 1983. Concepts of time in quaternary prehistory. *Annual Review of Anthropology* 12, 165–92.

Bailey, G.N. 1987. Breaking the time barrier. *Archaeological Review from Cambridge* 6, 5–20.

Binford, L.R. 1962. Archaeology as anthropology. *American Antiquity* 28, 217–25.

Binford, L.R. 1981. Behavioural archaeology and the 'Pompeii Premise'. *Journal of Anthropological Research* 37, 195–208.

Binford, L.R. 1983. *Working at Archaeology.* New York: Academic Press.

Binford, L.R. 1987. Data, relativism and archaeological science. *Man* 22, 391–404.

Foucault, M. 1981. *The History of Sexuality.* New York: Vantage.

Gillespie, N.C. 1977. The Duke of Argyll: evolutionary anthropology and the art of scientific controversy. *Isis* 68, 40–54.

Grayson, D. 1983. *The Establishment of Human Antiquity.* Orlando: Academic Press.

Hawkes, C.F.C. 1954. Archaeological theory and method: some suggestions from the Old World. *American Anthropologist* 56, 155–68.

Hodder, I. 1986. *Reading the Past.* Cambridge: Cambridge University Press.

Isaac, G. Ll. 1972. Chronology and the tempo of cultural change during the Pleistocene. In *Calibration of Hominoid Evolution*, W.W. Bishop and J.A. Miller (eds), 281–430. Edinburgh: Scottish Academic Press.

Isaac, G. Ll. 1981. Archaeological tests of alternative models of early hominid behaviour: excavation and experiments. In *The Emergence of Man*, J.Z. Young, E.M. Jope and K.P. Oakley (eds), 177–88. *Philosophical Transactions of the Royal Society,* Series B, 292

Lubbock, J. 1882. *The Origins of Civilization and the Primitive Condition of Man* (4th edn). London: Longmans, Green and Co.

Lubbock, J. 1971. *Prehistoric Times* (reprint of the 7th edn.). Freeport: Books for Libraries Press.

Miller, D. and C. Tilley 1984. Ideology, power and prehistory: an introduction. In: *Ideology, Power and Prehistory*, D. Miller and C. Tilley (eds), 1–15. Cambridge: Cambridge University Press.

Morgan, L.H. 1871. *Systems of Consanguinity and the Affinity of the Human Family.* Washington, D.C.: Smithsonian Institution.

Morgan, L.H. 1877. *Ancient Society.* London: Macmillan.

Murray, T. 1987. Remembrance of things present: appeals to authority in the history and philosophy of archaeology. Unpublished Ph.D. thesis, University of Sydney.

Schiffer, M.B. 1976. *Behavioural Archaeology.* New York: Academic Press.

Schiffer, M.B. 1985. Is there a 'Pompeii Premise' in archaeology? *Journal of Anthropological Research* 41, 18–41.

Schiffer, M.B. 1987. *Formation Processes of the Archaeological Record*. Albuquerque: University of New Mexico Press.

Shanks, M. and C. Tilley 1987a. *Re-constructing Archaeology. Theory and practice*. Cambridge: Cambridge University Press.

Shanks, M. and C. Tilley 1987b. *Social Theory and Archaeology*. Cambridge: Polity Press.

Tylor, E.B. 1865. *Researches into the Early History of Man*. London: John Murray.

Tylor, E.B. 1870. *Primitive Culture*. London: John Murray.

Tylor, E.B. 1893. On the Tasmanians as representatives of Palaeolithic man. *Journal of the Anthropological Institute* XXIII, 141–52.

Wylie, A. 1982a. Positivism and the New Archaeology. Unpublished Ph.D.. Thesis, SUNY Binghamton.

Wylie, A. 1982b. Epistemological issues raised by a structuralist archaeology. In *Symbolic and Structural Archaeology*, I. Hodder (ed.), 39–46. Cambridge: Cambridge University Press.

Wylie, A. 1985. Between philosophy and archaeology. *American Antiquity* 50, 478–90.

Index

agency: agents' expectations, discussion of the effects of on the dynamical behaviour of systems 118–40; Distributed Artificial Intelligence, its conceptualization of agents and agent systems 285, 286–7, 288; Hodder's theorization of the significance of purposive behaviour in structural transformation 4; post-processualism, critique of its account of social change as the outcome solely of reflexive social action 21; post-processualism, discussion of its use of Giddens's theorization of structuration 437

America: epidemic diseases, use of dynamic modelling to model the spread of into America 226–52; voyages of exploration to **8.1**, 219, 222; *see also* epidemics, Mesoamerica, North America

analogy: analogical reasoning, discussion of the debate on in archaeology 450; ethnographic analogy, discussion of the reasons for its use in archaeology for explaining socio-cultural change and variation 458

Annales School 4, 6: its non-linear conceptualization of historical process 6

archaeological theory: adoption of theory from other disciplines, discussion of 449–50; analogical reasoning, discussion of the debate on 450; archaeological approaches to prehistoric exchange systems,

discussion of 299–301; archaeological description of the long-term 4, 5, 9; archaeological epistemology, discussion of the problems of 21–2; the archaeology of power, its high profile in theories of socio-cultural change 298; artificial intelligence approaches, discussion of their potential for archaeological interpretation 169–70; its bias towards continuity as a narrative for describing the long-term 4–5; Catastrophe Theory, popularization of in archaeology 2, 25; character of paradigms in 1–2; cognitive archaeology, conceptualization of and discussion of its feasibility 171–3; discontinuity, critique of archaeological approaches to 33–4; Distributed Artificial Intelligence, discussion of its importance for the archaeological modelling of socio-cultural evolution 295–6; dynamic modelling, discussion of the role of Clarke and Doran in the development of in archaeology 15; ethnographic analogy, discussion of the reasons for its use in explaining socio-cultural change and variation 458; linear systems concepts, critique of the use of 14; natural sciences, discussion of the need to adopt insights from 20–1; metrology, discussion of in archaeology 426–45; non-linear modelling, discussion of the value of its use in archaeological interpretation 151–73; non-linear

data, discussion of archaeology's relationship with and the implications of 456

Europe: England, simulation of the spread of disease into the New World as emanating from **8.8**, **8.9**, 236, 238, 248; epidemic diseases, use of dynamic modelling to model the spread of from Europe into America 226–52; heterarchical and hierarchical structures, modelling the development of in later prehistoric temperate Europe 359, 363–6; instability in inter-regional trade, modelling the effects of on the settlement dynamics of later prehistoric temperate Europe 351–2, 355; inter-regional chaos, modelling the effects of on the settlement dynamics of later prehistoric temperate Europe 355–7, 359; Portugal, simulation of the spread of disease into the New World as emanating from **8.7**, 236, 248; Spain, simulation of the spread of disease into the New World as emanating from **8.5**, **8.6**, 231, 233, 236, 248; urban origins, modelling the dynamics of in temperate Europe in later prehistory 355–7, 359, 363–6

event: Prigogine's conceptualization of process and event, discussion of 2

evolution: artificial intelligence, discussion of the value of in modelling the evolutionary dynamics of societal systems 151–73; autonomous learning system, use of to investigate the relationship between the processes of biological and cultural evolution, discussion of 271–5, 278–9; biological and cultural evolution, discussion of the relationship between the processes of 269–75, 278–9; chaotic dynamics, evolutionary role of 12; comparison of clonal and non-clonal information strategies using an evolutionary automaton 260–8; critique of archaeological understandings of socio-cultural evolution 3–4; cultural evolution and the acceleration of the evolutionary process, discussion of 280–2; dynamical approach to

change, discussion of 39–55; environmental stability and the evolution of life 257–8; environmental stability, discussion of its relationship to the evolution of complexity in organisms 257–8; evolutionary approach to economics, definition and discussion of 50–1, 53; evolutionary approach to structural transformation, definition of 19–20; evolutionary dynamics of human behaviour, discussion of 54–5; evolutionary processes of non-linear systems 42–3; instability, evolutionary importance of 10–12; modelling of, discussion of 43–9; non-linear model of the evolutionary dynamics of urban systems in France 103–115; organism flexibility versus environmental stability, discussion of 258–9; physical sciences' approach to, discussion of 39–40; possibility space, role of in exploring change 43–9; qualitative dynamics of urban system evolution, discussion of 338–346; Shortugaï, discussion of the use of the expert system PALAMEDE to model the evolutionary dynamics of 156–71; *see also* cultural evolution, Darwinism, evolutionary drive, Lamarckianism, social evolution

evolutionary drive: definition and modelling of 43–9; and the modelling of the management of natural resources 49–50

exchange systems: archaeological approaches to, discussion of 299–301; chaotic dynamics of 303; Frankenstein and Rowlands's theory of the role of exchange relations in later prehistory, discussion of 299–300, 302; instability in inter-regional trade, modelling the effects of on the settlement dynamics of later prehistoric temperate Europe 351–2, 355; instability of 302–3; modes of exchange, discussion of 301–2; production dynamics, characterization and discussion of 303–15; Renfrew's theory of the role of exchange systems in developing social hierarchy during

MANW9781 3-25-97 Hill